D0026126

Clinical Handbook of Health Psychology

A Practical Guide to Effective Interventions

2nd revised and expanded edition

Edited by
Paul M. Camic, Ph.D. & Sara J. Knight, Ph.D.

With a Foreword by Robert D. Kerns, Ph.D.

Hogrefe & Huber

Library of Congress Cataloguing-in-Publication Data

is available via the Library of Congress Marc Database
under the LC Control Number 2002111970

National Library of Canada Cataloguing-in-Publication Data

Clinical handbook of health psychology : a practical guide to effective interventions /
Paul Camic & Sara Knight, editors. — 2nd rev. and expanded ed.

Includes bibliographical references and indexes.
ISBN 0-88937-260-8

1. Clinical health psychology. I. Knight, Sara J., 1952– II. Camic, Paul M. (Paul Marc), 1955–

R726.7.C54 2003   616'.001'9   C2003-906312-7

Copyright © 2004 by Hogrefe & Huber Publishers

PUBLISHING OFFICES
USA: Hogrefe & Huber Publishers, 875 Massachusetts Avenue, 7th Floor, Cambridge, MA 02139
             Tel. (866) 823-4726, Fax (617) 354-6875, E-mail info@hhpub.com
Europe: Hogrefe & Huber Publishers, Rohnsweg 25, 37085 Göttingen, Germany
             Tel. +49 551 49609-0, Fax +49 551 49609-88, E-mail hhpub@hogrefe.de

SALES AND DISTRIBUTION
USA: Hogrefe & Huber Publishers, Customer Service Department, 30 Amberwood Parkway,
             Ashland, OH 44805, Tel. (800) 228-3749, Fax (419) 281-6883
             E-mail custserv@hhpub.com
Europe: Hogrefe & Huber Publishers, Rohnsweg 25, 37085 Göttingen, Germany
             Tel. +49 551 49609-0, Fax +49 551 49609-88, E-mail hhpub@hogrefe.de

OTHER OFFICES
Canada: Hogrefe & Huber Publishers, 1543 Bayview Avenue, Toronto, Ontario, M4G 3B5
Switzerland: Hogrefe & Huber Publishers, Länggass-Strasse 76, CH-3000 Bern 9

Hogrefe & Huber Publishers
Incorporated and registered in the State of Washington, USA, and in Göttingen, Lower Saxony, Germany

No part of this book may be reproduced, stored in a retrieval system, or transmitted, in any form or by
any means, electronic, mechanical, photocopying, microfilming, recording or otherwise, without the
written permission from the publisher.

Printed and bound in the USA

Cover design based on artwork by Lawrence E. Wilson

ISBN 0-88937-260-8

Robert D. Kerns

Foreword

Looking back over a twenty-five year career as a clinical health psychologist, I can reflect on the relatively rapid emergence of a large and expanding body of knowledge about the role of psychological and interpersonal factors in the broadest possible array of health and illness issues and the ever-increasing influence the field has had on health practices and health policy. Our field has evolved into a sophisticated and rigorous science that now spans issues covering the entire life span and touching virtually every known health problem. Its influences on education from preschool through advanced professional and scientific training, almost regardless of the specific area of study, are increasingly apparent. Dissemination of knowledge informed by work in the field has garnered the public's interest in terms of lifestyle, prevention of illness and promotion of health, and expectations for healthcare. The breadth, and depth, of our field is enormous, and its promise for promoting quality of life, and even extending life, is compelling. Health psychology remains an exciting field, and one that captures the imagination and creativity of many who wish to influence the health and wellbeing of those around us.

Educating others about the breadth and complexity of the field of health psychology in a single text that is both meaningful and engaging clearly presents a series of challenges that few would have the nerve to undertake. Drs. Paul Camic and Sara Knight have once again risen to the occasion in their publication of this second edition of their previously successful book. Among all of the similar texts in the field, this one is at the top of my list.

The strengths of this text are numerous, but most important from my perspective is the success of these authors and their collaborators in capturing the excitement and enthusiasm that those of us who are immersed in this field continue to experience on a nearly daily basis. The editors' optimism about the potential of the field comes through loud and clear. In this sense the text stands to promote personal growth through an improved understanding of the interface between important psychological and interpersonal factors and health outcomes, and to encourage personal action informed by this knowledge and appreciation. At the same time it is likely to capture the attention of future scientists and health professionals and foster an interest in the pursuit of a deeper understanding of the potential relevance and importance of the field. For those considering a career in psychology, the text provides a sound foundation for future study and investigation by offering both information about the current state of the field and targets for future efforts to advance it.

Several additional strengths of the text are important to acknowledge. Contributing to the readers' understanding of even the most complex and challenging concepts are consistent efforts to promote integration and linkages across disparate domains and topics through the promotion of a unifying biopsychosocial perspective. This perspective serves as an important framework that will likely remain with the reader long after the course is completed. And, thankfully, and as opposed to many other texts in the field, the "social" dimension of the model is actually emphasized, rather than being given scant attention. The authors are to be commended for their routine consideration of cultural influences on health and behavior and of the cultural competence of practitioners. The concluding chapters that specifically address issues such as the role of the social context, spirituality and religion, and ethnic minorities help to reinforce this critical, but often neglected, dimension.

The first chapter of the book, authored by its editors, sets the stage for a sequential and graded consideration of the breadth of the field and provides a firm foundation for the chapters that follow. The chapter begins with a brief historical perspective that highlights the emergence of the field and the challenges in defining a new area of investigation and practice within the context of existing areas of inquiry and the contemporary healthcare industry. It is in this context that the biopsychosocial perspective is introduced as a unifying framework for the remainder of the text. Emerging themes in our field are also introduced in this chapter, including the concepts of environment of care, health and illness as a continuum, integration of art and science, complementary and alternative medicine perspectives and approaches, the social, cultural, and spiritual contexts of healthcare, and the influence of health economics. Discussion of these issues serves to encourage the reader to have an eye to the future when considering more specific topics and areas of interest. The second chapter on assessment similarly provides a critical foundation for the remainder of the text by discussing a series of key parameters of clinical assessment and the role of assessment in case conceptualization and in informing treatment planning.

The success of the authors of this text in providing an integration of the science of health psychology and practice is another noteworthy strength. This integrative perspective is represented by the editors of the volume and by the authors of each chapter. The scholarship represented in each of the chapters is clearly evident, and represents the current status of theory and empirical foundations. Just as important is the emphasis on the practitioner's perspective and experience. For example, Van Egeren's chapter on assessment in health psychology tackles practical issues such as the "reticent patient" that offer the reader insight into some of the complexities and challenges of translating state-of-the-art science and empirical evidence into practice. As already noted, the specific attention to the cultural context in considering these translations is critically important when considering the rapidly shifting demographics of our society and our emerging global perspective.

The editors have made a wise decision in offering a volume that is organized around the consideration of specific diseases or areas of inquiry and practice. Again, their success in engaging leading scholars and practitioners in authoring these chapters represents their appreciation of the trend toward specialization in the field of health psychology and the practical utility of this organizational approach. Chapters on diseases or problem domains in which health psychologists have had their greatest influence in terms of scientific advances, practice, and policy have been selected to substantially reflect the breadth of our field. Topics included are cardiology, pulmonary medicine, pain and pain management, dental medicine, diabetes mellitus, gastrointestinal disorders, human immunodeficiency virus, multiple sclerosis, obstetrics and gynecology, oncology, and urological disorders. The consistent organization of each chapter's content aids the reader in examining similarities and differences across these areas of inquiry and practice and encourages the development of a broad and well-informed perspective on the field.

Each chapter begins with a presentation of information that serves to build a foundation about the disease or problem from a medical perspective. A consideration of issues particularly relevant to the health psychologist is subsequently introduced in a manner that, once again, promotes integrative thinking and consideration of the practical interface of the practice of clinical health psychology within the broader healthcare system. Specific attention to the role of assessment, case conceptualization and treatment planning, and psychological intervention in the consideration of each disorder or problem domain is critical in further fostering this integrative and dynamic perspective. The presentation of a range of clinical problems that serve as targets for health psychological involvement within each domain serves to enhance the readers' awareness of the breadth of the field, opportunities for continued investigation, and the importance of continued efforts to promote change in our healthcare delivery system. The liberal use of tables helps to organize information. The routine inclusion of case examples serves to put a "real face" on the problems being addressed by clinical health psychologists. The consideration of specific professional practice issues in several of the chapters empha-

sizes the challenges being confronted by practitioners in the field and ongoing health policy issues.

All-in-all this is an exceptional volume that will appeal to educators and students alike. Congratulations to Drs. Knight and Camic and their coauthors for once again capturing the energy and excitement of the field of health psychology.

Robert D. Kerns, Ph.D.
Professor of Psychiatry, Neurology and Psychology
Yale University

Chief, Psychology Service
VA Connecticut Healthcare System

January 2004

Table of Contents

Section III: Health and Illness – Community, Social, Spiritual, and Creative Involvement

Paul M. Camic & Sara J. Knight

Preface to the Second Edition

The emergence of health psychology over 25 years ago, and its continuing growth and development as an area of research and an applied area of practice, mean that it is now well established as a distinct field within psychology. Significant contributions continue to be made in the areas of health promotion, disease prevention, health education, and treatment. With regards to treatment, health psychologists are currently involved with a wide range of disorders representing most of the body's physical systems. The focus of this book is on the treatment and assessment of these disorders, encompassing ten physical systems of the human body.

This book is intended to be a practical resource for clinicians, psychology interns, and advanced graduate students, providing a reference for both the classroom and clinical settings. While this book is not a basic introduction to clinical health psychology for undergraduates, it is suitable for graduates students as well as new- or established-practitioners. We assume the reader is somewhat familiar with the specialty of health psychology and the basics of clinical assessment, and is also knowledgeable about the key interventions used in health psychology (e.g., brief psychotherapy, autogenic techniques, progressive muscle relaxation, biofeedback, cognitive-behavioral therapy, learning and conditioning theories, fundamental psychodynamics, hypnosis, relapse prevention, supportive therapy, etc.). Our purpose is to assist the reader in the translation of research and theory in health psychology and medicine into evidenced-based clinical interventions. We hope this text will help clinicians understand not only the technical knowledge required to work with medical patients, but also help them value the process of healing.

The idea for the first edition of this book came about when we both expressed a desire for a clinical health psychology text suitable for advanced graduate students and interns. At the time both of us taught in clinical psychology doctoral programs, encompassing the scientist-practitioner (SJK) and scholar-practitioner (PMC) models, which offered health psychology training as a specialty track. We were frustrated that most of the texts in health psychology were either an introduction to the field, and thus overly broad, or highly specialized and not suitable to the general health psychology practitioner. While there had been rich theoretical and empirical innovations in health psychology, there was little published guidance for the new clinician on how to actually apply these concepts and findings in therapeutic relationships with patients from diverse backgrounds seen in complex, multidisciplinary clinical settings. Our hope at the time of developing the first edition was to provide a text that was solidly grounded in empirical science, but also one that left room for clinical insight and creativity and an appreciation of the *healing process*. The very positive response to the first edition of the *Clinical Handbook of Health Psychology* confirmed what we saw as a need to link empirical research findings, clinical practice, and the sometimes less than clear components of the culturally influenced phenomenon of healing. We have continued this perspective in the second edition. This new edition includes advancements made in health psychology assessment and treatment since the publication of the first edition in 1998 and involves new chapters and significant revisions of existing chapters.

We are asking that the users of this handbook think about the concept of healing as they consider an intervention strategy. Healing is after all, what our patients are seeking, in one way or another. Healing is also a difficult concept to measure. We believe healing takes place in all effective therapeutic relationships. Healing, for some, may mean being able to breathe without a ventilator and finally leaving the hospital. For others it may mean chemotherapy has stopped the progression of cancer cells and they are beginning to feel a bit of joy at being alive. For some of the people we work with, healing may mean coming to terms with dying or with pain that will always remain part of their lives.

In two initial organizing chapters, we introduce the concept of healing as an art and science. Here, we provide a context for the current practice of health psychology interventions and assessment in light of current trends and controversies. Chapters 3 through 12 are the primary focus of this handbook. Each chapter discusses the biopsychosocial aspects of an area of health psychology practice, including cardiovascular disease, respiratory illnesses, chronic pain, dental health, diabetes and other endocrine disorders, gastrointestinal disease, multiple sclerosis, human immunodeficiency virus, reproductive concerns, cancer, and urologic dysfunctions. For each, we consider referral questions, screening and psychological assessment, psychological interventions, and ethical and professional practice issues.

How to help someone heal is one of *the* most difficult questions we encounter in clinical practice. To begin to address the complexities of the healing process, our concluding chapters consider a number of themes that intersect the practice of health psychology–social relationships, spirituality, personal expression, and culture.

Certainly psychodynamic and humanistic psychotherapy as well as relaxation training, hypnosis, cognitive-behavioral therapy, and biofeedback can all help to reduce *symptoms,* but this may not be the same as helping someone to heal. Many turn to their belief in a higher power to help them do this. While many health psychology practitioners seem uncomfortable about an immeasurable "God" or a belief in spirituality, most other North Americans do not share this discomfort. Utilizing a patient's spiritual belief system is vitally important in the healing process for many people, whether the psychologist agrees with the beliefs or not. Chapter 15 considers this issue.

Another area that can contribute to healing is personal expression through the arts. Such well known institutions as Duke, UCLA, and the University of Florida Medical Center among many others, have formally developed arts-medicine programs for adult and pediatric medical patients. Expressive therapy training, which uses visual, movement, and sound arts, is rarely available in clinical or health psychology graduate programs. We have included a chapter introducing the field of medical art therapy. This chapter discusses basic tools such as imagery and visual expression that health psychologists can employ in their work.

Family, friends, and community can also be part of the healing process, and this is addressed in Chapter 14. A clinical intervention without considering the environment of the client may fail. The environment of one's family, friendship network, and living and working communities often needs to be *involved* in the process of helping the patient "to get better." The health psychologist's use of family and community should consider broadly the social network that is important to the patient's health and well-being: Inviting grandparents to a family session may help insure the success of a nutritional program for a Latino teenager recently diagnosed with AIDS more efficiently than a therapy using behavioral reinforcement; acknowledging a female patient's female partner (significant other) as a family member when the diagnosis of multiple sclerosis is given invites cooperation of that family member in the battle with this disease.

Finally, while we have much to offer our patients to alleviate suffering and to improve well-being, our interventions are only as effective as they are consistent with the culturally based preferences and values of patients and their families. The final chapter, Chapter 17, considers the cultural context of healing, and echoes our call for the inclusion of clinical material and research relevant to multicultural populations. This chapter discusses the challenges of involving minorities in health risk reduction interventions and provides a framework for insuring that our interventions reflect the concerns of individuals from diverse backgrounds.

We hope the information contained in the second edition of this text adds to your understanding of the physical systems and corresponding interventions that are the focus of the work of clinical health psychologists.

Health psychology is an exciting and expanding field. We have enjoyed our many years of involvement as participants in the birth and maturation of this specialty. Both of us have worked as clinicians, instructors, researchers, and supervisors and have many people to thank who have been helpful in our development along the way.

To the many patients who taught us about suffering and healing, to our supervisors and mentors, to our students and colleagues, to our partners and families, we thank each of you. We would also like to thank Larry Wilson for his artwork for the cover of this volume and our editors at Hogrefe & Huber for their continued support and confidence.

Paul M. Camic, Chicago, IL
Sara J. Knight, San Francisco, CA

About the Editors

Paul M. Camic, Ph.D., Professor of Psychology & Cultural Studies, Columbia College Chicago and adjunct Professor of Clinical Psychology, Chicago School of Professional Psychology. Recent publications include *Qualitative Research in Psychology: Expanding Perspectives in Methodology and Design* with J. Rhodes and L. Yardley (2003), American Psychological Association.

Sara J. Knight, Ph.D., is a faculty member in the Departments of Psychiatry and Urology at the University of California San Francisco and the San Francisco Department of Veterans Affairs Medical Center. Her work focuses on understanding patient preferences, medical decision-making, and comprehensive outcomes in cancer treatment, particularly prostate cancer, and in end of life care. She is the recipient of an Advanced Research Career Development Award from the Health Services Research and Development Service of the Department of Veterans Affairs. Grants from the Department of Veterans Affairs and the National Cancer Institute have supported her research. She lives in Belmont, California, with her husband Lynd D. Bacon, their dog Samantha, and Onion the cat.

Contributors

James E. Aikens, Ph.D.
Department of Family Medicine
University of Michigan
Ann Arbor, MI

William A. Ayer, D.D.S., Ph.D.
Department of Psychiatry and
Behavioral Sciences
Northwestern University Feinberg
School of Medicine
Chicago, IL

Albert J. Bellg, Ph.D.
Cardiac Psychology Services
Appleton Heart Institute
Appleton, WI

Paul M. Camic, Ph.D.
Department of Liberal Education
Columbia College Chicago
Chicago, IL

Darcy Cox, Psy.D.
Department of Neurology
University of California at San Francisco
San Francisco, CA

Marian L. Fitzgibbon, Ph.D.
Department of Psychiatry and
Behavioral Sciences
Northwestern University Feinberg
School of Medicine
Chicago, IL

Laura M. Gaugh, Psy.D.
Chicago School of Professional Psychology
Chicago, IL

Kimeron N. Hardin, Ph.D.
Bay Area Pain Center
San Jose, CA

Seth C. Kalichman, Ph.D.
Department of Psychology
University of Connecticut
Storrs, CT

Susan C. Klock, Ph.D.
Departments of Obstetrics and
Gynecology and Psychiatry
Northwestern University Feinberg
School of Medicine
Chicago, IL

Sara J. Knight, Ph.D.
Departments of Psychiatry and Urology
San Francisco Department of Veterans
Affairs Medical Center
University of California at San Francisco
San Francisco, CA

Susan M. Labott, Ph.D., ABPP
Department of Psychiatry
University of Illinois at Chicago
Chicago, IL

**Janet K. Long, M.A., M.F.C.C. (LMFT),
A.T.R.-B. C., C.T.P.**
California College of Arts and Crafts
California Institute of Integral Studies
Oakland, CA

David C. Mohr, Ph.D.
Departments of Psychiatry and Neurology
San Francisco Department of Veterans
Affairs Medical Center
University of California at San Francisco
San Francisco, CA

Robert J. Moretti, Ph.D.
Department of Psychiatry and
Behavioral Sciences
Northwestern University Feinberg
School of Medicine
Chicago, IL

Randolph G. Potts, Ph.D.
LeBonjeur Children's Medical Center
Memphis, TN

Jean E. Rhodes, Ph.D.
Department of Psychology
University of Massachusetts
Boston, MA

Lisa A. P. Sánchez-Johnsen, Ph.D.
Cancer Research Center of Hawai'i
University of Hawai'i at Manoa
Manoa, HI

Kathleen J. Sikkema, Ph.D.
Departments of Psychiatry, Psychology,
Epidemiology and Public Health
Yale University
New Haven, CT

Steven M. Tovian, Ph.D., ABPP
Department of Psychiatry and
Behavioral Sciences
Evanston Northwestern Healthcare
Northwestern University Feinberg
School of Medicine
Evanston, IL

Linda Van Egeren, Ph.D.
Department of Psychology
Minneapolis Department of Veterans
Affairs Medical Center
University of Minnesota
Minneapolis, MN

Lynne I. Wagner, Ph.D.
Center on Outcomes, Research and
Education
Evanston Northwestern Healthcare
Department of Psychiatry and
Behavioral Sciences
Northwestern University Feinberg
School of Medicine
Evanston, IL

Section I
Foundations of Practice

Sara J. Knight & Paul M. Camic

1

Health Psychology and Medicine: The Art and Science of Healing

A Brief Evolutionary History

The use of psychological therapies in the treatment of health problems has a very long history. Early Egyptians, Ancient Greeks, as well as Asian cultures believed imbalances within the mind and soul can cause physical illness. Pergamum, on the west coast of Asia Minor in approximately 100 B.C., offered treatments consisting of rest, massage, herbal potions, time spent at spas and more radically, a change in lifestyle for physical and mental distress. Many indigenous cultures in North and South America and Africa have had, as part of their belief systems, the importance of the soul's affect on the body. The attention and curiosity concerning what influences physical health, has been a matter of speculation and inquiry for nearly all cultures throughout recorded history.

The contemporary beginnings of health psychology as a discipline can be traced to the two leading psychologists of the early 20th century, William James at Harvard and G. Stanley Hall at Clark. James (1922) contended that the cause of work-related nervous problems was not the amount or nature of the work, but in the needless hurry, tension and anxiety produced by one's approach to the task. Hall (1904) believed health to be a medial value in development, and not something that should be left only to physicians. He was especially concerned with hygiene, preventive medicine and the concept of wholeness, all of which he felt to be embedded philosophically in the ideal of health.

The period between 1930 and the mid-1950s saw psychology nearly exclusively focus on the assessment of mental disorders and all things involving intelligence, motivation, memory and the mind. The problems of physical health and well-being were left to physicians and most notably to the emerging field of psychosomatic medicine. As psychosomatic medicine concepts grew in popularity, however, by the end of the 1950s, more psychologists began to investigate problems of mind-body interaction. Psychoanalytic theories strongly influenced psychosomatic medicine. While this theoretical view proved intellectually rich, few cures were produced. In contrast, the growing awareness of behaviorism in the 1950s and 1960s produced alternative, empirically-derived behavioral explanations for psychosomatic illnesses. Gradually, through the 1970s and 1980s, the underlying psychoanalytic perspective toward mind-body problems gave way to a more empirically supported psychophysiological approach.

The psychophysiological approach is based on a bidirectional model involving physiological factors, the immune system, behaviors, emotions and the environment (simply put, we are discarding the one-way cause and effect street for the avenue that is interactive and definitely two-way). The bidirectional model is the basis for the *clinical* method of assessment and treatment known as the biopsychosocial paradigm, which currently dominates clinical health psychology. As the name implies, a biopsychosocial approach takes into consideration the three domains of biological-physiological, psychological-behavioral and social-environmental, when evaluating clients. This paradigm allows clinicians to more fully consider complex interactions (e. g., the effects of racism, sexism or homophobia on emotions and physical functioning), in addition to assessing "traditional" biological and psychological domains. Inherent in this approach is the view that the health psychologist is a member of the health care team and has much to contribute to the wellbeing and welfare of people. Health psychologists are seen as health care, rather than mental health care, professionals thus dissolving the artificial boundary between problems of the mind and problems of the body.

The Healing Relationship

The biopsychosocial model became the focus of practitioners and scientists from a variety of disciplines — psychology, nursing, medicine, public health — who began to describe their work and its conceptual basis as behavioral medicine. The Yale conference on behavioral medicine in 1977 offered one of its first definitions as "the field concerned with the development of behavioral-science knowledge and techniques relevant to the understanding of physical health and illness and the application of this knowledge and these techniques to prevention, diagnosis, treatment, and rehabilitation. Psychosis, neurosis, and substance abuse are included only insofar as they contribute to physical disorders as an endpoint" (Schwartz & Weiss, 1977). While psychologists figured prominently in the inception of behavioral medicine, the field is inclusive of any discipline, including health psychology, that might play a role in its science and practice.

Health psychology evolved as a specialty within professional psychology. Beginning in the late 1970s as a Division within the American Psychological Association, the field has grown rapidly. In 1980, a definition of health psychology was adopted by the Division:

"Health psychology is the aggregate of the specific educational, scientific, and professional contributions of the discipline of psychology to the promotion and maintenance of health, the prevention and treatment of illness, the identification of etiologic and diagnostic correlates of health, illness, and related dysfunction, and the analysis and improvement of the health care system and health policy formation" (Stone, 1987). With minor modifications, this definition remains the "official" definition of the Division of Health Psychology.

This and other widely cited definitions of health psychology frame it in terms of its goals — the application of psychological theory and research in the prevention and treatment of medical disorders (Matarazzo, 1980; Millon, 1982). Other goals are directed to health care systems and health policy (Matarazzo, 1992). Whereas clinical psychology has its roots in inpatient psychiatry, health psychology is more identified with medicine and surgery. The focus of health psychology is not on treating mental illness. Rather, health psychology is oriented toward an integration of psyche and soma so as to bring about optimum health to those people with a medical illness or disease. It incorporates the social aspects of health and the health care system.

The goals outlined in these definitions of health psychology have given direction and focus to an emerging field. For clinical health psychologists working in medical settings, these goals have given shape to clinical services. The health psychologist's work is directed toward the health of the entire person. It is not limited by mind-body dualistic thinking but sees the mind very much connected to the body *and* sees the environment impacting on, and being impacted upon by, the patient.

Regardless of the setting where we meet with our patients, of the types of problems that we treat, or of the treatments we use, it is the quality of the relationship between professional and client that begins and sustains the healing process. It is this process of healing — meaning to restore to wholeness and health — that both mystifies and comforts us as clinicians. This is the process through which the clinical health psychologist, other health professionals, and the patient work together toward the goals of physical, psychological and social health implied in the biopsychosocial model. For clinical health psychologists, this is the process through which we translate theory and research into the art of care. Perhaps the Etruscan priests of 300 B. C. E. Tuscany, or the Hopi *tuhikya* of 1600 A. D. southwestern North America, or the present day Aztec *curanderos* of Mexico, all have this ability in common. Although the word *healing* has never appeared to our knowledge in any Division of Health Psychology, Society of Behavioral Medicine or American Psychosomatic Society journal, it is what we as health professionals *do*.

In a clinical guidebook for health psychology, we are especially interested in conveying the health psychologist's role in the healing process. By healing, however, we do not mean that it will always be possible for patient to attain a state of complete health. Throughout the text there are examples of healing that involve an individual's adjustment to chronic or life threatening disease and healing that occurs at the end of life. Our purpose in developing this text was to describe across a range of medical specialties the translation of health psychology to clinical practice. To establish our objectives and scope, we drew heavily from previous definitions of health psychology. To bring alive the science and art in clinical health psychology, however, we emphasize the health psychologist's contributions to the healing process. With these principles and goals, our working definition of clinical health psychology has been the integration of knowledge from behavioral, social, and biomedical sciences and from the clinical arts and the application of this knowledge to the healing of human beings — psychologically, physically, socially, and spiritually — at all points along the health and illness continuum.

Emerging Themes

The Environment of Care

With their work based on the biopsychosocial model, health psychologists are concerned with medical, psychological, social, community, and spiritual context of health care. The work of health psychologists, therefore, is not limited to the office setting, the traditional venue for clinical psychology. Health psychologists practice in medical and surgical clinics and inpatient units, in community health clinics, in schools, on reservations, in health maintenance organizations, on managed care boards, in rehabilitation settings and in nursing homes.

Outside the therapist's office, most clinical health psychologists find themselves working in complex, multidisciplinary environments. Those working in medical and surgical clinics and inpatient units, for example, are likely to interact with physicians from multiple specialties in medicine and surgery, nurses from multiple specialties, unit clerks, pharmacists, dieticians, occupational therapists, physical therapists, medical technicians, social workers, chaplains, hospital administrators, volunteers, and others. Add to that, in a teaching hospital, the clinical health psychologist works with physicians, nurses, and others at various levels of training and experience.

Intervention Targets Along the Health and Illness Continuum

The health psychologist's work is broad in scope. The focus of health psychology is not exclusively on the healthy individual. Health psychologists work with individuals of various levels of health and illness along a continuum from complete health to dying and death (Antonovsky, 1987). The health psychologist may direct an intervention to disease prevention in an individual who has not experienced an illness, but who engages in behaviors that present a risk for disease, such as smoking. Other health psychologists focus on existing symptoms, such as in a patient who experiences chronic pain or urinary incontinence. In chronic and life threatening illness, health psychologists may use psychological methods to reduce patient suffering and to promote adjustment to illness. Even at the end of a patient's life, a health psychologist may help an individual and family resolve conflicts or accomplish an important, yet unfulfilled, life goal.

Integrative Treatment

The tools employed vary nearly as much as the settings where patients are seen and the problems which patients bring to treatment. Supportive psychotherapy, behavior analysis, brief dynamic therapy, existential therapy, biofeedback, hypnosis, expressive therapy, a variety of stress reduction and relaxation training strategies, and cognitive-behavioral therapy, among others, are frequently used interventions. Health psychologists rely on a variety of treatment modalities as well. Individual, group, family, and couples therapies play important roles in the health psychologist's repertoire.

The biopsychosocial model considers patient needs as multifactorial and dynamic. Often the health psychologist integrates treatment systems and modalities to provide care as the patient's needs evolve during the course of an illness. Early in the course of a patient's illness, the health psychologist might use structured approaches, such as stress inoculation training, to strengthen the patient's ability to cope with disease and treatment. Later in the illness, the health psychologist might rely more on existential approaches as the patient's needs turn to understanding the meaning of surviving a life threatening event or of facing dying and death.

The very nature of health psychology practice and the integration of treatment modalities, brings health psychologists into situations in which they may assume multiple roles with patients. For example, the health psychologist meeting with the patient in a hospital room may interact with family members and other staff members involved in the patient's care. In such situations, health psychologists may incorporate multiple treatment modalities such as individual and family therapy. The clinical health psychologist's flexibility and ability to integrate treatment modalities may be important in providing timely, cost effective interventions that otherwise would not be possible due to lengthy referral processes and the expense of involving multiple professionals (Tovian, 1991). On the other hand, according to their professional and ethical standards, psychologists avoid multiple roles in their work with patients, especially where dual roles may compromise the best interest of the patient. Because of the adverse potential of dual roles, these situations require thoughtful consideration of professional standards and ethics, especially in evaluating the impact on patient well-being. Consequently, to avoid assuming multiple roles with a patient, the health psychologist may coordinate care across several health care professionals, each providing an aspect of care, such as group support, individual treatment, and marital therapy, all important in addressing the patient's complex needs.

The Art and Science of Care

While existing definitions of health psychology emphasize scientific and technical knowledge, Belar and Deardorf (1985) highlight the health psychologist's personal qualities, such as warmth, openness, flexibility, as crucial aspects of the practice of health psychology. Because of the centrality of the professional and patient relationship in health care, it is important for the health psychologist to understand and be aware of these personal qualities and their stimulus value that may assist or interfere with forming therapeutic relationships with patients. Each health psychologist will contribute a distinct set of skills, experiences, and personal qualities to the relationship with the patient. Each patient brings to the relationship distinct concerns, needs, and resources. Ultimately, this relationship forms the context within which the health psychologist translates theory, research, and clinical knowledge into practice. It is this relationship that makes health psychology an art, as well as a science.

Complementary and Alternative Therapies

Interest in complementary and alternative medicine (CAM) approaches is not new. In

North America, the last two centuries have seen spiritualists, herbalists, healers, homeopaths, naturopaths, osteopaths, hypnotherapists, acupuncturists, chiropractors, rolfers, acupressurists and psychologists, speak about their abilities to help people heal, cure, manage and cope with physical ailments. Recent interest in CAM encompasses entire systems of medicine such as Chinese medicine and Ayurvedic medicine as well as specific interventions such as botanicals, massage therapy, and imagery. Although many psychologists may bristle at the suggestion they are an "alternative" approach to traditional medical practices, this is how we are seen by many people seeking help for physical symptoms. Even when psychological intervention is not seen as an alternative therapy, but as *complimentary* treatment, it may be the psychologist whom the patient confides about their interest in alternative approaches. It is for these reasons that the health psychologist needs to be familiar with CAM.

A 1993 study by Eisenberg of over 1500 adults found extensive use of alternative therapeutic approaches. In this study, 34% reported using at least one unconventional (alternative) therapy. The most frequent use of alternative therapies was for back problems, anxiety, depression, headache, chronic pain and cancer. The most common therapies used were relaxation, massage, imagery, spiritual healing, weight loss programs, prayer and exercise programs. An earlier study by Verhoef (1990) reported on the extensive use of alternative medicine by patients with gastrointestinal disorders.

The interest in complementary and alternative therapies has not gone unnoticed by the National Institutes of Health with its establishment of the National Center for Complementary and Alternative Medicine. It is the responsibility of this office to develop basic and clinical research initiatives, educational grants and contracts, and outreach mechanisims to further study and educate professionals and the public about complementary and alternative approaches to medical therapies. In 1996 responding to both Federal governmental initiatives and popular demand, Kings County (Seattle) in Washington State, became the first municipality in the United States to open a publicly funded alternative medicine clinic. Clinics such as these do not disregard traditional allopathic medicine, but rather incorporate other approaches as complimentary.

Within the practice of clinical and counseling psychology, it is health psychology and behavioral medicine that are seen as alternative approaches. In addition, meditation, hypnosis, eye movement desensitization and retraining (EMDR), biofeedback, imagery and relaxation therapies are all viewed as alternatives to counseling and psychotherapy. An oncologist may be just as critical of a person with cancer seeing an herbalist as a psychoanalyst may be of someone seeking relaxation training for anxiety. It is not our position to either endorse or criticize alternative medicine approaches. Instead, we urge all health psychologists to be aware that many of our patients will engage in alternative treatments that either they have self-initiated or have sought out a professional. Helping the patient assess the quality and effectiveness of the alternative therapy is an important role of the health psychologist. Often, incorporating the alternative therapy as a complimentary approach, along side the traditional treatment, provides a good balance for patient and health care professionals.

Social, Cultural and Spiritual Considerations

The last ten years has seen a tremendous increase in interest in the health of diverse populations and in understanding the complex relationships among the interaction of social relationships, culture, spirituality, and health. It is as if psychology had just discovered the importance of these interrelationships, which have been known to anthropologists and sociologists since the beginning of the 20th century. As North America truly becomes more culturally diverse and, as a student described to one of us (PMC), much more like a salad than a melting pot, walking the line between what is politically correct in recognizing cultural differences and what is clinically useful, is not always uncomplicated. Seeking to help underserved and poorly served populations, while at the same time not wanting to clump all members of any cultural or ethnic group into one category (e. g., all Latinos value spirituality; all Asians prefer behavioral and medical explanations; all lesbians are monogamous, etc. ...) is challenging indeed. In developing this text, we asked each contributing author to include clinical examples utilizing members of different cultural groups when possible.

Finance and the Healing Process

The issue of whether a patient has a "physical" disorder or a "mental" problem continues to influence the delivery of health care services. Until recently, most insurance companies and managed care entities insisted that patients seen by a clinical health psychologist receive a Diagnostic and Statistical Manual (DSM) (i. e., psychiatric) diagnosis to obtain reimbursement. However, many of the patients seen in health care settings by clinical health psychologists are referred for treatment of the psychological and social dimensions of physical health problems, rather than for treatment of the psychiatric disorders that are represented in the DSM classification system. Consequently, although a health psychologist may be *directly* treating a medical condition, without an accompanying psychiatric diagnosis, treatment may not be approved and services may not be reimbursed. In the last several years, and after American Psychological Association Practice Directorate advocacy, the American Medical Association committee responsible to Current Procedural Technology (CPT) codes expanded this system to reflect psychosocial services to patients and families with physical health diagnoses. These health and behavior CPT codes provide a means for health psychologists to bill for assessment and intervention services that address the psychological, cognitive, behavioral, and social factors influencing a person's physical health and well-being. The health and behavior codes reflect a wide range of services provided by clinical health psychologists including individual, group, and family interventions used in the management of pain, fatigue, and other symptoms in cancer care or cognitive and behavioral approaches to dietary and exercise behaviors recommended in diabetes treatment.

While the new CPT codes represent a major shift in considering the psychological and social aspects of health, it unfortunately remains unusual outside of managed care settings to receive reimbursement for health promotion activities and other health enhancement strategies. Hence, the business of health care in the United States remains focused on treating illness, not on modifying behaviors, prevention, or on learning new coping skills. Although this volume does not have within its scope a discussion of health care policy or health promotion, clearly this is an important area for health psychology and medicine.

Health psychology has much to contribute regarding health promotion and health risk behaviors. Research continues to expand the intervention possibilities in these areas. However, without a change in current health care policy, promotion and prevention activities continue to be under financed. Sadly, nothing short of a fundamental shakeup of both organized medicine and the insurance industry will likely change this situation. Less money is to be made in health promotion and illness prevention activities and therefore less prestige is associated with these areas of research and intervention.

New Opportunities

As health psychology has evolved, new roles and opportunities for clinical practice have emerged. In the five years, since the first edition of the Clinical Handbook of Health Psychology, there has been greater recognition of the integral relationship between mental and physical health (Baum & Posluszny, 1999; U.S. Department of Health and Human Services, 1999; WHO, 2001). In 2001 the Accreditation Council for Graduate Medical Education (ACGME) instituted a requirement that residency programs develop pilot programs that promote an integrated collaborative approach to care, partnering with other health professionals such as psychologists. This has opened new opportunities for health psychologists in end-of-life care and palliative medicine (Twillman, 2002), primary care (McDaniel, Belar, Schroeder, Hargrove & Freeman, 2001), and geriatric medicine (Zeiss & Thompson, 2003) and other medical specialties that cut across the areas of practice represented in this edition of the Clinical Handbook of Health Psychology. Health psychologists find themselves as before practicing in an increasingly complex multidisciplinary environment and in unfamiliar clinical settings. This has led to examination of the current and potential contributions of psychologists to these areas and a delineation of the education and training needs of psychologists to equip them to work in these settings. While new opportunities are challenging, many health psychologists find the expansion and integration of behavioral health and medical care to be among the most exciting and rewarding aspects of this work.

Conclusion

Progress toward integrating a biopsychosocial paradigm in health care has been slow. The World Health Organization (WHO, 1997) has described the relationship between physical health and mental health services as often counterproductive and called for "a new alliance" between physical and mental health disciplines. In many ways, however, health psychology exemplifies the movement toward integrating psychological, social and biomedical knowledge.

The chapters which follow describe the health psychologist's participation in the patient's healing process. Each author provides a broad and rich view of the clinical practice of health psychology in their areas of practice within medicine. Each gives a brief introduction to the biomedical concepts basic to practice in the area. Each describes how the health psychologist might integrate behavioral and social science knowledge and methods in clinical practice. The chapters reflect the multidisciplinary context of the work of the health psychologist, the characteristic integration of treatment systems and modalities, and the psychologist's participation in healing relationships with patients. Four closing chapters discuss themes important to healing — social networks, spirituality, personal expression, and ethnic diversity.

Describing health psychology as involving a lifetime of learning, Miller (1987) emphasizes that it will be important for students of health psychology to have confidence in learning on their own. For most of us in health psychology, our careers started with the challenges of learning unfamiliar terms and protocols, developing relationships with professionals from diverse disciplines, and negotiating new environments outside the office setting. We struggled with the application of behavioral and social science knowledge in the context of rapid changes in medical technology and health care financing. For many of us, the continued learning is part of the appeal of clinical health psychology. For the reader, we offer the text in this spirit to provide a basis for and to capture the excitement of professional development in clinical health psychology.

References

American Psychological Association (1998). *Interprofessional health care services in primary care settings: Implications for the education and training of psychologists*. Washington, DC: American Psychological Association.

Antonovsky, A. (1979). *Health, stress, and coping*. San Francisco: Jossey-Bass.

Baum, A., & Posluszny, D.M. (1999). Health psychology: Mapping biobehavioral contributions to health and illness. *Annual Review of Psychology, 50*, 137–163.

Belar, C.D., & Deardorff, W.W. (1995). *Clinical health psychology in medical settings: A practitioner's guidebook*. Washington, DC: American Psychological Association.

Eisenberg, D., Kessler, R.C., Roster, C., Norlock, F.E., Calkins, D.R., & Delbanco, T.L. (1993). Unconventional medicine in the United States: Prevalence, costs, and patterns of use. *New England Journal of Medicine, 328*, 282–283.

Hall, G. (1904). *Health, growth and heredity*. New York: Teachers College Press.

James, H. (1922). *On vital reserves: The energies of men*. Cambridge: Harvard University Press.

McDaniel, S.H., Belar, C.D., Schroeder, C., Hargrove, D.S., & Freeman, E.L. (2002). A training curriculum for professional psychologists in primary care. *Professional Psychology: Research and Practice, 33*, 65–72.

Marwick, C. (1992). Alternative therapies study moves into new phase. *Journal of the American Medical Association, 268*, 3040.

Matarazzo, J.D. (1980). Behavioral health and behavioral medicine. *American Psychologist, 35*, 807–817.

Miller, N.E. (1987). Education for a lifetime of learning. In G. Stone, J. Matarazzo, N. Miller, J. Rodin, C. Belar, M. Follick , & J. Singer (Eds.), *Health psychology: A discipline and a profession*. Chicago: University of Chicago Press.

Millon, T. (1982). On the nature of clinical health psychology. In T. Millon, C.J. Green, & R.B. Meagher (Eds.), *Handbook of clinical health psychology*. New York: Plenum.

Schwartz, G.E., & Weiss, S.M. (1978). Behavioral medicine revisited: An amended definition. *Journal of Behavioral Medicine, 1*, 249–251.

Stone, G. (1987). The scope of health psychology. In G. Stone, J. Matarazzo, N. Miller, J. Rodin, C. Belar, M. Follick & J. Singer (Eds.), *Health psychology: A discipline and a profession*. Chicago: University of Chicago Press.

Tovian, S.M. (1991). Integration of clinical psychology into adult and pediatric oncology programs. In J.J. Sweet, R.H. Rozensky & S.M. Tovian (Eds.), *Handbook of clinical psychology in medical settings*. New York: Plenum.

Twillman, R.K. (2001). The role of psychologists in palliative care. *Journal of Pharmaceutical Care in Pain and Symptom Control, 9*, 79–83.

U.S. Department of Health and Human Services (1999). *Mental health: A report of the surgeon general*. Rockville, MD: U.S. Department of Health and Human Services, Substance Abuse and Mental Health Services Administration, Center for Mental Health Services, National Institutes of Health, National Institute of Mental Health.

Verhoef, M. (1990). Use of alternative medicine by patients attending a gastroenterology clinic. *Canadian Medical Association Journal, 142*, 121–125.

World Health Organization (1997). *The World Health Organization report: 1997*. Geneva: World Health Organization.

World Health Organization (2001). *World health report. Mental health: New understanding, new hope*. Geneva: World Health Organization.

Zeiss, A.M., & Thompson, D.G. (2003). Providing interdisciplinary geriatric team care: What does it really take? *Clinical Psychology: Science & Practice, 10*, 115–119.

Linda Van Egeren

Assessment Approaches in Health Psychology: Issues and Practical Considerations

The fundamental conceptual framework within health psychology is the biopsychosocial model (Belar & Deardorff, 1995; Smith & Nicassio, 1995). Engel (1977) in his landmark article described the limitations and inadequacies of the focus on biological processes and the exclusion of psychosocial factors in the traditional approach to medical care. He proposed the biopsychosocial model as an alternative. The biopsychosocial conceptual framework provides an integrated systems approach for the assessment of biological, psychological, and social factors that contribute to health and illness. This model assumes multifactorial, bi-directional, and indirect as well as direct causal mechanisms. Smith and Nicassio (1995) point out that the biopsychosocial model does not provide a unifying theory but rather a broad conceptual framework. Applying the biopsychosocial model to assessment means that health psychologists need to assess and utilize data across all three domains to provide a comprehensive understanding of the patient. Some of the assessment approaches and targets of assessment overlap with those familiar to mental health professionals. However, information related to the pathophysiology of medical diseases, medical procedures, the health care system, and the conceptual framework of health care providers are also essential elements of the assessment process and are unique to the medical setting (Smith & Nicassio, 1995). The challenge for the health psychologist is to truly integrate these different sources of information to provide an understanding of the interrelationship of biological, psychological, and environmental factors with the end result of increasing clinical utility.

In this chapter, I discuss issues and practical considerations in (a) conceptualizing the purpose of the assessment, (b) interviewing medical patients, (c) considering sociocultural issues in the assessment process, (d) the use of traditional assessment approaches with medical patients, and (e) the future of biopsychosocial assessment in health psychology. The intent of this chapter is to identify some organizing issues which are useful in guiding psychological assessment of medical patients. It is beyond the scope of this chapter to review specific assessment approaches in health psychology. Assessment strategies related to specific medical problems are detailed in chapters three through thirteen. The importance of assessing the social network of the patient will be discussed in chapter fourteen. Chapter fifteen introduces assessment issues concerning spirituality and religion. Chapter sixteen presents the emerging assessment possibilities of visual expression and imagery.

Purpose of the Assessment

The purpose for conducting an assessment focuses the content of the information being gathered and determines the selection of instruments and methods. The two most common purposes of psychological assessment are diagnosis and treatment planning. These two purposes are general functions of assessment shared with psychologists in mental health settings and have been identified by health psychologists as the two most frequent purposes for assessment (Stabler & Mesibov, 1984; Piotrowski & Lubin, 1990). In recent years, screening has become increasingly prevalent in medical settings and especially in primary care. Derogatis and Lynn (2000) note that screening is best described as a "preliminary filtering technique" that is designed to identify individuals in need of further evaluation. In addition to the function of assessment in diagnosis and treatment, the function of screening and its impact on the assessment process in health psychology will be discussed in this section.

Diagnosis

When the focus of assessment is diagnosis, typically this means diagnosis utilizing the *Diagnostic and Statistical Manual of Mental Disorders* (4th ed; DSM-IV; American Psychiatric Association, 1994). There has been widespread adoption by the mental health community in the United States of the DSM-IV as the diagnostic system for psychological disorders. Scientific journals and review boards for funding utilize DSM-IV categories (Follette & Hout, 1996). DSM-IV diagnoses are also widely used in clinical settings and are required for third-party reimbursement.

There are advantages to having a common system of classification which can be utilized for multiple purposes (e. g., treatment decisions, facilitating communication among professionals of different disciplines, administrative decisions). However, a number of problems have been noted with the DSM-IV system of diagnosis (see Follette, 1996). Regardless of your stance on the relative strengths and weaknesses of the DSM-IV, the DSM-IV is the classification system that is used in medical settings. The *International Classification of Diseases* (10th ed; ICD-10; World Health Organization, 1992) is the classification system used by physicians and is the system of classification for medical disorders that interfaces with the DSM-IV. Therefore, it is important to learn to use the DSM-IV system well and to be familiar with the ICD-10 system. I will discuss four diagnostic issues: the problem of tautological reasoning, limitations of the DSM-IV in conceptualizing problems from a biopsychosocial model, the problem of diagnostic categories that have pejorative connotations, and the limitations of a mental health nosological system when used in medical settings.

The problem of inferring causality to a diagnosis for the very symptoms that define the diagnostic category is an example of tautological reasoning. For instance, attributing a patient's angry outburst to the diagnosis of borderline personality disorder given that inappropriate anger was one of the symptoms that resulted in the diagnosis is tautological. The problem with tautological reasoning is that it gives an illusion of an explanation rather than a true understanding. The following example illustrates this point. A physician consulted with me regarding the diagnosis of a patient she had had a difficult interaction with during a medical appointment. The physician clearly wanted to understand this patient better so that she could work more effectively with her in the future. Instead of focusing on the issue of diagnosis, the consultation was focused on assessing the interaction with the patient and on developing a useful strategy for future visits.

Diagnoses that contribute to mind-body dualism are especially problematic from a biopsychosocial perspective. Mind-body dualism underlies referral requests for a psychological assessment of the functional etiology (as opposed to organic etiology) of the patient's physical symptoms. Toner (1994) has noted that "nearly every medical specialty has identified a functional somatic syndrome" (p. 157). The DSM-IV diagnostic category of *pain disorder associated with psychological factors* has replaced the earlier category of *psychogenic pain* and is a much-needed improvement. With this diagnostic category, it is possible to identify both psychosocial and medical factors as contributory to the pain. However, specific psychosocial factors and causal pathways are not identifiable with this system and therefore, limits its utility within a biopsychosocial framework.

Smith and Nicassio (1995) discussed the issue of psychiatric diagnosis from a biopsychosocial perspective. The authors argued that DSM-IV diagnostic categories such as *psychological factors affecting medical condition* are consistent with a biopsychosocial model. This diagnostic category identifies four possible pathways by which psychological factors can affect a medical condition. However, a limitation is the unidirectional causal linkage. For example, the diagnostic category of *psychological factors affecting medical condition* can be applied when anxiety and subsequent heightened arousal are conceptualized as contributory to irritable bowel syndrome. This diagnosis does not represent the reciprocal relationship between physiological and psychological factors for the patient who also experiences intense anxiety *because* of the irritable bowel syndrome. The authors note that the DSM-IV can be used to identify the effect of a medical condition on psychological functioning by utilizing the diagnostic category of *adjustment disorder* and identifying physical illness as a contributing factor (Smith & Nicassio, 1995). These examples illustrate that although it is possible to represent reciprocal causal linkages between psychosocial factors and medical conditions using the DSM-IV, the DSM-IV does not lend itself easily to a biopsychosocial conceptual framework.

The problem of some diagnoses having pejorative or moral connotations is not confined to the DSM-IV. Whether it is a DSM-IV diagnosis such as histrionic personality disorder or hypochondriasis, or a term used such as hysterical or somatization to label the patient's problem, the end result may be to contribute to the patient's fear that his or her physical symptoms are being trivialized or invalidated. This is also a gender issue in that women are more likely to receive such diagnoses and their symptoms are more likely to not be taken seriously by health care providers (Toner, 1994). While such psychiatric diagnoses can result in poor medical follow-up

and can contribute to a negative attitude toward the patient by medical and mental health care providers alike, such diagnoses can result in more appropriate medical follow-up (e. g., the avoidance of unnecessary medical diagnostic procedures) and in more satisfying interpersonal interactions with providers. The outcome should not be left to chance. It is important for the health psychologist to go beyond diagnoses and provide an empathic understanding of the patient and specific recommendations for health care providers. Working with health care providers to develop a collaborative plan which includes communicating to the patient that she or he is not being abandoned medically is an essential part of the assessment process when somatoform diagnoses are made.

When using the DSM-IV in the diagnosis of medical patients, it is important to recognize the limitations of this diagnostic system with a medical population. The DSM-IV was not designed to classify the wide range of psychological and behavioral problems that have been associated with medical disorders and physiological processes. It is not surprising that this classification system is inadequate in many important ways in the conceptualization of psychological problems experienced by medical patients. Problems such as emotional eating, nonadherence to a medical regimen, or a poor relationship with a health care provider are common targets for assessment by a health psychologist. To assign diagnoses to these problems when the patient has no significant psychopathology is not appropriate and should not be done.

Health care providers are increasingly providing mental health treatment to their medical patients. For instance, nonpsychiatric physicians write over 50 million antidepressant prescriptions whereas psychiatrists write about 33 million (as cited in Coyne, Thompson, Klinkman, & Nease, 2002). Yet, health care providers rarely use the DSM-IV to diagnose and to make decisions regarding treatment. DeGruy (1997) noted that the DSM-IV is too difficult to use for busy primary care providers and that it does not address the nature and type of emotional problems commonly seen in primary care. He noted that a major limitation of the DSM-IV is that there is no way to take into account the interplay between biomedical and psychological conditions and that this interplay may have important implications for treatment and management of these problems. DeGruy (1997) noted that depression in a patient who suffered a stroke is probably different in important ways from depression occurring without a chronic medical illness. DeGruy also noted that the DSM-IV does not describe mixed syndromes and subthreshold disorders that are very common in primary care and are often of great concern to primary care providers because of the functional impairment associated with these problems. There is a great need for a diagnostic system with clinical utility in primary care and other medical settings (Coyne, Thompson, Klinkman, & Nease, 2002; DeGruy, 1997). DeGruy (1997) mentioned that the ICD-10-PHC based on the ICD-10 and the DSM-IV-PC based on the DSM-IV are two promising systems in the process of development.

Selection of Treatment Interventions

A major purpose for diagnosis is to enhance treatment effectiveness by guiding the selection of interventions. The weak relationship between DSM-IV diagnoses and differential treatment outcome has been a major criticism of this classification system (Hayes, Wilson, Gifford, Follette & Strosahl, 1996; Koerner, Kohlenberg & Parker, 1996). Like diagnoses, assessment approaches can be evaluated in relation to their utility in contributing to the identification of effective treatments (Hayes, Nelson & Jarrett, 1987). In practice, clinicians do not always utilize assessment information to inform treatment, even when that was the original purpose of the assessment. If little of what is assessed affects decision making regarding treatment interventions, it is reasonable to question the value of the assessment and if the same general treatment approach is utilized regardless of the outcome of the assessment, then there

may be no reason to assess the patient at all. As there is increasing pressure for psychologists in medical settings to function efficiently, the treatment utility of assessments is likely to be an increasingly important issue. Another related and important purpose of assessment is to monitor treatment progress and assess treatment outcome. Outcome research regarding the effectiveness of psychological interventions with medical patients has not only increased knowledge in the field of health psychology but has also increased the credibility of health psychology with our medical colleagues and contributed to the growth in the number of health psychologists in medical settings.

A unique role of the health psychologist is to provide psychological assessment to improve the outcome of medical interventions. Health psychologists often are asked to evaluate medical patients prior to surgery (e. g., weight loss surgery, organ transplant) or other medical procedures (e. g., infertility treatment). An important purpose of these assessments is to identify psychological contraindications for the procedure. Another purpose of equal if not greater importance is to identify the need for psychological or other services prior to and/or after the medical intervention with the intention of improving the overall outcome for the patient. Such assessments require that the health psychologist has extensive understanding of the medical procedures involved, the associated coping issues, and the behavioral/cognitive demands of the medical regimen. In addition to assessing for severe psychopathology, active substance abuse, and significant cognitive deficits, these assessments usually include assessment of the patient's expectations, social support, and past compliance issues. A review of relevant research is needed to identify specific psychosocial predictors of outcome. For instance, depression may be a significant predictor of outcome for some medical procedures but not for others. There are often additional factors that are unique to the specific medical procedure that should be included in the assessment. For instance, it is important to assess for binge eating, a history of abuse, and eating habits that involve the consumption of high calorie beverages and sweet foods in evaluating patients for weight loss surgery because these factors can affect postsurgical outcome (Wadden, Sarwer, Womble, Foster, McGuckin, & Schmimmel, 2001).

Screening

Routine screening for mental health problems (e. g., depression, anxiety), substance abuse, health-related behaviors (e. g., smoking), and safety (e. g., domestic abuse, presence of firearms in the home) have increasingly become part of primary care. Screening may also be done in mental health settings (e. g., screening for sexual trauma) and in specialty medical settings (e. g., oncology, inpatient medical wards). Rather than screening all patients in a setting, subsets of patients may be screened only when a problem is suspected (e. g. cognitive screening of elderly individuals suspected of having a memory problem) or only with high-risk populations (e. g., screening for suicidal ideation in patients undergoing disfiguring cancer surgery). Health psychologists may be involved in assisting with the development and selection of screening instruments and procedures, and in educating and training medical staff in the screening procedure. Health psychologists may conduct the follow-up assessments of individuals who have screened positive and usually are responsible for providing any needed psychological treatments. It is important for health psychologists to be knowledgeable about psychometric properties of screening instruments, the empirical evidence regarding the effectiveness of screening, and the pragmatic issues involved in implementing screening procedures. Utilizing the example of screening for depression in primary care, I will briefly discuss some screening issues. The reader is referred to the reviews by Coyne, Thompson, Klinkman, and Nease (2002) and Derogatis and Lynn (2000), for more extensive information regarding screening in medical settings.

In selecting screening instruments, it is important to consider sensitivity (proportion of individual scoring above the cutoff score who have major depression), specificity (propor-

tion of individuals who do not have major depression and score below the cutoff), and positive predictive value (the probability that a person with a positive screen will have major depression). A frequently-used instrument for screening depression in primary care is the Center for Epidemiologic Studies Depression Scale (CES-D; Radloff, 1977) with sensitivity of 79.5%, selectivity of 71.1% and positive predictive value of 28.5% (as cited in Coyne et al., 2002). Summarizing the research on the psychometric properties of the CES-D, Coyne and colleagues (2002) noted that "the CES-D identified more than one in three patients as needing further evaluation, but less than one third of these were actually depressed, and 1 in 5 depressed patients would have been missed if a physician had relied exclusively on the screening to detect depression" (p. 800). Although the authors note that adjusting cutoffs and eliminating poor items may increase the performance of screening instruments, there are "inherent limitations" in using self-report screening instruments for depression.

When patients screen positive, they need to be assessed further and those who are found to have major depression are presumably treated or referred for mental health care. Research regarding treatment effectiveness indicate no or minimal short-term improvement in depression with no long-term benefit (Coyne et al., 2002). These results are often attributed to inadequate or under treatment by health care providers. However, the authors identified other likely contributing factors such as the patients' readiness to accept treatment or a referral for treatment, the likelihood that many of those screening positive do not need treatment in that they are only mildly depressed, and the over-reliance of medication as opposed to other options such as psychotherapy. Another issue to consider is the utilization of resources in following up false positives. Often this requires considerable professional time with no benefit to the patient. This is an especially important issue for health psychologists who may be involved in doing follow-up assessments of patients who have screened positive. It is also important to consider the impact of adding the demand of screening to the multiple competing demands of the primary care provider. In my experience, screening is often done poorly when there is no clear and obvious benefit either to the patient or the provider. This is not because providers are not dedicated professionals but rather the result of the understandable and pragmatic need to balance competing demands.

Interviewing Medical Patients

The clinical interview provides the foundation of the assessment process. Interviewing medical patients requires the same basic clinical skills needed in evaluating patients in any setting. Basic to all effective clinical interviews, the clinician must be able to empathize and develop rapport, gather relevant information, make adjustments as a function of process and patient characteristics, understand the importance of timing, and utilize a theoretical framework to guide the assessment process. This section will focus on interviewing issues that are especially important or are unique to working with medical patients. Table 1 provides a summary of common issues encountered in interviewing medical patients and associated strategies to address these issues during the referral process and assessment interview.

Settings and Accommodations of Physical Limitations

The setting in which the interview is being conducted has an impact upon the patient's perception of the interview and the health

Table 1. Strategies for addressing common issues in interviewing medical patients.

Issues	Strategies
Lack of privacy in inpatient setting	Inform ward staff of interview. Anticipate interruptions. Request visitors and roommate (if well enough) to temporarily leave room. Sit near patient and speak in a lowered voice if others are present. Acknowledge lack of privacy and assess patient's discomfort regarding the discussion of sensitive topics.
Physical limitations	Acknowledge physical limitations. Invite patients to let you know of their discomfort. Problem solve on how to help them be more comfortable during the interview. Accommodate patients by flexibility regarding the length (shorter), frequency, and scheduling (with other medical appointments) of sessions.
Sensory loss	*Hearing impaired:* Meet in a quiet room. Face patient when speaking. Speak distinctly, slowly, and only slightly louder. Use nonverbal cues and visual aids. When necessary, repeat words and phrases. *Visually impaired:* Meet in an adequately lit room. Sit near the patient. Written materials should be provided in large print.
The reticent patient	*Pre-Interview:* Educate referral source regarding your role and how to present the referral to the patient. Provide written materials regarding your role with medical patients. Be accessible for a brief meeting with the patient during a medical clinic visit. Participate on medical ward rounds. Meet jointly with patient and the patient's health care provider regarding the referral. *Interview:* Meet with the patient in a medical setting. Ask about patient's understanding as to the purpose of the referral. Clarify misunderstandings. Reassure patient of continued involvement by health care provider (assuming this is true). Normalize the reason for the assessment. Avoid behaving like a stereotypic mental health professional. Lighten the content of the interview. Use selective self-disclosure and respectful humor. Begin with problems that the patient is most receptive to discussing. Foster collaboration.
The somatically focused patient	The strategies suggested for the reticent patient are especially important. Initially focus on physical symptoms. Use medical terms and demonstrate an understanding of relevant medical problems. Listen to the patient's illness story. Elicit and negotiate the patient's health belief model. Use terms such as stress and quality of life. Take separate histories regarding the patient's physical problems and psychosocial issues.

psychologist's approach to the interview. Patients may be interviewed in a medical clinic, their hospital room, mental health clinic, private practice office, or in an emergency room. Patients who are requesting psychotherapy and perceive their problem as primarily psychological may be more comfortable being seen in a setting separate from their medical care. More typically, medical patients, for very understandable reasons, view their problems as primarily medical. Interviewing the patient in a medical setting in contrast to a mental health setting maintains the medical focus and therefore, is often more acceptable for the patient. The presence of a health psychologist in a medical setting especially when the psychologist is presented as part of the health care team communicates to patients that psychological concerns are relevant to health problems and that medical care includes addressing relevant psychosocial issues.

Patients may need to be interviewed in their hospital room or on a hospital ward. Often patients do not have private rooms. Belar and Deardorff (1995) stress the importance of attending to privacy. When the patient is not physically able to leave the hospital room, steps should be taken to increase the patient's privacy. For example, visitors and roommates who are well enough can be asked to leave the room for the duration of the interview. Visitors and roommates are usually very understanding of such requests. Prior to the interview, the psychologist should inform ward staff of the interview and request information regarding the patient's current medical status. Patients who are heavily sedated or are in intense pain will not be able to participate in an interview. Psychologists need to recognize that medical procedures take precedence over all other procedures and that the expectation is that the psychologist will work around interruptions and defer to medical procedures. If the patient needs to be interviewed while roommates or staff are present, sensitivity to privacy should be communicated to the patient. It is helpful to sit close to the patient, speak in a lowered voice, and assess the patient's discomfort about discussing sensitive concerns under these circumstances (Belar & Deardorff, 1995).

Flexibility in the length and number of assessment sessions is often necessary with patients who are in a great deal of physical discomfort, have cognitive impairments, or fatigue easily. Shorter more frequent appointments may be less exhausting and facilitate the patient's involvement in the assessment process. On the other hand, traveling for frequent appointments may also be difficult. A willingness to schedule sessions to coincide with other medical appointments can be helpful in reducing the disruption to the patient's life of numerous appointments. It is important to invite patients to generally let you know if they are in discomfort and problem solve about how to make the interview more comfortable or tolerable for them. Sensory loss has an impact on the patient's ability to communicate during an interview and is especially an issue with older patients (Patterson & Dupree, 1994). Such losses may not be initially apparent. With hearing-impaired patients, Patterson and Dupree (1994) recommend that the interviewer meet in a quiet room with minimal background noise, face the patient when speaking, and speak distinctly, slowly and only slightly louder. Using nonverbal cues, written and visual aids and when needed, repeating words and phrases are also helpful. With visually impaired patients, the authors recommend that the room be adequately lit, the interviewer sit near the patient, and that written materials be in large print.

The Reticent Patient

The patient's understanding of the purpose of the assessment and their feelings about the referral are important factors in the assessment process. One study (Hengeveld, Rooymans & Hermans, 1987) found that 41% of the patients had not been informed at all or had not been accurately informed as to the nature of the referral. The health care provider may perceive the health psychologist's professional role strictly from a mental health model and this will influence how the referral is presented to the patient. It can help to offer consultation to referral sources about strategies for presenting the referral to the patient. The health psychologist is likely to encounter patients who are reticent about a referral to a psychologist regardless of how it is presented. It is common for medical patients to never have had the experience of meeting with a psychologist. I have found it helpful to be available during medical visits to briefly meet the patient, introduce myself, explain my role in the clinic, and address any concerns the patient may have. It can also be helpful to meet jointly with the patient and the health care provider to discuss the referral. When I consulted to a cardiac surgical unit, I participated in weekly ward rounds in which the team introduced themselves to the patients. This brief contact was helpful in facilitating later referrals.

During the initial interview with a reticent patient, it is crucial that the following concepts are communicated to the patient. It is important that the patient understand that their health care provider will continue to be involved in the patient's care (assuming of course that this is true). It is equally important to normalize the contact with the psychologist in a way that makes sense to the patient. For some patients, it may be helpful to explicitly say that seeing a psychologist does not mean that she or he is crazy. Patients may also respond well to references to research findings, a discussion of the role of stress in medical disorders, or an everyday example which illustrates the relationship between psychosocial factors and health. It is important for the health psychologist to experiment with different strategies in order to identify those which are especially effective with their patient population. Last and probably most obvious, it is important that the health psychologist avoid behaving like a stereotypic mental health professional (e. g., focusing on emotional content, using psychological terminology, etc.). Many mental health professionals were trained to never disclose any information about themselves and to conduct the interview with a very serious demeanor (Turner & Hersen, 1994). Rapport with a reticent patient is more likely to be achieved by lightening up the interview.

The use of selective self-disclosure and respectful humor can facilitate familiarity between yourself and the patient and thus, help the patient feel more comfortable about seeing a psychologist. Patterson and Dupree (1994) noted that it is especially helpful with older patients to use a less formal approach such as sharing a common interest with the patient or offering a cup of tea while remaining respectful by using honorifics (e. g., Mrs. and Mr.) and requesting permission to interrupt in order to obtain needed information. It is important to stress that self-disclosure and well-timed humor are used sparingly for the purpose of enhancing rapport and should never be done in a way that invalidates the seriousness of the patient's problem (Turner & Hersen, 1994).

The Somatically Focused Patient

Patients who are somatically-focused can present a challenge in the assessment process. In addition to the methods for establishing rapport already discussed, it is important to initially focus on physical symptoms. Joining with the patient is facilitated by the health psychologist utilizing medical terms and generally demonstrating an understanding of the patient's medical problem and relevant medical procedures. McDaniel, Hepworth, and Doherty (1992) recommend listening carefully to the patient's "illness story" including experiences with the medical system. Patients are usually appreciative of the opportunity to be able to describe their experiences related to their physical symptoms and medical care. Belar and Deardorff (1995) recommend that the health psychologist "both elicit and negotiate the patient's health belief model" (p. 116). Is is helpful to focus on the patient's beliefs which are compatible with a biopsychosocial model (i. e., the common ground) and at the same time, communicate respect regarding the patient's beliefs that are incompatible with a biopsychosocial framework. The negotiating part which occurs later in the process involves looking for opportunities to present key biopsychosocial concepts in such a way that the patient can consider this alternative perspective given the patient's belief system and symptom experiences. In this way, the health psychologist and the patient begin to develop a compatible conceptualization of the nature of the patient's problem.

As the patient becomes more comfortable with the discussion, the health psychologist can proceed to assess psychosocial factors by using common, everyday terms such as stress and quality of life. Somatically-focused patients may be sensitive to the issue of possible psychosocial causes for their physical symptoms and therefore, may not want to acknowledge psychosocial concerns. Such patients, however, are usually willing to discuss the impact of their symptoms and health problems on their lives. They also may be more willing to acknowledge psychosocial stressors if the psychosocial history is taken separate from the history of the physical symptoms.

Case Example
A patient was referred for assessment of spells in which she felt dizzy, short of breath, sweaty, and generally out of control. She had had thorough cardiovascular and neurological evaluations with no abnormal findings. The patient was adamant that her spells were not related to any stressors in her life. However, when taking a separate history regarding her past relationships, she reported that she was dating a man who was controlling. She acknowledged that this disturbed her because she had been stalked years ago in another relationship and there were similarities between these two men although her current boyfriend was not physically or emotionally abusive toward her. The onset of this relationship coincided with the onset of her spells. It was difficult for her to consider a potential association between these two events because she minimized the significance of her emotional discomfort regarding this relationship. As her awareness of her discomfort increased, she was able to consider the possibility that her emotional reaction and her physical symptoms were related.

In summary, medical patients unlike mental health patients are less likely to accept psychological conceptualizations of their problems and more likely to question the involvement of a psychologist in their care. Rather than viewing the need to explain the psychologist's role to the patient as an obstacle in the assessment process, I view it as a valuable opportunity to begin to establish a collaborative relationship with the patient. Strategies can be helpful but it is the attitude of the health psychologist that will determine how the strategies are implemented. A collaborative, problem-solving attitude is the most important component of the assessment process.

Sociocultural Issues

Sociocultural factors influence patients' vulnerability to illness, their perception and interpretation of their symptoms, their help-seeking behaviors, and their relationship with health care professionals (Belar & Deardorff, 1995; Koss & Woodruff, 1991; Young & Zane, 1995). Most psychologists generally know it is important to understand the influence of the patient's social and cultural environment on the interviewing process, in the choice of assessment procedures, and in the interpretation of the assessment results. The reality is that these issues are highly complex and still poorly understood (Turner & Hersen, 1994). The incorporation of sociocultural factors into the assessment process is one of the major challenges of applying a biopsychosocial model. In this section, I will examine some implications of social and cultural issues for the assessment of medical patients. It is beyond the scope of this chapter to provide an extensive or comprehensive review of this important area. The purpose is to discuss selected issues as a way of generally illustrating the importance of sociocultural factors in the assessment process. Sociocultural issues discussed are ethnocultural factors, gender, ageism, and religion/spirituality.

Ethnocultural assessment biases can result in inappropriate diagnoses and treatment by (a) the pathologization of a culturally normative response or (b) the minimization of problems by assuming that they are consistent with cultural norms when in fact the behaviors are culturally deviant (Tanaka-Matsumi,

Seiden & Lam, 1996). It is just as important to recognize the differences in the degree of acculturation within a particular cultural group as is the differences between cultural groups. Tanaka-Matsumi and colleagues (1996) have provided an excellent conceptual framework for conducting a culturally sensitive cognitive behavioral interview. They recommend that acculturation be directly assessed using available acculturation scales and through the use of informants such as indigenous healers or mental health professionals from the patient's culture. The authors suggest the use of such instruments as the Racial Identity Attitude Scale for African Americans (Helms, 1986), the Suinn-Lew Asian Self-Identity Acculturation Scale (Suinn, Richard-Figueroa, Lew & Vigil, 1985), and the Multicultural Experience Inventory for Mexican Americans (Ramirez, 1984) for the assessment of acculturation.

Young and Zane (1995) have noted that ethnocultural disparities between the health care provider and the patient can result in inadequate assessment and nonadherence to medical regimens due to lack of self-disclosure on the part of the patient and cultural bias on the part of the health care provider. The authors also point out that when the culturally-influenced health belief system of the patient differs significantly from that of the health care provider, the practitioner's credibility with the patient may suffer and therefore, the patient may not adhere to treatment. The influence of cultural beliefs upon the patient's response to treatment recommendations is important to assess in understanding nonadherence problems.

Women and men inhabit a social world which includes different role expectations and these expectations influence their health experiences (Diamond & Levy, 1988). Women's caretaking role in the family contributes to stress and possibly somatization (Rodin & Ickovics, 1990). For some women, the only socially-acceptable way to be relieved of caretaking responsibilities is through incapacitating symptoms (Margolin & McIntyre-Kingsolver, 1988; Toner, 1994). Another part of women's social reality is that they are more likely than men to be subjected to domestic

abuse, sexual trauma, and sexual harassment (Rodin & Ickovics, 1990; Koss & Woodruff, 1991). These experiences have been associated with increased somatic symptoms in general and specifically, with gynecological problems such as chronic pelvic pain and gastrointestinal disorders such as irritable bowel syndrome (Koss & Heslet, 1992). Furthermore, women who have experienced physical or sexual trauma are more likely to seek help in a medical setting than in a mental health setting (Koss & Heslet, 1992). Health psychologists need to be aware of the importance of these social influences and assess the potential contribution of trauma to the health problems of their women patients.

Ageism can result in inadequate assessment of problems in older adults. The bias that treatable problems are due to aging, are inevitable, and are untreatable results in a self-fulfilling prophecy (Patterson & Dupree, 1994). Underdiagnosis of depression in older adults has been identified as a significant problem (La Rue & McCreary, 1991). This may be due in part to the tendency of older depressed patients to report somatic symptoms rather than emotional problems and to have more difficulty than younger individuals in describing their feelings, but it is also due to pessimistic attitudes on the part of practitioners regarding the likelihood and speed of change (Patterson & Dupree, 1994). Patterson and Dupree (1994) have argued that increased deficits in aged individuals and decreased competence (adaptive skills) result in the increased influence of environmental factors upon behaviors. Therefore, the authors stress the importance of assessing patient-environment interactions and focusing on assessment of factors with problem-solution potential when working with older adults.

Religion is a cultural factor that is not often discussed in relation to bias in assessment. Bias among mental health professionals and psychologists toward religion and beliefs about spirituality is an important issue and is especially relevant in working with medical patients (Larson & Milano, 1997). Religion and beliefs about spirituality are important aspects of most people's lives and yet often is not focused on in assessment. It has been my experience that religion or spirituality is rarely mentioned in psychological reports and when it is mentioned, it is usually in a negative context (e. g., psychotic religious delusions). Religion plays an important role in coping with chronic illness and death and dying (Zisook, Peterkin, Shuchter & Bardone, 1995; Larson & Milano, 1997). Religious beliefs are important coping resources that should be assessed in medical patients.

Use of Traditional Assessment Approaches in Health Psychology

In the following section, the use of traditional psychological assessment approaches with medical patients is examined. Surveys regarding the assessment practices of health psychologists (Piotrowski & Lubin, 1990; Stabler & Mesibov, 1984) indicated that the most frequently used instruments by health psychologists were those that measure psychopathology. These findings suggest the importance of examining the selection and use of traditional psychological instruments in the assessment of medical patients. Specifically, consideration of norms and base rates in the selection of instruments and the interpretation of results will be discussed.

Norms

Norms are important for interpreting an individual's response or score on standardized instruments by providing information regarding the individual's score relative to that of the normative group. Interpretations will vary as a function of the particular normative reference group that is utilized. There has been much debate about the use of traditional psychological assessment methods with medical patients because of concerns regarding the appropriateness of the norms (Turk & Kerns, 1985a; Bradley, McDonald-Haile & Jaworski, 1992). Derogatis, Fleming, Sudler, and DellaPietra (1995) have argued that the

appropriateness of the norm depends upon the question the clinician is asking. If the question is "how does this patient compare to patients with clinically-significant depression," then psychiatric norms are appropriate. Conversely, it has been argued that many of the symptoms of depression or other types of emotional dysfunction overlap with symptoms of chronic pain (Turk & Melzack, 1992), multiple sclerosis and Parkinson's disease (Rao, Huber & Bornstein, 1992), a variety of medical conditions seen in an inpatient setting (Clark, Cavanaugh & Gibbons, 1983), low back pain (Wesley, Gatchel, Polatin, Kinney & Mayer, 1991), and HIV (Kalichman, Sikkema & Somlai, 1995) which in turn results in overdiagnosis of psychopathology using instruments with psychiatric norms.

There are no simple answers to this dilemma. Derogatis and colleagues (1995) recommend the use of standardized instruments with psychiatric norms when the focus of the assessment is to determine the clinical significance of the patient's emotional distress. When the focus of the assessment is the patient's adjustment to illness, the authors suggest the use of instruments with relevant medical patient norms. Another approach is to develop normative samples for each specific group of medical patients (e. g., cancer patients, chronic pain patients, multiple sclerosis patients, etc.) for each measure of psychopathology. Derogatis and Spencer (1984) identified problems with this approach. They point out that it "is virtually impossible to develop a standardization sample that is representative concerning all the characteristics relevant to the attribute in question" (p. 2230). For instance, in cancer patients, the type of cancer, the stage of cancer, the prognosis, and the type and stage of treatment would all be relevant factors for stratification but would result in an unwieldy number of normative samples.

Data available regarding the use of an instrument with a specific group of medical patients can provide some guidance for interpreting scores (e. g., Clark et al., 1983; Wesley et al., 1991; Kalichman et al., 1995). However, typically for any specific medical disorder the number of studies is small and the data are not conclusive. Therefore, alterations in the interpretations based on such data should be done cautiously. A rational approach consisting of the deletion of specific items which overlap with symptoms of the patient's medical disorder and then recomputing the scores has some appeal. However, the problem with this approach is that the instrument is no longer standardized and it is likely to result in underdiagnosis. In deciding among options, it is important to consider the relative costs of underdiagnosis versus overdiagnosis.

Base Rates

Base rates of the assessment targets (e. g., psychopathology, behaviors) have important implications for the interpretation of testing results and clinical decision making. Base rates are the probability (expressed in percentages) of an event occurring. Different settings are likely to have different base rates. It is important to consider bases rates in the interpretation of test results. For instance, cutoffs for scale scores should be adjusted for the base rates of the particular setting (Finn & Kamphuis, 1995). There is also the issue of low base rates. There will be low positive predictive value, even with highly valid tests, when predicting low base rate events (Derogatis & Lynn, 2000).

Clinicians have subjective base rates which are developed over time as result of their experience with specific patient populations. Finn and Kamphuis (1995) note that a problem in clinical decision making occurs when clinicians develop their subjective bases rates in one setting and then apply them to another. This can happen when clinicians who were trained or have worked for a number of years in a mental health setting begin working in a medical setting. The base rates of serious psychopathology are very high in a mental health setting and by comparison, low in a medical setting. If the clinician does not readjust his or her subjective base rate, psychopathology will be overdiagnosed in the medical setting. It is important that health psychologists collect information regarding base rates for their particular setting and then consciously use this information in clinical decision making.

When encountering low base rate phenomenon, Finn and Kamphuis (1995) suggest using a debiasing strategy such as forcing yourself to think about alternative hypotheses regarding diagnoses and test interpretations. The authors gave the example of assessing a five year old with symptoms of a psychotic depression in an outpatient setting. The clinician had never before encountered a patient this young with these symptoms in this type of setting. The clinician did not accept his first impression and made himself think of alternative explanations for his findings. He sought consultation to explore other possible hypotheses. Through this process, it was identified that the child's symptoms were the result of an allergy medication overdose and drug interaction. This example demonstrates the value of seeking more supportive evidence than usual before arriving at a conclusion, when encountering low base rate phenomenon.

Biopsychosocial Assessment in Health Psychology

The biopsychosocial model allows for the identification of complex processes involving the interaction of biological, psychological, and social domains but the model does not prescribe the specific factors within each domain. The relevant factors will vary as a function of the health or illness issue and the characteristics of the patient. As a result, assessment methods in health psychology represent a considerable range of content areas and approaches. Although there is overlap across assessment methods utilized for different medical disorders and patient populations, Turk and Kerns (1985a) have noted that one trend in health psychology assessment has been to develop "high fidelity" approaches which focus on specific patient populations. In the remaining chapters of this book, valuable assessment approaches in relation to specific medical problems or specific content areas are presented.

It is important to recognize that much progress has been made in the development of instruments and assessment methods specifically for use with medical patients. However, the focus has been primarily on the assessment of intra-individual factors such as the physiological, affective, cognitive, and behavioral characteristics of the patient. One of the major challenges in implementing the biopsychosocial model is to incorporate family, social, and cultural factors into the assessment process. Kerns (1995) noted that health psychology as a field has been slow to recognize the role of families in conceptualizations of health and illness. The transactional cognitive behavioral model developed by Kerns and colleagues (Kerns & Weiss, 1994; Turk & Kerns, 1985b) holds considerable promise for the assessment of family functioning in relation to chronic illness. In subsequent chapters, issues related to the assessment of social networks and religion (i. e., two important sociocultural topics) will be presented. Although there has been progress in the assessment of family and sociocultural factors in health psychology, this continues to be a crucial area for further development in the implementation of the biopsychosocial model.

Another major challenge in implementing the biopsychosocial model is to develop assessment approaches that measure ongoing processes across all three domains. Computerized ambulatory monitoring which has the potential to provide simultaneous ongoing measurement of biological and psychosocial factors is a promising area of assessment in health psychology. With advances in computer technology and biotelemetry, ambulatory psychophysiological monitoring devices have been developed (Fahrenberg & Myrtek, 1996). For example, there are ambulatory devices to monitor transient ischemic states in patients with coronary heart disease (Kinne & Droste, 1996), blood pressure (Mussgay & Ruddel, 1996), and sleep-wake states (Tryon, 1991). Along with physiological responses, relevant ongoing psychosocial variables (e. g., moods, stressors, activities) can also be mon-

itored utilizing computerized devices (Van Egeren & Madarasmi, 1988; Perrez & Reicherts, 1996; Schandry & Leopold, 1996). Using palmtop computers, studies have been conducted on psychosocial factors and chronic low back pain (Jamison, Raymond, Levine, Slawsby, Nedeljkovic, Srdjan, & Katz, 2001), fibromyalgia (Affleck, Tennen, Urrows, Higgins, Abeles, Hall, Karoly, & Newton, 1998), and adolescent smoking (Whalen, Jamner, Henker, & Delfino, 2001). This is a new area of development that most health psychologists are only beginning to learn about.

We will continue to work toward the development of assessment approaches with empirically demonstrated psychometric properties and clinical utility that facilitate a conceptualization of health and illness from a biopsychosocial framework. As our knowledge base continues to expand and new assessment approaches continue to be developed, it will become increasingly challenging for health psychologists to maintain their knowledge and assessment skills. This challenge comes with considerable rewards and sources of satisfaction. The exciting and encouraging developments in the field of health psychology have provided intellectual stimulation for those of us in this field and additional options and ultimately, better care for medical patients who are the beneficiaries of these developments.

References

Affleck, G., Tennen, H., Urrows, S., Higgins, P., Abeles, M., Hall, C., Karoly, & Newton, C. (1998). Fibromyalgia and womens's pursuit of personal goals: A daily process analysis. *Health Psychology, 17,* 40–47.

American Psychiatric Association. (1994). *Diagnostic and statistical manual of mental disorders* (4th ed.). Washington, DC: Author.

Belar, C.D., & Deardorff, W.W. (1995). *Clinical health psychology in medical settings.* Washington, DC: American Psychological Association.

Bradley, L.A., McDonald-Haile, J., & Jaworski, T.M. (1992). Assessment of psychological status using interviews and self-report instruments. In D.C. Turk & R. Melzack (Eds.), *Hand-*

book of pain assessment (pp. 193–213). New York: Guilford.

Clark, D.C., Cavanaugh, S., & Gibbons, R.D. (1983). The core symptoms of depression in medical and psychiatric patients. *Journal of Nervous and Mental Disease, 171,* 705–713.

Coyne, J.C., Thompson, R., Klinkman, M.S., & Nease, D.E. (2002). Emotional disorders in primary care. *Journal of Consulting and Clinical Psychology, 70,* 798–809.

DeGruy, F.V. (1997). Mental healthcare in the primary care setting: A paradigm problem. *Families, Systems & Health, 15,* 3–26.

Derogatis, L.R., Fleming, M.P., Sudler, N.C., & DellaPietra, L. (1995). Psychological assessment. In P.M. Nicassio & T.W. Smith (Eds.), *Managing chronic illness: A biopsychosocial perspective* (pp. 59–116). Washington, DC: American Psychological Association.

Derogatis, L.R., & Spencer, P.M. (1984). Psychometric issues in the psychological assessment of the cancer patient. *Cancer, 53* (Suppl. 10), 2228–2232.

Derogatis, L.R., & Lynn, L.L. (2000). Screening and monitoring psychiatric disorder in primary care populations. In M.E. Maruish (Ed.), *Handbook of psychological assessment in primary care settings* (pp. 115–152). Mahwah, NJ: Lawrence Erlbaum.

Diamond, T., & Levy, J.A. (1988). Adulthood. In E.A. Blechman and K.D. Brownell (Eds.), *Handbook of behavioral medicine for women* (pp. 305–317). Elmsford, NY: Pergamon Press.

Engel, G.L. (1977). The need for a new medical model: A challenge to biomedicine. *Science, 196,* 129–136.

Fahrenberg, J., & Myrtek, M. (Eds.). (1996). *Ambulatory assessment: Computer-assisted psychological and psychophysiological methods in monitoring and field studies.* Kirkland, WA: Hogrefe & Huber.

Finn, S.E., & Kamphuis, J.H. (1995). In J.N. Butcher (Ed.), *Clinical personality assessment: Practical approaches* (pp. 224–235) New York: Oxford University Press.

Follette, W.C. (Ed.). (1996). Development of theoretically coherent alternatives to the DSM-IV [Special section]. *Journal of Consulting and Clinical Psychology, 64*(6).

Follette, W.C., & Hout, A.C. (1996). Models of scientific progress and the role of theory in taxonomy development: A case study of the DSM. *Journal of Consulting and Clinical Psychology, 64,* 1120–1132.

Hayes, S.C., Nelson, R.O., & Jarrett, R.B. (1987). The treatment utility of assessment: A functional approach to the evaluation of assessment quality. *American Psychologist, 42,* 963–974.

Hayes, S.C., Wilson, K.G., Gifford, E.V., Follette, V.M., & Strosahl, K. (1996). Experiential avoidance and behavioral disorders: A functional dimensional approach to diagnosis and treatment. *Journal of Consulting and Clinical Psychology, 64,* 1152–1168.

Helms, J.E. (1986). Expanding racial identity theory to cover the counseling process. *Journal of Counseling Psychology, 33,* 62–64.

Hengeveld, M.W., Rooymans, H.G.M., & Hermans, J. (1987). Assessment of patient-staff and intrastaff problems in psychiatric consultations. *General Hospital Psychiatry, 9,* 25–30.

Jamison, R., Raymond, S., Levine, J., Slawsby, E., Nedeljkovic, A., Srdjan, S., & Katz, N. (2001). Electronic diaries for monitoring chronic pain: One year validation study. *Pain, 91,* 277–285.

Kalichman, S.C., Sikkema, K.J., & Somlai, A. (1995). Assessing persons with human immunodeficiency (HIV) infection using the Beck Depression Inventory: Disease processes and other potential confounds. *Journal of Personality Assessment, 64,* 86–100.

Kerns, R.D. (1995). Family assessment and intervention. In P.M. Nicassio & T.W. Smith (Eds.), *Managing chronic illness: A biopsychosocial perspective* (pp. 207–244). Washington, DC: American Psychological Association.

Kerns, R.D., & Weiss, L. (1994). Family influences on the course of chronic illness: A cognitive-behavioral transactional model, *Annals of Behavioral Medicine, 16,* 116–121.

Kinne, G., & Droste, C. (1996). Psychophysiological monitoring of transient ischemic states in patients with coronary heart disease. In J. Fahrenberg and M. Myrtek (Eds.), *Ambulatory assessment: Computer-assisted psychological and psychophysiological methods in monitoring and field studies* (pp. 347–364). Seattle, WA: Hogrefe & Huber.

Koerner, K., Kohlenberg, R.J., & Parker, C.R. (1996). Diagnosis of personality disorder: A radical behavioral alternative. *Journal of Consulting and Clinical Psychology, 64,* 1169–1176.

Koss, M.P., & Heslet, L. (1992). Somatic consequences of violence against women. *Archives of Family Medicine, 1,* 53–59.

Koss, M.P., & Woodruff, W.J. (1991). Emerging issues in women's health. In J.J. Sweet, R.H. Rozensky & S.M. Tovian (Eds.), *Handbook of clinical psychology in medical settings* (pp. 201–222). New York: Plenum.

La Rue, A., & McCreary, C. (1991). Emerging issues in the care of the elderly. In J.J. Sweet, R.H. Rozensky & S.M. Tovian (Eds.), *Handbook of clinical psychology in medical settings* (pp. 223–248). New York: Plenum.

Larson, D.B., & Milano, M. (1997). Making the case for spiritual interventions in clinical practice. *Mind/Body Medicine, 2,* 20–30.

Margolin, G., & McIntyre-Kingsolver, K. (1988). Family relationships. In E.A. Blechman & K.D. Brownell (Eds.), *Handbook of behavioral medicine for women* (pp. 305–317). Elmsford, NY: Pergamon Press.

McDaniel, S.H., Hepworth, J., & Doherty, W.J. (1992). *Medical family therapy.* New York: Basic Books.

Mussgay, L., & Ruddel, H. (1996). Ambulatory blood pressure monitoring: Promises and limitations in behavioral medicine. In J. Fahrenberg & M. Myrtek (Eds.), *Ambulatory assessment: Computer-assisted psychological and psychophysiological methods in monitoring and field studies* (pp. 365–374). Seattle, WA: Hogrefe & Huber.

Nicassio, P.M., & Smith, T.W. (1995). Introduction. In P.M. Nicassio & T.W. Smith (Eds.), *Managing chronic illness: A biopsychosocial perspective* (pp. xiii–xxi). Washington, DC: American Psychological Association.

Patterson, R., & Dupree, L. (1994). Older adults. In M. Hersen & S. Turner (Eds.), *Diagnostic interviewing* (pp. 373–397). New York: Plenum.

Perrez, M., & Reicherts, M. (1996). A computer-assisted self-monitoring procedure for assessing stress-related behavior under real life conditions. In J. Fahrenberg & M. Myrtek (Eds.), *Ambulatory assessment: Computer-assisted psychological and psychophysiological methods in monitoring and field studies* (pp. 51–68). Seattle, WA: Hogrefe & Huber.

Piotrowski, C., & Lubin, B. (1990). Assessment practices of health psychologists: Survey of APA division 38 clinicians. *Professional Psychology: Research and Practice, 21,* 99–106.

Radloff, L.S. (1977). The CES-D scale: A self-report depression scale for research in the general population. *Applied Psychological Measurement, 1,* 385–401.

Ramirez, M. (1984). Assessing and understanding biculturalism-multiculturalism in Mexican American adults. In J.L. Martinez & R.H. Mendoza (Eds.), *Chicano psychology* (pp. 77–94). Orlando, FL: Academic Press.

Rao, S.M., Huber, S.J., & Bornstein, R.A. (1992). Emotional changes with multiple sclerosis and Parkinson's disease. *Journal of Consulting and Clinical Psychology, 60,* 369–378.

Rodin, J., & Ickovics, J.R. (1990). Women's health: Review and research agenda as we approach the 21st century. *American Psychologist, 45,* 1018–1034.

Schandry, R., & Leopold, C. (1996). Ambulatory assessment of self-monitored subjective and objective symptoms of diabetic patients. In J. Fahrenberg & M. Myrtek (Eds.), *Ambulatory assessment: Computer-assisted psychological and psychophysiological methods in monitoring and field studies* (pp. 393–402). Seattle, WA: Hogrefe & Huber.

Smith, T.W., & Nicassio, P.M. (1995). Psychological practice: Clinical application of the biopsychosocial model. In P.M. Nicassio & T.W. Smith (Eds.), *Managing chronic illness: A biopsychosocial perspective* (pp. 1–32). Washington, DC: American Psychological Association.

Stabler, B., & Mesibov, G.B. (1984). Role functions of pediatric and health psychologists in health care settings. *Professional Psychology: Research and Practice, 15,* 142–151.

Suinn, R.M., Richard-Figueroa, K., Lew, S., & Vigil, P. (1985). Career decisions and an acculturation scale. *Journal of Asian American Psychological Association, 10,* 20–28.

Tanaka-Matsumi, J., Seiden, D.Y., & Lam, K.N. (1996). The culturally informed functional assessment (CIFA) interview: A strategy for cross-cultural behavioral practice. *Cognitive and Behavioral Practice, 3,* 215–234.

Toner, B.B. (1994). Cognitive-behavioral treatment of functional somatic syndromes: Integrating gender issues. *Cognitive and Behavioral Practice, 1,* 157–178.

Tryon, W.W. (1991). *Activity measurement in psychology and medicine.* New York: Plenum.

Turk, D.C. & Kerns, R.D. (1985a). Assessment in health psychology: A cognitive-behavioral perspective. In P. Karoly (Ed.), *Measurement strategies in health psychology* (pp. 335–372). New York: Wiley.

Turk, D.C., & Kerns, R.D. (1985b). The family in health and illness. In D.C. Turk & R.D. Kerns (Eds.), *Health, illness, and families: A life-span perspective* (pp. 1–22). New York: Wiley Interscience.

Turk, D.C., & Melzack, R. (1992). The measurement of pain and the assessment of people experiencing pain. In D.C. Turk & R. Melzack (Eds.), *Handbook of pain assessment* (pp. 3–14). New York: Guilford.

Turner, S. & Hersen, M. (1994). The interviewing process. In M. Hersen & S. Turner (Eds.), *Diagnostic interviewing* (pp. 3–24). New York: Plenum.

Van Egeren, L.F., & Madarasmi, S. (1988). A computer-assisted diary (CAD) for ambulatory blood pressure monitoring. *American Journal of Hypertension, 1,* 179S–185S.

Wadden, T.A., Sarwer, D.B., Womble, L.G., Foster, G.D., McGuckin, B.G., & Schimmel, A. (2001). Psychosocial aspects of obesity and obesity surgery. *Surgical Clinics of North America, 81,* 1001–1024.

Wesley, A.L., Gatchel, R.J., Polatin, P.B., Kinney, R.K., & Mayer, T.G. (1991). Differentiation between somatic and cognitive/affective components in commonly used measurements of depression in patients with chronic low back pain—Let's not mix apples and oranges. *Spine, 16,* No. 6 Supplement, S213–S215.

Whalen, C., Jamner, I., Henker, B., & Delfino, R. (2001). Smoking and moods in adolescents with depressive and aggressive dispositions: Evidence from surveys and electronic diaries. *Health Psychology, 20,* 99–111.

World Health Organization. (1992). *International classification of diseases* (10th ed., clinical modification). Albany, NY: Author.

Young, K., & Zane, N. (1995). Ethnocultural influences in evaluation and management. In P.M. Nicassio & T.W. Smith (Eds.), *Managing chronic illness: A biopsychosocial perspective* (pp. 163–206). Washington, DC: American Psychological Association.

Zisook, S., Peterkin, J.J., Shuchter, S.R., & Bardone, A. (1995). In P.M. Nicassio & T.W. Smith (Eds.), *Managing chronic illness: A biopsychosocial perspective* (pp. 351–390). Washington, DC: American Psychological Association.

Section II
Physical Systems and Presenting Problems

Albert J. Bellg

3

Clinical Cardiac Psychology

Cardiac psychology is the study and application of psychological processes involved in the prevention and treatment of heart disease and in heart patients' adjustment to their illness and treatment. From a clinical perspective, there are three primary ways that psychological interventions can influence heart disease: 1) by facilitating health-promoting behavioral changes and adherence to recommended medical treatment; 2) by helping patients address illness-related issues and psychopathology; and 3) by having a direct effect on psychological factors and biological pathways influencing the onset and progress of disease. This last topic is especially promising, since few other areas in behavioral medicine have such a well-established association between psychological factors and physical disease.

The assumption that "cardiac psychology" is a subspecialty within health psychology is justified by the wide range of psychological theories, research, and clinical procedures that can be applied to cardiac patients. Although this chapter reviews the field of clinical cardiac psychology, space dictates that many details will be abbreviated or left out. A resource providing a more thorough treatment of the field and practice of cardiac psychology is *Heart and Mind: The Practice of Cardiac Psychology*, by Allan & Scheidt (1996a).

Biomedical Aspects

According to current estimates from the American Heart Association (2001a), slightly less than one in four Americans have some form of cardiovascular disease (CVD), the number one cause of death in the United States for every year since 1900, except 1918.[1] Nearly twice as many people die from CVD as from cancer, the second leading cause of death.

Four times as many heart attacks occur in men compared to women under age 65 (and *40 times* as many in men than women under age 45), primarily because of the protective effect of women's reproductive hormones. Overall, however, slightly more women than men die from all forms of CVD. The incidence of all forms of coronary heart disease (CHD) in women lags about 10 years behind that in men, and the incidence of acute events such as myocardial infarction (heart attack) and sudden death in women lags about 20 years behind that in men, although the gap narrows as men and women get older. For Americans under age 75, there is a higher proportion of CVD events due to coronary artery disease in men than in women, and a higher proportion of congestive heart failure (CHF) in women than in men.

There are also differences by race. The age-adjusted prevalence of CVD is 30.0% for white males and 23.8% for white females. In comparison with these base rates, the prevalence is 35.0% higher for African-American males and 4.0% lower for Mexican-American males than white males, and 66.4% higher for African-American females and 11.8% higher for Mexican-American females than white females.

There are three broad areas of biological

1 All disease-related statistics in this chapter are from the American Heart Association (2001a).

cardiovascular disease that a cardiac psychologist should be familiar with to successfully work with cardiology referrals and participate in a multidisciplinary treatment team for cardiac patients: 1) coronary artery disease (CAD); 2) heart failure; and 3) other forms of heart disease such as valvular disease and arrhythmias. The medical, psychological and neuropsychological consequences of stroke are usually addressed outside a cardiology practice, and will be briefly discussed here as CVD complications affecting cognitive function, adherence to treatment, and adjustment to illness. A concise source of information concerning CVD is *Cardiology* by Heger, Niemann, Roth, and Criley (1998). Additional information in the following section is from the American Heart Association (2001b) and Scheidt (1996).

Coronary Artery Disease

Coronary artery disease (CAD) is the atherosclerotic process that accounts for all but

about 1% of what is known as coronary heart disease (CHD) and about half of all deaths from CVD. CHD includes relatively rare syndromes such as cocaine-related spasm, endocarditis of the aortic valve, and congenital abnormalities. Although "coronary heart disease" is used in American Heart Association publications and in some of the research literature, "coronary artery disease" is more common in clinical settings and is the phrase of choice in this chapter. In similar fashion, it is useful to distinguish arteriosclerosis, which is a general term for the thickening and hardening of the arteries, from atherosclerosis, which comes from two Greek words meaning "paste" and "hardness." Atherosclerosis consists of hardened deposits (plaques) at specific locations on the inner lining of the arteries (the endothelium) that consist of fatty material, cholesterol, calcium, cellular waste products and fibrin, a clotting factor in the blood.

Why plaques occur is not well understood, although abnormalities and inflammation

Table 1. **Risk factors for atherosclerosis and related clinical syndromes: angina, MI, and sudden cardiac death.**

Unchangeable risk factors
- Increasing age
- Male gender
- Heredity

Changeable risk factors (per AHA)
- Smoking
- High overall or "bad" cholesterol (low density lipoprotein; LDL)
- Low "good" cholesterol (high density lipoprotein; HDL)
- Hypertension
- Diabetes mellitus
- Sedentary lifestyle
- Obesity 35% or more above ideal body weight
- Individual response to stress

Other changeable risk factors
- Pre-symptomatic atherosclerosis (per EBCT)
- Type A behavior, notably hostility
- Clinical depression
- Social isolation
- High triglycerides
- High blood viscosity

Adapted from American Heart Association (2001b) and Scheidt (1996).

of the endothelium, oxidative processes, and the effect of excess blood lipids on the lining of blood vessels are suspected. Risk factors for atherosclerosis are listed in Table 1. Risk factors toward the top of the list are generally better supported by research than those toward the bottom of the list.

The atherosclerotic process of CAD manifests as three progressively more severe clinical syndromes: angina pectoris, myocardial infarction, and sudden cardiac death. Less common presentations include silent ischemia, which is lack of blood to a portion of the heart muscle (the myocardium) without causing symptoms, and ischemic cardiomyopathy, where part of the heart becomes nonfunctional due to loss of blood flow (see Heart Failure below). The three major clinical syndromes are most likely to occur when there is a 70% or greater stenosis in at least one of the three main coronary vessels or their branches, although these syndromes can occur with less extensive blockage as well. The number of vessels involved is usually included in the characterization of the syndrome (e. g., "three-vessel disease").

CAD Clinical Syndromes

Angina pectoris. Ischemic pain results when there is insufficient blood flow and nutrients to muscle tissue. In the heart muscle, ischemia is called angina pectoris ("choking in the chest"). Ischemia is often described as chest "pain" or "pressure," and may be associated with a sensation of fullness. Physical activity or emotional arousal requiring increased blood flow can cause angina, or a temporary spasm of the coronary arteries may cause angina at rest. In some instances, angina can remain stable for years without much change in symptoms or acute events. Unstable angina may occur without provocation and can present with symptoms as severe as those of an MI, but does not result in permanent damage to the myocardium, although there is increased risk of acute events.

Myocardial infarction. An MI (heart attack) results when the blood flow is completely cut off following the formation of a blood clot (coronary thrombosis or occlusion) on the plaque's surface or when the plaque ruptures. A severe spasm can also cut off blood flow long enough for an MI to occur. The Framingham Heart Study found that 23% of initial MI's occurred in patients with a history of angina, and one in five MIs were silent or not identified by the patient from the presenting symptoms (Kannel & Feinleib, 1972).

Typical symptoms of a heart attack as outlined by the American Heart Association (2001b) include:
- Uncomfortable pressure, fullness, squeezing or pain in the center of the chest that lasts more than a few minutes, or goes away and comes back.
- Pain that spreads to the shoulders, neck or arms.
- Chest discomfort with lightheadedness, fainting, sweating, nausea, or shortness of breath.

Sudden cardiac death. The abrupt, unexpected loss of heart function can lead to sudden cardiac death (SCD). About half of all deaths from all types of heart disease occur suddenly. At least two major coronary arteries have atherosclerotic plaques in 90% of patients who have sudden death. The immediate cause of most sudden deaths, however, is ventricular tachycardia or ventricular fibrillation, a rapid or irregular heartbeat (American Heart Association, 2001b).

Diagnostic Procedures

Lab tests. Elevated cardiac enzymes, most notably creatine kinase (CK or CPK), and cardiac contractile proteins troponin T and I, indicate death of muscle tissue and are one of the first things examined when a patient is brought to the emergency room with a suspected MI. Serum electrolyte levels (potassium, calcium, and magnesium in particular) are also examined since abnormal levels may affect cardiac function and alter electrocardiogram readings.

Electrocardiogram (ECG). The ECG is a graphic representation of the electrical activity of the cardiac cycle or heartbeat. Alterations in ECG readings can assist in diagnosing a variety of heart disease, although an initial ECG may be non-diagnostic in 20-50% of cases of acute MI (McGuinnes, Begg & Semple, 1976). A Holter monitor is a portable ECG machine that can record heart activity during a patient's daily routine. This is usually done to assess for silent ischemia and arrhythmias.

Exercise stress test (EST). In patients with ischemic heart disease, coronary blood flow cannot increase to meet the heart's demand for oxygen. In an exercise stress test, patients are carefully monitored and given dynamic exercise up to a percentage of their age-predicted level of tolerance. Fatigue, dyspnea, tachycardia, angina, significant changes in BP, or ECG alterations may be indicative of ischemic heart disease. Women and patients with few or no cardiac risk factors have a higher likelihood of a false positive test.

Echocardiography. Echocardiography is a non-invasive procedure using ultrasound to provide moving images of cardiac structures. An "echo" can show cardiac valves, wall motion, flow-velocity patterns, and chamber dimensions and function. They are typically used in patients suspected of IHD, heart failure, valvular disease, and other cardiac diseases.

Nuclear imaging. A number of non-invasive imaging techniques using radioisotopes are used in cardiology. *Myocardial perfusion imaging* includes stress testing with thallium-201 or other radioisotopes that are absorbed by well-perfused areas of the myocardium; "cold spots" in the myocardium seen immediately following exercise but disappearing at rest indicate areas of decreased blood flow during exercise but adequate blood flow at rest. *Infarct avid imaging* uses an interaction between calcium and technetium pyrophosphate in damaged myocardial tissue to determine damage from an MI. *Radionuclide angiography* enables visualization of the atria and ventricles, calculation of ventricular ejection fractions, and identification of wall motion abnormalities and valvular disease. *Positron emission tomography (PET scans)* are also used to evaluate CAD and myocardium function and is especially helpful to assess for viable myocardial tissue. Computers are widely

used with all these techniques to refine and specify image data.

Magnetic resonance imaging (MRI) or nuclear magnetic resonance (NMR). Computer-generated MRI images can evaluate damage from an MI, diagnose some congenital heart defects, and evaluate disease of the larger blood vessels.

Cardiac catheterization. By passing a catheter through the femoral vein or artery, or through the brachial vessels, diagnostic information on a variety of heart functions can be obtained, including assessments of the coronary arteries, ventricular ejection fraction, myocardial wall motion, and valvular function. This procedure is relatively safe, with less than 1% morbidity (Hansing, 1979). Cardiac catheterization may also be used to biopsy transplanted hearts to test for rejection, and as an intervention for CAD (see below). From 1979 to 1999, the number of cardiac catheterizations has increased 355%.

Electron beam computed tomography (EBCT). "Ultra-fast" CT scans can rapidly produce an image of calcium deposits in the coronary arteries and have become increasingly popular for screening non-symptomatic men over age 40 and women over age 50 with no cardiac risk factors for CAD. Calcium deposits are highly correlated with atherosclerotic deposits, even at the early stages prior to any symptoms of CAD. For patients already diagnosed with CAD, however, EBCT provides no new information. EBCT and cardiac catheterization are the only tests (and EBCT is the only non-invasive test) that provides a pre-symptomatic early warning of CAD. However, the extent to which EBCT-identified calcium deposits are clinically significant and are associated with acute events and mortality remains controversial, with particular concern regarding patients who have a negative test yet develop symptoms of CAD within a year or two. Patients with a negative test and other changeable CAD risk factors may also erroneously use their negative EBCT results to avoid managing those risk factors.

Biomedical CAD Risk Factor Assessment and Treatment

In addition to performing the clinical tests for CVD noted above, the physician and other medical and technical staff can identify a variety of medical risk factors for CVD.

Dyslipidemias. Through the 1980's, it was unclear whether lowering total cholesterol (TC) would improve life expectancy. Since then, clinical trials of lipid-lowering medications have shown significant decreases in mortality for men with mildly to moderately elevated cholesterol (Shepherd, Cobbe & Ford, 1995) and in coronary events for post-MI patients with normal cholesterol (Sacks, Pfeffer, Moye, Rouleau, Rutherford, Cole, Brown, Warnica, Arnold, Wun, Davis & Braunwald, 1996).

Roughly half of all United States adults have total cholesterol (TC) above 200 mg/dl. So-called "good" cholesterol (high-density lipoprotein, or HDL) is considered normal at approximately 45 mg/dl for men and 55 mg/dl for women; each five-point reduction raises the risk of cardiac events by 10%. "Bad" cholesterol (low density lipoprotein, or LDL) is of concern when it exceeds 100 mg/dl for CAD patients, 130 mg/dl for those with multiple risks but no disease, and 160 mg/dl for those with no other risks. Another cause for concern is when the TC to HDL ratio exceeds 4 to 1. A variety of other lipid particles, including triglycerides (TG), have been implicated as risk factors for heart disease. Total cholesterol in women is higher on average than in men beginning about age 55.

A variety of medical treatments are available for lipid disorders. HMG CoA reductase inhibitors (the "statins"; e. g., pravastatin, simvastatin) are effective for reducing total cholesterol and LDL and are usually well tolerated. Some medications, notably the bile acid sequestrants and niacin, have significant side effects (e. g., flushing, paresthesias, nausea) that reduce patient tolerance and adherence. New formulations (such as time-release niacin) have an improved side effect profile and are better tolerated. Depressive symptoms have also been noted with highly reduced cholesterol (Schwartz & Ketterer, 1997). Behavioral treatments such as smoking cessation, exercise, and reduction in body weight and dietary fat are also recommended for management of dyslipidemias.

Hypertension (HTN). One in four American adults has high blood pressure (BP). Men are at greater risk of HTN than women until age 55; after age 74, women are at greater risk than men. However, HTN is 2 to 3 times more common in women taking oral contraceptives than in women not taking them. Blacks develop HTN earlier than whites, and have more severe HTN overall at any age. The overall death rate in 1999 from HTN in white males and females was 12.8 per 1000; for African-American males it was 46.8, and for African-American females it was 40.3.

Optimal BP is considered to be less than 130/85 mmHg (millimeters of mercury); hypertension is defined as a BP greater than or equal to 140/90 mmHg, and even mild HTN is associated with increased risk of CVD (JNC V, 1993). Lifestyle modifications for HTN (e. g., sodium restriction, weight reduction, and increased physical activity) are recommended for patients with any level of HTN as a first line of treatment. There is about a 1 mmHg decrease in both systolic and diastolic BP for each kilogram of weight lost (Blanchard, 1994). There is mixed evidence that smoking and caffeine use are associated with HTN. Antihypertensive drugs are administered if lifestyle modifications have not been successful at lowering BP sufficiently. The type of medication treatment depends on the constellation of risk factors and patient tolerance of side effects. Drugs usually tried first include diuretics, beta-blockers, calcium channel blockers, and ACE inhibitors; supplemental agents such as central alpha antagonists (e. g., Catapres, Aldomet), may also be used. Side effects may include metabolic disturbances such as dyslipidemias and glucose abnormalities, and quality of life effects such as fatigue, depression, insomnia and sexual dysfunction.

Insulin resistance syndrome (IRS). Also known as Syndrome X, IRS consists of three main elements: 1) significantly elevated serum insulin with normal or only slightly elevated glucose, indicating insulin resistance and impaired glucose metabolism; 2) normal TC, but low HDL and high triglycerides; and 3. abdominal obesity (Reaven, 1994). Serum insulin level is not routinely tested in cardiac patients, but IRS may be suspected if other characteristics are present. Patients with IRS have chest pain, normal angiograms, but abnormal exercise stress tests, which may be due to CAD in small cardiac vessels (microvascular angina) or spasms (Reaven, 1994; Poole-Wilson & Crake, 1989). Lifestyle modifications, such as increasing physical activity, lowering dietary fat, and reducing weight are recommended for treatment of IRS, partly because HTN may result from IRS, and HTN treatment with beta-blockers and thiazides can increase insulin resistance (Flack & Sowers, 1991).

Medical and Surgical Treatments

Medical treatment of angina. Angina is treated with three general classes of drugs: nitrates, beta-blockers, and calcium channel blockers. Nitrates (e. g., nitroglycerin, isosorbide) increase the supply of blood to the myocardium by decreasing the amount of work required by the left ventricle and by coronary vasodilation and improved collateral flow. Beta-adrenergic blocking agents (e. g., propranolol (Inderal), metoprolol (Lopressor)) block the action of catacholamines on the heart, reducing the amount of oxygen the heart requires by reducing heart rate and blood pressure, but also lowering myocardial contractility. Calcium channel blockers (e. g., nifedipine (Procardia), diltiazem (Cardizem)) can also reduce myocardial contractility and also inhibit coronary vasoconstriction. Percutaneous transluminal coronary angioplasty (PTCA) or coronary artery bypass graft surgery (CABG; see below) are often used to treat medically refractory angina.

Medical treatment of MI. The longer a coronary artery remains blocked, the more damage there is to the myocardium; fast response to an MI is critical. On reaching the emergency room, a clot-dissolving (thrombolytic) agent (e. g., streptokinase (SK), urokinase (UK), tis-

sue plasmogen activator (TPA)) is sometimes administered. Primary (direct) PTCA or emergency CABG surgery may immediately follow to also improve perfusion. Aspirin can reduce clotting mechanisms and stabilize plaques, reducing mortality and recurrence over the long term; short-term heparin use may help prevent reocclusion; long-term warfarin (Coumadin) use may reduce the chance of clots. Tissue recovery may be promoted by nitrates and beta-blockers; angiotensin-converting enzyme (ACE) inhibitors (e. g., captopril (Capoten), enalapril (Vasotec)) are vasodilators and also improve ventricular function. Follow-up treatment may also include PTCA or CABG surgery.

Percutaneous transluminal coronary angioplasty (PTCA). PTCA (balloon angioplasty) to dilate narrowed arteries is often used in patients with CAD. A guide wire is passed through the stenotic region of the coronary artery and a catheter with a narrow balloon on the end is threaded through the guide wire. The balloon is then inflated to compress the plaque and enlarge the lumen. Restenosis occurs in about 25% of patients within six months. Stents (mechanical devices to hold the lumen open), other catheterization procedures such as removing the plaque itself (atherectomy), anticoagulant medications (e. g., clopidogril bisulfate (Plavix)), and sometimes radiation are used to reduce the likelihood of restenosis.

Coronary artery bypass graft surgery (CABG). As previously noted, plaques almost always occur in well-defined locations. CABG surgery uses the patient's own saphenous vein to construct a pathway to bypass the stenosis. Multiple bypass grafts are typically constructed using one left internal mammary artery (LIMA) and several saphenous vein grafts (SVGs) as needed from the upper or lower leg. A recent variation on traditional CABG procedure is the minimally invasive coronary artery bypass (Mid CAB), which involves entering between the ribs instead of cutting the sternum and is a less physically stressful surgical procedure. Some CABG procedures are associated with increased risk of stroke.

CABG surgery undoubtedly relieves angina pain and improves exercise tolerance. It is less clear whether there is a significant increase in lifespan for CABG patients over those treated medically, although some subgroups such as patients with three vessel disease and left main disease do appear to live longer (Myers, Blackstone, Davis, Foster & Kaiser, 1999; Chaitman, Ryan, Kronmal, Foster et al., 1990)

Trans-myocardial laser revascularization (TMLR). This new procedure uses a laser to punch holes in areas of the myocardium which have been ischemically impaired. The myocardium is then perfused with blood directly from the inner chamber of the heart. TMLR is currently under investigation as an alternative treatment for patients with angina that is unable to be medically treated.

Heart Failure and Transplant

Heart failure results when the heart is damaged or overworked. *Congestive heart failure (CHF)* is the most common presentation, occurring in about 4,790,000 Americans and resulting in 50,824 deaths in 1999, an increase of almost 22% since 1993. It occurs when the heart is unable to pump efficiently. Blood returning to the heart backs up in the lungs and veins, causing shortness of breath (dyspnea) on exertion, swelling (edema), and inability to lie down (orthopnea). In CHF, the kidneys are no longer as efficient in removing sodium and water from the body, which aggravates the condition further. The New York Heart Association Functional Classification of heart failure is in Table 2.

Cardiomyopathy refers to a variety of diseases of the heart muscle. It occurs in over 3,000,000 Americans and was responsible for 27,260 deaths in 1999. Cardiomyopathy may be caused by ischemic heart disease, MI, congenital defects, hypertension, valvular disease, chronic alcohol use, or pulmonary hypertension. *Dilated cardiomyopathy* refers to an enlargement and weakening of the heart. *Hypertrophic cardiomyopathy* refers to a thickening of the left ventricle and the resulting dysfunction.

The area of the heart affected by cardiomyopathy or CHF will determine the symptoms reported. The right side of the heart leads to the lungs; right-sided heart failure results in fluid retention, edema, and dyspnea on exertion. The left side of the heart leads to the rest of the body; left-sided heart failure is associated with higher mortality than right-sided, and tends to produce pulmonary vascular congestion, dyspnea, orthopnea, and physical fatigue.

Diagnostic Procedures

Heart failure is usually diagnosed with assessment of physical symptoms, exercise stress test, echocardiogram, electrocardiogram, and chest x-ray. Of particular concern is identification of the functional classification of CHF, its anatomical classification, and precipitating cause. One key element is the ejection fraction (EF), or how much of the blood in the heart is expelled by the heart's contraction. A normal EF is 55–65%; heart transplant is usually considered in patients with an EF of 25% or lower and other clinical prognostic factors.

Table 2. **New York Heart Association (NYHA) functional classification in patients with heart failure.**

Class I:	No symptoms with ordinary activity, no limitations on activity.
Class II:	Slight to moderate symptoms with normal activity, slight limitation of activity; patient is comfortable at rest.
Class III:	Moderate symptoms with less than normal activity, marked limitation of activity.
Class IV:	Inability to carry on any physical activity without discomfort; symptoms may occur at rest.

Medical and Surgical Treatment

Medical treatment. If specific causes of CHF (e. g., hypertension, abnormal valves, etc) can be identified, their treatment may result in improvement of the CHF. Non-pharmacologic treatments such as salt and fluid restriction, and changes in physical activity level, may be sufficient for non-symptomatic Class I heart failure. Pharmacologic therapy for symptomatic CHF generally takes three forms: ACE inhibitors, diuretics (e. g., furosemide (Lasix)) which reduce the body's salt and fluid load, and inotropic agents (e. g., dopamine, dobutamine, amrinone, milrinone, digoxin (Lanoxin)), which improve the heart's pumping action. Vasodilators such as ACE inhibitors dilate blood vessels and decrease the blood pressure, reducing the effort required by the heart. Recent studies have also shown benefits from beta-blockers. Some of these medications cannot be administered adequately at home, and may require the patient to visit an infusion clinic at a hospital several times a week for four to eight hours.

Heart transplantation. A heart transplant may be considered when the myocardium is irreversibly and seriously damaged from cardiomyopathy, does not respond adequately to medical treatment, is unlikely to benefit from a bypass operation, and puts the patient at risk of dying. A total of 2,198 heart transplants were performed in the United States in 2000. However, 40,000 patients under the age of 65 (the usual cut-off age) could benefit from a transplant each year. The one-year survival rate for heart transplant is 84%, the three-year rate is 77%, and 69% of transplant patients survive for five years. Transplant patients typically must take eight to 12 medications per day for the rest of their lives to reduce the likelihood of rejection of the transplanted heart, combat infection, and control blood pressure. Many of these (see Table 5) may have significant effects on mood and mental status.

An alternative to transplantation currently under investigation for some cardiomyopathy patients is ventricular reduction surgery. Also, a left ventricular assist device (LVAD) can be used to temporarily assist ventricular function while a patient is waiting for a heart, and may in some cases be placed in patients who are not eligible for transplantation. Although this mechanical pump requires 24 hour monitoring, it may permit patients to leave the hospital and resume many of their normal activities.

Other Heart Disease

Valvular Disease

There are about 97,000 hospitalizations per year for valvular disease, nearly all for aortic or mitral valve disorders. Aortic valve disorders have about four times the mortality of mitral valve disorders. Valvular problems often cause dyspnea, fatigue or chest pain. They almost always produce additional heart sounds such as snaps or clicks, alteration in the intensity or timing of heart sounds, or heart murmurs resulting from turbulence caused by malformed valves.

Key types include aortic and mitral stenosis, aortic and mitral regurgitation (of which mitral valve prolapse is a common type and often associated with anxiety disorders), pulmonary valve disease, and tricuspid valve disease. Causes of valvular disease include infections such as rheumatic fever and congenital disorders of the valves. Medical intervention includes digoxin and inotropic medications. Surgical interventions involve valve replacement (with both porcine and mechanical valves) and surgically reconstructing the valve structure.

Arrhythmias

The electrical impulse that produces a heartbeat begins in the sinoatrial (SA or sinus) node of the heart. The impulse is transmitted to the atrial and ventricular muscle cells with precise timing, but can sometimes become disordered by: 1) abnormal electrolytes such as potassium, magnesium, and calcium; 2) addictive substances such as alcohol, nicotine, and recreational drugs; 3) medications such as digoxin and theophylline; and 4) other causes.

About 4.5 million Americans have arrhythmias, or irregular heartbeats, with 39,262 dying in 1999 of directly related problems. However, the great majority of the approximately 250,000 sudden cardiac deaths each year are also attributed to a type of arrhythmia, ventricular fibrillation. Bradycardia refers to a heart rate of less than 60 beats per minute; tachycardia refers to a heart rate of more than 100 per minute. Transient arrhythmias may not be picked up by a short-term ECG and may require a 24-hour or longer assessment with a Holter monitor.

Key types of arrhythmias include sinus arrhythmia, premature atrial contractions (PACs), premature ventricular contractions (PVCs), and atrial fibrillation. Atrial fibrillation is treated with electrical (and sometimes chemical) cardioversion to restore a normal heartbeat. Arrhythmias may be managed by medical therapy, or by a variety of implanted electrical cardiac pacemakers.

Pericardial Disease

The pericardium consists of a loose fibrous membrane covering the myocardium and a dense sac surrounding the heart that is filled with fluid and supports the heart within the chest. Pericardial disease most commonly results from infection, and symptoms can mimic an MI or CHF.

Endocarditis

Bacterial endocarditis results when an infection in the bloodstream begins to grow on valves of the heart. There are about 17,000 hospitalizations per year for endocarditis. Bacteria may enter the bloodstream during dental, gastrointestinal or urological procedures. The infection may grow for weeks or months before endocarditis is detected, and patients usually report symptoms of fever and fatigue. Treatment requires long-term high-dose antibiotics, and surgery is often necessary despite antibiotic therapy.

Aortic Aneurysms

About 63,000 hospitalizations per year occur for aortic aneurysms, with over a quarter of these cases resulting in death. An aneurysm is a ballooning (or pouching out) of the wall of a vein, artery, or part of the heart due to disease, injury or congenital abnormality. An aneurysm is especially critical in the aorta, which carries blood from the heart to the rest of the body. Treatment usually addresses high blood pressure and surgical patch of the weakened part of the artery.

Stroke

Stroke may be a complication of an MI, CABG surgery or surgery to remove plaques in the carotid arteries (endarterectomy), peripheral vascular disease, and other cardiac problems. A *cerebral thrombosis* or *embolism* is caused by a clot that blocks blood flow to the brain, and often results in the permanent death of brain tissue and loss of function. A *transient ischemic attack (TIA)* is a "mini" stroke that has minimal or transient effect on brain function. A *subarachnoid* or *cerebral hemorrhage* is caused by a burst blood vessel or aneurysm and may have more transient effects, since once the pressure on the brain is relieved, brain function may return.

Symptoms of stroke that may affect quality of life and functional ability are similar to the warning signs of stroke as outlined by the American Heart Association (2001b), which include:

- Sudden weakness or numbness of the face, arm, or leg on one side of the body.
- Sudden dimness or loss of vision, particularly in one eye.
- Loss of speech, or trouble talking or understanding speech.
- Sudden, severe headaches with no known cause.
- Unexplained dizziness, unsteadiness, or sudden falls.

Psychological Assessment and Treatment

Common Referral Questions

In a cardiology practice or preventive cardiology clinic, the standard psychological referral questions concern: 1) prevention associated with behavioral cardiovascular risk factors such as smoking, eating habits, and exercise; 2) adherence to medical treatment and cardiac rehabilitation; and 3) psychopathology and coping difficulties. Other specific referral questions may be noted by the physician, nurse practitioner, nutritionist or other health professional who sees the patient.

Referrals for Primary, Secondary and Tertiary Prevention

The perception of benefits, barriers and motivation affecting the patient's seeking and adhering to treatment and making healthy behavioral changes differs for primary, secondary, and tertiary prevention patients. For primary prevention patients, long-term lifestyle or medication control of risk factors (e. g., dyslipidemia) takes place in the absence of disease symptoms. Such patients frequently feel less urgency to address their risk factors, and are at higher risk of nonadherence to preventive medical treatment. Secondary prevention cardiology patients are symptomatic (e. g., with angina) without having had an acute event. Tertiary patients have diagnosed disease (e. g., cardiomyopathy) or have had an acute event (e. g., an MI). Although both secondary and tertiary prevention patients may have more initial motivation to engage in preventive treatment, successful long-term adherence to medication and a healthy lifestyle often depends on other psychological and behavioral factors.

Clinicians who follow a stages of change approach to behavioral change (Prochaska, Redding & Evers, 1997) need to make referral sources aware of the goals of stages of change intervention. Moving patients to a higher stage (e. g., precontemplation to contemplation) may temporarily be the only attainable goal for some patients. Since referring physicians may be expecting a more concrete behavioral outcome, however, they need to be informed of the patient's progress and the rationale for a stages of change intervention.

Referrals for Treatment Adherence

Adherence to treatment is a common concern and source of referrals in cardiology and preventive cardiology. However, although physicians will identify and refer patients for the most obvious cases of non-adherence, they can generally predict their patients' ad-

herence to treatment no better than chance (Roth & Caran, 1978), and frequently are not aware of factors in their patients' lives and experiences with medical caregivers that influence adherence. It is therefore necessary to keep adherence as an issue in any patient referral. Furthermore, although adherence to treatment is important in all areas of medical care, it is absolutely critical for two groups of cardiology patients: preventive cardiology patients, and heart failure patients, particularly those who are post-transplant.

In preventive cardiology patients, sustained long-term change to control risk factors is the only medically meaningful behavioral outcome. Short-term adherence to lifestyle changes or medication to manage chronic risk factors is essentially a failure of treatment. Similarly, in CHF patients a strict regimen of dietary and fluid restrictions and medication maintenance is necessary to control the progression of disease. Furthermore, successful adherence to a pre-transplant medical regimen is a prerequisite for heart transplant, since post-transplant patients are asked to maintain essentially perfect adherence to a complex treatment and monitoring regimen for the rest of their lives. Approaches to addressing long-term adherence is discussed later in this chapter.

Referrals for Psychopathology and Coping

Heart patients are generally good at hiding their poor adjustment to their illness. Heart patients tend to be older, and include more males than the traditional psychotherapy population. Both factors are associated with minimization of illness difficulties and resistance to recommendations for psychological services (Rybarczyk, 1994). Their resistance is aggravated by the lack of self-selection for psychological treatment.

For a successful referral for coping issues or psychopathology to occur with such patients, it is necessary to have the support of the referring physician. It is best for the physician to be forthright in explaining the reasons for the referral to the patient. In doing so, the physician may benefit from coaching by the psychologist to characterize psychological services accurately and non-threateningly, to underscore that psychological evaluation is both routine and necessary to provide the best medical care, and to deal with the patient's initial resistance (Bellg, 1993). Having the physician personally introduce the psychologist to the patient reinforces the physician's support for psychological services as part of the patient's medical care.

Assessment

Communication of findings and recommendations among members of a multidisciplinary treatment team is a key part of the process in caring for heart patients. The perspectives and language of cardiologists, nutritionists, exercise physiologists, and even consulting psychiatrists is significantly different than that of psychologists. It is therefore necessary for psychologist to develop familiarity with the treatment team's language and goals for patients. Furthermore, a psychological clinical interview often generates additional information that the treatment team may be unaware of, such as personal history or personally sensitive treatment side effects (e. g., sexual dysfunction), which needs to be communicated in the context of the broader goals for care of the patient. It is therefore helpful for the psychologist to be aware of the needs and language of the treatment team and the referring physician in case presentations, reports and chart notes.

General Cardiac Psychology Assessment

Screening questionnaires. Questionnaires may be useful to evaluate psychopathology symptoms, physical symptoms and functional ability, current life stressors, motivational style, perceived social support, or other areas of interest to the clinician. For sensitive issues such as substance abuse, patients are less likely to provide accurate information on a questionnaire and such issues are better explored in an interview.

Given the likely initial resistance of heart patients to psychology, the questionnaire burden is kept relatively low. The MMPI-2 and other extensive or too overtly "psychological" questionnaires that may evoke patient resistance are not administered for this reason. The two-page screening questionnaires we currently use begin with demographic information and an informal checklist of psychological symptoms, behavioral risk factors and life stressors. Checklist items are explored further in the interview and also provide a rough estimate of questionnaire self-report accuracy when compared with interview data. On the second page, patients fill out the 14-item Hospital Anxiety and Depression Scale (HADS; Zigmond & Snaith, 1983) to identify possible anxiety and depression, an 8-item social support scale adapted from the Interpersonal Support Evaluation List (ISEL; Cohen & Hoberman, 1983) to identify the perceived availability of emotional and tangible support relevant to the patient's illness or medical care, and two questions addressing previous treatment for mental health problems or for alcohol or drug use.

Other options that clinicians may wish to consider include the Brief Symptom Inventory (BSI; Derogatis, 1993), with 53 items in 10 subscales, as an overall screen for psychopathology; the Center for Epidemiological Studies Depression Scale (CESD; Radloff, 1977), slightly modified to a single page format (this may be preferable to the Beck Depression Inventory (BDI; Beck, 1972) in medical patients since it relies less on vegetative symptoms to assess depression); or the RAND 36-Item Health Survey Short Form (SF-36; Ware & Sherbourne, 1992) as a measure of patient functioning and quality of life in a variety of areas. Behavioral assessment questionnaires for specific behaviors (e. g., daily food records, exercise diaries) may also be helpful if the psychologist does not have the benefit of working with other professionals in these areas. Questionnaires and subscales are listed in Table 3.

Clinical interview outline. At our clinic, the interview with the psychologist generally follows evaluation by the nutritionist, exercise physiologist, and physician. Prior to the interview, the psychologist is briefed by the other professionals on their encounters with and recommendations for the patient. Ideally, the psychologist has information from the ques-

---

Table 3. **Suggested screening and evaluation instruments for heart patients.**

Screening Questionnaires
Demographic Information
Checklist of Psychological Symptoms, Risk Factor Behaviors and Life Stressors
Hospital Anxiety and Depression Scale (HADS, 14 items; Zigmond & Snaith, 1983)
Interpersonal Support Evaluation List (ISEL, 8 items; Cohen & Hoberman, 1983)

Other Questionnaires
Brief Symptom Inventory (BSI, 53 items; Derogatis, 1993)
Subscales: Depression, Interpersonal sensitivity, Anxiety, Phobic anxiety, Hostility,
Paranoid ideation, Somatization, Psychoticism, Obsessive-Compulsive, Other items
Center for Epidemiology Studies Depression Scale (CESD, 20 items; Radloff, 1977)
RAND 36-Item Health Survey Short Form (SF-36, 36 items; Ware & Sherbourne, 1992)
Subscales: Physical functioning, Role function affected by physical symptoms, Role
function affected by emotional symptoms, Social functioning, Pain, General health,
Health change, Energy/fatigue, Emotional well-being

Cognitive Assessment During Clinical Interview
Neurobehavioral Cognitive Status Exam (NCSE; Northern California Neurobehavioral Group,
1988)
Modified Mini-Mental State Examination (3MS; Teng & Chui, 1987)

---

tionnaires and the three other professionals prior to seeing the patient. In practice, the psychological interview often begins with less information than this.

Keeping in mind the need for long-term behavioral and psychological risk factor management, the interview needs to lay the foundation for a potential long-term (though perhaps intermittent) relationship with the patient. Discussion of the patient's reaction and adjustment to their illness and treatment is generally the entry point to the interview, and provides a context for developing empathy and rapport. Topics raised by the patient are pursued in depth, and additional topics are covered to complete the assessment. Interview topics include:

• Patient reaction and adjustment to illness and treatment, and the patient's perceptions of their caregivers.

• Treatment side effects and adherence, health-related lifestyle issues, health beliefs (e. g., benefits, barriers) regarding medication and lifestyle recommendations.

• Stage of change and motivation for risk factor modification.

• Coping style and resources such as social support, spiritual beliefs or practices, recreational activities.

• Accuracy of patient understanding of other health care professionals' recommendations.

• Symptoms of psychopathology.

• Substance use and dependence (alcohol, drugs, nicotine).

• Mental status and cognitive functioning.

Both anxiety and depression are common in heart patients, and depression may be found in 18 to 44 percent of cardiac patients over the course of their disease (Fernandez, 1993). Symptoms of psychopathology also may be atypical in these patients. Major depression manifesting as irritability or anger outbursts is more common than the average, as are anxiety disorders masked by legitimate illness concerns. Vegetative symptoms of depression must also be distinguished from illness symptoms or medication side effects. Psychiatric consultation with a psychiatrist familiar with heart patients and their medications and illness symptoms should be readily available if necessary.

Cognitive status may have been influenced by anoxia or an embolism, or more subtly by a TIA. A formal cognitive status screening exam is conducted with most secondary and tertiary prevention patients unless successful engagement in challenging life activities and patient report clearly indicates no functional impairment. Either the Neurobehavioral Cognitive Status Examination (NCSE; Northern California Neurobehavioral Group, 1988) or the Modified Mini-Mental State Exam (3MSE, an improvement on the commonly used Folstein Mini-Mental State Exam; Teng & Chui, 1987) may be used to screen for moderate or gross impairment of cognitive function. Neuropsychological evaluation may be appropriate for patients with more severe deficits.

Heart Transplant Assessment

In addition to a standard evaluation, potential heart transplant candidates require a more detailed assessment of factors that may affect their ability to take care of a new heart.

- History of adherence to medical treatment and tolerance of medication side effects.
- History of adherence to recommended lifestyle behavior changes. For instance, transplant patients often have difficulty controlling their weight following restoration of energy and return of appetite, which increases their medical risks.
- Patient attitudes toward medical caregivers, including trust and issues related to authority.
- Willingness and ability to change behaviors associated with substance abuse and dependence. Transplant programs typically require a person to be abstinent from questionable substances for at least six months to qualify for a transplant.
- Availability and capability of the patient's spouse, family, or companion to make a long term commitment to provide emotional and tangible support for the tasks associated with transplant (e.g., medication adherence, transportation to clinic).
- Ability to cope with major life changes.

Commonly agreed upon contraindications to transplantation include active suicidal ideation, current drug or alcohol use, acute psychosis, irreversible brain damage, and chronic non-adherence to treatment (Levinson & Olbrisch, 1993; Mai, 1993; Frierson & Lippman, 1987). Personality disorders generally do not rule out transplantation unless there is behavioral evidence that they affect the patient's ability to participate and engage successfully in their medical care. Poor treatment adherence is particularly important, and is responsible for a significant percentage of transplant rejections and up to 25% of deaths following the post-operative period (Dew, Roth, Thompson et al., 1996).

Psychosocial Risk Factor Assessment

As biological pathways for the action of psychological factors on the pathogenesis of CVD become more explicit and supported by experimental evidence, the association of psychosocial factors with CVD risk becomes more persuasive. Such pathways now include platelet and neuroendocrine activation, increased hypercholesterolemia, arrhythmogenesis, endothelial dysfunction and injury, and sympathetic nervous system activation exacerbated by individual differences (Rozanski, Blumenthal & Kaplan, 1999; Allan & Scheidt, 1996b). At this time, there are numerous studies showing a connection between psychosocial factors and CAD (e. g., Nunes, Frank & Kornfield, 1987), MI onset (e. g., Mittleman, Maclure, Sherwood et al., 1995), post-MI hospitalization time (e. g., Allison, Williams, Miller, Patten et al., 1995) and post-MI survival (e. g., Thomas, Friedmann, Wimbush & Schron, 1997). Furthermore, the addition of interventions for reducing psychosocial risk factors has an independent effect in reducing morbidity and mortality beyond that of standard cardiac rehabilitation regimens (Linden, Stossel & Maurice, 1996). Across a range of studies, the effects of psychosocial intervention have been found to be of similar or greater magnitude to those of medical preventive treatment in reducing non-fatal MIs and cardiac deaths in secondary prevention (Ketterer, 1993).

Depression. Assessment of psychosocial risks might start with a clinical interview for a diagnosis of clinical depression; depression has been shown to increase risk of mortality by five to six times within half a year following an MI (Frasure-Smith, Lesperance & Talajic, 1993). Non-clinical levels of depression on the BDI (scores ≥ 10) have also been associated with increased mortality at 18 months (Frasure-Smith, Lesperance & Talajic, 1995). Global emotional distress on the BSI is associated with increased risk of hospitalization within six months of an MI in cardiac rehabilitation patients (Allison et al., 1995). Although preliminary results of a major clinical trial of a cognitive intervention for depression and social isolation in CAD patients indicate no benefit on mortality or acute events (the ENRICHD trial; Blumenthal, 2002), results may have been influenced by minimal differences in depression change between the intervention and control groups.

Stress. Stress and job strain appear to influence CAD through a variety of biological pathways (Allan & Scheidt, 1996b). In particular, increased ischemia (mostly silent) has been associated with stressful daily life events (e. g., Barry, Selwyn, Nable, et al., 1988), and vasoconstriction has been demonstrated with psychological stressors (e. g., Feigl, 1987). Lipid levels can also be altered by neurogenic and behavioral stress, and may be of concern in people whose work or lives result in chronic stress (see Rosenman, 1997, for a review). Numerous animal studies have found increased atherosclerosis in stressed animals, although these results have been difficult to generalize to humans (Kaplan, Manuck, Williams & Strawn, 1993). Cardiovascular reactivity to stress has also become an active research area, particularly in identifying at-risk subgroups that may be more susceptible to the effect of stressful events on CVD. For instance, carotid atherosclerosis has been shown to progress more in men who have large changes in blood pressure in anticipation of a maximal exercise test (Everson, Lynch, Chesney, Kaplan et al., 1997); reactivity has also been measured in reaction to other stressors (e. g., Smith, Nealey, Kircher & Limon, 1997). Gender differences are also being explored, with men appearing to be more reactive to stressful tasks than women (Lawler, Wilcox & Anderson, 1995).

Type A behavior. Type A behavior pattern (TAPB) was initially defined as a drive for achievement, high competitiveness, involvement in multiple activities, a tendency to increase the rate of activities, extreme mental and physical alertness, and pervasive aggressive and hostile feelings (Rosenman, Swan & Carmelli, 1988). Although studies of TABP's association with coronary events have shown mixed results overall, group treatment of TABP in the Recurrent Coronary Prevention Project lowered the rate of non-fatal coronary recurrences by 44% in post-MI patients; patients who markedly reduced their TABP were substantially less likely to have a recurrence than those who did not reduce their TABP (Friedman, Thoresen, Gill, Ulmer, Powell, Price, Brown, Thompson, Rabin, Breall, Bourg, Levy & Dixon, 1986). In terms of assessment, TABP has been a better predictor of cardiovascular events when identified by an interview than a questionnaire (Allan & Scheidt, 1996b), and the latest tool for identifying TABP is the videotaped clinical examination (VCE; Friedman, Fleischmann & Price, 1996). The hostility component of TABP has been a stronger predictor of CHD events than a dichotomous characterization of Type A vs. Type B (Thoresen & Bracke, 1997). A hostility measure that assesses both affective and behavorial components is the Interpersonal Hostility Assessment Technique, which has been related to CAD severity (Barefoot, 1992).

Social isolation. Measured in terms of emotional support from close people and an extended social network, social isolation increased risk of acute events by a factor of four in a male Swedish population followed for six years (Orth-Gomer, Rosengren & Wilhelmsen, 1993). Other prospective studies of patients with CHD have also found increased risk of nonfatal or fatal events from living alone (Case, Moss, Case, McDermott & Eberly, 1992) and increased mortality from being unmarried and without a close confidant (Williams, Barefoot & Califf, 1992). Social isolation and support may also interact with other factors such as TABP and depression.

Treatment

Approaches to Long-Term Adherence and Health Behavior Change

Treatment adherence. Risk factor management and treatment adherence issues cannot be separated, and need to be addressed at all levels of the health care system. The American Heart Association has issued a "Multilevel Compliance Challenge" to patients, healthcare providers, and healthcare organizations to adopt strategies to improve the delivery of health care and behavioral risk-reducing strategies for heart patients (Miller, Hill, Kottke & Ockene, 1999). It has long been noted that treatment adherence has a significant effect on treatment efficacy; for example, patients who were more than 75% adherent to a lipid-lowering medication had 22% fewer coronary events than the average in the West of Scotland Coronary Prevention (WOS-COPS) study (Shepherd, 1996). Adherence may be influenced by general factors such as cognitive impairment and psychopathology, and by specific factors (e. g., stage of change, health beliefs regarding barriers, benefits and self-efficacy) associated with a particular medication or lifestyle change (see Bellg, Rivkin & Rosenson, 2002, for a review). Treatments that do not resolve patient-perceived symptoms and that also have significant side effects (e. g., hypertension treatment) also are associated with extremely low adherence (Sackett & Snow, 1979).

The main challenge for those promoting treatment adherence and healthy lifestyle change is that long-term maintenance of health behavior remains elusive. For example, patient adherence to cardiac rehabilitation services including exercise, dietary change, smoking cessation, and taking prescribed medications is only 25-40% after six months (U.S. Department of Health and Human Services, 1996). Adherence is consequently gaining increased attention, as evidenced by a symposium sponsored by the American Heart Association and the National Institutes of Health examining compliance issues and cardiac risk factor control (Burke & Ockene, 2001), and by an issue of *Health Psychology* [vol. 19, number 1 (Suppl); January, 2000] devoted to papers from a workshop held by the National Heart, Lung and Blood Institute (NHLBI) specifically focusing on maintenance of weight loss, smoking cessation, physical activity, and dietary behavior. The closing paper from that issue concluded that the NHLBI conference provided "a *starting point* (italics mine) for research on long-term maintenance of behavior change" (Wing, 2000). Clearly, there is much work to be done in this area.

Part of the strategy to improve delivery of risk-reducing interventions is to shift focus from short-term to long-term behavior change, and a variety of innovative approaches to accomplish this are being tested as of this writing (e. g., Behavior Change Consortium, 2002) or have been developed in the past decade (see *Health Behavior and Health Education* for a review; Glanz, Lewis & Rimer, 1997). The following theoretical and practical approaches have focused in different ways on this issue.

Stages of change approaches. Before patients can change their behavior, they often have to change their readiness to change. Stage of change (SOC) assessment and intervention (Prochaska, Redding & Evers, 1997; Prochaska, Velicer, Rossi, Goldstein et al., 1994) has been valuable in assisting this process. With cardiac patients, the stages of change model has been particularly useful in two areas. First, because of their general resistance to psychological treatment, the SOC model is helpful in assessing readiness to engage in psychological intervention for behavior change. Second, the SOC model can define readiness to engage in the specific behavioral goals of treatment (rather than as a preliminary global assessment of readiness to achieve general outcome goals). For instance, a patient who has been advised to quit smoking may be in the contemplation phase in relation to that general outcome goal, but may be in the action phase in terms of willingness to attend psychological sessions or in being willing to change to a brand of cigarettes with less nicotine.

Motivational approaches. Developing positive motivation for change is a key area for intervention. However, even the health benefits of making a change are often initially perceived as largely unsought and unpleasant advice. In helping patients internalize and integrate lifestyle changes, self-determined behaviors associated with positively experienced benefits are more likely to be sustained than extrinsically motivated behaviors experienced as being coerced by circumstances or other people (Botelho & Skinner, 1995; Bellg, Williams, Deci & Suchman, 1991), perhaps because they may be involved in assisting the process of integrated internalization and self-regulation (Bellg, 2003). Studies of self-determination in health behavior change have found promising results for adolescent health risk behaviors (Williams, Cox, Hedberg & Deci, 2001), long-term medication adherence (Williams, Rodin, Ryan, Grolnick & Deci, 1998), glucose control in patients with diabetes (Williams, Freedman & Deci, 1998), long-term adherence to exercise (Ryan, Frederick, Lepes, Rubio & Sheldon, 1997), long-term weight loss (Williams, Grow, Freedman, Ryan & Deci, 1996), and involvement and drop-out in alcohol treatment (Ryan, Plant & O'Malley, 1995).

Motivational interviewing is an effective way to implement a motivational approach. It is "a directive, client-centered counseling style for eliciting behavior change by helping clients to explore and resolve ambivalence" (Rollnick & Miller, 1995), and has been effectively adopted by therapists dealing with substance abuse and other behavioral problems such as risky sexual practices, compliance with medical recommendations, and eating disorders. Within this approach, there are five clinical strategies: 1) express empathy, 2) develop discrepancy, 3) avoid argumentation, 4) roll with resistance, and 5) support self-efficacy (Miller & Rollnick, 1991), all of which are intended to help patients identify and act upon their own reasons for engaging in a new behavior.

Cognitive-behavioral approaches. Although traditional cognitive-behavioral approaches are generally effective at helping patients initiate change, they have not been as successful in producing sustained health behavior change.

Nonetheless, some behavioral and cognitive techniques have worked well. For instance, behavioral self-management strategies involving a case management approach with personal contact and active long-term follow-up have been highly effective at promoting long-term change in CAD patients (Debusk, Miller, Superko, Dennis et al., 1994), although they require considerable resources and repeated patient contact. A case management telephone intervention has also been found highly successful with chronic heart failure patients at reducing rehospitalization rates and patient care costs (Riegel, Carlson, Kopp, LePetri et al., 2002).

In addition, cognitive strategies based on the Health Belief Model remain essential for understanding how patients think about their illness and how they engage with the health care system (Becker & Maiman, 1975; Strecher & Rosenstock, 1997). For instance, the perceived threat of cardiovascular disease is minimized by some patients, and the perceived benefits of preventive treatment may be unclear. Patients may also have barrier beliefs regarding medicines or a specific medicine (e. g., becoming "dependent" on it), concerns about medication interactions or taking too many medications, or misunderstandings about treatment (e. g., "When my labs are normal, I can quit my meds"). As for beliefs about healthy lifestyle change, misinformation is common (e. g., patients often are not aware that a modest weight loss or increase in exercise can be medically beneficial, or that even infrequent smoking increases risk of sudden cardiac death). Poor lifestyle assessment by patients is also common (e. g., patients often overestimate the amount of exercise they get on their job), and personal and cultural barrier beliefs about lifestyle changes may also need to be discussed (e. g., "If you're too thin, you're not healthy"), as will peer group beliefs and pressures. Finally, self-efficacy beliefs are important and are highly predictive of initial effort in making change (Turk & Meichenbaum, 1991). Low self-efficacy can be changed over time with education and positive experiences of success.

The following are some additional approaches to promote successful behavioral change in cardiac patients. These may be considered as ways to solve particular short-term behavioral problems, and need to be used within the context of a more comprehensive approach that facilitates long-term health behavior maintenance.

- Use counter-conditioning to deal with cravings. Relaxation training, distraction interventions, and substitute behaviors can help patients deal with urges for food or cigarettes.
- Develop stimulus control strategies. Help patients avoid tempting situations and manage their environments to reduce associations with negative behaviors.
- Reinforce positive behavior. Patient selection of a positive reward for success in achieving or maintaining a moderately difficult behavioral goal can support short-term change. Making the reinforcer relatively small but personal and genuinely appealing will help the process of internalization and support long-term change.

Risk Factor Management

Managing behavioral risk factors. Although the above approaches to health behavior change and risk factor management are very promising and currently under investigation, more traditional health behavior change theories and strategies have shaped many of the approaches to risk factor management currently being used. Some of the processes involved in behavioral interventions for smoking, weight loss, and cardiac rehabilitation are briefly described below.

Most smokers who eventually quit have tried more than once. There are few clinically meaningful differences in behavioral treatment options, with overall one-year quit rates of about 30% (Lichtenstein & Glasgow, 1992). Typical treatments include setting a "quit date," nicotine fading or use of nicotine replacement strategies, use of medications such as Zyban (bupropion), and group support or individual follow-up during initial phases of abstinence. More recent clinical trials show greater likelihood of smoking abstinence when behavioral treatments (e. g., Cinciripini, Cinciripini, Wallfisch, Haque & Van Vunakis, 1996) or minimum contact self-

help materials (Fortmann & Killen, 1995) are combined with nicotine supplements (i. e., transdermal patch, gum, or nasal spray). Nicotine supplements are particularly effective among depressed patients (Kinnunen, Doherty, Militello & Garvey, 1996). Nicotine supplements do not require a prescription, and do not increase cardiac events in patients with cardiac disease (Joseph, Norman, Ferry, Prochaska et al., 1996).

Achieving a reasonable weight goal can decrease blood pressure and risk of CAD. Abdominal fat is a particular risk factor for coronary events, and weight gain also needs to be addressed in many patients following heart transplantation. Controlling behavioral factors influencing weight is difficult, and regaining lost weight is highly likely. Key factors to prevent weight regain involve developing a regular exercise regimen (e. g., Dubbert, 1992) and finding acceptable substitutes for favorite foods that are unhealthy. Long-term medication interventions must be viewed with caution, particularly since some appetite-suppressant drugs in the mid-1990's (e. g., Redux, "fen-fen," fenfluramine) were associated with substantially increased risk of primary pulmonary hypertension, an uncommon but serious disease (Abenhaim, Moride, Brenot et al., 1996). Dietary changes that lower weight and improve other cardiovascular risks often focus on lowering fat and calories, and increasing fruits, vegetables and legumes (Singh, Rastogi, Rastogi et al., 1996).

Many of the principles for modifying single risk factors apply in promoting patient involvement and adherence to a cardiac rehabilitation program, which can influence a variety of coronary risk factors (Lavie & Milani, 1996). Patient motivation is often affected by their rehabilitation status. Phase 1 rehabilitation involves inpatients, and resistance often includes fear of further damage to the heart or feeling debilitated and frustrated by illness and treatment symptoms. Intervention focuses on improving coping and promoting self-efficacy by giving patients experiences that allow them to see their activity level improve. Phase 2 cardiac rehabilitation patients are in a specific, structured rehabilitation program to aid recovery following an acute event. Intervention often involves addressing barriers to treatment such as inconvenience, feeling different than the other cardiac rehabilitation patients (e. g., younger patients often feel out of place), having conflictual interactions with the rehabilitation staff, being uncomfortable with the experience of exercise, and having fatalistic beliefs ("if your number is up, it doesn't matter what you do"). Phase 3 cardiac rehabilitation involves ongoing maintenance of fitness status and healthy lifestyle behaviors, and is often conducted at home with only occasional visits to the rehabilitation center. Promoting adherence with Phase 3 patients is similar to promoting it for non-rehabilitation patients, with the benefit that they are receiving regular monitoring and feedback on their cardiovascular status.

Managing psychosocial risk factors. Although there is evidence that stress, Type A behavior, depression, and social isolation are risk factors for CVD of magnitude approaching that of biomedical risks, there have been fewer intervention studies showing that psychosocial disease risks may be reduced. However, a meta-analysis of studies examining interventions with psychosocial risk factors (Ketterer, 1993) showed positive effects on cardiovascular outcomes for treatment ranging from group therapy for TABP, group psychotherapy, stress monitoring, behavioral treatment, and relaxation training. Non-significant or negative intervention effects were found in educational discussion groups and exercise therapy counseling. A range of interventions in individual and group formats (Spira, 1997) formats therefore appears to be effective in addressing psychosocial risk factors.

One intervention addressing both the behavioral and psychosocial risks of heart disease was the Lifestyle Heart Trial (Ornish, Brown, Scherwitz, Billings et al., 1990). Patients in this study showed good adherence to rigorous regimen of lifestyle changes even after four years, as well as reduction of stenoses and fewer acute events. The program consisted of a low-fat (approximately 10%) vegetarian diet, moderate aerobic exercise, stress management, and group support. Along with adher-

ence issues, the groups were designed to address social isolation, improve communication skills, promote empathy and compassion, and encourage identification and expression of feelings (Billings, Scherwitz, Sullivan, Sparler & Ornish, 1996). Other psychosocial risk factor interventions have also been found to effectively reduce coronary prone behaviors, incorporating such strategies as "the hook" to raise awareness of the distinction between situations ("bait") and responses ("hooks"), daily drills to change one TABP behavior per day, strategies to improve relationships and social support, and relaxation techniques (Thoresen & Bracke, 1997).

Psychopathology and Adjustment to Illness
Coping with illness symptoms and treatment side effects. The pain, discomfort, and other symptoms of an MI may cause a great deal of fear and anxiety. Many patients also become sensitized to them, developing anxiety at each minor pain, and put constraints on their activities far more than may be justified by their illness. Some constraints may be justified, of course, and these often are associated with loss and a period of resentment or grieving. Cardiac medications may also produce uncomfortable physical and psychological side effects. Table 4 lists psychological side effects

Case Example
A 43 year old male cardiac rehabilitation patient was referred for non-adherence to recommended lifestyle changes to help control hypercholesterolemia and HTN, which were also being treated medically with no side effects. He had a significant family history of heart disease, with his father and uncle dying of MI's in their 50's, and a grandmother dying in her 60's. He tended to minimize the implications of his familial history of illness.

Initial attempts to change his diet through nutritional counseling were ineffective. He came to cardiac rehabilitation exercise sessions for three weeks, and then quit after he got a high pressure job selling and leasing commercial real estate. His eating habits were impulsive, and often included fast food. When he had lunches and dinners with colleagues, however, he was able to order appropriate low-fat meals.

He had been an athlete in college, but hadn't exercised regularly for 20 years. He also had many Type A characteristics: impatience, many projects going simultaneously, and explosive anger at subordinates. He was married, with two children, many acquaintances and a few close friends he saw infrequently. He did not smoke; he drank five drinks a week socially with colleagues and clients, and two six-packs of beer on weekends.

His risk reduction outcome goals consisted of obtaining better control over diet, increasing his exercise level, cutting his alcohol consumption, and reducing his TABP. Rapport was established easily, but developing a therapeutic alliance and agreeing on behavioral goals was more difficult. He made it clear he wanted to make changes without feeling he was depriving himself. Since he impulsively went to the same fast food restaurant near his office, he decided to change to a restaurant where he could order soups and salads he enjoyed. His fast food excursions dropped from daily to twice a week.

He also decided to walk up stairs at work at least twice a day instead of taking the elevator, and play softball on weekends. Although this was not a therapeutic level of exercise, he agreed

that developing an exercise habit would be a first step toward making more effective change. After a month of fair success at this, he began to take a daily 30 minute walk before work.

He was unwilling to change his drinking habits, since he felt that alcohol was an important part of his social life. Consequently, an initial thought of having him evaluated for an SSRI for his anger was postponed.

Over three months, his TABP changed slightly. He spent several weeks noting situations in which he was angry with his associates, and rated his anger at those times. He was surprised at the frequency of his anger. He was encouraged to verbalize his affection for his wife and children, and identify positive characteristics of his colleagues and give them more positive feedback. He initially had a difficult time with this, although he improved. He planned more unscheduled time during the day and on weekends, developed a practice of walking more slowly, and took a class in T'ai Chi.

He terminated treatment after nine sessions, deciding to resume periodically when he felt he needed help maintaining control of his lifestyle behaviors.

of cardiac medications, including those that are relatively infrequent. Surgical interventions such as CABG can also produce substantial postoperative changes in quality of life, mood, and cognitive status (Gold, 1996).

Coping with these difficult experiences can be aided with a variety of techniques. Cognitive restructuring (Beck & Emery, 1979) may be used to defuse helplessness and negative ideation associated with catastrophizing about symptoms. Assertiveness training may be effective in supporting the patient's self-efficacy in being able to deal with symptoms or treatment side effects. When alternatives to medications producing uncomfortable side effects are not available, patient tolerance may be increased by developing coping strategies to minimize the effect of specific symptoms (e. g., planning activities during times when medication-related drowsiness is not a problem). Postoperative coping may be fostered through promoting realistic expectations for postoperative functional status and time to recov-

ery, social support from family and friends, and CBT treatment for depression and other psychological symptoms (Gold, 1996). Group therapy to enhance coping may provide a supportive context for patients, facilitate emotional expression, promote active coping, and help patients reprioritize their goals and usual activities (Spira, 1997b).

In addition, psychologists can help patients cope with the difficulties of being an inpatient. Patients in a coronary care unit (CCU) may receive excellent care, but being surrounded by and connected to machines can be frightening. Patients also often feel depersonalized by hospital personnel and procedures. As anonymous inpatients, they become disconnected from the parts of their lives and their personal identities that have given them strength in the past (Rybarczyk & Bellg, 1997). The psychologist can encourage active coping by the patient and educate the staff on ways to promote patient choice and activity. Hospitalized patients with acute MIs have shorter stays when they are given infor-

Table 4. **Psychological side effects of medications commonly used with CAD and heart transplant patients.**

Medication class	Psychological side effects
Preventive Treatments	
Antihypertensives	depression, anxiety, sleep disturbances, sexual dysfunction
Lipid-lowering agents	depression, anxiety, sleep disturbances
Treatments for CAD	
Vasodilators	headache
Beta-blockers	depression, nightmares, insomnia, loss of libido, fatigue, delirium
ACE inhibitors	mania
Anticoagulants	none
Antiarrhythmics	depression related to thyroid dysfunction
Inotropic agents	sexual dysfunction, anxiety, delirium
Treatments for Heart Failure/Transplant	
Immunosuppressants	anxiety, delirium, hallucinations, delusions
Corticosteroids	anxiety, depression, increased appetite, weight gain, agitation, emotional lability, hypomania, insomnia, apathy, suicidal ideation, irritability, delirium
Sympathomimetics	mania, delirium
Antibiotics	hallucinations, fear of death, delirium
Antiviral drugs	irritability, hallucinations, delirium
Antifungal drugs	depression, hallucinations

Incidence of side effects may be low, and not all drugs in each class are associated with the indicated symptoms. Adapted from Tabrizi et al. (1996), Scheidt (1996), Wise and Rundell (1994), and Heather (1997).

mation about their condition and allowed to participate in their care (Cromwell & Levenkron, 1984). Other ways to buffer a negative hospital experience may involve facilitating and encouraging social support for the patient, identifying reasons for "bad" patient behavior (e. g., neediness, non-adherence) and communicating them to the staff, and conducting CBT around thoughts and feelings evoked by the hospital experience.

Psychopathology. For many patients, the diagnosis of CAD, the occurrence of an MI, or the chronic experience of symptoms of angina may trigger psychological processes leading to clinical depression or anxiety. Psychopathology may be effectively treated in these patients with a variety of cognitive-behavioral (e. g., Beck, Rush, Shaw & Emery, 1979; Beck & Emery, 1979) or other brief interpersonal approaches such as solution-focused therapy (Walter & Peller, 1992). Difficulties in treatment are similar to those in diagnosis, with

amelioration of symptoms of irritability or anger, social withdrawal, anhedonia and disinterest in usual activities as likely treatment goals for depression. Patterns of anxious ideation also need to be distinguished from reasonable concern and worry about their illness to help the patient develop awareness and monitor his or her progress. Referral sources need to be educated regarding appropriate patient response to illness and psychopathology, since physicians sometimes erroneously believe that if patients have a reason to be depressed or anxious, there is no reason to refer them for treatment.

Cardiac patients as a group tend to be older and have a larger proportion of men than the traditional psychotherapy population. As a result, presenting patients with an instrumental characterization of therapy ("to help you deal better with your situation") as opposed to a subjective one ("to help you feel better") is likely to be more successful in building a therapeutic alliance. Similarly, brief therapeutic approaches that pursue treatment with a goal clearly in mind are likely to be more successful, although patients can get considerable benefit just by being able to tell their stories to a receptive listener (Rybarczyk & Bellg, 1997). By encouraging reinvolvement in activities and social connections, therapeutic benefits can continue beyond the session.

Use of psychotropic medications is clearly indicated with many patients, and working with a psychiatrist who is familiar with cardiac patients and cardiac medications is a great benefit. You may also wish to consult with a psychiatrist regarding the use of SSRIs with hostile, TABP patients who are not clinically depressed. Hostility and impatience can be reduced in many such patients, even in the absence of vegetative symptoms of depression (Littman, 1993; Tollefson, 1995).

Precautions with psychotropic medications. Psychiatric monitoring of possible side effects from psychotropic medications in cardiac patients is important. However, it may be necessary to identify problematic psychotropic medications prescribed prior to diagnosis of heart problems. A few of the most serious precautions (from Tabrizi, Littman, Williams & Scheidt, 1995) are noted below.

- Tricyclic antidepressants (TCIs) are life-threatening in patients at risk of overdose (e. g., suicidal or cognitively impaired patients). They may also result in tachycardia during early phases of therapy, orthostatic hypotension, and ECG alterations.

- Trazodone (Desyrel) can cause orthostatic hypotension, which generally contraindicates its use in cardiac patients.

- Benzodiazepines (e. g., alprazolam [Xanax], lorazepam [Ativan], triazolam [Halcion]) may be helpful in controlling panic attacks, anxiety or insomnia, but can also cause delirium. Overdoses are life-threatening; withdrawal must be tapered, and withdrawal symptoms may include tachycardia.

- Lithium is relatively safe in patients with heart disease, but serum levels may be difficult to control in post-transplant pa-

tients; cyclosporin can raise lithium levels, and prednisone can decrease levels.

- Phenothiazine overdoses (e. g., Thorazine, Mellaril) can produce life-threatening arrhythmias.

SSRIs (notably fluoxetine [Prozac], sertraline [Zoloft], paroxetine [Paxil], citalopram [Celexa], and fluvoxamine [Luvox], among others) are generally safe in cardiac patients, although they can interact with and elevate levels of other medications such as beta-blockers, warfarin, and digoxin. Sertraline appears to be the least likely to cause such elevations. Bupropion (Wellbutrin) and mirtazapine (Remeron) are also non-cardiotoxic antidepressants, and are associated with less sexual dysfunction than SSRIs; however, mirtazapine may cause weight gain and elevated lipid levels. Buspirone (Buspar) can be used to treat generalized anxiety disorder and symptoms of hostility and irritability in cardiac patients. Valproic acid has no cardiac effects and may be an option for treatment of mania.

Case Example

A 68-year-old woman with hypercholesterolemia was referred to evaluate her recent weight gain. She had a TIA four months previously, and reported temporary impairment of short-term memory and ability to concentrate. She was on aspirin therapy and had successfully taken cholesterol-lowering medication.

She had gained 25 lbs. (to reach 180) in the previous two months. One year previously, she retired from a 70 hour per week practice as an architect. She had an active, driven personal style, and had had difficulty adjusting to the relative inactivity. She tried to remain busy during the day by working as a hospital volunteer, but felt "useless" and didn't want to be around sick people. After her TIA, she became less interested in her usual activities, and began to binge on "anything in sight," mainly cookies and high calorie foods. In the previous week, she had also binged on brandy and orange juice, drinking approximately 12 oz. of brandy with orange juice in two days. She had no previous history of an eating disorder or a drinking problem.

She reported no current difficulty with her

memory or concentration. Her thoughts were logical, but often somewhat tangential during the interview; her speech was coherent but mildly dysarthric. She reported being anxious and worried about her future, and denied feeling sad or having hopeless/helpless thoughts. She slept poorly, with difficult sleep onset due to "thinking too much" and several nocturnal awakenings with difficulty returning to sleep. Her depression scores on the intake questionnaires were only slightly elevated, but her Somatization score and the overall General Severity Index were substantially elevated on the Brief Symptom Inventory. She had two friends she could talk to "about anything," but both lived out of town.

She was diagnosed with Adjustment Disorder with Depressed Mood, and was interested in participating in psychotherapy. CBT included cognitive restructuring about her TIA, which had upset her so much she didn't want to discuss it during the first session, and cognitive re-

framing of her retirement to encourage her to be more active. She also learned a relaxation and meditation exercise, which she enjoyed and was willing to practice twice a day. Regarding her binges, after some negotiation, she agreed to sit while eating, pause frequently to ask herself if she wanted to continue, and eat slowly to enjoy the food as much as possible. She was also encouraged to develop new friends and social contacts.

Within a month, most of her depressive symptoms had resolved. Her ability to fall asleep easily and sleep through the night gradually improved; her binging was reduced in quantity and frequency immediately, and disappeared shortly after her sleep improved. She got involved in several arts and cultural groups that allowed her to build social relationships and take more of the leadership role she had been used to when working. She also reestablished friendships from her former job.

Other Treatment Issues

Treatment of non-cardiac chest pain. From 10 to 30% of patients with apparent symptoms of angina, and up to 60% of patients with other chest pain, have normal angiograms (Kemp, Vokonas, Cohn & Gorlin, 1973; Cannon, Quyyumi, Mincemoyer, Stine et al., 1994). Patients with panic disorders or clinical anxiety frequently experience chest pain as one of the diagnostic symptoms, as do patients with gastroesophageal reflux disease (GERD). Following five to 11 sessions of CBTcognitive behavior therapy (CBT) for anxiety and pain management in patients experiencing more than four episodes of chest pain per week, about one-third reported no symptoms, and another third reported fewer than four episodes (Klimes, Mayhou, Pearce, Coles & Fagg, 1990). Imipramine has produced a 52% reduction in episodes of non-cardiac chest pain (Cannon et al., 1994). Behavioral and psychopharmacological treatments for anxiety and panic disorders appear to be effective with many of these patients.

Case Example

A 55 year old man was referred by the heart failure team to evaluate psychological reasons for his frequent visits to the ER. He had dilated cardiomyopathy and CAD, had suffered an MI and was treated with PTCA two years previously. He had been listed for cardiac transplant, but improved under medical therapy and cardiac rehabilitation and was removed from the transplant list.

He had made 13 visits to the ER since his MI, each time complaining of overwhelming diffuse chest pain, stomach pains and fear of dying; no physical cause was found for these events. His chest pain always lessened and sometimes disappeared upon entering the ER, where he felt safe and believed "nothing could happen." He also was having "anxiety attacks" about twice a week, with fear and racing thoughts but no chest pain. He had a history of panic disorder that eight years previously been successfully treated with imipramine. He also had a history since his early 20's of fearing that he would be incontinent in public after he witnessed his grandfather's incontinence; as a result, he felt anxious and on the verge of incontinence whenever a restroom was unavailable. He had never had an incident, however.

He was highly somatically focused and tended to catastrophize about even minor symptoms. Following his MI, a physician told him that "30% of my heart is dead," which worried him constantly. Even so, he was able to describe numerous distinctions between the non-cardiac pain that sent him to the ER and the pain he had experienced during his MI. His symptoms were also different, however, than those he had experienced previously as panic attacks, which made it difficult for him initially to connect them with anxiety.

Therapy focused on relaxation training with a somatic focus (progressive relaxation training and abdominal breathing) to reduce and give him control over his physical symptoms of anxiety and panic, and cognitive therapy to help him distinguish panic from cardiac symptoms and defuse the negative attributions he associated with his symptoms. Also, after psychiatric evaluation, he was placed on Paxil 20 mg QD. Within two months his "anxiety attacks" had disappeared, and in the next six months he had one episode of chest pain which he was able to distinguish as non-cardiac and control with his relaxation exercises. He had no further visits to the ER. Without it being a specific focus of therapy, he also obtained almost complete relief of his fear of incontinence.

Professional Practice Issues

Age issues in psychological treatment. Cardiac patients and preventive cardiology patients tend to be middle-aged and older men and women. Such patients may be less likely to follow through with psychological treatment for illness adjustment problems, and may present with specific treatment difficulties in relation to health behavior change, seeing behavioral intervention as being contrary to their desire to be self-reliant. They are likely to be less experienced with and interested in psychological perspectives, less articulate about their internal experiences and feelings (with alexithymia resulting in reduced social skills [Lumley, Ovies, Stettner, Wehmer & Lakey, 1996]), and less inclined to look to others for support (Rybarczyk, 1994). However, chronological age is not a good predictor of emotional distress following an MI, and treatment expectations for cooperative older patients should not be lowered.

Gender issues. Gender plays an important role in identifying and treating risk factors for cardiac disease and dealing with its psychological consequences. Men have role barriers to identifying, expressing, and seeking help for behavior change and for psychopathology, including depression (Warren, 1983); white males over the age of 60 are four times more likely to commit suicide than any other group (National Center for Health Statistics, 1987). However, because men tend to be affected by heart disease earlier in their lives, women's concerns in prevention and treatment of heart disease have been underemphasized until recently and need to be specifically addressed. Surveys repeatedly show that women are more concerned about breast cancer than heart disease, even though only 1 in 30 women dies of breast cancer, and 1 in 2.4 women dies of cardiovascular disease (American Heart Association, 2001b). Women may consequently be less likely to participate in screening for cardiovascular disease and to address CVD risk factors. Women have a poorer prognosis following an MI than men (American Heart Association, 2001b) and certain risk factors such as smoking are more significant for women than men; a first MI occurs approximately seven years earlier in smoking men than nonsmoking men, but 19 years earlier in smoking women than nonsmoking women (Hansen, Anderson & Von Eyben, 1993). Women have also been underrepresented in treatment studies and in studies of psychosocial factors affecting CVD outcomes (e. g., Frasure-Smith, Lesperance & Talajic, 1995), in part because of lower illness rates in study populations including women. Jacobs and Sherwood (1996) note that men and women differ in cardiovascular reactivity, triggering events for MI, and types of stressors associated with CVD. There is a clear need to include more women in treatment and prevention studies and better understand cardiovascular risks among women (see Tsang, Barnes,

Gersh & Hayes, 2000, for an excellent review of women's risk factors).

Family therapy with heart patients. Some risk factors such as familial hypercholesterolemia (FH) run in families. Getting the cooperation of parents to change family patterns of eating or exercise in such cases is essential to making changes in behavioral patterns in children that may be already well-established at a young age. Patients under 10 years old are more amenable to their parents' input on meals, particularly if they see their parents eating in the same way. Teenagers have different challenges in dealing with lifestyle changes than do younger siblings or adults, such as peer pressure, developmental issues related to self-definition and self-acceptance, poor stimulus control, or frightened parents with controlling styles. Family therapy approaches are also useful in dealing with an acute health crisis or chronic illness in a family member, particularly when some family members are coping better than others or are carrying more of the caregiving burden than they can handle.

Development of new services. As was noted in the first edition of this chapter published in 1998, the clinical practice of cardiac psychology holds great promise, but is clearly underdeveloped. The same statement is true today. The current practice and future potential of cardiac psychology rests on the three components discussed in this chapter: 1) the generally under-utilized role of psychologists in treating traditional medical and behavioral cardiac risk factors, 2) the growing body of research supporting assessment and treatment of a range of psychosocial cardiac risk factors, and 3) the well-established role of psychologists in promoting illness adjustment and treating psychopathology.

There are many ways to advance the practice and profession of cardiac psychology. Identifying and treating patients associated with increased medical care costs, such as those with non-cardiac chest pain and psychosocial risk factors, can provide both a valuable service in a managed care environment and add to the professional credibility of the field. Publishing research in medical publications as well as in psychological journals will add to our interdisciplinary credibility as well. The field remains open for entrepreneurial health psychologists with the appropriate training to make contact with cardiology practices and hospital-based clinics and establish themselves - and their profession - as essential to the proper care of cardiac patients.

References

Abenhaim, L., Moride, Y., Brenot, F., Rich, S., Benichou, J., Kurz, X., Higenbottam, T., Oakley, C., Wouters, E., Aubier, M., Simonneau, G., & Begaud, B. (1996). Appetite suppressant drugs and the risk of primary pulmonary hypertension. *New England Journal of Medicine, 335,* 609–616.

Allan, R., & Scheidt, S. (Eds). (1996a). *Heart and mind: The practice of cardiac psychology.* Washington, DC: American Psychological Association.

Allan, R., & Scheidt, S. (1996b). Empirical basis for cardiac psychology. In R. Allan, & S. Scheidt (Eds), *Heart and mind: The practice of cardiac psychology.* Washington, DC: American Psychological Association.

Allison, T.G., Williams, D.E., Miller, T.D., Patten, C.A., Bailey, K.R., Squires, R.W., & Gau, G.T. (1995). Medical and economic costs of psychologic distress in patients with coronary artery disease. *Mayo Clinic Procedures, 70,* 734–742.

American Heart Association (2001a). *2002 Heart and stroke statistical update.* Dallas: Author.

American Heart Association (2001b). *Heart & stroke facts.* Dallas: Author.

Barefoot, J.C. (1992). Developments in the measurement of hostility. In H.S. Friedman (Ed.), *Hostility, coping and health.* Washington, DC: American Psychological Association.

Barry, J., Selwyn, A., Nabel, E., Rocco, M.B., Mead, K., Campbell, S., & Rebecca, G. (1988). Frequency of ST-segment depression produced by mental stress in stable angina pectoris from coronary artery disease. *American Journal of Cardiology, 61,* 989–993.

Beck, A., & Emery, G. (1979). *Cognitive therapy of anxiety and phobic disorders.* Philadelphia: Center for Cognitive Therapy.

Beck, A., Rush, A.J., Shaw, B.F., & Emery, G. (1979). *Cognitive therapy of depression.* New York: Guilford.

Becker , M.H., & Maimen, L.A. (1975). Sociobe-havioral determinants of compliance with health and medical care recommendations. *Medical Care, 13,* 10–25.

Behavior Change Consortium (2002). Conceptualizing health behavior change research: Theory comparison and multiple behavior intervention research from the NIH Behavior Change Consortium. In C.R. Nigg, J.P. Allegrante, & M. Ory (Eds), *Health Education Research, 17*(5).

Bellg, A.J. (2003). Maintenance of health behavior change in preventive cardiology: Internalization and self-regulation of new behaviors. *Behavior Modification, 27*(1), 103–131.

Bellg, A.J., Rivkin, S., & Rosenson, R.S. (2002). Adherence to lipid-altering medications and lifestyle recommendations. In B. Rose (Ed.), *Up to date in cardiovascular medicine* (Vol. 10(1)). Wellesley, MA: BDR, Inc.

Bellg, A.J. (1993, October). *The psychologist-physician partnership: Training physicians to conduct behavioral interventions with patients.* Poster presented at the conference on Partnerships in Health Care: The Means to Effective Reform, University of Rochester, Rochester, NY.

Bellg, A.J., Williams, G., Deci, E.L., & Suchman, A.L. (1991, March). *The influence of affects and perceptions on likelihood of compliance.* Paper presented at the Mid-Year Health Communication Conference, Monterey, CA.

Bergin, A.E., & Garfield, S.L. (Eds). (1994). *Handbook of psychotherapy and behavior change.* New York: John Wiley.

Billings, J.H., Scherwitz, L.W., Sullivan, R., Sparler S., & Ornish, D.M. (1996). The Lifestyle Heart Trial: Comprehensive treatment and group support therapy. In R. Allan, & S. Scheidt (Eds), *Heart and mind: The practice of cardiac psychology.* Washington, DC: American Psychological Association.

Blanchard, E.B. (1994). Behavioral medicine and health psychology. In A.E. Bergin, & S.L. Garfield (Eds), *Handbook of psychotherapy and behavior change.* New York: John Wiley.

Blumenthal, J.A. (2002, April). *ENRICHD and beyond: The role of psychosocial interventions in cardiac rehabilitation.* Paper presented at the Society of Behavioral Medicine Conference, Washington, DC

Botelho, R.J., & Skinner, H. (1995). Motivating change in health behavior: Implicatiions for health promotion and disease prevention. *Primary Care, 22,* 565–589.

Burke, L.E., & Ockene, I.S. (2001). *Compliance in healthcare and research.* American Heart Association Monograph Series. Armonk, NY: Futura Publishing.

Cannon, R.O. III, Quyyumi, A.A., Mincemoyer, R., Stine, A.M., Gracely, R.H., Smith, W.B., Geraci, M.F., Black, B.C., Uhde, T.W., Waclawiw, M.A., Maher, K. & Benjamin, S.B. (1994). Imipramine in patients with chest pain despite normal coronary angiograms. *New England Journal of Medicine, 330,* 1411–1417.

Case, R.B., Moss, A.J., Case, N., McDermott, M., & Eberly, S. (1992). Living alone after myocardial infarction: Impact on prognosis. *JAMA, 267,* 515–519.

Chaitman, B.R., Ryan, T.J., Kronmal, R.A., Foster, E.D., Frommer, P.L., & Killip, T. (1990). Coronary Artery Surgery Study (CASS): Comparability of 10 year survival in randomized and randomizable patients. *Journal of the American College of Cardiology, 16*(5), 1071–1078.

Cinciripini, P.M., Cinciripini, L.G., Wallfisch, A., Haque, W., & Van Vunakis, H. (1996). Behavior therapy and the transdermal nicotine patch: Effects on cessation outcome, affect, and coping. *Journal of Consulting and Clinical Psychology, 64,* 314–323.

Cohen, S., & Hoberman, H. (1983). Positive events and social supports as buffers of life change stress. *Journal of Applied Social Psychology, 13,* 99–125.

Cromwell, R.L., & Levenkron, J.C. (1984). Psychological care of acute coronary patients. In A. Steptoe & A. Mathews (Eds), *Health care and human behavior.* San Diego: Academic Press.

Debusk, R.F., Miller, N.H., Superko, H.R., Dennis, C.A., Thomas, R.J., Berger, W.E., Heller, W.E. III, Heller, R.S., Rompf, J., & Gee, D. (1994). A case-management system for coronary risk factor modification after acure myocardial infarction. *Annals of Internal Medicine, 120,* 721–729.

Dew, M.A., Roth, L.H., Thompson, M.E., Kormos, R.L., & Griffith, B.P. (1996). Medical compliance and its predictors in the first year after heart transplantation. *Journal of Heart and Lung Transplantation, 15,* 631–644.

Dubbert, P. (1992). Exercise in behavioral medicine. *Journal of Consulting and Clinical Psychology, 60,* 613–618.

Everson, S.A., Lynch, J.W., Chesney, M.A., Kaplan, G.A., Goldberg, D.E., Shade, S.B., Cohen, R.D., Salonen, R., & Salonen, J.T. (1997). Interaction of workplace demands and cardiovascular reactivity in progression of carotid ctherosclerosis: Population based study. *British Medical Journal, 314,* 553–558.

Feigl, E.O. (1987). The paradox of adrenergic coronary vasoconstriction. *Circulation, 76,* 737–745.

Fernandez, F. (1993). Depression and its treatment in cardiac patients. *Texas Heart Institute Journal, 20,* 188-193.

Flack, J.M., & Sowers, J.R. (1991). Epidemiologic and clinical aspects of insulin resistance and hyperinsulinemia. *American Journal of Medicine, 91,* 11S-21S.

Fortmann, S.P., & Killen, J.D. (1995). Nicotine gum and self-help behavioral treatment for smoking relapse prevention: Results from a trial using population-based recruitment. *Journal of Consulting and Clinical Psychology, 63,* 460-468.

Frasure-Smith, N., Lesperance, F., & Talajic, M. (1993). Depression following myocardial infarction: Impact on 6-month survival. *Journal of the American Medical Association, 270,* 1819-1825.

Frasure-Smith, N., Lesperance, F., & Talajic, M. (1995). The impact of negative emotions on prognosis following myocardial infarction: Is it more than depression? *Health Psychology, 14,* 388-398.

Friedman, M., Fleischmann, N., & Price, V.A. (1996). Diagnosis of Type A behavior pattern. In R. Allan, & S. Scheidt (Eds), *Heart and mind: The practice of cardiac psychology.* Washington, DC: American Psychological Association.

Friedman, M., Thoresen, C.E., Gill, J., Ulmer, D., Powell, L.H., Price, V.A., Brown, B., Thompson, L., Rabin, D., Breall, W.S., Bourg, W., Levy, R., & Dixon, T. (1986). Alteration of Type A behavior and its effect on cardiac recurrences in post-myocardial infarction patients: Summary results of the Recurrent Coronary Prevention Project. *American Heart Journal, 112,* 653-665.

Frierson, R.L., & Lippman, S.B. (1987). Heart transplant candidates rejected on psychiatric indications. *Psychosomatics, 28,* 347-355.

Glanz, K., Lewis, F.M., & Rimer, B.K. (Eds). (1997). *Health behavior and health education: Theory, research and practice.* San Francisco: Jossey-Bass.

Glassman, A.H., Helzer, J.E., Covey, L.S., Cottler, L.B., Stetner, F., Tipp J.E., & Johnson, J. (1990). Smoking, smoking cessation, and major depression. *JAMA, 264,* 1583-1584.

Gold, J.P. (1996). Psychological issues and coronary artery bypass surgery. In R. Allan, & S. Scheidt (Eds), *Heart and mind: The practice of cardiac psychology.* Washington, DC: American Psychological Association.

Hansen, E.F., Anderson, L.T., & Von Eyben, F.E. (1993). Cigarette smoking and age at first acute myocardial infarction, and influence of gender and extent of smoking. *American Journal of Cardiology, 71,* 1439-1443.

Hansing, C.E. (1979). The risk and cost of coronary angiography. *JAMA, 242,* 735-740.

Heather, J. (1997). *Psychiatric aspects of cardiac transplantation.* Unpublished manuscript, Rush-Presbyterian-St. Luke's Medical Center, Department of Psychiatry, Chicago.

Heger, J.W., Niemann, J.T., Roth, R.F., & Criley, J.M. (1998). *Cardiology* (4th edition). Baltimore: Lippincott Williams & Wilkins.

Jacobs, S.C., & Sherwood, J.B. (1996). The cardiac psychology of women and coronary heart disease. In R. Allan, & S. Scheidt (Eds), *Heart and mind: The practice of cardiac psychology.* Washington, DC: American Psychological Association.

JNC V (1993). The fifth report of the Joint National Committee on Detection, Evaluation, and Treatment of High Blood Pressure (JNC V). *Archives of Internal Medicine, 153,* 154-183.

Joseph, A.M., Norman, S.M., Ferry, L.H., Prochazka, A.V., Westman, E.C., Steele, B.G., Sherman, S.E., Cleveland, M., Antonnucio, D.O., Hartman, N., & McGovern, P.G. (1996). The safety of transdermal nicotine as an aid to smoking cessation in patients with cardiac disease. *New England Journal of Medicine, 335,* 1792-1798.

Kannel, W.B., & Feinleib, M. (1972). Natural history of angina pectoris in the Framingham Study. *American Journal of Cardiology, 29,* 154-162.

Kaplan, J.R., Manuck, S.B., Williams, J.K., & Strawn, W. (1993). Psychosocial influences on atherosclerosis: Evidence for effects and mechanisms in non-human primates. In J. Blascovich, & E.S. Katkin (Eds), *Cardiovascular reactivity to psychological stress and disease* (pp. 3-26). Washington, DC: American Psychological Association.

Kemp, H.G., Vokonas, P.S., Cohn, P.F., & Gorlin, R. (1973). The anginal syndrome associated with normal coronary arteriograms: Report of a six year experience. *American Journal of Medicine, 54,* 735-742.

Ketterer, M.W. (1993). Secondary prevention of ischemic heart disease. *Psychosomatics, 34,* 478-484.

Kinnunen, T., Doherty, K., Militello, F.S., & Garvey, A.J. (1996). Depression and smoking cessation: Characteristics of depressed smokers and effects of nicotine replacement. *Journal of Consulting and Clinical Psychology, 64,* 791-798.

Klimes, I., Mayhou, R.A., Pearce, M.J., Coles, L., & Fagg, J.R. (1990). Psychological treatment for atypical non-cardiac chest pain: A controlled evaluation. *Psychological Medicine, 20,* 605-611.

Kubansky, L.D., Kawachi, I., Spiro, A. III, Weiss,

S.T., Vokonas, P.S., & Sparrow, D. (1997). Is worrying bad for your heart? A prospective study of worry and coronary heart disease in the normative aging study. *Circulation, 95,* 818–824.

Lavie, C.J., & Milani, R.V. (1996). Effects of non-pharmacologic therapy with cardiac rehabilitation and exercise training in patients with low levels of high-density lipoprotein cholesterol. *American Journal of Cardiology, 78,* 1286–1289.

Lawler, K.A., Wilcox, Z.C., & Anderson, S.F. (1995). Gender differences in patterns of dynamic cardiovascular regulation. *Psychosomatic Medicine, 57,* 357–365.

Levinson, J.L., & Olbrisch, M.E. (1993). Psychiatric aspects of heart transplantation. *Psychosomatics, 34,* 114–123.

Lichtenstein, E., & Glasgow, R.E. (1992). Smoking cessation: What have we learned over the past decade? *Journal of Consulting and Clinical Psychology, 60,* 518–527.

Linden, W., Stossel C., & Maurice, J. (1996). Psychosocial interventions for patients with coronary artery disease: A meta-analysis. *Archives of Internal Medicine, 156,* 2302–2308.

Littman, A.B. (1993). Review of psychosomatic aspects of cardiovascular disease. *Psychotheraphy and Psychosomatics, 60,* 148–167.

Lumley, M.A., Ovies, T., Stettner, L., Wehmer, F., & Lakey, B. (1996). Alexithymia, social support and health problems. *Journal of Psychosomatic Research, 41,* 519–530.

Mai, F.M. (1993). Psychiatric aspects of heart transplantation. *British Journal of Psychiatry, 163,* 285–292.

Manton, K.G., Blazer, D.G., & Woodbury, M.A. (1987). Suicide in middle age and later life: Sex and race specific life table and cohort analysis. *Journal of Gerontology, 42,* 219–227.

McGuinnes, J.B., Begg, T.B., & Semple, T. (1976). First electrocardiogram in recent myocardial infarction. *British Medical Journal, 2,* 449–456.

Miller, N.H., Hill, M., Kottke, T., & Ockene, I., for the Expert Panel on Compliance (1997). The multilevel compliance challenge: Recommendations for a call to action. *Circulation, 95,* 1085–1090.

Miller, W.R., & Rollnick, S. (1991). *Motivational Interviewing: Preparing people to change addictive behavior.* New York: Guilford Press.

Mittleman, M.A., Maclure, M., Sherwood, J.B., Mulry, R.P., Tofler, G.H., Jacobs, S.C., Friedman, R., Benson, H., & Muller, J.E., for the Determinants of Myocardial Infarction Onset Study Investigators (1995). Triggering of acute myocardial infarction onset by episodes of anger. *Circulation, 92,* 1720–1725.

Myers, W.O., Blackstone, E.H., Davis, K., Foster, E.D., & Kaiser, G.C. (1999). CASS Registry long term surgical survival. Coronary Artery Surgery Study. *Journal of the American College of Cardiology, 33*(2), 488–498.

Northern California Neurobehavioral Group (1988). *Manual for the Neurobehavioral Cognitive Status Examination (NCSE).* CA: Fairfax.

Nunes, E.V., Frank, K.A., & Kornfield, D.S. (1987). Psychologic treatment for the type A behavior pattern and for coronary heart disease: A meta-analysis of the literature. *Psychosomatic Medicine, 48,* 159–173.

Ornish, D.M., Brown, S.E., Scherwitz, L.W., Billings, J.H., Armstrong, W.T., Ports, T.A., McLanahan, S.M., Kirkeeide, R.L., Brand, R.J., & Gould, K.L. (1990). Can lifestyle changes reverse coronary heart disease? The Lifestyle Heart Trial. *Lancet, 336,* 129–133.

Orth-Gomer, K., Rosengren A., & Wilhelmsen, L. (1993). Lack of social support and incidence of coronary heart disease in middle-aged Swedish men. *Psychosomatic Medicine, 55,* 37–43.

Poole-Wilson, P.A., & Crake, T. (1989). The enigma of syndrome X. *International Journal of Microcirculation, 8,* 423–432.

Prochaska, J.O., Redding, C.A., & Evers, K.E. (1997). The transtheoretical model and stages of change. In K. Glanz, F.M. Lewis, & B.K. Rimer (Eds), *Health behavior and health education: Theory, research and practice* (pp. 60–84). San Francisco: Jossey-Bass.

Prochaska, J.O., Velicer, W.F., Rossi, J.S., Goldstein, M.G., Marcus, B.H., Rakowski, W., Fiore, C., Harlow, L.L., Redding, C.A., Rosenbloom, D., & Rossi, S.R. (1994). Stages of change and decisional balance for 12 problem behaviors. *Health Psychology, 13,* 39–50.

Radloff, L.S. (1977). The CES-D Scale: A self-report depressive scale for research in the general population. *Journal of Applied Psychological Measurement, 1,* 385–401.

Reaven, G.M. (1994). Syndrome X: Is one enough? *American Heart Journal, 127,* 1439–1442.

Riegel, B., Carlson, B., Kopp, Z., LePetri, B., Glazer, D., & Unger, A. (2002). Effect of a standardized nurse case-management telephone intervention on resource use in patients with chronic heart failure. *Archives of Internal Medicine, 162,* 705–712.

Rollnick, S., & Miller, W.R. (1995). What is motivational interviewing? *Behavioural and Cognitive Psychotherapy, 23,* 325–334.

Rosenman, R.H. (1997). Neurogenic and behavioral influences on plasma lipids. In M. Hillbrand, & R.T. Spitz (Eds), *Lipids, health and behavior*. Washington, DC: American Psychological Association.

Rosenman, R.H., Swan, G.E., & Carmelli, D. (1988). Definition, assessment, and evolution of the Type A behavior pattern. In B.K. Houston, & C.R. Snyder (Eds), *Type A behavior patterns: Research, theory, and intervention*. New York: Wiley.

Roth, H.P., & Caran, H.S. (1978). Accuracy of doctors' estimates and patients' statements on adherence to a drug regimen. *Clinical Pharmacological Therapy, 23*, 361–367.

Rozanski, A., Blumenthal, J.A., & Kaplan, J. (1999). Impact of psychological factors on the pathogenesis of cardiovascular disease and implications for therapy. *Circulation, 99*, 2192–2217.

Rybarczyk, B.D. (1994). Diversity among American men: The impact of aging, ethnicity, and race. In C. Kilmartin (Ed.), *The masculine self*. New York: MacMillan.

Rybarczyk, B.D., & Bellg, A.J. (1997). *Listening to life stories: A new approach to stress management in the medical setting*. New York: Springer Publishing.

Ryan, R.M., Frederick, C.M., Lepes, D., Rubio, N., & Sheldon, K.M. (1997). Intrinsic motivation and exercise adherence. *International Journal of Sport Psychology, 28*, 335–354.

Ryan, R.M., Plant, R.W., & O'Malley, S. (1995). Initial motivations for alcohol treatment: Relations with patient characteristics, treatment involvement, and dropout. *Addictive Behaviors, 20*, 279–297.

Sackett, D., & Snow, J. (1979). The magnitude of compliance and non-compliance. In R. Haynes, D. Taylor, & D. Sackett (Eds), *Compliance in health care*. Baltimore: Johns Hopkins University Press.

Sacks, F.M., Pfeffer, M.A., Moye, L.A., Rouleau, J.L., Rutherford, J.D., Cole, T.G., Brown, L., Warnica, J.W., Arnold, J.M.O., Wun, C., Davis, B.R., & Braunwald, E. (1996). The effect of pravastatin on coronary events after myocardial infarction in patients with average cholesterol levels. *New England Journal of Medicine, 335*, 1001–1009.

Scheidt, S. (1996). A whirlwind tour of cardiology for the mental health professional. In R. Allan, & S. Scheidt (Eds), *Heart and mind: The practice of cardiac psychology*. Washington, DC: American Psychological Association.

Schwartz, S.M., & Ketterer, M.W. (1997). Cholesterol lowering and emotional distress: Current status and future directions. In M. Hillbrand, & R.T. Spitz (Eds), *Lipids, health and behavior*.

Washington, DC: American Psychological Association.

Shepherd, J. (1996). The West of Scotland Coronary Prevention Study (WOSCOPS): Benefits of pravastatin therapy in compliant subjects. *Circulation, 94*(Suppl), 539–543.

Shepherd, J., Cobbe, M., & Ford, I. for the West of Scotland Coronary Prevention Study Group (1995). Prevention of coronary heart disease with pravastatin in men with hypercholesterolemia. *New England Journal of Medicine, 333*, 1301–1307.

Sher, T.G., Bellg, A.J., Braun, L., Domas, A., Rosenson, R., & Canar, W.J. (2002). Partners for Life: A theoretical approach to developing an intervention for cardiac risk reduction. *Health Education Research, 17*(5).

Singh, R.B., Rastogi, V., Rastogi, S.S., Niaz, M.A., & Beegom, R. (1996). Effect of diet and moderate exercise on central obesity and associated disturbances, myocardial infarction and mortality in patients with and without coronary artery disease. *Journal of the American College of Nutrition, 15*, 592–601.

Smith, T.W., Nealey, J.B., Kircher, J.C., & Limon, J.P. (1997). Social determinants of cardiovascular reactivity: Effects of incentive to exert influence and evaluative threat. *Psychophysiology, 34*, 65–73.

Spira, J.L. (Ed.). (1997a). *Group therapy for medically ill patients*. New York: The Guilford Press.

Spira, J.L. (1997b). Understanding and developing psychotherapy groups for medically ill patients. In J.L. Spira, (Ed.), *Group therapy for medically ill patients*. New York: The Guilford Press.

Strecher, V.I., & Rosenstock, I.M. (1997). The Health Belief Model. In K. Glanz, F.M. Lewis, & B.K. Rimer (Eds), *Health Behavior and Health Education* (2nd ed.). San Francisco: Jossey-Bass.

Tabrizi, K., Littman, A., Williams, R.B. Jr., & Scheidt, S. (1996). Psychopharmacology and cardiac disease. In R. Allan, & S. Scheidt (Eds), *Heart and mind: The practice of cardiac psychology*. Washington, DC: American Psychological Association.

Teng, E.L., & Chui, H.C. (1987). The Modified Mini-Mental State (3MS) examination. *Journal of Clinical Psychiatry, 48*, 314–318.

Thomas, S.A., Friedmann, E., Wimbush, F., & Schron, E. (1997). Psychosocial factors and survivial in the cardiac arrhythmia suppression trial (CAST): A reexamination. *American Journal of Critical Care, 6*, 116–126.

Thoresen, C.E., & Bracke, P. (1997). Reducing coronary recurrences and coronary-prone behavior: A structured group treatment approach. In J.L. Spira (Ed.), *Group therapy for medically ill patients.* New York: The Guilford Press.

Tollefson, G.D. (1995). Anger, aggression, and depression. *Journal of Clinical Psychiatry, 56,* 404–418.

Tsang, T.S.M., Barnes, M.E., Gersh, B.J., & Hayes, S.N. (2000). Risks of coronary heart disease in women: Current understanding and evolving concepts. *Mayo Clinic Proceedings, 75,* 1289–1303.

Turk, D., & Meichenbaum, D. (1991). Adherence to self-care regimens. In J.J. Sweet, R.H. Rozensky, & S.M. Tovian (Eds), *Handbook of clinical psychology in medical settings.* New York: Plenum Press.

Walter, J.L., & Peller, J.E. (1992). *Becoming solution-focused in brief therapy.* New York: Brunner/Mazel.

Ware, J.E., & Sherbourne, C.D. (1992). The MOS 36-item short-form health survey (SF-36): I. Conceptual framework and item selection. *Medical Care, 30,* 473–483.

Warren, L.W. (1983). Male intolerance of depression: A review with implications for psychotherapy. *Clinical Psychology Review, 3,* 147–156.

Wenger, N.K., Speroff, L., & Packard, B. (Eds). (1993). *Cardiovascular health and disease in women.* Greenwich, CT: Le Jacq Communictions.

Williams, G.C., Cox, E.M., Hedberg, V.A., & Deci, E.L. (2001). Extrinsic life goals and health risk behaviors in adolescents. *Journal of Applied Social Psychology, 30,* 1756–1771.

Williams, G.C., Freedman, Z.R., & Deci, E.L. (1998). Supporting autonomy to motivate glucose control in patients with diabetes. *Diabetes Care, 21,* 1644–1651.

Williams, G.C., Grow, V.M., Freedman, Z.M., Ryan, R.R., & Deci, E.L. (1996). Motivational predictors of weight loss and weight-loss maintenance. *Journal of Personality and Social Psychology, 70,* 115–126.

Williams, G.C., Rodin, G.C., Ryan, R.M., Grolnick, W.S., & Deci, E.L. (1998) Autonomous regulation and long-term medication adherence in adult outpatients. *Health Psychology, 17,* 269–276.

Williams, R.B., Barefoot, J.C., & Califf, R.M. (1992). Prognostic importance of social and economic resources among medically treated patients with angiographically documented coronary artery disease. *JAMA, 267,* 520–524.

Wise, M.G., & Rundell, J.R. (1994). *A concise guide to consultation psychiatry* (2nd edition). Washington, DC: American Psychiatric Press.

Zigmond, A.S., & Snaith, R.P. (1983). The hospital anxiety and depression scale. *Acta Psychiatry Scandinavia, 67,* 361–370.

Susan M. Labott

4

COPD and Other Respiratory Diseases

Because the respiratory system is intimately involved in the body's functioning, diseases can cause significant physiological and psychological impairment and distress. In this chapter, I briefly review anatomy and respiratory functioning and characteristics of common pulmonary diseases. Next, I discuss reasons for a psychological referral, suggest assessment strategies, and describe major psychological problems associated with pulmonary diseases. I conclude with a discussion of relevant psychological treatment strategies, and a brief description of psychological issues that may present with pulmonary complaints.

Anatomy and Physiology of the Respiratory System

The respiratory system serves two purposes: to supply oxygen to cells and to remove carbon dioxide waste from the body. Air comes

Figure 1. **The respiratory system.**

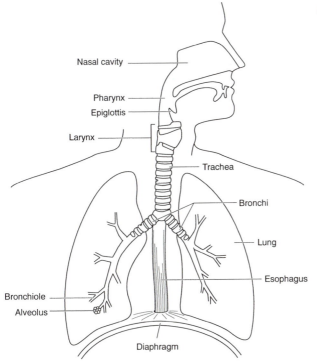

Nasal cavity

Pharynx

Epiglottis

Larynx

Trachea

Bronchi

Lung

Esophagus

Bronchiole

Alveolus

Diaphragm

into the body through the nostrils (see Figure 1). The nasal passages are covered with a ciliated mucous layer which traps foreign particles, and warms and moistens the air as it proceeds to the pharynx. A tube-like passageway, the lower portion is the laryngeal pharynx which separates the passageway into two sections. In front is the airway into the larynx; in back is the food path into the esophagus. The upper end of the larynx contains the vocal cords which vibrate to produce speech. The opening between the vocal cords is the glottis; the epiglottis is the flexible cartilage flap that closes the airway during swallowing.

The trachea connects to the larynx and transports air to the lungs; it extends to the center of the chest, behind the heart. It divides into two bronchi, the main air passageways that enter the lungs, one on each side. The lungs occupy most of the thoracic (chest) cavity, and are separated from the abdominal cavity by the diaphragm, the main inspiratory muscle. The base of each lung rests upon the diaphragm, and the lungs move up and down as respiration occurs.

As each bronchus enters a lung, it subdivides into smaller passageways; the smallest are bronchioles. Terminal bronchioles, those at the end of the passageway, are attached to clusters of air sacs called alveoli. Oxygen passes through the walls of the alveoli into red blood cells, attaches to hemoglobin, and is circulated throughout the body.

Respiration occurs due to air pressure changes and lung elasticity, or compliance. Inhalation is the active phase of breathing. When stimulated, the diaphragm contracts, enlarging the chest cavity. This decreases the pressure in the thorax, resulting in a partial vacuum. Air pressure in the alveoli becomes less than atmospheric pressure, causing air to flow in from outside the body until the internal pressure equals atmospheric pressure. Therefore, air rushes into the lungs.

Expiration is an inactive process. The muscles relax, lung tissues recoil, abdominal organs press up against the diaphragm, and air is pushed out. Here, alveolar pressure exceeds atmospheric pressure, forcing air out of the body, until inside pressure equals atmospheric pressure.

Lung compliance and airway resistance determine the energy it takes to maintain respiration (work of breathing). Factors which decrease lung compliance (e. g., emphysema) increase the work of breathing, as do factors which increase the resistance to air movement (e. g., asthma).

Breathing is regulated by a host of factors. The major neurologic regulation occurs in the medulla where inspiration and expiration are regulated. Other neurons in the pons work to regulate respiratory rhythm. Chemoreceptors, predominantly in the medulla, monitor changes in pH and in levels of blood oxygen and carbon dioxide, sending information to the medullary centers to modify rate and depth. Other factors, such as blood pressure changes, body temperature changes, and lung inflation, also play a role. Finally, respiration can be controlled voluntarily, overriding the respiratory centers temporarily. Voluntary control of breathing originates in the cerebral cortex, and enables us to hold our breath, or to change respiratory rate and depth.

Major Respiratory Disorders and Their Medical Treatment

Chronic Obstructive Pulmonary Disease (COPD)

The American Thoracic Society (ATS; 1995) defines COPD as "a disease state characterized by the presence of airflow obstruction due to chronic bronchitis or emphysema; the airflow obstruction is generally progressive" (p. S78). COPD is generally diagnosed from pulmonary function tests (PFTs) which assess lung capacity and gas transfer ability. Arterial blood gas (ABG) analysis is often performed to evaluate oxygenation.

COPD affects over 16 million Americans, and is the fourth leading cause of death, resulting in 110,000 deaths annually (Department of Health and Human Services, 1998).

This is the only type of lung disease in which white Americans are disproportionately affected. COPD is a chronic and progressive disease; there is no cure. The major cause of COPD is cigarette smoking which accounts for 80–90% of the risk for COPD (ATS, 1995). Other risk factors include occupational exposures to hazardous materials, and α_1-antitrypsin deficiency (a genetic abnormality accounting for 1% of COPD cases).

Individuals have generally smoked a pack of cigarettes per day for 20 years before problems develop. Typical symptoms include dyspnea (shortness of breath), cough, sputum production, airflow limitation, impaired gas exchange, and frequent respiratory infections. At severe levels, individuals must avoid exertion, and may need supplemental oxygen, continually.

COPD treatments are designed to slow its progression and to improve quality of life. The most important treatment is smoking cessation, accomplished through group programs, hypnosis, and nicotine patches. Community interventions are increasingly popular, and worksite smoking cessation programs are becoming common. The success of the various social and psychological treatments is reflected in national statistics, which indicate that smoking has decreased dramatically in the last 30 years (Fisher, Haire-Joshu, Morgan, Rehberg & Rost, 1990).

Pharmacotherapy is also a common component of COPD treatment. Metered dose inhaler bronchodilators, anticholinergic inhalers, or a combination, are often utilized for symptom relief; theophylline is used for some patients. Oral steroids are administered for exacerbations, although their complications often rule them out as a long-term treatment. Antibiotics are administered for infections, and alpha$_1$-antitrypsin augmentation treatment is useful for those suffering from the genetic version of COPD.

Oxygen therapy is another mainstay of COPD treatment, as COPD is often associated with decreased oxygenation of the blood (hypoxemia), which can cause cell and organ damage. Therefore, oxygen may be administered during exertion, during sleep, or continually, and is associated with improved mortality (see Rourke, Grant & Heaton, 1993).

Pulmonary rehabilitation involves an interdisciplinary team that works with patients and families to help them achieve the highest level of functioning possible (see Fishman, 1994). Most pulmonary rehabilitation programs have individual exercise programs as their major focus, see Table 1. Educational activities, through lecture or video, are common, as are support groups, smoking cessation programs, or individual psychotherapy. Many studies have documented positive outcomes of rehabilitation, generally in terms of exercise endurance and quality of life (e. g., Emery, Schein, Hauck, & MacIntyre, 1998; LacasseGuyatt, G.H., Goldstein, & Guyatt, 1997).Lung transplantation is also used to treat COPD, but it is not an option for many, due to organ shortage and the advanced age of most COPD patients. In lung volume reduction surgery, damaged tissue is removed. Preliminary results are promising, in terms of improvements in pulmonary function and exercise tolerance. The treatment, however, is controversial and new evidence indicates that some groups of patients may not benefit (National Emphysema Treatment Trial Research Group, 2001).

Table 1. **Components of a multi-dimensional pulmonary rehabilitation program.**

A. Exercise conditioning
 increase endurance
 decrease dyspnea
B. Educational techniques
 pursed-lip breathing
 cough training; postural drainage
 metered-dose inhaler usage
 nutrition
 medications
C. Psychological/behavioral interventions
 support groups
 individual treatment
 smoking cessation
 coping with chronic illness/cognitive
  problems
 family issues

Asthma

Asthma is a chronic lung disease, involving inflammation and narrowing of the airway, making breathing difficult. The narrowing is often reversible with treatment. Symptoms include wheezing, dyspnea, chest tightness, and cough. Asthma attacks are episodic and variable in terms of frequency, intensity, and duration. They may be triggered by a variety of factors (e. g., irritants, exercise, infection) or may have no apparent cause. Asthma affects approximately 15 million Americans, and occurs in both children (4.4 million) and adults (10.2 million; Department of Health and Human Services, 2001). Prevalence rates in children are higher in African Americans than in non-Hispanic whites. Diagnosis is often confirmed through PFTs or bronchial provocation.

A common treatment for asthma is bronchodilator therapy, or the inhalation of drugs that relax the bronchial muscles. Sympathomimetics are frequently used for this purpose. Corticosteroids may be used to suppress inflammation, but unwanted side-effects may rule out this treatment. Many patients are increasingly interested in complementary and alternative interventions such as chiropractic, acupuncture, and herbal remedies, but these have not demonstrated consistent effects (Angsten, 2000). Status asthmaticus occurs when severe asthma does not respond to outpatient treatment. Individuals are then treated on an inpatient basis, where they are given oxygen, intravenous corticosteroids, and may be intubated. A review of the development of knowledge about asthma for the past 2000 years from a biopsychosocial perspective can be found in Gregerson (2000).

Cystic Fibrosis

Cystic fibrosis(CF) is an autosomal recessive genetic disorder which results in abnormal mucous secretions which effect various organ systems, especially the respiratory system. Abnormal secretions in the respiratory tract make CF patients prone to chronic infections. CF may be diagnosed through PFTs or through use of the "sweat test" (which shows levels of sodium and chloride).

CF is the most common cause of chronic lung disease in white children in the United States, affecting 30,000 children; approximately 80% of the patients die from cardiorespiratory problems (FitzSimmons, 1993). As a result, until very recently, CF patients did not live to adulthood. However, of the 30,000 CF patients in the United States today, approximately 10,000 are over age 20 (Tierney, McPhee & Papadakis, 1997).

Therapy for CF begins by addressing the abnormal airway secretions, through mechanical and pharmacological avenues (Turpin & Knowles, 1993). Mechanical clearance of secretions is accomplished by chest physiotherapy techniques which include postural drainage and percussion, directed cough, and forced expiration. Other treatments include physical exercise, respiratory muscle conditioning, and inhaled bronchodilators. Nutrition and diet are also monitored and supplemented, as children with CF have difficulties with digestion and tend to be small. As the longevity of individuals with CF has increased, osteoporosis and diabetes have become more common (Nasr, 2000). Antibiotics are used to treat recurrent respiratory infections, and exacerbations may require hospitalization for the administration of intravenous antibiotics. Lung transplant is also used to treat CF, and trials of gene therapy are underway (see Jaffe, Bush, Geddes, & Alton, 1999).

Psychological Assessment and Treatment

Referrals

Table 2 outlines the referral questions and psychological concerns that health psychologists commonly receive from pulmonary medical teams. In the inpatient setting, consultation may be requested for acute concerns or chronic problems, generally dictated by the patient's current medical status, and the unit on which he/she is being treated. For

Table 2. Psychological referrals.

Acute medical phase—inpatient consultation
  anxiety/panic
  cognitive changes/delirium/competency
  failure to wean
  staff liaison issues

Chronic medical phase—outpatient treatment
  depression/anxiety
  adjustment to chronic illness
  noncompliance
  neuropsychological problems
  family/relationship issues
  somatization
  end of life decisions
  patient/health care provider relationship
    issues

Table 3. Initial evaluation of pulmonary patients.

A. Medical records review: history and course of medical problem, medication, current and past treatments, other relevant medical issues; PFT and laboratory results
B. Patient interview: psychological history and symptomatology, cognition, occupational status, substance use, stressors, social/familial situation and supports
C. Structured testing: mental status examination, specific areas of concern, overall adjustment, quality of life
D. Collateral information: school performance, peer relationships, family interactions

example, a patient in the intensive care unit may be seen for anxiety or for an evaluation of competency to make medical decisions, especially if withdrawal or withholding of life-sustaining treatment (e. g., a respirator) is a possibility. As the patient's condition improves, failure to wean from a ventilator or depression may become concerns.

Long-term psychological treatment may begin either inpatient or outpatient. If the patient is being treated for a new or worsening problem, issues of adjustment to chronic illness, smoking cessation, family or relationship conflicts, compliance with the medical regimen, somatization, and neuropsychological issues may be relevant. The presentation and treatment of these are, of course, colored by pre-existing cognitive and personality factors.

Assessment

Assessment of individuals with respiratory disease will depend upon the referral question, as well as the context. Most patients are initially seen in hospitals, making it difficult for the health psychologist to perform a complete psychological assessment battery. While a comprehensive evaluation is often

desirable, here I will discuss briefer screening methods that can be performed at the bedside. Table 3 contains relevant issues for an initial evaluation; the structure and content must be modified for the individual case.

Medical records contain the reports of other consultants, and may provide information of relevance to a psychological evaluation. Physicians often document impressions of the individual (e. g., looks depressed, is confused) which can help generate psychological hypotheses. However, medical records may contain mistakes. Therefore, it is best to use them only to generate ideas about the person and his or her history.

Patient interviews need to include psychological, cognitive, and social/familial components; these are usually the source of most of the information obtained. If the patient is able, he/she is the best source of psychosocial information.

Psychiatric history and symptomatology need to be assessed clearly and directly. A comprehensive evaluation of symptoms is warranted, with a focus on depression, anxiety, and psychotic symptoms. Differential diagnostic issues are especially important, e. g., in a COPD patient, weight changes, fatigue, decreased energy, and decreased concentration are not necessarily indicative of depression, as these are also symptoms that result from the physiological changes of COPD.

Table 4. **Assessment instruments for use with pulmonary patients.**

A. Cognitive screening
1. Mini-Mental State (MMS): brief screening device for cognitive changes (Folstein et al., 1975).
2. Strub & Black (1993) tasks: yield information on various aspects of cognitive functioning.

B. Psychological adjustment and coping
1. Psychosocial adjustment to illness scale (PAIS): Assesses adjustment to a chronic medical condition (Derogatis, 1986).
2. Millon Behavioral Health Inventory (MBHI): assesses psychological coping (Millon, Green & Meagher, 1979).
3. Beck Depression Inventory (BDI): screening measure for depression (Beck, Ward, Mendelson, Mock & Erbaugh, 1961).

C. Respiratory issues
1. Chronic Respiratory Questionnaire: an interview to assess functional ability (Guyatt, Berman, Townsend, Pugsley & Chambers, 1987).
2. COPD self-efficacy scale: assesses extent to which individuals can maintain comfortable breathing (Wigal, Creer & Kotses, 1991).
3. Asthma Symptom Checklist: provides a description of experience on several symptom clusters (Kinsman, Luparello, O'Banion & Spector, 1973).

D. Quality of life
1. St. George's Respiratory Questionnaire (Jones, Quirk, & Baveystock, 1991)
2. Quality-of-Life for Respiratory Illness Questionnaire (Maille, Koning, & Kaptein, 1994)
3. Living with Asthma Questionnaire (Hyland, Finnis, & Irvine, 1991)

However, these, with decreased interest, hopelessness, pessimism, and suicidal ideation, would be important in making a diagnosis of major depression. Similarly, dyspnea, choking, and chest pain would, in a healthy patient, probably form the basis for a diagnosis of anxiety or panic. In a pulmonary patient, these may be symptoms of respiratory disease. Respiratory and psychological symptoms often occur simultaneously, e. g., a patient with asthma may begin to panic, exacerbating the problem.

Assessing cognition in pulmonary patients is important, due to the deficits that occur if the individual's system is not delivering sufficient oxygen. Decreased oxygenation can result in changes in cognition that can significantly impact the individual's functioning. For example, individuals may have periods during which they are unable to understand medical instructions, to engage in a psychotherapeutic relationship, or to care for themselves properly. Patients vary in their willingness to admit to cognitive changes; but they should always be asked about changes in concentration and memory. However, a formal evaluation of mental status is critical, as subtle changes may not be apparent to the patient, family, or staff. The changes which can occur due to decreased oxygenation may be temporary or chronic – often requiring a repeat evaluation.

Administration of the Mini-Mental State (MMS; Folstein, Folstein & McHugh, 1975) is a brief, but thorough, way to obtain preliminary information on the client's cognitive functioning. The MMS consists of questions and tasks which evaluate issues such as orientation, attention, recall, and language usage. It requires less than ten minutes to administer, and provides a reliable and valid measure of the patient's ability. Often subtle changes, found on a brief mental status exam, are the earliest sign that the patient is in trouble, therefore, any question about the reason for an abnormality in mental status warrants a complete neuropsychological evaluation.

Assessment of psychological adjustment is aided by the administration of self-report inventories designed to evaluate a particular area, e. g., depression, adjustment to illness. Table 4 contains a list of some common instruments to evaluate psychopathology and adjustment, as well as issues specific to pulmonary disease. Many general and disease-specific measures of quality of life are now available; information on over 50 instruments is available on the ATS website at www.atsqol.org. Derogatis, Fleming, Sudler and DellaPietra (1995) and Sotile (1996) also provide options and details on assessment instruments for medical patients.

Finally, it is useful to interview a relative or friend of the patient, over the telephone, if necessary, to follow-up on concerns and hypotheses derived from earlier portions of the evaluation process. Relatives can often report a deterioration in mood or cognition that the patient can not. This also provides an opportunity to verify important information in cases in which patients may be motivated to provide inaccurate data.

Psychological Issues

Many studies have evaluated overall psychological adjustment in patients diagnosed with pulmonary disease, with a particular focus on depression and anxiety. Neuropsychological functioning has been a source of concern, particularly in COPD, while compliance is a problem in all of the disorders. Families and peer relationships are affected in CF and asthma, while marital and sexual issues are prevalent in CF and COPD.

Adjustment. For children with CF, age and gender are mediating factors in psychological adjustment. Cowen et al. (1985) reported no increases in behavior problems in CF children in comparison to healthy preschoolers, but studies of older children have shown more behavior problems in CF children when compared to their healthy siblings (Simmons et al., 1987) or to children with other illnesses (e. g., Thompson, Gustafson, Gil, Godfrey, & Bennett Murphy, 1998). Comparing adult CF patients to healthy controls, Shepherd et al. (1990) reported no significant differences on social support, self-esteem, or life satisfaction. Further, Anderson, Flume, and Hardy (2001) reported that a group of adult CF patients did not demonstrate significant levels of depression, anxiety, or other psychopathology on a battery of psychological tests. Vila, Nollet-Clemencon, deBlic, Mouren-Simeoni, & Scheinmann (2000) compared asthmatic children to healthy controls, and reported more anxiety symptoms and disorders in the children with asthma, but they were not more depressed, and their self-esteem was comparable. Anxiety disorders were also more prevalent in children with asthma than in those with diabetes, and the asthmatic children also had poorer self-esteem and social competence (Vila, Nollet-Clemencon, & Vera et al., 1999). Interestingly, researchers have found higher rates of familial depression, mania, substance use, and antisocial personality disorder in the families of adolescents with severe asthma, when compared to healthy controls (Wamboldt, Weintraub, Krafchick, & Wamboldt, 1996). Studies of adult asthmatics have reported significant depression (Thompson & Thompson, 1984), and a higher prevalence of agoraphobia and panic than in the general population (Shavitt, Gentil & Mandetta, 1992). In most cases, the asthma occurred before the panic (Perna, Bertani, Politi, Colombo, & Bellodi, 1997). Further, psychiatric disorders have been associated with increased hospitalizations and health care utilization (Ten Brinke, Ouwerkerk, Zwinderman, Spinhoven, & Bel, 2001).Within the COPD population depression is a significant problem, occurring in over 40% of patients (e. g., Aydin & Ulusahin, 2001; McSweeny, Czajkowski & Labuhn, 1996). COPD patients commonly feel depressed and pessimistic about the losses they have experienced as a result of their disease, and the massive adjustments they must make in their lives. They may feel worthless and burdensome to family members, and guilty about the years they smoked in the face of evidence that it was unhealthy. Weight and sleep changes, fatigue, and decreased concentration are also common, but it is important to remember that they may be symptoms of the physiological changes of COPD. Many COPD patients initially enter treatment with unwarranted optimism for its success at restoring their functioning; as they realize the limitations of treatment, suicide is a possibility (Sawyer, Adams, Conway, Reeves & Kvale, 1983).

Anxiety is a common problem in COPD; research shows rates from 34% to 96% (e. g., McSweeny et al., 1996). Breathlessness is a frequent experience, and one can easily see how this could predispose to anxiety disorders. However, dyspnea is not well correlated with changes in measures of respiratory functioning. Most dyspneic episodes are not life-threatening, but could lead to respiratory arrest if not addressed. Often an individual's fear of breathlessness exacerbates the problem. In individuals who live alone especially, dyspnea is associated with fears of dying because no one is there to help.

It has been suggested that emotions elicit breathing difficulty in COPD patients, causing individuals to avoid social and emotional situations — this has been termed the "emotional straitjacket" (Dudley, Wermuth & Hague, 1973). Recent research, however, has found that COPD patients are not socially isolated, nor are they less expressive in terms of weeping or laughter, but they do report less anger control and greater anger expression (Labott & Iannuzzi, 1994). Further, in a laboratory study of anger, the COPD patients did not report significantly less anger experience than controls, and did not demonstrate different patterns in physiological reactivity when angry (Labott, Sanjabi, Jenkins, & Iannuzzi, 2001).

Neuropsychological changes. Early studies of asthmatic children showed perceptual and motor impairments (Dunleavy & Baade, 1980); recent work has demonstrated that these are a short-term result of steroid use, and not associated with permanent changes in brain functioning (Suess, Stump, Chai & Kalisker, 1986). Bender (1999) reviews the literature on cognition in children with asthma, and concludes that brain development and neuropsychological functioning are not affected. However, secondary effects of asth-

ma, such as absences from school, not feeling at their best when at school, and sleep loss can result in difficulty learning. Similarly, in a study comparing CF children to healthy matched controls, no differences were found in intellectual, academic, or neuropsychological functioning (Stewart et al., 1995), although individuals with end-stage CF have been shown to have deficits in memory and executive functions (Crews, Jefferson, Broshek, Barth, & Robbins, 2000).

In COPD patients, neuropsychological changes have been repeatedly documented; the skills affected include abstraction, attention, and psychomotor speed and accuracy (e. g., Rourke et al., 1993). The cognitive deficits result from hypoxemia, and its severity is correlated with the degree of cognitive impairment. Supplemental oxygen treatment results in some improvement in neuropsychological functioning, especially if used continually (Heaton, 1988). Because neuropsychological changes can have important impacts on the patient's ability to participate in and benefit from psychological interventions, they need to be monitored closely.

Compliance. In asthmatic children, noncompliance with medication is 30–70% (see Creer & Bender, 1995). In children who died of asthma, Birkhead, Attaway, Strunk, Townsend, and Teutsch (1989) found near-zero theophylline levels, even through the patients had prescriptions for the medication. Nonadherence to inhaled corticosteroids has been associated with low levels of knowledge about asthma and family dysfunction (Bender, Milgrom, Rand, & Ackerson, 1998).

In CF, compliance is better, possibly because noncompliance has more immediate effects (Lask, 1995), although Stark, Jelalian, and Miller (1995) noted that nonadherence is a problem in certain areas, such as diet, exercise, and chest physiotherapy. Inadequate knowledge, psychosocial resistance, and educated nonadherence all exert effects on compliance with the CF regimen (Koocher, McGrath & Gudas, 1990), as do familial factors (e. g., Anthony, Paxton, Bines, & Phelan, 1999).

The focus of noncompliance research in

COPD has been on smoking cessation. As smoking is multi-determined, personality variables, peer support, and withdrawal are a few of the many factors to consider. Fisher et al. (1990) and Flaxman (1988) provide an overview of the issues and interventions in smoking cessation. Specific suggestions for patients are in Sotile (1996).

Relationships. Traditionally, it was believed that problems in the relationship with the mother were responsible for the development and maintenance of childhood asthma. Separation issues were paramount, and asthma attacks were conceptualized as a cry for the mother. Recent research, however, has demonstrated that asthma results from a host of allergic and immunologic factors.

However, some researchers have argued that either problems in the marital relationship (Askildsen, Watten & Faleide, 1993), or in the parent-child interaction (see Creer & Bender, 1995, for a review) are risk factors. Others have shown that family problems may follow the asthma symptoms (Gustafsson, Bjorksten & Kjellman, 1994). In a study of African-American and Hispanic families, financial burden, family isolation, and personal strain were correlated with asthma impact (Mailick, Holden & Walther, 1994). Conclusions are difficult to draw, but it is likely that, at the very least, family interactions play a role in the extent to which the child is compliant with medication and other treatment interventions which ultimately influence the course of the asthma (e. g., Meijer, Griffioen, vanNierop & Oppenheimer, 1995).

Cystic fibrosis places even more demands on the family than does asthma. Ievers and Drotar (1996) noted a variety of family stressors in the literature, e. g., the difficult treatment regimen, communication problems with family members, financial burdens, lack of information, and strained marital relationships. When CF parents were compared to parents of children with other illnesses, they reported higher levels of stress, generally due to the terminal nature of CF. However, studies of childrearing practices tended to show no differences between CF parents and controls.

As new medical developments have in-creased the life expectancy for those with CF, new issues have arisen. Children with CF may develop problems with body image because they are generally shorter and thinner and may have other characteristics that make them look different from their peers, e. g., puffy face, barrel-shaped chest, clubbed fingers (Bolyard, 2001). A group of women noted that having CF negatively influenced their relationships in adolescence (Johannesson, Carlson, Brucefors, & Hjelte, 1998). CF women also experience delayed puberty, irregular menstrual cycles and ovulation, and up to 20% have fertility problems (see Lemke, 1992, for a review of reproductive issues in CF adults). CF males may also experience delayed puberty, increased risk of genitourinary anomalies, and approximately 95%–98% are infertile (Bolyard, 2001). Concerns about the genetic make-up of the child and the expected shortened duration of the parent's life, make the decision to have children a difficult one, and health professionals often provide little information about these issues.

In the context of COPD, the marital relationship may become strained, resulting in disorganization, stability, or improved functioning as individuals work to adjust to new demands (Cannon & Cavanaugh, 1998). Sexual problems arise due to depression, fatigue, dyspnea, bronchospasms, or medication side-effects, and pre-existing sexual problems complicate the picture. Regardless of the level of impairment, various options for sexual intimacy are available to patients (e. g., Cole & Hossler , 1996; Selecky, 1993).

Psychological Treatment

The psychological treatment of the problems that occur in pulmonary diseases is consistent with current practice, i. e., commonly used techniques for the treatment of anxiety and depression are generally employed. Table 5 contains a summary of the major interventions for COPD, asthma, and CF. In COPD, work has focused on the rehabilitation programs. Devine and Pearcy (1996) reported on a meta-analysis of 65 studies of rehabilitation programs. These programs all included exercise and education, and most included

Table 5. **Psychological treatments in respiratory disease.**

A. Chronic obstructive pulmonary disease
1. Multidimensional rehabilitation
2. Individual cognitive and behavioral psychotherapy
3. Group therapy, self-help groups
4. Relaxation training
5. Psychoactive medications

B. Asthma
1. Self-management programs
2. Family therapy

C. Cystic Fibrosis
1. Group and individual disease management programs
2. Parent counseling

other treatments such as breathing exercises, psychological interventions, or vocational training. They reported positive impacts on psychological well-being, endurance, functional status, dyspnea, and adherence. The extent to which psychological interventions play a role in rehabilitation programs varies greatly, as do the specific interventions used.

Individual psychotherapy, group psychotherapy, vocational, and social counseling, and self-help support groups have all been included as components of pulmonary rehabilitation programs for COPD patients. Specific techniques include imagery, self-control strategies, goal-setting, and contracting. While the content and duration of the interventions differ, they tend to focus on the alleviation of depression and anxiety, adjustment, and improving compliance. Relaxation training (most often progressive muscle relaxation) and desensitization have been successfully used to treat the anxiety associated with dyspnea (e. g., McNabb & Elpern, 1991; Sotile, 1996). McNabb and Elpern (1991) provide a thorough description of the role of behavior in COPD, and also detailed behavior modification interventions that have proven useful. The uses of neuroleptics, antidepressants, and anxiolytics for COPD patients have been described by Dudley and Sitzman (1993). However, each of these can potentially compromise respiration, so all

must be used cautiously. By far, the most work has been done on asthma treatment. Creer (1991) summarizes a comprehensive self-management program which includes education about the contextual variables and antecedents of asthma attacks, and skill training in asthma management and control. Programs of this sort, especially for children, are common. A meta-analytic study of psychoeducational interventions for adults has also demonstrated improvements in a variety of dimensions, e. g., adherence, well-being, frequency of attacks (Devine, 1996). Family therapy has been a popular intervention for asthma patients, and research has shown positive effects (e. g., Gustafsson, Kjellman & Cederblad, 1986). Individual psychotherapy is useful for many asthmatic children, especially if they are significantly anxious or depressed, believe they have little control over the disease, and are erratic in their medication use (Creer & Bender, 1995). Tricyclics and antianxiety medications have been used with asthmatic patients with some positive results, but they have not been commonly used, and their long-term effects are unknown (Creer & Bender, 1995). See the case study below for an example of individual cognitive-behavioral treatment in an adult asthmatic patient.

Case Example

Background: Ms. S is a 32-year-old African American woman with severe asthma, who was referred by her pulmonologist for an evaluation of possible panic attacks. She was diagnosed with asthma as a child, but had minimal difficulty until three years prior to her evaluation. At that time, asthma attacks increased; she made repeated visits to the ER (approximately 15 per month), resulting in 12 admissions, and intubation on 4 occasions in the past three years. Her medications included theophylline, prednisone, several inhalers, and a nebulizer. Ms. S is single and has two children, ages 12 and 15. She has been unable to work the past few years, but would like to return to her work at a day care center. Ms S has completed some college, and has no history of substance abuse or of previous psychological treatment.

Assessment: Ms. S arrived on time, fashionably dressed and made-up. She was open and talkative, noting that a referral to psychology had been suggested in the past but she could see no point because the problem is her asthma. She denied problems with compliance, and described her frustration at the amount of time and money spent on treatments that do not seem to help. She denied depressed mood, indicated sleep is interrupted by shortness of breath at night, appetite increased (weight gain of 80 pounds since beginning prednisone), interest intact, no suicidal ideation. Patient denied anxiety, although noted feeling "hyper" as a result of the inhalers and theophylline. She described many episodes of shortness of breath that seemed to be elicited by a variety of stimuli such as smoke, wind, chemical smells, and exertion. Anger and frustration were also major antecedents of asthma attacks, and Ms S could describe situations in which arguing with her daughter was associated with asthma symptoms. She denied symptoms of panic, mania, paranoia, and reported no hallucinations.

A mental status exam revealed no gross cognitive problems. An MMPI-2 indicated she tends to be self-critical. The profile also indicated she is outgoing, with no significant anxiety, depression, turmoil, interpersonal difficulties, or somatic focus.

Formulation: Ms. S was a competent and independent woman who was able to provide for herself and her children until several years ago when the asthma symptoms increased. She now spends a great deal of time treating her symptoms, visiting physicians, sitting on the sidelines for activities she used to enjoy, and feeling unproductive. Further, her children are entering adolescence and are a source of frustration. Ms. S tends to be organized and efficient, and her inability to control either her body or her children distresses her. Our plan was to begin cognitive-behavioral therapy to help her learn to manage frustration and conflict in ways that would be less likely to elicit symptoms, and to seek strategies to maximize her productivity.

Treatment: Ms S attended weekly psychotherapy sessions for eight months. She was initially asked to monitor situations in which she had difficulty breathing. She reported instances in which she was exposed to smoke, chemicals, or humidity, and social conflicts. She knew to avoid the physi-

cal irritants, and how to properly used her inhalers, nebulizer, and oral medications. She was also quite aware of the physical sensations associated with the onset of breathing difficulty, so we worked to generate strategies to help her cope with the stressful situations. Ultimately, what worked for her was a combination of techniques, both cognitive and behavioral. That is, she learned to evaluate situations and to "choose her battles," rather than reacting to everything with strong affect. She learned to express strong feelings without physical exertion, e. g., no arm waving or yelling. She also become more assertive with others, increasing their understanding of her needs. When symptoms did occur, she learned to relax her body and use imagery to calm herself. The patient also developed the mindset that her mental health is a priority because it impacts her physical health.

One of Ms S's major frustrations was that she was unable to work, make money, and get ahead in life. As her asthma became more under control, she put more and more pressure on herself to go back to work. Given her medical history, her expectations for employment were surprisingly unrealistic. We discussed ways to gradually return to work, the types of employment to seek, and related issues. When faced with opportunities, however, she went for those that offered the most money, rather than those that were the most appropriate for her medical condition. At one point she took a job in construction. Her asthma worsened significantly, and she was unable to keep the job. This was very discouraging to her, although it provided her the opportunity to apply the strategies she had learned to deal with frustration. Treatment ended when the patient moved out of the area.

Outcome: The patient's episodes of severe shortness of breath decreased significantly (although not completely as she continued to have symptoms that were elicited by non-psychological factors). Her ER visits slowly decreased — she was ecstatic when she had not been to the ER in three weeks. In the six months after treatment ended, she made only two visits to the ER. She was hospitalized both times, and intubated once. She believes these had nothing to do with psychological issues. She uses the coping strategies on a daily basis and is quite happy with her results. She continues to look for work, and her goals have become somewhat more realistic.

The psychological treatments for CF are patterned after those for asthma. Therefore, group and individual programs have developed to educate children and parents, and to promote compliance with physiotherapy, medication, and diet programs (see Lask, 1995). Parent counseling is utilized, as parents must play an active role in the child's daily care (e. g., Brown, Krieg & Belluck, 1995). While these programs are promising, little controlled evaluation of them has been reported.

Respiratory Manifestations of Psychological Issues

Frequent symptoms presented to pulmonologists include cough, dyspnea, and stridor. In most cases, they are symptoms of either acute or chronic disease, but in some cases they are not. Clearly, anxiety disorders (i. e., panic) can present with respiratory symptoms, and often anxiety occurs secondary to respiratory disease; the distinction is often difficult to make.

Somatoform disorders can also present with respiratory symptoms. Medically unexplained symptoms (no apparent cause after a thorough medical work-up) were found in 2% of new patients presenting to a pulmonary subspecialty clinic over a two year period (Labott, Preisman, Popovich, & Iannuzzi, 1995). In a follow-up study with a subset of these patients, they had higher scores on scales measuring bodily preoccupation and hypochondriasis, as well as significantly more unexplained symptoms than a pulmonary control group (Labott, Preisman, Torosian, Popovich, & Iannuzzi, 1996).

Paradoxical vocal cord dysfunction (PVCD) presents with asthma symptoms, but provocation tests of airway hyperreactivity are negative. PVCD is produced by adduction of the vocal cords on inspiration, closing the airway when it should be open. Lacey and McManis (1994) present a review of cases of this type, noting that they tend to occur most frequently in women. Treatment generally involves behavioral techniques in which individuals learn to allow breathing to occur naturally.

Other possible somatoform disorders include psychogenic cough, functional aphonias and dysphonias, and paroxysmal sneezing. All are fairly rare, and have been successfully treated with behavioral methods. Finally, factitious disorders have presented with pulmonary symptoms, i.e., individuals voluntarily produce the symptoms to assume a patient role. An overview of the various types of functional respiratory problems can be found in Labott and Iannuzzi (1998).

Professional Issues

My work with respiratory patients and medical personnel has provided a host of challenges. Pulmonary physicians are generally quite aware of the psychological issues and frustrations that their patients face, however, they are often unaware of the role a health psychologist can play in the treatment of these difficulties. Further, most psychologists have little knowledge of pulmonary medicine, so they do not communicate well with physicians. Yet, because changes in a patient's medical status often have important implications for the psychological treatment, communication between the physician and the psychologist is essential. Education is necessary on both sides.

The specific issues that patients bring vary with the duration and severity of the illness, the family situation, and their own personalities. Although sometimes wary at first, patients generally appreciate a focus on the psychosocial issues. Initially, patients and families may be shocked by the diagnosis and frightened for the future. Here, information and support are most valuable. We can provide them with a sense of mastery and control over their illness that they desperately want. As the disease progresses, significant adjustments must be made, in the individual's life plan, in routine activities, and in the family system — many struggle with these adjustments throughout their lives. Here cognitive-behavioral treatment is most useful, and the treatment program must be adjusted as the patient's medical status and concerns change. Helpful information for patients (and professionals) can be found on the website for the American Lung Association (www.lungusa.org).

The final stages of illness provide new problems for patients, families, and psychologists, as individuals become more impaired. We may be asked to evaluate patients for competency to make decisions regarding the withholding or withdrawal of life-sustaining treatment. The social aspects are often problematic, especially when the patient's wishes are unclear and the family is conflicted. I have found these situations to be the most difficult, partly because medications and fluctuating degrees of consciousness make the evaluation complicated. It is difficult to watch individuals as they are weaned from life-sustaining equipment, knowing that this will result in their death. Our impact here is on the timing and circumstances surrounding the death, and we can add a component of humanity that might otherwise be missing in the sterile hospital environment. It is tempting to stop seeing the patient, but both patients and family members are in need of support and help coping.

On the brighter side, the treatment of pulmonary patients can be highly rewarding. Respiratory patients have significant breathing problems, yet most are willing to do what needs to be done to improve their quality of life. They have often not had any type of psychological treatment in the past, and are fresh and motivated. The resilience that people show in coming to grips with their illness, modifying their lifestyle, and coping with family and personal issues, is the most satisfying aspect of work with pulmonary patients.

References

American Thoracic Society (1995). Definitions, epidemiology, pathophysiology, diagnosis, and staging. *American Journal of Respiratory and Critical Care Medicine, 152,* S78–S83.

Anderson, D.L., Flume, P.A., & Hardy, K.K. (2001).

Psychological functioning of adults with cystic fibrosis. *Chest, 119,* 1079–1084.

Angsten, J.M. (2000). Use of complementary and alternative medicine in the treatment of asthma. *Adolescent Medicine, 11,* 535–546.

Anthony, H., Paxton, S., Bines, J., & Phelan, P. (1999). Psychosocial predictors of adherence to nutritional recommendations and growth outcomes in children with cystic fibrosis. *Journal of Psychosomatic Research, 47,* 623–634.

Askildsen, E.C., Watten, R.G., & Faleide, A.O. (1993). Are parents of asthmatic children different from other parents? *Psychotherapy and Psychosomatics, 60,* 91–99.

Aydin, I.O., & Ulusahin, A. (2001). Depression, anxiety comorbidity, and disability in tuberculosis and chronic obstructive pulmonary disease patients. *General Hospital Psychiatry, 23,* 77–83.

Beck, A.T., Ward, C.H., Mendelson, M., Mock, J., & Erbaugh, J. (1961). An inventory for measuring depression. *Archives of General Psychiatry, 4,* 53–63.

Bender, B.G. (1999). Learning disorders associated with asthma and allergies. *School Psychology Review, 28,* 204–214.

Bender, B., Milgrom, H., Rand, C., & Ackerson, L. (1998). Psychological factors associated with medication nonadherence in asthmatic children. *Journal of Asthma, 35,* 347–353.

Birkhead, G., Attaway, N.J., Strunk, R.C., Townsend, M.C., & Teutsch, S. (1989). Investigation of a cluster of deaths of adolescents from asthma. *Journal of Allergy and Clinical Immunology, 84,* 484–491.

Bolyard, D.R. (2001). Sexuality & cystic fibrosis. *American Journal of Maternal/Child Nursing, 26,* 39–41.

Brown, D.G., Krieg, K., & Belluck, F. (1995). A model for group intervention with the chronically ill. *Social Work in Health Care, 21,* 81–94.

Cannon, C.A., & Cavanaugh, J.C. (1998). Chronic illness in the context of marriage. *Families, Systems & Health, 16,* 401–418.

Cole, S.S., & Hossler, C.J. (1996). Intimacy and chronic lung disease. In A.P. Fishman (Ed.), *Pulmonary rehabilitation* (pp. 251–287). New York: Marcel Dekker.

Cowen, L., Corey, M., Keenan, N., Simmons, R., Arndt, E., & Levison, H. (1985). Family adaptation and psychosocial adjustment to cystic fibrosis in the preschool child. *Social Science and Medicine, 20,* 553–560.

Cowen, L., Corey, M., Simmons, R., Keenan, N., Robertson, J., & Levison, H. (1984). Growing older with cystic fibrosis: Psychologic adjustment of patients more than 16 years old. *Psychosomatic Medicine, 46,* 363-376.

Creer, T.L. (1991). The application of behavioral procedures to childhood asthma. *Patient Education and Counseling, 17,* 9-22.

Creer, T.L., & Bender, B.G. (1995). Pediatric asthma. In M.C. Roberts (Ed.), *Handbook of pediatric psychology* (2nd ed., pp. 219-240). New York: Guilford.

Crews, W.D., Jr., Jefferson, A.L., Broshek, D.K., Barth, J.T., & Robbins, M.K. (2000). Neuropsychological sequelae in a series of patients with end-stage cystic fibrosis. *Archives of Clinical Neuropsychology, 15,* 59-70.

Department of Health and Human Services (1998). *National Vital Statistics Report, 47*(4), Table E.

Department of Health and Human Services (2001). New Asthma Estimates, Fact Sheet, released 10/5/01. Retrieved 10/5/01 from http://www.cdc.gov/nchs/products/pubs/pubd/hestats/asthma/asthma.htm.

Derogatis, L.R. (1986). The Psychosocial Adjustment to Illness Scale. *Journal of Psychosomatic Research, 30,* 77-91.

Derogatis, L.R., Fleming, M.P., Sudler, N.C., & DellaPietra, L. (1995). Psychological assessment. In P.M. Nicassio & T.W. Smith (Eds.), *Managing chronic illness* (pp. 59-115). Washington, DC, American Psychological Association.

Devine, E.C. (1996). Meta-analysis of the effects of psychoeducational care in adults with asthma. *Research in Nursing & Health, 19,* 367-376.

Devine, E.C., & Pearcy, J. (1996). Meta-analysis of the effects of psychoeducational care in adults with chronic obstructive pulmonary disease. *Patient Education and Counseling, 29,* 167-178.

Dudley, D.L., & Sitzman, J. (1993). Psychobiologic evaluation and rehabilitation in pulmonary disease. In R. Casaburi & T.L. Petty (Eds.), *Principles and practice of pulmonary rehabilitation* (pp. 252-273). Philadelphia: Saunders.

Dudley, D.L., Wermuth, C., & Hague, W. (1973). Psychosocial aspects of care in the chronic obstructive pulmonary disease patient. *Heart and Lung, 2,* 389-393.

Dunleavy, R.A., & Baade, L.E. (1980). Neuropsychological correlates of severe asthma in children 9-14 years old. *Journal of Consulting and Clinical Psychology, 48,* 214-219.

Emery, C.F., Schein, R.L., Hauck, E.R., & MacIntyre, N.R. (1998). Psychological and cognitive outcomes of a randomized trial of exercise among patients with chronic obstructive pulmonary disease. *Health Psychology, 17,* 232-240.

Fisher, E.B., Haire-Joshu, D., Morgan, G.D., Reh-

berg, H., & Rost, K. (1990). Smoking and smoking cessation. *American Review of Respiratory Disease, 142,* 702-720.

Fishman, A.P. (1994). Pulmonary rehabilitation research. *American Journal of Respiratory and Critical Care Medicine, 149,* 825-833.

FitzSimmons, S.C. (1993). The changing epidemiology of cystic fibrosis. *The Journal of Pediatrics, 122,* 1-9.

Flaxman, J. (1988). Behavioral prevention of COPD: Smoking control. In A.J. McSweeny & I. Grant (Eds.), *Chronic obstructive pulmonary disease* (pp. 163-181). New York: Marcel Dekker.

Folstein, M.F., Folstein, S.E., & McHugh, P.R. (1975). Mini-mental state: A practical method for grading the cognitive state of patients for the clinician. *Journal of Psychiatric Research, 12,* 189-198.

Gregerson, B. (2000). The curious 2000-year case of asthma. *Psychosomatic Medicine, 62,* 816-827.

Gustafsson, P.A., Kjellman, N.-I.M., & Cederblad, M. (1986). Family therapy in the treatment of severe childhood asthma. *Journal of Psychosomatic Research, 30,* 369-374.

Gustafsson, P.A., Bjorksten, B., & Kjellman, N.-I.M. (1994). Family dysfunction in asthma. *Journal of Pediatrics, 125,* 493-498.

Guyatt, G.H., Berman, L.B., Townsend, M., Pugsley, S.O., & Chambers, L.W. (1987). A measure of quality of life for clinical trials in chronic lung disease. *Thorax, 42,* 773-778.

Heaton, R.K. (1988). Psychological effects of oxygen therapy for COPD. In A.J. McSweeny & I. Grant (Eds.), *Chronic obstructive pulmonary disease: A behavioral perspective* (pp. 105-121). New York: Marcel Dekker.

Hyland, M.E., Finnis, S., & Irvine, S.H. (1991). A scale for assessing quality of life in adult asthma sufferers. *Journal of Psychosomatic Research, 1,* 99-110.

Ievers, C.E., & Drotar, D. (1996). Family and parental functioning in cystic fibrosis. *Developmental and Behavioral Pediatrics, 17,* 48-55.

Jaffe, A., Bush, A., Geddes, D.M., & Alton, E.W. (1999). Prospects for gene therapy in cystic fibrosis. *Archives of Disease in Childhood, 80,* 286-289.

Janson, C., Bjornsson, E., Hetta, J., & Boman, G. (1994). Anxiety and depression in relation to respiratory symptoms and asthma. *American Journal of Respiratory and Critical Care Medicine, 149,* 930-934.

Johannesson, M., Carlson, M., Brucefors, A.B., & Hjelte, L. (1998). Cystic fibrosis through a female perspective. *Patient Education and Counseling, 34,* 115-123.

Jones, P.W., Quirk, F.H., & Baveystock, C.M. (1991). The St. George's Respiratory Questionnaire. *Respiratory Medicine, 85* (suppl), 25–31.

Kinsman, R.A., Luparello, T., O'Banion, K., & Spector, S. (1973). Multidimensional analysis of the subjective symptomatology of asthma. *Psychosomatic Medicine, 35,* 250–267.

Koocher, G.P., McGrath, M.L., & Gudas, L.J. (1990). Typologies of nonadherence in cystic fibrosis. *Developmental and Behavioral Pediatrics, 11,* 353–358.

Labott, S.M., & Iannuzzi, M.C. (1994). [Emotional expression in COPD]. Unpublished raw data.

Labott, S.M., & Iannuzzi, M.C. (1998). Respiratory manifestations of psychologic issues. *Pulmonary and Critical Care Update (online), 13,* lesson 9.

Labott, S.M., Preisman, R.C., Popovich, J., & Iannuzzi, M.C. (1995). Health care utilization of somatizing patients in a pulmonary subspecialty clinic. *Psychosomatics, 36,* 122–128.

Labott, S.M., Preisman, R.C., Torosian, T., Popovich, J., & Iannuzzi, M.C. (1996). Screening for somatizing patients in the pulmonary subspecialty clinic. *Psychosomatics, 37,* 327–338.

Labott, S.M., Sanjabi, P.B., Jenkins, N., & Iannuzzi, M.C. (2001). Anger experience and expression in chronic obstructive pulmonary disease. *Psychology, Health & Medicine, 6,* 481–486.

Lacasse, Y., Goldstein, R.S., & Guyatt, G.H. (1997). Respiratory rehabilitation in chronic obstructive pulmonary disease. *Reviews in Clinical Gerontology, 7,* 327–347.

Lacey, T.J., & McManis, S.E. (1994). Psychogenic stridor. *General Hospital Psychiatry, 16,* 213–223.

Lask, B. (1995). Psychological aspects of cystic fibrosis. In M.E. Hodson & D.M. Geddes (Eds.), *Cystic fibrosis* (pp. 315–327). London: Chapman & Hall Medical.

Lemke, A. (1992). Reproductive issues in adults with cystic fibrosis. *Journal of Genetic Counseling, 1,* 211–218.

Light, R.W., Merrill, E.J., Despars, J.A., Gordon, G.H., & Mutallipassi, L.R. (1985). Prevalence of depression and anxiety in patients with COPD. *Chest, 87,* 35–38.

Mailick, M.D., Holden, G., & Walther, V.N. (1994). Coping with childhood asthma. *Health and Social Work, 19,* 103–111.

Maille, A.R., Koning, C.J.M., & Kaptein, A.A. (1994). Developing a quality-of-life questionnaire for patients with respiratory illness. *Monaldi Archives of Chest Disease, 49,* 76–78.

McNabb, W.L., & Elpern, E.H. (1991). Behavior modification in COPD. In N.S. Cherniak (Ed.), *Chronic obstructive pulmonary disease* (pp. 535–541). Philadelphia: Saunders.

McSweeny, A.J., Czajkowski, S.M., & Labuhn, K.T. (1996). Psychosocial factors in the rehabilitation of patients with chronic respiratory disease. In A.P. Fishman (Ed.), *Pulmonary rehabilitation* (pp. 443–479). New York: Marcel Dekker.

Meijer, A.M., Griffioen, R.W., van Nierop, J.C., & Oppenheimer, L. (1995). Intractable or uncontrolled asthma: Psychosocial factors. *Journal of Asthma, 32,* 265–274.

Millon, T., Green, C.J., & Meagher, R.B., Jr. (1979). The MBHI: A new inventory for the psychodiagnostician in medical settings. *Professional Psychology, 10,* 529–539.

Nasr, S.Z. (2000). Cystic fibrosis in adolescents and young adults. *Adolescent Medicine: State of the art reviews, 11,* 589–603.

National Emphysema Treatment Trial Research Group (2001). Patients at high risk of death after lung-volume-reduction surgery. *New England Journal of Medicine, 345,* 1075–1083.

Perna, G., Bertani, A., Politi, E., Colombo, & Bellodi, L. (1997). Asthma and panic attacks. *Biological Psychiatry, 42,* 625–630.

Ries, A.L., Kaplan, R.M., Limberg, T.M., & Prewitt, L.M. (1995). Effects of pulmonary rehabilitation on physiologic and psychosocial outcomes in patients with chronic obstructive pulmonary disease. *Annals of Internal Medicine, 122,* 823–832.

Rourke, S.B., Grant, I., & Heaton, R.K. (1993). Neurocognitive aspects of chronic obstructive pulmonary disease. In R. Casaburi & T.L. Petty (Eds.), *Principles and practice of pulmonary rehabilitation* (pp. 79–91). Philadelphia: Saunders.

Sawyer, J.D., Adams, K.M., Conway, W.L., Reeves, J., & Kvale, P.A. (1983). Suicide in cases of chronic obstructive pulmonary disease. *Journal of Psychiatric Treatment and Evaluation, 5,* 281–283.

Selecky, P.A. (1993). Sexuality and the patient with lung disease. In R. Casaburi & T.L. Petty (Eds.), *Principles and practice of pulmonary rehabilitation* (pp. 382–391). Philadelphia: Saunders.

Shavitt, R.G., Gentil, V.V., & Mandetta, R. (1992). The association of panic/ agoraphobia and asthma. *General Hospital Psychiatry, 14,* 420– 423.

Shepherd, S.L., Hovell, M.F., Harwood, I.R., Granger, L.E., Hofstetter, C.R., Molgaard, C., & Kaplan, R.M. (1990). A comparative study of the psychosocial assets of adults with cystic fibrosis and their healthy peers. *Chest, 97,* 1310–1316.

Simmons, R., Corey, M., Cowen, L., Keenan, N., Robertson, J., & Levison, H. (1987). Behavioral adjustment of latency age children with cystic fibrosis. *Psychosomatic Medicine, 49,* 291–301.

Sotile, W.M. (1996). *Psychosocial interventions for cardiopulmonary patients.* Champaign, IL: Human Kinetics.

Stark, L.J., Jelalian, E., & Miller, D.L. (1995). Cystic fibrosis. In M.C. Roberts (Ed.), *Handbook of pediatric psychology* (2nd ed., pp. 241– 262). New York: Guilford.

Stewart, S., Campbell, R.A., Kennard, B., Nici, J., Silver, C.H., Waller, D.A., & Uauy, R. (1995). Neuropsychological correlates of cystic fibrosis in patients 5 to 8 years old. *Children's Health Care, 24,* 159–173.

Strub, R.L., & Black, F.W. (1993). *The mental status examination in neurology* (3rd ed.). Philadelphia: F.A. Davis.

Suess, W.M., Stump, N., Chai, H., & Kalisker, A. (1986). Mnemonic effects of asthma medication in children. *Journal of Asthma, 23,* 291–296.

TenBrinke, A., Ouwerkerk, M.E., Zwinderman, A.H., Spinhoven, P., & Bel, E.H. (2001). Psychopathology in patients with severe asthma is associated with increased health care utilization. *American Journal of Respiratory and Critical Care Medicine, 163,* 1093–1096.

Thompson, R.J., Jr., Gustfson, K.E., Gil, K.M., Godfrey, J., & Bennett Murphy, L.M. (1998). Illness specific patterns of psychological adjustment and cognitive adaptational processes in children with cystic fibrosis and sickle cell disease. *Journal of Clinical Psychology, 54,* 121–128.

Thompson, W.L., & Thompson, T.L. II (1984). Treating depression in asthmatic patients. *Psychosomatics, 25,* 809–812.

Tierney, L.M., Jr., McPhee, S.F., & Papadakis, M.A. (1997). *Current medical diagnosis and treatment* (36th ed.). Stamford, CT: Appleton & Lange.

Turpin, S.V., & Knowles, M.R. (1993). Treatment of pulmonary disease in patients with cystic fibrosis. In P.B. Davis (Ed.), *Cystic fibrosis* (pp. 277–344). New York: Marcel Dekker.

Vila, G., Nollet-Clemencon, C., deBlic, J., Mouren-Simeoni, M.-C., & Scheinmann, P. (2000). Prevalence of DSM IV anxiety and affective disorders in a pediatric population of asthmatic children and adolescents. *Journal of Affective Disorders, 58,* 223–231.

Vila, G., Nollet-Clemencon, C., Vera, M., Robert, J.J., deBlic, J., Jouvent, R., Mouren-Simeoni, M.C., & Scheinmann, P. (1999). Prevalence of DSM-IV disorders in children and adolescents with asthma versus diabetes. *Canadian Journal of Psychiatry, 44,* 562–569.

Wamboldt, M.Z., Weintraub, P., Krafchick, D., & Wamboldt, F.S. (1996). Psychiatric family history in adolescents with severe asthma. *Journal of the American Academy of Child & Adolescent Psychiatry, 35,* 1042–1049.

Wigal, D.K., Creer, T.L., & Kotses, H. (1991). The COPD self-efficacy scale. *Chest, 99,* 1193–1196.

Kimeron N. Hardin

5

Chronic Pain Management

Pain is a universal phenomenon. It is the most commonly reported symptom in medical offices and is responsible for billions of dollars of healthcare costs worldwide. Recent estimates suggest that between 10 to 30 percent of Americans, or about 24 to 80 million people, suffer from some type of pain (Turk & Nash, 1993). The economic consequences for this country are staggering with some estimates as high as 550 million lost workdays at a cost of over $100 billion per year (Turk & Nash, 1993), which includes the costs of medical care, lost income, disability income and legal issues related to pain. Beyond the economic costs, pain has a very significant and detrimental impact on a patient's psychological and social well-being. One third of sufferers reported in a recent survey that sometimes their pain is so severe and they feel so debilitated that they want to die (Foley, 2000).

The International Association for the Study of Pain (Merskey & Bogduk, 1994), a multidisciplinary organization of researchers and clinicians, defines pain as "... An unpleasant sensory and emotional experience associated with actual or potential tissue damage, or described in terms of such damage." The experience of pain is as unique to the individual as is their personality and upbringing. How, then, do health care providers begin to make sense of a person's "pain" and what is the role of a psychologist in the evaluation and treatment of this common problem?

This chapter is designed to provide the reader with a basic understanding of the medical and psychological aspects of the experience of chronic pain and specific information about how psychologists function in

a pain management center. As with any psychologist in a medical setting, a working knowledge of the physiological aspects of the condition, pain in this case, is essential. To this end, I will discuss the development of what is considered to be the best current theoretical representation of the experience of pain as we now know it. Following this brief review, commonly-used medical interventions for pain management will be discussed. I will then turn to the psychological assessment and treatment of patients with pain. In this section, I will examine the types of common referrals you will see for pain management and how to assess these patients adequately for both medical and psychological treatment needs. Finally, I will explore the formulation of a treatment plan, various treatment approaches and the various referral resources you may have available to you. This chapter will conclude with an example of a person who successfully manages her pain and her response to treatment.

The Perception of Pain

Pain is both a physiological and a psychological experience. Yet putting this realization into practice in treatment has not been simple, given the relative separation of traditional Western medicine and psychotherapy. The two fields have developed on separate tracts largely due to the pervasive influence of the work of Descartes, the 17th century philosopher who proposed a distinction between the mind and the body, known as *dualism*. This concept is an important one, since the modern biomedical model is still heavily weighted toward classifying problems as either "medical" or "psychological" (or "psychogenic"). The tendency to ignore psychosocial issues in the investigation and treatment of pain has in many ways added to the types of problems faced by people suffering with pain and will be necessary to address as a pain psychologist.

Physiological Theories of Pain

The recognition of pain as a complex mind-body phenomenon did not gain wide acceptance until relatively recently. Pain was first conceived as a simple, *stimulus-response* process known as "specificity theory" (Boring, 1942). This simple theory proposed that humans have free nerve endings in the skin that respond to specific types of stimulation and travel to the brain along specific pathways. This theory purports that different intensities of painful sensation are directly related to the amount of tissue damage caused by the stimulus. This way of conceptualizing pain has also influenced modern medicine's primary approach to pain in this century: find the cause of the pain and "fix" it with surgery and medication.

Pain that could not be explained by this and other biomedical theories, as well as the failure of traditional medical interventions to alleviate all pain, led to dissatisfaction with this model and to the development of a more complex theory by a psychologist, Ronald Melzack, and physiologist, Patrick Wall, called the "gate control" theory (Melzack & Wall, 1965). While this theory combined many components of previous models, it added the concept that pain signals were transmitted from the site of injury to the spinal cord where the signals are modulated before they go on to the brain for perception. The site in the spinal cord where this modulation occurs is referred to as the "gate," which can be affected not only by the intensity of the initial stimulation in the periphery, but also by factors in the spinal cord itself and by messages coming back from the brain.

In other words, the "gate" is controlled both by pain transmission along fibers that go from the site of injury to the spinal cord to the brain (afferent tracts), and by transmission of signals from the brain to the spinal cord that happens almost simultaneously (descending tract). This descending tract is presumably influenced by cognitive and/or emotional factors that may either assist in opening the gate to allow the perception of greater pain or in closing the gate, reducing the person's overall experience of pain. This important theory was among the first to consider the contribution of both mind and body to the experience of pain. As such it helped initiate the concept of multidisciplinary treatment of pain. The gate control theory continues to undergo revision as we increase our understanding of the anatomy and physiology of the nervous system and the contributions of the mind (Melzack, 1996).

In sum, often the treatment of pain requires the consideration of multiple factors including the type of stimulus that initiates pain (such as peripheral injury or systemic disease), the effectiveness of medical practitioners in reducing or eliminating this stimulus or its effects, and the cognitive/emotional/social makeup of the patient. It is commonly accepted that an individual's perception is a mediator of the experience of pain. Other factors, such as chronicity (or amount of time one experiences pain), and pain pattern, are also important factors to consider in the formulation of a treatment plan.

Acute vs. Chronic Pain

As discussed previously, most Western physicians are trained to detect the underlying cause of a symptom and direct treatment toward the cause in an attempt to eliminate suffering and/or produce a cure. When pain is the symptom, this "search and eliminate" mentality is shared in many cases by both the physician and patient. There are expectations of a "quick fix" in our culture as well, as evidenced by TV commercials with a "fast-fast-fast relief" emphasis.

When the pain is acute (like the pain you feel after you stub a toe), this type of approach makes sense. Acute pain is meaningful, telling us to stop what we're doing to avoid further harm and seek attention for the injury. Acute pain is often accompanied by a release of adrenaline, leading to increased muscle tension, heartrate, respiration, and stomach acid production. Emotionally, these changes are often experienced as anxiety/ fear/stress (Gil, 1992), which serves to motivate the person to move away from the source of the pain and provides the best physiological conditions for "fight or flight." Common medical interventions for acute pain include bedrest or reduced activity, pain medications, traction/ bracing/immobilization, heat or ice, and sometimes surgery.

Distinguishing acute from chronic pain has led to sweeping changes in modern thinking about pain treatment. Even while drug therapy continues to advance at an astounding pace, it is clear that drugs alone have not been able to control wide ranges of pain syndromes. Overuse of drugs and other acute pain treatments in fact are likely to exacerbate many chronic pain problems by adding gastrointestinal, physical deconditioning, cognitive or other side-effect stressors. In order to address chronic pain more effectively, our health care culture has had to look beyond the traditional biomedical model, which focuses on nerves and receptors, to the consideration of how the body, mind and society interact.

Pain is considered "chronic" presumably when the physician feels that enough time has elapsed for the normal healing process to have occurred. Generally, this has been estimated from one to six months, with even longer estimates for healing of neurological injuries. The term "chronic pain" is not dependent on the type of illness/injury or the prognosis, but simply is used to describe pain that has continued beyond what was expected and has shown few signs of going away. The term "benign" is often added if the pain is not due to a life-threatening illness, such as cancer or end-stage AIDS. Examples of chronic benign pain include low back pain, recurring or constant tension and migraine headaches, irritable bowel syndrome, postherpetic neuralgia (nerve damage due to shingles) and arthritis. Causes of chronic pain can include inflammation, scar tissue around a nerve root, instability of the spinal vertebrae, a damaged nerve (or neuropathic pain), and of course "unknown" factors.

Part of the frustration for many patients with chronic pain occurs when they fall into the last camp, that is, pain from no determinable cause, from a medical perspective. Other common psychological/emotional reactions to living with chronic pain include depression, anger/irritability, anxiety, lowered self-esteem, memory problems and suicidality. In a direct comparison between the emotional responses of acute and chronic pain patients, one recent study (Kinney, Gatchel, Polatin, Fogarty & Mayer, 1993) found that chronic pain patients were more likely to be depressed, to suffer from personality disorders, and to abuse drugs and alcohol than acute low back pain patients.

The Emotional Correlates of Chronic Pain

There is continued debate regarding whether psychological factors lead to the development of chronic pain or whether the majority of ad-

Severe
Premorbid
Psychopathology

Figure 1. **Pain patient, premorbid psychological functioning.**

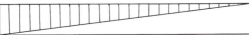

"Normal"
Premorbid
Functioning

verse psychological reactions are consequences of having chronic pain. Most chronic pain patients can be placed on a continuum between the patient with relatively "normal" premorbid function who goes on to become emotionally distressed after developing chronic pain and the chronic pain patient who had a history of psychological difficulties prior to developing chronic pain. See Figure 1 for a graphic representation of the continuum. Certainly where one falls on this continuum will directly impact treatment strategy.

Moving from Acute to Chronic Pain

More detailed explanations of how a patient moves from acute pain to chronic pain have been offered which present information useful in treatment planning. For example, Keefe (1982) defines three stages of pain: acute, prechronic and chronic. The acute pain stage, immediately following an injury, provides useful information to the patient to move away from the source of the injury and seek help. The prechronic pain stage is a critical time where the patient either begins to heal or to lose hope that the pain will decrease. This stage may be a crucial time to begin psychological intervention. The chronic pain stage then continues beyond the expected time course and develops its own cyclical pattern complicated by both psychological and social reinforcers. Gatchel (as cited in Gatchel, 1996), also proposes a three stage model presented in Figure 2, beginning with the initial reaction to pain of anxiety and fear in Stage 1, leading to further psychological consequences in Stage 2, and finally the acceptance of the "sick role" in Stage 3 and the development of habitual illness behaviors.

The role of the psychologist in the treatment of acute pain is valuable, particularly in teaching coping skills to reduce anxiety

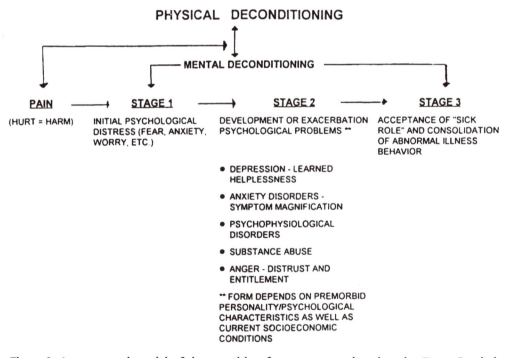

Figure 2. A conceptual model of the transition from acute to chronic pain. From Gatchel, R.J. (1996). Psychological disorders and chronic pain: Cause and effect relationships. In R.J. Gatchel & D.C. Turk (Eds.), *Psychological approaches to pain management: A practitioner's handbook* (pp. 33–52). New York: Guilford.

about both the experience of pain and interventional medical procedures. Techniques such as providing information about the procedures and natural course of the pain, relaxation and distraction, biofeedback and hypnosis are very useful in reducing anxiety associated with acute pain (Williams, 1996).

Maintaining and Exacerbating Cycles of Chronic Pain

Psychologists who work with chronic pain patients will recognize predictable patterns, known as "chronic pain syndrome," that develop as a patient with pain pursues medical intervention with little success, leading to frustration and a sense of despair, hopelessness and worthlessness. If continually treated with acute pain management methods, the pain appears to worsen. For example, while bedrest is an appropriate intervention immediately following an injury during the healing phase, over time, muscles quickly become atrophied and the person loses stamina. Loss of range of motion and muscle atrophy also occurs with prolonged bracing, which is meant to immobilize an area only during the healing phase.

On the border between iatrogenic harm and desperation, many pain patients seek out very aggressive or invasive interventions which carry little to no likelihood of improvement and, in fact, may carry a risk of further damage and more pain through the formation of scar tissue, accidental nerve damage, and even anesthesia overdose or medication toxicity. Frustration and anger increase muscle tension leading to more pain, leading to more anger. Chronic anger, muscle tension and atrophy lead to feelings of fatigue which in turn decreases motivation which in turn leads to passivity, more depression and a sense of hopelessness. Sleeplessness, another common complaint of the chronic pain patient, leads to depression, fatigue, multiple body aches, and so on. See Figures 3 and 4 for simplified drawings of pain cycles.

Another common cyclical problem for pain patients is the tendency to perform activities until the pain forces them to stop, particularly during periods when the pain is in-between "flare ups." They begin to associate activities that were previously pain-free with pain exacerbation and thereby avoid activity altogether or they persist in this reduced activity-overactivity pattern (Keefe, Beaupré & Gil, 1996; see Figure 5). These cycles are often maintained by rigid self-expectations that they should overcome the pain and thereby avoid feelings of "defeat," but in a larger sense, they may prolong the self-destructiveness of overdoing that leads to fatigue and depression.

It is a primary role of the psychologist to assess the factors contributing to this downward spiral into depression, passivity and hopelessness. The psychologist also will need to understand the patient's traditional coping mechanisms to see how they may be helpful to the patient in learning to successfully cope with pain. If the patient falls into the right side (lesser premorbid psychopathology) of the continuum in Figure 1, he or she may have many resources which can be fo-

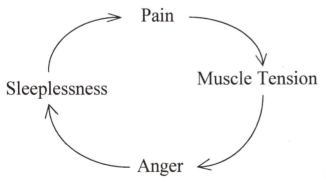

Figure 3. **Pain-agitation cycle.**

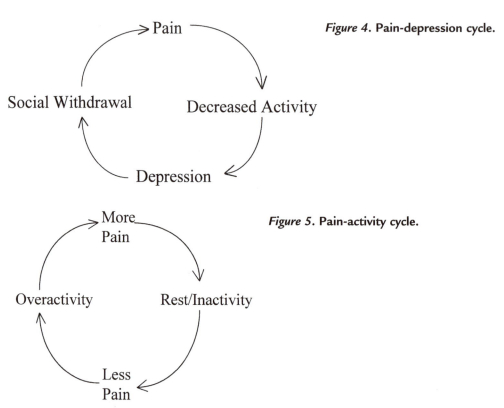

Figure 4. Pain-depression cycle.

Figure 5. Pain-activity cycle.

cused on managing pain more effectively. If the patient falls into the left side (greater psychopathology prior to pain), often old pathological or self defeating ways of coping with the world must be addressed before the patient can establish new and healthier ways of coping with pain.

The Assessment of the Chronic Pain Patient

Obviously, since the experience of pain is a result of physiological, cultural and perceptual factors, assessment from a biopsychosocial perspective is most desirable before forming a comprehensive treatment plan. The physicians role is to assess for underlying physical mechanisms contributing to the experience of pain. Common medical assessment procedures include a thorough physical examination and history, review of medical records, and ancillary testing. These tests include radiologic procedures (CAT scans, Magnetic Resonance Imaging (MRI), etc.), laboratory tests (blood work), pharmacologic blockade of nerves ("nerve blocks"), tests of autonomic function, and electrophysiological tests, such as electromyography (EMG) and evoked potential monitoring (Erickson, 1989).

The psychologist's role in a comprehensive assessment, based on a biopsychosocial model, involves evaluation across multiple systems, requiring flexibility of theoretical perspective. Whether the psychologist is working in isolation or as a part of a multidisciplinary team, becoming familiar with the work of other types of professionals in the treatment and management of pain is essential. Often the psychologist is in the best position to coordinate integrated care since he or she often spends a significant amount of time assessing the largest range of patient's needs through self-report, clinical interview, psychological testing, observation, and family input. Psychologists are also often primary conveyers of basic educational information about the self-management of chronic pain to patients and therefore our assessment allows us to detect knowledge deficits that may be acting as obstacles to treatment compliance or successful coping with pain. Normalizing the emotional experience of chronic pain patients is another valuable component of the initial assessment process provided by the psychologist. Understanding that depression, fear and irritability are common reactions to the experience of chronic pain can help the patient feel more comfortable with the assessment process and later intervention.

Characteristics of the Psychologist

Although it is part of the role of the psychologist during an interview to assess for overt psychopathology, related or unrelated to the pain, it is extremely important that one maintains an air of respect for the patient's experience of pain, physically or psychologically. Learning to think "holistically" (or about the patient' pain as a complex interaction between mind and body), rather than from either a "physical versus psychogenic" perspective, takes some practice and may be difficult initially. This is not to say that true psychogenic conditions don't exist, since you may well see the occasional conversion disorder or other somatoform disorder if you work frequently with a chronic pain population. However, in my experience, the true conversion disorder is quite rare. You will certainly see patients who may have enormous exacerbating or maintaining psychological factors affecting their pain experience, but these issues alone do not invalidate the possibility of underlying physiological processes as well. What is important to the patient is that you believe they are suffering and that you do not minimize the importance of this experience in their lives. Your warmth, respect and empathy play an important role in preventing or reducing patient resistance, both in the interview and in later treatment.

Referral Issues

As with any psychological assessment in a medical setting, the reason for referral is an important consideration in the psychological evaluation of these patients. For example, assessing the patient's appropriateness for a surgical procedure versus conservative (less invasive) intervention requires a slightly different focus than trying to decide whether the patient is ready for a rehabilitation program or vocational training. These and similar questions are necessary considerations before beginning the interview and may be helpful in structuring the evaluation itself.

Many times unfortunately, patients are referred to a psychologist as a "last resort" or to "help them learn to live with it," as is commonly reported by patients. They also are referred by physicians because of obvious emotional upset, most often signs of depression, anxiety or agitation. Occasionally, patients self-refer to a mental health professional because they have a sense that their emotional "suffering" is out of control or family stress has motivated them to seek help.

Common Pain Syndromes

In terms of specific pain syndromes (pain defined by the location of the pain or diagnosis), the most commonly reported type of pain is musculoskeletal, most specifically in the lower back, affecting from 50 to 75 percent of adults (Frymoyer, 1992; Skovron, 1992) at some point in their lives. Although only about 3 to 7 percent of acute low back sufferers go on to develop chronic pain problems, they account for more than three quarters of the cost of treatments (Nachemson, 1992). Other forms of musculoskeletal pain commonly presented for treatment include neck and shoulder pains, arthritis, fibromyalgia and myofascial pain syndromes. Also commonly seen are constant or frequently-occurring headaches (such as migraines, tension or cluster headaches), deep and chronic visceral pains (chest pain, orofacial pain, abdominal pain, gynecologic pain, and genitourinary pain), nerve and root injury pains (peripheral neuropathies, "phantom" pains, complex regional pain syndrome, and facial pain). For more detailed information regarding these conditions see Wall and Melzack's (1994) revision of the classic *Textbook of Pain*.

Regardless of the specific pain syndrome, many of the same emotional, behavioral and cognitive issues are shared by patients with chronic pain and can be approached in a similar way during the psychological evaluation. Since basic psychological assessment of the medical patient has been covered in detail in Chapters 2 and 3, I will cover primarily the factors unique to the assessment of the chronic pain patient.

Psychological Evaluation of the Chronic Pain Patient

There are three major sources of information that are essential in determining the cognitive, behavioral, intrapsychic, interpersonal, and psychophysiological factors influencing how a patient perceives and copes with pain. These include the clinical interview, medical records and psychological testing. Other helpful sources of information include discussion with the primary care physician, family interviews, and the keeping of a "pain diary" or log (Philips, 1988; Camic, 1989) by the patient of hourly pain intensity and associated behaviors, cognitions, emotions, medications, and interpersonal events that either precipitate, or are in response to, the pain.

The Clinical Interview

The structure of the initial interview with a chronic pain patient is extremely important for several reasons. First, although psychological or behavioral factors may be strongly related to the exacerbation or maintenance of the pain, many patients have been stigmatized by the medical system in the past and are expecting to hear that the pain is "all in their head." Beginning the interview in an unstructured, exploratory way may lead the patient to shut down, out of fear or resent-

ment. Second, it has been suggested that the somatizing patient (one who converts emotions into, or intensifies, bodily ills) may lack the appropriate language for emotional expression, a concept known as alexithymia. This form of somatization may be interpreted psychodynamically as a defense mechanism, cautioning the interviewer to move slowly into the emotional realm (see McDougall, 1989). Third, and relatedly, since many patients come to a psychologist upon the referral of a physician and may not understand clearly the role of the psychologist in their treatment plan, a semistructured interview with an initial emphasis on discussion of the role of the psychologist and pain may be useful in building patient trust.

The Semistructured Clinical Interview

The initial interview with a chronic pain patient may be highly stressful for the patient for several reasons. First, they often do not understand the role of the psychologist in the treatment of pain and therefore they see the visit as a threat to the validity of the pain complaint. Second, they may be referred to a psychologist by a medical provider who has implied, directly or indirectly, that the pain is "psychological" in nature. Finally, our culture still has a pervasive stigma against seeking mental health treatment and the patient may have only vague notions of what is expected of them in the session.

As a result of these perceptions, chronic pain patients may be guarded or even actively resistant or hostile to the interviewer, sometimes preventing the accurate assessment of factors important to the formulation of a treatment plan. I find it helpful to follow a semistructured interview format designed specifically to meet several basic goals, namely (1) reduction of patient resistance, (2) gathering essential information and (3) beginning positive transference for later treatment interaction.

Patient resistance often can be initially minimized by beginning the interview with an introduction to the role of the pain psychologist and a few words designed to alleviate their fears of being told the pain is "all in your head." A very brief discussion of the emotional impact of chronic pain on suffering works nicely, as well as a description of the various functions of the multidisciplinary team (if appropriate).

I then recommend beginning the actual interview with a complete pain history including pain location and quality (sensory and affective), exacerbating, alleviating and maintaining behaviors (including family responses), pain history (initial onset; course; medical, psychological and alternative interventions) and current pain beliefs and coping strategies. Beginning the interview with a discussion of the pain itself often puts the patient more at ease since your interest in this issue may be experienced as legitimizing. Since many pain patients are depressed, I incorporate an assessment for clinical depression during the pain history, especially addressing the vegetative symptoms in this phase.

From a behavioral perspective, the events or responses that follow a "pain behavior" (any observable behavior that signifies the experience of pain to others) have the potential to reinforce or reward the behavior (Fordyce, 1976; Romano et al., 1992) and are important to assess during the interview. Spouses or other family members may often feel helpless, but eager to reduce the pain experience of the family member in pain and may unknowingly establish new patterns of communication or family roles based on these responses. Fordyce identifies other potential systemic sources of reinforcement of pain behaviors or passiveness such as disability income, avoidance of responsibility and attention or sympathy from others (Fordyce, 1976, 1990). Obviously changes in the family system are crucial here as well. Patterson and Garwick (as cited in Kerns & Payne, 1996) have proposed a cognitively-mediated, Family Adjustment and Adaptation Response model that helps explain how families attempt to maintain balance or homeostasis when the role of a family member changes due to illness or pain.

While the initial and primary section of the semistructured interview is focused primarily on pain, the second section should broaden to address other health concerns and behaviors such as parental health/pain problems, smoking and alcohol/drug use, and may include caffeine intake or dietary habits. Identifying both healthy and maladaptive cognitions, beliefs and behaviors will be useful later in treatment planning.

Family health questions can lead to a discussion of childhood background including the experience of physical, sexual or emotional abuse, other family dysfunction and early models of maladaptive behaviors. I abbreviate or omit these questions at times depending on the patient's comfort level and tolerance during the initial interview with the goal of exploring them further as trust develops. From early childhood, I move forward into educational, vocational and relationship history and continue until we reach current functioning, living situation and stressors. As we discuss, I make an assessment of cognitive functioning, less formal if apparently intact and more formal if deficits are suspected. I also am attuned to unusual pain behaviors or other nonverbal cues.

Near the end of the interview, presumably when the patient has become the most relaxed with the process, I include a more thorough mood disorder assessment and suicide risk assessment. I usually end the interview with some words of hope through basic observations to the patient about behaviors that can be altered to improve pain coping skills, reduce pain or at least avoid further deterioration, and I give recommendations for further behavioral intervention.

An excellent example of a pain clinic psychologic evaluation form is included at the end of his chapter (Camic, 1989).

Psychological Testing

A significant portion of the assessment will be gathered through the clinical interview and behavioral observations, yet a more comprehensive picture may be gained through the addition of focused psychological testing. Commonly used psychological tests in the assessment of chronic pain patients range from those that deal with assessment of pain characteristics (such as pain intensity,

Table 1.

Test	Description	Psychometrics	Comments
Pain Measures			
VAS/0–10 scales	Subjective pain ratings on a continuum with bipolar anchors	Mixed data on reliability and validity. No normative data.	Limited sensitivity to tx induced changes. Scale cannot be assumed to be equal intervals.
McGill Pain Questionnaire (MPQ)	First attempt to measure perceptions of sensory, affective and intensity dimensions of pain experience.	Adequate reliability and validity.	Sensitivity to differences is questionable but is improved using Melzack's weighted-rank method.
Multi-dimensional Pain Inventory (MPI)	Based on cog-beh. model of chronic pain. Includes patient's percept. of pain, spouse's responses and activity levels.	Adequate reliability and validity. Normed on a male VA chronic pain population. No validity scales.	Useful for outcome studies. Very inexpensive to use and is computer-scored.
Behavioral Assessment of Pain Questionnaire (BAPQ)	Measures disability caused by sub-acute and chronic pain. Helps identify environmental and psych. factors that may maintain disability.	Adequate reliability and validity. Normed on a more varied chronic pain population.	Authors claim useful for making treatment decisions including appropriateness for a pain program or work hardening. Computer-scoring and reports are relatively expensive.
Pain Patient Profile (P³)	Designed to identify patients experiencing emotional distress associated with pain. Three scales include depression, anxiety and somatization.	Limited data suggests adequate reliability and validity. Offers a validity index.	Very brief. Better used as a screening tool.
Function and Disability Measures			
Oswestry Disability Index (ODI)	Simple, face-valid, self-report measure of daily function/activity level and use of pain meds.	Correlates with actual tests of function.	Useful as a screen for functional impairment and may suggest the need for a more extensive FCE.
Functional Capacity Evaluation (FCE)	A method, rather than a test, of directly assessing physical function and work capacities of an impaired patient usually by a physical therapist.	Little evidence available regarding validity or reliability.	Motivational factors may affect performance. Should include an interpretation by a psychologist in the final assessment report.
Personality Measures			
Minnesota Multiphasic Personality Inventor (MMPI; MMPI-2)	Most frequently used psychological test. Commonly use in pain pts. To screen for psychopathology and test-taking attitude.	Adequate reliability and validity. Has validity scales.	Pain research is conceptually flawed in trying to use it to distinguish between "psychogenic" and "physical" pain. May be too long for the average pain patient's attention span. Revision offers four "pain type" categories. Computer scoring and reports available.

Test	Description	Psychometrics	Comments
Millon Clinical Multiaxial Inventory (MCMI; MCMI-2,3)	Offers clinical scales for both Axis I and II. Includes Somatoform, PTSD and Alcohol/drug dependency scales.	Adequate reliability and validity. Has validity scales. Provides base rates instead of standard scores.	One major advantage is the shorter length (175 items) than the MMPI (566 items). Also more closely aligns with DSM-IV. Computer scoring and reports available.
Mood Measures			
Beck Depression and Anxiety Inventories (BDI; BAI)	Brief self-report inventories designed to assess severity of depression and anxiety in adolescents and adults.	Adequate test-retest reliability in a nonpatient population and adequate validity.	Useful for tracking changes in depressed pain patients and in pre-post, outcome-based studies.
Hamilton Anxiety and Depression Scales (HAM-A,D)	Brief observer-rating scales of anxiety and depression.	Adequate interrater reliability and adequate validity.	Useful as an adjunct to self-report measures. Useful in outcome-based research and in patient mood tracking.
Cognitive Measures			
Mini Mental Status Examination (MMSE)	Very brief, gross screen for disturbances in attention, consciousness, orientation and mental clarity. Multiple versions available.	Limited information on reliability or validity.	Recommended as part of each psychological assessment of pain patients given the potential for overmedication. Can help identify those who need full neuropsychological assessment.
Cognistat Neurobehavioral Cognitive Status Examination (NCSE)	Designed to assess intellectual functioning in five major areas: language, constructions, memory, calculations and reasoning.	Adequate reliability and validity.	Useful as a screen when cognitive deficits are suspected from medical history, family or self-report, or physician referral. Can help identify those who need full neuropsychological assessment.

pain beliefs and coping, and level of function) to more traditional psychological tests of personality, mood, cognitive functioning, and general illness attitudes or behaviors. Table 1 provides a quick reference guide to common psychological tests used to assess chronic pain patients.

Assessment of Pain

Although there is no way to measure pain directly, correlates of the experience of pain can be measured by (1) self-report, (2) behavioral, and (3) physiological techniques.

Brief, unidimensional self-report tests of pain perception include the Visual Analog Scales (which asks the patient to draw a line indicating where they think their pain falls between bipolar anchors) or alternately, asking the patient to rate their pain from "0" to "10," with 0 being "no pain" and 10 being the "worst pain imaginable" (see Figure 6). Other tests like the McGill Pain Questionnaire (Melzack; 1975, 1987), the Multidimensional Pain Inventory (WHYMPI; Kerns, Turk & Rudy, 1985), and the Behavioral Assessment of Pain Questionnaire (Tearnan & Lewandowski, 1992) were developed as attempts to measure the multidimensionality of pain.

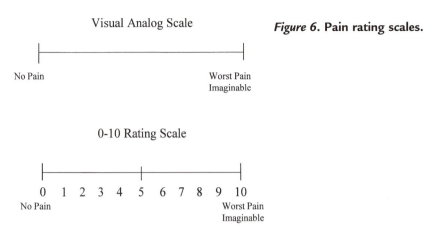

Figure 6. **Pain rating scales.**

Assessment of Disability and Function

Self-report of pain is not always the best measure of outcome in a psychological or behaviorally-focused treatment program. In fact, many programs, particularly those based on the operant principles of Fordyce, focus more on the functional levels of the patient rather than on decreasing subjective complaints of pain. One could argue that even if reduction in pain was a primary goal, one would expect activity levels to increase concurrently.

Disability level or functional activity levels are assesed by the Oswestry Disability Index (Fairbank, Davies, Couper & O'Brien, 1980; Baker, Pynsent & Fairbank, 1989), a simple, face-valid self-report measure with ten items that assess nine areas of daily function and activity level and the use of pain medication. The Functional Capacity Evaluation (FCE) is a method, rather than a specific test, of directly assessing the physical function (strength, endurance capacities) and work capacities (ability to push-pull, lift, etc.) of an impaired patient, usually by a physical therapist. These capacities are measured across several hours to days and often involve multiple trials of the same task to allow for error variance. Sometimes, these comprehensive evaluations include a portion conducted by a psychologist regarding emotional distress or behavioral factors affecting performance. Often, motivational factors play a significant role in the performance of the patient on these tasks. Some FCE's include data interpreting the motiva-

tion of the patient based on consistency or inconsistency of effort. These tests can therefore be harmful to the patient without proper interpretation by a psychologist familiar with the patient's background.

Assessment of Personality

Just as current perceptions of pain, emotional reactions to pain/disability and family factors affect adjustment to chronic pain, the role of the personality in coping with pain is an important one. Aside from Axis I disorders, the presence of an Axis II personality disorder is important for treatment planning and to the development of a relationship between the patient and his or her treating professionals. While no specific personality disorder has been found to predict pain chronicity better than others (Bigos et al, 1991), the presence of any personality disorder is generally a poor prognostic sign in pain management due to poor "life coping" skills.

Depending on the evaluation purpose, whether as a screen or as a comprehensive assessment, it may be helpful to include a formal personality inventory. The two most commonly used instruments are the MMPI (Hathaway & McKinley, 1951) and the MCMI (Millon, 1983). Generally, it appears that lower scores on the MMPI are predictive of better response to treatment. The MMPI-2 was introduced in 1989 with new scales and larger normative group. Based upon work by Costello, Hulsey, Schoenfeld and Ramamurthy (1987), computerized reports group chronic pain patients into four types: P — the most distressed patients, A — highly anxious and catastrophizing patients, I — agitated, depressed patients, and N — or normal patients. Newly added content scales can be very useful in determining the patient's most significant concerns. Special scales regarding potential substance abuse or dependency issues are also useful with this population. The MCMI-III has been judged by Green (as cited in Uomoto, Turner & Herron, 1988) to be more accurate in evaluating personality traits, coping styles, and interpersonal relationships (important issues with many chronic pain patients) compared to the MMPI.

I prefer to use the MCMI-III over the most recent revision of the MMPI (MMPI-2) for several reasons. First, the MCMI-III more closely aligns with the DSM-IV, allowing for more straightforward suggestions of diagnosis. Second, most pain patients are already highly suspicious of psychologists, and lengthy testing tends to encourage resistance. The MCMI-III has about two-thirds fewer items than the MMPI-2. Finally, the MCMI-III offers a number of specific scales of relevance to the assessment of chronic pain patients including the Somatoform, Alcohol/Drug Dependence, and Post-Traumatic Stress Disorder scales. A disadvantage of the MCMI-III include the potential overdiagnosis of personality disorders in pain patients (Repko & Cooper, 1985).

Other alternatives to the MMPI-2 and MCMI-III that may be useful in the chronic pain population include the Millon Behavior Health Inventory (MBHI; Millon, Green & Meagher, 1982) and the Millon Behavioral Medicine Diagnostic (MBMD; Millon et al., 2001).

The MBHI is a brief, self-report personality inventory that assesses psychological coping factors related to the health care of adult medical patients. It consists of 150 True-False items and while not specifically tailored to patients with chronic pain, it is useful in identifying potentially problematic responses to illness or treatment, developing rehabilitation programs for patients with chronic illnesses and identifying psychological issues that contribute to the maintenance or exacerbation of the disease or condition.

Scales include basic coping styles, psychogenic attitudes, psychosomatic correlates, prognostic indications and a validity index.

The MBMD is the newest of the Millon inventories and it contains 165 True-False items. It is normed on adult medical patients with a variety of medical problems. Scales include response patterns, psychiatric indications, coping styles, stress moderators, treatment prognostics, management guides, and negative health habits.

Both the MBHI and MBMD can be computer scored with options for either short profile reports or longer, interpretive reports.

Assessment of Mood and Cognition

The comprehensive assessment of a chronic pain patient may include other measures beyond pain instruments, disability or functional measures and a personality inventory. Often, it may be useful to include unidimensional scales of mood such as the Beck Depression Inventory (self-report) or the Hamilton Anxiety Scale (interviewer ratings). These instruments often supplement interview impressions and make very useful repeat measures to help monitor patient progress.

Given the possibility of cognitive deficits in this population (Jamison & Parris, 1988), due to the original injury, depression, surgical procedures with anesthesia, or overmedication, it is helpful to include at least an informal assessment of cognitive functioning. Commonly used measures include the Mini Mental State Examination (Folstein, Folstein & McHugh, 1975) and the Cognistat Neurobehavioral Cognitive Status Examination (Northern California Neurobehavioral Group, 1983).

Additional Assessment Measures

Pain produces both an emotional reaction and autonomic arousal, with one likely affecting the other. Attempts to correlate self-reported pain levels with measured physiological arousal has generally not been successful. However, three physiological variables — muscle tension, autonomic indices, and evoked potentials in the brain — have been explored as potential measures of pain.

Abnormal patterns of muscle tension have been measured with surface electromyography (EMG) in chronic pain patients. Level of muscle activity however does not correlate consistently with self-reported pain severity (Basmajian, 1978) and is generally not considered a valid index of pain. Autonomic indices, such as blood flow, pulse, hand temperature, and skin resistance (EDR) have also been measured in attempts to assess pain, again with some doubt about the usefulness of these measures. Evoked potentials or electrical signals generated by the brain in response to sensory stimuli, have shown some promise in differentiating patients with chronic pain and those who did not have pain, but again it is not precise or consistent enough for practical use according to Syrjala and Chapman (as cited in Brannon & Feist, 1996).

Behavioral observation techniques have been suggested as alternatives to self-report measures (Keefe & Block, 1982). Several behavior ratings systems (Keefe & Block, 1982; Follick, Ahern & Aberger, 1985) have been developed to observe the overt "pain behaviors" of the patient, or behaviors that signify that they are in pain or are suffering. Common pain behaviors include frowning, grimacing, groaning, limping, and crying and are subject to the same operant principles as all other behaviors. Aside from attempting to assess pain levels through rating scales, one can begin to determine what factors may be reinforcing or rewarding these behaviors such as avoidance of responsibilities, increasing attention or sympathy, and financial gain. Keefe and Block (1982) have found that decreases in pain behaviors were correlated with decreases in pain ratings. Behavioral observation scales are often more suitable to inpatient or highly structured environments, such as the workplace or physical therapy office.

Assessment Purpose

Selecting the proper tests depends primarily on the purpose of the assessment. For example, you may be consulted to determine a patient's readiness for an expensive and invasive medical procedure that may rely on rigid patient compliance with a postprocedure treatment plan. Recent consensus suggests that patients with active psychosis, untreated depression, active suicidal or homicidal behavior, serious alcohol or drug addiction problems, serious cognitive deficits or severe sleep disturbances (Nelson, Kennington, Novy & Squitieri, 1996) should probably be excluded from these procedures until they have been provided appropriate psychological intervention. Other exclusion or cautionary criteria include somatization disorder, involvement in pain-related litigation, and lack of social support. Additional factors to consider include constant pain ratings despite varying situations, certain personality disorders (paranoid, borderline, antisocial, etc.), patients with history of sexual and/or physical abuse, extremely elevated scores on the 1-2-3 neurotic triad scales of the MMPI, rigid concepts of pain or pain treatment ("pain is purely physical"), and unrealistic expectations of pain relief (Nelson et al., 1996).

Pre-surgical psychological assessments typically include an interview, objective and subjective pain measures, a personality inventory, a cognitive screen, a pain beliefs inventory and appropriate mood scales. An excellent guide to this process is provided by Andrew Block, Ph.D. (1996). The goal is to provide the surgeon with information that is relevant to the patient's predicted tolerance of the procedure, both during and after, their available social support, and their ability to comply with postsurgical instructions.

Another common purpose for assessment includes establishing appropriateness for participation in a multidisciplinary treatment program. These intensive programs, operating from a biopsychosocial model, may range from more operantly-based (Fordyce, 1976), to more eclectic approaches, and in both inpatient and outpatient settings. Programs are generally staffed by a team of professionals from various backgrounds including medicine, nursing, physical/occupational therapy, biotherapy and psychology. Each member of the team assesses the patient's appropriateness from that particular specialty's perspective and to make an assessment of the patient's overall level of motivation for change, realistic expectations and openness to accepting a more active role in the management of pain. Often the psychologist's assessment will focus on determining maladaptive behaviors that exacerbate or maintain the pain and that may be targeted for change, level of function, nonpain goals for improvement (less depression, more social activities), and obstacles (both psychological and physical) that might prevent full participation. Aside from initial pain measures and a personality inventory, measures of coping, level of function and mood are useful in this context.

Occasionally, you may be asked to perform an assessment as a consultation for insurance, legal purposes or establishment of disability status. In such cases, the psychologist must be aware that future psychological interventions are likely to be determined based on his or her evaluation report and recommendations. Keeping in mind that often in these cases, nonpsychologists will be making these determinations, such as case managers, attorneys or judges, the language of your report should be clear, understandable and not overly technical.

You may need to focus your assessment so that it communicates as accurately as possible about both the physical and psychological consequences of the pain and why it is necessary to include psychological services in any current treatment plan or the costs of such future treatment as a part of the financial settlement. A word of caution: many chronic pain patients will retain an attorney at some point, whether it is to sue for a personal injury, negotiate with worker's compensation, or file for social security disability. It is in your, and your patient's, best interest as a possible expert witness or treating professional to put only information that is relevant to the patient's pain in written documentation such as notes or reports, since this information will most likely surface in settings that could be potentially embarrassing or detrimental to the patient.

DeGood and Dane (1996) recommend that psychologists who are subpoened by the opposing attorney "stick as close to the facts as possible, offering minimal comment or interpretation." In support of their patients, however, they report that they often "add comments about the danger of stereotyping pain patients, point out potential abuses where they seem to occur, and emphasize where accusations made about the patient's motives and character seem improbable in light of his or her past social and work history."

Finally, specific psychotherapy recommendations may be reason for evaluation in itself. As mentioned previously, it is important to understand the effective treatment options for pain patients and where they are available, whether it be through a referral to a multidisciplinary clinic, or through provision of education, location of resources or individual, group or family psychotherapy. Usually it is helpful to provide brief explanations of how each treatment recommendation will be helpful in breaking the cycles of chronic pain and enhancing coping skills for the patient.

Treatment Considerations for Chronic Pain Patients

While the individual psychologist can be successful in helping the chronic pain patient to cope more effectively with pain, it is more recently accepted that the multidisciplinary treatment of pain is more effective because of the biopsychosocial focus on pain. At a minimum, this would mean that individual practitioners in solo practices, who concurrently treat a chronic pain patient, would communicate regularly with each other regarding goals, changes in treatment strategies, problems, etc. Optimally, these practitioners would function as a team, in the same facility or institution, and formulate integrated goals from an initial multidisciplinary assessment, providing the patient with specific, clear and consistent guidelines. As mentioned previously, such teams typically consist of a physician (usually an anesthesiologist, neurologist, or physiatrist), a psychologist, a physical/occupational therapist, a biotherapist (someone who provides mind-body techniques like biofeedback, relaxation training, imagery, etc.) and a nurse. Other teams may include practitioners such as acupuncturists, chiropractors or osteopathic physicians, massage therapists and yoga/meditation instructors. Before we move into the specifics of treatment from a psychologist's perspective, it will be helpful to have a basic understanding of the roles of the other team members.

Roles of Team Members in a Multidisciplinary Treatment Plan

The role of the physician in a team approach is multifaceted. First, the physician is often the gatekeeper to the participation of the patient in a multidisciplinary program. His or her role at this point is to communicate clearly to the patient the need for such an approach, emphasizing the complexity of chronic pain. Half of the battle in convincing the patient to consider nonmedical alternatives is won when the physician can communicate the need for psychological, social and behavioral change in a nonstigmatizing manner. Once this has been accomplished, the physician in the team continues to support the goals of the team with the patient while beginning his or her own specific part of the treatment plan. The physician, in this case, will focus primarily on the biomedical aspects of the pain problem, such as reviewing past medical records to determine whether basic, "firstline" treatments have been tried or tests have been done. Certainly, if a simple medical approach that would be effective has been missed, the physician may proceed with this before, or concurrently with, other team members' treatment. The physician may initiate relatively conservative medical interventions, such as medication management of the pain, or very aggressive interventions such as the implantation of pain medication pumps or spinal cord stimulators. Regardless of the intervention, the physician who functions as a part of a team will make this decision in coordination with both the other team members and the patient and will continue to support the approaches of the other team members.

Another very important member of the team is the physical or occupational therapist.

The guiding principle for these professionals is to increase the physical capacity and function of the patient. They will be able to explain to the patient the importance of remaining active, both physically and emotionally. Often, issues of motivation are discussed in this setting with frank discussions about fear of reinjury, "overdoing" on good days, activity pacing, good body mechanics, posture, and physical limit-setting. Typically, some type of gentle, graded exercise program is initiated, within the limits of the individual's capacity, with focus on setting small, achievable goals rather than larger, and potentially frustrating or demotivating, ones. Generally, the occupational therapist, in addition to re-establishing strength and stamina, will focus on helping the chronic pain patient to learn new ways of accomplishing daily tasks (such as dressing, grooming, household chores, etc.) within their physical or pain limitations.

The biotherapist is also often an important part of the multidisciplinary team, giving the patient a greater awareness of the impact of stress, pain and tension on the body. These professionals, often with varied types of backgrounds including nursing, counseling and other somatic therapies, accomplish this deeper awareness by focusing on training the chronic pain patient to use specific stress-reduction skills such as abdominal breathing, progressive muscle relaxation, biofeedback, bodywork, visualization and imagery.

Depending on the setting, the psychologist may often take on multiple roles, taking on the responsibility of coordinator of care as well as primary educator. Whether functioning independently or as a part of a larger team of professionals, there are specific approaches to working with a chronic pain patient that are effective. I will describe these in the following section.

Psychoeducation of the Chronic Pain Patient

One of the simplest, and often most effective, interventions that can be provided by a psychologist to reduce anxiety, confusion, and resistance, is education about chronic pain, including its physical and emotional conse-quences, natural course (without effective intervention) and available treatment options. In my experience, this information is best presented early and with the opportunity for questions and discussion. There are several ways that patients can be provided this information.

First, the information can be presented in a psychoeducational class or group format through formal lectures by either the psychologist alone or with each member of the team speaking from their particular perspective. For example, a typical program at a university-based medical center may offer an eight-week series of classes, with each class consisting of a one-hour lecture followed by an hour of support and discussion. Each class is organized by topic with each lecture provided by a different member of the multidisciplinary team. Topics include an introduction to the biopsychosocial aspects of pain, the basic neuroanatomy of pain, medication use (including a discussion of the concepts of addiction and tolerance), activity levels, stress and pain, cognitive aspects of pain, basic nutrition and sleep hygiene. The educational components of these groups are very helpful in empowering "defeated" or frustrated patients and encouraging a more active role in their own treatment planning.

Occasionally, it may be difficult to provide these types of classes for the patient. Psychologists may find limited numbers of patients available for a group, due to patient difficulties in traveling or limited financial resources of the patients. Also, patients with severe social anxiety may resist a referral to a group. In these cases, bibliotherapy may be an effective alternative that can be incorporated into the individual psychotherapy format. Two books for patients that include basic educational information, strategies and further references include Catalano and Hardin (1996) and Caudill (2002).

Stress Management

Everyone feels the impact of stress. Our bodies respond to perceived threats with a stress response, which involves excitation of the sympathetic nervous system, emotional arousal and cognitive interpretation. While this response, also known as "fight or flight," has adaptive purposes, particularly in avoiding imminent danger or further harm, remaining in this state chronically leads to wear and tear on the human body. For the chronic pain patient, there are many chronic or ongoing stressors, including the pain itself, loss of financial security, and family changes. The effect of living in this state often manifests as constant muscle tension, agitation, difficulty sleeping, fatigue, or exhaustion, other physical problems and depression (Sapolsky, 1998). All of these can lead to more pain.

Recent review articles on the effectiveness of relaxation training techniques (Lehrer, Carr, Sargunaraj & Woolfolk, 1994; National Institute of Health, 1996) found them to be effective adjuncts to the treatment of both chronic pain and insomnia. See Table 2 for common stress management techniques used with pain patients.

Stress management includes the above systematic approaches which help the chronic pain patient gain a sense of awareness and control over his or her psychophysiological responses to stress. However, effective stress management also should include broader discussions of changing or eliminating the sources of stress. For example, many pain programs help the patient distinguish between stress as a reaction to an external stressor, such as a noisy neighbor or rude salesman and internal stressors, such as the perception of pain, negative cognitions, or emotional distress.

In an effort to help a patient cope with external stressors, many programs offer classes in effective communication skills, such as assertiveness, other social skills training, or problem-solving training. Learning to eliminate or reduce the external stressors, or effectively detach from other stressors that cannot be reduced through the patient's effort, may help patients cope more effectively with the pain. Aside from techniques listed above, which help the patient reduce the effects of stress on the body and mind, and the learn-

Table 2. Stress management techniques for pain patients.

Technique	References	Comments
Abdominal breathing	Catalano & Hardin, 1996	Simple, effective beginning technique easily learned by most patients. Especially effective during acute pain flares and stress.
Progressive muscle relaxation (PMR) and **Autogenics**	Jacobsen, 1938; Bensen, 1975; Davis, Eschelman & McKay, 1995	Requires no special equipment. Patients can modify scripts and tapes to suit tastes. Enhances awareness of particular areas where tension is held in the body.
Biofeedback	Arena & Blanchard, 1996	Requires some equipment and training in their use. Patient-induced autonomic changes with visual/auditory feedback increases self-perception of control. Muscle imbalances can be isolated and addressed specifically.
Mindfulness meditation	Kabat-Zinn, 1991	Practiced regularly, can generalize across many life systems. Particularly effective for patients motivated to address existential fears.
Hypnosis	Syrjala & Abrams, 1996	Most useful when instructed in *self*-hypnosis to increase active coping strategies.
Guided imagery	Jaffe & Bresler, 1980	Individually-tailored images may increase effectiveness. Useful in reducing ego-alien images of pain.

ing of new skills with which to effect change in the environment, the effective modulation of cognitive distortion has been found to be extremely important in assisting patients toward effective coping with pain (Loscalzo, 1996; Bradley, 1996).

Cognitive-Behavioral Therapy (CBT)

Although the term "cognitive-behavioral therapy" has been applied to many different types of psychotherapy in widely varying settings, there are common features to all types of cognitive-behavioral therapy that are useful in the treatment of the chronic pain patient. Essentially, five assumptions underlie all CBT interventions according to Turk and Rudy (1989). These paraphrased assumptions are: (1) that people actively process information from their environment internally and behaviors are influenced by perceptions and expectations; (2) that thinking may alter behavior by eliciting emotions and

thoughts may be affected by physiological and emotional behaviors; (3) there is a reciprocally influencing relationship between behavior and the environment; (4) effective interventions must include emotional, cognitive and behavioral dimensions of the individual; and (5) individuals must be active participants in treatment in learning new ways of coping.

One reason that cognitive-behavioral treatment is rapidly becoming the treatment of choice for pain patients appears to be the obvious compatibility with the biopsychosocial model of pain used in many multidisciplinary settings. The experience of pain, whether acute or chronic, is an extremely emotional experience, leading to depression, anxiety, and anger. Activity levels are decreased in response to the pain due to fear of re-injury, avoidance of the pain itself and with increasing depression. Other changes in overt behaviors such as increased attention-seeking and pain behaviors are typically observed also. Along with these behavior changes, it follows, from a cognitive-behavioral perspective, that distorted beliefs, attitudes, and perceptions arise or intensify.

Typical CBT techniques include increasing the patient's awareness of distorted or irrational thoughts, teaching strategies for evaluating the accuracy of these thoughts, stopping or disputing them, and replacing the maladaptive ones with healthier, more realistic alternatives. Typical negative styles of thinking for pain patients include catastrophizing ("This pain will only get worse."), blaming ("It's all my doctor's fault."), and polarizing ("I'll either find a cure or die.") and lead to demotivation and depression.

Several specific cognitive-behavioral coping strategies have been developed for pain patients including self-efficacy training (Bandura, O'Leary, Taylor, Gauthier & Gossard, 1987); pain and stress inoculation techniques (Meichenbaum & Turk, 1976); and emotional expression (Pennebaker, Barger & Tiebout, 1989). Often, specific CBT interventions are combined in a multimodal way with basic patient education and social support (as mentioned previously), communication skill building, relaxation training/stress reduction, and relapse prevention. A significant and growing body of literature has demonstrated the effectiveness of cognitive-behavioral techniques with chronic pain patients (Bradley et al., 1987; Bru et al., 1994; Turk, 1996) in both individuals and groups.

Other Psychological Approaches

While the successful pain psychologist will be adept at the previously-mentioned strategies, an eclectic skill with other psychotherapeutic approaches is also essential in pain management. Family systems theory and family therapies, for example, have been applied to the changing dynamics within the families of patients with chronic pain and illness (Kerns & Payne, 1996). These approaches often focus on improving and clarifying the communication between family members and examining role changes (including acceptance of the "sick role").

Psychodynamic psychotherapy has been suggested for use with patients who have prior, unresolved trauma issues that maintain or exacerbate the pain, such as childhood physical or sexual abuse, or other co-existing psychopathology that responds effectively to psychodynamic approaches (Grzesiak, Ury & Dworkin, 1996). Internalization of the cultural and personal meanings of pain, such as perception of the pain as punishment for past transgressions, may require exploration of these meanings from both a cognitive and psychodynamic perspective. Although rare, hysterical conversion disorders, that may manifest with pain, are candidates for a psychodynamically-oriented approach as well. Psychodynamic theory has been applied to all of the currently-identified somatoform disorders.

Existential therapies have not appeared in the pain management literature. Yet, the typical chronic pain patient is faced with many existential issues. Many patients ask themselves questions like "What is the value of life with pain?" or "Is life worth living like this?." While one may apply a cognitive or other therapy approach to these questions, in my experience there is value, particularly in a group setting, in exploring these questions directly and overtly. In my experience, allowing the patient freedom to have these thoughts and feelings and to occasionally refer them for spiritual guidance, has been helpful. Awareness of cultural differences is particularly important in assessing and discussing existential issues since pain may have culture specific meanings (Weisenberg, Kreindler, Schachat & Werboff, 1975; Bates, 1996).

Group Psychotherapy with Chronic Pain Patients

All of the above-mentioned psychotherapeutic approaches to pain patients can be attempted in both individual and group formats. Several basic types of groups have emerged as particularly common, namely behavior change groups, psychoeducational groups, and support groups (Keefe, Beaupré & Gil, 1996). Behavior change groups focus on the acquisition of new coping skills, both behavioral and cognitive, and are generally short-term (6–10 weeks). Psychoeducational groups are organized under the assumption that information about chronic pain will both reduce anxiety and increase adjustment to pain and are typically led by a professional in the field of pain management. Support groups for pain patients have the effect of reducing feelings of social isolation, often reported by chronic pain patients. These types of groups may be facilitated by a psychologist or other professional, may be peer-led, or may be unfacilitated.

Two national organizations provide information to individuals regarding the location of local ongoing chronic pain support groups. They also provide information about how to start a support group for pain patients. These are: (1) the American Chronic Pain Association, P. O. Box 850 Rocklin, CA 95677, (916) 632–0922 and (2) the National Chronic Pain Outreach Association, Inc., 4922 Hampden Lane, Bethesda, MD 20814, (301) 652–4948. A complete list of other organizations that provide basic information or support to patients with specific pain syndromes is included in *The Chronic Pain Control Workbook* by Catalano and Hardin (1996).

There is evidence supporting the value of working with chronic pain patients in group settings. Keefe (as cited in Keefe, Beaupré & Gil, 1996), for example, found that behavior change oriented groups can reduce pain ratings and improve function. Psychoeducational groups that include cognitive-behavioral techniques appear more effective than education only groups (Holman, Mazonson & Lorig, 1989). Finally, while there is limited data available on the effectiveness of support groups, my professional experience over the past thirteen years with chronic pain groups suggests that patients experience decreased emotional distress and feelings of isolation, and decreased relapse following behavior change strategies, with regular participation in these groups. My own observation also is that peer-led groups are often difficult to sustain without the assistance of an institution or consulting health care professional.

The Process of Integration

Although I have covered treatment from several perspectives thus far, it may be helpful to briefly review the natural process of improvement in a chronic pain patient. Generally, moving a chronic pain patient from the "downward spiral" to "active coper" requires an awareness of common steps or stages in this process. These steps (very similar to Kühbler-Ross's stages of dying) include: denial, anger, bargaining, depression, acceptance. Patients move through these steps, not necessarily in order and they can experience multiple steps simultaneously. Western medicine in fact may play a role in keeping a chronic pain patient "stuck" in denial, offering hope after hope for cure in the form of new drugs, new procedures, and new research studies.

Patients describe the denial stage as a "never-ending rollercoaster or merry go round" with the "ups" of the promise of a cure and the "downs" of a failed drug or surgery. Some may stay in this stage for months or years until they either exhaust their financial resources, the doctors give up or they realize that the search for a fix is futile. Chronic pain patients may more actively resist working with a psychologist in the denial stages. Patients mired in this stage are often convinced that the right doctor, treatment or medical center will eventually take the pain away, thereby postponing the need to alter lifestyle. Since a primary role for the psychologist in a treatment team is to help a patient alter lifestyle, psychologists may be seen as an unwelcome or unnecessary presence. Your role in this stage, assuming you are allowed "in" may be simply to provide emotional support during the inevitable periods of despair and fatigue following unsuccessful medical intervention.

Another role is as coach to help the patient more effectively and assertively deal with the medical establishment. Sometimes a chronic pain patient can be "nudged" out of denial with frank discussions of the ineffectiveness of acute methods in treating a chronic problem, with concurrent offering of hope in the form of learning new behaviors that may help them reduce the pain or cope better with it.

They may also be forced from denial when the experienced pain physician explains to them that further treatment is not indicated, or when they otherwise realize that the pain will be an ongoing problem. Equally important is allowing yourself permission to "not help" the occasional patient stranded in denial, since attempting to uncover the denial may lead only to greater resistance and resentment. From denial, pain patients often move into an intense anger phase.

While the anger may be focused in multiple directions, directed at doctors, the insurance company or even themselves, this anger is often existentially fueled. Many pain patients who developed pain as a result of an injury may search for someone or something to blame: the presumed "cause" of the accident or injury, the supervisor, their family, or even God, again sapping energy and deepening depression. The effective therapist will allow the patient the opportunity to vent his or her frustrations and will often need to provide education about appropriate expression of anger and instruction in anger management skills. Assertiveness training is often offered to chronic pain patients, both to help those who tend to express anger too aggressively and to those with passive or passive-aggressive styles.

It is important to keep in mind that our society places a premium on "toughness" in the face of pain and adversity, often leading patients to expect stoicism from themselves even in the midst of confusion and anxiety. Stoicism is reinforced by family members or others in the environment who do not understand the experience of living with chronic pain and may directly or indirectly ignore, or even punish communication about the pain or emotional expression. Regardless of the emotional response to the pain, the chronic pain patient may not make the best use of available social support. Many need basic education about the value of support and how to ask for (and receive) support. Family therapy is very beneficial to the chronic pain patient in exploring the effect of changing family roles, increasing effective communication and maximizing mutual support.

For the dying patient, the third stage, bargaining, is an attempt to postpone death. For the pain patient however, bargaining is an attempt is both to postpone worsening of the pain and to receive a few, pain-free days. The patient may make one-sided deals with their "higher power" that they will comply with all physician or psychological treatments, "if only the pain will go away." Unfortunately, few chronic pain patients experience a complete remission of the pain, leaving them feeling hopeless, abandoned and skeptical about further intervention.

For a chronic pain patient, the fourth stage depression, can happen quickly and can be superimposed on the overall process. Fields (1991) has suggested that pain and depression are related at several levels including neurobiological, psychological and behavioral. Depression occurs rapidly because of the negative cycles mentioned previously, of increased and sustained stress responses, decreased sleep, limited activity, social isolation, etc. Grief may be a part of this stage related to the multiple losses the patient has suffered. Among these are the loss of income or previously-enjoyed activities, and also the loss of previously established identity and roles. The multidisciplinary team can play a primary role in this stage, with the psychologist providing appropriate individual psychotherapy, the physician prescribing antidepressant medication if necessary, the physical therapist encouraging activity, and a group providing social support.

Although some patients with good social support, premorbid coping skills, and other resources appear to eventually move into the final stage of acceptance of the pain on their own, it is only with the assistance of the psychologist and other multidisciplinary team member that other chronic pain patients reach this stage. In this case, acceptance means that the patient realizes that the pain they are experiencing is likely chronic and that they must play a more active role in managing their lifestyle in order to cope successfully. Emotionally, patients feel a combination of both relief, that the "rollercoaster ride" is ending as they view themselves and the process differently, and a sense of resignation, that the condition is now a part of their lives. At this stage, many patients are most able to fully incorporate new and more complex strategies for managing pain.

Case Example

Mary, a 52-year-old, white, married female with a 25-year history of low back pain, came to the UCSF/Mount Zion Pain Management Center complaining of both severe low back pain and frequent suicidal ideation. Mary had undergone numerous medical interventions over the years, including five major back surgeries, multiple injections, several courses of physical therapy, and trials of most classes of medications — all with minimal improvement in her pain. She self-referred to the pain management center after several years of haphazard care through a large HMO.

Although she had used Vicodin, a short-acting narcotic, in a very controlled and reliable way (4 per day) for most of 19 years to help her remain functional, after she switched insurance to the HMO, she was told that she could no longer have narcotic pain medications because she would become "addicted." Her pain management strategy when she first arrived at the center was to take Tylenol and to distract herself whenever possible through her work and home chores.

As a part of her initial assessment, Mary was evaluated by both a physician and a psychologist. During the semistructured psychological interview, Mary was found to be quite stoic emotionally and conservative in her social and religious values. She believed that her primary duty was to her husband, sons and work and that time focused on herself was "selfish." She often worked 8–10 hour days at her job, only to come home to cook and clean house until she went to bed, completely exhausted. She often then could not sleep well due to pain, increasing depression, anxiety and nightmares.

At the multidisciplinary team treatment planning meeting, a comprehensive plan was developed for Mary including medication changes, physical therapy, and individual psychotherapy, focused on increasing her coping skills and decreasing depression. With input from the psychologist about Mary's reliability and motivation, the physician decided to start Mary on a longer-acting narcotic, Methadone, which immediately allowed her to function with less pain and few side effects. She met with the physical therapist, also a specialist in chronic pain, who taught her graded exercises to slowly strengthen her body and improve flexibility.

The individual psychotherapy sessions began by providing her a supportive environment to discuss her fears about her future with the pain, her feelings of despair and hopelessness and her perception that she was "trapped" in a painful body with few options other than death. As trust was established, other information began to emerge about severe childhood abuse that likely led her to become passive-dependent and to defer to the desires of others in her relationships.

Through a combined cognitive-behavioral and humanistic approach, Mary began to change her self-perceptions and began to place her own needs higher on her list of priorities. She also learned how to appropriately assert these needs with her co-workers and family, setting limits with others who previously demanded that she attend to them, even at the expense of her own health.

She learned how to set limits with others, and she also became more aware of her own harsh internal expectations and how to change then to more reasonable ones. She later participated in the psychoeducational/support groups offered at the center and she learned excellent stress management skills through biofeedback sessions and classes on meditation.

At the end of treatment, Mary continued to have pain on a daily basis, but no longer felt continuously depressed, suicidal or "trapped." She eventually went on to quit her job to allow her to focus more on her health, and she entered couples' therapy with her husband, to work on their adjustment to the changes she had made in her life. Mary now recognizes that she can live with the pain and says now that she looks forward to the future with enthusiasm. "I still have my ups and downs," she says as she smiles, "but overall, even with the pain, the quality of my life is better than it's ever been."

References

Arena, J.G., & Blanchard, E.B. (1996). Biofeedback and relaxation therapy for chronic pain disorders. In R.J. Gatchel & D.C. Turk (Eds.), *Psychological approaches to pain management: A practitioner's handbook* (pp. 179–230). New York: Guilford.

Baker, D., Pynsent, P., & Fairbank, J. (1989). The Oswestry Disability Index revisited. In M. Roland & J. Jenner (Eds.), *Back pain: New approaches to rehabilitation and education* (pp. 174–186). Manchester, England: Manchester University Press.

Bandura, A., O'Leary, A., Taylor, C.B., Gauthier, J., & Gossard, D. (1987). Perceived self-efficacy and pain control: Opioid and nonopioid mechanisms. *Journal of Personality and Social Psychology, 53,* 563–571.

Basmajian, J.V. (1978). *Muscles alive: Their functions revealed by electromyography.* Baltimore: William & Wilkins.

Bates, M.S. (1996). *Biocultural dimensions of chronic pain: Implications for treatment of multi-ethnic populations.* New York: SUNY Press.

Benson, H. (1975). *The relaxation response.* New York: Morrow.

Bigos, S.J., Battie, M.C., Spengler, D.M., Fisher, L.D., Fordyce, W.E., Hansson, T.H., Nachemson, A.L., & Wortley, M.D. (1991). A prospective study of work perceptions and psychosocial factors affecting the report of back injury. *Spine, 16,* 1–6.

Block, A. (1996). *Presurgical psychological screening in chronic pain syndromes: A guide for the behavioral health practitioner.* Mahwah, NJ: Lawrence Erlbaum Associates.

Boring, E.G. (1942). *Sensation and perception in the history of experimental psychology.* New York: Appleton-Century.

Bradley, L.A. (1996). Cognitive-behavioral therapy for chronic pain. In R.J. Gatchel & D.C. Turk (Eds.), *Psychological approaches to pain management: A practitioner's handbook* (pp. 131–147). New York: Guilford.

Bradley, L.A., Young, L.D., Anderson, K.O., Turner, R.A., Agudelo, C.A., McDaniel, L.K., Pisko, E.J., Semble, E.L., & Morgan, T.M. (1987). Effects of psychological therapy on pain behavior of rheumatoid arthritis patients: Treatment outcome and six month follow-up. *Arthritis and Rheumatism, 30,* 1105–1114.

Brannon, L., & Feist, J. (1996). *Health psychology: An introduction to behavior and health.* Pacific Grove, CA: Brooks/Cole.

Bru, E., Mykletun, R.J., Berge, W.T., & Svebak, S. (1994). Effects of different psychological interventions on neck, shoulder and low back pain in female hospital staff. *Psychology and Health, 9,* 371–382.

Camic, P.M. (1989). Psychological assessment of the chronic pain patient: Behaviors, cognitions, and dynamics. In P.M. Camic & F.D. Brown (Eds.), *Assessing chronic pain: A multidisciplinary clinic handbook* (pp. 47–63). New York: Springer-Verlag.

Catalano, E.M., & Hardin, K.N. (1996). *The chronic pain control workbook.* Oakland, CA: New Harbinger.

Caudill, M.A. (2002). *Managing pain before it manages you.* New York: Guilford Press.

Chun, D.Y., Turner, J.A., & Romano, J.M. (1993). Children of chronic pain patients: Risk factors for maladjustment. *Pain, 52,* 311–317.

Costello, R., Hulsey, T., Schoenfeld, L., & Ramamurthy, S. (1987). P-A-I-N: A four cluster MMPI typology for chronic pain. *Pain, 30,* 199–209.

Davis, M.E., Eschelman, E., & McKay, M. (1995). *The relaxation & stress reduction workbook* (4th ed.), Oakland, CA: New Harbinger.

DeGood, D.E., & Dane, J.R. (1996). The psychologist as a pain consultant in outpatient, inpatient, and workplace settings. In R.J. Gatchel & D.C. Turk (Eds.), *Psychological approaches to pain management: A practitioner's handbook* (pp. 403–437). New York: Guilford.

Devor, M. (1994). The pathophysiology of damaged peripheral nerves. In P.D. Wall & R. Melzack (Eds.), *Textbook of pain* (pp. 79–100). London: Churchill Livingstone.

Engel, G.L. (1959). "Psychogenic pain" and the pain-prone patient. *American Journal of Medicine, 26,* 899–918.

Erickson, R.K. (1989). The physical examination of the patient in pain. In P.M. Camic & F.D. Brown (Eds.), *Assessing chronic pain: A multidisciplinary clinic handbook* (pp. 20–46). New York: Springer-Verlag.

Fairbank, J., Davies, J., Couper, J., & O'Brien, J. (1980). The Oswestry Low Back Pain Questionnaire, *Physiotherapy, 66,* 271–273.

Fields, H. (1991).Depression and pain: A neurobiological model. *Neuropsychiatry, Neuropsychology, and Behavioral Neurology, 4,* 83–92.

Foley, K. (2000). Chronic pain sufferers unsatisfied with pain treatments. *Newswise.* Retrieved July 15, 2003 from www.newswise.com/articles/view/?id=PAINPPH.

Follick, M.J., Ahern, D.K., & Aberger, E.W. (1985). Development of an audiovisual taxonomy of pain behavior: Reliability and discriminant validity. *Health Psychology, 4,* 555–568.

Folstein, M.F., Folstein, S.E., & McHugh, P.R. (1975). Mini-mental state: A practical method for grading cognitive states of patients for the clinician. *Journal of Psychiatric Research, 12,* 189–198.

Fordyce, W.E. (1976). *Behavioral methods for chronic pain and illness.* St. Louis: Mosby.

Fordyce, W.E. (1990). Learned pain: Pain as behavior. In J.J. Bonica (Ed.), *The management of pain* (2nd ed., pp. 291–299). Malvern, PA: Lea & Febiger.

Frymoyer, J.W. (1992). Predicting disability from low back pain. *Clinical Orthopaedics and Related Research, 279,* 101–109.

Gatchel, R.J. (1996). Psychological disorders and chronic pain: Cause and effect relationships. In R.J. Gatchel & D.C. Turk (Eds.), *Psychological approaches to pain management: A practitioner's handbook* (pp. 33–52). New York: Guilford.

Gil, K.M. (1992). Psychological aspects of acute pain. In R.S. Sinatra, A.H. Hord, B. Ginsberg, & L.M. Preble (Eds.), *Acute pain: Mechanisms and management.* St. Louis, MO: Mosby-Year Book.

Grzesiak, R.C., Ury, G.M., & Dworkin, R.H. (1996). Psychodynamic psychotherapy with chronic pain patients. In R.J. Gatchel & D.C. Turk (Eds.), *Psychological approaches to pain management: A practitioner's handbook* (pp. 148–178). New York: Guilford.

Hathaway, S.R., & McKinley, J.C. (1951). *The Minnesota Multiphasic Personality Inventory.* New York: The Psychological Corporation.

Holman, H., Mazonson, P., & Lorig, K. (1989). Health education for self-management has significant early and sustained benefits in chronic arthritis. *Transactions of the Association of American Physicians, 102,* 2204–2208.

Jacobsen, E. (1938). *Progressive relaxation* (2nd ed.). Chicago: University of Chicago Press.

Jaffe, D.T., & Bresler, D.E. (1980). The use of guided imagery as an adjunct to medical diagnosis and treatment. *Journal of Humanistic Psychology, 20*(4), 45–59.

Jamison, R.N., & Parris, W.C.V. (1988). The influence of problems with concentration and memory on emotional distress and daily activities in chronic pain patients. *International Journal of Psychiatry in Medicine, 18*(2), 183–191.

Kabat-Zinn, J. (1991). *Full catastrophe living: Using the wisdom of your body and mind to face stress, pain and illness.* New York: Delacorte.

Keefe, F.J. (1982). Behavioral assessment and treatment of chronic pain: Current status and future directions. *Journal of Consulting and Clinical Psychology, 50,* 896–911.

Keefe, F.J., Beaupré, P.M., & Gil, K.M. (1996). Group therapy for patients with chronic pain. In R.J. Gatchel & D.C. Turk (Eds.), *Psychological approaches to pain management: A practitioner's handbook* (pp. 55–77). New York: Guilford.

Keefe, F.J., & Block, A.R. (1982). Development of an observation method for assessing pain behavior in chronic low back pain patients. *Behavior Therapy, 13,* 363–375.

Kerns, R.D., & Payne, A. (1996). Treating families of chronic pain patients. In R.J. Gatchel & D.C. Turk (Eds.), *Psychological approaches to pain management: A practitioner's handbook* (pp. 283–304). New York: Guilford.

Kerns, R., & Rosenberg, R. (1995). Pain-relevant responses from significant others: Development of a significant other version of the WHYMPI Scales. *Pain, 61,* 245–250.

Kerns, R.D., Turk, D.C., & Rudy, T. (1985). The West Haven Yale Multidimensional Pain Inventory. *Pain, 23,* 345–356.

Kinney, R., Gatchel, R., Polatin, P., Fogarty, W., & Mayer, T. (1993). Prevalence of psychopathology in acute and chronic low back pain patients. *Journal of Occupational Rehabilitation, 3,* 95–103.

Lehrer, P.M., Carr, R., Sargunaraj, D., & Woolfolk, R.L. (1994). Stress management techniques: Are they all equivalent, or do they have specific effects?, *Biofeedback and Self-Regulation, 19,* 353–401.

Loscalzo, M. (1996). Psychological approaches to the management of pain in patients with advanced cancer. *Hematology/Oncology Clinics of North America, 10*(1), 139–155.

McDougall, J. (1989). *Theaters of the body: A psychoanalytic approach to psychosomatic illness.* New York: Norton.

Meichenbaum, D., & Turk, D.C. (1976). The cognitive-behavioral management of anxiety, anger and pain. In P.O. Davidson (Ed.), *The behavioral management of anxiety, depression, and pain,* New York: Brunner/Mazel.

Melzack, R.M. (1975). The McGill Pain Questionnaire: Major properties and scoring methods. *Pain, 1,* 277–299.

Melzack, R.M. (1987). The short form McGill Pain Questionnaire. *Pain, 30,* 191–197.

Melzack, R.M. (1996). Gate control theory: On the evolution of pain concepts. *Pain Forum, 5*(1), 128–138.

Melzack, R., & Wall, P.D. (1965). Pain mechanisms: A new theory. *Science, 150,* 971–979.

Merskey, H., & Bogduk, N. (Eds.). (1994). *Classification of chronic pain: Descriptions of chronic pain syndromes and definitions of pain terms* (2nd ed.). Seattle, WA: International Association for the Study of Pain Press.

Millon, T. (1983). *Millon Clinical Multiaxial Inventory Manual* (3rd ed.). Minneapolis: Interpretive Scoring Systems.

Millon, T., Antoni, M., Millon, C., Meagher, S., & Grossman, S. (2001). *Millon Behavior Medicine Diagnostic.* Minneapolis: National Computer Systems.

Millon, T., Green, C., & Meagher R. (1982). *Millon Behavioral Health Inventory.* Minneapolis: National Computer Systems.

Nachemson, A.L. (1992). Newest knowledge of low back pain. *Clinical Orthopaedics and Related Research, 279,* 8–20.

National Institute of Health Technology Assessment Panel on Integration of Behavioral and Relaxation Approaches into the Treatment of Chronic Pain and Insomnia. (1996). Integration of behavioral and relaxation approaches into the treatment of chronic pain and insomnia. *Journal of the American Medical Association, 276*(4), 313–318.

Nelson, D.V., Kennington, M., Novy, D.M., & Squitieri, P. (1996). Psychological selection criteria for implantable spinal cord stimulators. *Pain Forum, 5*(2), 93–103.

Northern California Neurobehavioral Group, Inc. (1995). *Manual for Cognistat (The Neurobehavioral Cognitive Status Examination).* Fairfax, CA: The Northern California Neurobehavioral Group.

Pennebaker, J.W., Barger, S.D., & Tiebout, J. (1989). Disclosure of traumas and health among holocaust survivors. *Psychosomatic Medicine, 51,* 577–589.

Philips, H.C. (1988). *The psychological management of chronic pain: A treatment manual.* New York: Springer Publishing Co.

Repko, G.R., & Cooper, R. (1985). The diagnosis of personality disorder: A comparison of MMPI profile, Millon Inventory, and clinical judgment in a worker's compensation population. *Journal of Clinical Psychology, 41,* 867–881.

Romano, J.M., Turner, J.A., Friedman, L.S., Bulcroft, R.A., Jensen, M.P., Hops, H., & Wright, S.F. (1992). Sequential analysis of chronic pain behaviors and spouse responses. *Journal of Consulting and Clinical Psychology, 60,* 777–782.

Sapolsky, R.M. (1998). *Why zebras don't get ulcers: An updated guide to stress, stress-related diseases and coping.* New York: W.H. Freeman Co.

Skovron, M.L. (1992). Epidemiology of low back pain. *Bailliére's Clinical Rheumatology,* 6, 559–573.

Syrjala, K.L., & Abrams, J.R. (1996). Hypnosis and imagery in the treatment of pain. In R.J. Gatchel & D.C. Turk (Eds.), *Psychological approaches to pain management: A practitioner's handbook* (pp. 231–258). New York: Guilford.

Tearnan, B.H., & Lewandowski, M.J. (1992). The Behavioral Assessment of Pain Questionnaire: The development and validation of a comprehensive self-report instrument. *American Journal of Pain Management, 2*(4), 181–191.

Tollison, C.D., & Langley, J.C. (1992). *The Pain Patient Profile.* Minneapolis: National Computer Systems.

Turk, D.C., Meichenbaum, D., & Genest, M. (1983). *Pain and behavioral medicine: A cognitive-behavioral perspective.* New York: Guilford Press.

Turk, D.C., & Nash, J.M. (1993). Chronic pain: New ways to cope. In D. Goleman & J. Gurins (Eds.), *Mind/body medicine: How to use your mind for better health* (pp. 111–130). Yonkers, NY: Consumer Reports Books.

Turk, D.C., & Rudy, T.E. (1989). A cognitive-behavioral perspective on chronic pain: Beyond the scalpel and syringe. In C.D. Tollison (Ed.), *Handbook of chronic pain management* (pp. 222–236). Baltimore: Williams & Wilkins.

Turk, D.C. (1996). Cognitive factors in chronic pain and disability. In K.S. Dobson & K.D. Craig (Eds.), *Advances in cognitive-behavioral therapy* (Vol. 2). Thousand Oaks, CA: Sage.

Uomoto, J.M., Turner, J.A., & Herron, L.D. (1988). Use of the MMPI and MCMI in predicting outcome of lumbar laminectomy. *Journal of Clinical Psychology, 44* (2), 191–198.

Von Korff, M., & Simon, G. (1996). The relationship between pain and depression. *British Journal of Psychiatry, 168* (Suppl. 30), 101–108.

Weisenberg, M., Kreindler, M.L., Schachat, R., & Werboff, J. (1975). Pain: Anxiety and attitudes in black, white and Puerto Rican patients. *Psychosomatic Medicine, 37*(2), 123–135.

Williams, D.A. (1996). Acute pain management. In R.J. Gatchel & D.C. Turk (Eds.), *Psychological approaches to pain management: A practitioner's handbook* (pp. 55–77). New York: Guilford.

Robert J. Moretti & William A. Ayer

6

Dental-Related Problems and Health Psychology

Dental disease is among the most expensive diseases in the United States. As far back as 1979, annual dental expenditures totaled over 15.9 billion dollars (Ayer, 1984), and by 1998, expenditures for dental services in the United States totaled 53.8 billion dollars, 48% of which was paid out of pocket. The annual cost of dental care very likely exceeded 60 billion dollars at the turn of the millennium (CDC, 2000).

Although most dental disease consists of caries and periodontal conditions, other diseases or dysfunctions also are significant, and include oral cancer, traumatic injuries, malocclusions, and oral habits. With some exceptions, most oral disorders can be prevented, reduced, or eliminated through changes in lifestyle behaviors and modifications of environmental factors. As a consequence, behavioral scientists and health psychologists have been increasingly involved in the research and treatment of dental disease. At programmatic levels these researchers and clinicians are involved in efforts to change behaviors in large groups of people. Prevention of disease via lifestyle modification (i. e., nutrition, brushing, flossing, fluoridation) is an example. While vitally important, such topics, along with the treatment of many oral diseases (caries, periodontal disease, cancer), will not be addressed here (the interested reader may consult Lipton, 1995). Our focus will be upon those aspects of dental disease and dysfunction that can be treated nonprogrammatically, by the individual health psychologist in a clinic or private practice setting.

As with much of clinical psychology as a whole, the early involvements of psychologists in dentally-related work were marked by a psychoanalytic emphasis. However, in a rather brief period of time psychological research and interventions in dental-related disorders took on a decidedly behavioral and cognitive behavioral orientation, long before such approaches achieved their current popularity. This reflects the efforts of health psychologists to focus upon practical, concrete interventions that effectively and rapidly make an impact upon the dental patient's problems. The National Institute of Dental Research has maintained a Behavioral Sciences section for many years, and has provided major funding for behavioral science initiatives, virtually all of which reflect a behavioral or cognitive behavioral emphasis. For some years now, it has been common for many dental schools to have formal programs of instruction in the behavioral sciences.

Dental Anxiety

Anxiety about going to the dentist is an extremely widespread problem. Extrapolating from survey research based upon a representative national sample, 45 million Americans report being very nervous or terrified about visiting the dentist, while 23 million are phobic and avoid going to the dentist because of their fear (Dionne, Gordon, McCullagh, & Phero, 1998). Although it is commonly as-

Figure 1. The Corah Dental Anxiety Scale.

Dental Questionnaire

Please respond to each of the following questions by drawing a circle around the letter which best describes your feeling. Your answers will help us provide you with better treatment.

1. If you had to go to the dentist tomorrow, how would you feel about it?
   a) I would look forward to it as a reasonably enjoyable experience.
   b) I wouldn't care one way or the other.
   c) I would be a little uneasy about it.
   d) I would be afraid that it would be unpleasant and painful.
   e) I would be very frightened of what the dentist might do.

2. When you are waiting in the dentist's office for your turn in the chair, how do you feel?
   a) Relaxed.
   b) A little uneasy.
   c) Tense.
   d) Anxious.
   e) So anxious that I sometimes break out in a sweat or almost feel physically sick.

3. When you are in the dentist's chair waiting, while he gets his drill ready to begin working on your teeth, how do you feel?
   a) Relaxed.
   b) A little uneasy.
   c) Tense.
   d) Anxious.
   e) So anxious that I sometimes break out in a sweat or almost feel physically sick.

4. You are in the dentist's chair to have your teeth cleaned. While you are waiting and the dentist is getting out the instruments which he will use to scrape your teeth around the gums, how do you feel?
   a) Relaxed.
   b) A little uneasy.
   c) Tense.
   d) Anxious.
   e) So anxious that I sometimes break out in a sweat or almost feel physically sick.

Thank you.

serted that dental anxiety occurs somewhat more frequently in females, presumably related to the tendency of females to report higher levels of all types of anxiety (Rankin & Harris, 1984), recent evidence indicates that men are actually more fearful of dentistry than women, at least within a European sample (Rowe & Moore, 1998). Fear of dentistry is not limited to any particular socioeconomic group (Gale & Ayer 1969), and it appears in all age groups, as well as cross-culturally. Personal traumatic dental experiences, quite often experienced in childhood, as well the stories told by significant others have been identified as common causes of dental anxiety (Kleinknecht, Klepac & Alexander, 1973; Jacobs & Nicastro, 1978; Dionne, Gordon, McCullagh, & Phero, 1998), although the individual's perception of what truly constitutes a trauma is an important variable. In that regard, some investigators once pointed out that dentally anxious individuals are often individuals who are anxious in general (Lautch, 1971). However, more recent data indicate that the overall trait anxiety of highly anxious dental patients does not differ from the trait anxiety of non-fearful patients (Kaufman, Bauman, Lichtenstein et al.,

---

Figure 2. **The Mount Sinai Hospital Dental Fear Inventory.**

On a scale of 0 to 100, where 0 is so relaxed you could fall asleep and 100 is the point when you are so fearful you might faint, become sick, or run out of the treatment room, please rate the following situations:

1. _____ Sitting in the dentist's waiting room.
2. _____ Smelling the "smell" of a dentist's office.
3. _____ Sitting up in a dental chair.
4. _____ Reclining in a dental chair.
5. _____ Seeing the needle and syringe for anesthesia.
6. _____ Receiving the anesthetic injection.
7. _____ Hearing the noise of the dentist's drill.
8. _____ Having a tooth drilled.
9. _____ Seeing the dental probes or instruments.
10. _____ Having the dental instruments manipulated in your mouth.
11. _____ The dentist walks into the treatment room.
12. _____ Having your teeth cleaned.
13. _____ Having dental X-rays taken.
14. _____ _____

1991). Current thinking distinguishes between those dental patients whose fear is the conditioned consequence of adverse treatment experiences (e.g., trauma) and those patients whose fear of dentistry is a cognitively learned reaction (e.g., fear of embarrassment). The former group constitutes the majority of fearful patients, those whose anxiety leads to greater avoidance of the dental situation; the latter group has higher overall trait anxiety (Berggren, Carlsson, Hagglin et al., 1997).

High levels of anxiety complicate the dentist's treatment efforts by increasing the length of treatment sessions (Filewich, Jackson & Shore, 1983), such that as many as a third of all dentists would prefer not to have to treat anxious patients. Moreover, there appears to be a substantial relationship between patient anxiety levels and patient dissatisfaction with dental treatment (Moretti, 1983). In a large-scale survey of dentists attending a meeting of the American Dental Association, 86% indicated that they usually try to find out whether a patient is anxious before treatment, yet only 43% actually asked the patient (Moretti, Ayer, Corah & O'Shea, unpublished data). While one might assume that it is easy to determine who is anxious by mere observation, this is not the case. Patients vary considerably in the man-

ner in which they express anxiety, and many anxious patients give little or no visible evidence of it. Consequently, the measurement of patient anxiety is required if the clinician is to get an accurate idea of its extent. Simple measurement methods have proven to be the best. The Corah Dental Anxiety Scale (Corah, Gale & Illig, 1978; Figure 1) can be completed in less than 60 seconds, and it provides an accurate assessment useful for treatment purposes. It remains the venerable standard against which newer measures are compared. An equivalent, modified version with more up-to-date language has been published as the Dental Anxiety Scale-Revised (Ronis, 1994; Ronis, Hansen, & Antonakos, 1995). Another new measure that purports to circumvent shortcomings of other dental anxiety questionnaires, with good psychometric properties that will interest the researcher, has been introduced as the Dental Anxiety Inventory (Stouthard, Hoogstraten, & Mellenbergh, 1995; Aartman, 1998). The Mount Sinai Dental Fear Inventory, in which patients rate 15 different dental treatment situations on a 0–100 scale of anxiety (Figure 2; Kaplan & Rubin, 1984), is mostly useful in developing anxiety hierarchies used in systematic desensitization treatment (see below).

The most feared aspects of dental treatment include having an injection, having a tooth extracted, and (surprising to many dentists) disapproval by the dentist (Gale 1972). Efforts by psychologists to address dental anxieties have been varied, including hypnosis (Morse, 1975, 1976; Nicolaou, 1991; Fabian & Fabian, 1998), modeling (Melamed, Weinstein, Hawes & Katin-Borland, 1975), paced respiration (Clark & Hirschman, 1980), providing distracting video games or taped instruction in progressive relaxation (Corah, Gale & Illig 1979a,b; Corah, Gale, Pace & Seyrek, 1982) and stress inoculation therapy (Klepac 1983). None of these methods is used with any substantive frequency by dental practitioners during actual treatment, probably because few dentists are trained in the techniques and because such interventions add to the time required for treatment. The health psychologist therefore has a very important role to play by teaching dental patients such self-regulation techniques. Truly optimal care will require cross-disciplinary efforts between the dentist and the health psychologist (Berggren, 2001).

Dental Phobia

Patients who totally avoid going to the dentist out of fear are designated as experiencing dental phobia. Dental phobia is a serious problem that leads dental conditions to go untreated for many years, greatly increasing severity and extensiveness of required treatment. Phobic patients who can be convinced to attempt treatment may require intravenous sedation or even general anesthesia in order for the treatment to be completed, increasing costs as well as risks to the patient. Moreover, these medication-based management techniques probably do nothing to eliminate the phobia itself. While some case studies suggest the possibility that anxiety desensitization may occur when patients are given conscious sedation during dental treatment (Moore, Peskin, & Pierce, 1990), the more carefully structured research studies have found something quite different. In research comparing psychological interventions vs. medication, one single session of

psychological treatment utilizing stress management techniques and imaginal exposure proved to be as effective as oral benzodiazepine medication in reducing the anxiety of dental phobics during treatment. Even more importantly, the follow-up data showed that the medication-treated patients had a relapse of their dental anxiety within two months, while the psychologically treated patients showed continued improvement and continued participation in dental treatment (Johren, Jackowski, Gangler et al., 2000; Thom, Sartory, & Johren, 2000).

Dental phobics, like other anxiety-disordered patients, engage in extreme catastrophic thinking (De Jongh, Muris, Schoenmakers, & Ter Horst, 1995). The cognitive behavioral methods that work well in general clinical practice are therefore aptly applied here as well. Nevertheless, in our opinion, the psychological treatment of choice for severe dental anxiety or dental phobia continues to be systematic desensitization. Consider the following:

Case Example
A 38-year-old woman presented for treatment with a dental phobia. She had not been to a dentist in 20 years, despite her obvious need to do so. Otherwise facially attractive, the woman's teeth had loosened and drifted from neglect, and presented an unsightly appearance. She was fearful of everything about dental treatment, but like most such phobic patients, her main fears were of injections and drilling. After taking a detailed history, the psychologist and the patient together formulated a hierarchy of her dental fears. She was then taught progressive relaxation (the method described by Bernstein & Borkovec, 1973). After attaining a relaxed state, the patient was asked to visualize, along with help from the psychologist, images of progressively more fearful items on her fear hierarchy. When she became significantly fearful, the imagery was immediately stopped, and relaxation instructions were reintroduced. By continuing in this fashion, the patient was able to actively imagine confronting all of the items on her hierarchy without significant anxiety after six office sessions. Subsequently, she enlisted the psychologist's help in making an appointment with a dentist, who was informed of the patient's anxiety so that proper consid-

eration would be given to it. She followed through with extensive dental treatment without significant problem (Case record, RJM).

While such rapid and dramatic relief of dental anxiety may not be typical, this example highlights the possibilities that systematic desensitization offers in the treatment of dental phobias and anxiety. The method used probably does not need to conform in all details to Wolpe's (1964; 1973) classical method. Gale and Ayer (1972) provide a slightly modified approach, which might lend itself to even further modification. The most essential element of the treatment quite likely is sufficient exposure to the feared stimulus. The relaxation technique offers a morale-enhancing supportive intervention that keeps the patient willing to attempt exposure, and also provides the patient with a means of self-regulating the symptoms of physiological arousal. The health psychologist should be prepared, if necessary, to provide *in vivo* desensitization in an actual dental setting for some patients. Because of the vividness of the *in vivo* experience, desensitization in such settings can be especially powerful.

Case Example
A 40-year-old male with dental phobia who had avoided going to the dentist for the past 8 years was seen for a series of systematic desensitization sessions by the health psychologist in a private practice setting. Though the patient felt increasing levels of confidence about eventually seeing a dentist, the imagery-based desensitization proved to be insufficient to help him take the next step of actually seeing a dentist. The health psychologist then made arrangements for the patient to meet him at a dental clinic, when no one else was present. The patient thereby became familiar with the sights and smells of a modern dental clinic, as well as with the feel of lying back in the chair. At any point when the patient reported experiencing at least moderate anxiety, relaxation instructions were given until the anxiety waned. After three of these *in vivo* desensitization sessions, the patient was successful in actually entering dental treatment.

Of course, a good working relationship with a dental office is necessary to provide opportunity for *in vivo* methods. In an attempt to increase the vividness of the stimulus without actually leaving the clinician's office, Carlsson (1977) in Sweden has developed an automated program for dental phobics. This method utilizes videotapes of dental treatment situations that are automatically switched on or off in response to the patient's autonomic nervous system arousal, as determined by psychophysiological monitors. A similar, but more complex computer program has been recently developed to deliver both *in vitro* and *in vivo* exposure therapy to patients having strong fears of dental injections (Coldwell, Getz, Milgrom et al., 1998). Virtual reality technology has been successfully applied to the treatment of other phobias (e.g., North, North, & Coble, 1998), where its capacity to realistically simulate *in vivo* exposure makes it a powerful component of therapy. However, to our knowledge it has yet to be applied to dental phobia. In any case, it seems likely that the costs of such technology will limit its application for some time to come. In the meantime, systematic desensitization provides a simple, low-tech, cost-effective form of treatment that is available to any practitioner.

Temporomandibular Disorders

Temporomandibular disorders (TMD) are a group of conditions related to functional problems associated with the temporomandibular joints (TMJ) and/or the muscles that move the jaw (masticatory muscles). Common signs and symptoms associated with TMD are limited range of mandibular movement, tenderness on palpation of the masticatory muscles and jaw joint, clicking sounds in the jaw joint on opening and/or closing the mouth, and pain during chewing. The most frequent symptom is pain in the TMJ region, which affects more than 10% of adults at any one time, and one in three adults over their life (NIH, 1996). There may also be problems in the surrounding musculature of the face, head, and neck.

Though TMD pain can be the consequence of a variety of different medical disorders too extensive to cover here, it is often exacerbated or even initiated by the clenching or grinding of teeth (bruxism), both during sleep and during waking hours. The chronic tensing of the musculature leads to muscle fatigue and soreness, so that eating may become a painful task. If the overworking of the muscles is intense, local ischemia can occur, resulting in painful spasm of the muscles. Pain is very common. The treatment of TMD by dentists and oral surgeons has encompassed a rather incredible variety of methods, each claiming to provide some degree of success. It is difficult to see what these various methods have in common, other than calling the patient's increased attention to the painful area. A recent committee of the National Institutes of Health concluded that TMD should be treated conservatively in the vast majority of cases, because of its tendency to improve on its own (National Institutes of Health, 1996). Interventions provided by the health psychologist for TMD are often effective, conservative treatments with demonstrated efficacy that are increasingly recognized as an important part of TMD treatment (Dworkin, 1996).

The psychologist is usually included in a comprehensive treatment approach to TMD in order to help the patient reduce bruxing and pain. Frequently the treating dentist will have prescribed medications intended to reduce the effects of the pain, and to relax the surrounding musculature. Such medications might include nonsteroidal anti-inflammatory drugs to reduce inflammation and pain in the joint itself; muscle relaxants to ease the chronic tension in the musculature; analgesic medications; and even psychotropic medications. Psychotropics are sometimes prescribed in order to reduce the underlying psychological stress that leads to the tensing of the musculature, and to provide additional actions as well. For example, the benzodiazepine class of anti-anxiety medications (e. g., diazepam, lorazepam, aprazolam, etc.) also has muscle-relaxing properties. Tricyclic antidepressants (e. g., amitriptyline, nortriptyline, desipramine, etc.) are used because they often have analgesic properties, and because they help to facilitate sound sleep with reduced clenching and bruxing. The psychopharmacologically informed psychologist can be of assistance in helping patients to understand the effects and side effects of such medications, and can be of assistance to the dentist through consultations about the appropriateness or inappropriateness of their use. For example, we have seen patients who were being treated by their dentists for chronic TMD pain with long-term use of benzodiazepines, which creates the likelihood of dependency. In one such case, the patient had been taking an older anti-anxiety medication for over 4 years, in gradually escalating dosages. When the dentist attempted to discontinue the drug, the patient underwent severe withdrawal crises, and ended up needing an exceedingly slow weaning from the drug.

Methods used in the treatment of TMD by psychologists include arousal-reduction therapies, such as biofeedback (especially EMG) and relaxation training (especially progressive relaxation); meditation; and cognitive behavioral therapy. There appears to be strong evidence that the various relaxation techniques being used effectively reduce the severity of chronic pain in a variety of disorders (NIH, 1995). These arousal reduction therapies are used to counteract the autonomic overarousal that leads to the muscle overactivity, and to teach the patient how to detect minute levels of muscle tension and reduce them before they escalate into pain. Meditation has relaxing properties of its own, but offers a more important benefit by helping patients to reduce the cycles of anxious mental rumination that can lead to bruxing and muscle tension. Similarly, cognitive behavioral therapy offers benefits in assisting patients to identify destructive thinking patterns that increase subjective stress and stress-related physical problems. In those cases where the TMD is chronic, cognitive behavioral therapy also offers patients the opportunity to learn to cope better with pain that cannot be completely eliminated or avoided. Each of these approaches is described below.

Arousal Reduction

EMG Biofeedback of the masseter muscles has been one of the main methods used by psychologists to treat TMD (Mealiea & McGlynn, 1987; Gervitz, Glaros, Hopper & Schwartz, 1995), although other sites such as the frontalis and temporalis regions are also used, often in combination with the masseters. Biofeedback offers some advantages over nonbiofeedback relaxation training in the treatment of TMD. With EMG biofeedback it is easy for the clinician to demonstrate to the patient how there are measurable changes in resting masseter muscle activity under conditions of psychological stress. For example, the patient can be given an anxiety-arousing mental performance task (such as mental arithmetic) while simultaneously being provided auditory EMG feedback of the musculature. This, then, is a useful first step: to help the patient see that muscle activity is subtly but measurably affected by anxious arousal. Subsequently, the patient can be taught through EMG biofeedback to achieve better conscious control of the masseters and other musculature. The biofeedback training then needs to be generalized from the doctor's office to the patient's everyday life, where the patent does not have the benefit of EMG information. That is, the patient should be trained to practice periodic observation and voluntary relaxation of muscle tension throughout the day. Various biofeedback protocols for the treatment of TMD have been provided by Rugh (1983), Schwartz (1995), and others.

Some of the most serious bruxingoften takes place during sleep. Rugh and Solberg (1974) have shown that masseter activity during sleep is correlated with the degree of psychological stress experienced by the patient during the waking day. To combat the nocturnal bruxing, patients are sometimes given portable EMG units fitted with alarms that are worn during sleep. Should the patient generate enough activity (via clenching or bruxing) during sleep, the alarm wakens the patient. While the portable EMG unit can effectively short-circuit episodes of clenching and grinding during its regular use, the underlying issues of psychological stress must be dealt with. If they are not, the clenching and bruxing return upon cessation of use of the portable EMG unit (Hudzinski & Walters, 1986; Hudzinski & Lawrence, 1992).

Why biofeedback is effective for the treatment of TMD remains unanswered. As with tension headache, patients may or may not show obvious EMG elevations while at rest. When EMG biofeedback training is provided, clinicians rarely attempt to train the patient to a particular criterion level of lowered arousal. At best, the patient seems to learn how to voluntarily relax the musculature, but not necessarily to relax it to levels that would account for the experienced reduction in pain. One explanation for this phenomenon is that in acquiring any degree of demonstrable voluntary control of the affected muscles, patients also acquire a sense of self-efficacy or capacity to self-regulate. This in itself may be therapeutic enough to reduce pain. Another explanation is that biofeedback simply increases the patient's awareness of muscular tension, enabling the patient to voluntarily release that tension before it reaches critical, painful levels (Dalen, Ellersten, Espelid & Gronningsaeter, 1986).

Even when biofeedback is the primary treatment, patients also need to be taught strategies they can employ during their everyday lives. That is, the clinician must be mindful of the necessity to create treatment effects that can be generalized beyond the biofeedback training situation. Many biofeedback clinicians teach patients established relaxation techniques, such as progressive relaxation, in addition to or instead of providing EMG training. For example, we have observed in our practice that patients experiencing chronic TMD-related pain can sometimes be taught in as few as 6 to 10 sessions of progressive relaxation to attain enough muscle control to significantly reduce their pain, even without EMG biofeedback. The method used in our offices is Jacobson's original progressive relaxation method (Jacobson 1929), which focuses much more intensely and extensively upon more discrete muscle sites, in contrast to the more widely used method popularized by Bernstein and Borkovec (1973), in which the entire body is relaxed in a single session. Of course, as with all self-regulation techniques, the adherence of the patient to daily practice of the methods taught is critical. Yet it must be said that the problem of adherence is also the same for patients treated with only EMG biofeedback. The progressive relaxation method has the advantage of immediately teaching patients a technique that is instantly employable outside the clinician's office.

While to our knowledge meditation has not been formally studied as an adjunctive treatment for TMD, the properties it has demonstrated in other research suggest that it would be helpful, and that is our clinical experience with the technique as well. Many TMD patients are individuals living extremely busy lives under intense time pressure. In the midst of trying to complete one task they are often already thinking about the several tasks that yet remain undone, increasing physiological arousal and accompanying muscle tension. Mindfulness meditation techniques (Kabat-Zinn 1990) reduce the stress that aggravates chronic pain by teaching individuals to focus more completely upon the experience of the present moment, without constant evaluations of the experience. Long-term follow-ups of pain patients who have undergone mindfulness meditation programs at the University of Massachussetts Medical Center have found that approximately 75% of patients report significant benefits, both immediately after training and up to 4 years later (Kabat-Zinn, Lipworth, Burney & Sellers, 1987). Yet clinicians who choose to use this method with their individual patients should be prepared for fairly high nonadherence rates or dropout rates. Even though patients have the best of intentions, they often are very resistant to scheduling meditation practice into their busy lives. Kabat-Zinn appears to have substantially reduced this nonadherence problem by employing instruction within the setting of a structured group.

Cognitive Behavioral Approaches

Mindfulness meditation is also an excellent starting point for cognitive behavioral psychotherapy, and is showing increasing promise in its application to depression (Segal, Williams, & Teasdale, 2002). Because chronic pain and depression are often bound together in a vicious circle, interventions that help depression often help with reducing pain as well. Through the practice of mindfulness meditation techniques, patients become more aware of the characteristic thoughts that pass through their minds, learning in the process that they have been automatically reacting to irrational or catastrophic thoughtsthey had not even been very consciously aware of before practice. The uncovering of such dysfunctional thinking is a very important first step in the cognitive behavioral method (Beck, 1995; Greenberger & Padesky, 1995). By learning to note or observe such thoughts, without judging them, patients also learn to treat dysfunctional cognitions as passing phenomena, similar to a repeating tape loop. They may not be able to stop the "tape," but they can learn not to attach meaning to it.

In a more general sense, we utilize two approaches in treating TMD with cognitive behavioral psychotherapy. In the first of these, the clinician focuses upon reducing the stress-producing cognitive patterns that give rise to the unconscious overuse of the musculature that leads to the development of the disorder in the first place. For example, patients are helped to identify the thoughts that rather automatically accompany moments when they feel stressed, such as when they feel pressured by time constraints. Frequently these thoughts reflect expectations that some catastrophe will result if work loads are not completed. In the vast majority of instances, patients are attempting in an unrealistic manner to fit too many tasks into too little time. Since they are literally expecting themselves to accomplish what is impossible, their expectations can be said to be irrational. The conscious realization by the patient that he or she is expecting to do what cannot be done is critical. Next, the expectation of a "Catastrophic" outcome if one fails to do the impossible is examined. Again, in the vast majority of instances, the outcome may be inconvenient, embarrassing, deflating, or costly; but only rarely is it truly catastrophic. Patients learn, through these examinations of cognitions, that if they fail to meet excessive expectations, they can survive the consequences and get on with their lives. A last step involves the behavioral implementation of these realizations. Since long-standing habits of dysfunctional thinking die hard, patients must be encouraged, under the therapist's direction, to put the new realizations into practice. In the example provided above, this might mean an actual cessation of an attempt to finish everything in too little time. The patient accepts that he or she will fail in the attempt to do the impossible, ceases efforts to work without needed rest or sleep, and accepts the noncatastrophic consequences. The therapist provides encouragement, support, and positive reinforcement for these efforts. The cognitive behavioral approach thus provides patients with an opportunity to change long-standing patterns that have led to the development of their physical symptoms, enabling them to live more reasonable lives.

A second approach to using cognitive behavioral therapy with TMD is most helpful in those instances where complete, lasting pain relief cannot be attained. Patients then need to learn to live with unavoidable pain. Here, the health psychologist helps the individual to learn to separate pain from suffering. "Pain" is the pure physical experience that cannot be avoided by the patient. "Suffering" is what the patient inadvertently creates by trying to avoid what cannot be avoided, and by getting caught up in wishes and expectations that things should be different than they are, that he or she should not have pain. The distinction is subtle, but clear: suffering can be avoided, while pain cannot. The goal of the therapy is to eliminate as much of the suffering as possible. Behaviorally, this means teaching patients, through the use of mindfulness meditation, not to fight against pain, but to "go with it," to enter into it experientially without judging what they feel. Though this may be counter-intuitive to patients at first, when they try it they are frequently rewarded by learning that the experience of the pain changes for them, becoming

more acceptable. The effectiveness of this approach partly lies in its elimination of the physical tension that accompanies efforts to fight off pain, aggravating it in the process, and partly in a readjustment of patients' attitudes toward their plight.

Oral Habits

Oral habits in children, such as thumb and finger sucking, are sometimes a cause for concern in parents and dentists because of their purported potential to produce problems in the occlusion of the teeth (e. g., protruding teeth). Though these habits are quite prevalent in infancy and childhood, there is no evidence that they cause permanent damage to the dentition, particularly if they are abandoned by about age four (Ayer, 1979). Health psychologists can treat these habits when they persist too long. Both aversive conditioning (punishing of undesired behavior) and positive reinforcement (rewarding of desired behavior) may be quite helpful. While behavior theorists have espoused the superiority of positive reinforcement as opposed to aversive conditioning, positive reinforcement requires almost complete control or monitoring of the individual's environment. Though effective, it is very time intensive and therefore sometimes impractical. Aversive procedures can be as innocuous as having an infant wear mittens (Benjamin, 1967), or as intrusive as having a child wear a mouth appliance that causes discomfort whenever thumbsucking occurs.

Baer (1962) provides an example that combines negative reinforcement (withdrawal of a reward) with positive reinforcement. A 5-year-old boy was shown cartoons that were removed when he put his thumb in his mouth (negative reinforcement). To see the cartoons, the child had to remove his thumb from his mouth (positive reinforcement). The more the child refrained from sucking his thumb, the more cartoons he was therefore permitted to view. Clinicians who are familiar with the basics of behavior modification theory will find it possible to creatively employ reinforcement procedures that fit the particular individual.

Facial Appearance Alterations

Orthodontic treatment is sought by many individuals not only for the improvement in oral function that results, but also because of its capacity to alter facial appearance in many cases. Research has indicated that individuals who experience problems in the anatomical relations and functioning of the teeth and adjacent facial structures (malocclusion) seem *primarily* interested in the issue of facial aesthetics (Albino 1981, 1984). The interest of patients in facial aesthetics is consistent with the considerable social psychological evidence that physical attractiveness is related to favorable perceptions by others, quantity and quality of social interactions, and even evaluations of intellectual expression. Consequently, it may make sense to assess the social pressures impinging upon the patient seeking orthodontic treatment (Albino 1984). The Orthodontic Attitude Survey (Fox, Albino, Green, Farr & Tedesco, 1982) can help the clinician assess the individual's attitudes regarding concern about appearance and function, desire for treatment, attitudes about the wearing of braces, relative value placed on obtaining treatment, and general attitude toward malocclusion. While the orthodontist might wisely use such a scale rather routinely, the health psychologist will likely use it in special instances when patients are upset about physical appearance and seeking an appearance change, or when patients seem conflicted about whether or not to pursue orthodontic treatment.

In cases of severe malocclusion, orthodontic treatment by itself is often not capable of producing sufficient improvement in function or appearance. Surgical intervention to reposition the lower or upper jaw, or to alter the dimensions of the jaws, is often undertaken in combination with orthodontic treatment to produce better outcome. This type of surgery is known as orthognathic surgery (Vig & Ellis 1989). It bears some resemblance to orthodontic treatment alone, in that it seeks to alter the occlusion of the patient in order to produce functional improvements. But orthognathic surgery also is similar to cosmetic facial plastic surgery, in that there is often a noticeable improvement in facial aesthetics following surgery. As with orthodontics, the patient's motives for seeking orthognathic surgery are often mixed. In the typical orthognathic case, the patient undergoes a period of orthodontic treatment to optimally position the teeth for surgery. The surgery that follows this period is itself a major procedure done under general anesthesia, and requiring a hospital stay of perhaps two days. Following surgery, many patients are again placed in orthodontic gear for a period of several months to over a year. Immediately following the surgery, the patient's face is often discolored, with considerable swelling. The swelling disappears considerably during the first two weeks after surgery, but thereafter only gradually. There is often minor swelling that persists 4 months postsurgery, and several additional months may pass before the facial tissues completely mold themselves to the new bone structure. This means that the patient does not know the final outcome in appearance until considerably after the surgery is performed, especially if he or she is required to wear orthodontic gear following surgery. During the first few weeks after surgery the patient experiences pain and must subsist on a largely liquid diet. There are often negative mood changes during this period, especially within the first few weeks.

A series of studies has shown that orthognathic surgery candidates are generally psychologically healthy, seek surgery for primarily aesthetic reasons, and have a high satisfaction rate with surgical outcome (Olson & Laskin, 1980; Kiyak, Hohl, Sherrick, West, McNeill & Bucher, 1981; Kiyak, McNeill, West, Hohl, Bucher & Sherrick, 1982; Kiyak, McNeill, West, Hohl & Heaton, 1986; Finlay, Atkinson & Moos, 1995). Is there a necessary role for the health psychologist? Despite the high satisfaction rate, the situation is not quite so simple as it at first appears. Increases in negative mood are some-

Case Example
It has been 10 weeks since surgery. It is amazing how quickly the conscious mind forgets a traumatic experience. And I have to say that having my mouth operated on was more traumatic than I ever expected. I tried hard to prepare myself for the surgery and the fixation of my jaws, but I didn't even come close. It was devastating both emotionally and physically ... I vaguely remember going up to surgery. I do remember having the Q-tips shoved up my nostrils. I remember thinking that this was not a good way to start your day! The next thing I remember is waking up in intensive care. One thing I'll never forget is when I threw up there. Talk about your whole life passing before your eyes [the patient's jaws were wired shut]! I really panicked, but they handled it beautifully. They calmed me down and suctioned my mouth, but the fear of throwing up stayed with me the entire time my jaws were fixated ... The depression really started when they transferred me to a regular room. The change in care [less attention] added to my depression ...

It wasn't bad enough that I had to feed myself through a syringe but all they served me were tasteless liquids ... I lost a lot of weight and strength ... Breathing wasn't all that simple either. It was very difficult no matter how often I used the decongestant spray ... Everything I did was an extra effort. My depression deepened after I got home. All of these things were contributing factors, the difficulty in breathing, eating, the swelling, the infection that set in, but most of all was the change in my appearance. I never really told anyone other than the surgeon that I was unhappy with the way I looked because I was ashamed of myself and embarrassed. So many people told me I was crazy for having this operation and that I looked fine the way I was ... So I kept everything to myself. I would go into the bedroom and shut the door and cry all by myself. I never regretted anything more in my life. I hated myself for being so vain. [This patient, despite experiencing a dramatic improvement in appearance, experienced a depression following the surgery that lasted 2 years.]

times dramatic, persisting long enough and with sufficient intensity to qualify as depressive disorders requiring treatment. These disorders may require further intervention such as psychotherapy and antidepressant medication. This is more likely when the patient has experienced depressive conditions at prior times in life. Also, there are instances of psychological reactions to the surgical outcome, even when favorable changes in appearance have occurred, that require supportive treatment, at a minimum, by the health psychologist. Moreover, such psychological reactions are disruptive to not only the patient, but also to the surgical team, which cannot readily understand why its

good surgical work is seemingly being unappreciated or even rejected. The description given above by a patient may provide some insight into the possible negative aspects of the orthognathic surgical experience.

The prevention or prediction of such outcomes is a valuable service that the health psychologist can render. Certain psychological measures have been shown to predict decreased satisfaction and greater negative mood change following surgery (see Table 1). The Somatic Anxiety Scale of the Millon Behavioral Health Inventory (1982) has been shown to marginally predict negative changes in mood in the aftermath of surgery, up to 4 months (Prose, 1987), as have the Pessi-

Table 1. Predicting psychological outcome in orthognathic surgery.

Predictors of negative mood following surgery:
- Somatic Anxiety Scale, Millon Behavioral Health InventoryMillon Behavioral Health Inventory
- Pessimism Scale, Millon Behavioral Health Inventory
- Future Despair Scale, Millon Behavioral Health Inventory

Predictors of overall satisfaction with surgery in first few months after surgery:
- Neuroticism Scale, Eysenck Personality Inventory (negative correlation)

Table 2. Presurgical assessment questions.

1. How do you feel your facial appearance affects your life? (This question is intended to elicit feelings regarding the degree of satisfaction with current appearance.)

2. How much of an impact do you believe this surgery will have upon your life? (Some patients experience very little impact, others experience profound impact. Patients who expect little impact may, in a few cases, be overwhelmed by the degree to which their life is affected. See the example below in this regard. Patients who expect a great impact are most often disappointed, and may even become depressed. The ideal patient is psychologically healthy enough to deal with either little impact or great impact.)

3. How do you feel others will respond to you after the surgery? (This is essentially an extension of the above issue.)

4. Is it possible that you might not be totally pleased with the results? How do you think will you respond? (Patients who are certain that they will be totally pleased may be being unrealistic. In any case, the mere asking of this question gives the patient the opportunity to do preparatory psychological work on an issue they might not otherwise even consider.)

5. Are there any other aspects of your appearance that you would like to change? (The patient should be prepared for the possibility that he or she may begin to focus upon other "defects" if their life does not change in the desired direction.)

mism Scale and Future Despair Scale (Connor, 1988). The Neuroticism Scale of the Eysenck Personality Inventory (Eysenck, 1968) also predicted negative mood changes in the weeks and months following surgery (Kiyak, McNeill, West, Hohl, Bucher & Sherrick, 1982). Neuroticism also negatively predicted overall satisfaction with surgery in the first few months after surgery. In clinical practice, we have used a series of interview questions before orthognathic surgery to help elucidate psychological issues that may prove to be important following surgery (see Table 2). The significance of being able to predict which patients will experience more negative mood changes and greater dissatisfaction lies in the relationship between these variables and increased interpersonal problems. Adaptation to changes in facial form and oral function produced by surgery take longer than patients expect, and impact upon the patient's relationships with friends and co-workers. Knowing in advance which patients are more likely to experience these problems makes it possible to prepare to intervene with postsurgical monitoring and counseling.

Orthognathic surgery, like all surgeries with cosmetic consequences, can stir up identity issues in patients, too:

Case Example
A 33-year-old married woman with a shy disposition planned for some time to undergo orthognathic surgery to advance her retrognathic mandible. Following the surgery, she hesitated about undergoing a second procedure, a chin augmentation, because she did not want to seem vain. Following the surgeries she presented her surgeon with a variety of complaints. But when questioned further by the health psychologist, the patient admitted she was actually upset about the manner in which people were treating her now that her appearance had considerably improved. Although pleased that others found her more attractive, she was angry that others gave her so much positive attention. After having been shy her entire life, she was having trouble coping with increased attention from other men as well as her husband. When she did not respond to positive attentions from others, people seemed to think she was now snobbish. Even on her job she found herself being treated better, and asked, "Why is everyone treating me different when I am the same person?" She was so distressed that she asked for and received a job transfer to a site where no one knew her pre-surgical appearance (Case record, RJM).

In cases such as the above, the health psychologist may be called upon to provide psychotherapy postsurgically for what is essentially a profound adjustment reaction. With rapid intervention, the psychotherapy may need to be only brief in nature.

Perhaps most importantly, patients should be prepared for the reality of the surgical experience and its sequelae. The research suggests that the patient may be better off knowing the various possibilities. If the negative experiences do not come to pass, the patient will be even more pleased, In particular, the patient should be advised of possible breathing difficulties in the immediate aftermath, swelling and its slow resolution, possible discoloration, pain, the stress of jaw fixation, intensification of negative mood, and the long period of time that is required for the final results to be apparent. Those patients who expect higher levels of pain than they actually experience are the most satisfied, while those who expect less pain than they actually experience are the least satisfied (Kiyak, McNeill, West, Hohl, Bucher & Sherrick, 1982; Finlay, Atkinson & Moos, 1995). As indicated above, there is a high likelihood that patients will be satisfied with the surgery in the long run (years later), but their degree of satisfaction in the months immediately following surgery will vary (Finlay, Atkinson & Moos, 1995), sometimes from month to month. Because there is often a period of further orthodontic treatment that follows the surgery, patients will not experience the "finished product" for perhaps a year or more following surgery. Consequently patients may feel dissatisfied in the short run, and their reactions to surgery may be complex. Despite the likelihood of overall satisfaction, research does not support the likelihood of increases in self-esteem in the short run of up to 9 months postsurgery (Kiyak, McNeill, West, Hohl & Heaton, 1986), even though body-image will be favorably affected. Friends, relatives, and acquaintances may or may not react differently to the patient after surgery. Even if the patient should be treated more favorably, it will take considerable time before this translates into increased self-esteem. Patients who have high expectations of improving their social lives and recreational activities are likely to be disappointed. Though patients often rate themselves as more extroverted following surgery, they in fact frequently return to pre-surgical levels of social and recreational functioning.

Conclusion

This chapter has covered a few of the primary roles that exist for health psychologists within dentistry. The clinical problems of dental phobia, dental anxiety, oral habits, temporomandibular disorders, and facial appearance alterations offer a wide range of opportunity, especially for those health psychologists who are comfortable with cognitive and behavioral treatment methods, and straightforward assessment techniques. Close collaborative relationships with practicing dental clinicians are necessary for optimal treatment of many of the conditions discussed, but such relationships are not difficult to establish if the health psychologist actively markets his or her skills to the dental community. Health psychologists do well to remember that dentists may be eager to know that there is a place to refer patients who need dentally-related psychological services. Finally, though not a topic of discussion in this chapter, there are also numerous opportunities within dentistry for the health psychologist to be involved in clinical research. Readers wishing to learn more about the area of behavioral dentistry should consult Cohen and Gift (1995), Okeson (1995), and Moretti and Ayer (1983).

References

Aartman, I.H. (1998). Reliability and validity of the short version of the Dental Anxiety Inventory. *Community Dentistry and Oral Epidemiology, 26*, 350–354.

Albino, J.E. (1981). *Development of methodologies for behavioral measurements related to malocclusion: Final report.* State University of New York at Buffalo and National Institute of Dental Research, Bethesda, Maryland.

Albino, J.E. (1984). Psychosocial factors in orthodontic treatment. *New York State Dental Journal*, October, 486–489.

Ayer, W.A. (1979). Thumb-, fingersucking, and bruxing habits in children. In P. Bryant, E. Gale & J. Rugh (Eds.), *Oral motor behavior: Impact on oral conditions and dental treatment*, pp. 3–22. National Institutes of Health publication no. 79-1845.

Ayer, W.A. (1984). Overview. In J.D. Matarazzo, S.M. Weiss, J.A. Herd & N.E. Miller (Eds.), *Behavioral health: A handbook of health enhancement and disease prevention, Chapter 58* (pp. 889–894). New York: Wiley.

Baer, D.M. (1962). Laboratory control of thumbsucking by withdrawal and representation of positive reinforcement. *Journal of the Experimental Analysis of Behavior, 5*, 525–528.

Beck, J.S. (1995). *Cognitive therapy: Basics and beyond.* New York: Guilford.

Benjamin, L.S. (1967). The beginning of thumbsucking. *Child Development, 30*, 1065.

Berggren, U. (2001). Long-term management of the fearful adult patient using behavior modification and other modalities. *Journal of Dental Education, 65,* 1357–1368.

Berggren, U., Carlsson, S.G., Hagglin, C., Hakeberg, M., & Samsonowitz, V. (1997). Assessment of patients with direct conditioned and indirect cognitive reported origin of dental fear. *European Journal of Oral Science, 105*, 213-220.

Bernstein, D.A., & Borkovec, T.D. (1973). *Progressive relaxation training: A manual for the helping professions.* Champaign, IL: Research Press.

Carlsson, S.G. (Ed.). (1977). Behavioral science approaches to dental clinical problems. *Reports from the Department of Applied Psychology, 2*(8), 2–17 (University of Goteborg, Sweden).

Clark, M., & Hirschman, R. (1980). Effects of paced respiration on affective responses during dental stress. *Journal of Dental Research, 59*, 1533.

Centers for Disease Control (2000). Oral Health 2000: Facts and Figures. Resource Library Fact Sheet.

Cohen, L.K., & Gift, H.C. (Eds.). (1995). *Disease prevention and oral health promotion: Socio-dental sciences in action.* Copenhagen: Munksgaard.

Coldwell, S.E., Getz, T., Milgrom, P., Prall, C.W., Spadafora, A., & Ramsay, D.S. (1998). CARL: A LabView 3 computer program for conducting exposure therapy for the treatment of dental injection fear. *Behaviour Research and Therapy, 36,* 429–441.

Connor, C. (1988). *Mood prediction in the orthognathic surgery patient.* Unpublished master's thesis,

Northwestern University Dental School, Chicago, IL

Corah, N.L., Gale, E.N., & Illig, S.J. (1978). Assessment of a dental anxiety scale. *Journal of the American Dental Association, 97*, 816–819.

Corah, N.L., Gale, E.N., & Illig, S.J. (1979a). Psychological stress reduction during dental procedures. *Journal of Dental Research, 58*, 1347–1351.

Corah, N.L., Gale, E.N., & Illig, S.J. (1979b). The use of relaxation and distraction to reduce psychological stress during dental procedures. *Journal of the American Dental Association, 98*, 390–394.

Corah, N.L., Gale, E.N., Pace, L.F., & Seyrek, S.K. (1982). *Patient preferences for relaxation or distraction used to reduce dental stress.* Paper presented at the 60th General Session of the International Association for Dental Research, New Orleans, March 19.

Dalen, K., Ellersten, B., Espelid, I., & Gronningsaeter, A.G. (1986). EMG feedback in the treatment of myofascial pain dysfunction syndrome. *Acta Odontologica Scandinavica, 44*, 279–284.

De Jongh, A., Muris, P., Schoenmakers, N., & Ter Horst, G. (1995). Negative cognitions of dental phobics: Reliability and validity of the dental cognitions questionnaire. *Behaviour Research and Therapy, 33*, 507–515.

Dionne, R.A., Gordon, S.M., McCullagh, L.M., & Phero, J.C. (1998). Assessing the need for anesthesia and sedation in the general population. *Journal of the American Dental Association, 129,* 167–173.

Dworkin, S.F. (1996). The case for incorporating biobehavioral treatment into TMD management. *Journal of the American Dental Association, 127,* 1607–1610.

Eysenck, H.J. (1968). *Manual for the Eysenck Personality Inventory.* San Diego: EDITS.

Fabian, T.K., & Fabian, G. (1998). Stress of life, stress of death: Anxiety in dentistry from the viewpoint of hypnotherapy. In P. Csermely (Ed.), *Stress of life: From molecules to man* (pp. 495–500). New York: New York Academy of Sciences.

Filewich, R.J., Jackson, E., & Shore, H. (1983). Effects of dental fear on efficiency of routine dental procedures. In R. Moretti & W.A. Ayer (Eds.), *The president's conference on the dentist-patient relationship and the management of fear, anxiety and pain* (pp. 41–42). Chicago: American Dental Association.

Finlay, P.M., Atkinson, J.M., & Moos, K.F. (1995). Orthognathic surgery: Patient expectations, psychological profile, and satisfaction with outcome. *British Journal of Oral & Maxillofacial Surgery, 33*, 9–14.

Fox, R.N., Albino, J.E., Green, L.J., Farr, S.D., & Tedesco, L.A. (1982). Development and validation of a measure of attitudes toward malocclusion. *Journal of Dental Research, 61*, 1039–1043.

Gale, E.N. (1972). Fears of the dental situation. *Journal of Dental Research, 51*, 964–966.

Gale, E.N., & Ayer, W.A. (1969). Treatment of dental phobias. *Journal of the American Dental Association, 78*, 1304–1307.

Gale, E.N., & Ayer, W.A. (1972). Treatment of dental phobias. In W.A. Ayer & R.D. Hirschman (Eds.), *Psychology and dentistry* (pp. 67–76). Springfield, IL: Charles C. Thomas.

Gervitz, R.N., Glaros, A.G., Hopper, D., & Schwartz, M.S. (1995). Temporomandibular disorders. In M.S. Schwartz & Associates, *Biofeedback: A practitioner's guide* (2nd ed., pp. 411–428). New York: Guilford.

Greenberger, D., & Padesky, C.A. (1995). *Mind over mood: A cognitive therapy treatment manual for clients*. New York: Guilford.

Hudzinski, L., & Lawrence, G. (1992). Effectiveness of EMG biofeedback in the treatment of nocturnal bruxism: A three-year retrospective follow-up. *Biofeedback and Self-Regulation, 17*, 312.

Hudzinski, L., & Walters, P. (1986). Use of portable electromyograms in determining and treating chronic nocturnal bruxism. *Psychophysiology, 23*, 442–443.

Jacobs, B.L., & Nicastro, J.D. (1978). Anxiety-stress or fear as related to dentistry in children and adults. *Dental Hygiene, 52*, 387–391.

Jacobson, E. (1929). *Progressive relaxation*. Chicago: University of Chicago Press.

Johren, P., Jackowski, J., Gangler, P., Sartory, G., & Thom, A. (2000). Fear reduction in patients with dental treatment phobia. *British Journal of Oral and Maxillofacial Surgery, 38*, 612–616.

Kabat-Zinn, J. (1990). *Full catastrophe living*. New York: Delacorte Press.

Kabat-Zinn, J., Lipworth, L., Burney, R., & Sellers, W. (1987). Four-year follow-up of a meditation-based program for the self-regulation of chronic pain: Treatment outcomes and compliance. *Clinical Journal of Pain, 2*, 159–173.

Kaplan, A.S., & Rubin, J.G. (1984). A dental phobia clinic. *New York State Dental Journal*, October, 491–492.

Kaufman, E., Bauman, A., Lichtenstein, T., Garfunkel, A.A., & Hertz, D.G. (1991). Comparison between the psychopathological profile of dental anxiety patients and an average dental pop-

ulation. *International Journal of Psychosomatics, 38*, 52–57.

Kiyak, H.A., Hohl, T., Sherrick, P., West, R.A., McNeill, R.W., & Bucher, F. (1981). Sex differences in motives for and outcomes of orthognathic surgery. *Journal of Oral Surgery, 39*, 757–764.

Kiyak, H.A., McNeill, R.W., West, R.A., Hohl, T., Bucher, F., & Sherrick, P. (1982). Predicting psychologic responses to orthognathic surgery. *Journal of Oral and Maxillofacial Surgery, 40*, 150–155.

Kiyak, H.A., McNeill, R.W., West, R.A., Hohl, T., & Heaton, P.J. (1986). Personality characteristics as predictors and sequelae of surgical and conventional orthodontics. *American Journal of Orthodontics, 89*, 383–392.

Kleinknecht, R.A., Klepac, R.K., & Alexander, I.D. (1973). Origins and characteristics of fear of dentistry. *Journal of the American Dental Association, 86*, 842–848.

Klepac, R. (1983). Stress inoculation to reduce fear of dental treatment. In R. Moretti & W.A. Ayer (Eds.), *The president's conference on the dentist-patient relationship and the management of fear, anxiety and pain* (pp. 59–61). Chicago: American Dental Association.

Lautch, H. (1971). Dental phobia. *British Journal of Psychology, 119*, 151–158

Lipton, J.A. (1995). Biobehavioral aspects of oral diseases. In L.K. Cohen & H.C. Gift (Eds.), *Disease prevention and oral health promotion: Socio-dental sciences in action*. Copenhagen: Munksgaard.

Mealiea, W.L., & McGlynn, F.D. (1987). Temporomandibular disorders and bruxism. In J.P. Hatch, J.G. Fisher, & J.D. Rugh (Eds.), *Biofeedback: Studies in clinical efficacy* (pp. 123–151). New York: Plenum.

Melamed, B.G., Weinstein, D., Hawes, R., & Katin-Borland, M. (1975). Reduction of fear related dental management problems with film modeling. *Journal of the American Dental Association, 90*, 822–826.

Millon, T., Green, C., & Meagher, R. (1982). *Millon Behavioral Health Inventory Manual* (3rd ed.). Minneapolis, MN: National Computer Systems.

Moore, P.A., Peskin, R.M., & Pierce, C.J. (1990). Pharmacologic desensitization for dental phobias: Clinical observations. *Anesthesia Progress, 37*, 308–311.

Moretti, R. (1983). Non-verbal communication skills of dentists, patient anxiety and patient satisfaction with treatment. In R. Moretti & W.A. Ayer (Eds.), *The president's conference on the dentist-patient relationship and the management of fear, anxiety and pain* (pp. 22–26). Chicago: American Dental Association.

Moretti, R., & Ayer, W.A. (Eds.). (1983). *The president's conference on the dentist-patient relationship and the management of fear, anxiety and pain.* Chicago: American Dental Association.

Moretti, R.J., Ayer, W.A., Corah, N.L., & O'Shea, R.W. (unpublished data). *Methods used by dentists in the management of patient anxiety.*

Morse, D.R. (1975). Hypnosis in the practice of endodontics. *Journal of the American Society of Psychosomatic Dentistry and Medicine, 22,* 17–22.

Morse, D.R. (1976). Use of a meditative state for hypnotic induction in the practice of endodontics. *Oral surgery, 41,* 664–672.

National Institutes of Health Technology Assessment Conference Statement. (1996). Management of temporomandibular disorders. In *Journal of the American Dental Association, 127,* 1595–1603.

National Institutes of Health Technology Assessment Conference Statement (1995). Integration of behavioral and relaxation approaches into the treatment of chronic pain and insomnia.

Nicolaou, P.E. (1991) Hypnosis in dentistry. In M. Heap & W. Dryden (Eds.), *Hypnotherapy: A handbook* (pp. 145–163). Bristol, PA: The Open University.

North, M.M., North, S.M., & Coble, J.R. (1998). Virtual reality therapy: An effective treatment for phobias. In G. Riva, B.K. Wiederhold et al. (Eds.), *Virtual environments in clinical psychology and neuroscience: Methods and techniques in advanced patient-therapist interaction* (pp. 112–119). Amsterdam: IOS Press.

Okeson, J.P. (1995). *Bell's orofacial pains* (5th ed.). Chicago: Quintessence.

Olson, R.E., & Laskin, D.M. (1980). Expectations of patients from orthognathic surgery. *Journal of Oral Surgery, 38,* 283–285.

Prose, S.E. (1987). *Mood changes in the orthognathic surgery patient.* Unpublished master's thesis, Northwestern University Dental School, Chicago, IL.

Rankin, J.A., & Harris, M.B. (1984). Dental anxiety: The patient's point of view. *Journal of the American Dental Association, 109,* 43–47.

Ronis, D.L. (1994). Updating a measure of dental anxiety: Reliability, validity, and norms. *Journal of Dental Hygiene, 68,* 228–233.

Ronis, D.L., Hansen, C.H., & Antonakos, C.L. (1995). Equivalence of the original and revised dental anxiety scales. *Journal of Dental Hygiene, 69,* 270–272.

Rowe, M.M., & Moore, T.A. (1998). Self-report measures of dental fear: Gender differences. *American Journal of Health Behavior, 22,* 243–247.

Rugh, J. (1983). Psychological factors in the etiology of masticating pain and dysfunction. In O. Laskin, W. Greenfield, E. Gale, J. Rugh, P. Niff, C. Alling, & W. Ayer (Eds.), *The president's conference on the examination, diagnosis and management of temporomandibular disorders.* Chicago: American Dental Association.

Rugh, J.D., & Solberg, W.K. (1974). Identification of stressful stimuli in the natural environment using a portable biofeedback unit. In *Proceedings of the 5th Annual Meeting of the Biofeedback Research Society, Colorado Springs.* Wheatridge, Colorado: Association for Applied Psychophysiology and Biofeedback.

Schwartz, M.S., & Associates. (1995). *Biofeedback: A practitioner's guide* (2nd ed.). New York: Guilford.

Segal, Z.V., Williams, J.M.G., & Teasdale, J.D. (2002). *Mindfulness-based cognitive therapy for depression: A new approach to preventing relapse.* New York: Guilford Press.

Shoben, E.J., & Borland, L. (1954). An empirical study of the etiology of dental fears. *Journal of Clinical Psychology, 10,* 171–174.

Stouthard, M.E.A., Hoogstraten, J., & Mellenbergh, G.J. (1995). A study on the convergent and discriminant validity of the Dental Anxiety Inventory. *Behaviour Research and Therapy, 33,* 589–595.

Thom, A., Sartory, G., & Johren, P. (2000). Comparison between one-session psychological treatment and benzodiazepine in dental phobia. *Journal of Consulting and Clinical Psychology, 68,* 378–387.

Vig, K.D., & Ellis, E. III. (1989). Diagnosis and treatment planning for the surgical-orthodontic patient. *Clinics in Plastic Surgery, 16,* 645–658.

Wolpe, J. (1964). Behavior therapy in complex neurotic states. *British Journal of Psychiatry, 110,* 28–34.

Wolpe, J. (1973). *The practice of behavior therapy* (2nd ed.). Elmsford, NY: Pergamon.

James E. Aikens & Lynne I. Wagner

7

Diabetes Mellitus and Other Endocrine Disorders

In this chapter, we aim to illuminate some of the many fascinating linkages between the worlds of Clinical Health Psychology and Endocrinology. First, most endocrine disorders have affective and behavioral features, some of which can be fairly dramatic. Second, medical management of the most prevalent endocrine disorder (diabetes) depends heavily upon patient behavior. Even though "psychological status" is the fifth leading predictor of mortality in diabetes (Davis, Hess, & Hiss, 1988), psychological variables tend to receive much less emphasis than biological assays that are actually less predictive of outcomes. Third, the personal burden of some endocrine disorders (e. g., diabetes) and endocrine treatments (e. g., steroid medications, replacement hormones) can create marked psychological effects which psychologists often need to anticipate, explain, and/or treat. Finally, there is increasing evidence for a genetic predisposition to the most prevalent type of diabetes. Although the accepted genetic analyses are still in the development stage, genetic screening for diabetes risk may well enter the clinical realm in the next decade. For the practicing psychologist, this can be expected to throw more grist into the mill: family issues, ethical concerns surrounding testing and disclosure of results, and practice issues related to modification of behavioral risk.

By way of overview, the endocrine system consists of the pancreas, thyroid, parathyroids, pituitary, adrenals, and additional glands that secrete hormones regulating numerous target organs. This chapter covers the three groups of endocrine disorders that would be of concern to most psychologists who practice in medical settings: (a) diabetes mellitus (DM), (b) thyroid hormone imbalances, and (c) the adrenal disorders. Of these, DM figures most prominently into psychological research and practice; therefore, we give it the most attention in this chapter. We will first cover the major reasons for psychological referral of endocrine patients and the basic medical features of each endocrine cluster. Next, we will cover various clinical problem areas which in our experience are prevalent reasons for psychological referral: poor medical regimen adherence, depressive disorders, anxiety disorders, physiological effects of stress, eating disorders, and cognitive impairment. Where applicable, we will cover the emerging ethical and psychological issues related to genetic testing, particularly for diabetes. Additional topics which we do not cover — but may be of interest to some clinical health psychologists — include post-partum depressive and psychotic disorders, PMS or "premenstrual dysphoric disorder," steroid-induced mental status changes, circadian rhythm dysregulation, psychoimmunology, endocrinologically-based obesity, Prader-Willi syndrome, and hemochromatosis.

Major Reasons for Psychological Referral

The reasons for the psychological referral of endocrine patients generally fall into the fol-

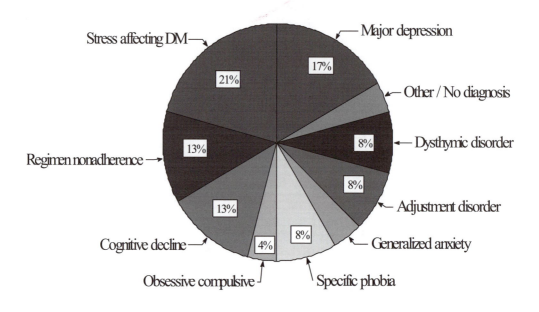

Figure 1. **Presenting problem in 65 consecutive endocrinology referrals.**

lowing categories: poor diabetes regimen adherence, poor adjustment to illness, stress exacerbating medical symptoms and/or self-care, psychiatric problems (especially mood and anxiety disorders), and cognitive problems. From a clinical series collected in the late 1990's, we classified 65 consecutive endocrine referrals seen through the Behavioral Endocrinology Service at the University of Chicago by primary-presenting-problem (or the corresponding DSM-IV diagnosis). Fifty-eight percent of these patients were African American, 35% were Caucasian, 6% were Hispanic, and 1% were Native American. Seventy-seven percent were female. Eighty-nine percent had DM, whereas virtually all of the rest had thyroid disorders. Our medical center sample seemed to have a longer illness duration (mean = 16.4 years), more complications (67% had ≥ 1), and more comorbid illnesses (75% had ≥ 1) than endocrine patients typically seen in community clinics or other general settings. Finally, actual reasons for referral probably vary from setting to setting due to the characteristics of referring physicians, differences in the accessibility of mental health services, and geographically-based cultural variations.

As seen in Figure 1, this clinical series suggests that the predominating reasons for psychological referral of endocrine patients are depressive disorders (with depression twice as common as dysthymia), life stress affecting illness, anxiety disorders, and poor medical regimen adherence. Cognitive impairment and adjustment disorders, while each comprising around 10% of referrals, are less typical reasons for referral. It must be emphasized that these data reflect referral patterns, not actual prevalences. For example, though adjustment disorders are more common than most other problems, they may seldom result in psychological referral because they are brief and comparatively mild.

As is true for any psychological referral, often the reason for referral is vague or unclear. For example, actual reasons for referral have included: "has death wish," "rejects diagnosis," "angry and uncooperative," "won't eat," "can't cope with disease." At other times referrals are expressed in a form which requests a specific course of action, e. g., "talk to patient about her anger," and "needs biofeedback." The clinician who receives these ill-defined reasons for referral is best-advised to contact the referring physician before evaluating (or even scheduling) the patient, with the goal of achieving a more thorough and useful understanding of the actual trigger for referral. If handled tactfully and diplomatically, this action can also educate and entrain the referring physician as to what health psychology services can and do provide.

Basic Medical Overview

Diabetes Mellitus (DM)

Insulin causes all of the body's cells to become more permeable to glucose, the primary "fuel" underlying normal metabolism. DM is characterized by insufficient pancreatic insulin production and/or insulin ineffectiveness (Pohl, Gonder-Frederick, & Cox, 1984), which results in abnormally elevated blood glucose (BG), or *hyper*glycemia. There are two major divisions of DM: insulin dependent (IDDM; also termed Type I or "juvenile onset" DM), and non insulin dependent (NIDDM; also termed Type II or "adult onset" DM). Their etiologies are both multifactorial, but differ considerably (Robbins & Kumar, 1987). In IDDM, the pancreas produces essentially no insulin, probably due to an autoimmune process (American Diabetes Association; ADA, 1996). In NIDDM, which is associated with obesity and genetic factors, the body becomes resistant to insulin and insulin production is insufficient to meet the body's requirements (ADA, 1996; Pohl et al., 1984). It was recently reported that a gene known as Calpain-10 increases the risk of NIDDM, and has given biomedical researchers new hope of understanding the genetics behind the disease. Although this knowledge may someday lead to new drugs or treatment options, screening for the associated mutations will probably not be practical or meaningful until more is learned about how the genetic abnormality influences DM risk.

According to the US Centers for Disease Control, diabetes was the seventh leading cause of death in the US in 1998, and in 1996 it was estimated that there are 7 million Americans with diabetes, about 95% of whom had NIDDM (National Center for Health Statistics, 1999). With the inclusion of probable undiagnosed NIDDM cases, total US DM prevalence has been estimated at least 6% (ADA, 1996) and is currently rising. NIDDM prevalence increases with age, and is more common among Native Americans and Americans of African or Hispanic descent. Gestational diabetes (GDM), which occurs in 2–5% of pregnancies and tends to remit afterwards, is associated with increased age of pregnancy, family DM history, and obesity (ADA, 1996).

DM can produce acute hyperglycemia, which can lead to visual disturbance, mood shifts, and even life-threatening tissue breakdown and dehydration (Pohl et al., 1984). Longstanding hyperglycemia is linked to blood vessel disease, neuropathy, renal dysfunction, visual impairment, and hypertension. Myocardial infarction is the most common cause of death in DM. The physiologically opposite state, acute *hypo*glycemia (dangerously low BG), can produce irritability, anxiety episodes, disorientation, and coma.

Metabolic control is assessed routinely by physicians as the major barometer of DM control, and it is complicated, multidimensional, and multiply-determined The two most commonly utilized specialized assays are glycosylated hemoglobin (HbA1c), which reflects the average BG control over the prior 6–12 weeks (ADA, 1996), and fasting BG, which indicates basal BG (Service, O'Brien, & Rizza, 1987). BG is often self-assessed by patients using portable reflectance meters, usually prior to meals or in response to the occurrence of unusual physical symptoms. The target BG range is 60 to 180 mg/dl, but actual clinical targets can vary widely across individual patients, depending on regimen, medical, lifestyle, and personal factors.

The DM treatment regimen typically includes a calorie-limited, balanced, scheduled diet. In NIDDM, an oral hypoglycemic or insulin-sensitizing agent is often included, while multiple daily insulin injections are prescribed for IDDM and more poorly-controlled NIDDM. The "tight control" DM management philosophy, which specifies a narrower BG target range and frequent regimen adjustments, was more recently supported by a large multi-site IDDM trial (DCCT Research Group, 1993) and is thus becoming widely adopted for standard IDDM management. Subcutaneous "smart" insulin pump delivery systems, which secrete small amounts of insulin as needed, are also being increasingly applied, and pancreatic cell transplantations are performed on some IDDM patients in the US (ADA, 1996), usually as a final resort. A recent, influential trial from the United Kingdom indicates that the control of hypertension is more important than previously recognized, in that lowering blood pressure to a mean of 144/82 mmHg was found to reduce the long term likelihood of stroke, diabetes-related death, heart failure, microvascular complications, and visual loss (UK Prospective Diabetes Study Group, 1998). This suggests that in NIDDM, hypertension control is more important for preventing premature death than blood glucose control is, and represents a major shift in the recommended goals for diabetes therapy.

Thyroid Disorders

The thyroid is located in the neck and produces thyroxine (T4) and triiodothyronine (T3), which regulate growth rate and general activity level. *Hyper*thyroidism (Grave's disease), or excessive thyroid hormone production, can cause dramatic behavioral and emotional abnormalities such as panic episodes, generalized anxiety, hyperactivity, attention deficit, tremors, insomnia, weight loss, irritability, restlessness, confusion, and psychosis (Slaby, Tancredi, & Lieb, 1981). Thyroid disorders are seven times more prevalent in women, who tend to experience onset between ages 30 to 50; men tend to develop hyperthyroidism at older ages. Treatment includes surgery and/or antithyroid medications. In contrast, *hypo*thyroidism refers to insufficient thyroid hormone, which can produce hypoactivity, weight gain, weakness, dermatological disturbances, memory deficits, general depressive symptoms, emotional lability, and psychosis (i. e., "myxedema madness"). Thyroid replacement medication is the usual treatment.

Adrenal Disorders

The adrenal glands are located superior to the kidneys and play a key role in regulating stress responses. They release corticosteroids, mineralcorticoids, androgens, epinephrine and norepinephrine. Excessive cortisol production (Cushing's syndrome) can produce a characteristic facial puffiness, hypertension, muscle wasting, and obesity, as well as decreased libido, weakness, irritability, insomnia, depression, and psychotic symptoms (Slaby et al., 1981). Fairly identical symptoms frequently occur in predisposed individuals taking steroid medication. Adrenomedullary hyperactivity may occur due to pheochromocytoma, which raises epinephrine and norepinephrine levels producing episodic hypertension, palpitations or tachycardia, anxiety, vomiting, headaches, dizziness, diarrhea, dilated pupils, and paresthesias. Cushing's syndrome occurs in all races, any age group, and both genders, but is most common in women between ages 20 and 60. Treatment usually entails tumor removal (Slaby et al., 1981). Adrenocortical insufficiency (Addison's disease) is rare, and can cause anorexia, weight loss, vomiting, diarrhea, hypotension, weakness, decreased libido, irritability, depression, apathy, psychosis, and/or delirium (Slaby et al., 1981). Treatment involves glucocorticoid and mineralcorticoid replacement therapy.

Diabetes Regimen Adherence and Self-Care Behavior

Because the DM regimen is burdensome, complex, intrusive, and lifelong, poor DM regimen adherence is a major clinical problem. Furthermore, there is little opportunity for immediate or direct feedback to guide effective self-management. Although regimen adherence improves BG levels and significantly reduces long term complication rates (DCCT Research Group, 1993), noncompliance with diet recommendations and insulin administration has been reported by most (58–80%) of DM patients (Sarafino, 1994). Poor adherence is associated with depression and anxiety, maladaptive personality traits (Lustman, Frank, & McGill, 1991), and poor coping skills (Delameter, Kurtz, Bubb, White, & Santiago, 1987). In accordance with models emphasizing health beliefs and self-efficacy factors, regimen behavior is predicted by patient illness attributions, perceived ability to self-manage DM, environmental adherence barriers, and the perceived costs versus benefits of the regimen. Social and family factors also appear to be relevant. Familial dysfunction is associated with poorer adherence in children and adolescents with IDDM (Anderson, 1990), whereas the lack of diabetes-specific, family support predicts nonadherence in adults with NIDDM (Glasgow & Toobert, 1988).

Assessment

Diabetes regimen adherence is somewhat challenging to assess, for three reasons. First, normal outpatient circumstances usually necessitate primary reliance upon self-report data. Second, there is no absolute or standard adherence criterion. Many patients simply do not receive explicit physician recommendations, especially in relation to diet and exercise. Third, regimen behavior has three or four dimensions which are only moderately intercorrelated. That is, medication-taking behavior may be unrelated to performance in another area, such as diet, which may in turn be unrelated to the consistency of BG testing (Glasgow, McCaul, and Schafer, 1987). In clinical interviews, each regimen component should thus be reviewed in isolation, with regards to frequency and consistency of medication administration, BG testing, physical activity, and relevant dimensions of eating behavior such as timing, amounts, meal composition, triggers for spontaneous eating, and consistency. Physicians, parents (for children and teens), and spouses are also interviewed whenever feasible, in order to obtain a more complete clinical understanding of regimen behaviors and the factors that influence them.

There are no universally accepted DM adherence measures, although research measures include self-report, self-monitoring, staff and spousal observation, and objective measures such as endocrine assays or electronic records of behavior. One of the most well validated instruments is the Summary of Diabetes Self Care Activity (see Toobert & Glasgow, 1993). This 12-item self-report instrument assesses diabetes self-care behavior over the preceding seven days, covering various relevant features of diet, exercise, BG testing, and medication administration. Its brevity, ease of scoring, and reference to specific behaviors make it particularly useful in the psychology practice environment.

Intervention

Several psychological interventions have been empirically shown to improve regimen adherence. For obese DM patients, eating behavior and weight loss are usually primary treatment goals, with the long-term goal of improved metabolic control. In general populations, effective behavioral programs typically include nutrition and exercise counseling, self-monitoring, stimulus control techniques, and contingency contracting (Sarafino, 1994; Masters, Burish, Hollon, & Rimm, 1987). Hartwell, Kaplan, and Wallace (1986) describe a behavioral dietary intervention for NIDDM patients featuring the identification and alteration of environmental cues associated with eating and health care behaviors, self-monitoring of medication and food intake, self-reinforcement of desired behavior changes using non-food positive reinforcers, modification of self-defeating cognitions related to the regimen, and an emphasis upon clear, discrete, verifiable, realistic goals for change. Presumably, it seems optimal to avoid a sole emphasis upon the target of weight loss per se, but to also emphasize the introduction and maintenance of healthy eating patterns. The psychological management of obesity can be a challenging and frustrating process, because progress may be slow and inconsistent. Therefore, each observable improvement should be heavily reinforced. Cox and Gonder-Frederick (1992) reviewed NIDDM specific behavioral weight-loss studies, concluding that men respond better to individual treatment, whereas women respond better to couples treatment, long-term medical improvement correlates with post-treatment weight loss, and the most effective treatments are those which incorporate routine physical exercise and very low calorie diets. Finally, maintenance differs by regimen area, with improved medication and BG monitoring tending to maintain better than changes in diet and exercise behavior (Rubin, Peyrot, & Saudek, 1989).

Depressive Disorders

Depression prevalence is elevated in IDDM and NIDDM, occurring at up to six times the rate normally observed in the general population (Lustman, Griffith, Clouse, & Cryer, 1986). However, it is not currently clear whether depression prevalence is higher in DM than in comparable chronic illnesses. Major depressive disorder is five times more likely among DM patients with a prior major depressive episode, and is associated with both poor illness control and increased reporting of clinical DM symptoms (Lustman, Griffith, Gavard, & Clouse, 1991).

Currently, there is no generally accepted explanation for the depression-DM association, but several possibilities exist. First, DM often introduces both episodic and chronic stressors, i. e., a fluctuating course superimposed over a relatively demanding (but permanent) lifestyle-oriented regimen. Second, the imperfect correlation between self-care behavior and health outcome can create a learned helplessness scenario. Third, numerous metabolic and hormonal abnormalities impinge upon the brain, which may alter emotional functioning at the neurophysiological level. Even transient BG fluctuation is associated with mood state in changes in IDDM, e. g., angry and sad moods correlate with high BG (Gonder-Frederick, Cox, Bobbitt, & Pennebaker, 1989). Thus, depression may possibly influence DM, or be influenced by DM.

Of the remaining endocrine disorders, hypothyroidism is most likely to be associated with depression. Irritability, low activity level, fatigue, and dysphoria can arise directly in response to low T3 and/or T4 levels, and depressive symptoms often improve when patients are medically restored to the euthyroid state. Little has been written about potential psychological mechanisms involved in hypothyroidism.

Assessment

The potential confounding of medical status and psychological symptoms is a core health psychology assessment issue, and one which especially applies to depression in endocrine populations. It should be verified through chart review or via the referring physician that hypothyroidism, adrenal medullary and cortical abnormalities, and other known depressogenic conditions have already been adequately assessed. If any of these conditions exist, the psychologist should obtain the physician's opinion regarding current degree of medical control, and the basis of this judgment (e. g., assay, physical exam, prospective knowledge). Patient reported medication regimen and laboratory results should be compared against physician assessments and/or medical records. Given the possibility that most depressive symptoms can be caused by hypothyroidism, a complete assessment should include ample verification that thyroid stimulating hormone (TSH) levels are normal. In DM, physical symptoms (weight loss, fatigue) and disrupted memory function could result from poorly controlled illness with persistent hyperglycemia. When any medically reversible states exist, the psychologist should conduct assessments both before and after reasonable medical interventions. Alternatively, the psychologist could simply postpone assessment until medical control is achieved, offering psychological support, reassurance, and close monitoring in the interim.

Assessment instruments developed on general psychiatric groups have been widely utilized to quantify distress in DM (Lustman, Griffith et al., 1986), although content overlap between DM symptoms and general psychiatric symptoms can lead to exaggerated psychopathology estimates (Bradley, 1994). The MMPI has been thus criticized as invalid for screening DM patients (Dunn & Turtle,

1981). The Symptom Checklist-90-Revised (Derogatis, 1977), while briefer, still contains at least 15 items rated by endocrinologists as attributable to DM or its treatment. These items cover content such as trembling, shakiness, faintness, bodily weakness, dizziness, numbness and tingling, sexual dysfunction, racing and pounding heart, chest pain, fatigue and low energy, appetite disturbances, sleep disruption, concerns over general somatic functioning, and so forth. While such indicators may overinflate psychopathology estimates, excluding them without careful consideration may decrease sensitivity and detection rates.

The Beck Depression Inventory (BDI; Beck & Steer, 1987) also has several items which may tap potential DM-related problems (e. g., diminished ability to work, sleep disruption, fatigue, appetite disturbance, weight loss, health worries, and sexual problems). However, Lustman, Freedman, Carney, Hong, and Clouse (1992) found that BDI item values for depressed DM patients closely resemble those of depressed psychiatric patients, with little resemblance to those of nondepressed DM patients, supporting its application to this population. The Well-Being Questionnaire (Bradley, 1984) has the advantage of being developed specifically for the DM population. Although its strengths also include good psychometric properties and the inclusion of a 16-item subscale assessing well-being, its depression subscale is limited to only 6 items. The interested reader is referred to Bradley (1994) for further psychometric information.

Symptom confound issues also apply to clinical interview techniques. The clinician must carefully weigh the possibilities that fatigue, sleep disturbance, sexual disturbance, and other somatic symptoms are attributable to DM, depressive disorder, or perhaps both. In this respect, Lustman, Harper, Griffith, and Clouse (1986) encourage the use of the standardized Diagnostic Interview Schedule (DIS; Robins, Helzer, Croughan et al., 1981) developed by the NIMH. Despite the fact that the DIS is designed to disregard possible psychiatric symptoms attributable to medical illness, it rarely fails to detect verified psychiatric disorder in DM patient samples.

Intervention

Because cognitive-behavioral therapy (CBT; see Beck, Rush, Shaw, & Emery, 1979) has been consistently demonstrated to be efficacious when applied to other medically ill populations such as rheumatoid arthritis (Young, 1992) and cancer (Anderson, 1992), it is reasonable to anticipate that CBT would benefit DM patients as well. One trial suggests that 10 weeks of CBT combined with intensive behavioral management of diabetes (IBMD) reduces depression more than IBMD alone (Lustman, Freedland, Griffith and Clouse, 1998a and 1998b). Patients with fewer diabetes complications and good adherence to BG self-monitoring improved more with CBT. A precautionary note is that interventions increasing activity level or general self-care may cause unanticipated improvements in BG control. Although such changes are medically therapeutic, medically supervised regimen adjustments may be necessary to prevent hypoglycemic episodes.

Oftentimes various illness-specific depressogenic cognitions and associated affective responses become evident during CBT with depressed diabetes patients. These can be targeted for change, but care must be taken to place them within the context of the variety and possibility inherent to diabetes. This implies, of course, that the therapist must be amply educated about diabetes. For example, patients may verbalize discouragement, helplessness, and even disgust toward their illness, its management demands, and its prognosis. We have clinically observed that this material is typically readily accessible and can be managed therapeutically by adapting the standard principles of classic CBT for depression. For example, the following depressogenic cognition was verbalized by a depressed 61-year old male with NIDDM: "Because of diabetes, I am going blind. I will die a miserable, lonely old man." Through several sessions of careful, open-ended questioning, collaborative empiricism, and structured between-session, behavioral experiments, all performed in an empathic therapeutic atmosphere. Through these efforts, he eventually began to experience a more accurate and functional thought,

i. e., "Diabetes takes a lot of my time, effort, and money to manage. It is affecting my vision. But even if I go blind, I can live with that. I will still be able to enjoy happy moments, although it will probably be more of a struggle." It can naturally be expected that patients who are already working very hard to cope with demanding medical problems may not progress in psychotherapy as quickly as a similarly depressed person who does not have the additional coping burden of a chronic medical problem. Psychotherapy with diabetes patients can be frequently interrupted by medical setbacks, and often patients go through a shift in which they suddenly do not consider their psychological difficulties as very important in comparison to the magnitude of their medical issues. We believe that the most effective psychologists are those who accept these realities, taking advantage of the "windows of opportunity" for psychological change (usually medically healthy periods), and following the patient's lead by providing a more purely supportive and flexible treatment during medical crises.

Antidepressant medications are potentially helpful, although currently only two controlled trials demonstrate efficacy (for fluoxetine and nortriptaline) in DM (Lustman, Freedland, Griffith, and Clouse, 2000). Additionally, certain complications are introduced by the nature of DM. Tricyclic antidepressant agents can occasionally produce hyperglycemia due to appetite stimulation, while selective serotonin reuptake inhibitors (SSRIs) possibly enhance insulin action enough to produce hypoglycemia (Goodnick, Henry, & Buki, 1995), and may require insulin adjustment by the physician. Drugs with anticholinergic properties may also cause painful symptom exacerbation among patients with autonomic neuropathy. In hypothyroidism, thyroid hormone replacement drugs are usually the most indicated approach.

Anxiety

Psychological research on anxiety in endocrine populations has focused almost exclusively on DM samples, despite the fact that anxiety is often a major clinical feature of hyperthyroidism and pheochromocytoma, and to a lesser extent, Cushing's syndrome. Generalized anxiety disorder (GAD) is the most common anxiety disorder among DM patients, and is associated with poor metabolic control (Turkat, 1982). The lifetime prevalence rate for anxiety disorders in DM is as follows: 40.9% for GAD, 26.3% for simple phobia, 15.8% for agoraphobia, 10.5% for social phobia, 3.5% for panic disorder, and 0.9% for obsessive-compulsive disorder (Lustman, Griffith, Clouse, & Cryer, 1986). Popkin, Callies, Lentz et al. (1988) found that anxiety disorder prevalence is lower in IDDM than in combined DM populations, although still higher than in the general population.

There are several possible explanations for the diabetes-anxiety association. Lustman (1988) speculates that anxiety symptoms can be produced by sympathetic nervous system responses to hyperglycemia. Alternatively, DM-related endocrine abnormalities might be exacerbated by normal physiological stress responses (Lustman, Griffith et al., 1986). A third reasonable possibility is that the psychological burden of adjusting to chronic illness and managing the daily self-care pressures of the DM may have a general negative impact upon coping effectiveness.

Finally, hypoglycemic fear (HF) is a significant difficulty for some IDDM patients, and is positively associated with other psychological variables, particularly trait anxiety (Polonsky, Davis, Jacobson, & Anderson, 1992). HF often has a realistic component, as hypoglycemia is usually a highly aversive subjective experience, which can exert extreme negative health consequences including unconsciousness, coma, and possibly even death. In response to HF, some DM patients develop elaborate hypoglycemia avoidance patterns that essentially raise BG to a subjectively "safe" range via adjustment of insulin, diet and activity level. If excessive, this can cause chronic hyperglycemia and perhaps long term complications. HF-related avoidance behavior correlates with past hypoglycemic episode frequency (Irvine, Cox, & Gonder-Frederick, 1992) and poor ability to discriminate between anxiety and hypoglycemic states. (Polonsky et al., 1992).

Assessment

Although hyperthyroidism, pheochromocytoma, and other major organic causes of anxiety have been typically been ruled out or medically controlled prior to psychological referral, psychologists should not automatically assume this to be the case. As asserted above with regard to depression, if such rule-outs are not overtly addressed in the medical record, then the psychologist should verify with the referring physician that such alternatives have been amply considered. Anxiety assessment in DM is also complicated by similarities between altered metabolism (especially low BG) and anxiety symptoms (Beardsley & Goldstein, 1993; Lustman, 1988). Symptom overlap may explain why anxiety disorders in DM have generally been underdetected by nonpsychiatric physicians (Lustman & Harper, 1987). To increase the accuracy of anxiety detection and diagnosis in endocrine patients, Jacobson (1996) suggests that clinicians assess only emotional and behavioral symptoms such as persistent fears, worries, and obsessions or compulsions, disregarding "physiological" symptoms such as palpitations, tremor, and perspiration.

As discussed above for depression, DM-specific assessment instruments may be the most valid. The aforementioned Well-Being Questionnaire (Bradley, 1994) also contains an anxiety subscale based on Zung's (1974) anxiety instrument. The Hypoglycemia Fear Survey (Cox, Irine, Gonder-Frederick, Nowacek, & Butterfield, 1987) measures hypoglycemia-related fear and avoidance behavior. Assessing psychiatric symptoms during episodes of relative metabolic control can also help differentiate metabolic and psychiatric symptoms. Finally, the Diabetes Quality of Life (DQOL) Questionnaire (DCCT Research Group, 1988), is psychometrically sound and has subscales differentiating between general and diabetes-related worry.

Intervention

As noted above, psychotherapeutic interventions for endocrine patient groups in general have not been widely examined. Given this knowledge gap, Rubin and Peyrot (1992) suggest that clinicians choose interventions with demonstrated efficacy in general psychiatric and community populations or preferably, in comparable medical patient samples. Well-validated CBT interventions for specific anxiety disorders in general populations are detailed elsewhere, i. e., for panic disorder and agoraphobia (Craske & Barlow, 1993), obsessive compulsive disorder (Riggs & Foa, 1993), social phobia (Hope & Heimberg, 1993), and GAD (Brown, O'Leary, & Barlow, 1993). Since all of these interventions directly teach specific coping skills and aim to alter maintaining factors rather than distal etiologies, it seems reasonable to suspect that they might be beneficial even if ongoing metabolic abnormalities are contributory.

For DM patients, cognitions to target for change can be detected through clinical interview as well as by carefully examining item responses on the DM-specific instruments cited above. For example, on the Bradley (1994) Well-Being Questionnaire, anxious DM patients tend to report more perceived barriers to treatment and fewer perceived treatment benefits, greater illness severity, and increased vulnerability to medical complications. Such areas could be further examined via open-ended cognitive interviewing (see Beck et al., 1979, for discussion of "Socratic" query and related techniques) to clarify their accuracy, function, and potentially anxiogenic impact. For example, patients are asked to clarify the meanings and implications of their illness-related beliefs and expectations. This method often involves questions such as "so when you say that being diagnosed with diabetes is worse than receiving a death sentence, what do you mean?" (to clarify *meaning* of cognitive material), and "when you have that thought, what (thought, feeling, or behavior) happens next?" (to clarify *function* of cognitive material). Standard CBT typically then involves a collaborative patient-therapist examination of the validity of problematic cognitions, primarily through retrospective examination of relevant evidence, further discussion of the implications of beliefs, and most importantly, behavioral experiments. In addition to cognitive mediation, it is also important to examine the role of learned anxiety avoidance behavior and its relationship to conditioning experiences. Patients may have had actual or vicarious exposure to anxiety-provoking DM-related morbidity and mortality via parents, siblings, or other relatives. They frequently acquire a repertoire of behavioral avoidance responses, which function to reduce further anxiety exposure; these usually need to be directly targeted for change via exposure and response prevention procedures. The clinician should appreciate that such learning history may have occurred back when DM treatment was literally limited to diet, bedrest, and opiates, and fear-provoking complications such as blindness and amputations were far more prevalent. In this respect, patient information pamphlets offered by the American Diabetes Association (Alexandria, VA, or regional affiliate) can be a potentially useful adjunct.

A caution is in order regarding relaxation training, frequently applied alone or with other components when treating anxiety disorders in general populations. Relaxation training has been occasionally reported to produce medically concerning levels of hypoglycemia in DM patients with well-controlled illness at baseline. Thus, it is advised that psychologists involve the internist or endocrinologist and patient in intensified blood glucose monitoring, so that potential hypoglycemia can be detected at an early stage, and appropriate medical compensations can be instituted (for details see below section, Physiological Effects of Stress on Diabetes). Furthermore, all of the reported studies involving relaxation training for DM patients involve non-psychiatric populations, i. e., patients who might report being under stress, but do not necessarily suffer from a clinically-significant anxiety disorder. The results discussed below thus may not readily generalize to patients with clinically significant anxiety problems such as generalized anxiety disorder, post-traumatic stress disorder, and so forth.

Pharmacological anxiety treatment in endocrine patients is relatively unexplored, and these therapies are not without risks. Lustman et al. (1995) reported that alprazolam generally improves glucose regulation, with benefits apparently independent of baseline anxiety level, regimen compliance, regimen changes, and weight alteration. Beta-blockers for physiological anxiety symptom management should be used cautiously with DM patients, because they might mask hypoglycemia symptoms (Jacobson, 1996). Potential problems with antidepressant agents are reviewed above (see Depressive Disorder).

Physiological Effects of Stress on Diabetes

Psychological stress is distinguished from clinical anxiety disorder by virtue of its ubiquitous, less-dramatic, and more normative nature. Presumably, most clinically anxious patients are also chronically stressed, while the majority of stressed individuals are free from significant anxiety disorder. It has often been suggested that stressful events can affect diabetes; in one study, 84% of IDDM patients reported that stress affects their glucose (Cox, Taylor, Nowacek, Holley-Wilcox, & Guthrow, 1984). One possibility, that stressful event occurrence disrupts DM control by interfering with regimen adherence, has not been widely supported (e. g., Aikens, Wallander, Bell, & Cole, 1992). A second possibility is that stress-related neurohormonal activity directly increases BG, since sympathetic nervous system activity functions to mobilize energy resources by inhibiting insulin production, blocking insulin action, and stimulating hepatic glucose release (Surwit, Schneider, & Feinglos, 1992).

Experimental stress exposure studies have yielded inconsistent BG effects in both IDDM and NIDDM, although BG effects appear stable within individuals with IDDM (see Cox & Gonder-Frederick, 1992; Surwit et al., 1992). Poor IDDM control is associated with increases in major life events stress (Grant, Kyle, Teichman, & Mendels, 1974) and minor everyday stress (Aikens, Wallander, Bell, & McNorton, 1994); similar associations with minor stress also exist in NIDDM patients (Aikens & Mayes, 1997; Aikens, Aikens, Wallander, & Hunt, 1997). While it is not altogether clear whether stress increases

BG, stress is undoubtedly produced by the abstract threat, lifestyle modifications, and frequently severe complications of DM.

Assessment

Clinical evaluation of stress as a factor in DM control should consider all relevant medical status variables, including DM type, duration, complications, regimen, hospitalizations, coexisting illnesses, and metabolic control (both HbA1c and daily BG). Since patient perceptions of a stress-BG correlation do not generally correspond to the actual correlation (Aikens et al., 1994), patients' self-monitoring of life stress and BG levels is highly advisable. The Daily Hassles and Uplifts Scale (Kanner, Coyne, Schaefer, & Lazarus, 1981) has been used in some DM research, and the Daily Stress Inventory (Brantley, Dietz, McKnight, Jones, & Tullery, 1988) covaries with stress hormone metabolites. A single item Likert or stress analog could be substituted, but the psychometric properties are usually unknown. Patients are often directed to fill out stress inventories each night, prior to bedtime; single items can be completed prior to each glucose test. While it is not always clinically feasible to obtain more than 14–21 daily observations on these measures, research protocols span 30 days or more. A plot (with respect to time) aids clinical interpretation and provides useful patient feedback (see clinical case, below). Data can also be subjected to single-case time series statistical analysis to yield a correlation coefficient indicating the strength and direction of stress-BG correspondence.

In one study of 25 adult IDDM females who monitored hassles and glucose for 30 days, two-thirds produced a "nonresponder" pattern (Aikens et al., 1994), i. e., weak stress-BG associations of no statistical or clinical significance. Such patients may actually be experiencing numerous everyday stressors, but they are simply unrelated to BG levels. Although no specific stress moderator variables have been identified, a variety of factors may be relevant: general coping effectiveness, diabetes management skills, reg-

imen adherence, depressive disorder, substance abuse, or manipulation of glucose levels for secondary gain. Interview data, behavioral observations, and psychometric findings can help evaluate such possibilities.

Intervention

Behavioral stress reduction studies in DM have also shown mixed results. Some show improvements following biofeedback-assisted progressive muscle relaxation training, while others show no change or inconsistent responses (see Cox & Gonder-Frederick, 1992; Surwit et al., 1992). While it is currently unclear whether relaxation training is generally efficacious, it possibly benefits NIDDM patients who have high baseline BG (Lammers, Naliboff, & Straatmeyer, 1984) or daily stress (Bradley, Moses, Gamsu, Knight, & Ward, 1985). Contradictory findings have been reported regarding the role of baseline anxiety symptoms in predicting treatment response (Aikens, Kiolbasa, & Sobel, 1997; Lane, McCaskill, Ross, Feinglos, & Surwit, 1993). In clinical practice, a variety of types of relaxation training can usually be expected to produce at least psychological benefits in most distressed medical patients who are not dissociative, actively psychotic, or severely depressed. Although the research has tended to focus on progressive muscle relaxation and frontalis EMG biofeedback, it is conceivable that benefit could also result from other stress management approaches such as imagery-based relaxation, autogenic training, cue-controlled relaxation, passive relaxation, mindfulness meditation, yoga, simple diaphragmatic breathing training, and a variety of other less standard stress management methods. We feel that a useful clinical approach is to initially apply the most well-validated methods, adding additional methods as needed if PMR or biofeedback are not amply helpful, or if the patient has a strong preconceived preference for a different approach. Typically, stress management and relaxation procedures are best taught directly in the office setting, with careful attention

Case Example

Although empirical support for a stress — BG relationship is somewhat mixed, our clinical experience suggests that a single-case approach to assessment and intervention is potentially helpful. I (JEA) evaluated and treated the patient (JH), who was a 27 year old single woman, attending graduate school in computer science, with a 19-year history of IDDM. Her prescribed daily DM regimen was a loosely-defined diet which was low in concentrated sugars and included small snacks between meals, and up to 4 daily injections of regular (also known as "R") insulin, with the timing and doses determined by the results of BG tests. JH's historically stable diabetes control deteriorated over the 3 months preceding referral, when she began showing elevated BG (over 200 mg/dl) at least 8 times per week. Her dietary adherence was reportedly fairly good, physical activity level was low but constant, insulin dosing was accurate, BG meter was functioning normally, and health was otherwise unremarkable except for a minor 4-day viral flu which resolved several weeks previously ago (is it okay to have this time-relative?). Clinical interview revealed no marked psychopathology or substance abuse, the BDI was non-elevated (raw score = 9), and that her SCL-90-R showed only one isolated, mild elevation (Anxiety; T = 65). Despite considerable exploration, the only recent major stressor JH reported was a lifestyle change; she had recently transitioned from primarily classroom-based learning to a routine in which she spent all her time on her dissertation project. She described the transition in this manner: "The move from classroom to lab was basically positive, and I have a lot more control over my time and learning pace, but I'm constantly preoccupied with my project now. You know, will it work? Will it be good enough? Will I make the grade?" She estimated that she was per-haps threefold-more prone to hyperglycemia compared to two months ago. I asked her to simply monitor her stress level (using a Hassles Scale) and her BG levels, both daily, for 2 weeks until her next appointment. This revealed that her average BG was 140 mg/dl and that it correlated moderately (across the 2 weeks) at +.48, with her stress level (see Figure 2). JH continued to monitor stress and BG while receiving four follow-up sessions of relatively straightforward progressive muscle relaxation training aimed at modifying her emotional and physiological reactions to job-related stress. The bulk of each session was spent reviewing her worries and concerns about her work, collaboratively generating alternative interpretations and options for coping, usually followed by brief guided relaxation practice. She was also provided with an audiotape of guided relaxation, which she reportedly practiced with about three to five times per week. At my suggestion, she eventually developed an audiotape made in her own voice (which I thought might promote generalization), although she usually preferred to use the original. By the fourth session, she was talking a lot less about the stress of her work, and noted that she took routine relaxation breaks during her long work periods. Eight weeks after finishing treatment, her BG averaged 118, which was a clinically significant reduction and also a return to her previous level of adequate BG control. This was also reflected in the elimination of her stress-glucose correlation (post-treatment r = +.04; see Figure 2). I had a brief follow-up visit from JH about nine months later, and found that she maintained good BG control, and she felt that her stress level continued to be much improved. This specific case example is provided to illustrate that for some patients with evidence of strong stress — BG associations, intervention can yield meaningful medical effects in addition to the presumed psychological benefits.

to undesirable side effects such as increased anxiety, self-generated performance pressure, physical discomfort, and so forth. Some patients may require several sessions using repetition of therapist-coached relaxation. Between-session practice is extremely helpful for promoting both skill acquisition and generalization, and this can be facilitated by providing patients with audiotaped instructions.

Eating Disorders, Obesity, and Diabetes

The combined effects of eating disorders and endocrinology are of concern in DM, given the dangerous impact of disordered eating behavior on metabolic control. In IDDM females (aged 13–45), Birk and Spencer (1989) estimated the respective prevalences of ano-

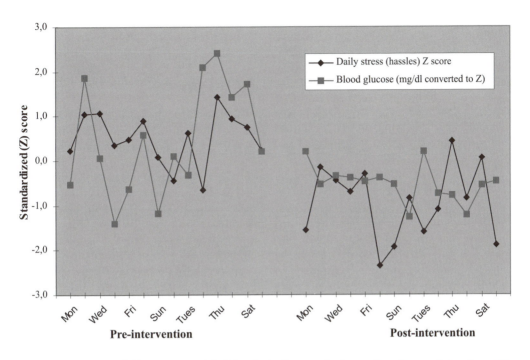

Figure 2. **Average daily stress and BG levels before and after relaxation training in a 27-year-old woman with IDDM.**

rexia nervosa and bulimia at 1% and 10%. Rydall, Rodin, Olmsted, Devenyi, and Daneman (1997) also examined adolescent females with IDDM and found that 29% had moderately high to highly disordered eating behavior. Of these patients, 11% had improved at 5-year follow-up and 18% continued to report disordered eating. Among patients who reported normal eating behaviors at initial assessment (71%), 15% had disordered eating at 5-year follow-up. Herpertz et al. (1998, 2000) examined IDDM and NIDDM patients and estimated the current prevalence of eating disorders to range from 5.9% to 9.0%. Estimates ranged from 10.3% to 14.0% for lifetime prevalence. These rates are in contrast to .5% and 1% in the general population (Fairburn & Beglin, 1990; Whitaker, Johnson, Staffer et al., 1990; APA, 1994). While most studies have demonstrated higher rates of eating disorders among DM patients, Meltzer et al. (2001) evaluated male and female adolescents with IDDM (ages 11–19 years) in comparison to a normative comparison sample and did not find differences between the two groups in disordered eating attitudes and behaviors.

Herpertz et al. (1998) found that 5.9% of IDDM and 2.2% of NIDDM patients intentionally omitted hyperglycemic medications for the purpose of weight reduction. Fourteen percent of female adolescents with IDDM reported the omission or underdosing of insulin for weight loss at baseline, increasing to 34% at five-year follow-up (Rydall et al., 1997). The frequency of insulin dose manipulation for weight loss purposes is much higher among DM patients with disordered eating behavior. Marcus and Wing (1990) found that 62% of eating-disordered IDDM females manipulate insulin dosing to promote weight loss, 75% are in poor metabolic control, and 48% have major IDDM complications. Meltzer et al. (2001) and Rydall et al. (1997) have demonstrated an inverse relationship between disordered eating behavior and glycemic control. Partial or complete insulin omission for weight loss purposes can produce hyperglycemia with diabetic ketoacidosis (DKA), and restricted food intake with unadjusted insulin administration can produce severe hypoglycemia. In DM, hypoglycemia is more likely in anorexia nervosa, whereas chronic hyperglycemia, recurrent DKA, and elevated HbA1c are more typical in bulimia nervosa (Rodin & Daneman, 1992). However, findings reported by Herpertz et al. (1998, 2000) did not indicate an association between disordered eating and glycemic control.

Timing of onset of eating disturbances in relationship to DM onset appears to differ for IDDM and NIDDM patients. For 90% of IDDM patients, an eating disorder developed after DM onset (Marcus & Wing, 1990). Numerous properties of IDDM may lower the threshold for eating disorder development in predisposed individuals (Rodin & Daneman, 1992), such as impaired awareness of hunger/satiety cues due to regimen-based dietary restraint, body dissatisfaction related to insulin-induced weight gain, and the availability of insulin manipulation to cause rapid weight loss. Life stress increases disordered eating in IDDM patients with poor eating inhibition (Balfour, White, Schiffrin, Dougherty, & Dufresne, 1993). Additional potential factors, which are not yet empirically supported, are food preoccupation promoted by the DM regimen, ongoing metabolic abnormalities, and altered family dynamics (Rodin & Daneman, 1992). In examining NIDDM patients with disordered eating, Herpertz et al. (1998) has found that most patients exhibiting eating disturbances prior to NIDDM onset. This observation has led to the suggestion that binge eating is a contributing cause to obesity, often preceding NIDDM onset.

Although obesity is not classified as an eating disorder in the DSM-IV (APA, 1994), obesity is a major risk factor for NIDDM development and progression to chronic complications. NIDDM prevalence is triple three times greater in people over 40% of recommended body weight (ADA, 1996), and 80% of NIDDM patients are obese (Herpertz et al., 2000; Robbins & Kumar, 1987). Yet 20% are nonobese, and many obese people do not develop NIDDM, suggesting that other factors are also relevant (e. g., genetic predisposition). Coverage of obesity treatment and re-

lated issues is provided above (see Regimen Adherence and Diabetes Self Care).

Assessment

Assessing eating disorders in DM is particularly challenging, due to content overlap between the DM diet and typical disordered eating patterns. The Eating Disorders Inventory (EDI; Garner, Olmsted, & Polivy, 1983) was used by Meltzer et al. (2001) to assess adolescents with IDDM. These authors recommended using the Bulimia subscale to screen patients attending DM clinics, with a clinical cutoff score of ≥ 5 to identify adolescents at risk for problems with glycemic control secondary to disordered eating habits. The Eating Attitudes Test (Garner, Olmsted, Bohr, & Garfinkel, 1982) is widely used to detect eating disorders in general populations, but has not yet been validly modified for DM application (Rodin & Daneman, 1992). Rodin and Daneman (1992) suggest screening for the following factors: refractory metabolic control (see also Fairburn, Peveler, Davies, Mann, & Mayou, 1991), binge-eating, weight preoccupation, insulin purging, laxative or diuretic abuse, and self-induced vomiting. The adoption of standard eating disorder criteria may be overly conservative, because even subclinical eating disorders can significantly alter DM control (Rubin & Peyrot, 1992).

Intervention

As with other disorders reviewed above, there is little research on the efficacy of eating disorders treatments in DM samples. Rodin and Daneman (1992) discuss CBT for eating-disordered IDDM patients, recommending self-monitoring (weight, insulin, food, BG, and HbA1c levels), dietary planning, discussing the relationship between disordered eating behavior and DM, and cognitive restructuring. Treatment should focus on modifying extreme beliefs regarding weight and body shape as well as dysfunctional attitudes concerning diabetes management. Alternative coping strategies, such as relaxation techniques, programmed mild aerobic exercise, and social support may be appropriate adjuncts for patients that eat in response to distress (Balfour et al., 1993). Family members could also be taught about the numerous biological and psychological factors maintaining problem eating behavior, including an overreliance upon food as the center of family rituals, the use of food to communicate positive feelings and/or exert interpersonal control, and other problematic family communication patterns thought to support disordered eating (Rodin & Daneman, 1992; Jacobson, 1996). Regarding medical management, Rodin and Daneman (1992) warn that overly rigid regimen plans may exacerbate binge eating in predisposed DM patients. Hospitalization is indicated for severe weight loss, severe hyperglycemia, or electrolyte abnormalities.

Cognitive Impairment

Numerous endocrine abnormalities can lead to impaired cognitive functioning, the nature of which depends upon the disorder. For example, hyperthyroid patients can display diminished concentration and memory, whereas hypothyroidism may produce mental slowing and decreased initiative, in addition to concentration and memory impairments (Dugbartey, 1998; for review see Erlanger, Kutner, & Jacobs, 1999). By contrast, cognitive disturbances with Cushing's syndrome and Addison's disease are typically mild in nature, and often attributable to affective distress (Lezak, 1995; Goldman, 1993)

In DM patients, BG abnormalities might disrupt cognition (Lezak, 1995; Goldman, 1993; Pohl et al., 1984). Experimentally induced hypoglycemia affects visual processing speed (Holmes, Koepke, & Thompson, 1986), visual tracking, visuomotor speed, concentration, and planning ability (Ewing, Deary, McCrimmon, Strachan, & Frier, 1998; Hoffman et al., 1989) independent of DM duration and metabolic control. In contrast, acute hyperglycemia is not clearly associated with cognitive impairments (Richardson, 1990; Lezak, 1995).

Research examining neuropsychological functioning among DM patients has produced mixed results. Strict regimen adherence over the 7-year DCCT intensive IDDM treatment study was unassociated with neuropsychological outcomes (DCCT, 1996). Lindeman et al. (2001) examined NIDDM patients 65 years of age and older and found no relationship between glycosolated hemoglobin levels and cognitive functioning. NIDDM patients did not differ from patients with normal glucose tolerance on neuropsychological performance. Scott, Kritz-Silverstein, Barrett-Connor, and Wiederholt (1998) reported similar findings among a community-dwelling sample of adults 55 years of age and older.

However, a good deal of evidence exists to indicate that chronic hyperglycemia and frequent severe hypoglycemic episodes are associated with cognitive deficits (Fontbonne, Berr, Ducimetiere, & Alperovitch, 2001; Gregg et al., 2000; Grodstein, Chen, Wilson, Manson, & Nurses' Health Study, 2001; Ryan, 1994). Strachan, Deary, Ewing, and Frier (1997) reviewed 19 controlled studies with NIDDM patients and found that in 13 studies, NIDDM patients demonstrated poorer performance on one or more cognitive assessment tasks than comparison groups. Cognitive functioning is differentially impacted by DM based on disease type, with NIDDM patients demonstrating greater severity of deficits (Bent, Rabbitt, & Metcalfe, 2000). Generally, IDDM patients are more likely to exhibit deficits in attention and psychomotor efficiency, with severe global deficits more probable if IDDM onset occurred prior to age five (Ryan, 1988). NIDDM patients are more likely to have learning and memory impairments and psychomotor slowing associated with chronically poor glycemic control (Perlmuter, Hokum, Hodgson-Harrington et al., 1984; Ryan & Geckle, 2000a, 2000b). The mechanism underlying observed neuropsychological deficits seem to be diffuse CNS pathology secondary to chronic metabolic abnormalities, as well as cerebrovascular disease (Biessels, 1999; Frier, 2001; Lezak, 1995).

Assessment

Whenever possible, cognitive assessment of endocrine patients should be performed by a psychologist with training in the cognitive evaluation of functional impairments resulting from underlying brain pathology. Erlanger, Kutner, and Jacobs (1999) provide guidelines for the neuropsychological assessment of patients with endocrine disorders. While standard neuropsychological batteries have been widely used in DM (Ryan, 1994; Lezak, 1995; Richardson, 1990), the potential effects of DM symptoms and complications must be carefully considered when interpreting performance. For example, numbness and pain related to peripheral neuropathy may slow motor speed, while retinopathy can obviously interfere with visual task performance. If possible, factors potentially interfering with valid assessment should be considered in the selection of assessment instruments and minimized prior to evaluation. The presence of cerebrovascular disease (and the possibility that a stroke may also be affecting cognition) should also be assessed prior to evaluation. Because of the elevated risk of vascular dementia and Alzheimer's disease among diabetes patients, Stewart and Liolitsa (1999) concluded that the existing classification scheme for dementia may not adequately account for diabetes patients, given the likely mixed pathogenesis of patients' cognitive deficits. Adequate eating and medication administration (i. e., per regimen) should be ensured during prolonged testing sessions, since impaired mental efficiency and other disruptions can occur with acute hypoglycemia (Hoffman et al., 1989; Richardson, 1990). For the same reasons patient BG self-monitoring should ideally be conducted before and periodically throughout the evaluation, to establish BG range during testing.

Intervention

When cognitive deficits are detected, patient and family supportive counseling is often a helpful forum for conveying this information. This should include a thorough, balanced discussion of implications for the patient's functioning in family relationships, work, daily responsibilities, self-care, and general psychological well-being. DM self-management should also be a focus. Sinclair, Girling, and Bayer (2000) found that DM patients with a Mini-Mental State Examination (MMSE) score of less than 23 were significantly less likely to monitor their disease. If appropriate, patient and family counseling also offers an avenue for teaching compensatory strategies such as using memory aids or safety precautions, and to arrange for any further necessary neuropsychological assessments. Finally, because cognitive declines are frequently accompanied by significant adjustment problems, the entire range of individual interventions such as supportive counseling, psychotherapy, behavior therapy, or medication may also be called for; these are described more thoroughly in above sections.

Case Example

GK is a 57-year-old, married, right-handed African American male with NIDDM who was referred by his endocrinologist for neuropsychological evaluation following recent abrupt-onset memory and concentration difficulties. A month prior to his referral, this gentleman had been first diagnosed with NIDDM as well as hypertension, although his medical records suggested that NIDDM had been suspected for at least five years prior to referral. GK's records also indicated poor chronic metabolic control, with his most recent HbA1c being 15.0% (severe range of hyperglycemia). However, it is important that we note that his BG varied within normal limits during the assessment (mean 140 mg/dl), because of the possibility that low BG could adversely affect test performance. During the interview, GK reported that he was currently employed as a full time salesman, had completed twelve years of education, and was experiencing the following psychiatric and neurological symptoms: bilateral lower extremity numbness, decreased visual acuity, sleep maintenance insomnia, extreme subjective anxiety, and daily episodes of dizziness and mild confusion prior to eating lunch. Also of note is the fact that he denied current or historical alcohol or substance abuse, traumatic head injury, seizures, and any history of loss of consciousness.

We present selected neuropsychological results in Table 1. GK displayed average general intellectual functioning, with no evidence of generalized cognitive decline. However, he displayed evidence of specific deficits in the following functions: problem-solving, verbal and nonverbal memory, confrontation naming, mental and motor speed, and concentration. We felt that these impairments were well beyond the level that would be attributable to GK's admittedly marked anxiety symptoms. Rather, GK's pattern of deficits suggests diffuse cerebral dysfunction, presumably secondary to NIDDM-related microvascular complications.

GK's case is an illustrative example of how cognitive function can decline for a variety of reasons. In his case, we conclude that his difficulties are attributable to the neurological impact of the illness itself as well as the cognitive effects of distress arising from a recent DM diagnosis. We followed up with a recommendation that GK promptly receive psychological intervention. The first intervention objective was to address the likely impact that his cognitive deficits probably have on his vocational performance. For example, when receiving feedback of his test results, he remarked that over the past two years he first began to have difficulty remembering new client's names, although he tended to "brush it off as a sign of getting old." In fact, though, his verbal memory problems progressed quickly over this two-year period and were well in excess of what would be predicted on the basis of the aging process alone. He also noted that his concentration ability deteriorated every afternoon. Because GK derived obvious satisfaction from continuing to work and his employer was also exceptionally willing to make adaptations, we decided against recommending that he retire suddenly. Instead, the therapist and GK were able to negotiate an abbreviated four-hour workday, a reduced client load, and increased prompting and supervision at work. These modifications indirectly helped us accomplish a sec-

Table 1. Selected neuropsychological findings from a 57-year-old NIDDM male with abrupt onset memory and concentration difficulties.

Construct measured	Instrument	Performance
General intellectual functioning	Wechsler Adult Intelligence Scale – Revised (WAIS-R)	Average
Problem solving, abstract reasoning, learning efficiency	Wisconsin Card Sorting Test	Moderately impaired
Memory Verbal memory Nonverbal memory	Wechsler Memory Scale – Form 1 Logical Memory Visual Reproduction	Moderately impaired Severely impaired
Concentration, attention	Trailmaking Test Stroop Color-Word Test WAIS-R Digit Span	Moderately impaired
Word finding, general language	Boston Naming Test	Mildly impaired Average
Visual perceptual skills (non-motor)	Judgment of Line Orientation	Average
Motor speed, manual dexterity	Grooved Pegboard	Mildly to moderately impaired
Depressive symptoms	Beck Depression Inventory	Moderately depressed
Current and chronic anxiety symptoms	State-Trait Anxiety Inventory	Severely anxious

ond major therapeutic goal, which was to promote GK's adjustment to his altered physical and cognitive status. In subsequent weekly psychotherapy sessions, the major focus was to promote his acceptance and understanding of his newly-diagnosed illness and the cognitive changes associated with it. This was an extremely important intervention, since the interview and testing data strongly suggested that some (but not all) of his cognitive difficulty was attributable to anxiety, secondary to recent DM diagnosis. Functional analysis of GK's anxiety revealed that he usually became acutely anxious upon spontaneously thinking about his diabetes (which reportedly happened at least once daily) or while testing his BG. He was first taught to distance himself from his anxious response, and eventually to question its validity. He also received training in applied relaxation, which he practiced with audiotaped guidance daily for three weeks and once weekly thereafter. Due to GK's memory difficulties, his relaxation audiotape use was usually cued by his wife, which fortunately turned out to be a workable arrangement for both he and his wife. After three months of intervention, he reportedly experienced spontaneous anxiety episodes only once a week or less, describing these remaining episodes as "mild and manageable." To promote maintenance and to monitor the need for neuropsychological re-assessment and further vocational modifications, GK continued to be followed by Behavioral Medicine on at least an every-other-month basis.

Closing Comments

This chapter covered current epidemiology, etiology, assessment, and psychological intervention for several emotional and behavioral problems associated with endocrine disorders. In summary, three general statements can be made. First, endocrinology provides some of the finest clinical examples of the widely-discussed "biopsychosocial" problem. This not only means that health psychologists working with endocrine patients must be facile with bidirectional mind-body interactions (not a problem for most), but also conversant in the mind-boggling language of glandular networks, hormones, dramatic, but often reversible medical crises, and endocrinology's endless list of "hypo's" and "hyper's." Second, endocrine disorders fit nicely with health psychology's general embracement of multidisciplinary care models. Good clinical outcomes hinge upon ongoing (and sometimes humbling) collaboration with endocrinologists, psychiatrists, internists, diabetes educators, nurses, dietitians, and other team members. As such, this specialty is not suitable for "lone ranger" psychologists, who may be long on projected confidence, but short on the team-mindedness needed for effective multidisciplinary interactions. Orthodox models need to be adapted to accomplish immediate goals, often in strange settings far from the comfort zone of the therapists' office, such as medical examining rooms, the hospital bedside, or over the telephone to the Emergency Room on a Sunday night. Third, considerable research obviously remains to be completed. Although relative progress has been made in prevalence, etiology, and assessment, the astute reader will quickly note that many of the interventions we recommend are merely untested extrapolations from non-DM research. We especially notice a lack of data on thyroid and adrenal disorders, which have been curiously of little historical interest to psychologists (yet strongly emphasized in psychiatric training). Although there is much we do not yet know, endocrinology presents diverse and interesting problems which can benefit from health psychology's unique scientific grounding, creativity, and professional diplomacy.

Acknowledgments

Helpful reviews of earlier versions of this manuscript were provided by Sara Knight, Ph.D., Paul Camic, Ph.D., Louis Philipson, M.D., Ph.D., Peter Vanable, M.A., Lance McCracken, Ph.D., Kathleen Shay Aikens, Ph.D., Neil Pliskin, Ph.D., Ivan Torres, Ph.D, Beth Duncan, Andrew Jun.

References

Aikens, J.E., Kiolbasa, T.K., & Sobel, R.S. (1997). Psychological predictors of glycemic change with relaxation training for non-insulin dependent diabetes mellitus (NIDDM). *Psychotherapy and Psychosomatics, 66,* 435–437.

Aikens, J.E., & Mayes, R. (1997). Elevated glycosylated albumin in NIDDM is a function of recent everyday environmental stress. *Diabetes Care, 20,* 1111–1113.

Aikens, J.E., Wallander, J.L., Bell, D.S.H., & Cole, J.A. (1992). Daily stress variability, learned resourcefulness, regimen adherence, and metabolic control in Type I diabetes mellitus: Evaluation of a path model. *Journal of Consulting and Clinical Psychology, 60,* 113–118.

Aikens, J.E., Wallander, J.L., Bell, D.S.H., & McNorton, A. (1994). A nomothetic-idiographic analysis of daily psychological stress and blood glucose in women with type I diabetes mellitus. *Journal of Behavioral Medicine, 17,* 535–548.

Aikens, K.S., Aikens, J.E., Wallander, J.L., & Hunt, S.L. (1997). Daily activity level buffers stress — glycemia associations in older sedentary NIDDM patients. *Journal of Behavioral Medicine, 20,* 371–388.

American Diabetes Association (ADA) (1996). *Vital Statistics.* Alexandria: American Diabetes Association.

American Psychiatric Association (1994). *Diagnostic and statistical manual of mental disorders* (4th ed.). Washington, DC: American Psychiatric Association.

Anderson, B.L. (1992). Psychological interventions for cancer patients to enhance quality of life. *Journal of Consulting and Clinical Psychology, 60,* 552–568.

Anderson, B.J., Miller, J.P., Auslander, W.F., & Santiago, J.V. (1981). Family characteristics of diabetic adolescents: relationship to metabolic control. *Diabetes Care, 4,* 586–594.

Anderson, B.J. (1990). Diabetes and adaptation in family systems. In C.S. Holmes (Ed.), *Neuropsychological and behavioral aspects of diabetes* (pp. 85–101). New York: Springer-Verlag.

Austin, E.J., & Deary, I.J. (1999). Effects of repeated hypoglycemia on cognitive function: A psychometrically validated reanalysis of the Diabetes Control and Complications Trial data. *Diabetes Care, 22,* 273–277.

Balfour, L., White, D.R., Schiffrin, A., Dougherty, G., & Dufresne, J. (1993). Dietary disinhibition, perceived stress, and glucose control in young, type 1 diabetic women. *Health Psychology, 12,* 33–38.

Beardsley, G., & Goldstein, M.G. (1993). Psychological factors affecting physical condition: Endocrine disease literature review. *Psychosomatics, 34,* 12–19.

Beck, A.T., Rush, A.J., Shaw, B.F., & Emery, G. (1979). *Cognitive therapy of depression.* New York: Guilford.

Beck, A.T., & Steer, R.A. (1987). *Manual for the Revised Beck Depression Inventory.* San Antonio, TX: Psychological Corporation.

Bent, N., Rabbit, P., & Metcalfe, D. (2000). Diabetes mellitus and the rate of cognitive ageing. *British Journal of Clinical Psychology, 39,* 349–362.

Biessels, G.J. (1999). Cerebral complications of diabetes: Clinical findings and pathogenetic mechanisms. *Netherlands Journal of Medicine, 54,* 35–45.

Birk, R., & Spencer, M.L. (1989). The prevalence of anorexia nervosa, bulimia, and induced glycosuria in IDDM females. *Diabetes Education, 15,* 336–341.

Bradley, C. (1994). *Handbook of psychology and diabetes: A guide to measurement in diabetes research and practice.* Chur, Switzerland: Harwood.

Bradley, C., Moses, J.L., Gamsu, D.S., Knight, G., & Ward, J.D. (1985). The effects of relaxation on metabolic control of type I diabetes: A matched controlled study. *Diabetes, 34,* 17A.

Brown, T.A., O'Leary, T.A., & Barlow, D.H. (1993). Generalized anxiety disorder. In D.H. Barlow (Ed.), *Clinical handbook of psychological disorders* (pp. 137–187.). New York: Guilford.

Cox, D., Irvine, A., Gonder-Frederick, L., Nowacek, G., & Butterfield, J. (1987). Quantifying fear of hypoglycemia: A preliminary report. *Diabetes Care, 10,* 617–621.

Cox, D.J., Taylor, A.G., Nowacek, G., Holley-Wilcox, P., & Pohl, S.L. (1984). The relationship between psychological stress and insulin-dependent diabetic blood glucose control: preliminary investigations. *Health Psychology, 3,* 63–75.

Cox, D.J., & Gonder-Frederick, L. (1992). Major developments in behavioral diabetes research. *Journal of Consulting and Clinical Psychology, 60,* 628–638.

Craske, M.G., & Barlow, D.H. (1993). Panic disorder and agoraphobia. In D.H. Barlow (Ed.), *Clinical handbook of psychological disorders* (pp. 1–47). New York: Guilford.

DCCT Research Group (1996). Effects of intensive diabetes therapy on neuropsychological function in adults in the Diabetes Control and Complications Trial. *Annals of Internal Medicine, 124,* 379–388.

DCCT Research Group (1993). Implications of

the Diabetes Control and Complications Trial. *Diabetes Care, 16,* 1517-1520.

DCCT Research Group (1988). Reliability and validity of a diabetes quality-of-life measure for the diabetes control and complications trial (DCCT). *Diabetes Care, 11,* 725-732.

Davis, W.K., Hess, G.E., & Hiss, R.G. (1988). Psychosocial correlates of survival in diabetes. *Diabetes Care, 7,* 538-545.

Delimiter, A.M., Kurtz, S.M., Bubb, J., White, N.H., & Santiago, J.V. (1987). Stress and coping in relation to metabolic control of adolescents with type I diabetes. *Developmental and Behavioral Pediatrics, 8,* 136-140.

Derogatis, L.R. (1977). *The SCL-90-R administration, scoring and procedures manual I.* Baltimore: Clinical Psychometric Research.

Dunn S.M., & Turtle, J.R. (1981). The myth of the diabetic personality. *Diabetes Care, 4,* 640-646.

Erlanger, D.M., Kutner, K.C., & Jacobs, A.R. (1999). Hormones and cognition: Current concepts and issues in neuropsychology. *Neuropsychology Review, 9,* 175-207.

Ewing, F.M., Deary, I.J., McCrimmon, R.J., Strachan, M.W., & Frier, B.M. (1998). Effect of acute hypoglycemia on visual information processing in adults with type 1 diabetes mellitus. *Physiology & Behavior, 64,* 653-660.

Fairburn, C.G., & Beglin, S.J. (1990). Studies of the epidemiology of bulimia nervosa. *American Journal of Psychiatry, 147,* 401-408.

Fairburn, C.G., Peveler, R.C., Davies, B., Mann, J.I., & Mayou, R.A. (1991). Eating disorders in young adults with insulin dependent diabetes mellitus: A controlled study. *British Medical Journal, 303,* 17-20.

Fontbonne, A., Berr, C., Ducimetiere, P., & Alperovitch, A. (2001). Changes in cognitive abilities over a 4-year period are unfavorably affected in elderly diabetic subjects: Results of the Epidemiology of Vascular Aging Study. *Diabetes Care, 24,* 366-370.

Frier, B.M. (2001). Hypoglycemia and cognitive function in diabetes. *International Journal of Clinical Practice, 123S,* 30-37.

Garner, D.M., Olmsted, M.P., & Polivy, J. (1983). Development and validation of a multidimensional eating disorder inventory for anorexia nervosa and bulimia. *International Journal of Eating Disorders, 2,* 15-34.

Garner, D.M., Olmsted, M.P., Bohr, Y., & Garfinkel, P.E. (1982). The Eating Attitudes Test: Psychometric features and clinical correlates. *Psychological Medicine, 12,* 871-878.

Glasgow, R.E., & Toobert, D. (1988). Social environment and regimen adherence among Type II diabetic patients. *Diabetes Care, 11,* 399-412.

Gonder-Frederick, L.A., Cox, D.J., Bobbitt, S.A., & Pennebaker, J.W. (1989). Mood changes associated with blood glucose fluctuations in insulin-dependent diabetes. *Health Psychology, 8,* 45-59.

Goldman, M.B. (1992). Neuropsychiatric features of endocrine disorders. In S.C. Yudofsky, & R.E. Holes (Eds). *The American Psychiatric Press textbook of neuropsychiatry.* Washington, DC: American Psychiatric Association Press.

Goodnick, P.J., Henry, J.H., & Buki, V.M.V. (1995). Treatment of depression in patients with diabetes mellitus. *Journal of Clinical Psychiatry, 56,* 128-36.

Gregg, E.W., Yaffe, K., Cauley, J.A., Rolka, D.B., Blackwell, T.L., Narayan, K.M., & Cummings, S.R. (2000). Is diabetes associated with cognitive impairment and cognitive decline among older women? Study of Osteoporotic Fractures Research Group. *Archives of Internal Medicine, 160,* 174-180.

Grodstein, F., Chen, J., Wilson, R.S., Manson, J.E., Nurses' Study (2001). Type 2 diabetes and cognitive function in community-dwelling elderly women. *Diabetes Care, 24,* 1060-1065.

Hartwell, S., Kaplan, R., & Wallace, J. (1986). Comparison of behavioral interventions for control of type II diabetes. *Behavior Therapy, 17,* 447-461.

Herpertz, S., Albus, C., Lichtblau, K., Kohle, K., Mann, K., & Senf, W. (2000). Relationship of weight and eating disorders in type 2 diabetic patients: A multicenter study. *International Journal of Eating Disorders, 28,* 68-77.

Herpertz, S., Albus, C., Wagener, R., Kocnar, M., Wagner, R., Henning, A., Best, F., Foerster, H., Schulze, S.B., Thomas, W., Kohle, K., Mann, K., & Senf, W. (1998). Comorbidity of diabetes and eating disorders. Does diabetes control reflect disturbed eating behavior? *Diabetes Care, 21,* 1110-1116.

Hoffman, R.G., Speilman, D.J., Hinnen, D.A., Conley, K.L., Guthrie, R.A., & Knapp, R.K. (1989). Changes in cortical functioning with acute hypoglycemia and hyperglycemia in Type I diabetes. *Diabetes Care, 12,* 193-197.

Holmes, C.S., Koepke, K.M., & Thompson, R.G. (1986) Simple versus complex performance at three blood glucose levels. *Psychoneuroendocrinology, 11,* 353-357.

Hope, D.A., & Heimberg, R.G. (1993). Social phobia and social anxiety. In D.H. Barlow (Ed.), *Clinical handbook of psychological disorders* (pp. 99-136). New York: Guilford.

Irvine, A.A., Cox, D., & Gonder-Frederick, L.

(1992). Fear of hypoglycemia: Relationship to physical and psychological symptoms in patients with insulin-dependent diabetes mellitus. *Health Psychology, 11,* 135–138.

Jacobson, A.M. (1996). The psychological care of patients with insulin-dependent diabetes mellitus. *New England Journal of Medicine, 334,* 1249–1253.

Lammers, C.A., Naliboff, B.D., & Straatmeyer, A.J. (1984). The effects of progressive muscle relaxation on stress and diabetic control. *Behavior Research and Therapy, 22,* 641–650.

Lane, J.D., McCaskill, C.C., Ross, S.L., Feinglos, M.N., & Surwit, R.S. (1993). Relaxation training for NIDDM: Predicting who may benefit. *Diabetes Care, 16,* 1087–1094.

Lezak, M.D. (1995). *Neuropsychological Assessment* (Third Edition). New York: Oxford University Press, Inc.

Lindeman, R.D., Romero, L.J., LaRue, A., Yau, C.L., Schade, D.S., Koehler, K.M., Baumgartner, R.N., & Garry, P.J. (2001). A biethnic community survey of cognition in participants with type 2 diabetes, impaired glucose tolerance, and normal glucose tolerance: The New Mexico Elder Health Survey. *Diabetes Care, 24,* 1567–1572.

Lustman, P.J., Griffith, L.S., Gavard, J.A., & Clouse, R.E. (1991). Depression in adults with diabetes. *Diabetes Care, 15,* 1631–1667.

Lustman, P.J., Frank, B.L., & McGill, J.B. (1988). Relationship of personality characteristics to glucose regulation in adults with diabetes. *Psychosomatic Medicine, 53,* 305–312.

Lustman, P.J., Griffith, L.S., Clouse, R.E., & Cryer, P.E. (1986). Psychiatric illness in diabetes mellitus: Relationship to symptoms and illness control. *The Journal of Nervous and Mental Disease, 174,* 736–742.

Lustman, P.J. (1988). Anxiety disorders in adults with diabetes mellitus. *Psychiatric Clinics of North America, 11,* 419–432.

Lustman, P.J., Griffith, L.S., Clouse, R.E., Freedland, K.E., Eisen, S.A., Rubin, E.H., Carney, R.M., & McGill, J.B. (1995). Effects of alprazolam on glucose regulation in diabetes. *Diabetes Care, 18,* 1133–1139.

Lustman, P.J., & Harper, G.W. (1987). Nonpsychiatric physicians' identification and treatment of depression in patients with diabetes. *Comprehensive Psychiatry, 28,* 22–27.

Lustman, P.J., Griffith, L.S., Freedland, K.E., Kissel, S.S., & Clouse, R.E. (1998). Cognitive behavior therapy for depression in type 2 diabetes mellitus. A randomized, controlled trial. *Annals of Internal Medicine, 129*(8), 613–621.

Lustman, P.J., Freedland, K.E., Griffith, L.S., &

Clouse, R.E. (1998). Predicting response to cognitive behavior therapy of depression in type 2 diabetes. *General Hospital Psychiatry, 20,* 302–306.

Lustman, P.J., Freedland, K.E., Griffith, L.S., & Clouse, R.E. (2000). Fluoxetine for depression in diabetes: A randomized double-blind placebo-controlled trial. *Diabetes Care, 23,* 618–623.

Marcus, M.D., & Wing, R.R. (1990). Eating disorders and diabetes. In C.S. Holmes (Ed.), *Neuropsychological and behavioral aspects of diabetes.* New York: Springer-Verlag.

Masters, J.C., Burish, T.G., Hollon, S.D., & Rimm, D.C. (1987). *Behavior therapy: Techniques and empirical findings* (3rd ed.). San Diego, CA: Harcourt Brace Jovanovich, Publishers.

Meltzer, L.J., Johnson, S.B., Prine, J.M., Banks, R.A., Desrosiers, P.M., & Silverstein, J.H. (2001). Disordered eating, body mass, and glycemic control in adolescents with type 1 diabetes. *Diabetes Care, 24,* 678–682.

National Center for Health Statistics, US Centers for Disease Control. (1999). *Vital and Health Statistics,* Series 10, No. 200.

Perlmuter, L.C., Hokum, M.K., Hodgson-Harrington, C., Ginsberg, J., Katz, J., Singer, D.E., & Nathan, D.M. (1984). Decreased cognitive function in aging non-insulin-dependent diabetic patients. *American Journal of Medicine, 77,* 1043–1048.

Pohl, S.L., Gonder-Frederick, L., & Cox, D.J. (1984). Area review: Diabetes mellitus. *Behavioral Medicine Update, 6,* 3–7.

Popkin, M.K., Callies, A.L., Lentz, R.D. et al. (1988). Prevalence of major depression, simple phobia, and other psychiatric disorders in patients with longstanding type I diabetes mellitus. *Archives of General Psychiatry, 45,* 64–70.

Richardson, J.T. (1990). Cognitive function in diabetes mellitus. *Neuroscience & Behavioral Reviews, 14,* 385–388.

Riggs, D.S., & Foa, E.B. (1993). Obsessive compulsive disorder. In D.H. Barlow (Ed.), *Clinical handbook of psychological disorders* (pp. 189–239). New York: Guilford.

Robbins, S.L., & Kumar, V. (1987). *Basic pathology* (4th ed.). Philadelphia, PA: W.B. Saunders.

Robins, L.N., Helzer, J.E., Croughan, J., & Ratcliff, K.S. (1981). National Institute of Mental Health Diagnostic Interview Schedule: Its history, characteristics, and validity. *Archives of General Psychiatry, 38,* 381–389.

Ryan, C.M., & Geckle, M.O. (2000a). Circumscribed cognitive dysfunction in middle-aged adults with type 2 diabetes. *Diabetes Care, 23,* 1486–1493.

Ryan, C.M., & Geckle, M. (2000b). Why is learning and memory dysfunction in Type 2 diabetes limited to older adults? *Diabetes/Metabolism Research Reviews, 16,* 308–315.

Ryan, C.M. (1988). Neurobehavioral disturbances associated with disorders of the pancreas. In R.E. Tarter, D.H. VanThiel, & K.L. Edwards (Eds), *Medical neuropsychology* (pp. 11–158). New York: Plenum.

Ryan, C.M. (1994). Measures of cognitive function. In C. Bradley (Ed.), *Handbook of psychology and diabetes.* Chur, Switzerland: Harwood.

Rydall, A.C., Rodin, G.M., Olmsted, M.P., Devenyi, R.G., & Daneman, D. (1997). Disordered eating behavior and microvascular complications in young women with insulin-dependent diabetes mellitus. *New England Journal of Medicine, 336,* 1849–1854.

Robertson, P., & Rosenvinge, J.H. (1990). Insulin-dependent diabetes mellitus: A risk factor in anorexia nervosa or bulimia nervosa? An empirical study of 116 women. *Journal of Psychosomatic Research, 34,* 535–541.

Rodin, G.M., & Daneman, D. (1992). Eating disorders and IDDM: A problematic association. *Diabetes Care, 15,* 1402–1412.

Rubin, R.R., & Peyrot, M. (1992). Psychosocial problems and interventions in diabetes: A review of the literature. *Diabetes Care, 15,* 1640–1657.

Sarafino, E.P. (1994). *Health psychology: Biopsychosocial interactions* (2nd ed.). New York: Wiley.

Scott, R.D., Kritz-Silverstein, D., Barrett-Connor, E., & Wiederholt, W.C. (1998). The association of non-insulin-dependent diabetes mellitus and cognitive function in an older cohort. *Journal of the American Geriatrics Society, 46,* 1217–1222.

Sinclair, A.J., Girling, A.J., & Bayer, A.J. (2000). Cognitive dysfunction in older subjects with diabetes mellitus: Impact on diabetes self-management and use of care services. All Wales Research into Elderly (AWARE) Study. *Diabetes Research & Clinical Practice, 50S,* 203–212.

Slaby, A., Tancredi, L., & Lieb, J. (1981). *Endocrine disorders. Clinical psychiatric medicine.* New York: Harper and Row.

Stewart, R., & Liolitsa, D. (1999). Type 2 diabetes mellitus, cognitive impairment and dementia. *Diabetic Medicine, 16,* 93–112.

Surwit, R.S., & Feinglos, M.N. (1983). The effects of relaxation on glucose tolerance in non-insulin-dependent diabetes. *Diabetes Care, 6,* 176–179.

Surwit, R.S., Feinglos, M.N., & Scovern, A.W. (1983). Diabetes and behavior: A paradigm for health psychology. *American Psychologist, 38,* 255–262.

Toobert, D.J., & Glasgow, R.E. (1994). Assessing diabetes self-management: The summary of diabetes self-care activities questionnaire. In C. Bradley (Ed.), *Handbook of psychology and diabetes* (pp. 351–375). Chur, Switzerland: Harwood.

Turkat, I.D. (1982). Glycosylated hemoglobin levels in anxious and nonanxious diabetic patients. *Psychosomatics, 23,* 1056–1058.

UK Prospective Diabetes Study Group (1998). Intensive blood-glucose control with sulphonylureas or insulin compared with conventional treatment and risk of complications in patients with type 2 diabetes. *Lancet, 352,* 837–853.

Whitaker, A., Johnson, J., Staffer, D., Rapoport, J.L., Kalikow, K., Walsh, B.T., Davies, M., Braiman, S., & Dolinsky, A. (1990). Uncommon troubles in young people: Prevalence estimates of selected psychiatric disorders in a nonreferred adolescent populations. *Archives of General Psychiatry, 47,* 487–496.

Young, L.D. (1992). Psychological factors in rheumatoid arthritis. *Journal of Consulting and Clinical Psychology, 60,* 619–627.

Zung, W.W.K. (1974). The measurement of affects: Depression and anxiety. In P. Pichot & R. Olivier-Martin (Eds), *Psychological measurement in psychopharmacology.* Basel: Karger.

Paul M. Camic and Laura M. Gaugh

8

Gastrointestinal Conditions and Disorders

The gastrointestinal system, also called the GI tract, is responsible for digestive and eliminatory functions. The ingestion of food and the act of chewing begin the digestive process. This process involves both smooth and striated muscles, sympathetic and parasympathetic innervation, hormones, and complex chemical messengers. These messengers might be a neurotransmitter, part of the endocrine or neuroendocrine systems or part of the paracrine system (Davenport, 1982). The gross anatomy of the GI system and its related structures includes the teeth and mouth, salivary glands, esophagus, stomach, gallbladder, liver, bile duct, pancreas, small intestine, colon, rectum and anus (Figure 1).

We have heard patients call the GI tract "gut," "down-there," "stomach," "tummy,"

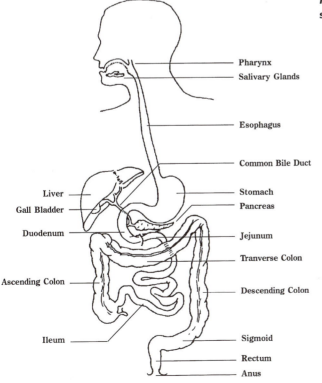

Figure 1. **The gastrointestinal system.**

Pharynx
Salivary Glands
Esophagus
Common Bile Duct
Liver
Stomach
Gall Bladder
Pancreas
Duodenum
Jejunum
Tranverse Colon
Ascending Colon
Descending Colon
Ileum
Sigmoid
Rectum
Anus

Table 1. Gastrointestinal disorders treated by health psychologists.

Disorders and conditions of the esophagus
Aerophagia
Dysphagia
Globus hystericus
Non-cardiac chest pain

Disorders and conditions of the upper GI tract
Cancer
Functional dyspepsia
Gastritis
Peptic ulcer disease
Vomiting disorders
    Anticipatory nausea and vomiting
    Rumination syndrome

Disorders and conditions of the lower GI tract
Cancer
Constipation
Crohn's disease
Fecal incontinence
Irritable bowel syndrome
Pelvic floor dyssynergia
Proctalgia fugax
Ulcerative colitis

highly spiced food, situational distress or other acute and transient situations. One common intervention is to do nothing. Employing a combination of treatments (including antacids, rest, increasing dietary fiber, altering food choices, using less caffeine and alcohol, stopping smoking, and reducing stress) is also usual. While acknowledging these symptoms to be uncomfortable and troublesome, they are not the focus of this chapter. Instead, we would like to focus on specific GI conditions which are recurring or chronic and to which a health psychologist can make a contribution (Table 1).

Digestion and Elimination

Biomedical Aspects

The gastrointestinal system is often divided into upper and lower GI tracts for diagnostic evaluation and easy description. These, however, are imprecise terms. Usually the upper GI tract refers to the stomach and sometimes to the esophagus and duodenum, while the lower GI tract refers to everything from the colon to the anus. Diagnostic studies such as colonoscopy, sigmoidoscopy, air contrast barium enema, upper gastrointestinal tract radiography, endoscopy, stool cultures, parasite studies, and lactose tolerance tests are common for patients with gastrointestinal distress (Latimer, 1983). This chapter will examine conditions affecting the gastrointestinal system including the esophagus, stomach, small intestine and colon, rectum and anal canal. A senior gastroenterologist once remarked half-jokingly to the first author, "If we could eliminate food, we could cure most GI disorders." Since the elimination of food is not possible for human beings and to help understand the digestive process, we will take you on a short voyage involving food's journey from ingestion to elimination. Along the way we will encounter the major organs involved in processing food and their associated GI disorders.

The best place to begin is with chewing. Food with all its essential nutrients for human survival, is taken into your mouth in

"my insides," "the cave," "hell" and "my bad and nasty parts" among others. Characterizations describing gastrointestinal distress include, "heartburn," "topsy-turvy," "tied-in-a-knot," "stopped-up," "acidy," "upside-down," "achy" and "downright painful." In our experience have also found that Asian, Hispanic and Native American patients may use words in their first languages, which more adequately describe GI symptoms for them. When a patient struggles to describe a symptom in English, consider encouraging them to name it in their first language. Translation, either through a dictionary, interpreter, or pictorial image has not proven difficult.

All of us, at one time or another, have probably experienced one or more of these GI symptoms. Perhaps they have been the result of a food toxin, one alcoholic beverage too many, too much food, not enough food, bites. Imagine a portion of food, say a healthy-sized bite of pizza, has just entered your mouth. It is here the piece of pizza begins to be prepared for absorption into your body. Through the action of chewing and mixing with saliva produced from the salivary glands, food is lubricated before continuing on its journey. The mechanisms that govern chewing are therefore partially voluntary and partially reflexive (Davenport, 1982).

The breaking down of food by chewing and saliva results in a mushy mass known as bolus. When the bolus is readied for swallowing, voluntary muscles thrust it into the pharynx, where involuntary muscle pressure takes over. Pushing the bolus toward the esophagus, the upper esophageal sphincter quickly opens to allow the bolus to pass through, thus engaging the swallowing reflex. The upper esophageal sphincter quickly closes when the bolus has passed to prevent regurgitation (Code & Schlegel, 1968). Through peristalsis (muscle contractions), distension of the esophagus and gravity, the bolus makes its way toward your stomach and the next part of the digestive process (Henderson, 1980). The function of the esophagus is to carry food to the stomach. No absorption or digestion takes place during transport. A health psychologist may encounter problems associated with the esophagus including aerophagia and the esophageal motility disorders of dysphagia, globus hystericus and noncardiac chest pain.

After leaving the esophagus and passing the lower esophageal sphincter, the bolus enters the small and relaxed stomach and begins to form layers in the body of the stomach. As the stomach is filling, the stomach's peristaltic waves become stronger. As they strengthen and engage the muscle of the antrum (lower chamber) to mix the stomach's contents with gastric secretions, chyme is produced. The breaking down of your piece of pizza continues as it is being prepared for absorption into the body. This muscle action slowly propels chyme into the duodenum thus beginning the emptying of the stomach (Figure 1). The rate of emptying the stomach is determined primarily by the volume of the

meal, the osmotic pressure in the stomach and the chemical composition of the chyme (Davenport, 1982, p. 61). Additional factors influencing the emptying of the stomach include pain, nausea and emotional disturbance (Abrahamsson, 1973). It is here in the stomach that intestinal gas first begins to accumulate from gas contained in foods and from saliva (Lasser et al., 1975). Problems associated with the stomach include gastritis, functional dyspepsia, peptic ulcer and abdominal bloating, and cancer.

In the duodenum, pancreatic and biliary secretions are added to the chyme, increasing the volume of fluid in the digesting food. The most significant part of digestion and absorption occurs in the duodenum and adjacent jejunum. Undigested and unabsorbed portions of chyme are delivered to the ileum for further absorption, with the remains being pushed into the ascending colon (Code, 1979; Davenport, 1982). Fermentation of yet to be absorbed food in the small intestine may lead to the production of intestinal gas in larger volumes than usual. This may cause sensations of bloating, discomfort and possibly pain (Berk, 1968).

The small intestine is made up of the duodenum, jejunum and ileum. Motility (spontaneous movement) in the intestine takes place by way of segmentation (Code et al., 1968). To help understand the process, picture yourself slowly pushing toothpaste out of its tube from the middle, leaving a double-humped camel shape. Replace the cap and again push the toothpaste, but this time push from the end of the tube. Then follow up with a gentle push in the middle. This slowly contracting and expanding motion is similar to the action of segmentation in the duodenum, jejunum and ilium. At the end of the ileum is the ileocecal sphincter that separates the ileum from the colon (or large intestine as it is often called). This sphincter is normally closed. When opened, it allows the colon of an adult to receive an average of between 400 and 2,500 ml of chyme each day (Davenport, 1982). The chyme at this point in the digestive process consists of undigested and unabsorbed food, water and electrolytes. Further absorption takes place throughout the chyme's movement through the colon. What is not absorbed in the ascending, transverse, and descending parts of the large intestine moves toward the sigmoid colon and rectum for eventual elimination (Holzl & Whitehead, 1983). Problems associated with the colon include cancer, irritable bowel syndrome, ulcerative colitis and Crohn's disease.

As the chyme is pushed forward through the ignoid colon and into the sigmoid colon, it triggers the distension of the rectum, and the defecation reflex is aroused. This often occurs soon after a meal (Davenport, 1982). The act of defecation requires movement of both voluntary and involuntary muscles of the rectum and anus. Tension felt in the wall of the rectum is a sensation that triggers preparatory elimination behaviors by an individual. Successful elimination results in passing feces through the rectum into the anal canal. This triggers the relaxation of the anal sphincter muscles discharging anal fecal matter out of the body. Ignoring these sensations contributes to fecal incontinence (Whitehead & Drossman, 1996). The rectum eventually relaxes and the feces are returned to the sigmoid colon. If feces remain in the sigmoid colon they may dry out and become hard masses (Cerulli et al., 1979). This causes constipation and may contribute to cancers of the colon and rectum. Besides constipation and cancer other problems associated with the rectum and anus include proctalgia and pelvic floor dyssynergia (Whitehead et al., 1990). This concludes the (simplified) voyage of your piece of pizza.

Psychological Factors

The psychological literature addressing GI disorders is amazingly varied and at times quite contradictory. One perspective looks at the antecedents and consequences of the symptom to determine the effects of learning or conditioning (Miller, 1970). Another position concerns the importance of discovering a unifying psychological etiology for each GI disorder (Graham et al., 1958; Folks & Kinney, 1992). The hunt for a predisposing personality or a cluster of personality traits to

describe what was thought to be a psychosomatic process is first described by Alexander (1950). This quest often reminds me of the chicken and the egg question, and more distressingly of a Cartesian world view. Attempts to classify gastrointestinal disorders as *either* a medical or a psychological problem continue in the way third party payers reimburse clinical health psychology services. Insurance companies continue to insist that the GI disorders must have a DSM diagnosis in order for a health psychologist to receive reimbursement. This type of thinking is particularly problematic. For many GI conditions, recent research does not support a clear differentiation of etiological factors into a problem of the mind *or* a problem of the body.

More than 40 years of research, investigating psychological factors and gastrointestinal problems, has yet to find empirical support for a psychological etiology, or a unifiable role for psychosocial factors (Cassileth & Drossman, 1993). More recently, however, the search for a single psychological factor is abating. Researchers and clinicians are now examining GI conditions within a biopsychosocial context (Smith & Nicassio, 1995). This context acknowledges the patient is part of a system that involves many factors. This includes the varying genetic material each of us inherits, the lifestyles we live, the social support we perceive, the psychological distress or illness we experience, the cultural factors in our lives, our gender and our sexual orientation (Markus & Kitayama, 1991; Rhodes, this volume). Current psychological assessment of GI conditions, which is discussed later in the chapter, has developed from a biopsychosocial approach to evaluation and treatment (Weiner, 1977; Gatchel & Blanchard, 1993).

This change in perspective acknowledges a bidirectional interaction between behaviors, emotions, environmental factors, immune functioning (Maier et al, 1994) and susceptibility to GI disorders (Fullwood & Drossman, 1995). Cognitive and emotional centers in the brain are linked by bidirectional pathways with the neuroendocrine axis, immune system and enteric nervous system (Mayer & Raybould, 1990). Neural connections from higher centers permit external (smell, vision, etc.) and internal (emotions, thoughts, memories, etc.) information to affect GI sensation, motility and secretion (Fullwood & Drossman, 1995, p. 491). In turn, changes in GI sensation and motility affect internal information and behaviors. This emerging biopsychosocial-bidirectional paradigm provides a developing methodology for improving assessment and treatment strategies on the part of both medical and psychological professionals working with individuals with gastrointestinal disorders (Drossman, 1998). New research initiatives are needed to further investigate these connections.

Gastrointestinal Disorders Seen by Health Psychologists

This section identifies the gastrointestinal disorders and conditions that are currently treated by health psychologists. This list should not be viewed as exclusive or permanent, but as an indication of the current treatment literature.

Aerophagia is swallowing excessive amounts of air. Usually, 2–3 ml of air enters the stomach with each swallow (Calloway, 1969). Frequent swallowing or gulping large amounts of air are the principal mechanisms by which the stomach becomes distended (Whitehead & Schuster, 1985) causing belching, bloating, abdominal pain and flatulence (Whitehead, 1992b). Frequent swallowing is often triggered by anxiety and stress where 3–4 times as much air is swallowed as compared with nonanxious individuals (Maddock et al., 1949). It has also been seen as a voluntary response in severely intellectually impaired individuals who swallow air and then belch or regurgitate (Whitehead & Schuster, 1985). In addition, patients with hiatal hernia and duodenal ulcer have been observed to swallow air more than nonpatients leading to speculation that aerophagia may contribute to the

etiology of these disorders (Calloway et al., 1982).

Constipation is the infrequent or difficult evacuation of feces from the rectum and is experienced at one time or another by many people, usually of short duration. It is a symptom sometimes seen in irritable bowel syndrome, rectal pain, pelvic floor dyssynergia, proctalgia and fecal incontinence (Pilling et al., 1972; Whitehead & Schuster, 1985; Whitehead, 1992a). Constipation can also be the result of a diet low in fiber as well as a symptom due to other dietary and medical origins. It should always be evaluated by a physician before the health psychologist begins treatment.

Crohn's disease (CD) is, along with *Ulcerative Colitis*, a subtype of *Inflammatory Bowel Disease (IBD)*. Crohn's Disease can affect any part of the GI tract. It involves a progressive inflammatory process that begins under the mucosa and can spread to all layers of the bowel causing thickening of the bowel wall, scaring and possible bowel obstruction. The symptoms of Crohn's disease are abdominal pain, anorexia and weight loss, diarrhea and fever (Kirsner & Shorter, 1982). No physiological mechanisms have yet been identified by which the inflammatory process occurs. Whitehead and Schuster (1985, p. 128) propose three etiological hypotheses: infection, abnormal motility and abnormal immune responses. The latter two hypotheses support a place for a psychophysiological mechanism. Crohn's disease, like ulcerative colitis, may go into remission for many years only to emerge "with vengeance that can be overwhelming, like a tidal wave," as described to me by a patient. The course of CD can be erratic with increases and decreases in symptoms over a lifetime.

Crohn's disease substantially increases the risk of bowel cancer, particularly after the disease has been present for more than 20 years (McIllmurray & Langman, 1975). Additional complications of Crohn's include bowel obstruction caused either by the build up of scar tissue or inflammation. Bowel obstruction can lead to a distension of the bowel with a risk of bowel rupture, leading to bacterial contamination that can be fatal (Kirsner & Short, 1982). Obstruction of the bowel is the precipitating basis for the surgical procedure (resection) of the small bowel or colon (Whitehead & Schuster, 1985).

CD can also produce significant psychosocial stressors for the individual. These can include problems in interpersonal relationships, work restrictions, embarrassing bowel discharges, worries about the possibility of surgery and concerns about cancer. Psychological problems produced by this chronic disease can include an increase in dependency needs, depression, anxiety and an over-attention to physical symptoms. The more severe the symptoms and resulting complications, the more likely that psychosocial and psychological problems will develop.

Functional dyspepsia (FD) is a frequent complaint in GI clinics (up to 40% of visits) and one that accounts for 3–4% of all general practice visits (Edwards et al., 1985; Warndorff et al., 1989). Symptoms include upper abdominal pain, nausea and upper GI discomfort, bloating and early satiety with relief sometimes occurring after meals. FD is also called nonulcerative dyspepsia, gastritis, nonorganic dyspepsia, nervous dyspepsia and x-ray negative dyspepsia. Differential diagnosis between FD, reflex esophagitis and peptic ulcer is important and should be made by the gastroenterologist before the health psychologist begins treatment. While these three disorders have similar symptomatology and may be misdiagnosed, their etiologies and medical treatment are quite different. The accurate diagnosis of FD requires the physician to rule out peptic ulcer, reflex esophagitis, gallstone disease, Crohn's disease, gastric cancer, and chronic pancreatitis among others (Berstad, 1993). The accurate determination of FD can be quite costly, requiring upper alimentary endoscopy and possibly abdominal ultrasonography (Johannessen et al., 1990).

The etiology of FD is not clear but involves gastric acidity and disturbances in upper gastrointestinal motility. Stress may play a role by activating reactions in the central nervous system that may modify afferent and efferent impulses both to and from the peripheral organs (Berstad, 1993; Maier et al., 1994). The stomach is one such peripheral organ where disturbances in motility (dysmotility) can be easily manifested as a reaction to stress. Psychological hyperresponsiveness, as measured by the Eysenck Personality Questionnaire (EPQ), has been found to be higher in FD patients than in peptic ulcer patients or among a control group (Haug et al., 1992).

FD patients have also been observed through ultrasonographic studies to have a wider gastric antrum (chamber in lower stomach before the duodenum) with weaker antral motility than healthy controls (Hausten & Berstad, 1992). Additional observations support the idea that there is a problem with gastric adaptation in these patients as compared to healthy individuals. People with FD have abnormal food distribution in the stomach with more food being pushed into the antrum (Magnall et al., 1991). It has also been revealed that these patients have weak vagal control (related to the vagus nerve) of the gastroduodenal motor function. Weak vagal tone has been positively correlated with high psychological hyperresponsiveness on the EPQ (Hausken et al., 1993). It is possible that weak vagal control of this motor function, which is influenced by psychological hyperresponsiveness, may cause both the meal related discomfort and disturbances in motility seen with these patients (Berstad, 1993).

Although one study has shown FD patients with no greater levels of psychopathology than peptic ulcer patients (Morris et al., 1992), an earlier and better designed study by Bennett and associates (1991) revealed higher levels of anxiety, depression, and neuroticism in these patients, thus supporting the weak vagal tone-psychological hyperresponsiveness hypothesis. It seems likely that there is an interaction between psychological hyperresponsiveness (seen here as a personality trait), stressful events, visceral perception, and lowered vagal tone (Lehmann et al., 1991). A recent study suggested that when narrow criteria ruling out esophageal motility and gastroesophageal reflux were applied to a diagnosis of FD, patients displayed higher levels of depression in relation to a control group, but not higher levels of anxiety. However, on other symptom measures these same FD patients reported significantly more anxiety, depression, and somatization than did controls (Lee, Park, Choi, Abbey, & Rodin, 2000). Lee et al. (2000) further suggested that coping styles differed between FD patients and controls, relating the finding that FD patients reported significantly less problem focused coping, but equitable emotion-focused coping than did controls. The pathogenesis of FD proposed by Berstad (1993, p. 51) involves chronic emotional stress taxing the person's coping capability beyond his or her ability. This in turn activates mechanisms that render the individual hypersensitive to both visceral and psychological stimuli, possibly reducing vagal tone. Reduced vagal tone is accountable for disturbances in gastric adaptation to ingested food. The resulting poor adaptive gastric relaxation and a dilated gastric antrum produce symptoms localized to the stomach. It is hypothesized that the stomach distress is overly perceived by the individual and cognitively mislabeled, thus contributing to the cycle of distress. Further research supports the hypothesis of cognitive mislabeling and resulting challenges to ability to cope for persons with FD. Cheng, Hui, and Lam (1999) found that persons in Hong Kong with FD tended toward coping patterns involving action-oriented, direct control over stressors, while subjects from two control groups (one without health symptoms, one with rheumatic illness) discriminated use of coping strategies across different stressful situations. Cheng et al. (1999) hypothesized that non-discriminatory, action-oriented approaches to cope with stress may actually produce more anxiety surrounding stressful life events, or constant action-oriented coping may be psychologically taxing over time, increasing the perception of stress and hopelessness in patients with FD.

Esophageal motility disorders include dysphagia, globus hystericus, and noncardiac chest pain.

Dysphagia refers to difficulty in swallowing and may be related to esophageal spasm, stress, anxiety, esophagitis, hiatal hernia and 20 other medical disorders (Epstein et al., 1993). Our discussion will focus on esophageal spasm, stress and anxiety. The etiology of an esophageal spasm is not known. Mellow (1977) states that some type of vagal nerve degeneration is responsible in some cases. Spasms, which are of greater than normal amplitude and are sometimes accompanied by pain, can occur spontaneously and may be brought on during periods of stress and anxiety (Jacobson, 1927; Earlham, 1975). There is significant support for an association between this condition and psychological stress, worry, and anxiety (Clouse & Lustman, 1983; Waterman et al., 1989). Both classical and operant conditioning models and psychodynamic models can help explain the development of symptoms. Stress and anxiety are correlated with increases in swallowing difficulty, increasing muscle contractions, but not with the severity of a spasm (Whitehead and Bosmajian, 1982). EMG biofeedback has been successful in reducing muscle contractions and anxiety associated with swallowing (Haynes, 1976).

Globus hystericus (GH) is the sensation of an unidentified object or lump in the pharynx that is nearly always present. The sensation disappears however during eating and crying and does not result in any difficulty swallowing. Although there is no reported medical or structural etiology responsible for this condition, it has been suggested to be related to hiatal hernia, reflex esophagitis, peptic ulcer disease and cervical spinal disorder (Malcomson, 1966). It is estimated that between 18–46% of the general population experiences this condition at least once (Thompson & Heaton, 1982). When another GI disorder has been ruled out, careful questioning by the health care provider may reveal a mild to moderate upsetting event occurred concomitantly with onset. If treatment is necessary, reassurance, support, autogenic training (Luthe, 1970), and systematic desensitization (Wolpe & Lazarus, 1966) should result in relief of symptoms.

Fecal incontinence is associated with weakness of the external anal sphincter muscle, impaired ability to sense rectal distension, abnormal patterns of motility in the distal colon and overflow incontinence associated with the development of fecal impaction. It can be a symptom of Crohn's disease, ulcerative colitis, cancer of the colon and rectum, diabetes mellitus, spinal cord transsection (Whitehead & Drossman, 1996) and occasionally, irritable bowel syndrome.

Gastritis is inflammation of the stomach. It is often used as a global description for upper GI tract or stomach distress and sometimes used synonymously with functional dyspepsia. Gastritis can be acute or chronic with a variable etiology including infection, poison or a corrosive agent. It can involve atrophy of the mucus membrane, erosion of the gastric surface, infiltration and enlargement of the glands, abscesses in the stomach walls, and hypertrophy of the gastric mucosa with excessive secretion of mucus (Whitehead & Schuster, 1985). Some types of acute gastritis are treated with over-the-counter medications while others will require intervention by a physician.

Irritable bowel syndrome (IBS) is one of the most widely studied GI conditions. It was once believed to be the result of abnormal motility patterns in the colon exacerbated by psychological factors. The motility hypothesis has gathered little continued support and the focus of clinical research has turned toward abnormal pain perception as an explanation for the symptoms of IBS (Whitehead, 1992b; Drossman, 1998; Crowell & Barofsky, 1999). Those patients with higher pain sensitivity are likely to report greater psychological discomfort and seek out more medical services than patients with lower pain sensitivity. Over time, diagnostic criteria has evolved into an increasingly restrictive and specific format (Blanchard & Scharff 2002). The most recent (Rome II) criteria require the presence of symptoms of abdominal discomfort or pain for at least 12 weeks (not necessarily consecutive) of the past 12 months. Two of the following symptoms of abdominal pain

must be present: pain relieved by defecation, and or onset associated with a change in either frequency or form of stool. In addition, IBS might be indicated by cumulative symptoms, such as: abnormal stool frequency, form or passage, feeling of incomplete evacuation, passage of mucus, and bloating or feeling of abdominal distension (Blanchard, 2001).

For many years it was assumed that IBS was a psychosomatic disorder. Studies involving the natural history of IBS have discovered, however, that 70–80% of people with IBS do not have a need to consult a physician. These individuals were more psychologically healthy than the 20–30% of individuals who consulted a physician for IBS (Drossman et al., 1988; Whitehead et al., 1988). Psychological symptoms appear not to cause IBS, but do influence the decision to consult a physician (Smith et al., 1990). The association between psychological symptoms and IBS seen in previous reports seems to have been the result of sampling error (Whitehead, 1992b). Although many IBS patients report more stressful events than healthy individuals, the correlation between stress and IBS symptoms is quite low, allowing for only 10% of the variance in bowel symptoms attributed to stress (Whitehead, 1992b, p. 606). Current research further suggests a relationship between Central Nervous System (CNS) responses to perceived stress and CNS reactions to learned fear, which subsequently is suggested to play a role in increasing perception of anxiety and onset of symptoms of IBS (Mayer, Craske, and Naliboff, 2001). Although patients diagnosed with IBS may not display diagnostically significant symptoms of anxiety or depression, it is suggested that there are similarities in autonomic response and regional brain activity between IBS patients and individuals diagnosed with anxiety, depression and Post Traumatic Stress Disorder (Ballenger, Davidson, Lecrubier, & Nutt, 2001). In combination with the hypothesis of altered visceral perception and possible hypervigilance to stress and pain perception, this relationship between CNS arousal and perception of stress in some persons diagnosed with IBS contributes support for therapeutic intervention that combines management of anxiety and affective symptoms with approaches to health management (Ballenger et al., 2001; Crowell & Barofsky, 1999; Mayer et al., 2001). Increasingly, research has pointed toward an association between IBS and childhood trauma, such as the loss of a parent through death or marital separation and physical or sexual abuse (Hill & Bledis, 1967; Hislop, 1979; Drossman et al., 1990). Loss and separation issues in childhood and conflicted or dependent parental relationships with children are more frequently reported by IBS patients seeking medical treatment than IBS individuals not seeking medical treatment (Lowman et al., 1987; Whitehead et al., 1988). The illness behavior of IBS individuals seeking treatment may also be related to social learning. IBS patients report more severe bowel problems, more doctor visits in childhood and more pain associated with current bowel symptoms than IBS nonpatients or peptic ulcer patients (Whitehead et al., 1982; Folks & Kinney, 1992).

Non-cardiac chest pain (NCCP) refers to pain often accompanied by a burning sensation in the esophagus. It is distinguished by chest pain that may follow a meal, physical activity, or bending over and is described as burning. It may be accompanied by dysphagia, nausea, and vomiting and sour and bitter tasting material refluxed into the throat (Whitehead & Schuster, 1985). The majority of patients with this disorder do not have abnormal gastric or esophageal motility, suggesting anxiety and depression play a role in its etiology (Hewson et al., 1990). This condition is also described as "nutcracker esophagus," referring to the high-amplitude peristaltic contractions in the esophagus (Browning, 1990). In addition, stress-induced laboratory studies have shown that increases in psychological stress induces an alteration in esophageal pressure producing NCCP (Anderson et al., 1989).

Peptic ulcer disease (PUD) is caused by exposure to gastric acid and pepsin. The mucosa of the intestines or stomach are inadequately protected from the effects of exposure. This may be caused by excess secretion of acid, decreased emptying of the stomach, inadequate secretion of mucus or secretion of abnormal mucus (Whitehead & Schuster, 1985, p. 98). Tobacco use and alcohol, two substances that often increase in use during stressful times, are associated with a slower rate of healing of ulcers. The most effective and economical treatment for PUD is to keep the gastric juice neutralized with antacids or pharmacologically to block the secretion of gastric acid (Peterson et al., 1977; Winship, 1978; Whitehead, 1992b).

There is a wide difference in how PUD patients respond to stress with no predictable responses to specific stressors. There is also no more psychopathology in PUD patients than in other chronic medical populations. Psychological and environmental factors have been linked to PUD, however. People with PUD tend to be reserved, inhibited and socially conforming. Other factors include living in an urban environment, loss of a father during childhood (for a male child), occupations involving danger or high stress, and living in a war zone (Whitehead & Bosmajian, 1982; Whitehead & Schuster, 1985; Whitehead, 1992b).

Pelvic floor dyssynergia (PFD) involves a paradoxical contraction, rather than relaxing, of the pelvic floor muscles while straining to defecate. These contractions make defecation very difficult or impossible, thus resulting in constipation. This is thought to be an inappropriately learned response (Whitehead & Drossman, 1996), possibly from a history of painful bowel movements and unusually large stools, childhood sexual abuse or inflammation. PFD may account for 30–50% of the cases of constipation seen in GI clinics (Whitehead, 1992a).

Proctalgia fugax (PF) is a sudden, severe and fleeting pain in the anal area that lasts from a few seconds to several minutes (Thompson, 1981). Partially due to the infrequent occurrence of PF (no more than 5–6 times per year in a given patient), there are no controlled studies examining health psychology interventions. Proctalgia has been reported in patients with irritable bowel syndrome, peptic ulcer, ulcerative colitis and Crohn's disease and as a primary symptom (Thompson, 1984). It was initially speculated that PF was a form of irritable bowel syndrome where the pain from sigmoid motor activity is referred to the rectum or anal canal (Harvey, 1979; Whitehead & Schuster, 1985, p. 172).

The psychological mechanisms involved are unclear but were first believed to be similar to irritable bowel syndrome. This hypothesis was initially supported by a study using the MMPI and a structured interview where 67% of patients were discovered to be perfectionistic, 73% to be anxious and 40% to be hypochondriacal (Pilling et al., 1972). This preliminary study lent support to the roles of anxiety, stress and worry in contributing to PF. In the absence of a recognized disease, more recent evidence supports overly controlled pelvic floor muscles as causative (West et al., 1990). It is possible that anxiety and stress contribute to the extreme contracting of the pelvis floor muscles resulting in the symptom of pain.

Ulcerative colitis (UC) like Crohn's disease is an inflammatory bowel disease. It involves inflammation and ulceration of the inner lining of the colon. Involvement of the rectum and sigmoid colon are likely and potentially the entire colon, but UC does not extend to the small intestine. Symptoms include abdominal pain, anorexia, diarrhea, rectal bleeding, vomiting and fever (Lewkonia & McConnell, 1976). Colon cancer is the most serious complication of UC. Unlike Crohn's disease, UC can be cured by colectomy (Folks & Kinney, 1992).

The etiology of UC and the role of psychological factors continues to be uncertain (Helzer et al., 1982). UC patients appear to have no more psychopathology than other people with a chronic medical condition. Although they may have elevated scores on measures of depression and anxiety, these elevated scores are probably reactions to coping with a chronic disease rather than predisposing factors (Tarter et al., 1987; Andrews et al., 1987). More recent research has pointed to the possibility that autoimmune determi-

nants may be etiological triggers (Folks & Kinney, 1992), but findings as of this date are inconclusive. The belief that UC is a psychosomatic illness, in the psychoanalytic conceptualization of illness, continues to have little support among well-controlled studies.

Vomiting Disorders

Rumination syndrome is a disorder primarily occurring in infants and severely intellectually impaired adults. It is characterized by chewing, swallowing and re-chewing food followed by either re-swallowing or expectorating (DSM-IV, 1994). *Anticipatory nausea and vomiting* are seen primarily in patients undergoing chemotherapy treatment for cancer. It is also sometimes seen in patients who become highly anxious before engaging in a feared or noxious activity. It is treated through systematic desensitization therapy (Wolpe & Lazarus, 1966).

Cyclic Vomiting Syndrome (CVS) is characterized by recurrent, discrete episodes of vomiting that are repetitive with regard to onset, symptoms and duration, intervals of normal health between episodes, and the absence of clinical findings that would support a biological cause. Patients with CVS episodes may become dehydrated, and symptoms may be accompanied by a low-grade fever and diarrhea, leading to initial misdiagnosis as frequent episodes of stomach flu or food poisoning. Distinctions between the flu or food poisoning and CVS include severe palor (as though the individual were in shock), as well as frequency and duration of vomiting episodes. Although this disorder is most frequently diagnosed in young childhood and is hypothesized to diminish by adulthood, findings suggest a link between childhood CVS and adult-onset migraine with gastrointestinal symptoms. New research suggests that there may also be a subgroup of adults who suffer from CVS without migraines. A relationship between family history of migraine headaches and CVS lends further support for the migraine/CVS relationship. Treatment is similar for individuals suffering from migraine, including preventive measures such as avoidance of stress, excitement and excess sensory stimulation (Li & Howard, 2002). The disabling and unpredictable nature of this disorder may recommend CVS patients to health psychologists to help with coping strategies and family impact. Biofeedback can also be used in combination with relaxation techniques to manage migraine symptoms and may be indicated for patients with CVS to manage migraine-like symptoms (Cottraux, 1998).

Other Gastrointestinal Concerns

Individuals may also be referred due to attribution of gastrointestinal symptoms to food allergies and/or chemical sensitivity that has not been supported by clinical evidence, such as skin and enzyme absorption testing. Because skin testing evidences poor correlation to symptom severity in patients with diagnosable food allergies, review of patient diet, and symptom onset helps lead to plausible diagnoses of food allergy. For patients without consistent correlation between ingestion and symptom onset, medical staff may arrive at a diagnosis of "pseudo-food allergy". In these cases, it is hypothesized that gastrointestinal symptoms are more closely attributable to depression, anxiety and other psychological disorders. Recommended treatment includes monitoring and aid in management of diet to prevent nutritional deficiency (from patient diet restriction) in combination with therapeutic approaches to manage psychological symptomatology (Epstein et al., 2002).

Psychological Assessment

In this section we present a psychological assessment protocol that has been effectively used in both clinic and hospital settings and in independent practice. Close cooperation with the referring gastroenterologist or other health care provider is important, if not essential, for treatment success. It is assumed that a gastroenterologist, internist or other medical doctor has evaluated the individual and made the referral. If this is not so, prior to or soon after the health psychology assessment, a referral should be made to a physician knowledgeable about GI conditions. Table 2 lists the components of the assessment protocol this section addresses.

The Referral and Initial Contact

Upon speaking with a patient for the first time, either on the telephone, in your office or at a hospital or clinic, learning the individual's understanding about the reason for referral is important. This is an opportunity to clarify your role on the health care team and to understand what the patient has been told about her or his condition. It is also the time to begin the education process about mind-body interaction and the biopsychosocial approach to assessment and treatment.

The patient's understanding about why they have been referred to a health psychologist, and what you have been told by the referring physician, may be quite disparate. Seeking clarification from the patient's physician in these circumstances is critical. For example, within the past 4 years the first author has been asked to see people with GI distress because they "are nuts," "bothersome to the nursing staff," "complainers," "whiners," and just "difficult to work with." None of these patients knew why they had been referred. Understanding the patient's working medical diagnosis, treatment to date, the physician's treatment expectations, and the problems encountered thus far in the treatment, are important domains to examine, if only briefly, with the referring provider. This can be accomplished if necessary, by an exchange of voice-mail or E-mail messages. Speaking directly with a physician may not always be possible, but discerning both the surface and underlying reasons for referral is requisite. Likewise, for those patients who are self- referred, obtaining permission to speak with the individual's physician is highly recommended. Self-referred individuals are more likely to be experiencing greater levels of acknowledged psychological distress than physician-referred patients and may already perceive the relevance of health psychology treatment for their problem.

When it is possible, we send patients an in-

Table 2. Health psychology assessment protocol for GI patients.

Introductory assessment packet mailed to patient
  Information about biopsychosocial approach
  Brief clinician biographical statement and role in patient's care
  General Health Questionnaire-30 (GHQ-30)
  Health history questionnaire

Semi-structured clinical interview
  History of current problem
    How is the GI problem incorporated into the patient's life?
    Has it become the primary focal point in his/her life?
    What role does the distress play?
    How have others (family, friends, employer, health care) responded?
  Assess for psychiatric co-morbidity
    Anxiety and depression for immediate evaluation and treatment
    Personality style for organizing treatment plan

GI symptom diary

Food diary

Psychometric testing
  Beck Depression Inventory (BDI)
  State Trait Anxiety Inventory (STAI)
  Digestive Symptoms Inventory (DSI)
  Additional Psychometric Measures:
    Psychological General Well-Being Index
    Gastrointestinal Symptom Rating Scale
    Psychosocial Adjustment to Illness Scale
    Minnesota Multiphasic Personality Inventory-2 (MMPI-2)
    Symptom Checklist-90-Revised (SCL-90-R)

Biofeedback assessment (as indicated for specific GI conditions)
  Electromyograph (EMG) for muscle contraction and general relaxation
  Galvanic skin response (GSR) to assess immediate psychophysiological responses
  Skin temperature (thermal) for autonomic nervous system measurement and general relaxation

troductory assessment packet before the first interview. This includes information about the assessment process (much of which we have reviewed on the telephone), a two-paragraph introduction to the biopsychosocial approach to health care, and a one-paragraph statement outlining our role in their care. In this paragraph, we describe the collaborative nature of the assessment and treatment process and provide some brief biographical information about our training and experience. In addition to this information, we also include the General Health Questionnaire-30 (Goldberg & Blackwell, 1970; Goldberg, 1983) and a health history questionnaire asking for the following information: current symptoms, patient's medical history, family health history, current and previous medications, education background and previous five year-employment history.

The Clinical Interview

The clinical interview has undergone many revisions from its inception as a psychoanalytic tool. Contributions from ego psychology, object relations, self psychology, behavioral analysis, phenomenology and cognitive therapy, as well as from the psychosomatic and psychophysiological approaches, have increased our ability to better evaluate clients. The interview is not only a time to gather information, but also begins to establish a relationship between you and your patient. The quality of this relationship, like scientific knowledge, is important to the assessment process. Relationship building within the context of assessment and treatment is usually not mentioned in behavioral medicine and health psychology texts. Often the focus is exclusively on the technical or procedural components of treatment, overlooking that we are working with human beings, not instruments or constructs.

We prefer to see our clients as collaborators (Heron, 1996) and the assessment process is introduced to them in this manner. This sets the tone of the interview as one where their active participation is welcome and necessary. A semi-structured, rather than an open-ended or structured interview (Rogers, 1995), is recommended. This type of interview enables the clinician to ask specific questions consistently across patients, allowing for comparisons between patients, and easier evaluation of treatment effectiveness. A semi-structured, rather than a structured interview, also gives patients the opportunity to complement the structured questioning with additional information that is likely to be useful to the assessing clinician.

Current problem. After introductions and welcoming the patient into the office or inquiring if we may enter their inpatient room, the interview begins by asking about their symptoms and present condition. The goal is to listen carefully to both *what* the patient describes and *how* they describe it. We want to know how they are currently affected by this problem and what the symptoms mean to them. As a way to help organize the life history of the patient and their symptoms, we use the metaphor "illness as a journey." *How* has this individual traveled on her or his journey to the time and place they are right now? *What* has happened along the way? The use of metaphor helps sift through the sometimes voluminous data of symptoms, previ-

ous doctors, medications, patient beliefs about the problem, etc. This is not a metaphor shared with the patient. We use "illness as a journey" to help us develop a story about this person's life, much like a story that might be told around a kitchen table to a family member (Remen, 1996). We do not find much clinical value in simply collecting "facts" about symptoms, behaviors and treatments. Before a treatment plan can be developed and implemented successfully, we need to know what role the GI condition plays in the patient's life (Slavney & McHugh, 1984). These questions address the issues of quality of life and adjustment to illness, areas in which health psychologists are well-prepared to intervene.

If the patient does not volunteer, we ask about their family's response to the problem (Kerns, 1995), whom have they told, how it has affected their schooling or work, and if applicable, the relationship with their significant other. We are listening to how the client creates her life. Questions we ponder include: How is the GI distress incorporated into the person's life? Has it become the primary focal point in his or her life? What character, if any, does the distress play on the lifestage? How does the patient expect others to respond to their problem? These questions are relevant regardless whether the problem has an organic etiology or appears chiefly functional.

This portion of the interview is likely to take 15 to 30 minutes. The length of time will depend on several factors including the person's comfort level at revealing personal information, severity of the problem, cooperation, knowledge of English, cultural differences, cognitive and personality style, and psychiatric co-morbidity.

Psychiatric disorders or *psychiatric co-morbidity*, in particular anxiety and depression, has been cited as occurring in 10–50% of patients presenting with GI disorders. Prevalence rates vary depending upon the GI condition or disorder but there is continuing support that of those patients seeking medical intervention many will present with a DSM diagnosis (APA, 1994). If possible, the first interview should answer the question, "Does this patient have a working DSM diagnosis in addition to the presenting medical diagnosis?" For many patients, if a psychiatric disorder is present, it will need to be addressed along with the GI condition to increase the likelihood of treatment success (Blanchard, 1993). Rather than attempt to determine if the psychiatric condition is causing the GI disorder, we have found it more beneficial to assess whether the psychiatric condition in any way exacerbates the GI problem. If treatment is indicated for the psychiatric problem, should it be done before or concurrently with the presenting GI problem? Ignoring psychiatric disorders in some GI patients may account for dropouts and treatment failures that would otherwise have benefited from a health psychology intervention (Blanchard, 1993). This is particularly the case when a GI patient also presents with a personality style involving narcissistic, borderline, histrionic or other possibly disruptive behaviors. Although the assessing clinician may choose not to treat the personality disorder, understanding the manifestations of different personality styles can better prepare the clinician for the best approach suited for a particular patient.

GI symptom diary is a useful and necessary component in the assessment of all GI conditions. It can provide both the clinician and patient information about the type, intensity and duration of GI symptoms and how much distress they cause (Blanchard, 1993). It is also an effective way to quantify treatment progress, one that is visual and easily measured. A general GI symptom diary (Table 3) may be easily modified to measure specifically the symptoms of any GI condition discussed in this chapter. Leave room on the diary for the patient to add symptoms that may not have been discussed during the initial assessment interview. The diary is introduced to patients near the end of our first meeting.

Our instructions to patients are: *"Complete the diary at the time the symptom occurs, or as soon as possible, but please do not wait until the end of the day."* End of the day summarizing may distort actual symptoms by over-or-under-reporting and lessen the efficacy of the diary. Ask patients to keep a daily diary for two weeks during the assessment. For many years the first author requested all patients to continue the symptom diary throughout treatment. This sometimes had a paradoxical and

---

Table 3. GI symptom diary.

Date:_____ Day:_____ Medications Taken:_____

Severity and Distress Level:

Symptom	None/Mild/Moderate/Severe/Debilitating				
Abdominal tenderness	1	2	3	4	5
Belching	1	2	3	4	5
Bloating	1	2	3	4	5
Cramping	1	2	3	4	5
Constipation	1	2	3	4	5
Diarrhea	1	2	3	4	5
Difficulty swallowing	1	2	3	4	5
Fecal incontinence	1	2	3	4	5
Flatulence	1	2	3	4	5
Nausea	1	2	3	4	5
Vomiting	Time:_____				

Other symptoms:

_____	1	2	3	4	5
_____	1	2	3	4	5

unintended effect of bringing unnecessary attention to symptoms at a time in treatment when patients were developing new ways of coping. Distraction from over-attention to bodily processes is necessary for some, and the GI symptom diary inhibited this. In a more collaborative approach, we ask patients how best can we help them measure progress during therapy. Some choose to keep a symptom diary, others use visual measures (Malchiodi, 1993) and others use narrative means in the form of a diary.

Food diary. Although it is not an essential part of assessment for every patient, a daily food diary, kept for two weeks, can provide useful nutritional and dietary content information. Immediately after the GI Symptom Diary is explained, introduce the Food Diary. Instructions to patients are, *"Please write down everything you eat or drink over the next two weeks, no matter how small an amount. Next to the food or beverage write how much you consumed and the time of day. Use a page for each day of the week."* The quantity and quality of a patient's diet are believed to play a role in irritable bowel, dyspepsia, gastritis and peptic ulcer disease. An alteration in fiber content, for example, may help reduce constipation, bloating and diarrhea. Regularly scheduled, smaller meals may also lessen cramping and pain and decrease constipation. Knowledge of basic nutrition and the effect of certain food groups on the digestive process will add to the health psychologist's repertoire in working with GI conditions.

A food diary is also useful in revealing how a patient uses food. A 27-year-old Asian gentleman, who was referred to the first author for stress related to his ulcerative colitis and Crohn's Disease, had decreased the vegetable content in his food dramatically. He believed vegetables caused dysmotility and led to loss of bowel control, which he had experienced embarrassingly three times. The unusual constipation he experienced was due in part to a diet of almost all chicken and fish and a small amount of grain. Constipation was gradually eliminated by providing dietary education, slowly altering his diet in consultation with his physician, and helping him in-crease control of his anal sphincter muscles through EMG biofeedback.

Psychometric Testing

To the best of our knowledge, except for Irritable Bowel Syndrome, no psychometric norms exist for GI disorders (Blanchard, 1993). Unfortunately, without specific normative data the utility of psychological testing is reduced. The lack of normative data is particularly troublesome when personality measures and measures of general psychological functioning are used. Somatic symptoms, such as those experienced by people with GI distress, are recorded as positive symptoms of psychopathology on the MMPI-2. This assessment problem has arisen because most psychometric instruments are normed on psychiatric populations, the assumption being, paraphrasing Gertrude Stein, "A patient is a patient is a patient … A symptom is a symptom is a symptom." If psychological testing is used with GI patients, it will be important that the clinician be knowledgeable about the usual and expected symptoms that accompany the disorder. For example, a patient had been referred to the first author for treatment of somatization disorder. Daily vomiting was one of her symptoms. She also had elevated scores on Subscales One and Three of the MMPI. The referring psychologist had not been aware that vomiting is a serious and potentially dangerous symptom of peptic ulcer disease. The patient's endorsement of MMPI items paralleled many expected symptoms of poorly controlled PUD. Diagnosing her with somatization disorder, based on MMPI results, was not accurate and clearly resulted from a lack of knowledge about this GI disorder.

Standard psychometric battery. A cautious approach to psychometric evaluation will demand that the clinician never base a diagnosis or treatment plan solely on test results. We primarily use testing as a screening tool and to help confirm hypotheses that develop in the clinical interview. Testing can also be useful when a patient's response to medical treatment has been particularly problematic and there are indications that personality style is a complicating factor. A part of routine assessment of GI patients should include a measure of depression and anxiety. The Beck Depression Inventory (BDI) is a well established measure for assessing depression in medical populations (Beck et al., 1961; Latimer, 1983; Haug et al., 1994). Likewise, the State-Trait Anxiety Inventory (STAI) is a well-studied instrument for the measure of anxiety (Spielberger et al., 1970; Latimer, 1983; Blanchard, 1993). The BDI and the STAI can be readministered throughout therapy to assess change in depression and anxiety levels. Together with physiological measures and self-report, they are also good treatment outcome measures. Both are easily administered in an outpatient or inpatient setting.

The Digestive Symptoms Inventory (DSI) (Latimer et al., 1981; Latimer, 1983) is a Likert-type measure of numerous GI symptoms (Likert, 1932), making it a useful tool for assessing all GI disorders. The advantage of this type of measure is that it does not appraise symptoms as absolute categories (i. e., "you have it or you don't") but uses a dimensional approach in assessing gradations of symptom severity. A patient may have a particular symptom but reports a low level of discomfort or lack of interference with life activities, therefore not making it a consideration for treatment. We have also found the DSI to be a useful tool in evaluating change in symptoms during treatment. Easily administered in outpatient and inpatient settings, the DSI is not intrusive and takes about 10 to 15 minutes to complete.

When a general measure of personality traits or psychopathology is warranted, the MMPI-2 is frequently utilized. While there are other instruments commercially available, the MMPI-2 and its predecessor, the MMPI, are well known across many medical populations. As previously discussed, the results of the MMPI-2 should be interpreted cautiously so as not to psychopathologize a physical symptom. It has been our experience that many medical patients resist and frankly do not like completing either MMPI. A concern we have often heard is "now my doctor thinks its all in my head." Using this instrument can convey the message that the health care team is viewing the patient's problem as a psychological one and discounting the physical and medical complaints that have brought them to seek treatment. The administration of the MMPI-2 can also be frustrating, angering and disheartening to patients because of its focus on psychopathology, unusual behaviors and thoughts. In addition, the time needed to complete it is significant.

The General Health Questionnaire (GHQ-30) is a screening instrument developed to identify psychiatric complaints in an adult medical population (Goldberg & Blackwell, 1970; Goldberg, 1985; Haug et al., 1994; Derogatis et al., 1995). It is a tool that can be easily administered routinely to patients. This instrument provides information concerning psychiatric symptoms that can be evaluated further, in the clinical interview, with additional psychometric testing or during treatment (Corney et al., 1991). The Symptom Checklist-90 Revised (SCL-90R) (Peveler & Fairburn, 1990) is also a test frequently used in medical clinics to assess psychiatric symptoms. It takes longer to complete than the GHQ-30 but likewise, is easy to administer. Along with the BDI, STAI and DSI, the GHQ-30 completes the standard psychometric battery we would suggest as part of your routine assessment protocol. Depending on the reading ability, educational level and personal investment of a patient, this battery can be completed in 30 to 45 minutes. These tests have all been translated into different languages and have been utilized on a cross-section of North American and European cultural groups.

Additional psychometric measures. Additional domains requiring assessment often include quality of life and adjustment to illness. Although these are areas that are usually address in the clinical interview, they are not routinely evaluated in psychological testing. If a patient presents with GI symptoms or a diagnosed GI disorder that is long-standing, assessing the patient's quality of life and adjustment to illness should be undertaken. The ability to help quantify change in treatment is an advantage of psychometric testing. While this is obviously helpful to both patient and clinician, it can also be a measure useful to demonstrate treatment effectiveness for managed care and other third party payers. Quality of life measures employed with GI patients include the Psychological General Well-Being Index (Dupuy, 1984; Diminäs et al., 1993), Gastrointestinal Symptom Rating Scale (Svedfund et al., 1988; Diminäs et al., 1993) and Psychosocial Adjustment to Illness Scale (Derogatis et al., 1983; Derogatis, 1986; Wilhelmsen, 1995).

The global assessment of a specific symptom (e. g., pain, bloating, etc.) or certain aspects of quality of life (e. g., social, marital, spiritual, physical, etc.) can also be measured by a visual analog scale (VAS) (Eggebrecht et al., 1989; Wilhelmsen, 1995). The VAS is a reliable, discriminating and easy instrument to use (May et al., 1986). A scale is drawn on paper that is 100 mm in length where zero is the optimal level and 100, the most severe level. A patient is instructed to place an "x" on the line at the location that corresponds to their current feelings. This measure can be repeated on a daily or weekly basis and can be used for multiple symptoms or problem areas. For example, a patient presenting with symptoms of pain and bloating complains that the symptoms occur at the same time and always at a high level of intensity. She can be asked to complete a VAS for both symptoms. This measure, with the aid of the assessing clinician, can help the patient begin to differentiate between the symptoms of pain and bloating that have been perceptually linked together as one symptom. In addition the VAS can assist the clinician in determining which symptom or problem area should be a target of initial intervention.

Biofeedback Assessment

Biofeedback assessment can provide the clinician additional information about the patients' psychophysiological responses. This is particularly useful when anxiety and stress play a role in the exacerbation of symptoms (Whitehead & Schuster, 1985). Biofeedback is also effective in combination with cognitive therapy in a multi-component approach

to assessment and treatment (Neff & Blanchard, 1987; Schwartz et al., 1990). Electromyographic (EMG) biofeedback has shown promising treatment results in patients with fecal incontinence (Engel et al., 1974; Wald & Tunuguntla, 1984; Bassotti & Whitehead, 1994), pelvic floor dyssynergia (Turnbull & Ritvo, 1992; Whitehead & Drossman, 1996), levator ani syndrome (Grimaud et al., 1991; West et al., 1992) and aerophagia (Calloway et al., 1983; Whitehead, 1992a; 1992b).

Biofeedback is no longer recommended for the direct control of gastric acid secretion in peptic ulcer disease, due to the high cost involved compared to pharmacologic therapy (Whitehead, 1992b). It is also no longer suggested as a treatment for inflammatory bowel disease because the link between psychosocial stressors and symptom increase has not been consistently supported (Whitehead & Schuster, 1985; Whitehead, 1992b). Colonic dysmotility was once considered a primary factor in irritable bowel syndrome and biofeedback was regarded as a treatment to decrease dysmotility. This in no longer thought to be the case. Biofeedback is now considered useful for the management of pain associated with IBS and in use with relaxation training.

Evidence-Based Health Psychology Treatments

This final section will discuss interventions for several GI disorders addressed in this chapter: Aerophagia, Crohn's Disease, Fecal Incontinence, Functional Dyspepsia, Irritable Bowel Syndrome, Pelvic Floor Dyssynergia, Peptic Ulcer Disease and Ulcerative Colitis. Regardless of the presenting GI problem, by the time treatment begins you should have the following information available from your assessment: working medical diagnosis; demographic, cultural, and other background data; a patient's understanding of their condition and motivation for therapy; completed GI symptom and food diaries; history of the problem; coping abilities of the patient, their adjustment to the illness and current quality of life; tentative DSM diagnosis if appropriate; and if applicable, a completed biofeedback assessment showing the patient's reactivity to stress and ability to relax through a psychophysiologic measure. This information provides appropriate documentation for evidence-based treatment decisions.

Aerophagia. There are few controlled outcome studies examining aerophagia (Whitehead et al., 1991). This is both unfortunate and surprising considering the prevalence of aerophagia in the GI clinic population. It is a condition ideal for health psychology intervention, involving behavioral and physiological mechanisms. Stress and anxiety have also been associated with its development and exacerbation. A study by Calloway and associates (Calloway et al., 1983) supports the use of progressive muscle relaxation training (PMR), galvanic skin response biofeedback (GSR) and auditory biofeedback in its treatment.

The goal of the first phase of treatment is to help the patient learn that they can induce a state of physical and emotional relaxation. This is accomplished by training the patient in PMR relaxation and providing further information about mind-body interaction. This usually takes 3–5 sessions. The second phase involves the use of auditory feedback (AF) according to Calloway's method. A microphone is placed on the patient's throat amplifying swallowing sounds. The goal of this phase is to substitute the newly learned relaxation response in the place of "automatic" swallowing. EMG biofeedback is also effective. The EMG electrodes are placed on the throat bilaterally and midway between the shoulders and chin (EMG biofeedback is more readily available than AF biofeedback and should be considered. When using EMG biofeedback, the auditory, rather than the visual mode of feedback is less distracting).

The length of treatment averages 12 sessions including assessment. In addition to the biofeedback component of therapy, the clinician should be aware of any emotionally distressing events that the patient is currently experiencing. These may be exacerbating factors. You may either want to encourage the patient to use therapy to work on these problems or consider a referral toward the conclusion of treatment, to a psychotherapist.

Cancer of the Gastrointestinal System. Persons diagnosed with colorectal, gastric, esophageal, pancreatic, and biliary cancers are increasingly seen for psychological intervention in combination with medical treatment for management of symptoms and promotion of healing (Speca, Carlson, Goodey, & Angen, 2000). Physical symptoms of GI cancers vary depending on the location, stage and treatment phase of cancer, and may include GI pain, dysphagia, painful swallowing, changes in frequency and consistency of defecation, fatigue, weight loss, nausea, vomiting, and occasionally respiratory and vocal changes (Brooks-Brun, 2000; Wasteson, Nordin, Hoffman, Glimelius, & Sjoden, 2002). Prognostic outcomes for gastrointestinal (GI) cancers vary significantly depending on location of the cancer, from approximately 5% survival rate for pancreatic cancer to approximately 50% survival rate for colorectal cancer (Brooks-Brun, 2000; Wasteson et al., 2002).

Given the potentially life-threatening outcome, it is typical for individuals who have been recently diagnosed with GI cancers to experience an initial state of crisis, reacting with denial and increased depression. Although it is hypothesized that patients may experience anxiety symptoms, research does not support significantly higher levels of anxiety in individuals recently diagnosed with cancer than in normal controls (Wasteson et al., 2000; Nordin, Wasteson, Hoffman, Glimelius & Sjoden, 2001). Higher levels of depression and anxiety are found in spouses and caregivers of patients with non-curable cancers than in patients themselves (Maguire, 1999; Nordin et al., 2001). Recent research focuses on the relationship between coping strategies and perception of emotional well-being, rather than on psychopathology in GI cancer patients. According to Nordin et al. (2001), patients with confronting (fighting for survival) coping styles experience less emotional distress than patients whose coping includes focus on anxiety and hopelessness or helplessness. Nordin et al. (2001) also found that patients who find ways to reduce the discrepancy between attainment and importance of values related to quality of life tend to adapt best to diagnosis of cancer of the GI system, regardless of the terminal or non-terminal nature of the disorder.

Psychotherapeutic approaches for patients with GI cancers include relaxation training, cognitive-behavioral techniques focused on coping style (Emmelkamp & Van Oppen, 1998), mindfulness meditation (Speca et al., 2000), and supportive interventions for both patients and families (Nordin et al., 2001, Wasteson et al., 2000). While psychological intervention may be useful to help individuals with GI cancers develop effective coping strategies and manage states of crisis following initial diagnosis, psychologists should also be attentive to potential need for additional therapeutic support for spouses and caregivers of patients with GI cancers.

Crohn's disease and ulcerative colitis. The reasons for referring a person with CD or UC to a health psychologist are likely due to one of the following: problems coping with medical complications of the disease; anxiety, stress or depression; lack of compliance with medical treatment and psychological sequelae of surgery. Schwartz & Blanchard (1991) present a comprehensive review of the treatment of both CD and UC. They concluded that people with CD have more psychopathology that those with UC. Drossman and associates (1991) report however that psychopathology increases only when physical symptom severity is taken into consideration.

There are also contradictory findings regarding stress management training. A study by Milne and colleagues (1986) reports an improvement in physical and psychological symptoms after a stress management group. Another study (Shaw & Ehrlich, 1987) discovered patients with UC, who received relaxation training, reported reductions in pain. Schwartz and Blanchard (1990) however, found stress management training did not improve symptoms but rather exacerbated them. This rather surprising finding has not been reported elsewhere. Whitehead (1992b,

p. 609) concludes there is no evidence, as of yet, that psychological interventions are effective at improving the physical symptoms of CD. What does improve with psychological treatment is the patient's subjective sense of well-being, affecting their quality of life and adjustment to the illness.

When compared to other groups experiencing a chronic medical problem, CD and UC patients are no more likely to receive a psychiatric diagnosis (Fava & Davan, 1976; Whitehead & Schuster, 1985). There is little supporting evidence to prove claims of Engel (1954; 1955) and others that these disorders are psychosomatic diseases. Rather, it appears more likely that elevations on the MMPI-2 (especially scales 1 and 3) and illness behaviors observed in some of patients, are the results of the disease — or the interaction of disease and personality — and not its cause.

A number of prevention-focused approaches for IBD patients are discussed in recent literature, including education about the disorder, enhancement of problem-solving coping, facilitation of mourning/grief related to diagnosis, and increasing social support (Dudley-Brown, 2002; Maunder & Esplen, 1999). These approaches are suggested for persons with CD or UC that do not initially have significant concomitant psychiatric symptoms.

Treatment recommendations additionally include supportive psychotherapy (Freyberger, 1975) that consists of psychoeducation about the mind-body relationship, providing support, encouragement and advice, positive reinforcement, and help in coping with the disease. Insight oriented therapies that initially increase anxiety and stress are contraindicated (Groen & Bastiaans, 1951). Although not consistent for all patients, empirical evidence for supportive-educational psychotherapy has been impressive for improving emotional well-being and reducing psychological symptoms (Grace et al., 1954; Karush et al., 1977; Freyberger et al., 1984; Schwartz & Blanchard, 1991). This type of therapy begins initially on a weekly basis utilizing individual or group approaches. Family involvement is recommended during assessment and treatment as necessary. Although there are no outcome-dose studies suggesting optimal treatment, once the patient is coping better with the disease, often after 10–12 individual or 10 group sessions, less frequent meetings can be arranged.

Autogenic training (AT), a technique developed for the treatment of psychophysiological disorders (Schultz, 1929), increases blood flow and provides subjective feelings of calmness, warmth, and relaxation. In addition to these subjective feelings, AT effects can be measured physiologically (Luthe, 1970). Initial studies confirmed beneficial effects for managing UC symptoms (Schaeffer, 1966; Luthe & Schultz, 1969; DeGossely et al., 1975). These promising earlier studies have disappointedly not been continued, thus leaving empirical uncertainty about AT. The first author's own experience has shown AT is a technique easily taught to patients with both CD and UC, with good results in reducing both anxiety and some of the physical distress associated with these disorders. Although not a controlled study, of the over 125 patients he has seen with inflammatory bowel disease, nearly 80% have reported AT as helpful in symptom distraction, increasing relaxation and/or reducing worry. In particular, distraction from pain and lessening the worry about fecal incontinence are areas of success for AT and pain management therapy. Self-help groups are an additional source of assistance and can be located through the National Foundation for Ileitis and Colitis (1983).

Many people with UC and CD will need to have a diseased portion of their colon removed; for UC patients this is the only way to cure the disease and reduce the risk of colon cancer. Likewise, many people with CD will also receive a colectomy if diseased portions of the colon are obstructed, increasing the risk of rupture of the bowel. Briefly, there are two primary operations to be considered. Historically, the most common procedure has been a practocolectomy. This is the removal of the entire colon and creation of an ileostomy. The ileostomy brings the small intestine through the abdominal wall and allows for the continual collecting of liquid fecal matter into a plastic bag (Whitehead & Schuster, 1985). The second type of surgery is a partial colectomy, leaving a portion of the colon intact. This allows for discharge of formed stools, rather than liquid stools, into a colostomy bag that hangs at the side of a person, under their clothing.

The psychological impact of either ileostomy or colectomy surgery is significant. Patients may initially react with fear, disgust, a poor body image and develop problems with sexual intimacy. Sexual partners may also have difficulty in adjusting to these changes. Depression and anxiety are not uncommon reactions. Suicidal ideation should be assessed, both pre and post surgery. Post surgical work restrictions and changes in recreational activity may also be necessary, thus requiring patients to make yet another lifestyle adjustment. Health psychologists should be aware that leakage and the routine of emptying the colostomy bag can result in unpleasant odors and the need for cleanup. Feelings of embarrassment and shame are common and need to be responded to with empathy, support and understanding by the psychologist. Exploring possible countertransference toward patients who have had these procedures is advised (Druss et al., 1968), to help avoid reinforcing messages of rejection and shame.

Helping patients adjust, both emotionally and physically, are the tasks for the health psychologist, post surgery. Supportive psychotherapy at first, followed by autogenic training for relaxation, and visual imagery to help develop coping responses, are suggested as a possible treatment protocol. Help with sexual intimacy through individual or couples therapy may also be necessary. In addition to therapy, volunteer self help groups have also evolved with the support of the National Ostomy Association, with chapters throughout the country.

Fecal incontinence. A training protocol has been developed that involves either anal canal pressure or pelvic floor EMG biofeedback (Whitehead & Drossman, 1996). Sensors are either taped to the skin adjacent to the anus to record the muscle activity of the external anal sphincter (Cox et al., 1994) or a plastic plug with sensors attached is placed in the anal canal (Whitehead and Thompson, 1993). The goal of therapy is to help patients learn to contract the anal sphincter correctly with the biofeedback device attached so they can practice without the device at home. Practice should be on a daily basis with biofeedback sessions twice per week until continence is restored. It is important that the patient *not* contract other muscle groups simultaneously, but remained focused contracting only the sphincter muscles (Whitehead and Drossman, 1996). If incontinence is due to the inability to perceive rectal distension, sensory retraining is indicated. This is a more complex procedure requiring a catheter containing a balloon and should be performed in an outpatient clinic setting. Whitehead and Drossman (Whitehead, 1992b; Whitehead & Drossman, 1996) explain this procedure in detail.

Functional dyspepsia. Although patients with FD have been shown to have elevations in anxiety, worry, depression, pain and irritability, health psychology researchers have all but ignored this problem (Whitehead, 1992b). There is an overlap of many symptoms between FD and IBS suggesting that similar approaches to treatment may be useful (Svedlund et al., 1985). In particular, a pain management approach (Camic, 1989; Hardin, this volume) similar to that used in IBS management (Corney et al., 1991), exhibits promise in reducing psychological and physical symptoms. One of the few controlled studies with FD (Haug et al., 1994) utilizes cognitive therapy (Persons, 1989) and pain management (Skinner et al., 1990). Reductions on several physical symptoms (pain, nausea, heartburn, constipation, diarrhea) are maintained at one year follow-up. A recent study by Cutts and associates (1996) utilizes prokinetic pharmacologic therapy. This study is promising in two ways. First, it demonstrates that a pharmacologic agent is useful in reducing physical symptoms and second, a reduction in physical symptoms significantly reduces psychologic distress. This study also illustrates that psychological distress is a result of GI distress, rather than part of its cause, offering further evidence that psychosomatic/psychoanalytic theories of GI distress are not supportable. Recent research by Hamilton and colleagues (2000) suggests that brief psychotherapy from an interpersonal model contributed to significant amelioration of somatic and psychological symptoms. However, Hamilton and colleagues (2000) report that this approach was not found to be effective for individuals whose functional dyspepsia symptoms were accompanied by severe heartburn.

Irritable bowel syndrome. A minority of the patients with IBS are psychologically distressed and may require treatment. Brief psychodynamic therapy (Svedlund et al., 1983; Guthrie et al., 1991), hypnotherapy (Whorwell et al., 1984; Harvey et al., 1989; Covino & Frankel, 1998), multi-component cognitive-behavioral therapy (Lynch & Zamble, 1989; Drossman & Thompson, 1992) and cognitive therapy (Greene & Blanchard, 1994) have all been superior to routine medical care or a control group monitoring symptoms (Blanchard & Malamood, 1996; Blanchard & Scharff, 2002). Behavioral psychotherapy alone has not been shown to improve IBS symptoms in comparison to a control group of routine medical treatment (Corney et al., 1991). Corney's study did demonstrate however, a correlation between improvement in bowel symptoms and an improvement in psychological symptoms, as measured by the Clinical Interview Schedule (CIS) (for the CIS see Goldberg et al., 1970). Of these psychologically based treatments, cognitive therapy, through modifying Beck's (1976) method for the treatment of depression, has yielded stronger and more consistent results for both GI symptom relief and improvement in psychological functioning (Payne & Blanchard, 1995). There have not however, been controlled comparison studies between these four approaches. The cost-effectiveness of any of these approaches has also not been determined (Blanchard & Malamood, 1996). Nonetheless, these psychologically-based interventions, which vary from five to twenty visits including booster sessions, are all less costly than routine medical treatment for IBS.

Pelvic floor dyssynergia. A treatment protocol utilizing EMG biofeedback and modified PMR relaxation training has been reported by Whitehead and Drossman (1996) to be cost effective when compared to medical and environmental interventions for PFD. This type of EMG biofeedback treatment requires specialized training beyond the more customary biofeedback training in graduate school or internship. Treatment should be conducted in an outpatient medical or health psychology clinic rather than an office setting. A sensor is inserted into the anal canal and connected to a feedback device that will amplify the electrical potentials in the pelvic floor muscle. Cox and associates report (1994) that electrodes can also be externally placed next to the anus with good results. The purpose of training is to teach the patient to relax the pelvic floor muscles prior to and during defecation.

Peptic ulcer disease. Compliance to the pharmacologic regimen is essential to the treatment of this disease. Where compliance is a problem, a health psychologist can work with the patient and if needed, with her or his family to improve this. Stopping smoking and reducing alcohol use can also help decrease ulcers and promote healing. While psychological factors have been identified in the development of PUD, psychological treatment has proven too costly as compared to pharmacologic therapy, perhaps explaining the lack of continued research in this area (Whitehead, 1992b). However, combining psychiatric intervention with therapeutic intervention to help patients learn to manage stress is recommended for patients with a clear relationship between symptom recurrence and stress, anxiety and depression (Epstein et al., 2002).

Proctalgia fugax. There are few reported outcome studies using psychological interventions with this disorder (Whitehead, 1992b). As mentioned earlier, preliminary studies support the roles of stress, worry and anxiety and the role of contracted pelvic floor muscles. In a study involving EMG biofeedback and PMR training, pain relief was obtained in association with relaxation training for all 12 subjects in the study. Pain relief was sustained at 16-month follow-up for 11 of the subjects (Grimaud et al., 1991). An earlier study by West and associates (1990) also supported a reduction in pain complaints after EMG biofeedback and relaxation training. These are preliminary yet promising studies that lend support to combining EMG and PMR therapies. As yet there are no published medical or pharmacologic interventions for PF, thus making these results particularly promising (Whitehead, 1992b).

References

Abrahamsson, H. (1973). Studies on the inhibitory nervous control of gastric motility. *Acta physiology Scandinavia, 1,* 390.

Alexander, F. (1950). *Psychosomatic medicine.* New York: Norton.

American Psychiatric Association. (1994). *Diagnostic and statistical manual: Fourth edition.* Washington, DC: Author

Anderson, K., Dalton, C., & Bradley, L. (1989). Stress induces alteration of esophageal pressures in healthy volunteers and noncardiac chest pain patients. *Digestive Diseases and Sciences, 34,* 83–89.

Andrews, H., Barczak, P., & Allen, R. (1987). Psychiatric illness in patients with inflammatory bowel disease. *Gut, 28,* 1600–1604.

Ballenger, J., Davidson, J., Lecrubier, Y., & Nutt, D. (2001). Consensus statement on depression, anxiety and functional gastrointestinal disorders. *Journal of Clinical Psychiatry, 62,* 48–51.

Bassotti, G., & Whitehead, W. (1994). Biofeedback as a treatment approach to gastrointestinal tract disorders. *American Journal of Gastroenterology, 89,* 158–164.

Beck, A. (1976). *Cognitive therapy and the emotional disorders.* New York: International Universities Press.

Beck, A., Mendelsohn, M., Mack, J., & Erbaugh, J. (1961). An inventory for measuring depression. *Archives of General Psychiatry, 4,* 561–571.

Bennett, E., Beaurepaire, J., Landeluddecke, P., Kellow, J., & Tennant, C. (1991). Life stress and nonulcer dyspepsia: A case control study. *Journal of Psychosomatic Research, 35,* 579–590.

Berk, J. (1968). Gastrointestinal gas. *Annals of the New York Academy of Sciences, 150.*

Berstad, A. (1993). Non-ulcerative dyspepsia and

gastritis: Clinical aspects. *Journal of Physiology and Pharmacology, 44 (Suppl. 1)*, 41–59.

Blanchard, E. (1993). Irritable bowel syndrome. In R. Gatchel & E. Blanchard (Eds.), *Psychophysiological disorders: Research and clinical applications.* Washington, DC: American Psychological Association.

Blanchard, E. (2001). *Irritable bowel syndrome: Psychological assessment and treatment.* Washington, DC: American Psychological Association.

Blanchard, E., & Malamood, H. (1996). Psychological treatment of irritable bowel syndrome. *Professional Psychology: Research and Practice, 27*, 241–244.

Blanchard, E., & Scharff, L. (2002). Psychosocial aspects of assessment and treatment of irritable bowel syndrome in adults and recurrent abdominal pain in children. *Journal of Consulting and Clinical Psychology, 70* 725–738.

Brooks-Brunn, J. (2000). Esophageal Cancer: An overview. *MedSurg Nursing, 5* [On line] Location: http://FirstSearch.oclc.org

Browning, T. (1990). Members of the patient care committee of the American Gastroenterological Association. Diagnosis of chest pain of esophageal origin. *Digestive Diseases and Sciences, 35*, 289–293.

Calloway, D. (1969). Gas in the alimentary canal. In C. Code (Ed.), *Handbook of physiology, Section 6: Alimentary canal, Volume 4: Motility.* Washington, DC: American Physiological Society.

Calloway, S., Fonagy, D., & Pounder, R. (1982). Frequency of swallowing in duodenal ulceration and hiatus hernia. *British Medical Journal, 285*, 23–24.

Calloway, S., Fonagy, D., Pounder, R., & Morgan, M. (1983). Behavioral techniques in the management of aerophagia in patients with hiatus hernia. *Journal of Psychosomatic Research, 27*, 499–502.

Camic, P. (1989). Psychological assessment of the chronic pain patient: Behaviors, cognitions and dynamics. In P. Camic & F. Brown (Eds.), *Assessing chronic pain: A multidisciplinary clinic handbook.* New York & Berlin: Springer-Verlag.

Cassileth, B., & Drossman, D. (1993). Psychological factors in gastrointestinal illness. *Psychotherapy and Psychosomatics, 59*, 131–143.

Cerulli, M., Nikoomanesh, P., & Schuster, M. (1979). Progress in biofeedback conditioning for fecal incontinence. *Gastroenterology, 76*, 742–746.

Cheng, C., Hui, W., & Lam, S. (1999). Coping style of individuals with functional dyspepsia. *Psychosomatic Medicine, 61*, 789–795.

Clouse, R., & Lustman, P. (1982). Psychiatric illness and contraction abnormalities of the esophagus. *New England Journal of Medicine, 309*, 1337–1342.

Code, C. (1979). The interdigestive housekeeper of the gastrointestinal tract. *Perspectives in Biological Medicine, 22*, 49.

Code, C., Marlett, J., & Szurszewski, J. (1968). A control concept of gastrointestinal motility. In C. Code (Ed.), *Handbook of physiology: Section 6, alimentary canal. Volume 5.* Washington, DC: American Physiology Society.

Code, C., & Schlegel, J. (1968). Motor action of the esophagus and its sphincters. In C. Code (Ed.), *Handbook of physiology: Section 6, alimentary canal: Volume 5.* Washington, DC: American Physiology Society.

Corney, R., Stanton, R., Newell, R., Clare, A., & Fairclough, P. (1991). Behavioral psychotherapy in the treatment of irritable bowel syndrome. *Journal of Psychosomatic Research, 35*, 461–469.

Cottraux, J. (1998). Behavioral psychotherapy applications in the medically ill. In G. Fava & H. Freyberger (Eds.), *Handbook of psychosomatic medicine* (pp. 519–539) Madison, CT: International Universities Press, Inc.

Covino, N., & Frankel, F. (1998) Hypnosis and relaxation in the medically ill. In G. Fava & H. Freyberger (Eds.), *Handbook of psychosomatic medicine.* (pp. 541–566) Madison, CT: International Universities Press, Inc.

Cox, D., Sutphen, J., Borowitz, S., Dickens, M., Singles, J., & Whitehead, W. (1994). Simple electromyographic biofeedback treatment for chronic pediatric constipation/encopresis: Preliminary report. *Biofeedback and Self Regulation, 19*, 41–50.

Craig, T., & Brown, G. (1984). Goal frustration and life events in the etiology of painful gastrointestinal disorder. *Journal of Psychosomatic Research, 28*, 411–421.

Crowell, M., & Barofsky, I. (1999). Functional gastrointestinal pain syndromes. In A. Block, E. Kremer, & E. Fernandez (Eds.), *Handbook of pain syndromes: Biopsychosocial perspectives* (pp. 475–496). Mahwah, NJ: Lawrence Erlbaum Associates, Inc.

Cutts, T., Abell, T., Karas, J., & Kuns, J. (1996). Symptom improvement from prokinetic therapy corresponds to improved quality of life in patients with severe dyspepsia. *Digestive Diseases and Sciences, 41*, 1369–1378.

Dancey, C., Fox. R., & Devins, G. (1999). The measurement of irritable bowel syndrome (IBS)-related misconceptions in people with IBS. *Journal of Psychosomatic Research, 4*(7), 269–276.

Davenport, H. (1982). *Physiology of the digestive tract: An introductory text. Fifth edition.* Chicago: Year Book Medical Publishers.

DeGrossely, M., Koninok, N., & Lengant, H. (1975). La recto-colite hemorrogique: Training autogene. *Acta Gastro-Enterologica Belgica, 38,* 454–462.

Derogatis, L. (1986). The psychosocial adjustment to illness scale (PAIS). *Journal of Psychosomatic Research, 30,* 77–91.

Derogatis, L., Fleming, M., Sudler, N., & DellaPietra, L. (1995). Psychological assessment. In P. Nicassio & T. Smith (Eds.), *Managing chronic illness: A biopsychosocial perspective.* Washington, DC: American Psychological Association.

Derogatis, L., & Lopez, M. (1983). *PAIS and PAIS-SR. Administration, scoring and procedure manual.* Baltimore: Johns Hopkins University School of Medicine.

Dimenäs, E., Glise, H., Halleback, H., Hernquist, J., Svedlund, J., & Wiklund, L. (1993). Quality of life in patients with upper gastrointestinal symptoms: An improved evaluation of treatment regimens? *Scandinavian Journal of Gastroenterology, 28,* 681–687.

Drossman, D. (1998). Presidential address: Gastrointestinal illness and the biopsychosocial model. *Psychosomatic Medicine, 60,* 258–267.

Drossman, D., Leserman, J., Mitchell, C., Li, Z., Zagami, E., & Patrick, D. (1991). Health status and health care use in persons with inflammatory bowel disease: A national sample. *Digestive Diseases and Sciences, 36,* 1746–1755.

Drossman, D., Leserman, J., Nachman, G., Li, Z., Gluck, H., Toomey, T., & Mitchell, C. (1990). Sexual and physical abuse in women with functional or organic gastrointestinal disorders. *Annals of Internal Medicine, 113,* 828–833.

Drossman, D., McKee, D., Sandler, R., Mitchell, C., Cramer, E., Lowman, B., & Burger, A. (1988). Psychosocial factors in irritable bowel syndrome. A multivariate study of patients and nonpatients. *Gastroenterology, 95,* 701–708.

Drossman, D., & Thompson, G. (1992). The irritable bowel syndrome: Review and a graduated multicomponent treatment approach. *Annals of Internal Medicine, 116,* 1009–1016.

Drossman, D., Thompson, G., Tally, N., Funch-Jensen, P., Janssens, J., & Whitehead, W. (1990). Identification of subgroups of functional gastrointestinal disorders. *Gastroenterology International, 3,* 159–172.

Druss, R., O'Connor, J., Prudder, J., & Stern, L. (1968). Psychologic response to colectomy. *Archives of General Psychiatry, 18,* 53–59.

Dudley-Brown, S. (2002). Prevention of psychological distress in persons with inflammatory bowel disease. *Issues in Mental Health Nursing, 23,* 403–422.

Dupuy, H. (1984). The psychological general well-being index. In N. Wenger, M. Mattson, C. Furnberg & J. Ellison (Eds.), *Assessment of quality of life in clinical trials of cardiovascular therapies.* Paris: Le Jacq.

Earlham, P. (1975). Clinical tests of oesophageal spasm: An evaluation of suggestion-therapy as determined by means of the esophagoscope. *Psychosomatic Medicine, 2,* 139–140.

Edwards, M., Forman, W., & Walton, J. (1985). Audit of abdominal pain in general practice. *Journal of the Royal College of General Practice, 35,* 235–238.

Eggebrecht, D., Bautz, M., Brenig, M., Pfingsten, M., & Franz, C. (1989). Psychometric evaluation. In P. Camic & F. Brown (Eds.), *Assessing chronic pain: A multidisciplinary clinic handbook.* New York & Berlin: Springer-Verlag.

Emmelkamp, P., & Van Oppen, P. (1998). Cognitive interventions in behavioral medicine. In A. Block, E. Kremer, & E. Fernandez (Eds.), *Handbook of pain syndromes: Biopsychosocial perspectives* (pp. 567–591). Mahwah, NJ: Lawrence Erlbaum Associates, Inc.

Engel, B., Nikoomanesh, P., & Schuster, M. (1974). Operant conditioning of rectosphincteric responses in the treatment of fecal incontinence. *New England Journal of Medicine, 290,* 646–649.

Engel, G. (1954). Studies of ulcerative colitis I. Clinical data bearing on the nature of the somatic process. *Psychosomatic Medicine, 16,* 231–256.

Engel, G. (1955). Studies of ulcerative colitis III. The nature of the psychological processes. *American Journal of Medicine, 17,* 231–256.

Epstein, S., Meguid, A., & Wise, T. (2002). Psychiatric Aspects Of Gastroenterology. In N. Stotland (Ed.), *Cutting-edge medicine: What psychiatrists need to know (Review of Psychiatry Series, Volume 21, Number 1; Oldham J M., & Riba, MB, series editors)* (pp. 23–65) Washington, DC: American Psychiatric Publishing.

Epstein, S., Wise, T., & Goldberg, R. (1993). Gastroenterology. In A. Stoudemire & B. Fogel (Eds.), *Psychiatric care of the medical patient. Second edition.* New York & London: Oxford University Press.

Fava, G., & Pavan, L. (1976). Large bowel disorders I. Illness configuration and life events. *Psychotherapy and Psychosomatics, 27,* 93–99.

Folks, D., & Kinney, F. (1992). The role of psychological factors in gastrointestinal conditions. *Psychosomatics, 33,* 257–270.

Freyberger, H. (1975). Supportive psychotherapeutic techniques in primary and secondary alexithymia. *Psychotherapy and Psychosomatics, 86*, 348.

Freyberger, H., Kuensebeck, H-W., Lempa, W., Wellman, W., & Avenarius, J.-J. (1985). Psychotherapeutic interventions in alexithymic patients with special regard to ulcerative colitis and Crohn-patients. *Psychotherapy and Psychosomatics,44*, 72–81.

Fullwood, A., & Drossman, D. (1995). The relationship of psychiatric illness with gastrointestinal disease. *Annual Review of Medicine, 46*, 483–496.

Gatchel, R. (1993). Psychophysiological disorders: Past and present perspectives. In R. Gatchel & E. Blanchard (Eds.), *Psychophysiological disorders: Research and clinical applications*. Washington, DC: American Psychological Association.

Goldberg, D. (1985). Identifying psychiatric illness among general medical patients. *British Medical Journal, 291*, 161–162.

Goldberg, D., & Blackwell, B. (1970). Psychiatric illness in general practice: A detailed study using a new method for case identification. *British Medical Journal, 2*, 439–443.

Goldberg, D., Cooper, B., Eastwood, M., Kenward, H., & Sheperd, M. (1970). A psychiatric interview suitable for using in community surveys. *British Journal of Preventive Medicine, 24*, 18–26.

Grace, W., Pinksy, R., & Wolff, H. (1954). Treatment of ulcerative colitis II. *Gastroenterology, 26*, 462–468.

Graham, D., Stern, J., & Winokur, R. (1958). Experimental investigation of the specificity hypothesis in psychosomatic disease. *Psychosomatic Medicine, 20*, 446–457.

Greene, B., & Blanchard, E. (1994). Cognitive therapy for irritable bowel syndrome. *Journal of Clinical and Consulting Psychology, 62*, 576–582.

Grimaud, J.-C., Bouvier, M., Naudy, B., Guien, C., & Salducci, J. (1991). Manometric and radiographic investigations and biofeedback treatment of chronic idiopathic anal pain. *Diseases of the Colon and Rectum, 34*, 690–695.

Groen, J., & Bastiaans, J. (1951). Psychotherapy of ulcerative colitis. *Gastroenterology, 17*, 344- 352.

Guthrie, E., Creed, F., Dawson, D., & Tonenson, B. (1991). A controlled trial of psychological treatment for the irritable bowel syndrome. *Gastroenterology, 100*, 450–457.

Hamilton, J., Guthrie, E., Creed, F., Thompson, B., Bennett, R., Moriarty, K., Stephens, W., & Liston, R. (2000) Alimentary tract: A randomized controlled trial of psychotherapy in patients with functional dyspepsia. *Gastroenterology, 119*, 661–669.

Harvey, R. (1979). Colonic motility in proctalgia fugax. *Lancet, 713–714*.

Harvey, R., Hinton, R., Gunary, R., & Barry, R. (1989). Individual and group hypnotherapy in treatment of refractory irritable bowel syndrome. *Lancet, 424–425*.

Haug, T., Wilhelmsen, I., Svebak, S., Berstad, A., & Ursin, H. (1994). Psychotherapy in functional dyspepsia. *Journal of Psychosomatic Research, 38*, 735–744.

Hausken, T., Svebak, S., & Wilhelmsen, I. (1993). Low vagal tone and antral dysmotility in patients with functional dyspepsia. *Psychosomatic Medicine, 19*, 12–22.

Hausken, T., & Berstad, A. (1992). Wide gastric antrum in patients with nonulcer dyspepsia. *Digestive Diseases and Sciences, 32*, 924.

Haynes, S. (1976). Electromyographic biofeedback treatment of a woman with chronic dysphagia. *Biofeedback and Self Regulation, 1*, 121–126.

Helzer, J., Stillings, W., & Chammas, S. (1982). A controlled study of the association between ulcerative colitis and psychiatric diagnosis. *Digestive Diseases and Sciences, 27*, 513–518.

Henderson, R. (1980). *Motor disorders of the esophagus* (2nd ed.). Baltimore: Williams & Wilkins.

Heron, J. (1996). *Co-operative inquiry*. London: Sage.

Hewson, E., Dalton, C., Hackshaw, B., Wu, W., & Richter, J. (1990). The prevalence of abnormal esophageal test results in patients with cardiovascular disease and unexplained chest pain. *Archives of Internal Medicine, 150*, 965–969.

Hill, O., & Blendis, L. (1967). Physical and psychological evaluation of "nonorganic" abdominal pain. *Gut, 8*, 221–229.

Hislop, I. (1979). Childhood deprivation: An antecedent of the irritable bowel syndrome. *Medical Journal of Australia, 1*, 372–374.

Holzl, R., & Whitehead, W. (1983). Psychophysiology of the gastrointestinal tract: Experimental and clinical applications. New York: Plenum.

Jacobson, E. (1927). Spastic esophagus and mucus colitis: Etiology and treatment by progressive relaxation. *Archives of Internal Medicine, 39*, 433–445.

Johannessen, T., Peterson, H., & Kleveland, P. (1990). The predictive value of history in dyspepsia. *Scandinavian Journal of Gastroenterology, 27*, 689–697.

Karush, A., Daniels, G., O'Connor, J., & Stern, L. (1968). The response to psychotherapy in chronic ulcerative colitis I. Pretreatment factors. *Psychosomatic Medicine, 30*, 255–276.

Kellner, R. (1994). Psychosomatic syndromes, somatization and somatoform disorders. *Psychotherapy and Psychosomatics, 61*, 4–24.

Kerns, R. (1995). Family assessment and intervention. In P. Nicassio & T. Smith (Eds.), *Managing chronic illness: A biopsychosocial perspective.* Washington, DC: American Psychological Association.

Kirsner, J., & Shorter, R. (1982). Recent developments in "nonspecific" inflammatory bowel disease. *Gastroenterology, 75*, 540–511.

Lasser, R., Bond, J., & Levitt, M. (1975). The role of gastrointestinal gas in functional abdominal pain. *New England Journal of Medicine, 293*, 524.

Latimer, P. (1983). *Functional gastrointestinal disorders: A behavioral medicine approach.* New York: Springer-Verlag.

Latimer, P., Sarna, S., Campbell, D., Latimer, M., Waterfall, W., & Daniel, E. (1981). Colonic motility and myoelectrical activity: A comparative study of normal subjects, psychoneurotic patients and patients with irritable bowel syndrome. *Gastroenterology, 80*, 893–901.

Lee, S., Park, M., Choi, S., Nah, Y., Abbey, S., & Rodin, G. (2000). Stress, coping, and depression in non-ulcer dyspepsia patients. *Journal of Psychosomatic Research, 49*, 93–99.

Lehmann, M., Dederding, J., Flourie, B., Franchisseur, C., Rambaud, J., & Rian, R. (1991). Abnormal perception of visceral pain in response to gastric distension in chronic idiopathic dyspepsia. *Digestive Diseases and Sciences, 36*, 1249–1254.

Lewkonia, R., & McConnell, R. (1976). Progress report: Familial inflammatory bowel disease- heredity or environment? *Gut, 17*, 235–243.

Li, B., & Howard, J. (2002). New hope for children with cyclic vomiting syndrome. *Contemporary Pediatrics* [On line] Location: http://FirstSearch.oclc.org.

Likert, R. (1932). A technique for measuring attitudes. *Archives of Psychology, 55*, 140.

Lowman, B., Drossman, D., Crammer, E., & McKee, D. (1987). Recollection of childhood events in adults with irritable bowel syndrome. *Journal of Gastroenterology, 9*, 324–330.

Luthe, W. (1970). *Autogenic therapy. Volume IV.* New York: Grune & Stratton.

Luthe, W., & Schultz, J. (1969). *Autogenic therapy. Volume I.* New York: Grune & Stratton.

Lynch, P., & Zamble, E. (1989). A controlled behavioral treatment study of irritable bowel syndrome. *Behavior Therapy, 20*, 509–523.

Maddock, W., Bell, J., & Tremaine, M. (1949). Gastro-intestinal gas: Observations on belching during anaesthesia, operations and pyelography, and rapid passing of gas. *Annals of Surgery, 130*, 512–535.

Magnall, Y., Houghton, L., Bread, N., & Johnsen, A. (1991). Non-ulcer dyspepsia: Pattern of emptying fatty liquids from the proximal and distal stomach. *European Journal of Gastroenterological Hepatology, 3, (Suppl. 1)*, 9.

Maguire, P. (1999). Physical and psychological needs of patients dying from colo-rectal cancer. *Palliative Medicine, 13*, 45–50.

Maier, S., Watkins, L., & Flesher, M. (1994). Psychoneuroimmunology: The interface between behavior, brain and immunity. *American Psychologist, 49*, 1004–1017.

Malchiodi, C. (1993). Medical art therapy: Contributions to the field of arts medicine. *International Journal of Arts Medicine, 2*, 28–31.

Malcomson, K. (1966). Radiographic findings in globus hystericus. *British Journal of Radiology, 39*, 583–586.

Markus, H., & Kitayama, S. (1991). Culture and the self: Implications for cognition, motivation and emotion. *Psychological Reviews, 98*, 224–253.

Maunder, R., & Esplen, M. (1999). Facilitating adjustment to inflammatory bowel disease: A model of psychosocial intervention in non-psychiatric patients. *Psychotherapy and Psychosomatics, 68*, 230–240.

May, P., Smedby, B., & Wetterberg, L. (1986) (Eds.). Perceptions of the values and benefits of research: A report by an international study group. *Acta Psychiatry Scandinavia, 74 (Suppl.)*, 331.

Mayer, E., Craske, M., & Naliboff, B. (2001). Depression, anxiety and the gastrointestinal system. *Journal of Clinical Psychiatry, 62*, 28–36.

Mayer, F., & Raybould, H. (1990). Role of visceral afferent mechanisms in functional bowel disorders. *Gastroenterology, 99*, 1688–1704.

McIllmurray, M., & Langman, M. (1975). Large bowel cancer: Causation and management. *Gut, 17*, 815–820.

Mellow, M. (1977). Symptomatic diffuse esophageal spasm: Manometric follow-up and response to cholinergic stimulation and cholinesterase inhibition. *Gastroenterology, 73*, 237–240.

Miller, N. (1977). Effect of learning on gastrointestinal functions. *Clinical Gastroenterology, 6*, 533–546.

Milne, B., Joachim, G., & Niedhart, J. (1986). A stress management programme for inflammatory bowel disease patients. *Journal of Advances in Nursing, 11*, 561–567.

Morris, C., Chapman, R., & Mayou, R. (1992). The outcome of unexplained dyspepsia: A questionnaire follow-up study of patients after endoscopy. *Journal of Psychosomatic Research, 36*, 751–757.

National Foundation for Ileitis and Colitis (1983). *The crohn's disease and ulcerative colitis fact book.* New York: Scribner's.

Neff, D., & Blanchard, E. (1987). A multicomponent treatment for irritable bowel syndrome. *Behavior Therapy, 18*, 70–83.

Nemiah, J. (1975). Denial revisited: Reflections on psychosomatic theory. *Psychotherapy and Psychosomatics, 26*, 140–147.

Nordin, K., Wasteson, E., Hoffman, K., Glimelius, B., & Sjoden, P. (2001). Discrepancies between attainment and importance of life values and anxiety and depression in gastrointestinal cancer patients and their spouses. *Psycho-Oncology, 10*, 479–489.

Payne, A., & Blanchard, E. (1995). A controlled comparison of cognitive therapy and self-help support groups in the treatment of irritable bowel. *Journal of Consulting and Clinical Psychology, 63*, 779–786.

Persons, J. (1989). *Cognitive therapy in practice: A case formulation approach.* New York: W.W. Norton.

Peterson, W., Sturdevant, R., Frankl, H., Richardson, C., Isenberg, J., Elashoff, J., Sones, J., Gross, R., McCallum, R., & Fordtran, J. (1977). Healing of duodenal ulcer with an antacid regimen. *New England Journal of Medicine, 297*, 341–345.

Peveler, R., & Fairburn, C. (1990). Measurement of neurotic symptoms by self-report questionnaire: SCL-90-R. *Psychological Medicine, 20*, 873–879.

Pilling, L., Swenson, W., & Hill, J. (1972). The psychological aspects of proctalgia fugax. *Diseases of the Colon and Rectum, 8*, 372–376.

Remen, N. (1996). *Kitchen table wisdom.* New York: Riverhead Books.

Rogers, R. (1995). *Diagnostic and structured interviewing.* Odessa, FL.: Psychological Assessment Resources.

Schaeffer, G. (1966). Autogenic training with ulcerative colitis. In J. Lopez Ibor (Ed.), *IV world congress of psychiatry, Madrid, 5–11, September.* Amsterdam: Excerpta Medica Foundation, International Congress Series, 117.48.

Schultz, J. (1929). Autogenes Training. *Medizinische Welt, 47.*

Schwartz, S., & Blanchard, E. (1990). Inflammatory bowel disease: A review of the psychological assessment and treatment literature. *Annals of Behavioral Medicine, 12*, 95–105.

Schwartz, S., & Blanchard, E. (1991). Evaluation of psychological treatment for inflammatory bowel disease. *Behaviour Research and Therapy, 29*, 167–177.

Schwartz, S., Taylor, A., Scharff, L., & Blanchard, E. (1990). A four year follow-up study of behaviorally treated irritable bowel syndrome patients. *Behavior Research and Therapy, 28*, 331–335.

Shaw, L., & Ehrlich, A. (1987). Relaxation training as a treatment for chronic pain caused by ulcerative colitis. *Pain, 29*, 287–293.

Skinner, J., Erskine, A., Pearce, S., Rubenstein, I., Taylor, M., & Foster, C. (1990). The evaluation of a cognitive behavioral treatment programme in outpatients with chronic pain. *Journal of Psychosomatic Research, 34*, 13–19.

Slavney, P., & McHugh, P. (1984). Life stories and meaningful connections: Reflections on a clinical method in psychiatry and medicine. *Perspectives in Biological Medicine, 27*, 279–288.

Smith, R., Greenbaum, D., Vancouver, J., Henry, R., Reinhart, M., & Greenbaum, R. (1990). Psychosocial factors associated with health seeking rather than diagnosis in irritable bowel syndrome. *Gastroenterology, 98*, 293–301.

Smith, T., & Nicassio, P. (1995). Psychological practice: Clinical application of the biopsychosocial model. In P. Nicassio & T. Smith (Eds.), *Managing chronic illness: A biopsychosocial perspective.* Washington, DC: American Psychological Association.

Speca, M., Carlson, L., Goodey, E., & Angen, M. (2000). A Randomized, wait-list controlled clinical trial: The effect of mindfulness meditation-based stress reduction program on mood and symptoms of stress in cancer outpatients. *Psychosomatic Medicine, 62*, 613–622.

Spielberger, C., Gorsuch, R., & Lusken, R. (1970). *Manual for the State-Trait Anxiety Inventory.* Palo Alto, CA.: Consulting Psychologists Press.

Svedlund, J., Sjodin, I., & Doteval, G. (1988). A clinical rating scale for gastrointestinal symptoms in patients with irritable bowel syndrome and peptic ulcer disease. *Digestive Diseases and Sciences, 33*, 129–134.

Svedlund, J., Sjodin, I., Ottosson, J.-O., & Dotevall, G. (1983). Controlled study of psychotherapy in irritable bowel syndrome. *Lancet*, 589–592.

Tarter, R., Switala, J., & Carra, J. (1987). Inflammatory bowel disease: Psychiatric status of patients before and after onset. *International Journal of Psychiatry and Medicine, 17*, 173–181.

Thompson, W. (1981). Proctalgia fugax. *Digestive Diseases and Sciences, 26*, 1121–1124.

Thompson, W. (1984). Proctalgia fugax in patients with irritable bowel syndrome, peptic ulcer or inflammatory bowel disease. *American Journal of Gastroenterology, 79,* 450–452.

Thompson, W., & Heaton, K. (1982). Heartburn and globus hystericus in apparently health people. *Journal of the Canadian Medical Association, 126,* 46–48.

Turnbull, G., & Ritvo, D. (1992). Anal sphincter biofeedback relaxation treatment for women with intractable constipation symptoms. *Diseases of the Colon and Rectum, 35,* 530–536.

Wald, A., & Tunuguntla, A. (1984). Anorectal sensorimotor dysfunction in fecal incontinence and diabetes mellitus: Modification with biofeedback therapy. *New England Journal of Medicine, 310,* 1281–1287.

Warndorff, D., Knottnerus, J., Huijnen, L., & Starmrans, R. (1989). How well do general practitioners manage dyspepsia? *Journal of the Royal College of General Practice, 39,* 499–502.

Wasteson, E., Nordin, K., Hoffman, K., Glimelius, B., & Sjoden, P. (2002). Daily assessment of coping in patients with gastrointestinal cancers. *Psycho-oncology, 11,* 1–11.

Waterman, D., Dalton, C., Ott, D., Castell, J., Bradley, L., Castell, D., & Richter, J. (1989). Hypersensitive lower esophageal sphincter: What does it mean? *Journal of Clinical Gastroenterology, 11,* 139–146.

Weiner, H. (1977). *Psychobiology and human disease.* New York: Elsevier Science.

West, L., Abell, T., & Cutts, T. (1990). Anorectal manometry and EMG in the diagnosis of the levator ani syndrome. *Gastroenterology, 98,* A401.

West, L., Abell, T., & Cutts, T. (1992). Long-term results of pelvic floor muscle rehabilitation of constipation. *Gastroenterology, 102,* A533.

Whitehead, W. (1992a). Biofeedback treatment of gastrointestinal disorders. *Biofeedback and Self Regulation, 17,* 59–76.

Whitehead, W. (1992b). Behavioral medicine approaches to gastrointestinal disorders. *Journal of Clinical and Consulting Psychology, 60,* 605–612.

Whitehead, W., & Bosmajian, L. (1992). Behavioral medicine approaches to gastrointestinal disorders. *Journal of Clinical and Consulting Psychology, 50,* 672–683.

Whitehead, W., Bosmajian, L., Zonderman, A., Costa, P., & Schuster, M. (1988). Symptoms of psychological distress associated with irritable bowel syndrome. Comparison of community and medical clinic samples. *Gastroenterology, 95,* 709–714.

Whitehead, W., Chami, T., Crowell, M., & Schuster, M. (1991). Aerophagia: Association with gastrointestinal and psychological symptoms. *Gastroenterology, 100,* A508.

Whitehead, W., Crowell, M., & Schuster, M. (1990). Functional disorders of the anus and rectum. *Seminars in Gastrointestinal disease, 1,* 64–84.

Whitehead, W., & Drossman, D. (1996). Biofeedback for disorders of elimination: Fecal incontinence and pelvic floor dyssynergia. *Professional Psychology: Research and Practice, 7,* 234–240.

Whitehead, W., & Schuster, M. (1985). *Gastrointestinal disorders: Behavioral and physiological basis for treatment.* Orlando, FL.: Academic Press.

Whitehead, W., Winget, C., Fedoravicius, S., Wodey, S., & Blackwell, B. (1982). Learned illness behavior in patients with irritable bowel syndrome and peptic ulcer. *Digestive Diseases and Sciences, 27,* 202–208.

Whorwell, P., Prior, A., & Colgan, S. (1987). Hypnotherapy in severe irritable bowel syndrome: Further experience. *Gut, 28,* 423–425.

Wilhelmsen, I. (1995). Quality of life in upper gastrointestinal disorders. *Scandinavian Journal of Gastroenterology, 30 (Suppl. 211),* 21–25.

Winship, D. (1978). Cimetidine in the treatment of duodenal ulcer: Review and commentary. *Gastroenterology, 74,* 402–406.

Wolpe, J., & Lazarus, A. (1966). *Behavior therapy techniques.* New York: Pergamon.

Seth C. Kalichman and Kathleen J. Sikkema

9

Human Immunodeficiency Virus Infection and Acquired Immune Deficiency Syndrome

Introduction

The AIDS epidemic poses complex and ever-changing challenges to clinical health psychologists. In its beginning, AIDS only occurred in large urban areas with sizable numbers of gay men and injection drug users.[1] Within a few short years, Human Immunodeficiency Virus (HIV, HI-virus) spread to most cities and rural areas in North America. AIDS now affects persons in most every socio-demographic level. AIDS is most concentrated, however, at lower socioeconomic strata, disproportionately affecting the most disadvantaged and underserved populations. The HI-virus is transmitted through sexual and drug using behaviors, challenging us to openly discuss what remain some of the most personal and often socially stigmatized behaviors. HIV-AIDS is a global pandemic, which also challenges us to reach across cultures to find solutions.

Although still incurable, there are now several options for treating and controlling HIV infection and the opportunistic illnesses that define an AIDS diagnosis. However, treatments for HIV and its associated illnesses are not universally available, with the most socioeconomically disadvantaged persons - those who are most afflicted by AIDS — being the least likely to access care and adequate treatment (Palacio et al., 1999; Shapiro et al., 1999). When HIV treatments are available they demand strict adherence to what are often complicated multi-drug regimens (Ostrow & Kalichman, 1998). Because HIV is transmitted through only a few well identified behaviors and because the success of medical interventions for HIV-AIDS is determined by specific health practices, clinical health psychologists play a significant role in the care of people living with HIV-AIDS.

In this chapter, we provide an overview of the clinical manifestations and medical management of HIV infection. First, we provide a brief discussion of the human immune system, highlighting the components of immune system functioning most relevant to HIV-AIDS. We then discuss how HIV affects the immune system, causes disease, and ultimately causes AIDS. We also briefly review medical treatments for HIV and the lifestyle challenges often posed by these regimens. Our attention is then shifted to the psychological assessment and treatment of people living with HIV-AIDS.

---

1 HIV-AIDS is a global public health crisis with the vast majority of AIDS cases occurring in developing countries throughout Africa and Asia. However, this chapter focuses on the North American HIV epidemic to fit the practices of clinical health psychologists practicing in the United States and Canada.

The Human Immune System

The chief function of the immune system is to defend the body against microorganisms and toxins, ultimately preventing disease. The human immune system has evolved to recognize foreign agents and mount a defensive response to eliminate from or clear the body of potential hazards. To achieve successful immune responses, the immune system launches a series of complex and highly interactive chains of biological events. An immune response is accomplished through a highly complex and dynamic system that consists of specialized cells and lymphoid organs. A healthy functioning immune system recognizes its own cells as self, through a process of recognizing highly specific self-identifying markers. Non-self or foreign agents that are capable of triggering an immune response are called antigens. In the case when the ability to recognize self from non-self agents does not function adequately, there is an increased vulnerability to infection, allergy, or cancer.

The lymphoid organs compose the major components of the immune system. Of greatest importance are bone marrow, the thymus, lymph nodes, and spleen. Some immune system cells are derived from stem cells that originate in bone marrow, developing into bone marrow originating lymphocytes, or B-lymphocytes (B-cells). Another type of lymphocyte, the T-lymphocytes (T-cells), originates from precursor cells in the thymus gland. B-cell and T-cell lymphocytes work together and in complimentary ways to mount a protective immune response. B-cell immunity is also known as humoral immunity and is mediated by antibodies — protein molecules that protect against foreign materials that invade outside of cells, such as bacteria or parasites. B-cells make specific antibodies that bind to or fit specific antigens. The fitting of antibodies to antigens is analogous to a key — and — lock to illustrate the high-degree of specificity of the immune system. T-cell immunity is called cell-mediated immunity and protects against intracellular agents, such as viruses. There are two principle types of T-cells: (a) regulatory T-cells that include T-helper cells and T-suppressor cells, and (b) cytotoxic T-cells also called natural killer cells.

After a foreign agent invades the body, the immune system reacts with both nonspecific and specific immune mechanisms. Immune mechanisms in the skin and mucous membranes offer a first-line defense against disease. Immune cells are directed toward the site of invasion and mount an initial response to destroy and remove non-self material. Two types of cells that play instrumental roles in these initial immune responses are Langerhans cells and M-cells. When these surface oriented responses cannot successfully remove the foreign agent, the immune system responds with a second tier response that includes phagocytosis and inflammatory processes that attempt to keep the non-self material from proceeding into body systems. When these systems fail, humoral/B-cell and cellular/T-cell immune mechanisms are called into play.

Humoral and cellular immunity compose the acquired or adaptive immune response. These processes develop overtime because they are specific to non-self agents. When adaptive immunity is disabled, such as when HIV invades and destroys T-cells and other components of the immune system, the immune system itself fails and leaves the body vulnerable to disease.

HIV Transmission and the Onset of HIV Infection

There are four primary modes of HIV transmission: (a) person-to-person through fluid-exchanging sexual behaviors; (b) use of HIV-contaminated injection equipment; (c) mother to infant during pregnancy, labor and delivery, or breast-feeding; and (d) through transfusion with infected blood or blood products (see Table 1).

When HIV exposure occurs through mucous membrane contacts, such as during sexual transmission of HIV, initial immune mechanisms launched by the skin, mucous membranes, and inflammatory processes

Table 1. **Routes of HIV transmission.**

Route	Transmission mechanism
Anal intercourse	Infected semen or blood enters the anal/rectal mucosa or penis through absorption or micro-openings. Varies with presence of blood, STIs, lacerations, and stage of HIV infection.
Vaginal intercourse	Infected vaginal fluids, semen, or blood enters the vaginal or penile mucosa or through micro-openings. Varies with presence of blood, STIs, lacerations, and stage of HIV infection.
Oral-genital contact	Infected semen or vaginal fluids enter blood stream through micro-openings in oral cavity or infected cells enter vagina or penis through micro-openings.
Perinatal transmission	Transplacental transfer of virus during gestation, transfer of virus or maternal blood during labor/delivery, breast feeding.
Injection drug use with sharing	Use of needles and other injection equipment previously used by an infected person exposes HIV directly to the blood stream.
Needlestick injury	Occupational injury in medical setting.
Blood transfusion	Principle risk in U.S. occurred prior to 1984 blood screening programs, blood or blood parts from an infected person enter blood stream.

Table 2. **Activities by which HIV destroys the immune system.**

Mechanism	Description
HIV Budding	HIV reproduced in cells erupt and infect a multitude of new target cells
Syncytia	HIV envelope proteins adhere to the receptor area of one cell which then adheres to another until a cluster of immune cells are bound together
Binding with proteins (gp120)	HIV envelope proteins bound to the cell membrane can cause impaired cell functioning
Autoimmune Responses	Virus components bound to cell membranes can trigger an immune response which eventually attacks the infected immune cells

may effectively destroy and remove the HI-virus before it establishes infection. However, HIV selectively binds to cells that carry the CD4 molecule on their surface membranes. Unfortunately, the CD4 molecule is found on the surface of Langerhans cells and M-cells, both of which are found in mucous membranes as part of the initial immune response (Soto-Ramirez et al., 1996). HIV therefore binds to the very cells whose purposes are to clear potential causes of disease from mucous linings and carry them to the immune system. In the next line of defense, T-helper lymphocyte cells respond to foreign agents and direct immune reactions to neutralize potential causes of disease. T-helper cells also carry the CD4 molecule on their surface membranes and it is these cells that are the principle target of the HI-virus. HIV infects and destroys T-helper cells and other cells that protect the body from viruses and other infectious agents, systematically disabling the very mechanisms designed to destroy it and effectively prevent other diseases. Table 2 summarizes the various ways that HIV destroys cells as a part of its invasion and replication processes.

Significant loss of T-helper cells was the

Table 3. Areas of the brain most commonly affected by HIV.

Structures	Disrupted functions
Frontal Lobes	Apathy, depression, trouble concentrating, loss of organizational skills
Limbic System & Temporal Lobes	Memory loss and language impairment
Basal Ganglia	Impaired eye-movements, involuntary movements, tremor
Brain Stem	Disturbed gait, eye-movement dysfunctions, visual disturbances
Demyelination	Delayed information processing, slowed responses, impaired motor skills

earliest and most widely recognized immune system abnormality resulting from HIV infection, and it is the depletion to T-helper cells that results in the profound immune suppression that causes AIDS. When untreated, T-helper cells rapidly decline by a factor of one third in the first 12 to 18 months after the onset of HIV infection, with a subsequently slower rate of cell loss, approximately 80 T-helper cells per unit measure per year. A second accelerated period of T-helper cell loss occurs prior to the onset of clinical AIDS. The close associations between duration of HIV infection, loss of T-helper cells and immune suppression clearly shows that HIV causes AIDS. In healthy immune systems, there are about 1000 T-helper cells per blood unit (mm^3). After years of HIV infection, T-helper cell counts fall below 200 cells/mm^3 and this level of immune destruction is taken as a reliable marker for the development of AIDS (Schoub, 1994). In fact, medical diagnoses of AIDS now include T-helper cell counts of 200 cells/mm^3 as a diagnostic criterion for AIDS even in the absence of clinical illness.

In addition to absolute counts of T-cells, the proportion of T-helper to T-suppressor cells is a key indicator of immune system functioning. In the case of a healthy immune system, T-helper lymphocytes outnumber T-suppressor cells, with 60% of peripheral lymphocytes being T-helper cells and 30% T-suppressor cells (Fauci et al., 1984). The immune system is therefore activated rather than suppressed. However, with HIV infection, the proportion of T-helper to T-suppressor can be-

Table 4. AIDS-related conditions of the central nervous system.

Manifestation	Disease causing agent
Opportunistic Viral Infections	Cytomegalovirus Herpes Simplex I & II Herpes Zoster Papovavirus (PML)
Fungal and Protozoan Infections	Toxoplasmosis Cryptococcus Candida Mycobacterium
Malignancies	Primary lymphoma Metastatic lymphoma Metastatic Kaposi's sarcoma
Cerebrovascular	Hemorrhage Infarction

come inverted. Greater T-suppressor cells than T-helper cells signals a hallmark of immune suppression because of the loss of T-helper cells as opposed to an increase in T-suppressor cells. The inverted ratio of T-helper and -suppressor cell abnormality further suppresses immunity and results in a substantial increase in susceptibility to infectious diseases.

In addition to the loss of T-helper lymphocyte cells, several other branches of immunity are indirectly affected by the HI-virus. Although there is not a significant loss of T-suppressor cells or natural killer cells, the functions of these immune cells are coordinated by T-helper cells. HIV also affects monocyte macrophages, which also express the CD4 surface molecule to which HIV se-lectively binds. Monocyte macrophages are phagocytes — with the specific function of engulfing and destroying infectious agents. Thus, the HI-virus can enter and infect mac-rophages by either binding with their CD4 surface molecule or by infecting the cells by being engulfed as part of the immune re-sponse against the virus. HIV-infected mac-rophages are disabled, unable to attack and destroy other microorganisms and HIV can become harbored inside of host macrophage cells protected from further immune re-sponses. Further, HIV infected macrophages may be disseminated to multiple organ sys-tems, particularly infiltrating the lungs and brain (Fauci, 1986, 1988; Sande & Volber-ding, 2000). With respect to the brain, HIV itself does not infect neurons, the fundamen-tal cells of the central nervous system. How-ever, toxins emitted by dying macrophages, disrupted immune systems, and loss of sup-port cells can have severe adverse effects on central nervous system functioning. Table 3 summarizes the major areas of the brain af-fected by HIV and Table 4 presents the com-mon neurological disorders associated with AIDS.

The Medical Management of HIV-AIDS

The first 30 years of HIV-AIDS saw dramatic evolutions and revolutions in the develop-ment of medications to effectively slow the course of HIV infection. The early days of the U.S. HIV-AIDS epidemic presented a disease trajectory that was characterized by a slow and progressive decline of the immune sys-tem with only the hope of preventing the op-portunistic illnesses that occur when adap-tive immunity is disabled. The advent of the first class of anti-HIV medications, reverse transcriptase inhibitors, helped slow the pro-gressive loss of immune cells by interfering with a specific enzyme (reverse transcriptase) that is necessary for replication of the HI-vi-rus. Continued progress in the treatment of HIV infection resulted from the development of new classes of drugs that inhibit other en-zymes essential to the HIV replication pro-cess, particularly protease inhibiting agents. Combinations of at least three drugs that in-clude either a protease inhibitor or a non-nu-cleoside analog reverse transcriptase inhibi-tor constitutes highly active antiretroviral

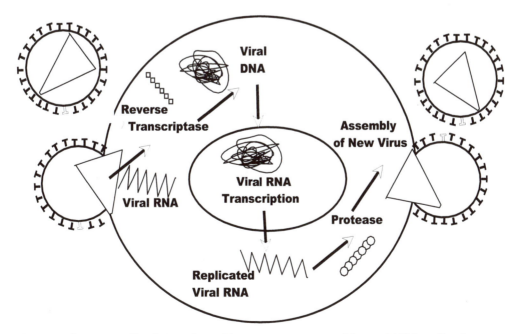

Figure 1. The HIV replication cycle and key enzymes targeted by anti-HIV medications.

therapy (HAART). Figure 1 shows the critical features of the HIV replication process and the enzymes that are targeted by various classes of HIV-targeting medications. Remarkable progress in the development of antiretroviral drugs continues as well as the development of novel approaches to treating HIV (Eron & Vernazza, 2001).

The availability of multiple drugs used in combination treatment regimens has modified the disease trajectory of HIV-AIDS. Effective multiple drug treatment regimens that include reverse transcriptase inhibitors and protease inhibitors have proven to lengthen the overall duration of treatment, delay the onset of symptoms, and extend the spacing between opportunistic illnesses (Egger, Junghans, Friis-Moller, & Lundgren, 2001). However, effective HIV treatments require strict adherence to what have been complex regimens of multiple medications (Brook et al., 2001; Chesney et al., 2000). Although changes in dosing schedules and the advent of multi-drug combination pills has eased the burden of HIV treatment, people undergoing anti-HIV therapies must achieve at least 90% medication adherence to maintain suppression of HIV replication (Stone et al., 2001). HIV treatment demands among the most strict medication adherence because the HI-virus rapidly mutates and adapts to pressures asserted by enzyme inhibitors (Larder, 2001). Rates of HIV replication and mutation translate to several thousands of generations of virus particles over a 10 year period, representing as much genetic change as humans may experience over the course of a million years (Nowak & McMichael, 1995), showing that HIV's mutation rate creates a survival advantage; the production of new genetic strains that can evade drug mechanisms and eventually overwhelm the immune system. Treatment resistant strains of HIV are transmissible to others (Hecht et al., 1998) and it is possible that as many as 50% of new U.S. HIV infections involve genetic variants of HIV that are resistant to anti-HIV medications (Richman, Bozette, Morton, Chien, Wrin, Danson, & Hellman, 2001).

Following severe suppression of the immune system, which can take between 8 and 20 years depending on immune reactions, medications, and viral strains, the body becomes susceptible to disease. AIDS is diagnosed when an HIV infected person either experiences immune suppression marked by T-helper cell count under 200 cells/mm^3 or falls ill with any one of several opportunistic illnesses. However, persons diagnosed with AIDS can experience full recovery from opportunistic illnesses and can even experience a rebound in T-helper cells above 200 cells/mm^3. Psychologically, an AIDS diagnosis is a significant event for people living with HIV because an AIDS diagnosis marks the end-stage of HIV infection. Unfortunately, as many as 40% of people who test HIV positive do so within one year of being diagnosed with AIDS, leaving little time for emotional adjustment and leaving no time for early medical intervention (Valdessari, 2001).

Psychological Assessment of People Living with HIV-AIDS

The psychological assessment of people living with HIV- AIDS must take into account the characteristics of populations most represented in the HIV epidemic — populations typically not included in measurement, standardization and normative studies. The populations most affected by AIDS overlap with persons living in poverty and therefore raise questions about how scores from many clinical instruments should be interpreted. In North America, the majority of AIDS cases have occurred among gay and bisexual men, while assessment instruments are inherently biased toward heterosexual relationships. In addition, racial and ethnic minorities account for a significant number of AIDS cases in the United States, with the relative proportion of minorities with AIDS increasing each year. Thus, instruments may yield invalid results when they do not take into account cultural differences in social structures, roles, and language. The psychological assessment of people living with HIV-AIDS must also consider the life-altering context of combination anti-HIV therapies (Rabkin & Ferrando, 1997). Another important factor in assessing people with HIV-AIDS is reading literacy. Research in urban centers suggests that as many as one in four people living with HIV-AIDS experiences significant difficulty reading and comprehending basic medical information (Kalichman et al., 2000). Reading and comprehension problems observed in HIV infected patients can prohibit the use of self-administered tests and can impede the reliability and validity of interview-administered diagnostic instruments due to limited comprehension skills.

Clinical assessments of persons with HIV infection must also consider potential cultural differences when evaluating scores against existing norms. Populations most affected by the HIV epidemic have been among the most under-represented in normative samples. Cultural and gender differences in symptom expression and sub-population base-rates of psychological distress must be considered in clinical evaluations. These issues underscore the importance of collecting convergent and divergent sources of clinical information when evaluating persons with HIV infection.

Of particular importance in people living with HIV-AIDS is screening for clinical depression and anxiety. Use of most standardized inventories for the detection of depression and anxiety may result in high false positive rates because of overlapping symptoms of emotional disorders and HIV infection. Several aspects of HIV disease must be considered when persons with HIV infection are clinically assessed for depression and anxiety. The overlapping relationships between symptoms of chronic medical illnesses, medication side effects, and physical symptoms of emotional distress that can be manifested chronic medical patients have been well recognized. HIV disease and emotional distress share several co morbid symptoms that pose problems in assessing clinical depression. For example, seven of the twenty-one items of the Beck Depression Inventory (BDI, Beck & Steer, 1993) reflect symptoms of depression that are also characteristic of HIV infection.

Overlap occurs for problems in mental concentration and decision making, negative changes in physical appearance, increased difficulty in social and occupational functioning, sleep disturbances, increased fatigue, loss of appetite, and excessive weight loss (Kalichman, Rompa, & Cage, 2000). Additional items on the BDI and other measures of depression reflect concerns about

Table 5. **Clinical responses on the Beck Depression Inventory by a person with advanced HIV disease.**

BDI Item	Scored response
I feel sad	1
I feel discouraged about the future	1
I do not feel like a failure	0
I don't enjoy things the way I used to	1
I don't feel particularly guilty	0
I don't feel I am being punished	0
I am disappointed in myself	1
I don't feel I am any worse than anybody else	0
I don't have any thought of killing myself	0
I don't cry anymore than usual	0
I get annoyed or irritated more easily than I used to	1
I am less interested in other people than I used to be	1
I make decisions about as well as I ever could	0
I am worried that I am looking old or unattractive	1
I have to push myself very hard to do anything	2
I don't sleep as well as I used to	1
I get tired from doing almost nothing	2
My appetite is not as good as it used to be	1
I have lost more than 10 pounds	2
I am worried about physical problems such as aches and pains; or upset stomach; or constipation	1
I am less interested in sex than I used to be	1

Note: Items in italics overlap with HIV-related symptoms.

physical health and physical attractiveness, declining sexual interests, and excessive guilt, all of which may be a part of HIV-AIDS-related experiences. Table 5 presents a clinical case example of a BDI obtained from a person with advanced HIV infection, illustrating the divergence of clinical responses among cognitive and affective symptoms in contrast to somatic symptoms. This individual's score on the BDI was 17, indicating mild depression, with nearly two-thirds of the total depression score in this case attributable to somatic symptoms that overlap with HIV disease.

Overlapping symptoms of depression and HIV infection occur in other common depression assessment instruments, such as the Centers for Epidemiological Studies Depression Scale (CESD, Radloff, 1977). In factor analytic studies of BDI and CESD scores with independent measures of mental health and HIV disease-related measures, Kalichman et al. (2000) found that the somatic depression symptoms of the BDI and the CESD were most closely associated with an index of HIV symptoms. In contrast, negative affective and negative cognition components of the BDI and CESD corresponded with independent measures of pessimistic beliefs, borderline personality, obsessive compulsive thinking, and trait-anxiety. Assessing depression in people living with HIV-AIDS is therefore most accurate when co morbid physical symptoms are accounted for.

Similar problems occur when assessing anxiety. The Trait Anxiety Inventory, for example, includes items that reflect fatigue and cognitive confusion and the Hamilton Rating Scale for Anxiety includes items related to autonomic reactivity, including gastrointestinal distress and fatigue, symptoms that may also be indicative of progressing HIV infection. Screening for depression and anxiety in HIV positive persons should therefore use instruments that do not include physical symptoms as benchmarks for depression and anxiety such as Hospital Anxiety and Depression Scale (Zigmond & Snaith, 1983).

The neuropsychological assessment of people with HIV-AIDS is a common referral request because of the potential disruptions

in neuropsychological functioning that can occur with HIV infection. Mild to moderate cognitive, affective, and motor disturbances can occur early in HIV infection, with individuals at later stages of AIDS experiencing more such symptoms. Subtle signs of cogni-

Table 6. **Neuropsychological test battery recommended by Butters et al. (1990).**

Cognitive Function	Assessment Instrument
Premorbid intelligence	* WAIS-R Vocabulary National Adult Reading Test
Attention	WMS-R Digit Span * WMS-R Visual Span
Processing Speed	Sternberg Search Task Simple and Choice Reaction Time * Paced Auditory Serial Addition Test
Memory	* California Verbal Learning Test Working Memory Test Modified Visual Reproduction Test
Abstraction	Category Test Trails Making Test A and B
Language	Boston Naming Test Letter and Category Fluency Test
Visual Spatial Ability	Embedded Figures Test Money's Standardized Road-Map Test of Direction Sense Digit Symbol Substitution
Construction Ability	Block Design Test Tactile Performance Test
Motor Abilities	Grooved Pegboard Finger Tapping Test Grip Strength
Psychological Distress	Diagnostic Interview Schedule * Hamilton Depression Rating Scale * State-Trait Anxiety Inventory Mini-Mental Status Examination

Note: WMS-R = Wechsler Memory Scale – Revised; WAIS-R = Wechsler Adult Intelligence Scale – Revised, * recommended tests for an abbreviated battery.

tive dysfunction that appear earlier in the course of disease can include difficulty-maintaining concentration, memory problems, and motor disturbances, including slowing of arm, leg, and eye movements (Sande & Volberding, 2000). Demyelinating neuropathologies can also occur early in infection, resulting in impaired sensory and motor functioning (Price, 2000). Neurological disease is usually diagnosed when symptoms become moderate to severe and disrupt occupational, basic self-care, intellectual, social, or motor functioning. The toxic effects of HIV infection of the brain noted earlier can cause a cascade of neurological problems. Clinical symptoms of HIV are almost always caused by diffuse brain damage rather than focal lesions (Price, 2000). Some degree of neurological impact occurs in as many as 90% of HIV-infected individuals, although functional impairment ranges from none to profound. The assessment of neurological disturbances requires rather comprehensive batteries to differentiate between potential effects of HIV from opportunistic illnesses, pre-morbid brain damage resulting from trauma, toxic exposures, and drug abuse. Table 6 presents the tests included in a long established battery for assessing neuropsychological functioning in people living with HIV-AIDS (Butters et al., 1990). Newer editions and revisions of recommended tests should be substituted when available. In addition, tests that are suggested for use in an abbreviated battery are marked in Table 6.

Psychological Interventions for People Living with HIV-AIDS

Several approaches to the psychological treatment of people living with HIV-AIDS have been described, including individual, couples, and group therapies (see Kalichman, 1998 for a review of psychotherapies for people living with HIV-AIDS). Below we briefly overview these most common approaches.

Individual Psychotherapy

Research has suggested that individual counseling and psychotherapy can be effective in treating depression in HIV infected persons. Markowitz et al. (1995) provided evidence for the effects of interpersonal psychotherapy on depression in people living with HIV infection. Depressed clients explored affectively laden life situations and reframed these difficulties into one of four problem areas: grief, role dispute, role transition, or interpersonal deficits. Focusing on the here and now, therapists highlighted the client's goals and strategies for achieving these goals. The study demonstrated reductions in depression among treated clients relative to a supportive psychotherapy control condition. Thus, mental health counseling and therapy conducted in both group and individual sessions have demonstrated positive outcomes with people living with HIV-AIDS. These services should therefore be considered the treatments of choice for people living with HIV infection and suffering from psychological distress, particularly when antidepressant and anti-anxiety medications interact with antiretroviral medications. Thus, individual psychotherapy offers a viable means of delivering mental health services to some HIV infected persons.

Couples Counseling

The issues confronting couples affected by AIDS and counseling models adapted for couples where at least one partner is HIV positive have been described (Remien, Carballo-Dieguez, & Wagner, 1995). Kain (1996), for example, identified themes that arise in counseling HIV affected couples. Of particular concern are issues facing couples where one partner is HIV positive and the other is HIV negative, referred to as HIV serodiscordant couples. The very nature of an HIV serodiscordant relationship can lead to both partners feeling isolated and misunderstood. Fear of HIV transmission within the relationship, either through sexual contact or perhaps irrational fears of casual contagion, impedes intimacy in serodiscordant relationships. Additional fears that both partners may experience include fear of dependency, loss, or abandonment. The following case illustrates some of the challenges faced in conducting couples counseling with HIV serodiscordant partners.

Case example

Mark and Cynthia were in their mid-twenties, both were white, and of lower-to-middle incomes. They had been friends since their late teens and only started dating after graduating high school. Mark and Cynthia had been dating for four years and living together as a couple for a little over two years. They had recently planned to marry. Mark worked in food services and Cynthia was a day care worker. For as long as they knew each other Mark and Cynthia were active and enjoyed good health. But Mark became sick and developed a chronic cough. His breathing and fever became increasingly worse and he eventually had to be hospitalized for a bronchial pneumonia that would not respond to antibiotics. While Mark was in the hospital lab tests showed that he was severely immune impaired. His immune system impairment drew his doctor's attention and prompted him to test Mark for HIV. The test was positive and Mark was subsequently diagnosed simultaneously with HIV infection and AIDS. Mark was not surprised that he was HIV positive. He had been sexually involved with men in his late teens and he had tried injecting heroin with friends. In fear of losing his relationship with Cynthia, Mark had never shared this history with Cynthia or nearly anyone else.

Despite his lack of surprise, Mark was emotionally devastated when he learned his HIV test results and felt that he had no one to turn to except Cynthia. But Cynthia did not react sympathetically. She recognized that she was now at risk for HIV and immediately sought the support of her friends and family. She had many people to provide emotional support, but their pressure for her to leave Mark, now referred to as the 'man who gave her AIDS', also stressed her. Cynthia had never even considered the possibility that she could be exposed to HIV and had never been tested. Now, however, Cynthia did get tested and she tested HIV positive. Cynthia was devastated. Although Cynthia felt betrayed by Mark for not warning her of his past risks, she also felt badly for the man she loved

because he had gotten so ill so quickly and she wanted to care for him. These conflicted feelings were very difficult for Cynthia to reconcile. Nevertheless, Cynthia was committed to staying with Mark, in part because she loved him, and in part because she felt she now had no options. Cynthia believed that no other man would now have her.

HIV-AIDS changed everything about Mark and Cynthia's relationship. Mark was burdened by guilt for not having owned the truths of his past and sharing them with Cynthia. He also felt ashamed that he ha never been tested for HIV, removing any chance that he could have acted to protect Cynthia from the virus. Mark blamed himself for Cynthia contracting HIV. And Cynthia often reminded Mark about her HIV status, frequently acting out her anger with sarcastic remarks and temper outbursts. Mark's HIV infection advanced despite his taking anti-HIV medications and he became disabled and unable to work, with financial concerns exerting added stress in the relationship. Although Cynthia continued to work at the day care center, she became increasingly involved in Mark's medical care.

In counseling, Mark and Cynthia identified a mutual need to reconcile the events surrounding their discovery of HIV and the toll it has taken on their relationship. They specifically wanted to heal their guilt, sense of betrayal, and anger. Both Mark and Cynthia were open and honest and willing to do the hard work often demanded in couples counseling. Consistent with common issues identified by Kain (1996) in his work with HIV positive couples, it was important for Mark work through his feelings of blame associated with being the source of Cynthia's HIV infection. Cynthia dealt with her concerns about Mark's advancing illness and the likelihood that she would survive him. She also worked through issues related to her role as Mark's primary caregiver. Couples counseling occurred over the course of four months with several signs of success, including improved communication, relationship satisfaction, and stability.

Group Therapies

The most extensively tested models of mental health interventions for people living with HIV infection have been based on cognitive-behavioral therapy approaches and have been delivered in group settings. Coates, McKusick, Kuno, and Stites (1989) offer an early example of these interventions. In this study, group therapy consisted of eight 2-hour weekly sessions and emphasized instruction in systematic relaxation, health habit change such as smoking and alcohol reduction, increasing rest and exercise, and other stress-management skills. Coates et al. reported successful outcomes in improved mental health benefits among the group participants. Another treatment approached based on cognitive-behavioral therapy was tested by Antoni et al. (1991). This group intervention included the following: behavioral stress management, relaxation skills training, self-monitoring of environmental stressors, stress reappraisal, active coping, enhancing self-efficacy, and expanding social networks. This multi-component cognitive-behavioral-stress-management (CBSM) model produced significant reductions in emotional distress among men who tested HIV positive. Other variations on the CBSM group intervention for people living with HIV-AIDS have shown successful outcomes in subsequent studies by Antoni and his University of Miami colleagues (e. g., Lutgendorf et al., 1997) as well as other research groups (e. g., Eller, 1995; Miller & Cohen, 2001).

Kelly et al. (1993) also tested an intensive cognitive-behavioral therapy group for depressed HIV-positive clients. In a three condition study, Kelly et al. (1993) randomly assigned 68 HIV-positive (non-AIDS) men with heightened depressed mood to receive either: (a) cognitive-behavioral treatment group; (b) social support group; or (c) individual psychotherapy. As described by Kelly et al., the cognitive-behavioral groups focused on the use of cognitive and behavior strategies to reduce maladaptive anxiety and depression. Each session had a behavioral or skill training theme and the sessions involved teaching participants the skill, group discussion of potential uses and benefits of the skill, and weekly review of success in implementation. Skill areas included modification of cognitions that exacerbate anxiety or depression, progressive muscle relaxation, controlled relaxation, disclosure of serostatus and safer sex practices if sexually active, and establishment of a network of socially supportive relationships. Participant questions, concerns, and problems in implementation of change were handled from a cognitive problem-solving perspective. Most sessions also included at-home practice assignments. Results of the study showed that both group interventions positively affected group members relative to the individual therapy control condition. However, the social support group appeared to have the greatest benefit over a 3-month follow-up period. Eighty-six percent of the social support group participants demonstrated clinically significant improvement on an index of distress severity, whereas two thirds of the comparison condition showed clinical deterioration, regressing below baseline levels. Although members of the cognitive-behavioral group demonstrated a pattern of clinical change that was intermediate between the social support groups and the control condition, cognitive-behavioral group participants did decrease their use of illicit substances to a greater degree than the other two groups.

Coping effectiveness training is another group-based cognitive behavioral intervention approach that emphasizes fitting coping strategies to specific problem situations. Chesney, Folkman, and Chambers (1996) described coping effectiveness training that consisted of ten 90-minute sessions, with an additional day long-retreat between the fourth and fifth sessions. The training included six central elements: (a) appraisal of stressful situations; (b) problem and emotion focused coping; (c) determining the fit between coping strategies and controllable versus uncontrollable stressful situations; (d) maximizing use of social support; (e) training in maintenance of stress reduction through effective coping; and (f) effectively using a series of workbook exercises. The training emphasizes both problem-focused and adaptive emotion-focused coping strategies with an attempt to fit specific coping strategies to specific situations. Thus, coping effectiveness training offers a specific and well-defined approach to enhancing coping capacities that can be applied across a variety of stressful situations. Similar cognitive-behavioral intervention elements have demonstrated effectiveness with adolescents whose parents are HIV positive (Rotheram-Borus, Stein, & Lin, 2001).

Case example

The goal of the group therapy was to reduce distress and increase adaptive coping among people with HIV infection who are also experiencing with AIDS-related bereavement. The intervention approach is based on the cognitive theory of stress and coping (Lazarus & Folkman, 1984) and supportive approaches to bereavement (Sikkema et al., 1995). The group was co-led by female therapists, experienced in issues related to HIV/AIDS, and was conducted on a weekly basis over three months.

Group members

Ethel is a 48-year-old, African American with a longstanding history of alcohol and substance abuse. Her primary loss was her cousin, with whom she was very close emotionally, but also introduced to the "drug scene" and shared injection equipment. She blames herself for her cousin's death, as does her family. Ethel has five children, from who she is estranged. She currently lives with a physically abusive male partner and had attempted suicide just prior to enrolling in the group program.

Cynthia is a 42-year-old, college-educated white woman who lost her husband two years ago, and recently lost her son to suicide following the progression of a mental illness. She experiences depressive episodes, guilt, and a deep sense of loss. Cynthia currently lives with her elderly parents, to whom she has not disclosed her HIV status.

Dana is a 28-year-old Latina who lost her husband within the past year. She has a longstanding history of substance use, and credits her husband with helping her to get off drugs and improve her life. He was HIV positive when they met, but she attributes her infection to her own previous injection drug use. They moved from her home of origin as his disease progressed, as he wanted to be closer to his family. Dana now finds herself feeling alone and disconnected from her previous family and social support system, and has a strong desire to return to her home. She previously lost custody of her daughter, and has not been in touch with her for several years.

Gloria is a 37-year-old African-American woman, who recently completed a drug rehabilitation program and is transitioning to independent living. She lost her fiancé and is currently in a relationship with an emotionally and physically abusive man she met through drug treatment. Gloria lost custody of her two young children, but has recently obtained visitation rights, as they live with her ex-husband. She is in regular contact with and seeking to establish a better relationship with them. Gloria was recently hospitalized and learned that her physical condition is deteriorating.

Mary is a 33-year-old white woman, with advanced HIV disease and other debilitating health problems. She is a strong advocate of her own health care and actively utilizes alternative forms of medicine (e. g., acupuncture, hypnosis). Mary's parents' currently have custody of her two children, one of whom is HIV positive, and she is in a hostile legal battle with them as she wants to regain custody, though her parents are seeking permanent guardianship.

Janine is a 38-year-old African American woman, with a longstanding history of substance abuse, violence, and incarceration. She has four children, two in foster care and two in the custody of her mother. Janine has frequent interaction with two of her daughters, both teenagers, and they are a frequent source of her anger and occasional rage. Janine lost a brother to AIDS, and has three others substance abusing siblings. They commonly shared injection equipment, and all are HIV positive.

Diane is a 41-year-old white woman, infected by her previous husband, who has since died. She is quite attractive, and works hard to present herself in a positive light. She has a son in college and is currently living with a verbally abusive husband, who abuses alcohol. Diane feels trapped in the relationship, because he provides for her and her son. She has a history of depression and avoidance of dealing with issues of conflict. Diane hopes to become independent, but has yet been able to do so.

While few research studies have targeted women in testing mental health interventions, peer-led support groups are frequently offered to women through community-based organizations. The following case description illustrates issues that women with HIV infection commonly face. The case description is accurate with respect to clinical details, with identifiable characteristics altered to protect the client's identity.

Intervention Content and Process. The focus of the initial group sessions was on the development of social support and group cohesion. All group members were encouraged to share their loss history and the stressors experienced related to HIV/AIDS, and AIDS-related loss. A key part of the initial process was the identification and expression of emotions, such as: sadness, depression, anger, guilt, helplessness, frustration, loneliness, abandonment and resentment. Group members were asked to identify stressors and coping difficulties related to HIV/AIDS and the losses they had experienced. While sometimes a challenge, group members were assisted in identifying specific stressors and the ways in which they currently coped, whether adaptive or maladaptive. Types of stressors the women experienced included: intense sadness and despair, with occasionally immobilizing grief; unpredictability of abusive partner's behavior; estrangement from or conflicted relationships with children, due primarily to consequences of substance abuse or HIV disease; and, loneliness and inability to initiate new relationships. Group members then identified current coping strategies, and set goals for achieving more adaptive way of coping. A stress and coping model (Folkman et al, 1991) was presented to group members, including an approach for determining the difference between emotion-focused and problem-focused way of coping, and the selection of an appropriate goal for coping with HIV and loss. A visual representation of this model was distributed to group members, to be used as a prompt when experiencing stressful situations outside of the group setting. The remainder of the group intervention was focused on the implementation of selected coping strategies, appraisal of their impact on distress, and modification of goals and coping strategies to most effectively cope with ongoing stressors experienced throughout the group treatment. Since the intervention was time-limited, the goal was for group members to enhance adaptive coping skills specific to selected stressors, and develop the ability to utilize this approach for coping with stress and loss when it was experienced in the future.

The diversity and support of the group was critical in developing group cohesion and generating adaptive coping strategies to complex situations. However, this type of group intervention was challenging to conduct, due to a variety of reasons. The task of balancing the issues related to loss and bereavement with those encountered by living with HIV/AIDS was at times difficult. This is further complicated by the daily life stressors encountered by some of the women in the group, including domestic violence, homelessness, poverty, child care, and legal issues related to child custody. These stressors are in addition to those faced to due HIV disease, such as medication side effects and navigating the health care and social service systems. Psychiatric co morbidity frequently added another layer to the complexity of the group process, with the majority of participants experiencing mood or anxiety disorders, substance abuse or dependence, and characteristics of personality disorders.

However, often those in greatest need have a strong motivation to decrease distress and improve coping. A few success stories are worth noting. Ethel faced additional stressors during the course of the group, including the loss of her apartment in a fire and continued harassment and abuse from her partner. The importance of identifying a specific stressor and attempting a more adaptive way of coping was the critical element in her use of the coping model. Rather than returning to substance use when she was overwhelmed by the loss of her apartment, she sought help from a social service agency in finding her temporary shelter. Her resulting increase in self-confidence then empowered her to resist the pressures of her abusive partner, and end the relationship. In addition, with the support of the group, she was able to accept the loss of her cousin and work through the guilt she felt in relation to her death. Dana was able to share her feelings of loneliness and grief related to her husband's death, and accept that it was important to her own well-being to return to her own family of origin, and care for her parents as well as herself. She was developing a moving plan at the close of the group intervention. Gloria was able to stay off drugs throughout the duration of the group therapy. Based on what she learned from the group about sexually transmitted diseases, she attempted to negotiate condom use with her current partner. Unfortunately, he beat her up for asking him to use condoms and implying that he could not be trusted. This experience, combined with knowledge of her disease progression, led Gloria to end their relationship, and she was also able to establish consistent visitations with her children.

Ethical and Professional Issues. A number of ethical and professional issues surfaced throughout the group therapy. As described above, two women reported experiencing partner violence and risk of violence toward others had to be evaluated in one instance. One participant who had difficulties with anger management also indicated that she had access to a gun, and a plan for removing the firearm from her home was successfully implemented. One woman requested that the group therapists support her in a legal battle for custody of her children. We decided to refer her to our consultant psychiatrist for a full psychiatric evaluation, which was presented by the psychiatrist as part of the court case. Lastly, one woman died suddenly, within one week after completion of the group therapy. The therapists informed all group members of her passing, and offered follow up support, if needed.

In summary, coping with HIV disease in combination with AIDS-related loss and bereavement is a challenge for women with HIV/AIDS, especially in the face of daily life stressors such as substance use and psychiatric co morbidity, family concerns, poverty, and disease progression. Given the multitude of these losses and the complexity of the women's lives, it is also imperative that the therapist recognizes that working with this population requires awareness of the potential personal impact and the need to maintain appropriate professional boundaries, while providing empathy and support.

Conclusions

Not so long ago clinical health psychologists did not come into contact with AIDS patients. Whether working on psychiatric services, providing consultation to general medical services, or treating behavioral disorders, the sheer limits to the epidemiology of HIV insulated all but only a few psychologists from the devastating effects AIDS. Today AIDS is commonly encountered in most every urban medical center. Clinical health psychologists play integral roles in the interdisciplinary care of people living with HIV infection from its onset which is determined almost entirely by the practice of sexual and drug use behaviors, to the decision to seek diagnostic testing, to the emotional adjustment to living with a chronic illness, to adhering to complex medication regimens, to preparing for end of life. For the clinical health psychologist working in AIDS there is always something new. AIDS is a dynamic problem; everything about AIDS is always changing. The virus itself mutates, the social conditions surrounding AIDS change, the people affected by AIDS change, and the strategies necessary to effectively intervene must change. AIDS therefore challenges to adapt and develop in our efforts to prevent new HIV infections and assist those living and coping with HIV-AIDS.

Author Notes

Preparation of this chapter was supported by funding from the National Institute of Mental Health Grants R01 MH63666 and R01 MH/NR 62287. We thank Wendy L. Nelson for generously allowing us to adapt the section on the human immune system from excellent chapter in the previous edition of this book.

Correspondence should be addressed to Seth C. Kalichman, Department of Psychology, University of Connecticut, Storrs, CT 06269, Phone 860 208-3706, Fax 860 486-4876, e-mail seth.k@uconn.edu

References

Antoni, M.H., Baggett, L., Ironson, G., LaPerriere, A., August, S., Klimas, N., Schneiderman, N., & Fletcher, M.A. (1991). Cognitive-behavioral stress management intervention buffers distress responses and immunologic changes following notification of HIV-1 seropositivity. *Journal of Consulting and Clinical Psychology, 59*, 906–915.

Beck, A.T., & Steer, R.A. (1993). *BDI: Beck Depression Inventory manual.* New York: Psychological Corporation.

Brook, M.G., Dale, A., Tomlinson, D., Waterworth, C., Daniels, D., & Forster, G. (2001). Adherence to highly active antiretroviral therapy in the real world: Experience of twelve English HIV units. *AIDS Patient Care and STDs, 15*, 491–494.

Butters, N., Grant, I., Haxby, J., Judd, L.L., Martin, A., McClelland, J., Pequegnat, W., Schacter, D., & Stover, E. (1990). Assessment of AIDS-related cognitive changes: Recommendations of the NIMH workshop on neuropsychological assessment approaches. *Journal of Clinical and Experimental Neuropsychology, 12*, 963–978.

Chesney, M., Folkman, S., & Chambers, D. (1996). Coping effectiveness training for men living with HIV: preliminary findings. *International Journal of STD & AIDS, 7*(Suppl 2), 75–82.

Chesney, M.A., Ickovics, J., Chambers, D., Gifford, A., Neidig, J., Zwickl, B., Wu, W. et al. (2000). Self-reported adherence to antiretroviral medications among participants in HIV clinical trials: The AACTG adherence instruments. *AIDS Care, 12*, 255–266.

Coates, T., McKusick, L., Kuno, R., & Stites, D. (1989). Stress reduction training changed number of sexual partners but not immune function in men with HIV. *American Journal of Public Health, 79*, 885–886.

Eller, L.S. (1995). Effects of two cognitive-behavioral interventions on immunity and symptoms in persons with HIV. *Annals of Behavioral Medicine, 17*, 339–348.

Eron, J.J. & Vernazza, P. (2001). Alternative strategies for anti-HIV treatment. *AIDS, 15*(suppl), S161–S169.

Fauci, A.S. (1986). Current issues in developing a strategy for dealing with the acquired immunodeficiency syndrome. *Proceedings of the National Academy of Sciences, 83.*

Fauci, A.S. (1988). The human immunodeficiency virus: Infectivity and mechanisms of pathogenesis. *Science, 239*, 617–622.

Fauci, A.S., Macher, A.M., Longo, D.L., Lane, H.C., Rook, A.H., Masur, H., & Gelmann, E.P. (1984). Acquired immunodeficiency syndrome: Epidemiologic, clinical, immunologic, and therapeutic considerations. *Annals of Internal Medicine, 100*, 92–06.

Kain, C. (1996). *Positive: HIV affirmative counseling.* Alexandria, VA: American Counseling Association.

Kalichman, S.C. (1998). *Understanding AIDS: Advances in treatment and research* (2nd edition). Washington, DC: American Psychological Association.

Kalichman, S.C., Rompa, D., & Cage, M. (2000). Distinguishing between overlapping somatic symptoms of depression and HIV disease in people living with HIV-AIDS. *Journal of Nervous and Mental Diseases, 188*, 662–670.

Kalichman, S.C., Benotsch, E., Suarez, T., Catz, S., & Miller, J. (2000). Health Literacy and Health-Related Knowledge Among Men and Women Living with HIV-AIDS, *American Journal of Preventive Medicine, 18*, 325–331.

Kelly, J., Murphy, D., Bahr, G., Kalichman, S., Morgan, M., Stevenson, L., Koob, J., Brasfield, T., & Bernstein, B. (1993). Outcome of cognitive-behavioral and support group brief therapies for depressed persons diagnosed with HIV infection. *American Journal of Psychiatry, 150*, 1679–1686.

Larder, B. (2001). Mechanisms of HIV-1 drug resistance. *AIDS, 15*(suppl), S27–S34.

Lazarus, R.S., & Folkman, S. (1984). *Stress, appraisal, and coping.* New York: Springer-Verlag.

Lutgendorf, S.K., Antoni, M.H., Ironson, G., Klimas, N., Kumar, M., Starr, K., McCabe, P., Cleven, K., Fletcher, M.A., & Schneiderman, N. (1997). Cognitive-behavioral stress management decreases dysphoric mood and herpes simplex virus-type 2 antibody titers in symptomatic HIV-seropositive gay men. *Journal of Consulting and Clinical Psychology, 65*, 31–43.

Markowitz, J.C., Klerman, G.L., Clougherty, K.F., Spielman, L A., Jacobsberg, L.B., Fishman, B., Frances, A.J., Kocsis, J.H., & Perry, S.W. (1995). Individual psychotherapies for depressed HIV-positive patients. *American Journal of Psychiatry,* *152,* 1504–1509.

Miller, G.E. & Cohen, S. (2001). Psychological interventions an the immune system: A Met-Analytic Review and critique. *Psychological Bulletin,* *20,* 47–63.

Nowak, M.A., & McMichael, A.J. (1995). How HIV defeats the immune system. *Scientific American,* *8,* 58–65.

Palacio, H., Shiboski, C., Yelin, E., Hessol, N., & Greenblatt, R. (1999). Access to and utilization of primary care services among HIV-infected women. *JAIDS, 21,* 293–300.

Price, R.W. (2000). Management of the neurologic complications of HIV-1 infection and AIDS. In M.A. Sande & P.A. Volberding, *The medical management of AIDS* (6th ed.). Philadelphia: W.B. Saunders.

Rabkin, J.G., & Ferrando, S. (1997). A 'second life' agenda: Psychiatric research issues raised by protease inhibitor treatments for people with human immunodeficiency virus or the acquired immunodeficiency syndrome. *Archives of General Psychiatry, 54,* 1049–1053.

Radloff, L.S. (1977). The CES-D Scale: A self-report depression scale for research in the general population. *Applied Psych Measurement, 1,* 385–401.

Remien, R.H., Carballo-Dieguez, A., & Wagner, G. (1995). Intimacy and sexual behavior in sero-discordant male couples. *AIDS Care, 7,* 429–438.

Rotheram-Borus, M.J., Stein, J.A., & Lin, Y.Y. (2001). Impact of parent death and an intervention on the adjustment of adolescents whose parents have HIV/AIDS. *Journal of Consulting and Clinical Psychology, 69,* 763–773.

Sande, M.A. & Volberding, P.A. (2000). *The medical management of AIDS* (6th edition). Philadelphia: W.B. Saunders.

Shapiro, M.F., Morton, S., McCaffrey, D., Senterfitt, W., Fleishman, J., Perlman, J., Athey, L., Keesey, J., Goldman, D., Berry, S., & Bozzette, S. (1999). Variations in the care of HIV-infected adults in the United States: Results from the HIV Cost and Service Utilizations Study. *JAMA,* *281,* 2305–2315.

Schoub, B.D. (1993). *AIDS & HIV in perspective.* New York: Cambridge University Press.

Sikkema, K.J., Kalichman, S.C., Kelly, J.A., & Koob, J.J. (1995). Group intervention to improve coping with AIDS-related bereavement: Model development and an illustrative clinical example. *AIDS Care, 7,* 463–475.

Soto-Ramirez, L., Renjifo, B., McLane, M., Marlink, R., O'Hara, C., Sutthent, R., Wasi, C., Vithayasai, P., Vithayasai, V., Apichartpiyakul, C., Auewarakul, P., Cruz, V., Chui, D., Osathanondh, R., Mayer, K., Lee, T., & Essex, M. (1996). HIV-1 langerhans cell tropism associated with heterosexual transmission of HIV. *Science, 271,* 1291–1293.

Spielberger, C.D., Gorsuch, R., Lushene, P., Crane, P., Jacobs, G., & Warden, T. (1983). *Manual for the State-Trait Anxiety Inventory.* Palo Alto, CA: Consulting Psychologists Press.

Stone, V., Hogan, J., Schuman, P., Rompalo, A.M., Howard, A., Korkontzelou, C., & Smith, D. (2001). Antiretroviral regimen complexity, self-reported adherence, and HIV patients' understanding of their regimens: Survey of women in the HER Study. *Journal of Acquired Immune Deficiency Syndromes, 28,* 124–131.

Valdessari, R. (2001). HIV Testing and Counseling and HIV Prevention. National HIV Prevention Conference, Atlanta, GA.

Zigmond, A.S., & Snaith, R.P. (1983). The Hospital Anxiety and Depression Scale. *Acta Psychiatrica Scandinavica, 67,* 361–370.

David C. Mohr & Darcy Cox

10

Multiple Sclerosis

This chapter will examine the clinical health psychologist's role in the care of patients with multiple sclerosis (MS). First, the disease will be described, followed by a discussion of psychological and neuropsychological assessment, a review of the empirical literature of the treatment of psychological disorders in MS, and finally a discussion of issues of caregiving.

Natural History

MS is a chronic autoimmune disease in which the myelin sheath surrounding the axons of nerve cells in the central nervous system (CNS) becomes damaged. The damaged areas are referred to as *lesions* or *plaques*. Demyelination associated with MS diminishes the cell's ability to transmit information (Raine, 1990), which can result in a wide variety of physical problems. Some of the more common impairments include numbness and tingling in the limbs, loss of function or sensation in the limbs, spasticity, pain, sexual dysfunction, loss of balance, visual impairment or blindness, debilitating physical fatigue and weakness, cognitive impairment, and mood disturbance including depression or euphoria. While symptoms can be quite severe, patients' lives are usually not substantially shortened (Goodkin, 1992; Mohr & Cox, 2001). MS affects approximately 350,000 people in the United States (Anderson et al., 1992), and, as is common in autoimmune diseases, has about twice the prevalence in women compared to men.

Little is known about the etiology of MS. Several lines of evidence suggest a genetic susceptibility is involved. MS is more common in Caucasians but occurs more rarely in native Africans, Asians, or Native Americans, even when they live in the same community (Sibley, Poser & Alter, 1989). Risk of developing the disease is 2–3% if the individual has an immediate relative with MS. There is also support for environmental agents. For example, the further north one spends their childhood, the greater the likelihood of developing MS as an adult. This has been interpreted as evidence for a virus as a causal factor. In summary, while we do not yet understand the origins of MS, it does appear to have a complex etiology, involving numerous factors.

The course of MS can vary considerably from patient to patient. There are a number MS disease types which are characterized by variations in the symptom course (Lublin & Reingold, 1996). Approximately 10–15% of all patients initially have a *benign course*, with little disease activity. However, over the course of years, a number of these patients go on to develop one of the three most common disease presentations. Between 65–70% have a *relapsing-remitting* course marked by periodic disease exacerbations (sudden increases in the number and/or intensity of symptoms which last for at least 24 hours and can persist up to several months). Between exacerbations, patients can return to their baseline levels of functioning, or experience some residual symptoms. Roughly half of patients with an initial relapsing-remitting course will then transition into a *secondary-progressive* course, which is characterized by a steady worsening of symptoms, that may or may not also include exacerbations. Approximately 10-15% of patients have a *primary progressive* course in which there is a steady worsening of symptoms with no exacerbations. The *relapsing-progressive* course, which affects fewer than 5% of patients, begins with progression and is later accompanied by exacerbations. A *malignant* course, characterized by rapid deterioration resulting in death, is very rare.

Medical Intervention

Until the last decade, neurologists were unable to slow the course of the disease and were only able to treat the symptoms. At that time, MS was one of the most disabilitating neurological diseases, with 81% of all patients out of the workforce (U.S. Bureau of the Census, 1982). While the risk of permanent disability is still high for MS patients, there are now a number of medications which slow the progression of the disease and reduce the number of exacerbations. Interferons, chemotherapy agents, and other medications can all slow the course of the disease and preserve function. The disease is also still treated symptomatically. Exacerbations are treated with oral or intravenous corticosteroids, which greatly reduce the severity and duration of the exacerbation. The medications used to treat MS, while changing the course of the disease and reducing the risk of permanent disability, can produce significant side effects which can prove challenging to patients as well. The experience of patients with MS has changed significantly over the last two decades, and is likely to continue to change rapidly over the next several as our understanding of genetics, autoimmunity, and psychoneuroimmunology lead to new treatments. These changes will impact the psychological experience of patients living with MS.

Neuropsychological Assessment

A primary assessment referral to psychologists for MS patients is for neuropsychological assessment. Neuropsychological problems in MS can best be characterized as heterogeneous (Ryan, Clark, Klonoff, Li, & Paty, 1996), with no single pattern of deficits. Many MS patients exhibit a pattern of deficits characterized as a *subcortical dementia* (Cummings, 1986). Subcortical dementia has several specific features, including memory retrieval failure with intact coding and storage, impaired conceptual-reasoning skills within a near normal level of intellectual functioning, slowed information-processing time, the absence of aphasia, and personality disturbance characterized by apathy, depression, or euphoria (Rao, 1986). However, other patients showing memory problems associated with encoding are also frequently seen. Word-finding deficits and problems with verbal fluency are also seen, both with and without associated dysarthria (Basso, Beason-Hazan, Lynn, Rammohan, & Bornstein, 1996; Rovaris et al., 1998; Thornton & Raz, 1997). Visual-spatial encoding and memory, visuoperceptive organization, and visual-spatial construction can also be impacted (DeLuca, Barbieri-Berger, & Johnson, 1994). Executive functioning, defined as patients' ability to reason, sequence, problem-solve, and shift sets can also be impacted, either in conjunction with memory deficits or in the context of an intact memory (Beatty & Monson, 1994; Foong et al., 1997: Zakzanis, 2000 #809). The most common neuropsychological symptoms are deficits in processing speed and attention (Brassington & Marsh, 1998; Grant, McDonald, & Trimble, 1989b; Kail, 1998; Kujala, Portin, Revonsuo, & Ruutiainen, 1995; Zakzanis, 2000). While cognitive dysfunction in MS can meet the diagnostic criteria for Dementia due to MS (severe, disability deficits in memory and at least one other area of functioning), most patients with deficits better fit the criteria characterized as a Cognitive Disorder NOS due to MS (American Psychiatric Association, 1994).

Table 1. Neuropsychological functioning and assessment in patients with multiple sclerosis.

Area of Neuropsychological Function and Common Assessment Instruments	Common Findings Among MS patients
Attention and Concentration - Digit Span & Visual Memory Span (Wechsler Memory Scale – Revised; Wechsler, 1987) - Stroop Test, (Golden, 1978)	MS patients usually do not show deficits in attention and concentration to simple tasks (e. g., digits forwards) but often show deficits on more complex tasks (e. g., digits backwards, or Stroop; Rao et al., 1991)
Speed of Information Processing - Symbol Digit Modalities Test (Smith, 1973)	Cognitive slowing is one of the most common deficits seen in MS (Beatty et al., 1989)
Language - Boston Naming Test (Kaplan et al., 1983) - Controlled Oral Word Association Test (Benton & Hamsher, 1989)	While aphasia, alexia and agraphia are rare, patients with MS frequently show word impairments on tests of confrontation naming (Beatty et al., 1988) but rarely show overt word finding problems in ordinary conversation.
Visual Functioning - Judgment of Line Orientation (Benton et al., 1983) - Hooper Visual Organization Test (Hooper, 1958)	MS patients may show deficits in judgment of line orientation, as well as facial recognition and discrimination of forms, but tend to retain the ability to perform mental construction tasks (Rao et al., 1991)
Memory - California Verbal Learning Test (Delis et al., 1987) - Wechsler Memory Scale–Revised (Wechsler, 1987) - 7/24 Spatial Recall Test (Rao et al., 1991)	While true amnestic disorders are less common, MS patients suffer a variety of memory difficulties. Most commonly MS patients show fewer deficits in perceiving and storing information, but have significant difficulties retrieving the information. Implicit or procedural memory appears to be preserved in MS (Rao, 1990).
Problem Solving - Wisconsin Card Sorting Test (Heaton, 1981) - Standard Raven Progressive Matrices (Raven, 1960) - Booklet Category Test (DeFilippis & McCampbell, 1979)	Many patients show a loss in problem solving abilities across many different types of tasks. Problems solving problems are often related to a pattern of perseverative responding despite negative feedback about errors (Rao, 1990; Rao et al., 1991).

Table 1 displays the types of cognitive impairments seen in MS and neuropsychological tests commonly used in the assessment of those functions.

Cognitive deficits are estimated to afflict 43–65% of all MS patients depending on sampling and definition of cognitive impairment. There is little correlation between physical impairment and cognitive impairment (Heaton, Nelson, Thompson, Burks & Franklin, 1985; Peyser, Rao, LaRocca & Kaplan, 1990; Rao, Leo, Bernardin & Unverzagt, 1991). Neuropsychological dysfunction correlates moderately with the volume of brain lesions caused by MS (Camp et al., 1999; Comi et al., 1995; Foong et al., 2000; Rovaris et al., 1998; Sperling et al., 2001). A number of other disease processes in MS, including brain atrophy, axonal degeneration, and other changes in normal-appearing white matter also correlate moderately with cognitive dysfunction (Barkhof et al., 1998; Foong et al., 1999; Foong et al., 2000; Van Buchem, McGowan, & Gossmann, 1999). For some individuals cognitive impairment may occur early in the disease, often before any marked physical symptoms (Grant, McDonald, Trimble, Smith & Reed, 1984; Amato et al., 1995), while other individuals may experience profound physical symptoms with no significant cognitive changes.

Cognitive impairment has a significant impact on the quality of life for MS patients. Patients who exhibit cognitive impairment are less likely to be working, engage in fewer social activities, report more sexual dysfunction, and experience greater difficulty with household tasks (Rao, Leo, Ellington, Nauertz, Bernardin & Unverzagt, 1991). While some studies have not found any relationship between cognitive dysfunction and depression (Jouvent et al., 1989; Möller, Wiedemann, Rohde, Backmund & Sonntag, 1994), others have found depression to be related to long-term memory problems (Gilchrist & Creed, 1994) and problem-solving deficits (Filippi et al., 1994).

Neuropsychological assessment is frequently ordered for disability evaluations. In such evaluations it is important to conduct a detailed task analysis of job demands and an analysis of the work place environment (e. g., noise level, number of interruptions, distracting stimuli, etc.) in addition to a neuropsychological and psychological test battery. If adjustments to the work environment or job description can be made which will allow the person to continue working productively, these should be recommended before considering disability. Sometimes patients who transition to a less challenging position or from full-time to part-time work are able to continue working. Maintaining employment under reasonable and achievable expectations can preserve an important part of an individual's social network, self-esteem, self-image, and personal and financial independence. On the other hand, patients with significant cognitive impairment or severe depression may not be able to accurately judge their ability to continue to work, or may deny the impact of their symptoms on their work performance. If disability is the only alternative, adjustment problems should be anticipated with the patient, and referral sources and support services should be identified and put in place.

Physicians and allied healthcare professionals frequently refer patients to psychologists. Neurologists sometimes seek to document and identify patients' cognitive impairments. Such documentation may be used for treatment planning, such as assessing a patient's ability to adhere to a medical regimen or in arranging for patient care. Physical and occupational therapists often find neuropsychological assessment useful in determining how to present new information. For example, visual memory may be less impaired than verbal, suggesting the use of visual rather than verbal memory cues when teaching patients new exercises or skills. Some patients may have lost the ability to mentally rotate images, in which case instruction should be carried out side-by-side rather than standing opposite the patient. Social workers may use neuropsychological evaluations to identify patient needs for services and in making decisions in the event a patient requires placement into a home or nursing facility.

Neuropsychological evaluation can also serve as the basis for improving the patient's quality of life. Most patients with cognitive impairment notice changes in thinking and memory but are unaware that these represent symptoms of MS. Many patients fear they are going crazy, blame themselves in some way for their cognitive failures, or worry that they are developing another disease as well as MS, such as Alzheimer's. For such individuals a neuropsychological evaluation can reduce the amount of distress and anxiety the patient experiences by providing concrete information. Furthermore, with awareness of the specific nature of the deficits and of areas of preserved functioning, the patient, with the neuropsychologist's help, can begin to develop compensatory strategies which utilize preserved functioning and avoid functions which are impaired.

Neuropsychological evaluations can also improve family functioning. It is not uncommon for families to attribute cognitive problems such as inattentiveness or forgetfulness as a willful uncaring act. Neuropsychological assessments can help families understand what changes in a person's behavior are due to cognitive impairment. When family functioning is part of the purpose of the evaluation, it is best to conduct collateral interviews with other members of the family in order to obtain a variety of perspectives on the patient's functioning within the context of the family system.

Counseling on adaptation to cognitive impairment is an important component of neuropsychological intervention. Neuropsychological test results should be used to develop specific recommendations to help the patient compensate for his or her specific areas of weakness using any remaining areas of strength. Managing physical and cognitive fatigue, improving organization and redundancy, and reducing environmental distractions are helpful for almost all patients. If the patient lives with others, it is very important to elicit their aid in implementing these strategies. Managing fatigue requires both the patient to develop an appropriate schedule of periods of rest and activity, and the need for others to respect and support that schedule. Improving organization frequently includes keeping the home clean, ensuring that "everything has its place" in the home, keeping a large family calendar, using message boards, personal organizers, and phone logs, and developing and maintaining routines. Electronic personal organizers with alarm functions can be particularly helpful because the patient can set the alarm as a reminder for numerous things throughout the day. Reducing distractions can include turning off the TV, particularly during conversations and meals, and teaching children to accommodate the needs of the parent with MS.

Cognitive Rehabilitation

Currently, there is a great deal of hope that medications developed for use in other progressive dementias will be useful in MS patients with cognitive dysfunction, and research in this area is on-going. Donepezil hydrochloride, currently approved for use with Alzheimer' disease, was recently shown to be effective in improving cognitive function in an open trial with 17 MS patients (Greene et al., 2000).

There has been little research in the area of cognitive rehabilitation for patients with MS-related cognitive difficulties, and the research thus far finds limited benefits. An initial small trial of a cognitive rehabilitation program found no improvement in cognitive functioning associated with treatment other than reduced depression (Jønsson, Korfitzen, Heltberg, Ravnborg, & Byskov-Ottosen, 1993). Based upon the cognitive rehabilitation findings from other disorders, Plohmann and colleagues believed that attention would be the area most likely to respond to remediation (Plohmann et al., 1998). They found evidence that a computer-based attention cognitive rehabilitation program produced significantly improved alertness, divided attention, and selective attention among mildly-attention impaired MS patients. Self-report measures obtained from these patients suggested that these improvements were generalized to their daily lives. Another approach to cognitive rehabilitation is to teach compensatory strategies. Canellopoulou (Canellopoulou & Richardson, 1998) examined the ability of MS patients to learn to use mnemonic strategies. In a research setting patients were able to learn new and more effective mnemonics from examiners, and thus to improve their scores on measures of memory. However, patients were not able to independently develop these mnemonics effectively. This suggests that patients may require on-going guidance in the development and selection of compensatory strategies for memory.

While the findings in cognitive rehabilitation research have not been highly encouraging, this area of research remains largely unexplored. One potentially useful but unexamined area of intervention is managing cognitive fatigue. Cognitive fatigue refers to a patient's decline in performance on an effortful task over time due to the fatigue associated with the task. Patients with MS have been shown to fatigue cognitively much more quickly than healthy people. Krupp and Elkins (Krupp & Elkins, 2000) found that MS patients fatigue cognitively much more quickly than medically healthy controls, demonstrating a global decline on a battery of cognitive measures following 4 hours of a continuous cognitive effort, while the control group demonstrated improvement due to learning effects. By managing cognitive and physical fatigue through scheduled periods of rest and activity, MS patients may be able to reduce the functional impact of cognitive deficits.

Psychological Assessment

Depression

Patients with MS experience a wide variety of psychological disorders at a rate higher than the general population. It is widely agreed that depression is one of the more common symptoms in MS (Anderson & Goodkin, 1996; Schapiro, 1994; Thompson, 1996). Lifetime prevalence of major depressive disorder (MDD) following MS diagnosis is approximately 50% (Joffe, Lippert, Gray, Sawa, & Horvath, 1987; Minden, Orav, & Reich, 1987; Sadovnick, Eisen, Ebers, & Paty, 1991). Point-prevalence rates have ranged from 14%–57% (Schiffer, Caine, Bamford, & Levy, 1983; Schubert & Foliart, 1993; Surridge, 1969; Whitlock & Siskind, 1980) however these data are generally poor, using small samples that are not necessarily representative. Several studies have found that rates of depression are higher in MS than in other chronic illnesses (Minden et al., 1987; Surridge, 1969) and other neurological disorders (Rabins et al., 1986; Whitlock & Siskind, 1980).

The high prevalence of depression may reflect a variety of potential etiologies. Depression in MS clearly has psychosocial origins. Loss of function in MS is unpredictable, and for many patients, unrelenting. While absolute level of cognitive or physical impairment is not necessarily related to adjustment or depression (McIvor, Riklan, & Reznikoff, 1984; Millefiorini et al., 1992; Rabins et al., 1986; Rao, Leo, Bernardin, & Unverzagt, 1991; Whitlock & Siskind, 1980), patient's perceptions of the uncertainty (Wineman, Schwetz, Goodkin, & Rudick, 1996), variability in disease (Schiaffino, Shawaryn, & Blum, 1998), and the perceived intrusiveness of disease on daily activities (Devins et al., 1993a; Devins et al., 1993b; Devins et al., 1996) are all related to depression and adjustment. Loss of social support and social role functioning associated with the disease has also been shown to be

associated with depression (Barnwell & Kavanagh, 1997; Gilchrist & Creed, 1994; Gulick, 1997; Pakenham, 1999).

While the psychological sequelae of MS are associated with depression, this alone would not account for rates of depression that may be higher than rates found in other progressive diseases. We therefore speculate that depression may be related to MS-specific disease processes (Mohr & Cox, 2001). For example, depression may result from immune dysregulation associated with MS. There is evidence that depression is strongly associated with disease exacerbation, which is the result of proinflammatory disease activity, measured both clinically and by magnetic resonance imaging (MRI) (Dalos, Rabins, Brooks, & O'Donnell, 1983; Fassbender et al., 1998). Depression has also been associated with specifically located brain lesions (Franklin, Heaton, Nelson, Filley, & Seibert, 1988a; Pujol, Bello, Deus, Marti-Vilalta, & Capdevila, 1997). Thus, depression may be a product of specific MS-related autoimmune disease processes, as well as the neurological damage caused by these processes in the form of brain lesions. This would indicate that depression can be both a complication associated with MS, as well as a symptom of MS.

There has been some speculation that new onset or increased depression may be an iatrogenic effect associated with some of the medications commonly used to treat MS. There are five disease-modifying medications used to treat MS, three of which are interferon drugs. While initial uncontrolled studies found increases in depression following the initiation of interferons (Mohr et al., 1996; Mohr et al., 1998; Neilley, Goodin, Goodkin, & Hauser, 1996), subsequent studies have found no increased risk of depression associated with these drugs (Borràs et al., 1999; Mohr et al., 1999b). However, MS exacerbations are frequently treated with either oral or IV steroids, which are known to produce changes in mood and cognition (Medical Economics, 1998).

Diagnosis of affective disorders is complicated because many of the symptoms of psychiatric diagnosis are confounded with the symptoms of MS. In depression, for example, four of the nine symptoms needed for a DSM-IV diagnosis of Major Depressive Disorder (MDD) are also common symptoms associated with MS, including insomnia or hypersomnia, fatigue, psychomotor agitation or retardation (often the sequelae of fatigue), and diminished ability to think or concentrate. Four methods of addressing the problem of overlapping symptoms have been suggested, and have been termed *inclusive, exclusive, etiologic* and *substitution* approaches (Cohen-Cole & Harpe, 1987). The inclusive approach makes the psychiatric diagnosis on the basis of all symptoms present, including those which may be secondary to the medical disorder. While reliable, this method has a high false positive rate since MS patients could conceivably only need one of the non-confounded depressive symptoms to be positive for depression. The exclusive approach excludes all potentially confounded symptoms in making a psychiatric diagnosis. This method, also reliable, is likely to have a high false negative rate since an MS patient would have to have all of the nonconfounded depressive symptoms to qualify for a diagnosis. The etiologic approach asks the clinician to decide whether to use a confounded symptom by determining its origin. If reliability can be maintained, this method has the potential for more accurate diagnoses. The substitution method requires that other criteria be substituted for the confounded symptoms, for example social withdrawal might be substituted for fatigue. Alternative symptoms have been identified for diagnosing depression in MS (Mohr, Goodkin, Likosky, Beutler, Gatto & Langan, 1997), however such diagnostic criteria have not been validated.

Often self-report measures such as the Beck Depression Inventory (BDI; Beck et al., 1961) or the Center for Epidemiologic Studies Depression Scale (CES-D; Radloff, 1977) are used to assess depressive symptoms. As with diagnostic criteria, many of the items on these questionnaires may be confounded. Mohr et al. (1997) have identified three BDI items which are more related to MS than to depression, including fatigue, work difficul-

ty, and health concerns. However, as others have found that these items are sensitive to depression in MS (Aikens et al., 1999), alteration of existing measures should only be undertaken after careful consideration.

While depression among nonmedical patients tends to improve with time even if left untreated, there is some indication that this is not the case in MS (Mohr & Goodkin, 1999). Two controlled studies of psychotherapy found that self-reported depression among MS patients in no-treatment or waitlist control groups increases over 6–10 weeks (Crawford & McIvor, 1987; Larcombe & Wilson, 1984). Thus, MS patients who report depression may be at risk for deterioration and should be referred for treatment.

Pathological Laughing and Crying, and Euphoria

Pathological laughing and crying (PLC) has been used synonymously with pseudobulbar affect. PLC is defined as bouts of uncontrollable laughing, crying, or both in response to non-specific stimuli in the absence of a matching mood state (Poeck, 1969). It is estimated that PLC occurs in approximately 5-10% of MS patients (Feinstein, Feinstein, Gray, & O'Connor, 1997; Surridge, 1969). It is generally associated with greater physical and cognitive disability. PLC is often responsive to fluoxetine (Seliger, Hornstein, Flax, Herbert, & Schroeder, 1992) and fluvoxamine (Iannaccone & Ferini-Strambi, 1996). Euphoria is a similar condition in which the patient's mood is consistently cheerful and s/he is seemingly unaware of or unconcerned with his/her condition. Estimates of the prevalence of euphoria vary from 5-48%, although in our experience the lower number is likely more accurate. Euphoria is a symptom of MS as is associated with greater lesion load in the brain (Kahana, Leibowitz, & Alter, 1971; Rabins et al., 1986; Surridge, 1969). Extreme caution should be used in ascribing symptoms such as PLC or euphoria to psychological causes such as repression or denial, particularly in patients with substantial cognitive impairment.

Anxiety Disorders

Compared to depression, little has been written on anxiety in MS. The available literature on the prevalence of anxiety is generally not good, with small sample sizes and a lack of consistency in methods of assessment across studies. Existing work suggests that the point-prevalence of anxiety ranges from 19% to 34% (Feinstein, O'Connor, Gray, & Feinstein, 1999; Minden & Schiffer, 1991; Pepper, Krupp, Friedberg, Doscher, & Coyle, 1993; Stenager, Knudsen, & Jensen, 1994) and may be higher than in the general population (Maurelli et al., 1992).

Uncertainty and perceived potential threats, hallmarks of MS, are likely to contribute to anxiety (Wineman, 1990; Wineman, Durand, & McCulloch, 1994; Wineman et al., 1996; O'Conner, Detsky, Tansey, Kucharczyk & Rochester-Toronto MRI Study Group, 1994). There are, however, many other potential sources of anxiety. One of the common medications used to treat MS, glatiramer acetate, can produce episodes of tachycardia resembling panic attacks in some patients (Johnson et al., 1995). Other commonly used medications, such as corticosteroids, can also produce symptoms of anxiety.

Anxiety may also be associated with the act of injecting some of the commonly used medications. The most common and effective medications currently available to slow MS progression require injection. Patients are usually encouraged to learn to self-inject. Between a third and one-half of all patients patients experience significant anxiety or phobia associated with self-injection. Such injection-anxiety has been shown to contribute to a failure to adhere to injectable medications (Mohr, 2001).

Anger

Anger has also been noted frequently by clinicians as a reaction to MS (Minden, 1992; Pollin, 1995) however there is to date little empirical literature examining this area. While anger may be an appropriate response to the frustrations of having a chronic illness and encountering new physical limitations, it can become problematic when the intensity of the anger creates distress, or when the anger is displaced onto other people. Anger may be misdirected toward the healthcare system and toward healthcare professionals and is also frequently directed toward family and friends of the patient. Given the potential for anger to disrupt the patient's social support system it remains an important but underinvestigated area .

Stress and Disease Activity

Many patients report that stress results in disease exacerbation. This notion was first considered by Charcot, one of the earliest investigators of MS, who speculated that grief, vexation, and adverse changes in social circumstance were related to the onset of MS (Charcot, 1877). While early case-control studies failed to detect a significant relationship between stressful life events, psychological distress, and first symptom or clinical exacerbations of MS (Antonovsky et al., 1968; Pratt, 1951), more recent studies have supported these observations. Patients with MS are more likely to report stressful life events prior to the first identified symptom compared to patients experiencing the first symptom of other neurological disorders or rheumatoid arthritis (Warren, Greenhill, & Warren, 1982), or healthy controls (Grant et al., 1989a). Both case control and longitudinal studies have shown that stress increases the risk of experiencing a disease exacerbation (Ackerman et al., 2000; Franklin, Nelson, Heaton, Burks, & Thompson, 1988b; Sibley, 1997; Warren, Warren, & Cockerill, 1991).

Data also suggest that different types of stress may have differential effects. While Sibley (Sibley, 1997) found marital and job-related stress was followed by clinical exacerbation, major negative life events, such as a death in the family, were not. MS patients in a clinical trial in Israel showed a decreased exacerbation rate while under actual or threatened missile attack during the Persian Gulf War and for the two-month period thereafter (Nisipeanu & Korczyn, 1993). This suggests that it may be important to differentiate between relatively severe stressors and moderate, but more chronic stressors, when examining the relationship between stress and disease activity.

We had an opportunity to follow 36 patients who received gadolinium enhanced MRI scans every four weeks for 28–100 weeks (gadolinium is a contrast agent that permits visualization of the breakdown in the blood-brain-barrier). Assessing mood and stress at each MRI scan, we found that increased stress due to increased conflict and disruption in routine predicted the risk of developing a new brain lesion eight weeks later (Mohr et al., 2000a). As predicted, there was no effect for severe life stressors. This study supported the notion that different types of stressors have different effects. Furthermore, this was the first study to suggest a biological pathway. This study suggested that stress may affect MS by increasing permeability of the blood-brain-barrier.

There are several caveats that should be mentioned regarding the literature on stress and MS. First, the relationship between stress and MS exacerbation is not consistent either within or across patients. For some people stress never seems to result in exacerbation. For others stress at one point may be followed by exacerbation and at another point it is not. The process by which stress might affect MS is not understood.

Finally, it should be remembered that having MS and experiencing disease exacerbations may be stressful events in themselves. Thus, rather than thinking of stress and disease activity as simple, one-way causal effects, dynamic reciprocal models of stress and MS must be developed. Such models would serve to guide future research in this area.

Coping

Impairment, strictly defined as problems in body function or structure that affect one's ability to function and participate in life (World Health Organization, 1999), is not associated with decreased adaptation (Provinciali, Ceravolo, Bartolini, Logullo, & Danni, 1999). On the other hand, limitations in a person's ability to engage in normal activities or societal roles are associated with decreased well-being and psychological adaptation. For example, not being able to walk does not affect well-being in and of itself. However, loss of ambulation can reduce well-being when it prevents completion of a desired task or increases the effort required to participate in activities. A person who is able to minimize the effects of impairment on his/her ability to perform activities and engage in life will experience the impairments as less stressful. This suggests that coping plays a substantial role in adaptation.

The vast majority of coping research in MS has utilized Lazarus and Folkman's model, which defines coping as "constantly changing cognitive and behavioral efforts to manage specific external and/or internal demands that are appraised as taxing or exceeding the resources of the person" (Lazarus & Folkman, 1984) (p. 141). Much of the work in MS has relied on assessment instruments developed by Folkman (Folkman & Lazarus, 1986; Folkman & Lazarus, 1988) which broadly classify coping strategies into problem-focused and emotion-focused strategies, based upon the targets of the coping behaviors.

Problem-Focused Coping

Problem-focused coping, such as confrontive coping or problem-solving, tends to be associated with well-being in people without chronic physical illness (Folkman & Lazarus, 1986; Lazarus & Folkman, 1984; Zeidner & Saklofske, 1996). This relationship is less clear in MS, with some studies finding a positive relationship between adaptation and problem-focused coping (Aikens, Fischer, Namey, & Rudick, 1997; Mohr, Goodkin, Gatto, & Van Der Wende, 1997a; O'Brien, 1993; Pakenham, Stewart, & Rogers, 1997) and others finding no relationship (Beatty et al., 1998; Hickey & Greene, 1989; Jean, Beatty, Paul, & Mullins, 1997; Jean, Paul, & Beatty, 1999). However, such main-effects analyses may miss important relationships. For example, different aspects of the disease may require different coping strategies. We have found that problem-solving is related to lower levels of psychological distress in patients with high levels of physical impairment but is unrelated to distress in patients with less impairment (Mohr et al., 1997a). Thus, the utility of some problem-focused strategies may be moderated by impairment, and possibly other disease related variables.

Specific forms of problem-focused coping may also be more helpful than others. For example, behavioral coping strategies that are focused on achievable health maintenance goals (e. g. moderate levels of exercise tailored to the person's physical capacities, such as maintaining a healthy diet and appropriate weight, adherence to medical regimens) or behavioral compensation (e. g. compensating for fatigue by building rest periods into one's daily schedule, proper use of ambulation aids or other adaptive devices, shopping at non-peak hours) are associated with higher quality of life (QOL) in MS in cross-sectional studies (Gulick, 1997; Stuifbergen, 1995). Mediational analyses suggest that health behaviors mediate the effects of disability on QOL (Stuifbergen & Roberts, 1997). However, when behavioral strategies are focused on alleviating problems that cannot be resolved (e. g. attempts to return physical functioning to a pre-MS baseline despite progressed disability), coping efforts are likely to result in frustration (Maes, Leventhal, & DeRidder, 1996). While there is little empirical data on this, our clinical experience suggests that such fruitless coping strategies are commonly employed by MS patients who are having difficulty accepting their disease and/or impairments.

Cognitive coping strategies such as cognitive reframing, information gathering, planning, and goal setting have generally been associated with better adaptation to MS (Aikens et al., 1997; Baker, 1998; Mohr et al., 1997a). Cognitive reframing is a way of re-conceptualizing a problem from something considered impossible to solve into something for which other coping strategies may be helpful. For example, if an untreatable memory disorder can be reframed as an organizational problem, this can allow the patient to utilize other strategies such as information gathering, planning and goal setting

(e. g. develop systems of reminders, use an organizer, keep "to do" lists) that can reduce the impact of the impairment on role performance (Canellopoulou & Richardson, 1998) (Allen, Goldstein, Heyman, & Rondinelli, 1998).

Positive reframing, a specific form of cognitive coping, is related to better adaptation in MS (Aikens et al., 1997; Mohr et al., 1999a; Mohr et al., 1997a). Positive reframing can be a complex and profound coping strategy. In a recent study, in which we asked patients how MS had affected their lives, we found that patients not only reported a variety of demoralizing consequences, but the majority also reported a variety of benefits they had derived from the disease (Mohr et al., 1999a). The benefits included such things as improved relations with family, increased compassion, enhanced appreciation of life, as well as other benefits. Benefit-finding was associated positive reappraisal. These findings are consistent with findings from other populations with medical illnesses (Affleck & Tennen, 1996; Folkman, 1997; Taylor, 1983).

Emotion-Focused Coping

Consistent with research from other chronic illnesses, both cross-sectional and longitudinal studies in MS have found that passive, avoidant, emotion-focused coping strategies (e. g. wishful thinking, self-blame, avoidance) are related to poorer adjustment and lower levels of QOL (Aikens et al., 1997; Buelow, 1991; Mohr et al., 1997a; O'Brien, 1993; Pakenham, 1999; Pakenham et al., 1997).

There has been little focus on emotion-focused coping, compared to problem-focused coping. This may be due in part to the widespread belief that emotion-focused coping is associated with poor outcomes. However, in a progressive disease with limited treatment options, emotion-focused coping strategies may account for a substantial portion of a patient's coping efforts. Furthermore, not all emotion-focused coping is necessarily deleterious. Clinicians have touted the salutary effects of acceptance (Minden, 1992; Pollin, 1995). One of the longest longitudinal studies examining psychosocial functioning in

MS found that acceptance was related to adaptation in MS up to seven years later (Brooks & Matson, 1982; Matson & Brooks, 1977). Interpretation of these results is complicated by the finding that "fighting" MS was also related to subsequent adaptation and that the use of religion or family as major coping strategies was associated with decreases in adjustment. While this study is important, it did not have the benefits of improvements in assessment methodologies that have occurred over the past 25 years, particularly in coping. The adaptive use of emotion-focused coping strategies, such as acceptance, remains a significant hole in the MS coping literature

Psychological Intervention

The prevalence of psychological distress among MS patients has long been recognized, and led to several early reports of group psychotherapies lasting from 6 months to 2½ years (Barnes, Busse, & Dinken, 1954; Bolding, 1960; Day, Day, & Herrmann, 1953). While objective outcomes are lacking in these early reports, authors reported decreased depression, increased self-reliance, and decreased utilization of overly used medical services.

The empirical literature has examined cognitive-behavioral therapies (CBT), relaxation, supportive or insight oriented group psychotherapy, and antidepressant medications (see Mohr and Goodkin, 1999 for a review). Larcombe and Wilson (1984) described the first controlled, randomly assigned treatment study employing a 6-week group-administered CBT. The study was small, with 9 active patients and 10 controls, but nevertheless showed a large reduction in depression for CBT, compared to an increase in depression for the control group. Subsequently Foley et al. (1987) compared 18 patients who received a six-week individually-administered "stress-inoculation" program based on CBT principles to 18 patients receiving a Treatment as Usual (TAU) control that included some supportive therapy for some patients. Foley reported significant reductions in depression

and anxiety for the active treatment group and no change for the control group. These changes were maintained at 6-month follow-up. Crawford and McIver (1987) compared a 13-session group CBT stress management program administered to 23 patients to 21 control patients. The group CBT treatment was effective at reducing depression and anxiety. Similar to Larcombe and Wilson's findings, the control group worsened.

Many patients with MS have mobility impairments or experience fluctuations in symptoms that prevent them from attending a clinic on a regular basis. Others may live far from specialized treatment. Alternative treatment delivery methods via telephone or the internet might increase access to mental health treatment for these patients. A recent small trial found that an 8-week manualized telephone-administered CBT significantly reduced depressive symptoms compared to patients receiving treatment as usual through a large HMO (Mohr et al., 2000b). Moreover, adherence to disease modifying medications was better for the active treatment group than the control condition.

Several other forms of therapy have also been evaluated. A 50-week insight oriented group psychotherapy was compared to a current events group and a no-treatment control group (Crawford & McIvor, 1985). The insight oriented group showed significant reductions in depression compared to the other two groups. However, this effect size was significantly smaller than the effect sizes seen in briefer CBT interventions (Mohr & Goodkin, 1999). One report of a group psychotherapy employing relaxation, visualization and art therapy reported declines in depression and improvements in verbal learning and abstraction, however, inadequate statistical analyses made it impossible to determine if these changes were significantly different from the wait list control group (Maguire, 1996).

Antidepressant medication is likely the most widely administered treatment (Mohr et al., 1997b) because it can be easily administered by neurologists. Both desipramine (Schiffer & Wineman, 1990) and sertraline (Mohr et al., 2002) have been shown to be effective in reducing depression in clinical trials.

Retrospective chart review has shown a wide variety of antidepressant medications to be effective (Scott, Allen, Price, McConnell, & Lang, 1996). However, because many physicians may not adequately monitor antidepressant use and effectiveness after prescribing, patients treated with antidepressants in general medicine or neurology clinics are likely underdosed, and have high rates of non-adherence. Properly taken in sufficient doses, antidepressant medication is a useful tool that should be considered by patients and the mental health professionals treating them.

Many MS patients are reluctant to take antidepressant medications. Many feel they are already taking too many medications, while others see taking mood-modifying medication as a personal failure. Patients may also be sensitive to being labeled a somatisizer by health care providers, and may perceive a prescription for antidepressants as an indication their physician isn't taking their disease seriously. Medications may be useful for patients and should be carefully considered by both patients and therapists. However, medication is not a substitute for individual psychotherapy to help patients develop skills to cope with emotions, thoughts, adjustment and MS symptoms.

Most of the clinical literature and the efficacy studies to date focus on three different forms of treatment: coping and skills training, emotional expression and enhancement of social support, and medication. We have recently completed the first comparative trial examining individual CBT, supportive-expressive group psychotherapy (Spiegel & Classen, 2000), and the antidepressant sertraline for the treatment of major depressive disorder in MS (Mohr et al., 2002). Using the BDI (Beck, Ward, Medelson, Mock, & Erbaugh, 1961) as the primary outcome measure, a significant difference was found between the treatments, with supportive-expressive group therapy being less effective than CBT or sertraline. This suggests that CBT or antidepressant therapy should be considered first as treatments for major depressive disorder and that groups focusing on support or emotional expression are not as useful for treatment major depressive disorder in MS.

It should be noted, however, that many of the group therapy patients reported that the group was meaningful and valuable to them in many other ways. Indeed, a wide variety of other quality of life measures have failed to find a difference between these three treatments. Thus, supportive expressive groups may be useful in helping patients adapt; they are simply less likely to be effective in treating major depressive disorder.

Other Psychotherapy Findings

Psychotherapy has also been used to address sexual dysfunction among MS patients. In a recent survey of MS patients, 78% of men and 45% of women reported some form of sexual dysfunction, primarily erectile dysfunction and problems with vaginal lubrication, respectively (Mattson, Petrie, Srivastava & McDermott, 1995). Of 60 patients, six reported having tried counseling, and of those, four reported that counseling was helpful. The finding that psychotherapy can improve erectile functioning, even when the etiology is organic, has been previously reported among other populations such as diabetics (Mohr & Beutler, 1990). These findings suggest that psychotherapy for sexual dysfunctions may be an underutilized resource for MS patients.

Issues in the Treatment of MS Patients

The patient's experience is not solely of a symptom, or an emotional reaction and treatment rarely focuses on one symptom to the exclusion of everything else. The patient's experience is the intersection of many different events, including symptoms, changes in the environment (e. g., divorce, loss of job), emotional reactions, and coping behaviors to name a few. Although largely neglected in the empirical literature, these intersections of experience are central to the patient and to psychotherapy. These intersections of experience have been termed "issues in chronic illness" (Pollin, 1995). Clinicians (some of whom are active researchers) have tended to identify several issues among MS patients including fear of loss of control, independence vs. dependence, self-image, fear of abandonment, and isolation (Minden, 1992; Pollin, 1995).

Fear of Losing Control

Fear of losing of control is pervasive in MS. The diagnosis of MS is often accompanied by a flood of feelings and thoughts that feel out of control. While this panic subsides, the fear of loss of control usually does not. Realistically, most patients will eventually lose some control of their physical strength, limbs, bowels, bladder, and/or cognitive abilities. MS is a disease characterized by uncertainty, and the unpredictable nature of symptom onset and remission makes it very difficult to accurately guess what the future will hold. While a patient may focus on worsening symptoms, the loss of physical control is often a metaphor for the loss of a sense of control over one's destiny. Not being able to predict one's level of functioning from one year to the next makes the planning of families or careers difficult at best. The person with MS can no longer expect wellness. Many people with MS have long periods of stability in their symptoms, and the fear of loss of control and anticipatory grief about feared losses can be quite problematic even during periods of stability.

Fear of loss of control in some realms of life can often lead to damaging over-compensation in others. For example, the person who has lost use of his or her legs may become bossy or controlling with others, insisting that they help immediately, or perform tasks in exactly the same manner as the MS patient would, if he or she could. This is frequently an attempt to use others as "surrogate limbs" to be able to control the environment, but such attempts can often result in increased interpersonal tension, leaving the patient feeling even more helpless.

Independence vs. Dependence

Many people, particularly those who have prided themselves on their autonomy and self-sufficiency, experience dependency fears, which can manifest either as the fear of loss of autonomous functioning, or the fear of becoming a burden on others. In our experience, these patients often feel infantilized by others' attempts to help. Patients who are struggling with these issues are often at risk for physical injury as they attempt to push themselves past their endurance. For example, patients may refuse to request help with household duties, and push themselves to the point of collapse and injury. Because these patients are unwilling to balance periods of rest and activity and to accept help, and therefore are more fatigued, they may in fact create conditions that lead to their greater functional dependence. Struggles with increasing dependency often result in increased family tensions, as the patient becomes angry at others' attempts to be helpful.

Less frequent, but also common, is the patient who readily accepts dependency. For this person, the illness provides the perfect excuse to expect and receive care and attention the patient has craved. With such patients, secondary gain is a common problem. However, the gratification of these wishes eventually results in the patient losing his or her role in the family along with a sense of alienation and increased depression. In addition, these patients risk increased caregiver burnout. Regardless of the type of conflict around independence and dependence, it is frequently helpful to involve the family in any psychotherapy to help the patient and the family retain expectations of the patient which preserve the patient's role in the family, but which do not include demands of physical or cognitive functions which are beyond the patient's capabilities.

Self-Image

A person's self-image often changes after receiving a diagnosis of chronic illness. On a most basic level, the person's self-image must shift from seeing one's self as healthy to seeing one's self as having a chronic illness. However, specialists in MS have noted that people who begin seeing themselves as "sick"can begin seeking special attention and consideration, and can also give up large parts of life (Minden, 1992). The person who sees themselves as "sick" risks becoming consumed by the illness; that is, they have a hard time differentiating the illness from who they are.

However, the person who refuses to acknowledge changes can also be at risk. An individual must acknowledge losses and changes. The long distance runner may need to mourn the loss of his/her sport; the family may need to mourn the loss of family hiking trips; the energetic entrepreneur may need to mourn the loss of unbridled energy or cognitive flexibility. If the individual attempts to hold onto a former and currently inaccurate self-image, the person is at risk for a variety of problems. As with dependency issues, the person may place themselves in physically dangerous situations to prove to themselves that they still have capacities which are lost. People who cannot incorporate changes into their self-image often begin to withdraw socially to avoid confrontation with their limitations. For example, a runner who can no longer run may completely stop exercising at all, rather than switching to an activity that is still possible, like yoga, swimming, biking, or water aerobics. People who either completely deny or completely embrace the reality of their MS may also put themselves at risk by making life decisions such as giving up a job, taking on debt, or not having children based on an unrealistic appraisal of their level of health. People should not stop living because they have MS, but neither should they make decisions which ignore their condition.

Ideally the individual with MS would acknowledge that MS has become a part of their life, be able to talk about the implications of having MS, make any necessary adjustments in plans, goals, and life style, and to do all this without necessarily giving in to the disease. Rather than achieving this ideal, it is more helpful to view coping with MS as an ongoing process of incorporating the disease into one's life. Continual changes must be made as the individual changes developmentally, and as the disease progresses. For patients who see themselves as doing battle with the disease, we often use the metaphor that staging well thought out tactical retreats

is not the same as surrender, and may actually lead to a strengthened position vis-a-vis the MS. For patients with less combative stances, discussing when to accept and let go may be more helpful.

Stigma

Living in a society which prizes youth and health, people with chronic illnesses often suffer the consequences of stigma. This is real and the clinical health psychologist can help the patient by allowing him/her to talk about the feelings, and to develop ways of coping and understanding the stigma. However, the health psychologist should also be sensitive to the fact that it is not uncommon for patients to perceive stigma where there is none. Patients often have their own prejudices against illness and disability, and often project these prejudices onto others. Sorting out real stigma from projection can be difficult for some patients. In exploring this, it is often helpful for the patients to become aware of their attitudes toward illness and disability in others prior to their diagnosis. MS patients who use visible aids, such as canes, crutches, scooters, or wheelchairs, face a number of difficulties in our society, which does not ensure access for people who are not completely independent in mobility. However, because MS can also be an invisible disease, many patients may fear that others consider them to be faking it, malingering, or seeking out unfair special treatment. Symptoms such as fatigue, weakness, pain, cognitive problems, and bladder or bowel problems are not immediately visible, and patients who require accommodations on the basis of these symptoms (such as handicapped parking permits or additional time on tests) can face questions from employers, educators, and strangers about the nature of their disability. Patients, particularly those with few or no visible symptoms, and those who are working, often have a great deal of concern about to whom and when to disclose their disease status. Patients may fear, in some cases rightly, that they will face stigma if they disclose their MS to employers, educators, potential or current romantic partners, or others. Some patients may fear that if they leave an unsatisfactory employer they will never be able to get another job or get health insurance in the future.

Fear of Abandonment and Isolation

Fear of abandonment and the ensuing loneliness are some of the most frightening issues confronting people with MS. Patients often fear their spouses will leave them; people who are not married wonder if they will ever find a partner. The specter of loneliness often lurks in every shadow.

In our experience, loss of social supports is multi-faceted. Virtually every patient experiences losses in friends and family over the course of their illness. Some friends disappear after they are informed of the diagnosis. Other relationships may disappear as a person loses functioning. Some people are uncomfortable around people with disabilities, and other times relationships end when a common activity (e. g., sports) is lost due to MS.

But patients also frequently create their isolation. Patients withdraw for fear of confronting changes in relationships with friends or extended family. Some people, anticipating rejection by others, become angry and push others away. And perhaps most commonly, patients withdraw as they experience depression and demoralization in the face of MS-related losses.

Caregiving in MS

The unpredictable, yet progressive, nature of MS often requires that family members be ready to provide both personal care to the individual as well as assume the household responsibilities of the ill family member. This responsibility of providing care generally falls to the spouse. Unlike the caregivers of Alzheimer's Disease or stroke patients, the MS caregiver is more likely to be a young adult, to have children at home, to be in an early part of career development, or to be not quite finished with his/her education (O'Brien, 1993c). Therefore, the demands of caring for a spouse in this stage of illness of-

ten result in reduced time for the caregiver's own personal needs, reduced availability to meet the needs of children that may be in the home, and economic strain on the family with the possible loss of employment for either the MS patient or the caregiver (O'Brien, 1993c).

Chronic Sorrow

Two reported emotional consequences of the MS caregiving experience are chronic sorrow and caregiver burden. Chronic sorrow is a pervasive sadness that is permanent, periodic, and progressive in nature (Hainsworth, 1996). It is described as a normal reaction to significant loss in either an individual or a caregiver (Burke, Hainsworth, Eakes & Lindgren, 1992; Hainsworth, 1994; 1996). Therefore, it is distinct from both acute grief from an immediate loss, or depression. Chronic sorrow is a chronic state of grief, where the illness becomes a constant reminder of loss. In general, chronic sorrow is experienced by individuals who are otherwise highly functional (Burke, Hainsworth, Eakes & Lindgren, 1992).

Hainsworth (1996) asked a small group of 10 caregivers to respond to open-ended questions of how their spouse's MS affects their lives and how they cope with the course of this disease. Despite this small sample size, and the nature of the qualitative design, the caregivers' reports of "chronic sorrow" encourage controlled studies of this phenomenon as well as urge health care providers to investigate the emotional status of family caregivers of MS patients. Assessing the emotional state of family caregivers within this population is especially important because chronic sorrow may exist even when the caregiver appears to have strong coping skills. No studies of treatment for chronic sorrow have been documented.

Caregiver Burden

Caregiver burden, long discussed in the Alzheimer's Disease literature, results when the responsibilities assumed by the caregiver exceed the caregiver's resources (Zarit et al.,

1980; Rabins et al., 1982; Cantor, 1983; Gallagher, 1985; Horowitz, 1985a,b). As this concept begins to get attention in the MS caregiving population, the findings are quite similar. O'Brien (1993c) described that in her sample of caregivers (n = 20), the vast majority reported that the demands of caregiving disrupted their obligations to friends, family or their career, resulted in feelings of confinement because they were unable to leave their care-recipient alone, as well as resulted in financial burdens to the family which ultimately limited their resources to obtain help. In a sample of 61 MS patients and their caregivers, caregiver burden explained a large portion of variance in caregiver health, mood, and life satisfaction (O'Brien, Wineman & Nealon, 1995). This study also found that perceptions of burden differed such that MS patients believed that their caregivers were experiencing less burden than was endorsed by the caregiver. This finding of unequal reports of perceived burden has since been corroborated by a survey study in Canada investigating the needs of caregivers and their use of support services (Aronson, Cleghorn & Goldenberg, 1996). Consequently, the discrepancy in perceptions of burden might perpetuate caregiver burden and stress, as the care recipient and the caregiver are not in agreement as to when to introduce outside services. In this circumstance, it is likely that the care receiver would not support the needs of the caregiver to take a break. Thus, the cycle of burden continues, perhaps to the point where the caregiver experiences either chronic sorrow or depression.

MS caregivers tend to cope with burden using problem-focused coping strategies (O'Brien, 1993c). Yet, despite caregivers' ability to find and develop new strategies to solve problems around providing care, few formal support services are utilized by this population (Winslow & O'Brien, 1992; Aronson, Cleghorn & Goldenberg, 1996).

Caregiver burden may be reduced or buffered when perceptions of social support among family caregivers are high (Pearlin, Mullan, Semple & Skaff, 1990; Rivera, Rose, Futterman, Lovett, Gallagher-Thompson,

1991; O'Brien, Wineman & Nealon, 1995). Similarly, as found in the Alzheimer's Disease literature, there are gender differences in perceptions of social support between male and female caregivers with male caregivers reporting far fewer resources and lower perceptions of social support (Rivera et al., 1990; O'Brien, 1993a; Good, Bower & Einsporn, 1995). Lower perceptions of social support were also reported for caregivers who have small children in the household, suggesting that as the number of people increases for whom the caregiver is responsible, it becomes more difficult to perceive that they have external supporters as resources.

Caregiving can also affect the physical health of the caregiver. When caregiving duties become overwhelming, it is common for caregivers to neglect their own health while addressing the needs of their care-recipients (Gaynor, 1990). O'Brien (1993a) explored the relationship between dependency needs of the MS spouse and the health promoting behaviors of the caregiver. Twenty spousal caregivers responded to a health promoting lifestyle questionnaire. The results indicated that as dependency needs increased in the MS patient, caregivers paid less attention to their own health. O'Brien also found that this effect was greater for the male caregivers as they were older, the majority worked full time, and they provided care longer than female caregivers. These findings urge health care providers to continually inquire about the health status of the caregivers they see as well as encourage them to take care of their own health needs. While these findings offer practical advice for the caregiver and the health care provider, longitudinal investigations are needed to identify the actual changes in health status of the non-MS spouse during the caregiving process.

There are no controlled studies on interventions for the MS spousal caregiver. Yet, results from the Alzheimer's Disease literature clearly report that services such as psychotherapy are quite beneficial for alleviating depression in family caregivers of Alzheimer's patients (Gallagher & Steffen, 1994).

In summary, MS caregivers report significant sources of stress in the areas of changing roles, reduced social contacts, economic strain, possible reduction in occupational status as well as often raising children while caring for a spouse. As a result of these changes in lifestyle, both caregiver burden and chronic sorrow can emerge as emotional reactions to the continued losses of the MS patient as well as the losses experienced by the couple or family. The investigations of the existence of caregiver burden and chronic sorrow are limited but consistent; and no controlled intervention studies for the caregiver of an MS patient exist. Given that the emotional and physical needs of the spouse of an MS patient are on the line as caregiving duties increase, health care providers should include an inquiry into the emotional and physical state of the caregiver as well as encourage the caregiver to take care of him/herself.

Summary

MS is is a complex illness that can potentially have a broad and profound effect on an individual's functioning. In addition to the potential physical impairments, many patients experience declines in cognitive functioning and increased psychological distress, particularly depression. Many patient's experience considerable losses in their social environment including loss of employment and increased social isolation. Furthermore, MS affects those close to the patient who take on caregiving roles. These caregivers can experience increased burden and sorrow.

Working with MS patients and their families is often very rewarding for a variety of reasons. Intellectually, the work is challenging. The disease is complex and affects virtually every area of a person's life, including their physical health, cognitive functioning, social roles, psychological well-being, sense of self, family, work, and social environment. It calls on a wide range skills from the psychologist, including individual, group, and family psychotherapy, patient education, neuropsychology, and consultation with oth-

er health professionals. However, it is also personally quite rewarding. Many of these individuals, in the face of potential or actual assaults on virtually every area of their lives, are nevertheless able to adapt, and to find pleasure and meaning in life. We often find ourselves asking if we, in their shoes, could do so well. At those times, humbled by the quiet potential of the human spirit, it seems these patients have more to offer us than we could hope to offer them.

References

Ackerman, K.D., Martino, M., Heyman, R., Moyna, N.M., & Rabin, B.S. (1996). Immunologic response to acute psychological stress in MS patients and controls. *Journal of Neuroimmunology, 68*, 85–94.

Ackerman, K.D., Martino, M., Heyman, R., Moyna, N.M., & Rabin, B.S. (1998). Stressor-induced alteration of cytokine production in multiple sclerosis patients and controls. *Psychosomatic Medicine, 60*, 484–491.

Ackerman, K.D., Rabin, B., Heyman, R., Frank, E., Anderson, B., & Baum, A. (2000). Stressful life events precede multiple sclerosis disease exacerbations. *Psychosomatic Medicine, 62*, 147.

Affleck, G., & Tennen, H. (1996). Construing benefits from adversity: Adaptational significance and dispositional underpinnings. *Journal of Personality, 64*, 899–922.

Aikens, J.E., Fischer, J.S., Namey, M., & Rudick, R.A. (1997). A replicated prospective investigation of life stress, coping, and depressive symptoms in multiple sclerosis. *Journal of Behavioral Medicine, 20*, 433–445.

Aikens, J.E., Reinecke, M.A., Pliskin, N.H., Fischer, J.S., Wiebe, J.S., McCracken, L.M., & Taylor, J.L. (1999). Assessing depressive symptoms in multiple sclerosis: Is it necessary to omit items for the original Beck Depression Inventory? *Journal of Behavioral Medicine, 22*, 127–142.

Allen, D.N., Goldstein, G., Heyman, R.A., & Rondinelli, T. (1998). Teaching memory strategies to persons with multiple sclerosis. *Journal of Rehabilitation Research and Development, 35*, 405–410.

Alter, M., Antonovsky, A., & Leibowitz, V. (1968). Epidemiology of multiple sclerosis in Israel. In M. Alter & J. Kurtzke (Eds.), *The epidemiology of multiple sclerosis* (pp. 83–109). Springfield, IL: Thomas.

Amato, M.P., Onziani, G., Pracucci, G., Bracco, L., Siracusa, G., & Amaducci, L., (1995). Cognitive impairment in early-onset multiple sclerosis: Pattern, predictors, and everyday impact in a 4-year follow-up. *Archives of Neurology, 52,* 168–172.

American Psychiatric Association. (1994). *Diagnostic and statistical manual of mental disorders* (4th Edition). Washington, DC: American Psychiatric Association.

Anderson, D.W., Ellenberg, J.H., Leventhal, C.M., Reingold, S.C., Rodriguez, M., & Silberberg, D.H. (1992). Revised estimate of the prevalence of multiple sclerosis in the United States. *Annals of Neurology, 31,* 333–336.

Anderson, P.-B., & Goodkin, D.E. (1996). Current pharmacologic treatment of multiple sclerosis symptoms. *Western Journal of Medicine, 165,* 313–317.

Antonovsky, A., Leibowitz, U., Medalie, J.M., Smith, A., Halpern, L., & Alter, M. (1968). Reappraisal of possible etiologic factors in multiple sclerosis. *American Journal of Public Health, 58,* 836–848.

Aronson, K.J., Cleghorn, G., & Goldenberg, E. (1996). Assistance arrangements and use of services among persons with multiple sclerosis and their caregivers. *Disability and Rehabilitation, 18,* 354–361.

Baker, L.M. (1998). Sense making in multiple sclerosis: The information needs of people during acute exacerbation. *Qualitative Health Research, 8,* 106–120.

Baldwin, B.A. (1988). The stress of caring: Issues confronting mid-life caregivers. *Caring,* March, 16–19.

Barkhof, F., Elton, M., Lindeboom, J., Tas, M., Schmidt, W., Hommes, O., Polman, C., Kolk, A., & Valk, J. (1998). Functional correlates of callosal atrophy in relapsing-remitting multiple sclerosis patients. A preliminary MRI study. *Journal of Neurology, 245,* 153–159.

Barnes, R.H., Busse, E.W., & Dinken, H. (1954). The alleviation of emotional problems in multiple sclerosis by group psychotherapy. *Group Psychotherapy, 6,* 193–201.

Barnwell, A.M., & Kavanagh, D.J. (1997). Prediction of psychological adjustment to multiple sclerosis. *Social Science and Medicine, 45,* 411–418.

Basso, M.R., Beason-Hazan, S., Lynn, J., Rammohan, K., & Bornstein, R.A. (1996). Screening for cognitive dysfunction in multiple sclerosis. *Archives of Neurology, 53,* 980–984.

Beatty, W.W., Goodkin, D.E., Monson, N., & Beatty, P. (1989). Cognitive disturbances in patients with relapsing remitting multiple sclerosis. *Archives of Neurology, 46,* 1113–1119.

Beatty, W.W., Goodkin, D.E., Monson, N., Beatty, P.A., & Hertsgaard, D. (1988). Anterograde and retrograde amnesia in patients with chronic progressive multiple sclerosis. *Archives of Neurology, 45,* 611–619.

Beatty, W.W., Hames, K.A., Blanco, C.R., Williamson, S.J., Wilbanks, S.L., & Olson, K.A. (1998). Correlates of coping style in patients with multiple sclerosis. *Multiple Sclerosis, 4,* 440–443.

Beatty, W., & Monson, N. (1994). Picture and motor sequencing in Multiple Sclerosis. *Journal of Clinical and Experimental Neuropsychology, 16,* 165–172.

Beck, A.T., Rush, A.J., Shaw, B.F., & Emery, G. (1979). *Cognitive therapy of depression.* New York: Guilford.

Beck, A.T., Ward, C.H., Mendelson, M., Mock, J., & Erbaugh, J. (1961). An inventory for measuring depression. *Archives of General Psychiatry, 4,* 561–571.

Benton, A.L., & Hamsher, K.D.S. (1989). *Multilingual aphasia examination.* Iowa City, IA: AJA Associates.

Benton, A.L., Hamsher, K.d.S., Varney, N.R., & Spreen, O. (1983). *Contributions to neuropsychological assessment: A clinical manual.* New York: Oxford University Press.

Billings, A.G., & Moos, R.H. (1984). Coping, stress and social resources among adults with unipolar depression. *Journal of Personality and Social Psychology, 46,* 877–891.

Bolding, H. (1960). Psychotherapeutic aspects in the management of patients with multiple sclerosis. *Diseases of the Nervous System, 21,* 24–26.

Borràs, C., Río, J., Porcel, J., Barrios, M., Tintoré, M., & Montalbon, X. (1999). Emotional state of patients with relapsing-remitting MS treated with interferon beta-1b. *Neurology, 52,* 1636–1639.

Brassington, J.C., & Marsh, N.V. (1998). Neuropsychological aspects of multiple sclerosis. *Neuropsychological Review, 8,* 43–77.

Brooks, N.A., & Matson, R.R. (1982). Social-psychological adjustment to multiple sclerosis: A longitudinal study. *Social Science and Medicine, 16,* 2129–2135.

Buelow, J.M. (1991). A correlational study of disabilities, stressors and coping methods in victims of multiple sclerosis. *Journal of Neuroscience Nursing, 23,* 247–252.

Burke, M.L., Hainsworth, M.A., Eakes, G.G., & Lindgren, C.L. (1992). Current knowledge and research on chronic sorrow: A foundation for inquiry. *Death Studies, 16,* 231–245.

Camp, S., Stevenson, V., Thonspon, A., Miller, D., Borras, C., Auriacombe, S., Brochet, B., Falautano, M., Filippi, M., Herisse-Dulo, L., Montalban, X.E.P., Polman, C., De Sa, J., & Langdon, D. (1999). Cognitive function in primary progressive and transitional progressive multiple sclerosis: A controlled study with MRI correlates. *Brain, 122*, 1341–1348.

Canellopoulou, M., & Richardson, J.T.E. (1998). The role of executive function in imagery mnemonics: Evidence from multiple sclerosis. *Neuropsychologia, 36*, 1181–1188.

Cantor, M.H. (1983). Strain among caregivers: A study of the experience in the United States. *The Gerontologist, 23*, 597–604.

Charcot, J.M. (1877). *Lectures on diseases of the nervous system* (G. Sigerson, Trans.). London: New Sydenham Society.

Cohen-Cole, S.A., & Harpe, C. (1987). Diagnostic assessment of depression in the medically ill. In A. Stoudemire & B.S. Fogel (Eds.), *Principles of medical psychiatry*, (pp. 23–36). New York: Grune & Stratton.

Comi, G., Filippi, M., Marinelli, V., Campi, A., Rodegher, M., Alberoni, M., Sirabian, G., & Canal, N. (1995). Brain MRI correlates of cognitive impairment in primary and secondary progressive multiple sclerosis. *Journal of the Neurological Sciences, 132*, 222–227.

Cottrell, S.S., & Wilson, S.A.K. (1926). The affective symptomatology of disseminated sclerosis. *Journal of Neurology and Psychopathology, 7*, 1–30.

Coyne J.C., Aldwin C., & Lazarus, R.S. (1981). Depression and coping in stressful episodes. *Journal of Abnormal Psychology, 90*, 439–447.

Crawford, J.D., & McIvor, G.P. (1985). Group psychotherapy: Benefits in multiple sclerosis. *Archives of Physical Medicine Rehabilitation, 66*, 810–813.

Crawford, J.D., & McIvor, G.P. (1987). Stress management for multiple sclerosis patients. *Psychological Reports, 61*, 423–429.

Cummings, J.L. (1986). Subcortical dementia. Neuropsychology, neuropsychiatry, and pathophysiology, *British Journal of Psychiatry, 149*, 682–697.

Dalos, M.P., Rabins, P.V., Brooks, B.R., & O'Donnell, P. (1983). Disease activity and emotional state in multiple sclerosis. *Annals of Neurology, 13*, 573–583.

Day, M., Day, E., & Herrmann, R. (1953). Group therapy of patients with multiple sclerosis. *Archives of Neurology and Psychiatry, 69*, 193–196.

DeFilippis, N.A., & McCampbell, E. (1979). *The Booklet Category Test manual*. Odessa, FL: Psychological Assessment Resources.

Delis, D.C., Kramer, J.H., Kaplan, E., & Ober, B.A. (1987). *California Verbal Learning Test: Adult version*. San Antonio: The Psychological Corporation.

DeLuca, J., Barbieri-Berger, S., & Johnson, S.K. (1994). The nature of memory impairments in multiple sclerosis: Acquisition versus retrieval. *Journal of Clinical and Experimental Neuropsychology, 16*, 183–189.

Devins, G.M., Edworthy, S.M., Paul, L.C., Mandin, H., Seland, T.P., Klein, G., Costello, C.G., & Shapiro, C.M. (1993a). Restless sleep, illness intrusiveness, and depressive symptoms in three chronic illness conditions: Rheumatoid arthritis, end-stage renal disease, and multiple sclerosis. *Journal of Psychosomatic Medicine, 37*, 163–170.

Devins, G.M., Edworthy, S.M., Seland, T.P., Klein, G.M., Paul, L.C., & Mandin, H. (1993b). Differences in illness intrusiveness across rheumatoid arthritis, end-stage renal disease, and multiple sclerosis. *Journal of Nervous and Mental Disease, 181*, 377–381.

Devins, G.M., & Sedlund (1987). Emotional impact of multiple sclerosis: Recent findings and suggestions for future research. *Psychological Bulletin, 101*, 363–375.

Devins, G.M., Styra, R., O'Connor, P., Gray, T., Seland, T.P., Klein, G.M., & Shapiro, C.M. (1996). Psychosocial impact of illness intrusiveness moderated by age in multiple sclerosis. *Psychology, Health, and Medicine, 1*, 179–191.

Eakes, G.G. (1993). Chronic sorrow: A response to living with cancer. *Oncology Nursing Forum, 20*, 1327–1334.

Endicott, J. (1984). Measurement of depression in patients with cancer. *Cancer, 53*, 2243–2248.

Fassbender, K., Schmidt, R., Mößner, R., Kischka, U., Kühnen, J., Schwartz, A., & Hennerici, M. (1998). Mood disorders and dysfunction of the hypothalamic-pituitary-adrenal axis in multiple sclerosis. *Archives of Neurology, 55*, 66–72.

Feinstein, A., Feinstein, K., Gray, T., & O'Connor, P. (1997). Prevalence of neurobehavioral correlates of pathological laughing and crying in multiple sclerosis. *Archives of Neurology, 54*, 1116–1121.

Feinstein, A., O'Connor, P., Gray, T., & Feinstein, K. (1999). The effects of anxiety on psychiatric morbidity in patients with multiple sclerosis. *Multiple Sclerosis, 5*, 323–326.

Filippi, M., Alberoni, M., Martinelli, V., Sirabian, G., Bressi, S., Canal, N., & Comi, G. (1994). *European Neurology, 34*, 324–328.

Flax, J.W., Gray, J., & Herbert, J. (1991). Effect of

fluoxetine on patients with multiple sclerosis. *American Journal of Psychiatry, 148,* 1603.

Folkman, S. (1997). Positive psychological states and coping with severe stress. *Social Science Medicine, 45,* 1207–1221.

Folkman, S., & Lazarus, R.S. (1986). Stress processes and depressive symptomatology. *Journal of Abnormal Psychology, 95,* 107–113.

Folkman S., & Lazarus, R. (1988). *Manual for the Ways of Coping Questionnaire.* Palo Alto, CA: Consulting Psychologists Press.

Foley, F.W., Bedell, J.R., LaRocca, N.G., Scheinberg, L.C., & Reznikoff, M. (1987). Efficacy of stress-inoculation training in coping with multiple sclerosis. *Journal of Consulting and Clinical Psychology, 55,* 919–922.

Foong, J., Rozewicz, L., Bavie, C.A., Thompson, A.J., Miller, D.H., & Ron, M.A. (1999). Correlates of executive function in multiple sclerosis: The use of magnetic resonance spectroscopy as an index of focal pathology. *Journal of Neuropsychiatry and Clinical Neurosciences, 11,* 54–50.

Foong, J., Rozewicz, L., Chong, W., Thompson, A., Miller, D., & Ron, M. (2000). A comparison of neuropsychological deficits in primary and secondary progressive multiple sclerosis. *Journal of Neurology, 247,* 97–101.

Foong, J., Rozewicz, L., Quaghebeur, G., Davie, C., Kartsounis, L., Thomson, A., Miller, D., & Ron, M. (1997). Executive function in multiple sclerosis: The role of frontal lobe pathology. *Brain, 120,* 15–26.

Franklin, G.M., Heaton, R.K., Nelson, L.M., Filley, C.M., & Seibert, C. (1988a). Correlation of neuropsychological and MRI findings in chronic/progressive multiple sclerosis. *Neurology, 38,* 1826–1829.

Franklin, G.M., Nelson, L.M., Heaton, R.K., Burks, J.S., & Thompson, D.S. (1988b). Stress and its relationship to acute exacerbations in multiple sclerosis. *Journal of Neurologic Rehabilitation, 2,* 7–11.

Gallagher, D. (1985). Intervention strategies to assist caregivers of frail elders: Current research status and future research directions. In M.P. Lawton & G. Maddox (Eds.), *Annual review of gerontology and geriatrics, 5.* New York: Springer Press.

Gallagher, D., Rose, J., Rivera, P., Lovett, S., & Thompson, L.W. (1989). Prevalence of depression in family caregivers. *The Gerontologist, 29,* 449–455.

Gallagher, D., & Steffen, A.M. (1994). Comparative effects of cognitive-behavioral and brief psychodynamic psychotherapy for depressed

caregivers. *Journal of Consulting and Clinical Psychology, 62,* 543–549.

Gaynor, S.E. (1990). The long haul: The effects of home care on caregivers. *Image, 22,* 208–212.

Gilchrist A.C., & Creed, F.H. (1994). Depression, cognitive impairment and social stress in multiple sclerosis. *Journal of Psychosomatic Research, 38,* 193–201.

Golden, C.J. (1978). *Stroop Color and Word Test.* Chicago: Stoelting.

Good, D.M., Bower, D.A., & Einsporn, R.L. (1995). Social support: Gender differences in multiple sclerosis spousal caregivers. *Journal of Neuroscience Nursing, 27,* 305–311.

Goodkin, D.E. (1992). The natural history of multiple sclerosis. In R.A. Rudick & D.E. Goodkin (Eds.), *Treatment of multiple sclerosis: Trial design, results, and future perspectives* (pp. 17–45). New York: Springer-Verlag

Grant, I., Brown, G.W., Harris, T., McDonald, W.I., Patterson, T., & Trimble, M.R. (1989a). Severely threatening events and marked life difficulties preceding onset or exacerbation of multiple sclerosis. *Journal of Neurology, Neurosurgery, and Psychiatry, 52,* 8–13.

Grant, I., McDonald, W.I., & Trimble, M. (1989b). Neuropsychological impairment in early multiple sclerosis. In K. Jensen, L. Knudsen, E. Stenager, & I. Grant (Eds.), *Mental Disorders and Cognitive Deficits in Multiple Sclerosis* (pp. 17–26). London: John Libbey.

Grant, I., McDonald, W.I., Trimble, M.R., Smith, E., & Reed, R. (1984). Deficient learning and memory in early and middle phases of multiple sclerosis. *Journal of Neurology, Neurosurgery, and Psychiatry, 47,* 250–255.

Greene, Y., Tariot, P., Wishart, H., Cox, C., Holt, C., Schwid, S., & Noviasky. (2000). 12-week, open trial of donepezil hydrochloride in patients with multiple sclerosis and associated cognitive impairments. *Journal of Clinical Psychopharmacology, 20*(3), 350–356.

Gulick, E.E. (1997). Correlates of quality of life among persons with multiple sclerosis. *Nursing Research, 46,* 305–311.

Hainsworth, M.A. (1994). Living with multiple sclerosis: The experience of chronic sorrow. *Journal of Neuroscience, 50,* 237–240.

Hainsworth, M.A. (1996). Helping spouses with chronic sorrow related to multiple sclerosis. *Journal of Psychological Nursing, 34,* 36–40.

Heaton, R.K. (1981). *Wisconsin Card Sorting Test manual.* Odessa, FL: Psychological Assessment Resources.

Heaton, R.K., Nelson, L.M., Thompson, D.S., Burks, J.S., & Franklin, G.M. (1985). Neuropsychological findings in relapsing-remitting and chronic-progressive multiple sclerosis. *Journal of Consulting and Clinical Psychology, 53*, 103–110.

Hickey, A., & Greene, S.M. (1989). Coping with multiple sclerosis. *Irish Journal of Psychological Medicine, 6*, 118–124.

Honer, W.G., Hurwitz, T., Li, D.K.B., Palmer, M., & Paty, D.W. (1987). Temporal lobe involvement in multiple sclerosis patients with psychiatric disorders. *Archives of Neurology, 44*, 187–190.

Hooper, H.E. (1958). *Hooper Visual Organization Test manual.* Los Angeles: Western Psychological Services.

Horowitz, A. (1985a). Family caregivers to the frail elderly. In M.P. Lawton & G. Maddox (Eds.), *Annual review of gerontology and geriatrics, 5.* New York: Springer Press.

Horowitz, A. (1985b). Sons and daughters as caregivers to older patients: Differences in role performance and consequences. *The Gerontologist, 25*, 612–617.

Iannaccone, S., & Ferini-Strambi, L. (1996). Pharmacologic treatment of emotional lability. *Clinical Neuropharmacology, 19*, 532–535.

Jean, V.M., Beatty, W.W., Paul, R.H., & Mullins, L. (1997). Coping with general and disease-related stressors by patients with multiple sclerosis: Relationships to psychological distress. *Multiple Sclerosis, 3*, 191–196.

Jean, V.M., Paul, R.H., & Beatty, W.W. (1999). Psychological and neuropsychological predictors of coping patterns by patients with multiple sclerosis. *Journal of Clinical Psychology, 55*, 21–26.

Joffe, R.T., Lippert, G.P., Gray, T.A., Sawa, G., & Horvath, Z. (1987). Mood disorder and multiple sclerosis. *Archives of Neurology, 44*, 376–378.

Johnson, K.P., Brooks, B.R., Cohen, J.A., Ford, C.C., Goldstein, J., Lisak, R.P., Meyers, L.W., Panitch, H.S., Rose, J.W., Schiffer, R.B., Vollmer, T., Weiner, L.P., Wollinsky, J.S., & Group, C.M.S.S. (1995). Copolymer 1 reduces relapse rate and improves disability in relapsing-remitting multiple sclerosis: Results of a phase III multicenter, double-blind, placebo-controlled trial. *Neurology, 45*, 1268–1276.

Jønsson, A., Korfitzen, E.M., Heltberg, A., Ravnborg, M.H., & Byskov-Ottosen, E. (1993). Effects of neuropsychological treatment in patients with multiple sclerosis. *Acta Neurologica Scandinavica, 88*, 394–400.

Jouvent, R., Montreuil, M., Benoit, N., Lubetzki, C., Tournier-Lasserve, E., des Lauriers, A., Widlocher, D., Lhermitte, F., & Lyon-Caen, O. (1989). Cognitive impairment, emotional disturbances and duration of multiple sclerosis. In K. Jensen, L. Knudsen, E. Stenager & I. Grant (Eds.), *Mental disorders and cognitive deficits in multiple sclerosis* (pp. 139–145). London: John Libbey.

Kahana, E., Leibowitz, U., & Alter, M. (1971). Cerebral multiple sclerosis. *Neurology, 21*, 1179–1185.

Kail, R. (1998). Speed of information processing in patients with Multiple Sclerosis. *Journal of Clinical and Experimental Neuropsychology, 20*(1), 1–9.

Kaplan, E., Goodglass, H., & Weintraub, S. (1983). *Boston Naming Test.* Philadelphia, PA: Lea & Febiger.

Krupp, L.B., & Elkins, L.E. (2000). Fatigue and declines in cognitive functioning in multiple sclerosis. *Neurology, 55*, 934–939.

Kujala, P., Portin, R., Revonsuo, A., & Ruutiainen, J. (1995). Attention related performance in two cognitively different subgroups of patients with multiple sclerosis. *Journal of Neurology, Neurosurgery, and Psychiatry, 59*, 77–82.

Larcombe, N.A., & Wilson, P.H. (1984). An evaluation of cognitive-behaviour therapy for depression in patients with multiple sclerosis. *British Journal of Psychiatry, 145*, 366–371.

Lazarus, R.S., & Folkman, S. (1984). *Stress, appraisal, and coping.* New York: Springer Publishing Inc.

Lazarus, R.S., & Launier, R. (1978). Stress-related transactions between person and environment. In L.A. Pervin & M. Lewis (Eds.), *Internal and external determinants of behavior* (pp. 287–327). New York: Plenum.

Logsdail, S.J., Callanan, M.M., & Ron, A. (1988). Psychiatric morbidity in patients with clinically isolated lesions of the type seen in multiple sclerosis. *Psychological Medicine, 18*, 355–364.

Lublin, F.D., & Reingold, S.C. (1996). Defining the clinical course of multiple sclerosis: Results of an international survey. *Neurology, 46*, 907–911.

Maes, S., Leventhal, H., & de Ridder, D.T.D. (1996). Coping with chronic diseases. In M. Zeidner & N.S. Endler (Eds.), *Handbook of coping: Theory, research, application.* New York: Wiley.

Maguire, B.L. (1996). The effects of imagery on attitudes and moods in multiple sclerosis. *Alternative Therapies, 2*, 75–79.

Matson, R.R., & Brooks, N.A. (1977). Adjusting to multiple sclerosis: An exploratory study. *Social Science and Medicine, 11*, 245–250.

Mattson, D., Petrie, M., Srivastava, D.K., & McDermott, M. (1995). Multiple sclerosis: Sexual dysfunction and its response to medications. *Archives of Neurology, 52*, 862–868.

Maurelli, M., Marchioni, E., Cerretano, R.,

Bosone, D., Bergamaschi, R., Citterior, A., Martelli, A., Sibilla, L., & Savoldi, F. (1992). Neuropsychological assessment in MS: Clinical neuropsychological and neuroradiological relationships. *Acta Neurologica Scandinavica, 86,* 124–128.

McIvor, G.P., Riklan, M., & Reznikoff, M. (1984). Depression in multiple sclerosis as a function of length and severity of illness, age, remissions, and perceived social support. *Journal of Clinical Psychology, 40,* 1028–1033.

McLaughlin, J., & Zeeberg, I. (1993). Self-care and multiple sclerosis: A view from two cultures. *Social Science Medicine, 3,* 315–329.

Medical Economics (1998). *Physicians' desk reference* (52nd Edition). Montvale, NJ: Medical Economics Data Production Company.

Meichenbaum, D. (1977). *Cognitive behavior modification: An integrative approach.* New York: Plenum.

Millefiorini, E., Padovani, A., Poszzilli, C., Oriedo, C., Bastianello, S., Buttinelli, C., Di Piero, V., & Fieschi, C. (1992). Depression in the early phase of MS: Influence of functional disability, cognitive impairment and brain abnormalities. *Acta Neurologica Scandinavica, 86,* 354–358.

Minden, S.L. (1992). Psychotherapy for people with multiple sclerosis. *Journal of Neuropsychiatry, 4,* 198–213.

Minden S.L., Orav, J., & Reich, P. (1987). Depression in multiple sclerosis. *General Hospital Psychiatry, 9,* 426–434.

Minden, S.L., & Schiffer, R.B. (1991). Mood disorders in multiple sclerosis. *Neuropsychiatry, Neuropsychology, and Behavioral Neurology, 4,* 62–77.

Mishel, M.H. (1988). Uncertainty in illness. *Image: Journal of Nursing Scholarship, 20,* 225–232.

Möller, A., Wiedemann, G., Rohde, U., Backmund, H., & Sonntag, A. (1994). Correlates of cognitive impairment and depressive mood disorder in multiple sclerosis. *Acta Psychiatrica Scandinavica, 89,* 117–121.

Mohr, D.C. (under review). *Assessment and treatment of depression in multiple sclerosis: Review and meta-analysis.*

Mohr, D.C., Baumann, K., Lopez, J., Likosky, W., & Goodkin, D.E. (1997, April). *Physician role in mediating coping and anger among multiple sclerosis patients.* Presented at Society of Behavioral Medicine, San Francisco.

Mohr, D.C., & Beutler, L.E. (1990). Erectile dysfunction: A review of diagnostic and treatment procedures. *Clinical Psychology Review, 10,* 123–150.

Mohr, D.C., Boudewyn, A.C., Goodkin, D.E., Siskin, L.P., Epstein, L., Cheuk, W., & Lee, L.

(2002). Comparative outcomes for individual cognitive-behavioral therapy, supportive-expressive group therapy, and sertraline for the treatment of depression in multiple sclerosis. *Journal of Consulting and Clinical Psychology, 69,* 94–949.

Mohr, D.C., Boudewyn, A.C., Likosky, W., Levine, E., & Goodkin, D.E. (2001). Injectable medication for the treatment of multiple sclerosis: The influence of expectations and injection anxiety on adherence and ability to self-inject. *Annals of Behavioral Medicine, 23,* 125–132.

Mohr, D.C., & Cox, D. (2001). Multiple sclerosis: Empirical literature for the clinical health psychologist. *Journal of Clinical Psychology, 57,* 479–499.

Mohr, D.C., Dick, L.P., Russo, D., Pinn, J., Boudewyn, A.C., Likosky, W., & Goodkin, D.E. (1999a). The psychosocial impact of multiple sclerosis: Exploring the patient's perspective. *Health Psychology, 18,* 376–382.

Mohr, D.C., Dick, L., & Van Der Wende, J. (1997, March). *Uncertainty in illness, anxiety, and the mediating effects of perceived spousal and physician support among multiple sclerosis patients.* Paper presented at the American Psychosomatic Society, Santa Fe, NM.

Mohr, D.C., & Goodkin, D.E. (1999). Treatment of depression in multiple sclerosis: Review and meta-analysis. *Clinical Psychology: Science and Practice, 6,* 1–9.

Mohr, D.C., Goodkin, D.E., Bacchetti, P., Boudewyn, A.C., Huang, L., Marrietta, P., Cheuk, W., & Dee, B. (2000a). Psychological stress and the subsequent appearance of new brain MRI lesions in MS. *Neurology, 55,* 55–61.

Mohr, D.C., Goodkin, D.E., Gatto, N., Likosky, W., & Baumann, K. (1997). Treatment of depression enhances adherence to interferon β-1b among multiple sclerosis patients. *Archives of Neurology, 54,* 531–533.

Mohr, D.C., Goodkin, D.E., Gatto, N., & Van Der Wende, J. (1997a). Depression, coping, and level of neurological impairment in multiple sclerosis. *Multiple Sclerosis, 3,* 254–258.

Mohr, D.C., Goodkin, D.E., Likosky, W., Beutler, L.E., Gatto, N., & Langan, M.K. (1997). Identification of Beck Depression Inventory Items related to multiple sclerosis. *Journal of Behavioral Medicine, 20,* 405–412.

Mohr, D.C., Goodkin, D.E., Likosky, W., Gatto, N., Baumann, K.A., & Rudick, R.A. (1997b). Treatment of depression improves adherence to interferon beta-1b therapy for multiple sclerosis. *Archives of Neurology, 54,* 531–533.

Mohr, D.C., Goodkin, D.E., Likosky, W., Gatto, N.,

Neilley, L.K., Griffen, C., & Stiebling, B. (1996). Therapeutic expectations of patients with multiple sclerosis upon initiating interferon beta-1b: Relationship to adherence to treatment. *Multiple Sclerosis, 2,* 222–226.

Mohr, D.C., Likosky, W., Boudewyn, A.C., Marietta, P., Dwyer, P., Van Der Wende, J., & Goodkin, D.E. (1998). Side effect profile and compliance in the treatment of multiple sclerosis with interferon beta-1a. *Multiple Sclerosis, 4,* 487–489.

Mohr, D.C., Likosky, W., Dick, L.P., Van Der Wende, J., Dwyer, P., Bertagnolli, A.C., & Goodkin, D.E. (2000b). Telephone-administered cognitive-behavioral therapy for the treatment of depressive symptoms in multiple sclerosis. *Journal of Consulting and Clinical Psychology, 68,* 356–361.

Mohr, D.C., Likosky, W., Dwyer, P., Van Der Wende, J., Boudewyn, A.C., & Goodkin, D.E. (1999b). Course of depression during the initiation of intrferon beta-1a for multiple sclerosis. *Archives of Neurology, 56,* 1263–1265.

Neilley, L.K., Goodin, D.S., Goodkin, D.E., & Hauser, S.L. (1996). Side effect profile of interferon beta-1b in MS: Results of an open label trial. *Neurology, 46,* 552–554.

Nisipeanu, P., & Korczyn, A.D. (1993). Psychological stress as risk factor for exacerbations in multiple sclerosis. *Neurology, 43,* 1311–1312.

Noy, S., Achiron, A., Gabbay, U., Barak, Y., Rotstein, Z., & Sarova-Pinhas, I. (1995). A new approach to affective symptoms in relapsing-remitting multiple sclerosis. *Comprehensive Psychiatry, 36,* 390–395.

O'Brien, M.T. (1993a). Multiple sclerosis: Health-promoting behaviors of spousal caregivers. *Journal of Neuroscience Nursing, 25,* 105–112.

O'Brien, M.T. (1993b). Multiple sclerosis: The relationship among self-esteem, social support, and coping behavior. *Applied Nursing Research, 6,* 54–63.

O'Brien, M.T. (1993c). Multiple sclerosis: Stressors and coping strategies in spousal caregivers. *Journal of Community Health Nursing, 10,* 123–135.

O'Brien, R.A., Wineman, N.M., & Nealon, N.R. (1995). Correlates of the caregiving process in multiple sclerosis. *Scholarly Inquiry for the Nursing Practice: An International Journal, 9,* 323–338.

O'Conner, P., Detsky, A.S., Tansey, C., Kucharczyk, W., & Rochester-Toronto MRI Study Group. (1994). Effect of diagnostic testing for multiple sclerosis on patient health perceptions. *Archives of Neurology, 51,* 46–51.

Olshansky, S. (1962). Chronic sorrow: A response to having a mentally defective child. *Social Casework, 43,* 191–193.

Pakenham, K.I. (1999). Adjustment to multiple sclerosis: Application of a stress and coping model. *Health Psychology, 18,* 383–392.

Pakenham, K.I., Stewart, C.A., & Rogers, A. (1997). The role of coping in adjustment to multiple sclerosis-related adaptive demands. *Psychology, Health, and Medicine, 2,* 197–211.

Pearlin, L.I., Mullan, J.T., Semple, S.J., & Skaff, M.M. (1990). Caregiving and the stress process: An overview of concepts and their measures. *The Gerontologist, 30,* 583–594.

Pepper, C.M., Drupp, L.B., Friedberg, F., Doscher, C., & Coyle, P.K. (1993). A comparison of neuropsychiatric characteristics in chronic fatigue syndrome, multiple sclerosis, and major depression. *Journal of Neuropsychiatric and Clinical Neurosciences, 5,* 200–205.

Peyser, J.M., Rao, S.M., LaRocca, N.G., & Kaplan, E. (1990). Guidelines for neuropsychological research in multiple sclerosis. *Archives of Neurology, 47,* 94–97.

Plohmann, A.M., Kappos, L., Ammann, W., Thordai, A., Wittwer, A., Huber, S., & Bellaiche, Y. (1998). Computer assisted retraining of attentional impairments in patients with multiple sclerosis. *Journal of Neurology, Neurosurgery, and Psychiatry, 64,* 455–462.

Poeck, K. (1969). Pathophysiology of emotional disorders associated with brain damage. In P.J. Vinken & G.W. Bruyn (Eds.), *Handbook of Clinical Neurology* (pp. 343–367). Amsterdam: North Holland Publishing.

Pollin, I. (1995). *Medical crisis counseling: Short-term therapy for long-term illness.* New York: Norton.

Pratt, R.T.C. (1951). An investigation of the psychiatric aspects of disseminated sclerosis. *Journal of Neurology, Neurosurgery, and Psychiatry, 14,* 326–336.

Provinciali, L., Ceravolo, M.G., Bartolini, M., Logullo, F., & Danni, M. (1999). A multidimensional assessment of multiple sclerosis: Relationships between disability domains. *Acta Neurologica Scandinavica, 100,* 156–162.

Pujol, J., Bello, J., Deus, J., Marti-Vilalta, J.L., & Capdevila, A. (1997). Lesions in the left arcuate fasciculus region and depressive symptoms in multiple sclerosis. *Neurology, 49,* 1105–1110.

Rabins, P.V. (1990). Euphoria in multiple sclerosis. In S.M. Rao (Ed.), *Neurobehavioral aspects of multiple sclerosis* (pp. 180–185). New York: Oxford University Press.

Rabins, P.V., Brooks, B.R., O'Donnell, P., Pearlson, G.D., Moberg, P., Jubelt, B., Boyle, P., Dalos, N., & Folstein, M.F. (1986). Structural brain correlates of emotional disorder in multiple sclerosis. *Brain, 109*, 585–597.

Rabins, P., Mace, N., & Lucas, M. (1982). The impact of dementia on the family. *Journal of the American Medical Association, 248*, 333–335.

Radloff, L.S. (1977). The CES-D Scale: A self-report depression scale for research in the general population. *Applied Psychological Measurement, 1*, 385–401.

Raine, C.S. (1990). Neuropathology. In S.M. Rao (Ed.), *Neurobehavioral aspects of multiple sclerosis* (pp. 15–36). New York: Oxford University Press.

Rao, S.M. (Ed.). (1990). *Neurobehavioral aspects of multiple sclerosis*. New York: Oxford University Press.

Rao, S.M., Leo, G.J., Bernardin, L., & Unverzagt, F. (1991). Cognitive dysfunction in multiple sclerosis: I. Frequency, patterns, and prediction. *Neurology, 41*, 685–691.

Rao, S.M., Leo, G.J., Ellington, L., Nauertz, T., Bernardin, L., & Unverzagt, F. (1991). Cognitive dysfunction in multiple sclerosis: II. Impact on employment and social functioning. *Neurology, 41*, 692–696.

Raven, J.C. (1960). *Guide to the Standard Progressive Matrices*. London: H.K. Lewis.

Rivera, P.A., Rose, J.M., Futterman, A., Lovett, S.B., & Gallagher-Thompson, D. (1991). Dimensions of perceived social support in clinically depressed and nondepressed female caregivers. *Psychology and Aging, 6*, 232–237.

Rogers, D., Khoo, K., MacEachen, M., Oven, M., & Beatty, W.W. (1996). Cognitive therapy for multiple sclerosis: A preliminary study. *Alternative Therapies, 2*, 70–74.

Ron, M.A., & Logsdail, S.J. (1989). Psychiatric morbidity in multiple sclerosis: A clinical and MRI study. *Psychological Medicine, 19*, 887–895.

Rosenthal, R. (1995). Progress in clinical psychology: Is there any? *Clinical Psychology: Science and Practice, 2*, 133–150.

Rovaris, M., Filippi, M., Falautano, M., Minicucci, L., Rocca, M., Martinelli, V., & Comi, G. (1998). Relation between MR abnormalities and patterns of cognitive impairment in multiple sclerosis. *Neurology, 50*, 1601–1608.

Ryan, L., Clark, C.M., Klonoff, H., Li, D., & Paty, D. (1996). Patterns of cognitive impairment in relapsing-remitting multiple sclerosis and their relationship to neuropathology on magnetic resonance images. *Neuropsychology, 10*, 176–193.

Sabatini, U., Pozzilli, C., Pantano, P., Koudriavtseva, T., Padovani, A., Millefiorini, E., Di Biasi, C., Fualdi, G.F., Salvetti, M., & Lenzi, G.L. (1996). Involvement of the limbic system in

multiple sclerosis patients with depressive disorders. *Biological Psychiatry, 39*, 970–975.

Sackheim, H.A., Greenberg, M.S., Weiman, A.L., Gur, R.D., Hungerbuhler, J.P., & Geschwind, N. (1982). Hemispheric asymmetry in the expression of positive and negative emotions. *Archives of Neurology, 41*, 210–218.

Sadovnick, A.D., Eisen, K., Ebers, G.C., & Paty, D.W. (1991). Cause of death in patients attending multiple sclerosis clinics. *Neurology, 41*, 1193–1196.

Schapiro, R.T. (1994). Symptom management in multiple sclerosis. *Annals of Neurology, 36*, S123–S129.

Schiaffino, K.M., Shawaryn, M.A., & Blum, D. (1998). Examining the impact of illness representations on psychological adjustment to chronic illness. *Health Psychology, 17*, 262–268.

Schiffer, R.B. (1987). The spectrum of depression in multiple sclerosis: An approach for clinical management. *Archives of Neurology, 44*, 596–599.

Schiffer, R.B., Caine, E.D., Bamford, K.A., & Levy, S. (1983). Depressive episodes in patients with multiple sclerosis. *American Journal of Psychiatry, 140*, 1498–1500.

Schiffer, R.B., Herndon, R.M., & Rudick, R.A. (1985). Treatment of pathologic laughing and weeping with amitriptyline. *New England Journal of Medicine, 312*, 1480–1482.

Schiffer, R.B., Weitkamp, L.R., Wineman, N.M., & Guttormsen, S. (1988). Multiple sclerosis and affective disorder: Family history, sex, and HLA-DR antigens. *Archives of Neurology, 45*, 1345–1348.

Schiffer, R.B., & Wineman, N.M. (1990). Antidepressant pharmacotherapy of depression associated with multiple sclerosis. *American Journal of Psychiatry, 147*, 1493–1497.

Schiffer, R.B., Wineman, N.M., & Weitkamp, L.R. (1986). Association between bipolar disorder and multiple sclerosis. *American Journal of Psychiatry, 143*, 94–95.

Schubert, D.S.P., & Foliart, R.H. (1993). Increased depression in multiple sclerosis patients: A meta-analysis. *Psychosomatics, 34*, 124–130.

Scott, T.F., Allen, D., Price, T.R.P., McConnell, H., & Lang, D. (1996). Characterization of major depression symptoms in multiple sclerosis patients. *Journal of Neuropsychiatry and Clinical Neurosciences, 8*, 318–323.

Seliger, G.M., Hornstein, A., Flax, F., Herbert, J., & Schroeder, K. (1992). Gluoxetine improves emotional incontinence. *Brain Injury, 6*, 267–270.

Sherbourne, C.D., Wells, K.B., Hays, R.D., Rogers, W., Burnam, M.A., & Judd, L.L. (1994). Subthreshold depression and depressive disorder: Clinical characteristics of general medical and mental health specialty outpatients. *American Journal of Psychiatry, 151*, 1777–1784.

Shnek, Z.M., Foley, F.W., LaRocca, N.G., Smith, C.R., & Halper, J. (1995). *Journal of Neurologic Rehabilitation, 9*, 15–23.

Sibley, W.A. (1997). Risk factors in multiple sclerosis. In C.S. Raine, H.F. McFarland, & W.W. Tourtellotte (Eds.), *Multiple sclerosis: Clinical and pathogenetic basis* (pp. 141–148). London: Chapman & Hall.

Sibley, W.A., Poser, C.M., & Alter, M. (1989). Multiple Sclerosis. In L.P. Rowland (Ed.), *Merritt's textbook of neurology* (8th ed, pp. 741–765). Philadelphia, PA: Lea & Febiger.

Smith, A.A. (1973). *Symbol Digit Modalities Test Manual*. Los Angeles: Western Psychological Services.

Sperling, R.A., Guttmann, C.R., Hohol, M.J., Warfield, S.K., Jakab, M., Parente, M., Diamond, E.L., Daffner, K.R., Olek, M.J., Orav, E.J., Kikinis, R., Jolesz, F.A., & Weiner, H.L. (2001). Regional magnetic resonance imaging lesion burden and cognitive functioning in multiple sclerosis: A longitudinal study. *Archives of Neurology, 58*, 115–121.

Spiegel, D., & Classen, C. (2000). *Group psychotherapy for cancer patients*. New York: Basic Books.

Stenager, E., Knudsen, L., & Jensen, K. (1993). Multiple sclerosis: Correlation of anxiety, physical impairment and cognitive dysfunction. *Italian Journal of Neurological Sciences, 15*, 99–103.

Stuifbergen, A.K. (1995). Health-promoting behaviors and quality of life among individuals with multiple sclerosis. *Scholarly Inquiry for Nursing Practice: An International Journal, 9*, 31–50.

Stuifbergen, A.K., & Roberts, G.J. (1997). Health promotion practices of women with multiple sclerosis. *Archives of Medical Rehabilitation, 78*, S3–S9.

Surridge, D. (1969). An investigation into some psychiatric aspects of multiple sclerosis. *British Journal of Psychiatry, 115*, 749–764.

Taylor, S.E. (1983). Adjustment to threatening events: A theory of cognitive adaptation. *American Psychologist, 38*, 1161–1173.

Thompson, A.J. (1996). Multiple sclerosis: Symptomatic treatment. *Journal of Neurology, 243*, 559–565.

Thornton, A.E., & Raz, N. (1997). Memory impairment in multiple sclerosis: A quantitative review. *Neuropsychology, 11*, 357–366.

Tsolaki, M., Drevelegas, A., Karachristianou, S., Kapina, K., Divanlogou, D., & Routsonis, K. (1994). Correlation of dementia, neuropsychological and MRI findings in multiple sclerosis. *Dementia, 5*, 48–52.

U.S. Bureau of the Census. (1982). *1980 Census of Population, Alphabetical Index of Industries and Occupations* (PHS 80-R3). Washington, DC.

Van Buchem, M.A., McGowan, J.C., & Gossmann, R.I. (1999). Magnetization transfer histogram methodology: Its clinical and neuropsychological correlates. Neurology, 53(S3), S23–S28.

Warren, S., Greenhill, S., & Warren, K.G. (1982). Emotional stress and the development of multiple sclerosis: Case-control evidence of a relationship. *Journal of Chronic Disease, 35*, 821–831.

Warren, S., Warren, K.G., & Cockerill, R. (1991). Emotional stress and coping in multiple sclerosis exacerbations. *Journal of Psychosomatic Research, 35*, 37–47.

Wechsler, D. (1987). *Wechsler Memory Scale — Revised manual*. New York: Harcourt Brace Jovanovich.

Whitlock, F.A., & Siskind, M.M. (1980). Depression as a major symptom of multiple sclerosis. *Journal of Neurology, Neurosurgery, and Psychiatry, 43*, 861–865.

Wineman, N.M. (1990). Adaptation to multiple sclerosis: The role of social support, functional disability, and perceived uncertainty. *Nursing Research, 39*, 294–299.

Wineman, N.M., Durand, E.J., & McCulloch, B.J. (1994). Examination of the factor structure of the Ways of Coping Questionnaire with clinical populations. *Nursing Research, 43*(5), 268–273.

Wineman, N.M., Durand, E.J., & Steiner, R.P. (1994) A comparative analysis of coping behaviors in persons with multiple sclerosis and spinal cord injury. *Research in Nursing and Health, 17*, 185–194.

Wineman, N.M., Schwetz, K.M., Goodkin, D.E., & Rudick, R.A. (1996). Relationships among illness uncertainty, stress, coping, and emotional well-being at entry into a clinical drug trial. *Applied Nursing Research, 9*, 53–60.

Winslow, B., & O'Brien, R. (1992). Use of formal community resources by spouse caregivers of chronically ill adults. *Public Health Nursing, 9*, 128–132.

World Health Organization. (1999). *International classification of functioning and disability (beta-2 draft)*. Geneva: World Health Organization.

Zakzanis, K. (2000). Distinct neurocognitive profiles in multiple sclerosis subtypes. *Archives of Clinical Neuropsychology, 15*(2), 115–136.

Zarit, S.H., Reever, K.E., & Bach-Peterson, J. (1980). Relatives of the impaired elderly: Correlates of feelings of burden. *The Gerontologist, 20,* 649–655.

Zarit, S.H., Todd, P.A., & Zarit, J.M. (1986). Subjective burden of husbands and wives as caregivers: A longitudinal study. *Gerontologist, 26,* 260–266.

Zeidner, M., & Saklofske, D. (1996). Adaptive and maladaptive coping. In M. Zeidner & N.S. Endler (Eds.), *Handbook of coping: Theory, research, applications* (pp. 505–531). New York: Wiley.

Susan C. Klock

11

Obstetric and Gynecological Conditions

Introduction

The obstetrician or gynecologist is often a woman's primary care provider and may be the first person she consults for medical and psychological problems. Due to the obstetrician's role as a primary care provider many obstetric and gynecology practices now employ a mental health professional as a consultant to their patients. A psychologist in this role needs to be conversant with the physiological aspects of women's health and a specialist in the psychological, social and cultural influences that converge to impact a woman's health.

As Mathis (1967) noted three decades ago, "Sex, reproduction, and the reproductive system are almost synonymous with emotional reactions in our culture ... The physician who assumes this responsibility automatically becomes involved in emotional processes unequaled in any other branch of medicine." Unfortunately, in the current health care environment, the physician is usually limited in the amount of time he or she can spend to help the patient with her psychological distress. Additionally, most physicians are not trained in behavioral medicine and may be ill-prepared to deal with the psychological needs of their patients. Therefore, the role of the psychologist in the obstetric and gynecology practice has become more active in recent years.

Since the advent of modern medical and anesthetic practices normal reproductive events have become "diseases" in the medical nomenclature. In fact, as advances in technology continue, the medicalization of a woman's reproductive life has become more common. With the discovery of anesthetics and antiseptics, pregnancy has become a medically mediated event. The creation of the assisted reproductive technologies have made infertility a disease with a wide variety of hormonal and surgical treatments. Even the cessation of a woman's reproductive life is now medicalized with the recent trend to prescribe hormone replacement therapy to women to prevent the menopause-related changes in bone density and cardiovascular function.

The medicalization of women's reproductive functioning has had both positive and negative effects on women's quality of life. It has lead to a greater need for women to be informed decision-makers and have active participation in their health care (Boston Women's Health Book Collective, 1992). It has also led to greater identification and treatment of the psychological conditions associated with reproduction. The purpose of this chapter is to describe the common conditions seen by the health psychologist working in the obstetrics and gynecology service and to summarize how the health psychologist can contribute to the evaluation and treatment of the obstetrics and gynecology patient.

Biomedical Aspects

The Female Reproductive System and Menstrual Cycle

In order to understand the medical issues in obstetrics and gynecology a basic understanding of the female reproductive cycle is needed. For a complete description of the reproductive endocrinology cycle see Guyton and Hall (1996) and Speroff, Glass and Kase (1989). The following is a basic summary of the reproductive cycle (Guyton & Hall, 1996).

The principal organs of the female reproductive tract are the ovaries, fallopian tubes, uterus and vagina (Figure 1). Reproduction is dependent on the development of ova in the ovaries, with one mature ovum being released each month. The ovum travels from the ovary, through the fallopian tubes to the uterus where it may be fertilized by sperm from the male. If the ovum is fertilized it can implant in the uterine wall were it develops into a fetus, placenta and fetal membranes. A female infant is born with approximately 2 million ova, this decreases to approximately 300,000 at the time of puberty when she becomes fertile. Throughout the course of a woman's reproductive life only about 450 mature ova are released and potentially fertilized, the rest degenerate. At the time of menopause, only a few ovum remain and they soon become atretic due to lack of hormonal stimulation.

The female reproductive cycle has three levels of hormones controlling the release of the ovum. At the first level is the hypothalamus. It releases a hormone called luteinizing hormone- releasing hormone (LHRH). LHRH acts at the anterior pituitary where it prompts the release of two additional hormones, follicle-stimulating hormone (FSH) and luteinizing hormone (LH). FSH prompts the development of follicles, which contain the ova, in the ovary and LH is needed for the release of the ova from the follicle, ovulation, and the development of the corpus luteum. After ovulation, the remaining cells of the follicle become the corpus luteum, a group of cells that secrete progesterone (P) and estrogen (E). The P and E prepare the body for possible pregnancy. They also provide negative feedback to the anterior pituitary to stop the release of FSH and LH. If fertilization and implantation do not take place, the corpus luteum degenerates, E and P levels drop and menstruation begins. The levels of these hormones at various times in the menstrual cycle are illustrated in Figure 2. The average duration of the menstrual cycle is 28 days, with day 1 indicated by the first day of bleeding. A single mature ovum is released each month around day 14. The corpus luteum degenerates over the course of the next 12 days if pregnancy does not take place, then menstruation begins approximately 2 days later. The ova remains viable and capable of being fertilized probably no longer than 24 hours.

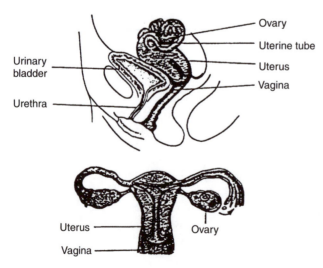

Figure 1. Anatomy of the female reproductive system. From Guyton, A.C., & Hall, J. (1996). *Textbook of medical physiology* (9th ed., pp. 1005–1037). Philadelphia: W.B. Saunders. Reprinted with permission.

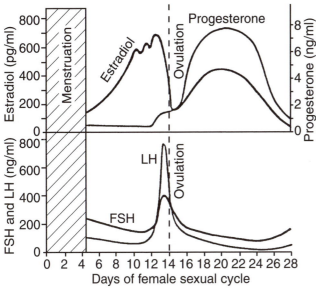

Figure 2. Hormonal levels during the menstrual cycle. From Guyton, A.C., Hall, J. (1996). *Textbook of medical physiology* (9th ed., pp. 1005–1037). Philadelphia: W.B. Saunders.

Sperm remains viable in the female reproductive tract approximately 24–72 hours, therefore sperm must be available shortly after ovulation in order for fertilization to occur.

Major Gynecologic Events

The female reproductive life cycle is marked by several major events. Menarche, or the onset of menstruation at puberty, around the age of 11, signifies the beginning of the woman's reproductive potential. The onset of sexual activity marks a second psychological and developmental milestone. By the age of 20 the majority of American youths have become sexually active, with 23% becoming sexually active by their 16th birthday and 53% becoming sexually active by their 18th birthday (Allgeier & Allgeier, 1989).

Pregnancy and the transition to first-time parenthood is another important event, both physically and psychologically. Approximately 50% of pregnancies are unintentional (Goldberg, 1988) and in the past two decades the rates of teenage pregnancy have risen dramatically. Whether unintentional or intentional, pregnancy represents a pivotal physical and emotional challenge to most women.

Menopause is the final milestone for a woman's reproductive life. Menopause is the cessation of the menstrual cycle and associated reproductive capacity. It occurs in the United States at the average of 51 years of age. In Western cultures menopause is associated with numerous physical and psychological complaints for some women, but in other cultures it is a developmental phase that is greatly anticipated for the increased social and familial status it entails (Van Keep & Kellerhals, 1974; Wilbush, 1982).

Current Medical Management of Pregnancy, Infertility and Menopause

Pregnancy

Pregnancy can first be detected approximately 10 days after ovulation by levels of a hormone called human chorionic gonadotropin (hcg). More often though, pregnancy is suspected when a woman misses her menstrual period and takes a home pregnancy test. Pregnancy occurs approximately 25% of the time with appropriately timed intercourse between two fertile individuals. About 20% of all pregnancies miscarry, usually due to genetic reasons, during the first 12 weeks of pregnancy, although miscarriage rates increase with maternal age. Female fertility is at its peak from 18 through 34 years of age, with stepwise declines at 35 and 40 years of ages.

Medical care during pregnancy is critical

for the assurance of the health and safety of the mother and the developing fetus (American Medical Association, 1996). Pregnancy is 40 weeks in duration, calculated from the first day of the last menstrual period (not the estimated date of conception). The pregnancy is divided into three, 13 week trimesters. The first trimester is the most critical in terms of the health of the baby's development. By the end of the first trimester all of the baby's major organs and extremities are fully formed. During this time the fetus is especially vulnerable to external agents, such as drugs or alcohol, environmental toxins or infections. During the first trimester women experience a variety of symptoms including tiredness, nausea ("morning sickness"), breast tenderness, frequent urination, and food cravings or aversions. The first prenatal visit with the doctor or midwife is usually scheduled during the end of the first trimester. At that visit the doctor takes the medical history, performs a physical exam, establishes a due date, plans for upcoming appointments and discusses prenatal testing.

The second trimester is usually most enjoyable for the woman. Nausea has usually subsided, the pregnancy becomes visibly apparent and quickening is detected around the 16th week. Around the fifth month the fetus has a growth spurt and will be about 11 to 14 inches long and weigh 1 to 1½ pounds. Given the growth of the fetus, the woman's body changes to accommodate it and some of these changes are uncomfortable. During the second trimester, the woman is seen by her midwife or doctor on a monthly basis. At 28 weeks the visits are scheduled for every 2 to 3 weeks, then at 36 weeks the visits are weekly until the time of delivery. During the visits, weight and blood pressure are measured as well as the growth of the uterus and the fetal heartbeat. During the 6th month, the woman will have a glucose tolerance test to determine if she has developed gestational diabetes.

Between 15 and 18 weeks, most women are offered the alpha-fetoprotein (AFP) test, which is a blood test to determine if the fetus has a neural tube defect (developmental failure in the brain or spinal cord). The AFP test has a high false positive rate, therefore most positive tests are followed up with additional testing. If the AFP is positive, then an ultrasound may be recommended to visualize the fetus. Also, an amniocentesis test may be used. The amniocentesis is usually performed during the 14th to 18th weeks to analyze the amniotic fluid. The amniotic fluid contains genetic material that is tested for genetic abnormalities including neural tube defects, Down's syndrome, cystic fibrosis, and sickle cell anemia. Amniocentesis is routinely recommended for women 35 years or older due to the increased risk of genetic abnormalities among older women. The risk of miscarriage after amniocentesis is 1 in 200.

Another prenatal test to detect genetic abnormalities is chorionic villus sampling (CVS). CVS takes a sample of the placental tissue for use in genetic testing. The major advantage of CVS over amniocentesis is that it can be done earlier in the pregnancy (10th to 12th week). Earlier diagnosis of a genetic abnormality may lead to earlier resolution of the pregnancy. The major disadvantage of CVS is the slightly higher rate of miscarriage, 1 in 100.

Throughout the pregnancy ultrasound testing may be used to determine the position of the fetus and other physical signs. The ultrasound is a painless and safe imaging procedure that uses sound waves to create a picture of the fetus and placenta. The decision to have an amniocentesis or CVS, as well as other prenatal tests, is up to the woman. Knowledge about the woman's religious, moral, and ethical beliefs are critical in helping counsel here regarding the utility of prenatal testing.

During the third trimester the woman usually becomes uncomfortable due to the added weight and size of her abdomen. During this time the fetus grows from approximately 3 pounds to its final birth weight of 6 to 9 pounds. Due to fetal size, movement and sleeping become more difficult for the woman. The average range of weight gain for a healthy pregnancy is 25–35 pounds. The woman may experience symptoms of tiredness, swollen feet or ankles, and mild contractions during this time. Labor usually begins in the 37th to 42nd week.

Labor is divided into three stages, dilation and effacement (opening and thinning of the cervix), delivery of the baby and delivery of the placenta. The duration of labor is highly variable, from 1 hour to 24 hours. Labors usually shorten in length with subsequent births. During the dilation and effacement phase, the cervix changes to allow the delivery of the baby. Full effacement is 100% and progress toward full effacement is described in percentages. Dilation is measured in centimeters, with 10 centimeters indicating full dilation. Dilation and effacement do not necessarily occur together. The first phase of labor is over when dilation is 10. When the cervix is fully dilated the delivery phase has begun and the doctor or midwife instructs the woman to begin pushing. Contractions come every 2–5 minutes and last 1–1½ minutes. This stage of labor usually lasts 1–2 hours for a first delivery. This stage ends when the baby is born. The last stage of labor is the delivery of the placenta. After the baby is delivered, the placenta detaches from the uterine wall and passes out of the body. This usually happens within 30 minutes after the baby is delivered.

Infertility

The medical management of infertility has increased greatly in the past two decades. As the baby boom cohort of women reached their reproductive years in the 1980s and 1990s, the utilization of infertility treatment rose dramatically. It is estimated that 15% of couples are infertile (Mosher, 1988) although only a minority (24%) of these couples seek medical treatment (Wilcox & Mosher, 1993). Those most likely to obtain specialized services are Caucasian, 30 years of age or older, nulliparous, married and of higher socioeconomic status. The initial phases of the infertility work-up and treatment can be time-consuming, anxiety-provoking and frustrating. A couple who has been unsuccessful at achieving a pregnancy after 12 months of appropriately timed intercourse may be seen by their gynecologist or reproductive endocrinologist.

A series of tests will be performed, most on the woman, to determine the cause of the problem. About 35% of fertility problems are attributable to male factor, 20% to ovulatory problems, 20% tubal factor, 5% cervical factor, 10% endometriosis and 10% unexplained. About 25% to 35% of infertility problems have multiple causes. Causes of male infertility include anatomic factors, such as a varicocele, endocrine problems, genetics, inflammatory factors, sexual dysfunction and exogenous agents such as medication, radiation, substance abuse or excessive heat. Causes of female infertility can be categorized as ovulatory dysfunction, cervical factors, tubal and peritoneal factors (blocked tubes, pelvic adhesions and endometriosis) and uterine factors. The goals of the initial infertility evaluation are to (1) identify the cause of the problem; (2) provide and discuss treatment options; (3) provide a reasonable prognosis; and (4) to provide emotional support (Rein & Schiff, 1996).

In terms of diagnostic tests, the male has a semen analysis to determine the number, shape and motility of his sperm. This test requires the man to produce a semen sample in the clinic, via masturbation, and can be anxiety producing for some men. The female partner may undergo a variety of diagnostic tests to determine the cause of the infertility. One of the most basic is the basal body temperature chart, that is daily taking of the temperature upon waking to determine the time of the mid-cycle rise in temperature associated with ovulation. The woman may also have blood tests to determine levels of the reproductive hormones. The postcoital test, hysterosalgingogram, endometrial biopsy, and laparoscopy are other diagnostic procedures used to determine the cause of the infertility. The postcoital test is a sampling of the cervical mucus several hours after intercourse to determine the number of viable sperm in the cervical area. A hysterosalpingogram is a radiological procedure in which dye is introduced through the uterus to determine if it flows freely throughout the uterine cavity and fallopian tubes. This test is used to determine if there is tubal blockage. An endometrial biopsy is a sampling of the endometrial tissue in the uterus 2 to 3 days prior to menses to determine if the endometrium is appropriately developed. A laparoscopy is commonly used to diagnose pelvic adhesions, endometriosis or anatomical factors that may be preventing pregnancy.

The completion of the diagnostic tests can take 2 to 3 months. Following the completion of the tests the majority of couples can expect to have a diagnosis for the fertility problem and a treatment plan. Anovulation or oligoovulation (irregular ovulation) may be treated with ovulation induction agents such as clomiphene citrate or human menotrophin gonadotrophins. The side effects of ovulatory stimulation medications include abdominal bloating, pelvic discomfort, breast tenderness and for some women emotional lability and short term memory problems. These medications are usually tried for four to six cycles with intrauterine insemination. Success rates for these treatments are variable. If ovulation induction treatment does not work, then couples may consider in vitro fertilization.

In vitro fertilization (IVF) was developed in the mid 1970s and the first IVF baby was born in the United Kingdom in 1978. Since that time it has been widely used for the treatment of infertility. In this procedure the woman undergoes ovulation induction with transvaginal retrieval of the eggs. The eggs are fertilized and after 2 days the developing embryos are transferred back to the woman's uterus. The couple waits two weeks for a pregnancy test. Extra embryos are frozen for use in subsequent cycles or donated to research or to another couple if the originating couple has completed their family. The average success rate for the procedure is 21% per cycle. Multiple pregnancies (twins, triplets, quadruplets, etc.) are more likely with IVF pregnancies. The procedure usually costs between $8000 and $10,000 per cycle. Variations on IVF can be used, such as IVF with donor sperm or egg donation from a known or anonymous egg donor in cases of advanced maternal age. With all the varied options for assisted reproduction, the emotional, ethical and legal issues are myriad. Society's ability to keep pace with the technological developments in reproduction has been limited. Also the lack of regulation of

these treatments in the United States has left the market open to a wide range of clinical practices.

Menopause
Menopause is the permanent cessation of menses. The mean age of women at menopause is 51 years (Walsh, 1996). The age of menopause is not related to the number of pregnancies a woman has had or previous use of oral contraceptives. As women's life expectancies have increased so too has the amount of time women live postmenopausally. Now a woman can expect to live one third of her life after menopause. For years prior to menopause, estrogen and progesterone levels decline despite the continuation of ovulatory cycles. The decrease in estrogen and progesterone lead to feedback to the hypothalamic-pituitary system and results in an increase in follicle stimulating hormone (FSH). The remaining ovarian follicles have a decreased response to the increasing FSH levels and in turn less estrogen and progesterone are released. Menopause is diagnosed by the documentation of an elevated FSH level.

The prominent symptom of menopause is vasomotor flushes. Approximately 80% of women experience vasomotor flushes within 3 months of menopause. Vasomotor flushes are episodes with a prodromal phase of palpitations or sensation of pressure in the head, weakness or faintness followed by a sensation of intense warmth lasting a few minutes. They end with a period of sweating and a cold sensation. They occur more frequently at night. Vasomotor flushes are the result of the withdrawal of estrogen from the women's system.

Osteoporosis is another consequence of menopause. It is a progressive reduction in bone mass due to estrogen depletion. Women lose approximately 4% of bone mass each year for the 6 years following menopause. Caucasian and Asian women are at greater risk than African American women. Thin women are at greater risk than obese women. Women who are sedentary, smoke, drink alcohol or drink more than two cups of coffee per day generally lose bone mass more quickly than women who do not engage in these behaviors. Once osteoporosis has occurred it cannot be significantly reversed. It is usually diagnosed by a measure of bone density at regular intervals to determine if bone mass is being lost and at what rate. Because the condition cannot be reversed, prevention rather than treatment is usually recommended by the physician. The use of estrogen replacement and calcium supplements can be used to prevent bone loss, in conjunction with stopping at risk behaviors.

Cardiovascular disease (CVD) is another problem for postmenopausal women. Over 50% of postmenopausal women will develop CVD. It is believed that estrogen plays a role in protecting women from CVD in the premenopausal years and that the protective effects of estrogen can return with the use of hormone replacement therapy (Walsh, 1996).

Genital atrophy is another change associated with menopause. The tissue of the vagina, labia and urethra are estrogen dependent therefore the decrease of estrogen during menopause causes the tissue to become less vascular, thin and less elastic. Women usually complain of vaginal dryness, dyspareunia and vaginismus which can alter sexual functioning and can decrease sexual desire or performance.

Treatment of menopausal changes with hormone replacement therapy is becoming more common. Estrogen or estrogen in combination with progesterone can be given to alleviate menopausal changes. Natural and synthetic hormone preparations are available. The specific regime for hormone replacement treatment needs to be individualized by a woman's physician to take into consideration her current situation and health history. Side effects of estrogen treatment include nausea, headache, and mood changes. Side effects of progesterone include abdominal bloating, headaches, mood changes and acne. Use of unopposed estrogen (not in combination with progesterone) may be associated with endometrial hyperplasia. This risk is reduced when estrogen is given in combination with progesterone. The risk for other types of cancer, such as ovarian and breast cancers, may be increased with es-

trogen administration, but this relationship is not definitive.

In decades past, menopause was not considered a medical condition, it was considered a normal phase of a women's reproductive life; the end of her reproductive capacity and the beginning of her middle age. In the past several decades with the advances in reproductive endocrinology has come the increased usage of hormone replacement therapy to alleviate the symptoms of menopause. Hormone replacement therapy can reverse the negative effects of estrogen depletion, including hot flashes, osteoporosis and cardiovascular changes, but it does not regenerate a woman's reproductive capacity. At this time there appears to be a consensus that hormone replacement therapy is of benefit to menopausal women in reducing vasomotor changes, preventing osteoporosis and decreased risk of CVD. These benefits need to be balanced with the possible increased risk of endometrial, ovarian and breast cancer. These risks and benefits need to be discussed with the woman's physician in conjunction with consideration of her individual health and history factors.

Psychological Assessment and Treatment

Introduction to Common Referral Problems

The following is a description of four common referral problems seen by the author over the past 10 years in her role as a psychologist in obstetrics and gynecology services. These problems are premenstrual syndrome (PMS), postpartum depression, infertility and adjustment to menopause.

PMS

Premenstrual syndrome was described over 50 years ago by Frank (1931) when he reported women's experience of an "indescribable tension" in the late luteal phase of the menstrual cycle. He reported that the tension increased during the late luteal phase and remitted with the onset of menses. Since the publication of Frank's article, there have been thousands of studies investigating various aspects of PMS. In 1987, in an attempt to clarify this clinical phenomenon, the American Psychiatric Association included late luteal phase dysphoric disorder (LLPDD) in the DSM-III-R as a provisional diagnosis in need of further study (American Psychiatric Association, 1987). These same criteria are also included in the DSM-IV under the diagnosis of premenstrual dysphoric disorder (PDD) (American Psychiatric Association, 1994).

The definition and diagnostic criteria of the disorder have evolved significantly in the past 20 years When doing an evaluation of PMS/PDD the first issue to consider is the differentiation of normal *premenstrual changes* from problematic *premenstrual symptoms* (Blechman, 1982). Blechman defined *premenstrual changes* as any physical or behavioral experience that is discriminably different during the premenstruum compared to other times in the menstrual cycle. Premenstrual changes can be either positive or negative. It is estimated that 80% of women experience some type of premenstrual change (Magos, Brincat & Studd, 1986). *Premenstrual symptoms* are those changes that are perceived by the woman to be severe, negative or of such significance as to limit her functioning. Over one hundred symptoms have been identified as a part of PDD (Rubinow & Roy-Byrne, 1984). Symptoms can be in several categories, such as affective, cognitive, pain, neurovegetative, autonomic, fluid/electrolyte and behavioral. Common symptoms include feelings of depression or irritability, decreased concentration, increased food and alcohol consumption, breast pain, edema, headaches, and fatigue. Although some researchers have argued that there are several subtypes of PDD, most patients present with a unique combination of symptoms that vary in degrees of intensity and duration (Halbreich & Endicott, 1982; Abraham, 1983).

Despite widespread recognition of PMS/PDD and its inclusion in the psychiatric nomenclature, the etiology of the disorder is unclear. Common hypotheses about the cause include excess estrogen, progesterone deficiency, fluid retention, hyperprolactinemia, vitamin B6 deficiency, prostaglandin deficiency, endogenous opioid malfunction, and psychogenic. Several thorough reviews of the etiology of PDD are available (Reid & Yen, 1981; Rubinow & Roy-Bryne, 1984; Smith &Schiff, 1989; Steiner & Pearlstein, 2000).

In terms of the intensity and duration of symptoms, according to Rubinow and Roy-Bryne (1984) the definition of PMS/PDD is, "the cyclic recurrence in the luteal phase of the menstrual cycle of a combination of distressing physical, psychologic, and/or behavioral changes of sufficient severity to result in deterioration of interpersonal relationships and/or in interference with normal activities." PDD should be diagnosed only if the symptoms: (1) are reliably related to the luteal phase of the menstrual cycle; (2) remit shortly after the onset of menses; (3) are separate from a preexisting psychiatric disorder and; (4) significantly impair the women's functioning (Steege, 1989). It is estimated that 3%–8% of women have some form of PDD although rates vary depending on the stringency of the diagnostic criteria and the accuracy of assessment (Steiner & Pearlstein, 2000).

Criteria for PDD can be found in the Diagnostic and Statistical Manual of the Mental Disorders DSM-IV (American Psychiatric Association, 1994). These criteria specify that a woman must have at least one prominent mood symptom, four other somatic or behavioral symptoms, and the symptoms must be prospectively confirmed via daily symptom ratings for at lease two cycles. There must be at least 1 year's duration of symptoms that begin in the luteal phase and remit during the follicular phase in order to meet stringent diagnostic criteria (Endicott, 2000). It is estimated that 5% of women from the general population and 24% of women from a psychiatric population meet the diagnostic criteria for PDD (Eckerd, Hurt & Severino, 1989; Rivera-Tovar & Frank, 1990). In a multicenter study the prevalence of PDD was estimated from a sample of 670 women seeking evaluation for PMS (Hurt, Schnurr, Severino, Freeman, Gise, Rivera-Tovar, 1992). The typical patient in this study was 34 years old, Caucasian, employed, and college educated with two children and had an 8 year history of premenstrual difficulties. Using three different scoring methods for daily symptoms the rates of PDD varied from 14% to 38%. Twenty seven percent of the sample had a preexisting psychiatric disorder and 50% had a history of psychiatric illness. Others have noted the high prevalence of personality and other psychiatric disorders among patients presenting for an PDD evaluation (Eckerd et al., 1989; Hair, Schramm, Caruso & Hale, 1990).

Given the recent evolution of the diagnostic criteria for PMS/PDD, it is not surprising that the assessment of PDD has undergone significant changes over the past three decades. In the 1960s, Dalton (1964) simply asked women if they had symptoms that varied with their menstrual cycle. Unfortunately, it has been found that retrospective reports of premenstrual symptomatology are inaccurate (Ruble, 1977), therefore daily symptom charting for at least two menstrual cycles is needed before a diagnosis of PDD can be made.

Others measures such as the Premenstrual Assessment Form and Daily Rating Form (Halbreich, Endicott & Nee, 1982), the Moos Menstrual Distress Questionnaire (Moos, 1969) and visual analog scales are available (Casper & Powell, 1986). Other psychometric tests such as the MMPI can determine the presence of coexisting psychopathology (Choung, 1988).

The psychological evaluation of the PDD referral should contain the following. First, a thorough psychological intake interview should be conducted with special emphasis on the onset, duration, intensity and symptom course. Crucial to this assessment is the discovery of the consequences of the symptoms in the woman's life. This is to determine if the consequences of the symptoms are in some way reinforcing the reoccurrence of the symptoms month after month. Also important at this phase is to determine the impact of the woman's symptoms on others, including her partner, children, other family members, co-workers and friends. Often, the premenstrual symptoms can prompt changes in

these relationships which may also serve to reinforce the continuation of the symptoms. Last, the woman should be asked how she has attempted to cope with or treat the symptoms herself. Has she made any accommodations for herself, either positive or negative, during the premenstruum that alters her symptomatology in any way? If she has, were these measures successful?

Following completion of the interview, the patient should be given a daily rating form to keep track of her symptoms. This form should be completed each day. The woman should note the severity of each symptom listed, days of the menstrual cycle, unusual events (at work, in relationships, etc.) and the use of alcohol or other substances. The woman should be seen for additional follow-up appointments at two week intervals to complete the history taking, to discuss events of importance and to develop rapport while the daily symptoms ratings forms are completed for at least two menstrual cycles. After the forms are complete, it is helpful for the clinician to graph the symptom changes as a function of the menstrual cycle. This can be done manually or by a simple computer graphics program. The visual display of the symptoms and their relationship to the woman's menstrual cycle is a powerful tool to provide the woman with feedback. Usually there are one of three outcomes: (1) the patient does not keep the daily diary and does not return for evaluation; (2) the patient keeps the diary and finds out that the symptoms are not related to her menstrual cycle and; (3) the patient keeps the diary and finds out that her symptoms are related to her menstrual cycle. Approximately 50% of cases fit in category one. A second subgroup of women find out that their symptoms are not related to their menstrual cycle. This opens the door to discussion of other factors that might be affecting their symptoms. Any number of these causes could be identified and dealt with in psychotherapy. For the woman who has documented PDD several recommendations can be made to alleviate the symptoms. First, the acknowledgment and validation of PDD can be a great relief and reassurance for the woman. This may change her mental outlook and make her feel that the symptom onset and duration is predictable and controllable, therefore her general attitude may improve. Second, behavioral modifications such as regular aerobic exercise, a well-balanced diet, 8 hours of sleep, limited caffeine use and abstinence from alcohol may all prove to be helpful (Steege, 1993). The use of progesterone and other hormonal preparations, such as the oral contraceptive, have not proven to be effective in treating PDD. In the only double-blind, placebo controlled study of progesterone, a common past treatment for PDD, Freeman, Rickels, Sondheimer & Polansky (1990) demonstrated that progesterone was ineffective in treating PDD. Several studies have demonstrated the effectiveness of selective serotonin reuptake inhibitors (SSRIs) for treating PDD. These medications appear to be effective at doses given during

Case example

Ms. P is a 34-year-old married mother of two who was referred to me by her gynecologist for an evaluation of premenstrual dysphoria. Ms. P reports that for the past 2 years, since the birth of her last child, she has experienced debilitating premenstrual symptoms the week prior to her menses. She reports becoming a "raving maniac" with little tolerance for her husband, children or co-workers. Recently her employer commented to her that her usual calm composure was deteriorating. She reports that by the end of the day, during the premenstruum, she feels unable to cope with the demands for attention by her children and with the interactions with her husband. As she described her situation she said, "All I want to do is to be alone, with a bar of chocolate and a bag of potato chips." When her children or husband express a need to her, she becomes irritable and often explodes with anger, then feels remorseful. The patient believes that the family is learning to leave her alone during these times. She also notes that her husband becomes more active in child care and household duties during these times in order not to aggravate her. The patient has not made any attempts to alter her behaviors to try accommodate the premenstrual symptoms. The patient's psychiatric history is unremarkable.

I began the assessment with an intake interview including a description of the symptom pattern. I gave her the daily rating form for her to begin keeping track of her symptoms. She agreed to begin daily symptom charting and return in two weeks for a follow-up visit. At the follow-up visit Ms. P told me how interesting it was for her to notice the symptom changes over the course of the week. As she kept the daily symptom diary she became more aware of the nonmenstrually related events that irritated her. She also discussed the competing demands of raising a family, maintaining a marriage and working outside the home. I continued to see her every two weeks until 2 months of symptom ratings were completed. I graphed the symptom pattern across the days of her cycle on a chart for her. This demonstrated that Ms. P had some somatic symptoms that were related to her menstrual cycle but the emotional symptoms were related to disruptive events at home or work, such as conflicts with her husband or project deadlines at work. Ms. P was surprised and a little dismayed that it was, as she put it, "all in my head." I reframed her interpretation to suggest that the problems were not in her head but in her life; external events that placed pressure on her that she had not developed adequate coping mechanisms for. I focused the therapy on examining the sources of stress and a review of the patient's priorities. During this process Ms. P rearranged her schedule and modified her circumstances in order to minimize stress. A second component of the treatment focused on teaching the patient how to manage her time, assert her wishes and regulate her behavior to help her feel as if she has more control over the events in her day. I also wanted to determine if there was reciprocity in her relationships with others. Often women feel that they are in the caregiver role in many relationships and this leaves them little time to take care of themselves. This in turn makes them feel angry, irritable and resentful of others who they are taking care of. Over the course of several weekly visits Ms. P learned to re-organize her time and become more organized at home and work. She also learned to prioritize her time with her children and to state her needs more effectively to her husband. These changes lead to greater feelings of control and competency which helped the patient deal more effectively with the stressors her life.

the luteal phase and are well-tolerated (Steiner & Pearlstein, 2000). Psychotherapeutic interventions include stress management techniques such as assertiveness training, time management, progressive relaxation and guided imagery (Goodale, 1990). Alternative therapies, such as herbal remedies, dietary supplements and massage therapies have all been used but have not been proven more effective than placebo in double-blind, controlled trials (Stevinson & Ernst, 2001).

Postpartum Depression

Pregnancy and childbirth are significant developmental milestones for most women. Physical, intrapersonal, and relationship adaptations are needed to successfully adjust to pregnancy and new motherhood. The stresses that a new mother faces are numerous and include disruption in routine, sleep deprivation, decreased independence, social isolation, and changes in status at the workplace. The well-adjusted woman is able to anticipate these changes and prepare for them accordingly. Unfortunately, a minority of women may experience postpartum depression, a serious disorder that afflicts the new mother. Postpartum depression should be assessed and treated as soon as possible because of the deleterious consequences it can have on the mother and the newborn. The adverse impact of postpartum depression on infants has been noted (Robson & Kumar, 1980; Cooper, 1988; Murray, 1988).

Postpartum depression is characterized by depressed affect, loss of interest in activities, change in appetite, fatigue, sleep difficulties, difficulty caring for the baby, guilt, low self-esteem, difficulty concentrating, psychomotor retardation or agitation, and suicidal ideation. It is more serious and persistent than the "maternity blues" which is a transient emotional reaction that women experience shortly after birth that subsides without intervention in the two weeks following delivery (Hopkins, Marcus & Campbell, 1984). Postpartum depression begins at least two weeks after delivery and can persist for several months (Hayworth, Little, Bonham-Carter, Raptopoulos, Priest, & Sandler, 1980). Estimates of the prevalence of postpartum depression vary depending on the method of assessment. Based on self-report data, Dalton reported that 7% of women become depressed during the postpartum (Dalton, 1971). Others report rates vary from 3.5% to 26% (Cutrona, 1983; O'Hara, Neuhaber & Zekoski 1984; Gotlib, Whiffen, Mount, Milne & Cordy, 1989). Considering all studies, the base rate of postpartum depression is approximately 10% (O'Hara, 1989). Routine screening of all postpartum women with the Edinburgh Postnatal Depression Scale, a 10 item self-report questionnaire, has been recommended to allow greater identification of women at risk (Georgiopoulous et al., 1999).

Postpartum psychosis can be considered the most serious type of postpartum depression in which a woman's thinking becomes impaired. This is a rare disorder occurring in approximately 1 or 2 per 1000 women (0.1%–0.2%). It usually develops rapidly and is associated with depressed or euphoric mood, disorganized behavior, delusions, hallucinations and infanticidal thoughts. Postpartum psychosis is considered a psychiatric emergency and almost always requires hospitalization and medication management (Kendall et al., 1987). Women with a history of postpartum psychosis have an approximately 70% relapse rate; women with a past episode of postpartum depression have a 50% recurrence rate (Nonacs & Cohen, 1998).

Several factors have been investigated as possible causes of postpartum depression. Biologic variables, including hormones and neurotransmitters, have been investigated. One prospective study found that estradiol levels were significantly lower in depressed women than in nondepressed women (O'Hara, Schlechte, Lewis & Varner, 1991). Others have studied the relationship between postpartum depression and tryptophan levels (the precursor to serotonin) and have had equivocal results (Treadway, Kane, Jarrahi-Zadeh & Lipton, 1969; Handley, Dunn, Baker, Cookshott & Gould, 1977; Handley, Dunn, Waldron & Baker, 1980).

The relationship between postpartum depression and psychosocial variables has been studied by numerous investigators. Hopkins et al. (1984) summarize these data by concluding that there appears to be a relationship between postpartum depression and marital relationship quality. Several studies have found that poor martial relationships precede postpartum depression (Watson, Elliott, Rugg & Brough, 1984; Kumar & Robson, 1984; O'Hara, 1986). Cutrona reported that a lack of perceived social support during pregnancy was associated with the degree of later postpartum depression (1983). Another significant predictor of postpartum depression is depression during pregnancy (Cutrona, 1983; O'Hara, Rehm & Campbell 1983; O'Hara, Neuhaber & Zekoski, 1984).

Gotlib, Whiffen, Mount, Milne and Cordy (1989) followed a group of 360 pregnant women during and after pregnancy to determine the predictors of postpartum depression. They found that 10% of women met criteria for depression during pregnancy and 7% were depressed during the postpartum. Only half of the cases of postpartum depression were new onset; the remainder of the women, who were depressed during the postpartum, were also depressed during pregnancy. Also, these investigators found that variables that predicted depression during pregnancy differed from those that predicted postpartum depression. Factors associated with depression during pregnancy were young age, less education, multiparity and lack of outside employment. These variables were not significant predictors of postpartum depression. Gotlib, Whiffen and Wallace (1991) studied a group of 730 women during pregnancy and found that 10% developed a depression during pregnancy and an additional 5% became depressed during the postpartum. Variables related to postpartum depression included depressive symptoms during pregnancy, high perceived stress during pregnancy, lower levels of marital satisfaction, and use of escape as a coping strategy.

In a unique matched control group study, O'Hara, Zekoski, Phillips and Wright (1990) compared a group of pregnant women with a group of nonpregnant controls to determine if pregnancy and the postpartum were times of increased stress and depression for women. Results indicated that 8% of the pregnant women were depressed during pregnancy, compared to 6% of the control women during the same time period. At the 9 week postpartum assessment, 10% of the postpartum women were depressed compared with 8% of the control subjects. The rates, times of onset, and duration of depression were not significantly different between the two groups. During the postpartum assessment, 26% of the pregnant women had the "maternity blues," compared to 8% of the controls having the "blues." The authors concluded that the prevalence of clinical depression may not significantly increase after childbirth but depressive symptoms are much more likely to occur.

O'Hara, Schlechte, Lewis and Varner (1991) have proposed a diathesis-stress model of postpartum depression. In this model, diatheses (vulnerability factors) such as familial predisposition for depression, history of depressive episodes or dysfunctional cognitive attributional style may predispose a woman to depression which then emerges as the woman has to cope with the stressors related to pregnancy and new motherhood. Common stressors during pregnancy and the postpartum are given in Table 1. These stressors have been demonstrated to be related to postpartum depressive mood (Powell & Drotar, 1992).

Table 1. Postpartum stressors.

Disruption in sleep
Physical changes associated with delivery
Physical discomfort
Learning to breastfeed
Decreased independence
Loss of work status
Loss of salary while on leave
Increase expenses (supplies, childcare)
Social isolation
Monotonous schedule
Less time for spouse
Lack of equal sharing of childcare responsibilities with spouse
Changes in self-esteem
Ideal expectation versus real experience with infant
Worry over the health of the infant
Less sexual desire/ interaction
Learning how to set limits with infant

Treatment for postpartum depression is similar to the treatment of others types of depression, but with special appreciation for the stresses of new motherhood and the role of relationship issues. After a thorough psychological intake interview the first decision is whether to hospitalize the patient or not. Hospitalization is indicated when the woman is delusional, suicidal or infanticidal. In these rare cases commitment may be needed to protect both the mother and baby. The second decision is regarding the use of antidepressants in order to provide relief from incapacitating symptoms. Sichel (1992) recommends early antidepressant medication use to stabilize the patient. Some breastfeeding mothers may worry about the transmission of the medication through the

Case example

Ms. L is a 34-year-old married woman who recently had her first child after a four year history of infertility treatment and one miscarriage. Ms. L has been married for 7 years and describes her marriage as a good one. Prior to delivery Ms. L was a vice president of a financial institution and is currently on maternity leave. Ms. L is pleased that she had a baby but now reports feelings of severe depression, uncontrollable episodes of crying, feeling "this was not what I expected," being tired, irritable and alone the majority of the time. She reports being disgusted with herself for not having lost twenty additional pounds she gained during pregnancy. She feels that pregnancy and childbirth have fundamentally changed her and that she doesn't know who she is anymore. Attempts by her husband to comfort her are met with annoyance and resentment because she feels he cannot understand the significant changes she has gone through. In terms of her daily functioning, Ms. L is breastfeeding every 2 to 3 hours and is sleep deprived. She reports an increase in her food and caffeine intake to make it through the days. She reports that she is able to care for the baby but at times feels that she cannot. She is not able to do anything else during the day. She cannot concentrate on reading or television and feels the days "slip away," each one the same as the one before.

Ms. L was open to the suggestion of beginning an antidepressant in order to help stabilize her mood. I referred her to a psychiatrist for the medication and monitoring. In addition, we reviewed the patient's daily schedule, and I identified some additional sources of support for her. We worked with the patient's husband to arrange for him to get up once a night for a bottle feeding in order to provide the patient 5 or 6 consecutive hours of sleep. Her husband was initially resistant but when I pointed out the relatively unequal contributions to childcare tasks, the husband agreed to take the night feeding responsibility. Additionally, childcare provided by a neighbor was arranged by the patient to enable her to come to weekly psychotherapy appointments. I advised her not to bring the infant to the psychotherapy due to her need for time alone. During the psychotherapy I prompted the patient to examine her expectations regarding motherhood. Given her infertility history, the patient felt she could not allow herself to feel any negative reactions to motherhood. She had imagined motherhood to be something out of a dream, with only good and happy moments, with none of the monotony and irritation that she had experienced. Once she identified the inherent ambivalence in motherhood she felt less guilty about her emotions and more able to talk about them. She also discussed the traditional roles she and her husband maintained in their relationship. Although she heard her husband say that he would accommodate his work schedule to spend more time at home, she had not seen any evidence of this and felt that she was the only one who had changed her worklife to accommodate the demands of parenthood. This inequity made her angry and resentful of her husband and began blocking their attempts at open communication. Last, the patient felt that her major source for self-esteem, her work, had been taken away from her. Prior to having the baby she believed that she should be a full-time parent. Now she wondered about returning to work part-time but felt guilty about thinking about part-time work because she did not want to leave the baby that she had waited so long for. All of these themes emerged at various points and new solutions were generated by the patient. The patient continued to work through changes in her self-esteem and incorporate her new role as a mother into her existing roles as she continued to care for her baby and maintain her marriage.

breast milk. They should be referred to a psychiatrist who is familiar with the impact of antidepressants on breastfeeding and provide routine screening of the mother and infant to determine blood levels of the medication. Studies investigating the efficacy of antidepressant treatment have demonstrated that the SSRIs are effective and well-tolerated (Nonacs & Cohen, 1998). Psychotherapy is also an effective means of treatment. A recent study by O'Hara et al. has demonstrated that interpersonal psychotherapy, for 12, one hour weekly sessions significantly reduced depressive symptomatology (O'Hara et al., 2000).

Infertility

Fertility is highly valued in most cultures and the wish for a child is one of the most basic of all human motivations. For women, pregnancy and motherhood are developmental milestones highly emphasized by our culture. When attempts to have a child fail it can be an emotionally devastating experience (Mahlstedt, 1985; Daniluk, 1988).

Infertility is defined as 12 months of appropriately timed intercourse that does not result in conception. Approximately 15% of couples in the United States have difficulty conceiving (National Center for Health Statistics, 1982). The apparent rise in infertility in the past 15 years is an artifact of the large cohort of women born during the baby boom who entered their reproductive years during the past decade and a half. The rate of infertility has remained relatively stable in the United States, but the absolute number of people seeking infertility treatment rose during the 1980s and early 1990s and will taper off again as the baby boom cohort enters menopause (Mosher & Pratt, 1990).

Approximately 40% of infertility problems are attributable to the female, 40% to the male and 20% to both partners or of unknown etiology. For decades clinicians have believed that infertility, particularly unexplained infertility, could be *caused* by psychological distress or other psychological factors (Benedek, 1952; Sandler, 1968; Mai, Munday & Rump, 1971). In the absence of any data to support this hypothesis, others began to reconceptualize the interaction between infertility and psychological distress and posited that psychological distress is a *consequence* of infertility and its treatment.

Hundreds of studies have focused on psychological variables related to infertility (American Society for Reproductive Medicine, 1996). A sampling of those studies indicates that infertility and its treatment, particularly in vitro fertilization (IVF) is extremely stressful. Freeman, Boxer, Rickels, Tureck and Mastroianni (1985) found that 18% of men and 16% of women in their sample of

---

Table 2. Comprehensive Psychosocial History for Infertility (CPHI). From Burns, L.H., & Greenfeld, D.A. (1991). *The Comprehensive Psychosocial History for Infertility (CPHI). Mental Health Professional Group.* Birmingham, AL: American Society for Reproductive Medicine.

This is not a psychometric test. Instead, it is a comprehensive psychological and social history of infertility designed to be used by a mental health or medical professional. It should provide the clinician with a global impression of the patient's history, stressors, functioning and current psychosocial status relevant to infertility. Although the history provides guidelines for potentially disruptive responses, there are some areas that are red flags and indications for referral for more complete psychological evaluation and intervention. They include: (1) uses or consideration of a donor/surrogate program, (2) prior psychiatric illness, (3) change in current mental status and/or exacerbation of prior psychiatric symptoms, (4) history of pregnancy loss, (5) history of cancer, (6) history of rape, (7) ambisexual patterns, and (8) current problems with substance abuse.

I. Reproductive History
   A. Infertility

  1. Current infertility: primary or secondary
  2. History of past infertility
 B. Pregnancy
  1. Living children (stepchildren, adopted, donor offspring, placed for adoption)
  2. Therapeutic abortion(s)
  3. Spontaneous abortion(s)
  4. Other perinatal loss: SIDS, death of a child
  5. High risk pregnancy
 C. History of Genetic/Chromosomal Abnormalities
  1. Cancer of the reproductive tract and/or chemotherapy
  2. DES exposure
  3. Congenital anomalies of the reproductive tract
II. Mental Status
 A. Psychiatric History
  1. Hospitalization for psychiatric illness
  2. Psychiatric treatment
  3. Treatment with psychotropic medication
  4. Substance abuse
 B. Current Mental Status
  1. Symptoms of depression
  2. Symptoms of anxiety/panic attacks
  3. Symptoms of obsession
  4. Current use of psychotropic medications
  5. Current problem with substance abuse
 C. Change in mental status
 D. Exacerbation of prior psychiatric symptoms
III. Sexual history
 A. Frequency and response
 B. Function/dysfunction
 C. Religious or cultural influence on sexual patterns or reproduction beliefs
 D. Sexual history
  1. Function/dysfunction
  2. Sexually transmitted disease
  3. Prior sperm donor/surrogate mother/consideration of use of donor gametes
  4. Homosexual or ambisexual patterns
  5. History or rape or incest
 E. Changes in any sexual patterns secondary to infertility or medical treatment
IV. Relationship status
 A. Marital
  1. History or marriages/divorces
  2. History or marital discord/therapy
  3. Extramarital relationships
  4. Current satisfaction/dissatisfaction
  5. Ambivalence about medical treatment and reproductive technologies
 B. Familial
  1. History of dysfunctional family of origin
  2. Recent deaths or births in family
  3. History of numerous familial losses
 C. Social
  1. Available social support
  2. Career disruptions or pressures

200 IVF patients reported significant levels of psychological distress including high levels of depressive symptoms. Many reported that infertility was the most stressful experience of their life. Baram, Tourtelot, Muechler and Huang (1988) surveyed couples after they had completed one IVF cycle. As an indirect measure of how stressful the procedure was, couples were asked if they would undergo IVF again. They found that 38% of the couples would not undergo IVF again because it was too expensive, the success rate was too low and the emotional pain of the procedure was too intense. In addition, 18% of couples reported that infertility had negatively impacted their marriage, 66% of women reported that they became depressed after the procedure and 13% of the women reported becoming suicidal after an unsuccessful cycle. This study underscores the significant psychological component of infertility.

Infertility and its treatment often lead to depressive symptoms and clinical depression. Two studies have investigated the stress of infertility using a stress and coping model. Litt, Tennen, Affleck and Klock (1992) assessed several variables to determine their contribution to post-IVF distress. These variables included demographic and reproductive history, optimism, situational appraisal, and coping skills. Following an unsuccessful cycle of IVF, 20% of women had a reactive depression. Results indicated that the general optimism and perceived low responsibility for the cause of the infertility were protective against post-IVF distress. Feelings of loss of control, perceived contribution to the IVF failure, and the use of escape as a coping mechanism were associated with increased post-IVF distress.

In a cross-sectional study of infertile patients investigators found that for women the most important factors related to psychological distress were perceived personal control, optimism that they will eventually have a child, and intensity of motivation to have a child (Abbey, Halman & Andrews, 1992). High levels of perceived personal control and optimism were related to lower distress levels and high levels of motivation to have a child were associated with increased distress. According to this study, the more important it was for the woman to have a child, the more distress she reported related to the infertility experience.

Several recent papers have tried to demonstrate a relationship between psychological status and pregnancy outcome (Edelmann, 1991; Moller & Fallstrom, 1991; Strauss, Appel & Ulrich, 1992). These studies have found no significant relationship between pretreatment psychological variables and subsequent pregnancy outcome. Although claims for improved pregnancy rates after a course of relaxation therapy have been made (Domar, Seibel & Benson, 1990; Domar, Clapp, Slawsby et al., 2000), these studies have significant methodological problems that preclude support for this assertion. Women continue to struggle with the role, if any, of psychological stress in their infertility.

In terms of psychological intervention with infertility patients, some programs mandate a psychological interview prior to the first IVF cycle or when donor sperm or egg are used. It is widely accepted that psychological counseling should be available to any infertile couple in treatment. Guidelines for the provision of these services are described elsewhere (Klock & Maier, 1991; Klock, 1998). In general, infertility should be considered a couple's issue with the couple seen together for the initial consultation. A structured interview for use with infertility patients has been developed (Burns & Greenfeld, 1991; cf. Table 2) and should be used to address specific reproductive and sexual history issues relevant to the infertility problem. In addition to the clinical interview, some clinicians working with infertile patients routinely use psychological tests, usually personality tests, to obtain further information about the individual. While numerous measures, including the Minnesota Multiphasic Personality Inventory (MMPI), Symptom Checklist 90 (SCL-90), Spielberger's State Trait Anxiety Inventory (STAI) and Beck Depression Inventory (BDI), have been used to evaluate infertile patients' in clinical research, their utility in the clinical context for predictive purposes has not been demonstrated.

The goal of the psychological evaluation is to prepare the patient for the treatment they are about to undergo, to raise emotional and ethical treatment issues that the individual(s) may not have considered, to screen for individuals who may benefit from psychological treatment either before or during infertility treatment and to evaluate patents for any preexisting psychopathology that would preclude infertility treatment. Specific questions related to the couple's social, cultural, religious and moral beliefs are needed in order to determine how they feel about the various treatment options such as cryopreservation of embryos, multifetal pregnancy, multifetal pregnancy reduction, nongenetic parenting via donor sperm or oocyte, privacy or disclosure about infertility and possible legal entanglements over the custody of created embryos. In addition, the consultation provides the couple with an opportunity to discuss the treatment success rates, answer questions about the informed consent process and to provide an initial contact with a trained mental health professional who can serve as a resource in the future if problems develop or if infertility treatment ends and counseling regarding adoption or child free living is needed.

Most couples seen in the context of infertility treatment are high functioning and psychologically minded therefore the psycholo-

Case example

I saw Mr. and Mrs. S for a routine psychological consultation prior to beginning IVF. Mr. S was a 36-year-old Catholic man with no previous psychiatric history. He was employed as a stockbroker. His wife, Mrs. S was 34 years old and had a previous pregnancy termination at age 21. As the result of a pelvic infection, Mrs. S's tubes were blocked therefore IVF was needed. I noticed that Mr. and Mrs. S were in disagreement with one another about whether to begin IVF. Mr. S stated that he felt they should adopt a child because using the medications and interventions to conceive was going "against God's will." Mrs. S on the other hand was a highly successful advertising agent who was used to setting a goal and working hard to achieve it. She now viewed pregnancy as an "achievement" which she had to attain. She stated that she was willing to go to any length to have a child. As we discussed the IVF treatment, Mr. S became uncomfortable with the concepts of out of body fertilization, embryo cryopreservation and the chance for multiple pregnancy and fetal reduction. During the interview the couple began arguing about whether to pursue the treatment or not.

It was clear to me that the couple was not ready to begin treatment because of their different perceptions of the treatment and motivation. Mr. S was uncomfortable with the treatment from a religious and moral perspective. Mrs. S seemed to have denied all the emotional consequences of the infertility and subordinated them to her desire to "achieve" a pregnancy. The couple's communication had broken down due to these differences. I recommended that the couple begin short term counseling prior to deciding on treatment. Although initially angry, Mrs. S agreed because she was physically exhausted from the treatment she had undergone. The couple agreed to take a two month break. During that time I met with them weekly improve their communication and to help them come to a consensus about whether to proceed with IVF. I pointed out each partner's perspective of the IVF to help them have empathy for one another. I also reframed Mrs. S view of pregnancy from a "goal" to a process. I also reminded her that she had to consider Mr. S's religious beliefs as they influenced his perspective of the treatment. I reiterated to both partners that the treatment was a joint decision. I asked both spouses to discuss their priorities in life and the role of parenting and the continuation of their marriage among these priorities. They also discussed the relative contributions of genetics versus the environment in their beliefs about parenting. This helped them deemphasize the technological aspects of pregnancy and refocus on the importance of the emotional and social aspects of parenting. Both partners became more willing to consider adoption if they were unable to have a biological child. Last, I urged both partners to discuss how much treatment they were willing to undergo and when they would stop treatment. This helped contain the affect about the treatment by providing an endpoint at which time they could move on to another option, such as adoption or child free living.

gist may only need to remind them about adaptive coping skills, provide them with information regarding the treatment and offer further follow-up as needed. Unfortunately there are a minority of cases in which infertility treatment may be contraindicated. In general, infertility treatment is contraindicated and may be denied or postponed when: (1) treatment or pregnancy may significantly worsen an active psychiatric illness; (2) active substance dependence with concomitant chaotic lifestyle is evident; (3) one partner is coercing the other to proceed with treatment; (4) one or both partners are unable or unwilling to provide consent for the treatment; (5) a legal history relevant to child endangerment or abuse is discovered; (6) infertility treatment is used to compensate for a sexual dysfunction; (7) the use of a family member gamete donor would cause significant familial discord; (8) custody arrangements for the potential child of a known gamete donor cannot be agreed upon by all parties. If one of these situations is discovered, then an appropriate treatment plan needs to be developed and presented to the couple.

Menopause

Significant biological and psychological changes occur for women in mid-life (Hutchinson, 1993). Menopause is the time when a woman's menstrual cycle ends because of estrogen deficiency. This deficiency also produces vasomotor instability (hot flushes) and changes in bone density. With these biological changes, significant psychosocial events may also occur, such as changes in relationships with children, loss or illness of parents, and marital instability or widowhood. Menopause has been described as a psychologically difficult time during which women are subject to moodiness, depression and irritability (Strickler, Borth, Cecutt, Cookson, Harper, Potvin, & Riffle, 1977). In the late nineteenth century psychiatrists Maudsley and Kraepelin both described a clinical syndrome of depression or melancholia that occurred during menopause (Schmidt & Rubinow, 1989). It was widely assumed in psychiatry and psychology that depression was a normal part of the menopause experience. It was not until a

landmark study by Weissman (1979) was conducted that the myth of "involutional melancholia" was put to rest. In her study Weissman found no difference in the prevalence of depression between women who were less than 45 years of age compared with women 45 years of age and older. Winokur (1973) also found that there was no greater risk for a depressive episode during menopause compared with other times during a woman's life.

Despite these findings many attempts have been made to establish a link between menopause and depressive symptoms. Researchers have hypothesized that depressive symptoms during menopause are caused by declining levels of gonadal hormones or are secondary to fatigue and loss of sleep from nocturnal hot flushes (Schmidt & Rubinow, 1989; Hutchinson, 1993). Sherwin's (Sherwin & Gelfand, 1985; Sherwin, 1988; Sherwin, 1991) work has been instrumental in clarifying the relationship between hormonal status and depressive symptoms during menopause. In two methodologically rigorous studies of the effects of exogenous hormones on menopausal mood symptoms Sherwin found that the placebo group reported higher levels of depressive symptomatology and had corresponding lower levels of estrogen than did treatment groups. A second study found that there was a significant correlation between estrogen levels and psychological state. Women receiving estrogen posthysterectomy reported greater feelings of composure, elation, energy, and confidence than women receiving placebo. In the past two decades hormone replacement therapy (HRT) has become a common "treatment" for the normal changes associated with menopause. Outcome studies investigating the risks and benefits of HRT continue to emphasize the importance of individualized decision-making between a woman and her physician regarding the use of HRT. Studies discussing the cognitive and mood effects of HRT continue to show a mixed picture in terms of the benefits (Hogervorst, Williams, Budge et al., 2000; Pearlstein, Rosen & Stone, 1997).

In addition to hormonal changes, psychological changes take place during menopause. Dennerstein and Burrows (1978) noted nervousness, irritability, depression and decreased social adaptation among menopausal women. Another factor that may influence the occurrence of psychological changes associated with menopause is the negative expectations about menopause that are prevalent in our culture. Women may dread the changes that they have heard about from others and this may make them more susceptible to those changes. Interestingly, cross-cultural studies have shown that women in other, non-Western cultures do not have significant menopausal psychological difficulty. In some cultures where a woman's status rises after menopause, there are no noted negative psychological changes in functioning (Van Keep & Kellerhals, 1974; Davis, 1982; Wilbush, 1982).

Some have speculated that the loss of the traditional role as mother and childrearer is particularly difficult during the menopause (Deutsch, 1945). The "empty nest" problems of loss of role and identity is a popular clinical myth but there is little scientific support for this view. In fact some studies have found that women report relief and satisfaction after their child had left home (Glen, 1975; Lowenthal, Thurnher & Chiriboga, 1975).

Changes in sexual desire and functioning may impact a woman's mental health during menopause (Bachmann, 1985; Sarrel, 1990). These investigators have reported increased referrals for sex therapy among menopausal women and that approximately 20% of a sample of menopausal women reported decreases in sexual desire. Overall, four major changes in sexual functioning

Case example

Mrs. G is a 52-year-old married, Catholic woman who was referred to me by her husband because he believed she was "going crazy." He reported that his wife cried "all day" and was no longer completing household tasks and social obligations as she once had. This behavior began 6 months ago after the patient had an unexpected hysterectomy. I evaluated Mrs. G and found her to be emotionally labile, depressed, tearful and angry at her husband. Her thoughts were logical and sequential with no evidence of delusions or hallucinations. She reported symptoms of depression including excessive sleep, overeating with a thirty pound weight gain, decreased concentration and general inability to work or function at home. She cried as she told me about her hysterectomy because she felt that she had no say in whether the hysterectomy took place. She also reported significant guilt at a previous elective abortion that she had at age 46. She was ambivalent about the unplanned pregnancy but her husband "forced" her to have the termination. Since that time she has feared "God's retribution" for the abortion.

I began seeing Mrs. G in weekly psychotherapy. She started on hormone replacement therapy to treat the vascular changes of menopause and to prevent further bone loss. She expected that the

hormone therapy would "cure" her but instead she found that while she felt better physically she was still not able to function as well as she had in the past. Over the course of 2 years of weekly psychotherapy I learned a lot about the impact of the subordination of thoughts and feelings among women of Mrs. G's generation. Mrs. G told me how angry she was about the hysterectomy which she felt was another example of men having control over women's bodies. This led to further discussion of the abortion and her belief that her husband exerted his influence and forced her to end the pregnancy. This led to further discussions and working through of issues in her family of origin including a conflicted relationship with her father and a sexual molestation perpetrated by a relative. All of these experiences had lead her to believe that she specifically and women in general were powerless in relationships and society. I focused on pointing out areas in which she had control to express her thoughts and feelings. We then role-played various situations to improve her communication skills to effectively articulate her wants and needs. We also worked to create experiences in which the patient had power over her actions and outcomes. Over time, these experiences and the subsequent change in attitudes coincided with the resolution of her depression.

may take place during menopause. These are diminished sexual responsiveness, dyspareunia, decreased sexual frequency, and decreased sexual desire (Sarrel, 1990). These changes are multidetermined by the hormonal, psychological and social changes that take place during this phase of life. Physically, the decreases in gonadal hormones causes decreased genital vascularity, delayed clitoral reaction time and decreased vaginal secretions. Psychological and social changes that impact sexuality include loss or unavailability of a partner, changes in body image and expectations of loss of sexuality in later life.

The evaluation and treatment of a menopausal women who is referred for an evaluation of depressive or other psychological symptoms is straight forward. Daily symptom charting and ratings of severity are useful to help the patient see the correlation between hot flushes, sleep deprivation and psychological symptoms. Depending on the woman's history, the physician may prescribe hormone replacement therapy to alleviate the hot flushes and other vasomotor changes. This generally minimizes the psychological symptoms attributable to sleep deprivation related to nocturnal hot flushes and also may improve the woman's mood.

If depressive symptoms persist after the initiation of hormone replacement therapy, then a standard evaluation for depression is indicated. Special attention can be paid to causes of depression during mid-life, such as changes or losses of relationships, the stress of being a caregiver to a spouse or parent, conflicted relationships with adult children or financial pressures. As with other types of depression, the use of a standard psychological measure may be useful to assess the initial level of depression and document treatment progress. Cognitive behavioral interventions may be particularly helpful in order to help change negative attributional styles and to demonstrate to the woman her ability to change her behavior and thinking.

Professional Practice Issues

A key component to becoming an integral member of the treatment team is to be available and helpful when asked to consult on a case. The psychologist's task is to help the patient deal with her problem and to let the physician know about the psychologist's contribution to the resolution of the patient's problem. The most important aspect of developing a strong consultative relationship is providing excellent clinical care. This includes taking care of the patient and giving appropriate feedback to the referring physician. It is also important to be available, by phone, beeper or with an open office door. If the psychologist has a choice, he or she should be located as close to the clinical practice area as possible. This allows for informal "curbside consults" that help the psychologist get to know the staff and the staff to know the psychologist.

When working as a consultant in a medical service, the psychologist has to be aware of the difference between psychological and medical records. In some states there are different laws governing the release of psychiatric records, therefore the consultant needs to check whether the psychological notes should be kept in the general medical record, with relatively less confidentiality, or in a separate section of the chart to preserve confidentiality of the psychological records. In addition the boundaries of confidentiality need to be clarified for the patient and the referring doctor. The patient needs to give her consent prior to sharing information with the referring physician.

In an obstetrics and gynecology service the role of the psychologist can be interesting, meaningful and highly satisfying. While many of the situations are not life threatening, they are life changing and often require significant change on the part of the woman, her partner and family. The convergence of physical and psychosocial issues often complicate the patient's problem but effective listening, knowledge about reproductive events and good psychotherapeutic skills can help identify the problems and generate the solutions for a woman's effective adaptation throughout her reproductive life.

References

Abbey, A., Halman, L., & Andrews, F. (1992). Psychosocial, treatment and demographic predictors of the stress associated with infertility. *Fertil. Steril.*, *57*, 122–127.

Abraham, G. (1983). Nutritional factors in the etiology of premenstrual syndromes. *J. Reprod. Med.*, *28*, 446–450.

Allgeier E.R., & Allgeier, R. (1991). *Sexual interactions* (3rd ed., p. 330). Lexington, MA: D.C. Heath.

American Medical Association (1996). *Complete guide to women's health* (R.I. Slupik, Ed.). New York: Random House.

American Psychiatric Association (1987). *Diagnostic and statistical manual of mental disorders: Third edition – revised*. Washington, DC: American Psychiatric Association.

American Psychiatric Association (1994). *Diagnostic and statistical manual of mental disorders: Fourth edition*. Washington, DC: American Psychiatric Association.

American Society for Reproductive Medicine (1996). *Bibliography from the Mental Health Professional Group*, Birmingham, AL.

Arrizmendi, T., & Affonso, D. (1987). Stressful events related to pregnancy and postpartum. *J. Psychosm. Res.*, *31*, 743–742.

Bachmann, G. (1985). Correlates of sexual desire in postmenopausal women. *Maturitas*, *7*, 211–217.

Baram, D., Tourtelot, E., Muechler, E., & Huang, K. (1988). Psychosocial adjustment following unsuccessful in vitro fertilization. *J. Psychosm. Obstet. Gynecol.*, *9*, 181–190.

Benedek, T. (1952). Infertility as a psychosomatic defence. *Fertil. Steril.*, *3*, 527–532.

Blechman, E. (1988). Premenstrual syndrome. In E. Blechman & K. Brownell (Eds.), *Handbook of behavioral medicine for women*. New York: Pergamon.

Boston Women's Health Book Collective (1992). *The new our bodies, ourselves*. New York: Touchstone.

Burns, L.H., & Greenfeld, D.A. (1991). *The Comprehensive Psychosocial History for Infertility (CPHI)*. Mental Health Professional Group. Birmingham, AL: American Society for Reproductive Medicine.

Casper, R., & Powell, A.M. (1986). Premenstrual syndrome: Documentation by linear analog scale compared with two descriptive scales. *Am. J. Obstet. Gynecol.*, *155*, 862–863.

Choung, C. (1988). The MMPI as an aid in evaluating patients with premenstrual syndrome. *Psychosomatics*, *29*, 197–200.

Cooper, P. (1988). Nonpsychotic psychiatric disorders after childbirth: A prospective study of prevalence, incidence, course and nature. *Br. J. Psychiatr.*, *152*, 799–804.

Cutrona, C. (1983). Causal attributions and perinatal depression. *J. Abnormal Psychol.*, *92*, 161–172.

Dalton, K. (1964). *The premenstrual syndrome*. Springfield, IL: Thomas.

Dalton, K. (1971). Prospective study into puerperal depression. *Br. J. Psychiatr.*, *118*, 689–692.

Daniluk, J. (1988). Infertility: intrapersonal and interpersonal impact. *Fertil. Steril.*, *49*, 982–986.

Davis, D. (1982). Women's status and experience of the menopause in a Newfoundland fishing village. *Maturitas*, *4*, 207–211.

Dennerstein, L., & Burrows, G. (1978). A review of studies of the psychological symptoms found at menopause. *Maturitas*, *1*, 55–61.

Deutsch, H. (1945). *The psychology of women, Vol. 2*. New York: Grune & Stratton.

Domar, A., Seibel, M., & Benson, H. (1990). The mind/body program for infertility: A new behavioral treatment approach for women with infertility. *Fertil. Steril.*, *53*, 246–249.

Domar, A., Clapp, D., Slawsby, E., Dusek, J., Kessel, B., & Freizinger, M. (2000). The impact of group psychological interventions on pregnancy rates in infertile women. *Fertil. Steril.*, *73*, 805–811.

Eckerd, M., Hurt, S., & Severino, S. (1989). Late luteal phase dysphoric disorder: Relationship to personality disorder. *J. Personality Disorder*, *3*, 338–344.

Edelmann, R. (1991). Psychogenic infertility: Some findings. *J. Psychosom. Obstet. Gynecol.*, *12*, 163–172.

Endicott, J. (2000). History, evolution, and diagnosis of premenstrual dysphoric disorder. *J. Clin. Psychiatry*, *61*(suppl 12), 5–8.

Frank, R. (1931). The hormonal cause of premenstrual tension. *Arch. Neurol. Psychiatr.*, *26*, 1053–1057.

Freeman, E., Boxer, A., Rickels, K., Tureck, R., & Mastroianni, L. (1985). Psychological evaluation and support in a program of in vitro fertilization and embryo transfer. *Fertil. Steril.*, *43*, 48–53.

Freeman, E., Rickels, K., Sondheimer, S., & Polansky, M. (1990). Ineffectiveness of progesterone suppository treatment for premenstrual syndrome. *JAMA, 264,* 349–353

Georgiopoulous, A.M., Bryan, T.L., Yawn, B.P., Houston, M., Rummans, T.A., & Therneau, T.M. (1999). Population-based screening for postpartum depression. *Obstet. Gynecol., 93,* 653–657.

Glen, N. (1975). Psychological well being in the postparental stage. *J. Marr. Fam, 37,* 105–111.

Goldberg, W.A. (1988). Perspectives on the transition to parenthood. In G.Y. Michaels & W.A. Goldberg (Eds.), *The transition to parenthood: Current theory and research* (pp. 1–20). New York: Cambridge University Press.

Goodale, I., Domar, A., & Benson, H. (1990). Alleviation of premenstrual syndrome symptoms with the relaxation response. *Obstet. Gynecol., 75,* 1649–1652.

Gotlib, I., Whiffen, V.E., Mount, J.H., Milne, K., & Cordy, N.I. (1989). Prevalence rates and demographic characteristics associated with depression in pregnancy and the postpartum. *J. Consult. Clin. Psychol., 57,* 269–274.

Gotlib, I., Whiffen, V.E., & Wallace, P. (1991). Prospective investigation of postpartum depression: Factors involved in onset and recovery. *J. Abnorm. Psychol., 100,* 122–132.

Guyton, A.C., & Hall, J. (1996). *Textbook of medical physiology* (9th ed., pp. 1005–1037). Philadelphia: W.B. Saunders.

Hair, C., Schramm, R., Caruso, S., & Hale, M. (1990). Premenstrual syndrome in a psychiatric setting. In *New Research Abstracts,* 143rd Annual Meeting of the American Psychiatric Association, Washington, DC.

Halbreich, U., & Endicott, J. (1982). Classification of premenstrual syndromes. In R. Friedman (Ed.), *Behavior and the menstrual cycle.* New York: Marcel Dekker.

Halbreich, U., Endicott, J., & Nee, J. (1982). The diversity of premenstrual changes as reflected in the Premenstrual Assessment Form. *Acta Psychiatr. Scand., 65,* 46–65.

Handley, S., Dunn, T., Waldron, G., & Baker, J. (1980). Tryptophan, cortiol, and puerperal mood. *Br. J. Psychiatr., 136*: 498–506.

Handley, S., Dunn, T., Baker, J., Cookshott, C., & Gould, S. (1977). Mood changes in puerperium and plasma tryptophan and cortisol concentrations. *Br. Med. J., 2,* 18–22.

Harrison, W., Endicott, J., & Nee, J. (1989). Treatment of premenstrual depression with nortriptyline: A pilot study. *J. Clin. Psychiatr., 5,* 136–139.

Harrison, W., Endicott, J., & Nee, J. (1990). Treat-ment of premenstrual dysphoria with alprazolam. *Arch. Gen. Psychiatry, 47,* 270–272.

Hayworth, J., Little, B.C., Bonham Carter, S., Raptopoulos, P., Priest, R.G., & Sandler, M. (1980). A predictive study of postpartum depression: Some predisposing characteristics. *Br. Med. J., 53,* 161–167.

Hopkins, J., Marcus, M., & Campbell, S. (1984). Postpartum depression: A critical overview. *Psychol. Bull., 95,* 498–530.

Hurt, S., Schnurr, P., Severino, S., Freeman, E., Gise, L., Rivera-Tovar, A., & Steege, J. (1992). Late luteal phase dysphoric disorder in 670 women evaluated for premenstrual complaints. *Am. J. Psychiatr., 149,* 525–530.

Hogervorst, E., Williams, J., Budge, M., Riedel, W., & Jolles, J. (1997). The nature of the effect of female gonadal hormone replacement therapy on cognitive function in post-menopausal women: A meta-analysis. *Neuroscience, 101,* 485–512.

Hutchinson, K. (1993). Psychological aspects of menopause. *Infertil. Reprod. Med. Clin. N. Am., 4,* 503–515.

Kendall, R.E., Chalmers, J.C., & Platz, C. (1987). Epidemiology of puerpal psychoses. *Br. J. Psychiatry, 150,* 662–673.

Klock, S.C. (1998). Psychological evaluation of the infertile patient. In S. Covington & L.B. Burns (Eds.), *Infertility counseling: A comprehensive handbook.* Pearl River, NY: Parthenon.

Klock, S., & Maier, D. (1991). Guidelines for the provision of psychological services for infertility patients at the University of Connecticut Health Center. *Fertil. Steril., 56,* 680–685.

Kumar, R., & Robson, K. (1984). A prospective study of emotional disorders in childbearing women. *Br. J. Psychiatr., 144,* 35–39.

Litt, M., Tennen, H., Affleck, G., & Klock, S. (1992). Coping and cognitive factors in adaptation to in vitro fertilization failure. *J. Behav. Med, 15,* 171–183.

Lowenthal, M., Thurnher, M., & Chiriboga, D. (1975). *Four stages of life.* San Francisco: Jossey-Bass, 1975.

Magos, A., Brincat, M., & Studd, J. (1986). Trend analysis of the symptoms of 150 women with a history of premenstrual syndrome. *Am. J. Obstet. Gynecol., 155,* 335–340.

Mahlstedt, P. (1985). The psychological component of infertility. *Fertil. Steril., 43,* 335–341.

Mai, F., Munday, R., & Rump, E. (1972). Psychosomatic and behavioral mechanisms in psychogenic infertility. *Br. J. Psychiatr., 120,* 199–201.

Mathis, J. (1967). Psychiatry and the obstetrician-gynecologist. *Med. Clin. N. Amer., 51*, 1375–1382.

Menkes, D., Taghavi, E., Mason, P., Spears, G., & Howard, R. (1992). Fluoxetine treatment of severe premenstrual syndrome. *Br. Med. J., 305*, 346–347.

Moller, A., & Fallstrom, K. (1991). Psychological consequences of infertility: A longitudinal study. *J. Psychosom. Obstet. Gynecol., 12*, 27–35.

Moos, R. (1969). The development of a menstrual distress questionnaire. *Psychosom. Med, 30*, 853–867.

Mosher, W. (1988). Fertility and family planning in the United States: Insights from the National Survey of Family Growth. *Fam. Plan. Perspect., 20*, 207–211.

Mosher, W., & Pratt, W. (1990). Fecundity and infertility in the United States, 1965–1988. *Advance Data, 192*, 1–16.

Murray, L. (1988). Effects of postnatal depression on infant development. In R. Kumar & I. Brockington (Eds.), *Motherhood and mental illness* (Vol. 2). London: John Wright.

National Center for Health Statistics (1982). *Reproductive impairments among married couples.* United States Vital Health Statistics, Public Health Service, Washington, DC, U. S. Government Printing Office.

Nonacs, R., & Cohen, L. (1998). Postpartum mood disorders: Diagnosis and treatment guidelines. *J. Clin. Psychiatry, 59*(suppl 2), 34–40.

O'Hara, M., Rehm, L., & Campbell, S. (1983) Predicting depressive symptomatology: Cognitive behavioral models and postpartum depression. *J. Abnorm. Psychol., 91*, 457–461.

O'Hara, M., Neuhaber, D., & Zekoski, E. (1984). Prospective study of postpartum depression: prevalence, course and predictive factors. *J. Abnormal Psychol., 93*, 158–171.

O'Hara, M. (1986). Social support, life events, and depression during pregnancy and the puerpium. *Arch. Gen. Psychiatr., 43*, 569–573.

O'Hara, M. (1989). Psychologic and biologic factors in postpartum depression. In J. McGuire, A. Phillips & D. Rubinow (Eds.), *Premenstrual, postpartum and menopausal mood disorders*. Baltimore: Urban & Schwarzenberg.

O'Hara, M., Schlechte, J.A., Lewis, D.A., & Varner, M.W. (1991). Controlled prospective study of postpartum mood disorders: Psychological, environmental, and hormonal variables. *J. Abnorm. Psychol., 100*, 63–73.

O'Hara, M., Zekoski, E., Phillips, L.H., & Wright, E.J. (1990). Controlled prospective study of postpartum mood disorders: Comparisons of childbearing and nonchildbearing women. *J. Abnorm. Psychol., 99*, 3–15.

O'Hara, M.W., Stuart, S., Gorman, L., & Wenzel, A. (2000). Efficacy of interpersonal psychotherapy for postpartum depression. *Arch. Gen. Psychiatry, 57*, 1039–1045.

Pearlstein, T., Rosen, K., & Stone, A.B. (1997). Mood disorders and menopause. *Endocrinol. Metabol. Clin. N. America, 26*, 279–294.

Powell, S., & Drotar, D. (1992). Postpartum depressed mood: The impact of daily hassles. *J. Psychosom. Obstet. Gynecol., 13*, 255–267.

Reid, R., & Yen, S. (1981). Premenstrual syndrome. *Am. J. Obstet. Gynecol., 139*, 85–104.

Rein, M., & Schiff, I. (1996). Evaluation of the infertile couple. In K. Ryan, R. Berkowitz & R. Barbieri (Eds.), *Kistner's gynecology* (6th ed., pp. 278–304). St. Louis: Mosby.

Rivera-Tovar, A., & Frank, E. (1990). Late luteal phase dysphoric disorder in young women. *Am. J. Psychiatr., 147* 1634–1636.

Robson, K., & Kumar, R. (1980). Delayed onset of maternal affection after childbirth. *Br. J. Psychiatr., 136*, 347–354.

Rubinow, D., & Roy-Byrne, P. (1984). Premenstrual syndromes: Overview from a methodologic perspective. *Am. J. Psychiatr., 141*, 163–172.

Ruble, D. (1977). Premenstrual symptoms: A reinterpretation. *Science, 197*, 291–292.

Sandler, S. (1968). Emotional stress and infertility. *J. Psychosom. Res., 12*, 51–60.

Sarrel, P. (1990). Sexuality and menopause. *Obstet. Gynecol., 75* (Suppl.), 26–30.

Schmidt, P., & Rubinow, D. (1989). Menopausal mood disorders. In L. Demars, J. McGuire, A. Phillips & D. Rubinow (Eds.), *Premenstrual, postpartum and menopausal mood disorders* (pp. 193–204). Baltimore: Urban & Schwarzenberg.

Sherwin, B., & Gelfand, M. (1985) Sex steroids and affect in the surgical menopause: A double-blind cross-over study. *Psychoneuroendocrinology, 10*, 325–335.

Sherwin, B. (1988). Affective changes with estrogen and androgen replacement therapy in surgically menopausal women. *J. Affect. Dis., 14*, 177–187.

Sherwin, B. (1991). The impact of different doses of estrogen and progestin on mood and sexual behavior in postmenopausal women. *J. Clin. Endocrin. Metab., 72* 336–343.

Sichel, D. (1992). Psychiatric issues of the postpartum period. *Current Issues Affect. Illness, 11*, 5–16.

Smith, S., & Schiff, I. (1989). The premenstrual syndrome—diagnosis and management. *Fertil. Steril., 52*, 527–543.

Speroff, L., Glass, R.H., & Kase, N.G. (1989). *Clini-*

cal gynecologic endocrinology and infertility (4th ed.). Baltimore: Williams & Wilkins.

Steege, J. (989). Symptom measurement in premenstrual syndrome. In L. Demars, J. McGuire, A. Phillips & D. Rubinow (Eds.), *Premenstrual, postpartum and menopausal mood disorders* (pp. 53–64). Baltimore, Urban & Schwarzenberg.

Steege, J., & Blumenthal, J. (1993). The effects of aerobic exercise on premenstrual symptoms in middle aged women. *J. Psychosom. Res., 37*, 127–134.

Steiner, M., & Pearlstein, T. (2000). Premenstrual dysphoria and the serotonin system: Pathophysiology and treatment. *J. Clin. Psychiatry, 61*(suppl 12), 17–21.

Stevinson, C., & Ernst, E. (2001). Complementary/alternative therapies for premenstrual syndrome: A systematic review of randomized controlled trials. *Am. J. Obstet. Gynecol., 185*, 227–235.

Strauss, B., Appel, H., & Ulrich, D. (1992). Relationship between psychological characteristics and treatment outcome in female patients from an infertility clinic. *J. Psychosom. Obstet. Gynecol., 13*, 121–130.

Strickler, R., Borth, R., Cecutt, H., Cookson, B.,

Harper, J., Potvin, R., & Riffel, P. (1977). The role of estrogen replacement in the climacteric syndrome. *Psychol. Med., 7*, 631–639.

Treadway, R., Kane, F., Jarrahi-Zadeh, A., & Lipton, M. (1969). A psychoendocrine study of pregnancy and puerperium. *Am. J. Psychiatr., 125*, 86–92.

Van Keep, P., & Kellerhals, J. (1974). The impact of socio-cultural factors on symptom formation. *Psychother. Psychosom., 23*, 251–260.

Walsh, B. (1996). Menopause. In K. Ryan, R. Berkowitz & R. Barbieri (Eds.), *Kistner's gynecology* (6th ed., pp. 437–460). St. Louis: Mosby.

Watson, J., Elliott, P., Rugg, S., & Brough, D. (1984). Psychiatric disorders in pregnancy and the first postnatal year. *Br. J. Psychiatr., 144*, 453–462.

Weissman, M. (1979). The myth of involutional melancholia. *JAMA, 242*, 742–745.

Wilbush, G. (1982). Climacteric expression and social context. *Maturitas, 4*, 195–201.

Wilcox, L.S., & Mosher, W. (1993). Use of infertility services in the United States. *Obstet. Gynecol., 82*, 122–125.

Winokur, G. (1973). Depression in the menopause. *Am. J. Psychiatr., 130*, 92–94.

Sara J. Knight

12

Oncology and Hematology

Cancer is the second leading cause of death in the world's developed countries, with undeveloped countries showing a similar trend in rates. Cancer occurs in people of all ages, but the incidence increases with age. In 2002, worldwide, ten million individuals were newly diagnosed with cancer, 6.2 million people died of cancer, and over 20 million individuals were living with cancer (World Health Organization, 2002).Psychological, behavioral and social factors play critical roles in cancer biology and its treatment, and are instrumental in an individual's adjustment to cancer. Health psychologists have made important contributions to both cancer control and cancer care (Derogatis, 1986a; Andersen, 1992). In cancer control, this work has advanced knowledge of cancer risk behaviors (e. g., smoking, diet, sun exposure) and early detection behaviors (e. g., genetic testing, colon cancer screening). In cancer care, health psychologists have developed and adapted psychological assessment and treatment approaches to address the psychosocial needs of individuals diagnosed with cancer and their families. This work has lead to greater understanding of the psychological and social processes influencing cancer biology and health outcomes (Andersen, Kiecolt-Glaser & Glaser, 1994). In this chapter, I discuss topics relevant to cancer care, especially those issues of interest to the clinical health psychologist working with adults diagnosed with cancer and cared for in a clinical setting.

Biomedical Aspects of Cancer and its Treatment

The following section provides an overview of cancer biology, diagnosis, and treatment to introduce the reader to basic concepts. Readers who are interested in pursuing additional information will find a comprehensive review in DeVita, Hellman and Rosenberg (2001).

Cancer Biology: Risk, Development, and Progression

The term cancer is used to represent over one hundred different diseases. Each has its associated etiology. Rates of cancer differ across gender, race, socioeconomic status, culture, and geographic region. Behavioral and psychosocial factors (e. g., diet, sun exposure, smoking) influence cancer risk. Other factors include genetic influences (e. g., inherited mutations, mutations that occur from metabolism), immune conditions, exposure to exogenous and endogenous hormones (e. g., estrogen), radiation, infectious organisms, and chemicals. What is common to all cancers is the abnormal regulation of cell growth and reproduction. Cancer cells may have other abnormalities, such as genetic instability, loss of the ability to differentiate, increased motility (invasiveness), and decreased drug sensitivity. Kastan and Skapek (2001) note that a common misunderstanding is that cancer cells grow more rapidly than normal cells. The basic abnormality, however, involves lack of control responses in cellular development. These responses would normally signal the cell to stop its passage through the cycle of growth and reproduction. Cancer cells originate when mutations occur in genes that normally control these regulatory signals.

When cancer is diagnosed, it usually is made up of multiple subpopulations of cells with heterogeneous genetic, biochemical, immunologic, and biologic characteristics. As it develops, it may spread outside its original site (e. g., breast, lung, skin) to nearby tissue and eventually to distant regions of the body.

Metastasis refers to the spread of cancer from a primary tumor to distant sites. To metastasize, tumor cells have to complete a number of steps without being destroyed by the host. Initially, to grow to a size of 1 to 2 mm, the primary tumor must receive nutrients via blood. This is possible through a process termed angiogenesis in which a network of capillaries develops around the tumor. Some tumor cells have increased motility and detach from the primary tumor. These enter the circulatory and lymphatic systems, but many are destroyed by physical trauma in transport and by the host's immune responses. Those cells that survive adhere in nearby and distant capillary beds. Some of these cells penetrate blood vessel walls and attach themselves to distant organs. Similar to the growth process of the primary tumor, angiogenesis must occur for the metastatic tumor to grow. As the metastasis grows, its cells can create new metastases.

Cancer Diagnosis

The diagnosis of cancer is accomplished through a medical history interview and physical examination. Blood tests, radiographic procedures, ultrasound examinations, nuclear scans, computerized tomography (CT) scans, magnetic resonance imaging (MRI) scans and endoscopic examinations complete the work-up. From the time a person seeks help for a suspicious symptom, she or he will undergo a series of interactions with physicians and technicians that may last, if there is no delay, several days to several weeks.

As a part of the work-up, a needle or surgical biopsy may be conducted. In a needle biopsy, a fine needle or core cutting needle is inserted into the tumor and a sample of tissue is withdrawn. Incisional and excisional biopsies are surgical procedures that involve taking a portion of the tumor (incisional) or all of the tumor (excisional) for analysis.

One way that cancer is defined is by the site of its primary origin. Solid tumors include breast, lung, kidney, bladder, prostate, colon, pancreatic, esophageal, and ovarian. Cancers of the lymph system are called lymphomas and include Hodgkin's disease and non-Hodgkin's lymphoma. Cancers of the blood include acute and chronic leukemias. Metastatic disease is defined by the primary site. For example, breast cancer that has metastasized to the bone, brain, or lung is considered breast cancer. It is possible, however, for a person to develop two or more primary cancers—breast cancer and colon cancer, for instance.

Cancer stage and histologic type are determined through the visual inspection of the pathologic anatomy of the tumor and through the pathologist's histologic evaluation of cancer cells. Cancer staging systems vary with the type of cancer (e.g, breast, prostate, lung). Across cancers, three general terms may be used to describe the stage of disease. *Localized* disease refers to an invasive cancer that appears confined to the organ of its origin. *Regional* disease describes a cancer that has extended beyond the organ to surrounding tissues, lymph nodes, or organs. When the cancer has spread to remote sites in the body, it is considered *distant* disease.

The pathologist's histologic evaluation (i. e., examination of cancer cells under the microscope) provides information about the cancer's histologic type. This classification distinguishes between epithelial and nonepithelial tumors (carcinomas versus sarcomas) and across grades (well differentiated to undifferentiated). Different histologic types, even at the same site, have different properties, such as drug sensitivity and invasiveness, resulting in different prognoses. As understanding of cancer biology has increased, pathologic evaluations have become highly refined, yielding information about the cancer's growth rate, sensitivity to endogenous and exogenous substances, and genetics. The pathology data provide guidance in selection, timing and dose of treatments, determining prognosis, and in considerations of familial risk (Percy et al., 1995).

Cancer Treatment

Patients often find hope in the rapid development of cancer treatments, such as gene therapy, cancer vaccines, hormonal therapies, antimetastasis, antiangiogenesis, monoclonal antibody therapy. Also, advances in supportive care have contributed to improved management of pain, fatigue, and nausea and vomiting. These innovations have contributed to shifts in the psychosocial consequences of cancer treatment. Indeed, the number of available treatments presents the individual diagnosed with cancer with complex and difficult decision making tasks.

Contemporary cancer treatment is multimodal, involving various combinations and sequences of surgeries, chemotherapies, radiation therapies, bone marrow transplantation, biologic therapy, and hormonal therapies. Treatments include *local* interventions, such as surgery to remove a tumor from the colon, or radiation therapy to a surgical scar to reduce the possibility of a recurrence at that site. Treatments are considered *systemic*, such as chemotherapy, when they circulate through the entire body.

Surgery

Surgical treatment plays a role in cancer prevention, diagnosis, cure, rehabilitation, and in palliation. Consequently, surgeons are involved with cancer care throughout the disease trajectory (Rosenberg, 2001b). Research and refinements in surgical techniques have led to modifications in surgeries for cancer, especially to reduce the amount of tissue removed thereby preserving organ function, to spare nerves, and to reconstruct the area affected by removal of the tumor. For example, nerve sparing, radical prostatectomies are possible for many men diagnosed with pros-

tate cancer, reducing the incidence of erectile and urinary dysfunction. Surgery for prevention has been accepted for some cancers (e. g., multiple endocrine neoplasia types II and III) but is controversial for others (e. g., breast). When underlying conditions (e. g., ulcerative colitis) and genetic traits (e. g., familial colon cancer) are associated with high incidence of subsequent cancer, especially in nonvital organs, surgery to remove the organ is considered. When the risk of cancer is increased over normal risk, but does not approach 100%, the decision to undertake surgery is more complex. This is the case for familial breast cancer where counseling is suggested regarding decision to undertake prophylactic mastectomy or increased surveillance (Lerman & Croyle, 1995; Lerman et al., 1996; Burke et al., 1997a; Burke et al., 1997b).

Advances in reconstructive surgery have been important in preserving body image where the cancer surgery to remove the tumor would cause a visible deformity, as with breast cancer and head and neck cancer. Although reconstructive surgery involves additional risk of morbidity and mortality (from longer or additional surgeries), studies have documented its psychological benefits (Wellisch, Schain, Noone & Little, 1985; Rowland, Holland, Chaglassian & Kinne, 1993).

Cancer surgeons play an important role in palliative care. Surgeons place central line catheters for the administration of chemotherapy drugs, nutrition support, and pain medication. They excise tumors to reduce pain, airway obstruction, or gastrointestinal pressure.

Chemotherapy

The treatment of cancer with cytotoxic drugs is a relatively new development during this century. Early discoveries included the effects on tumors of anti-infectious agents and alkylating agents (nitrogen mustard used in World Wars I and II) (Chu & DeVita, 2001). The number of chemotherapy drugs under investigation and in use has increased dramatically. At this time chemotherapy is curative for several types of cancer, such as Hodgkin's disease. Knowledge in molecular biology has contributed to new understanding of the mechanisms through which chemotherapy works to kill cancer cells and through which cancer cells develop resistance to chemotherapy drugs. This has advanced the development of new drugs, dosage schedules, and support technology.

Chemotherapy is used as the principal treatment in advanced cancer when alternative treatment (radiation, surgery) will not effectively control the tumor. When cancer progresses after earlier therapy, chemotherapy is used as a *salvage* treatment. Chemotherapy serves as an *adjuvant* treatment when it is used after the primary tumor has been controlled by local treatments (e. g., surgery, radiation therapy). *Neoadjuvant* chemotherapy refers to its use as the initial treatment for a locally advanced cancer for which an alternative, but less than completely effective, treatment exists. An advantage of neoadjuvant treatment is that it allows for evaluation of the tumor's drug responsiveness.

Chemotherapy typically involves a combination of drugs that vary in terms of their effectiveness across different cancer cells. The combination of drugs, each acting differently against tumor cells, contributes to maximal destruction of cancer cells across drug-resistant cell lines. The dosage and schedule of combination chemotherapies is guided by established principles. One of the most important factors in determining the schedule is the time required for recovery of the patient's bone marrow. In a typical chemotherapy schedule, patients receive treatment over one or more days followed by several weeks to allow for immune system recovery.

Many chemotherapy drugs affect cells in the body, other than cancer cells, contributing to side effects and toxicities, and limiting the dosage which can be safely given. Many cytotoxic drugs affect the lining of the mouth and gastrointestinal tract so that patients develop mouth sores, nausea, and diarrhea. Another dose limiting toxicity is immunosuppression. Side effects include hair loss, fatigue, and diminished concentration. Fortunately, in the last 10 years, advances in supportive technologies—anti-emetics for nausea and vomiting, colony-stimulating factors for immune system recovery, drug delivery methods for pain management — have reduced the impact of chemotherapy-related side effects.

Radiation Therapy
Radiation therapy in the treatment of cancer involves the application of energized particles directed to the cancer site and surrounding tissue. Radiation may be used as a local treatment with a curative, adjuvant, or palliative purpose. The precise mechanisms through which radiation works to kill cancer cells are not clear and cell death from radiation might occur through a number of pathways (Hellman, 2001).

Two radiation therapy types are used in the clinical setting. *Brachytherapy* involves the use of radiation implanted within or close to the tumor. An example is radiation implant treatment of cervical cancer and prostate cancer. In these situations, a small amount of radioactive material is placed in the cervix or close to the prostate. Treatment with radioactive isotopes or implants may involve hospitalization over several days and, because of the danger of exposing others to radiation, may require special precautions and isolation from others. *External beam radiation* involves a source located a short distance from the patient. This type of radiation may be focused over a primary cancer site to prevent recurrence. It may be used over a broad area, such as in the case of whole body radiation.

Before the start of radiation treatment, procedures are performed to localize, or identify, the tumor and the surrounding normal tissue. The radiation dose that may be safely delivered is limited by the tolerance of normal tissue in the path of the radiation beam. The *localization* process will involve a minimum of a clinical examination, radiography, ultrasonography, and computed tomography.

Once localization is accomplished, the radiation oncologist, working with a physicist, dosimetrist, and technicians develop a *treatment plan*. This involves determination of the radiation beam distribution and the dosage. To maximize effectiveness and reduce side effects, it is critical that the radiation dose affect only the designated area.

After formulating a treatment plan, the radiation oncologist conducts a simulation to test and refine the approach. Temporary and permanent markings (tattoos) are made on the individual's skin to ensure accuracy in dosage and delivery. Treatment commences after the *simulation*. In external beam radiation, each treatment is brief, lasting minutes. The schedule for the total treatment, however, may include daily sessions for five to six weeks.

Toxicities from radiation therapy depend on the dosage and the site that receives radiation. Common side effects include fatigue and redness of the skin at the site of radiation exposure. Depending on the site (e. g., cranium, neck, pelvis), radiation side effects may include nausea, anorexia, diarrhea, immunosuppression, dry mouth, change in taste, and alopecia (Johnson, Nail, Lauver, King & Keys, 1988; Johnson, Lauver & Nail, 1989;). Late side effects include secondary malignancies, radiation fibrosis, and sterility (Greenberg, 1998)).

Biologic Therapies
Biologic therapies or immunotherapies are recently developed major oncologic and hematologic treatments. These approaches act on an individual's immune system to activate her or his natural defense mechanisms to eliminate cancer cells. The immune system is an organized network of circulating cells, not in constant contact with each other, but acting in integrated ways to protect the body from pathogens. Immune system cells secrete two proteins—antibodies and cytokines. Many of the approaches to biologic therapy are based on these proteins and their tumor cell destruction abilities (Rosenberg, 2001a).

Two major approaches are used in biologic therapy. *Active* approaches are those which elicit an immune response to eliminate tumor growth. These include treatment with interferon, interleukin-2 (IL-2), and immunization with tumor antigen vaccines. *Passive* approaches to biologic therapy are those which use previously sensitized immunologic reagents that have their own anti-tumor effects. These therapies include treatments with monoclonal antibodies. Toxicities and side effects vary with the type of immunotherapy. For example, IL-2 side effects include flu-like symptoms, concentration and attention difficulties, nausea and vomiting, diarrhea, cardiac arrhythmia, respiratory distress, and anemia.

Bone Marrow Transplant
Bone marrow transplant refers to treatments in which the intervention, usually a combination of high dose chemotherapy and radiation therapy, suppresses or abolishes the bone marrow and, consequently, reduces immune function . Immune system recovery is accomplished through reinfusion with the patient's own bone marrow or peripheral stem cells, referred to as an *autologous* transplant, or through the infusion of the bone marrow of a related or unrelated bone marrow donor, termed an *allogeneic* transplant. Allogeneic bone marrow transplants, because the marrow is harvested from a donor, are used when it is not possible to use the patient's own bone marrow or peripheral stem cells. Because of the possibility of rejection of the donor marrow, termed *graft versus host disease*, allogeneic transplants, as compared to autologous transplants, involve greater risk of mortality and morbidity for the patient.

Advances in support technology have led to significant decreases in risk of morbidity and mortality with bone marrow transplant treatments. The development of technology to extract stem cells from the peripheral blood and the commercial development of growth factor have greatly reduced the time needed for recovery of the bone marrow. Also, improvements in pain management, control of nausea and vomiting, mouth care, and dietary and exercise regimens have reduced discomfort and disability from drug side effects and graft versus host disease. Outpatient transplant programs are now available (Meisenberg et al., 1997). This setting may further improve patient quality of life, as patients are able to maintain more normal diet, activity levels, and sleep than they would during a prolonged hospitalization.

Psychological Assessment and Treatment

Psychological Referrals in Cancer Care

Responding to Referral Questions

Referrals for psychological evaluation cover a wide range of concerns of cancer caregivers, patients, and family members. These include anxiety, depression, delirium, adjustment to illness, self-esteem, treatment side effects, family relationship, patient professional communication, and treatment compliance

(Stam, Bultz & Pittman, 1986; Cull, Stewart & Altman, 1995; Fincannon, 1995). The cancer treatment team may underestimate the presence of psychosocial problems among their patients (Cull et al., 1995). Also, the oncology treatment professional's view of the patient's needs and priorities may be different from that of the patient (Bennett et al., 1997; Crawford et al., 1997).

In receiving a referral, it is important to understand the perspectives of the interested parties and to clarify what is seen as the problem and what help is wanted. It is important especially to understand the concern from the patient's point of view. In the initial interview,

Table 1. **Psychosocial issues across the course of illness.**

Symptom detection	Anxiety Search for providers for diagnostic work-up Delay in seeking diagnosis
Diagnosis and pretreatment	Shock, numbness, relief (with clarification of symptom), anxiety, anticipatory grief, anger Search for second opinion Treatment decision making Adjustment of roles and responsibilities
Treatment	Investment of energy in fighting cancer Anxiety, grief with loss of well-being Side effects and conditioned aversive responses Communication with health providers Dependence on health providers and social network
Post-treatment	Fear of recurrence Anxiety as health care team is less available for support Feeling of accomplishment Negotiation of roles and responsibilities Re-evaluation of life priorities
Recurrence and disease progression	Disappointment, guilt, anxiety, anger, grief Search for new medical opinions Treatment decision making Psychological adaptation to ongoing treatment and follow-up evaluation Participation in experimental and alternative medical therapies
Palliative care and end-of-life care	Fear of abandonment and suffering, anxiety and illness sadness related to loss of control, anticipatory grief Communication with health care providers about pain and discomfort Resolution in important relationships Life review, re-evaluation of life meaning

Source: Adapted from Holland (1989) and Tovian (1991).

I request the patient's permission to speak with the oncology treatment team. Contact with the other health care professionals is important in understanding how they see the presenting problem and what they expect for the patient's recovery, prognosis, and treatment. This contact further serves to alert the rest of the health care team about the involvement of the health psychologist. For example, my informing other members of the oncology team about my work with a patient has contributed to the team keeping me informed of changes in the patient's health status, treatment options, and psychosocial situation. My frequent interactions with other members of the health care team has, in turn, allowed me to foresee impending stressors that a patient will face, to evaluate the basis of a patient's fears about treatment or prognosis, and to assess problems of communication with the health care team.

Referral Concerns

Psychosocial concerns vary according to where a person is along the disease course (Holland, 1989a). A person going through a work-up for cancer experiences responses and needs that are different from the person who is undertaking treatment. The concerns of the person who has survived without a recurrence for three years differ from person who has progressing, recurrent cancer. Table 1 lists psychosocial issues according to the course of the disease and treatment.

Psychiatric Disorders and Psychological Distress. Evidence suggests that the prevalence of psychiatric disorders among cancer patients is higher than in the general population (Derogatis et al., 1983; Stefanek, Derogatis & Shaw, 1987; Zabora, Brintzenhofeszoc, Curbow, Hooker & Prantadosi, 2001). Similar rates have been observed in samples from India and Japan (Alexander, Dinesh & Vidyasagar, 1993; Minagawa, Uchitomi, Yamawaki & Ishitani, 1996). In a study of 215 cancer patients, Derogatis and colleagues (1983) found that the most common group of psychiatric disorders observed included the adjustment disorders with a rate of 32%. Major

depression and anxiety disorders are common at 6% and 2%, respectively. Others, however, have noted a higher incidence of anxiety and distress, with rates of 44% in outpatients (Schag & Heinrich, 1989). Rates of psychological distress and psychiatric disorders appear to increase with severity of illness (Hardman, Maguire, Crowther, 1989; Pasacreta & Massie, 1990; Kaasa et al., 1993). The revision of the Diagnostic and Statistical Manual of Mental Disorders, Fourth Edition, (DSM-IV) expanded the criteria for anxiety disorders to include post-traumatic stress disorder (PTSD) in response to life threatening illness such as cancer. Consequently, the prevalence of anxiety disorders may be higher than previously reported (Andrykowski, Cordova, McGrath, Sloan & Kenady, 2000; Cordova, Andrykowski, Kenady, McGrath, Sloan, Redd, 1995; Kelly, Raphael, Smithers, Swanson et al., 1995).

The rates of other psychiatric disorders, including organic mental disorders and organic mood disorders, are lower than that of adjustment disorders, with estimates of 4% (Derogatis et al., 1983). Nonetheless, the health psychologist will need to be prepared to evaluate individuals experiencing severe depression and other, less common, psychopathology. This is particularly important when the psychologist works on an inpatient medical oncology unit. Medications (e. g., steroids), metabolic conditions (e. g., hypercalcemia), metastatic disease in the central nervous system, hormone secreting tumors, and other factors can contribute to mental status changes. Several studies of referrals to consultation liaison psychiatry services suggest that the rates of severe depression and organic mental disorders on these units are 9% to 56% and 20% to 40%, respectively (Levine, Silberfarb & Lipowski, 1978; Bukberg, Penman & Holland, 1984; Massie, Holland & Breitbart, 1989). On an inpatient medical oncology unit, when the diagnosis is severe depression or an organic disorder, the health psychologist may suggest a referral to a psychiatrist for evaluation and medication management.

Marital and Family Distress. Marital and family concerns are common with a diagnosis and treatment for cancer (Pederson & Valanis, 1988; Andersen, Anderson & deProsse, 1989; Keitel, Cramer & Zevon, 1990; Compas et al., 1994). Spouses and families may express more worry about the health of patient than does the patient (Davis-Ali, Chesler & Chesney, 1993; Jansen, Halliburton, Dibble & Dodd, 1993). However, spouses and family members often receive less support than the patient receives. Studies have focused on the impact of cancer on family caregivers, highlighting their distress and need for support for themselves (Schumacher, Dodd & Paul, 1993; Taylor, Ferrell, Grant & Cheyney, 1993).

Wortman and Dunkel-Schetter have suggested that family patterns of coping may have a detrimental effect on the patient (1979). For example, family members may invest energy in work, withdrawing support from the patient, in order to modulate their own sadness and anxiety. While empirical evidence suggests that loss of social support is not common among individuals diagnosed with cancer (Bloom & Kessler, 1994), the health psychologist may see examples of diminished social support during prolonged illness.

Coping and support. Contemporary cancer patients show a concern about the impact of stress, psychological state, and social support on survival. Many cancer patients seek counseling after a cancer diagnosis to reassure themselves that they are coping well and doing everything possible from a psychological and social perspective. Some patients and family members may experience guilt that, through past distress and conflict, they have contributed to the development of the cancer. As patients experience what is understandable sadness, anxiety, and anger, some individuals fear that the negative emotions may cause the cancer to spread. The evidence for the relationship between psychological factors and cancer treatment outcome is suggestive, but not conclusive, at this time (Ironson, Antoni & Lutgendorf, 1995). In particular, the mechanisms through which psychological factors might influence health outcomes have not yet been delineated (Kiecolt-Glaser & Glaser, 1992; Andersen et al., 1994).

When patients seek psychological services, such as visualization, to improve health outcomes, it is important to present an accurate view of the scientific data. It is equally important to encourage patients in all their efforts to enhance well-being. One way to accomplish this balance is to discuss with the patient the biopsychosocial model (e. g., Andersen et al., 1994), pointing out the pathways through which psychological and social interventions might improve health. The health psychologist can present an accurate view of the research, dispelling guilt and blame, but reinforcing the value of the patient's psychological efforts.

Compliance. Noncompliance in cancer care is a problem when a patient does not take prescribed medication at the recommended times, stops treatment before the recommended dose is attained, neglects recommended self-care activities, or fails to change health habits that may interfere with treatment (e. g., smoking, alcohol use).In the oncologic setting, noncompliance can be life threatening as when an immunosuppressed patient fails to follow infection control guidelines.. While there is evidence that compliance is high in cancer treatment (Taylor, Lichtman & Wood, 1984), other data suggest that the rates vary according to treatment type, treatment side effects, socioeconomic status, and psychological distress (Love, Leventhal, Easterling & Nerenz, 1989, Ayres et al., 1994; Jacobs et al., 1994; McDonough, Boyd, Varvares & Maves, 1996; Urguhart, 1996).

Multiple factors contribute to noncompliance: (1) fatigue due to treatment; (2) low motivation due to depression; (3) severity of side effects and toxicities; (4) anticipatory anxiety about the recommended treatment; (5) lack of patient understanding of the purpose of the chemotherapy or radiotherapy schedule; (6) communication problems between the patient and health care team; (7) lack of support for the recommended treatment from family members. Noncompliance, albeit potentially destructive to health outcomes, may be one of the few ways the individual undergoing treatment for cancer has to exert and maintain a sense of control in her or his life (Taylor, 1979).

Psychosocial Problems Related to Treatment and Diagnostic Procedures. These problems include conditioned responses to chemotherapy (e. g., anxiety, nausea, vomiting) (Carey & Burish, 1988; Jacobsen, Bovbjerg & Redd, 1993), sleep disturbances (Silberfarb, Hauri, Oxman & Lash, 1985; Silberfarb, Hauri, Oxman & Schnurr, 1993), pain and discomfort (Jay, Elliott & Varni, 1986; Dorrepaal, Aaronson & van Dam, 1989), and disturbance in body image and body integrity (e. g., hair loss, scarring, skin discoloration) (Hopwood & Maguire, 1988). Fatigue is reported to be a common and distressing side effect of a variety of cancer treatments, including chemotherapy, radiation therapy, and biologic therapy (Love et al., 1989; Tierney, Taylor & Closs, 1992; Longman, Braden & Mishel, 1996).

Sexual dysfunction may occur as a result of treatment and its side effects (e. g., Schover, Fife & Gershenson, 1989; Schover, 1993). The stress of having a chronic and life-threatening illness compounds problems of sexual desire, arousal, and orgasm (Auchincloss, 1991; Ofman & Auchincloss, 1992).

Finally, many patients report experiencing cognitive disturbances during and following cancer treatment, including loss of attention, concentration, and memory (Meyers, 2000). Loss of cognitive abilities may make it difficult for patients to fulfill their normal work and family responsibilities, to understand and retain important information about their condition and treatment, and to distract themselves from treatment related side effects through reading and other activities.

Psychosocial Concerns of Recurrent and Advanced Cancer. Advanced cancer contributes to many psychosocial issues for patients and their families (Mahon & Casperson, 1995; Pinder et al., 1993). Individuals with relapsing or progressing disease face pain with repeated diagnostic tests, the discomfort and inconvenience of ongoing chemotherapy and radiotherapy, anxiety with uncertainty about the rapidity of progression, disappointment over the failure of the initial treatments, and guilt

related to attributions of personal responsibility for the cancer progression. Nonetheless, many patients with recurrent and advanced cancers adjust, psychologically, and are able to engage in meaningful activities and function well in their lives (Payne, 1992).

Survivorship Issues. As cancer treatment ends, many individuals experience renewed anxiety about their longevity, a consideration of the meaning of their experience with cancer, and a reevaluation of their lives (Cella & Tross, 1986; Schag, Ganz, Wing, Sim & Lee, 1994; Kurtz, Wyatt & Kurtz, 1995; Wyatt & Friedman, 1996). Some survivors experience intense fears of recurrence. Others consider change in jobs, leisure activities, and family relationships at this time. One qualitative study suggests that the time following treatment marks a transition for survivors, involving awareness of physical hardship, loss, mortality, and uncontrollability (Ferrell & Dow, 1996). However, recent perspectives on cancer survivorship emphasize the possibilities for personal growth and appreciation of life as well as what might be considered negative outcomes (Cordova, Cunningham, Carlson & Andrykowski, 2001).

Cancer Risk Concerns. Advances in understanding familial patterns of cancer and the role of genetics in cancer risk have contributed to an upsurge of interest in genetic testing for various cancers (Lerman, Seay, Balshem & Audrain, 1995). This in turn has lead to individuals making decisions to undergo genetic testing, increased surveillance, and prophylactic intervention for cancer. The disclosure of abnormal findings in genetic testing has been linked to increased psychological distress (Croyle, Smith, Botkin, Baty & Nash, 1997). It is important for the health psychologists to be aware of the psychosocial and ethical issues, such as employment and insurance discrimination, involved in genetic testing (Lerman, Rimer & Engstrom, 1991; Lerman & Croyle, 1995).

Care During Dying and Grief. Referrals to the health psychologist in end of life care include those related to patient anxiety about dying and death, patient and family decision making regarding treatment and advance directives, anticipatory grief on the part of patient and family, caregiver burden and burnout, and concerns about children coping with parental death (Koocher, 1986; Lentz & Ramsey, 1988). Medical and nursing schools have incorporated curricula on death and dying.End of life care, however, remains stressful for health care professionals as well as for patients and their families (Dickinson, 1988; Spencer, 1994; Swenson & Dimsdale, 1989).

Assessment

The health psychologist's assessment of the individual with cancer provides data critical in determining the focus and type of psychosocial intervention. Also, the assessment functions as an intervention. It provides an opportunity for the individual to tell her or his story in the presence of an interested, yet impartial, observer whose concern is the individual's well-being. The assessment serves to make more understandable to the individual her or his emotional response to the disease. The structure of the assessment may provide the individual with an experience of organization and control in the face of extreme uncertainty and uncontrollability.

The health psychologist will need to consider the patient's medical condition in planning the length of the initial interview and in selecting measures to use for psychological assessment. As previously discussed, it is vital that the psychologist gather information on both the patient's understanding of the problem and the oncology health care professional's point of view. In addition, it is often important to understand the concerns of the patient's significant others. Family members and friends may influence the patient's confidence in the psychological intervention. Their support of psychological intervention often may be crucial in its success.

Interview

In setting the appointment for an initial interview, I talk to the patient to identify expectations and misconceptions about the meeting, and to establish realistic goals. Many patients

fear that, if they talk with a psychologist, their medical doctors will not take them seriously or will neglect to treat symptoms such as pain, nausea, or fatigue. In light of concerns such as these, Holland (1997) suggests that psychological assessment in cancer care focus on "distress" as a term that is not highly stigmatizing, yet is comprehensive, subsuming a range of psychological needs and responses.

In the initial contact, I emphasize that most people have an emotional response to a cancer diagnosis and that sometimes emotions about cancer are strong. If a patient has concerns about the severity of psychological distress, I explain that, because receiving a cancer diagnosis and undergoing cancer treatment are stressful, people may experience stress responses, such as anxiety and depression. Rather than attempting to "normalize" the emotional response, I direct my comments to making emotions about cancer understandable to the patient. Also, I express my confidence that psychological and psychiatric treatment can help a person feel better, even when anxiety and depression are severe.

I typically start the interview with the patient's report of concerns and follow the patient's lead. In my questions, I attempt to understand as completely as possible the presenting problem, including its severity, frequency, and related antecedent and consequent events. Also, I collect information on the patient's and significant others' reaction to the problem, the patient's resources to cope with or resolve the problem, and the patient's expectations for change.

In addition to conducting a thorough behavioral investigation of the problem, I use the interview to make a psychiatric diagnosis. This is important not only for billing purposes, but to determine whether I will suggest further evaluation for psychiatric medication as a treatment option or adjunct. My questions include inquiry about suicidality and homicidality, even in patients who have received a "good prognosis." During the interview, it is important for the health psychologist to inquire about factors that might increase the patient's risk of experiencing psychological distress with cancer (e. g., Weis-

Table 2. **Risk factors for psychological distress.**

Patient	Young age
	Current and previous psychiatric disorder or substance abuse
	Concurrent stress
	Previous adverse experience with cancer
	Difficulty accepting change in physical appearance and function
	Pessimism
	Suppresses negative feelings
	Avoidant coping
Social	Pre-existing problems in significant relationships (e. g., marriage)
	Lack of social support
	Lack of involvement in satisfying or meaningful activities
Disease and treatment	Treatment with cytotoxic drugs
	Treatments associated with visible physical deformity
	Physical symptoms at diagnosis
	Poor prognosis

Source: Adapted from Carver et al., 1993; Ganz et al., 1993; Vinokur et al., 1989; Weisman, 1979.

man, 1979a; Bukberg et al., 1984; Schag & Heinrich, 1989; Vinokur, Threatt, Vinokur-Kaplan & Satariano, 1990; Schag et al., 1993). These include young age, previous psychiatric disorders, poor prognosis, treatments associated with physical deformities, aggressive cytotoxic treatment, concurrent stress, marital distress, pessimism, and lack of social support. Evaluation of risk factors for distress is important when the health psychologist is conducting the assessment to determine need for psychological follow-up during treatments, such as bone marrow transplant. See Table 2 for a summary of risk factors for psychological distress. The mechanisms through which these risk factors influence psychological distress are not well understood. For example, Oktay and Walter (1991) and Rowland (1989) suggest that developmental stage mediates or moderates the relationship between age and psychological distress with cancer diagnosis and treatment, but this is yet to be evaluated.

In discussing the presenting concern, the patient often will describe previous experience with cancer (e. g., cancer in a family member, a previous diagnosis of cancer) and the meaning they ascribe to their cancer diagnosis and treatment. If not, I explore these areas as well. Understanding the patient's

previous experience of cancer may help explain the intensity of the patient's emotional response to the diagnosis and treatment.

The meaning that the patient takes from the cancer diagnosis and treatment can influence the patient's view of cancer as a stressor, but it can represent a coping resource to the patient. For the patient who sees cancer as a challenge to be undertaken, it is a manageable stressor that can be dealt with through medical treatment and personal efforts. In contrast, the patient who considers cancer as a punishment may respond with guilt and hopelessness..

I inquire about coping strategies and styles to identify potential strengths and factors associated with psychological morbidity. Those strategies and styles that have been associated with psychological distress, include escape avoidance coping and pessimism (e. g., Carver et al., 1993; Stanton & Snider, 1993; Manne et al., 1994; Classen, Koopman, Angell & Spiegel, 1996; Mytko et al., 1996). Current perspectives on adaptation to cancer suggest that an individual's goals in life influence the beneficial or harmful impact of coping (Scheier & Carver, 2001). Understanding a person's purpose in life, including religious and spiritual beliefs (Jenkins & Pargament, 1995; Potts, 1996)provides a context from which to understand their ability to withstand the disruption and losses associated with cancer. During the interview, I assess the patient's understanding of their treatment and their expectations for the future. In addition to discussion of conventional medical treatment, I ask about their interest in and use of alternative therapies. In evaluating the patient's view of their cancer treatment and their future, I consider how realistic the expectations appear in light of what I learn from the medical team. This will help me gauge potential disappointments and challenges that that patient is likely to experience with the disease and treatment. I have learned, however, not to base my own expectations for patients entirely on clinical information that they may have rapidly progressing or widespread disease. Many individuals with advanced cancer survive beyond expectations to accomplish important life goals.

Because cancer is often seen as a life-threatening illness, it is important to allow discussion of dying and death even if this is not the reason for referral. These discussions can be initiated with open-ended questions about the patient's previous understanding of cancer, the patient's familiarity with others who have had cancer, and the patient's expectations for their future. While these conversations may be distressing for some individuals, many patients are relieved to find that they can talk about dying and death, and their fears about their own mortality, with a health care professional who is comfortable with this topic.

The patient's description of the relationship with the oncology treatment professionals is critical in my assessment. Often, patients find that the relationship with the oncologist involves frequent contact, discussion of emotionally charged issues, and dependency. The patient's oncology treatment team will consist of members from multiple disciplines. I assess the patient's understanding of their treatment team and of how the members can help them. I ask the patient about their communication with their oncologists and other the team members. These questions help me anticipate communication problems that might interfere with can-

cer care and the patient's ability to use the oncology treatment team as a social support resource. Information on the patient's use of alternative therapies helps me identify other treatment professionals in the patient's network.

In addition to interviewing the patient, I speak to the medical team. I typically ask about their observations of the patient's behavior and their communication with the patient. Also, I inquire about their interest in participating in the psychological intervention. This is particularly important when the patient is an inpatient. On an inpatient unit, staff members influence many antecedent and consequent events associated with patient behavior and can serve as powerful sources of reinforcement and support for the patient.

Assessment Instruments

Some of the most useful measures in the psychological assessment of cancer patients include brief distress scales. These include the Hospital Anxiety and Depression Scale (HADS) (Zigmond & Snaith, 1983; Carroll et al., 1993), the Profile of Mood States (McNair, Lorr & Droppleman, 1971), and the Brief Symptom Checklist (Derogatis & Melisaratos, 1983). The National Comprehensive Cancer Network (2002) suggests the use of a simple visual analog scale ("Distress Thermometer") in the psychological assessment. The brevity of these instruments is important as many patients do not have the physical stamina to complete lengthy measures. Use of these instruments in the diagnosis of anxiety and depression may be problematic due to their inclusion of somatically focused items (see chapter two in this volume). Nonetheless, scores on these scales can provide a benchmark from which to gauge treatment progress. Measures of stressful events (e. g., Sarason, Johnson & Siegel, 1978) and everyday hassles (e. g., Kanner, Coyne, Schaefer & Lazarus, 1981) may provide additional information. It is possible to obtain normative information for these instruments across cancer types, stages, treatments, and points in the disease trajectory. Gotay and Stern (1995) provide an excellent review of the assessment of psychological functioning in patients diagnosed with cancer.

Quality of life instruments, although developed primarily as outcome measures in clinical trials, provide important information for psychological intervention. Quality of life refers to a multidimensional construct that reflects an individual's subjective experience of well-being (Donovan, Sanson-Fisher & Redman, 1989; Cella & Tulsky, 1990; Gotay, Korn, McCabe, Moore & Cheson, 1992). The dimensions assessed vary across instruments. Most instruments measure physical status (e. g., pain, discomfort, nausea), functional status (e. g., ability to work, ability to perform responsibilities), psychological status (e. g., worry, sadness), and social status (e. g., ability to spend time with significant others). Other dimensions include relationship with health care professionals, satisfaction with care, financial status, spirituality, and existential meaning. Some quality of life measures have added subscales to assess dimensions such as spirituality and religiosity (Mytko & Knight, 1999). Other instruments include disease or treatment specific modules to assess concerns unique to cancer type and treatment. Quality of life measures specific to cancer include the Functional Assessment of Cancer Therapy Scale (FACT) (Cella et al., 1993), the Functional Living Index–Cancer (FLIC) (Schipper, Clinch, McMurray & Levitt, 1984), the Cancer Rehabilitation Evaluation System (CARES) (Schag & Heinrich, 1990), the European Organization for Research and the Treatment of Cancer Quality of Life Questionnaire (EORTC-QLQ) (Aaronson et al., 1993), and the Quality of Life Index (Spitzer et al., 1981). Generic measures include the Psychosocial Adjustment to Illness Scale (PAIS) (Derogatis, 1986b) and the Short Form-36 (SF-36) (McHorney, Ware & Raczek, 1993).

In health psychology interventions in cancer care, quality of life measures are particularly useful in the assessment of the patient's physical and functional status. The sensitivity of emotional and social subscales to psychological intervention is as yet undetermined; nonetheless, quality of life instruments may prove helpful in the design of psychosocial treatment.

Psychological Interventions

A meta-analysis analysis of studies of psychological interventions in cancer care supports their efficacy in improving emotional and functional adjustment and in reducing disease symptoms and treatment side effects (Meyer & Mark, 1995). Also, recent studies suggest that the effects of psychological interventions for cancer patients include enhanced immune function and health outcomes (Spiegel, Bloom, Kraemer & Gottheil, 1989; Fawzy, Kemeny, Fawzy, Elashoff et al., 1990). However, another rigorous review of the literature suggests that, while a number of interventions (i. e., group therapy, education, structured and unstructured counseling, cognitive behavioral therapy) appear to improve psychosocial outcomes, only relaxation training and guided imagery have a beneficial impact on conditioned and physical side effects of cancer treatment (Newell, Sanson-Fisher & Savolainen, 2002). While the beneficial effects of psychosocial interventions in cancer care and the mechanisms of these effects are not yet clearly delineated, the evidence is suggestive that psychological intervention has an important role in the psychological and physical well-being of cancer patients. (Ironson et al., 1995; Redd, 1995).

Intervention Strategies

Many patients come to the health psychologist with concerns amenable to a cognitive and behavioral treatment, such as depression and conditioned aversive response to chemotherapy. Also, patients may need to express emotion, to explore the meaning of cancer, and to experience interpersonal support. For these reasons, psychological intervention in cancer care often integrates supportive and expressive therapies with cognitive and behavioral approaches (Worden & Weisman, 1984; Spiegel, 1985; Moorey & Greer, 1989a; Fawzy & Fawzy, 1994).

Moorey, Greer, and colleagues (Moorey & Greer, 1989; Moorey, 1996; Moorey & Greer, 2002) have adapted cognitive therapy for patients with cancer. This approach allows for greater attention to the patient's emotional expression than otherwise would be typical in cognitive therapy. The therapist encourages emotional expression and helps the patient develop ways of containing affect, such as the scheduling of worry and grief. It incorporates cognitive restructuring with an emphasis on helping the patient to manage emotions, such as fear and sadness, that are often realistic and understandable in the context of the cancer diagnosis. The cognitive strategies involve understanding the personal meaning of thoughts about the illness, treatment, death and dying. The therapist engages the patient in evaluating thoughts in terms of their usefulness and their basis in reality. Through treatment, the patient learns to identify and challenge those beliefs that represent distortions of reality and that are destructive to the patient's well-being.

Behavioral techniques—relaxation, attentional distraction, activities scheduling — are incorporated as a part of treatment. Relaxation techniques include progressive muscle relaxation training and passive relaxation used in managing stress and treatment side effects. Attentional distraction serves to focus the patient's awareness on engaging and enjoyable activities, such as computer games, crafts, or puzzles. Activity planning is used to help patients increase their involvement in enjoyable and rewarding pursuits. The patient and therapist collaborate on developing a list of activities, including those that provide a sense of mastery and those that provide a pleasurable experience.

Other psychological interventions in cancer care include training in problem solving, social skills, and coping (Sobel & Worden, 1982; Worden & Weisman, 1984; Telch & Telch, 1985; Golden, Gersh & Robbins, 1992; Fawzy, Fawzy, Hyun & Wheeler, 1996; Nezu, Nezu & Faddis, 1998). Supportive expressive and existential approaches to group psychotherapy with patients with cancer have been described by Spira and Spiegel (Spira & Spiegel, 1993; Spira, 1997; Spira & Reed, 2002). Existential therapies focus on the meaning of the patient's experience with cancer and on the patient's personal growth toward living in the present in spite of facing losses and the possibility of death. Spira points out that the support available in a group facilitates the existential therapy process: The involvement of others in the same situation reduces social isolation and offers support in confronting difficult issues, such as loss of health and disability. The therapist working from this perspective asks leading questions to assist patients as they explore their experiences. The treatment focus varies, including diverse topics such as coping with treatment, re-evaluating life priorities, and considering death and dying.

Specific Intervention Targets

Conditioned Aversive Responses. These include conditioned anxiety, taste aversion, nausea, vomiting, and immunosuppression, occurring in response to chemotherapy (Andrykowski, 1986; Carey & Burish, 1988). Conditioned anxiety may develop in response to painful or uncomfortable medical procedures, such as to needle sticks, bone marrow biopsy, or MRI scans. Treatment of conditioned aversive responses to chemotherapy involves the use of relaxation training often in conjunction with systematic desensitization (Redd, 1989). Other approaches, such as stress inoculation (e. g., cognitive coping statements), hypnosis, and preparative information, have been employed as well (see Morrow, 1986; Andrykowski & Redd, 1987; Kaye, 1987; Burish & Tope, 1992; Vasterling, Jenkins, Tope & Burish, 1993).

Pain. Cancer pain can be related to a diagnostic test, treatment toxicities, or tumor invasion of bones, nerves, or organs (Foley, 1987). Two thirds of patients with advanced disease experience pain (Grond, Zech, Diefenbach, Radbruch & Lehmann, 1996). Pain control is usually accomplished through medical management, including pharmacological therapy and palliative surgery, radiation, and chemotherapy. Cleeland, Syrjala, and others have developed behavioral approaches to cancer pain management (Cleeland & Tearnan, 1986; Syrjala, Cummings & Donaldson, 1992; Syrjala, Donaldson, Davis, Kippes & Carr, 1995). These incorporate relaxation, visualization, hypnosis, distraction, music, and cognitive coping. Because many patients and families misunderstand and fear addiction to opioids used in cancer pain relief (Glajchen, Fitzmartin, Blum & Swanton, 1995), education of the patient to increase compliance with pain medication schedules may be an important part of a psychological intervention (Rimer et al., 1987).

Sleep Disturbance. Evidence suggests that insomnia is common among patients with cancer. In a sample of 1579 patients in five major oncology centers, 48% of the prescribed medications were hypnotics, and 44% of psychotropic prescriptions were written for sleep (Derogatis et al., 1979). Insomnia in cancer patients may be related to pain, depression, or hot flashes, requiring medical and psychiatric treatment. Psychological interventions include education about sleep hygiene, schedule and environmental adjustment (e. g., regular sleep onset and awakening times, quiet sleep environment), stimulus control (e. g., limit bed to sleep activities), relaxation, and focused attention (Cannici, Malcolm & Peek, 1983; Stam & Bultz, 1986; Hu & Silberfarb, 1991). In addition, it may be helpful to educate patients about the effects that their cancer treatments may have on sleep (e. g., agitation related to steroids).

Sexual Dysfunction. Some types of cancer and cancer treatment have profound effects on a couple's sexual functioning and relationship (Schover et al., 1989; Schover, 1991; Andersen, Woods & Copeland, 1997). Couples therapy focuses on helping the couple to understand change in sexual function with the cancer and its treatments. It can help a couple continue their affectional relationship when treatment related fatigue or injury to sexual organs limits sexual activity. During the patient's recovery from cancer treatment, the health psychologist may use sexual dysfunction treatment approaches, such as sensate focus as the couple gradually resumes greater sexual activity. Schover and Jensen (1988) have written an outstanding reference on sexuality and chronic illness, including cancer.

Grief and Bereavement. Worden's 's (1982) tasks of mourning model may be helpful in working with patients experiencing grief and anticipatory grief. These tasks are: (1) accepting the reality of the loss; (2) experiencing the pain of grief; (3) adjusting to an environment in which the deceased is missing; (4) withdrawing emotional energy from the deceased and reinvesting it in other relationships. Following this model, the therapist supports the patient in the awareness of the loss and allows for emotional expression. Later in the course of treatment, the therapist may use structured approaches, such as social skills training and activities planning, as the patient resumes normal responsibilities and roles without the deceased. Many patients find comfort and stability in understanding the intensity, duration, and breadth of the feelings associated with grief. Education about process of adjustment during mourning is helpful. After the death of a loved one, psychological intervention often is enough support for patients to reorganize their resources and to resume their lives. Although many of the symptoms of depression are normal during bereavement, some individuals experience clinical depression and may need referral for anti-depressant medication.

Patient and Professional Communication Problems. These problems influence medical decision making, compliance with treatment, psychological distress, and quality of life (Thorne, 1988; Siminoff, 1989; Schain, 1990; Steptoe, Sutcliffe, Allen & Coombes, 1991). Both patients and professionals contribute to communication problems; but in working with the patient, an important goal for the health psychologist is to help patients improve their ability to communicate with their physicians. Table 3 lists possible activities of the health psychologist, addressing patient and professional communication problems. These start with encouraging the patient to interact, directly, with the professional. If the patient appears to lack knowledge or skills in health care interactions, education, modeling, and role playing may be helpful. In some situations, I may attend a doctor's appointment with the patient or organize a patient and professional meeting in order to facilitate communication between patient and the oncology team.

Table 3. **Activities to promote patient provider communication.**

Patient interventions	Identify communication needs
	Educate about cancer care team — its members and their roles
	Encourage and reinforce efforts to communicate directly with providers
	Help structure interactions with providers (e. g., writing down questions, asking significant other to attend provider visit)
	Use role playing and modeling to assist communication efforts
Provider interventions	Feedback about patient concerns and efforts to participate in treatment
	Encourage provider in efforts to communicate with patient
Patient and provider interventions	Attend patient visit with provider (with permission of both parties)
	Arrange patient, family, provider meeting
Health care system interventions	Participate in patient care rounds
	Provide grand round presentations focusing on patient provider communication
	Send research reports on patient concerns to providers
	Request library subscription to journals which cover psychosocial issues in cancer care
	Conduct or participate in research on psychosocial concerns of cancer patients

Selected Intervention Modalities

Group Interventions. Considerable research evidence exists on the efficacy of support groups, psychotherapy groups, and coping skill groups in improving psychological and social well-being in cancer patients (Cella & Yellen, 1993; Fawzy, 1994). Growing evidence suggests that groups may have a beneficial impact on immune functioning and health outcomes (Spiegel et al., 1989; Fawzy et al., 1990). In spite of these benefits, some patient populations are underrepresented in groups. For example, in one study of fourteen groups, women participants outnumbered men by three to one and most had a high socioeconomic status (Deans, Bennett-Emslie, Weir, Smith & Kaye, 1988). There appears to be little difference in outcome for group participants, however, across most sociodemographic and medical factors, such as gender, age, marital status, education, and health status (Cunningham, Lockwood & Edmonds, 1993).

Therapists may use many of the same psychological interventions in individual and group therapy. Groups, however, have the advantage of providing feedback and support from others who are experiencing cancer and its treatment–a powerful source of affirmation and communion.

Spira (1997) has described central considerations for developing and providing therapy groups for patients with cancer. An important question in forming a group is whether to mix individuals with different times since diagnosis, cancer types, and stages in the same group. Individuals with localized cancer often have different concerns than those with advanced cancer. People who are newly diagnosed with cancer even when the disease is localized may experience intense emotional reactions, make complex decisions about treatments, learn to cope with symptoms and side effects, and develop new relationships with medical treatment professionals. In contrast, people with advanced disease face greater awareness of the possibility of death and greater uncertainty about their ability to engage in meaningful life activities. Compared to the individual with new or localized disease, the person with advanced cancer may receive more aggressive and more experimental treatments, along with an indefinite treatment duration. It may be difficult, if not impossible, to meet the diverse needs of those with new and localized disease and those with advanced cancer in the same group.

Another issue is group size. Seven to twelve participants often is thought to be the optimal number for meaningful group interaction. With cancer patients, group size often fluctuates from session to session, because of participant illness, medical treatments, and hospitalization. With too few members, group participants may be discouraged when only one or two show up for a session because the rest are too sick to attend. On the other hand, waiting to start the group until enough participants of the same cancer type and stage are available may not be practical. Some potential participants will experience a decreased need for the group by the time it commences. Other considerations are whether the group should be structured or unstructured and time limited (e. g., ten to twenty sessions) or open ended. The health psychologist may base decisions regarding structure on the type of participants and where the participants are in the cancer trajectory. For example, patients with new diagnoses may need to learn stress and side effect management, coping skills, and communication skills. Consequently, these participants may benefit from a group that offers skill building and allows time for emotional expression. Participants who are at the end of treatment and defining themselves as cancer survivors or those with advanced disease and dealing with existential issues may need time for open ended discussion. Setting a time limit for the group can help the participants and facilitator work toward an end point. For skill building groups, this is often helpful. A flexible time limit in an open ended group gives the participants and facilitator a designated point to reevaluate participant needs and goals before continuing.

The decision to keep an ongoing group open to new participants depends on the type of group. Another important consideration is the screening of potential participants. Many educational groups and peer facilitated support groups do not screen participants, allowing participants to attend as many or as few groups as they would like. Psychotherapy groups, however, are often based on the development of group cohesion and do not work as well as with participants dropping in and out of the sessions. Members who show little commitment to the group and who frequently do not show up for sessions due to reasons other than illness erode the trust and safety experienced by other members. Particularly in a psychotherapy group, screening can serve to help clarify potential members' expectations for the group. Individuals who see the group as not providing for their needs typically decide not to participate.

Partner and Family Treatment. Often the health psychologist will find that the request for help comes from the cancer patient's partner or family member. Tovian (1991) suggests that the health psychologist may want to be flexible about combining individual and family therapy when appropriate. This reduces delay in treatment, excessive referrals, and fragmentation of treatment.

Family members and partners have exposure to extreme stress similar to that of the cancer patient. When family member or partner distress is high, psychological intervention for that individual can provide support and clarification of emotional responses. In family and couple sessions, the therapist may intervene to increase communication, appreciation, and affection and warmth. Kerns (1995) describes the importance of the family maintaining enjoyable activities and negotiating roles and responsibilities disrupted by illness.

Psychological Preparation for Cancer Treatment. Health psychologists have developed interventions to prevent high levels of distress associated with cancer treatment (Burish, Snyder & Jenkins, 1991; Dodd, 1987; Rainey, 1985; Worden & Weisman, 1984). These programs target patients undergoing surgery, chemotherapy, and radiation therapy. An advantage of preparative interventions is that they may reduce rates of psychological morbidity.

The content of preparative programs may include education about the upcoming treatment, relaxation training, hypnosis, attentional distraction, and cognitive restructuring. Table 4 gives an example intervention outline. The provision of preparative information regarding what the patient might ex-

Table 4. **Preparation for breast cancer chemotherapy: intervention outline.**

Before chemotherapy	Build rapport and relationship
	Assess psychosocial needs
	Train in relaxation and guided imagery for management of stress and treatment side effects
	Introduce distraction activities
	Introduce cognitive coping
During chemotherapy	Reinforce use of relaxation, distraction, and cognitive coping
	Identify and reinforce existing coping efforts
	Identify social support network
	Discuss the impact of the diagnosis and treatment on family and other relationships
	Discuss change in roles and responsibilities during treatment
	Identify preferred types of social support
	Discuss communication with medical oncology team
	Introduce problem solving for decisions about activities and responsibilities during treatment (e. g., disability)
After chemotherapy	Discuss expectations for the future
	Identify needs for support after treatment
	Discuss use of cognitive coping to manage fear of recurrence
	Explore the meaning of survivorship

pect in the medical or surgical treatment is a unique aspect of these programs. Informational interventions typically inform the patient about what they might expect in the upcoming medical or surgical treatment, especially regarding its intent, duration, side effects, and recovery period.

Innovative Approaches. The health psychologist will need to adapt psychological interventions to meet the evolving needs of the patient as the cancer progresses. The psychologist may find, for example, that the patient with advanced cancer becomes too weak or has too much pain to travel for an office visit. Flexibility in working with the patient with cancer is critical in the patient's getting psychological care in advanced cancer or at the end of life. In these situations, the health psychologist may offer to provide treatment through a hospital visit or home visit.

Telephone contact (Mermelstein & Holland, 1991; Alter, Fleishman, Kornblith, Holland et al., 1996; Carlsson, Strang & Lindblad, 1996; Colon, 1996; Marcus, Garrett, Cella, Wenzel, Brady, Crane, McClatchey, Kluhsman & Pate-Willig, 1998) and comput-

er linkages (Fieler & Borch, 1996; Weinberg, Schmale, Uken & Wessel, 1996; Knight, Nathan, Siston, Kattan, Elstein, Collela, Wolf, Slimack, Bennett & Golub, 2002; Rawl, Given, Given, Champion, Kozachik, Kozachik, Barton, Emsley & Williams, 2002) are innovative ways of providing support and psychological intervention to cancer patients. These modalities have special characteristics, advantages, and limitations. For example, telephone counseling offers greater immediacy, anonymity, and convenience than face-to-face sessions. It can provide a means of maintaining therapeutic contact with patients when office sessions are not an option. However, the limited nonverbal data available over the telephone is a disadvantage It is important for the health psychologist to consider the professional and ethical issues involved in hospital sessions, home visits, and telephone and computer interaction. In a home visit, for example, the psychologist may experience difficulty maintaining patient confidentiality when family members are present. .

Belar and Deardorff (1995) provide an excellent discussion of the ethical and professional issues involved in contact with the patient outside the therapist's office, especially in the context of the inpatient medical unit. Many of the considerations they raise are applicable to home visits and telephone counseling.

Treatment Considerations

In psychological intervention with the patient with cancer, the health psychologist will need to pace each treatment session according to the patient's physical and mental stamina. Also, in teaching, the psychologist should gauge the presentation of information based on the patient's ability to attend and concentrate. Attention and concentration deficits may occur due to intensity of emotional response, level of concurrent stress, and treatment side effects. For this reason, it may be helpful to use a multimedia approach, using written handouts, books, audio and video tapes, and pictures to supplement the discussion in the treatment session.

One Patient's Story

Presenting Concern: M, a 47-year-old African American man, was diagnosed with renal cell cancer and referred to the psycho-oncology service for evaluation and treatment of "anxiety during MRI scan" and "difficulty coping." He worked as a university administrator and lived nearby with his Danish wife and 5-year-old son. His 19-year-old son and 22-year-old daughter from a previous marriage lived with their mother in another neighborhood. He had completed most of his work toward a doctorate, but had left his graduate studies to support his siblings after his mother's death.

Initial Assessment: I was immediately struck by the contrast between M's size (6'4") and his soft voice. His description of the time leading up to the discovery that he had cancer was articulate and insightful. He had felt tired, nauseated, and depressed for six months before his diagnosis. While he was devastated to learn that he had kidney cancer, he was relieved to have an explanation for his symptoms. However, during a MRI scan, M be-

came very anxious and was unable to complete the procedure. He noted, "I felt like I was suffocating" and "I couldn't make myself to do one more test."

He reported no previous psychiatric or medical problems, but described symptoms of fatigue, loss of appetite, loss of interest in usually enjoyable activities, hopelessness, and guilt about burdening his family. Although symptoms such as fatigue and loss of appetite may be associated with cancer, guilt is less likely to have a strong physiologic basis and, taken together with the other symptoms, suggested the possibility of depression. He denied suicidal and homicidal ideation and intent.

In terms of his social network, M described close relationships with his wife, children, and siblings, but noted a strained relationship between his wife and his family—"they have never really accepted her." He expressed respect for his oncologist and described a good working relationship with the cancer care team.

Treatment: The initial treatment plan included 1) referral to a psychiatrist for evaluation regarding use of medication, 2) relaxation training and systematic desensitization to reduce anxiety, and 3) supportive psychotherapy directed toward M's effort to understand his emotional response to the losses associated with his illness, and to regain a sense of control in his life.

As we started treatment, I discussed the plan of psychological care with M's medical oncologist and with the psychiatrist who had recommended an antidepressant. I initiated relaxation training and systematic desensitization focusing on anxiety about medical procedures particularly scans. By the end of a month in treatment, he had been able to complete his MRI scan and his depression and anxiety had improved markedly. However, M continued to struggle with fatigue in spite of medical treatment targeting this symptom. Using a cognitive behavioral approach, we focused on identifying his patterns of energy and adapting his expectations and activities to accommodate his reduced stamina (e. g., ensuring that his schedule allowed for relaxation and sleep, maintaining regular physical activity, re-evaluating expectations for work and home responsibilities). As his ability to predict and modulate his energy improved, M was able to work out an arrangement so that he could return to work.

As we continued to meet, we devoted time in each session to understanding M's view of the meaning of cancer in his life. In these discussions, M explored different perspectives on his illness, especially focusing on how cancer allowed him to slow down in his work life and enjoy family and friends. However, he was still troubled by the family tension that had contributed to increasing arguments between M and his wife. M's wife attended several sessions with M and, for the first time in many years, M and his wife were able to discuss the struggles they experienced as an interracial and multicultural couple. We discussed ways that M could set limits when his family criticized his wife. As his wife felt more supported by M, she expressed greater understanding of M's need to spend time with his adult children and brothers and sisters. Also, in these sessions, M and his wife discussed their concerns about the changes in their sexual relationship that had occurred during the course of his medical treatment.

We closed treatment approximately a year after M had been diagnosed. The cancer was in remission and M's anxiety and depression were much improved. In our closing session, M remarked on the opportunities that his cancer had opened up for him especially in terms of the renewed sense of meaning in his life and closeness with his wife and family.

Postscript

Approximately 5 years after I first saw M, he called me to request that we meet again. His cancer had recurred with metastatic disease in his brain. While he maintained some optimism that treatment would prolong his life, he questioned how much time he had left.

At this point, treatment addressed the many losses that M was experiencing—his deteriorating physical condition, his difficulty with short-term memory, his inability to work or coach his son's soccer team. We also discussed M's fear and sadness about dying.

During these discussions, M noted that he had often regretted leaving school to support his family, but now was able to appreciate the courage that he had in doing so and the benefits that his brothers and sisters had realized from his support.

As M approached the end of his life, the conflict between M's wife and one of his sisters reemerged as the family struggled to make decisions about M's care. After discussion with M, I arranged a meeting between M's oncologist and several members of the cancer care team and M and his family including his wife, his sister and several other siblings, and his adult children. The meeting was useful in a number of respects. The family had an opportunity to review with M his wishes about his end of life care including his choice of his wife as surrogate decision maker. Each family member was able to express concerns and ask questions about what to expect for M over the next few weeks. While the longstanding family issues were not resolved, the meeting went a long way to help the family put aside their differences to provide the support that M needed as he was dying, and to develop the intimacy that was important to the entire family in their grieving.

In my last meeting with M, he reflected on how important it had been that I had facilitated this meeting and had served as a witness. We shared feelings of loss, and appreciation to have known each other through this therapeutic work. We said good-bye a last time.

Concluding Remarks

This case illustrates the importance of a multimethod and multidisciplinary approach to assessment and treatment and the need to adapt treatment to emerging patient needs. Also, it highlights the need for a flexible, but reasoned, approach to confidentiality and professional boundaries. It shows several important countertransference issues — the therapist's grief and the therapist's gratification in sharing moments with an individual and family as they face some of life's most challenging experiences. It is

---

Table 5. **Resources for psychooncology.**

Readings
Psychooncology—Holland (1998)
Helping Cancer Patients Cope: A Problem-Solving Approach—Nezu, Nezu & Faddis (1998)
Group Therapy for Cancer Patients: A Research-Based Handbook of Psychosocial Care—Spiegel & Classen (2000)
Psychosocial Interventions for Cancer—Baum & Andersen (2001)
Cognitive Behavior Therapy for People with Cancer—Moorey & Greer (2002)

Journals
Psychooncology
Journal of Psychosocial Oncology
Cancer Practice
Journal of Pain and Symptom Management

Organizations
National Cancer Institute—www.nci.nih.gov
American Cancer Society—www.cancer.org
National Comprehensive Cancer Network—www.nccn.org
American Society for Preventive Oncology—www.aspo.org
American Psychosocial Oncology Society—www.apos-society.org
International Psycho-oncology Society—www.ipos-aspboa.org

Internet
www.oncolink.com
www.canceradvocacy.org

---

beyond the scope of this chapter to discuss in depth the professional issues involved in clinical practice of health psychology on an oncology and hematology service. The reader will find excellent discussion of these considerations in Belar and Deardorff (1995) and Tovian (1991). Table 5 lists additional resources relevant to psychological services in cancer care.

Belar and Deardorff and Tovian point to qualities of the health psychologist important in work with cancer patients. They cite flexibility, high frustration tolerance, the ability to interact with professionals from many disciplines, and the capacity to quickly form relationships with patients. In addition, they emphasize that the health psychologist will need preparation to work with suffering, dying, and death. I would add to this list the ability to cope with ambiguity and to see possibilities for human growth and development throughout the course of illness.

Redd (1995) has described research in psychological interventions in cancer as a model for health psychology—"Quite simply, by in-

creasing compliance and reducing distress, psychosocial interventions help oncologists do their jobs." The health psychologist's participation in the care and healing of cancer patients is a critical contribution to cancer care. That participation is one of its most meaningful rewards.

References

Aaronson, N.K., Ahmedzai, S., Bergman, B., Bullinger, M., Cull, A., Duez, N.J., Filiberti, A., Flechtner, H., Fleishman, S.B., de Haes, J.C. et al. (1993). The European Organization for Research and Treatment of Cancer QLQ-C30: A quality-of-life instrument for use in international clinical trials in oncology. *Journal of the National Cancer Institute, 85*, 365–376.

Alexander, P.J., Dinesh, N., & Vidyasagar, M.S. (1993). Psychiatric morbidity among cancer patients and its relationship with awareness of illness and expectations about treatment outcome. *Acta Oncologica, 32*, 623–626.

Alter, C.L., Fleishman, S.B., Kornblith, A.B., Holland, J.C. et al. (1996). Supportive telephone intervention for patients receiving chemotherapy. *Psychosomatics, 37,* 425–431.

American Cancer Society (2003). *Cancer facts & figures: 2003.* Atlanta, GA.

Andersen, B.L. (1992). Psychological interventions for cancer patients to enhance the quality of life. Special Issue: Behavioral medicine: An update for the 1990s. *Journal of Consulting & Clinical Psychology, 60,* 552–568.

Andersen, B.L., Anderson, B., & deProsse, C. (1989). Controlled prospective longitudinal study of women with cancer: II. Psychological outcomes. *Journal of Consulting & Clinical Psychology, 57,* 692–697.

Andersen, B.L., Kiecolt-Glaser, J.K., & Glaser, R. (1994). A biobehavioral model of cancer stress and disease course. *American Psychologist, 49,* 389–404.

Andersen, B.L., Woods, X.A., & Copeland, L.J. (1997). Sexual self-schema and sexual morbidity among gynecologic cancer survivors. *Journal of Consulting & Clinical Psychology, 65,* 221–229.

Andrykowski, M.A. (1986). Definitional issues in the study of anticipatory nausea in cancer chemotherapy. *Journal of Behavioral Medicine, 9,* 33–41.

Andrykowski, M.A., Cordova, M.J., McGrath, P.C., Sloan, D.A., & Kenady, D.E. (2000). Stability and change in posttraumatic stress disorder symptoms following breast cancer treatment: A 1-year follow-up. *Psychooncology, 9,* 69–78.

Andrykowski, M.A., & Redd, W.H. (1987). Life-threatening disease: Biopsychosocial dimensions of cancer care. In A.S.B. Randall & L. Morrison (Eds.), *Medical factors and psychological disorders: A handbook for psychologists.* New York: Plenum.

Antoni, M.H. & Smith, R. (2002). *Stress management intervention for women with breast cancer.* Washington, DC: American Psychological Association.

Auchincloss, S. (1991). Sexual dysfunction after cancer treatment. *Journal of Psychosocial Oncology, 9,* 23–42.

Ayres, A., Hoon, P.W., Franzoni, J.B., Matheny, K.B., Contanch, P.H., & Takayanage, S. (1994). Influence of mood and adjustment to cancer on compliance with chemotherapy among breast cancer patients. *Journal of Psychosomatic Research, 1994,* 393–402.

Baum, A. & Andersen, B.L. (2001). *Psychosocial interventions for cancer.* Washington, DC: American Psychological Association.

Beck, A.T. (1972). *Depression: Causes and treatment.* Philadelphia: University of Pennsylvania.

Belar, C.D., & Deardorff, W.W. (1995). *Clinical health psychology in medical settings: A practitioner's guidebook* (rev. ed.). Washington, DC: American Psychological Association.

Bennett, C.L., Chapman, G., Elstein, A.S., Knight, S.J., Nadler, R.B., Sharifi, R., & Kuzel, T. (1997). A comparison of perspective on prostate cancer: Analysis of utility assessment of patients and physicians. *European Urology, 32*(suppl. 3), 86–88.

Bloom, J.R., & Kessler, L. (1994). Emotional support following cancer: A test of the stigma and social activity hypotheses. *Journal of Health & Social Behavior, 35,* 118–133.

Bukberg, J., Penman, D., & Holland, J.C. (1984). Depression in hospitalized cancer patients. *Psychosomatic Medicine, 46,* 199–212.

Burish, T.G., Snyder, S.L., & Jenkins, R.A. (1991). Preparing patients for cancer chemotherapy: Effect of coping preparation and relaxation interventions. *Journal of Consulting & Clinical Psychology, 59,* 518–525.

Burish, T.G., & Tope, D.M. (1992). Psychological techniques for controlling the adverse side effects of cancer chemotherapy: Findings from a decade of research. *Journal of Pain & Symptom Management, 7,* 287–301.

Burke, W., Daly, M., Garber, J., Botkin, J., Kahn, M.J.E., Lynch, P., McTiernan, A., Offit, K., Perlman, J., Petersen, G., Thomson, E., & Varricchio, C. (1997a). Recommendations for follow-up care of individuals with an inherited predisposition to cancer: BRCA1 and BRCA2. *Journal of the American Medical Association, 277,* 997–1003.

Burke, W., Petersen, G., Lynch, P., Botkin, J., Daly, M., Garber, J., Kahn, M.J.E., McTiernan, A., Offit, K., Thomson, E., & Varricchio, C. (1997b). Recommendations for follow-up care of individuals with an inherited predisposition to cancer: I. Hereditary nonpolyposis colon cancer. *Journal of the American Medical Association, 277,* 915–919.

Cannici, J., Malcolm, R., & Peek, L.A. (1983). Treatment of insomnia in cancer patients using muscle relaxation training. *Journal of Behavior Therapy & Experimental Psychiatry, 14,* 251–256.

Carey, M.P., & Burish, T.G. (1988). Etiology and treatment of the psychological side effects associated with cancer chemotherapy: A critical review and discussion. *Psychological Bulletin, 104,* 307–325.

Carlsson, M.E., Strang, P.M., & Lindblad, L. (1996). Telephone help line for cancer counseling and cancer information. *Cancer Practice, 4,* 319–323.

Carroll, B.T., Kathol, R., & Noyes, R. (1993).

Screening for depression and anxiety in cancer patients using the hospital anxiety and depression scale. *General Hospital Psychiatry, 15,* 69–74.

Carver, C.S., Pozo, C., Harris, S.D., Noriega, V., Scheier, M.F., Robinson, D.S., Ketcham, A.S., Moffat, F.L., Jr., & Clark, K.C. (1993). How coping mediates the effect of optimism on distress: A study of women with early stage breast cancer. *Journal of Personality & Social Psychology, 65,* 375–390.

Cella, D.F., & Tross, S. (1986). Psychological adjustment to survival from Hodgkin's disease. *Journal of Consulting & Clinical Psychology, 54,* 616–622.

Cella, D.F., & Tulsky, D.S. (1990). Measuring quality of life today: Methodological aspects. *Oncology, 4,* 29–38, discussion 69.

Cella, D.F., Tulsky, D.S., Gray, G., Sarafian, B., Linn, E., Bonomi, A., Silberman, M., Yellen, S.B., Winicour, P., Brannon, J. et al. (1993). The Functional Assessment of Cancer Therapy scale: Development and validation of the general measure. *Journal of Clinical Oncology, 11,* 570–579.

Cella, D.F., & Yellen, S.B. (1993). Cancer support groups: The state of the art. *Cancer Practice, 1,* 56–61.

Cordova, M.J., Cunningham, L.L., Carlson, C.R., & Andrykowski, M.A. (2001). Posttraumatic growth following breast cancer: A controlled comparison study. *Health Psychology, 20,* 176–185.

Chu, E., & DeVita, V.J., Jr. (2001). Principles of cancer management: Chemotherapy. In V.J. DeVita Jr., S. Hellman & S.A. Rosenberg (Eds.), *Cancer: Principles and practice of oncology* (5th ed.). Philadelphia: Lippincott-Raven.

Classen, C., Koopman, C., Angell, K., & Spiegel, D. (1996). Coping styles associated with psychological adjustment to advanced breast cancer. *Health Psychology, 15,* 434–437.

Cleeland, C.S., & Tearnan, B.H. (1986). Behavioral control of cancer pain. In A.D. Holzman & D.C. Turk (Eds.), *Pain management.* New York: Pergamon.

Colon, Y. (1996). Telephone support groups: A nontraditional approach to reaching underserved cancer patients. *Cancer Practice, 4,* 156–159.

Compas, B.E., Worsham, N.L., Epping-Jordan, J.E., Grant, K.E., Mireault, G., Howell, D.C., & Malcarne, V.L. (1994). When mom or dad has cancer: Markers of psychological distress in cancer patients, spouses, and children. *Health Psychology, 13,* 507–515.

Cordova, M.J., Andrykowski, M.A., Kenady, D.E.,

McGrath, P.C., Sloan, D.A., & Redd, W.H. (1995). Frequency and correlates of posttraumatic-stress-disorder-like symptoms after treatment for breast cancer. *Journal of Consulting and Clinical Psychology, 63,* 981–986.

Crawford, D.E., Bennett, C.L., Stone, N.N., Knight, S.J., DeAntoni, E., Sharp, L., Garnick, M.B., & Porterfield, H.A. (1997). Comparison of perspectives on prostate cancer: Analyses of survey data. *Urology, 50,* 366–372.

Croyle, R.T., Smith, K.R., Botkin, J.R., Baty, B., & Nash, J. (1997). Psychological responses to BRCA1 mutation testing: Preliminary findings. *Health Psychology, 16,* 63–72.

Cull, A., Stewart, M., & Altman, D.G. (1995). Assessment of and intervention for psychosocial problems in routine oncology practice. *British Journal of Cancer, 72,* 229–235.

Cunningham, A.J., Lockwood, G.A., & Edmonds, C.V.I. (1993). Which cancer patients benefit most from a brief, group, coping skills program? *International Journal of Psychiatry in Medicine, 23,* 383–398.

Davis-Ali, S.H., Chesler, M.A., & Chesney, B.K. (1993). Recognizing cancer as a family disease: Worries and support reported by patients and spouses. *Social Work in Health Care, 19,* 45–65.

Deans, G., Bennett-Emslie, G.B., Weir, J., Smith, D.C., & Kaye, S.B. (1988). Cancer support groups—who joins and why? *British Journal of Cancer, 58,* 670–674.

Derogatis, L.R. (1986a). Psychology in cancer medicine: A perspective and overview. *Journal of Consulting & Clinical Psychology, 54,* 632–638.

Derogatis, L.R. (1986b). The Psychosocial Adjustment to Illness Scale (PAIS). *Journal of Psychosomatic Research, 30,* 77–91.

Derogatis, L.R., Feldstein, M., Morrow, G., Schmale, A., Schmitt, M., Gates, C., Murawski, B., Holland, J., Penman, D., Melisaratos, N., Enelow, A.J., & Adler, L.M. (1979). A survey of psychotropic drug prescriptions in an oncology population. *Cancer, 44,* 1919–1929.

Derogatis, L.R., & Melisaratos, N. (1983). The Brief Symptom Inventory: An introductory report. *Psychological Medicine, 13,* 595–605.

Derogatis, L.R., Morrow, G.R., Fetting, J., Penman, D., Piasetsky, S., Schmale, A.M., Henrichs, M., & Carnicke, C.L., Jr. (1983). The prevalence of psychiatric disorders among cancer patients. *Jama, 249,* 751–757.

DeVita, V.J., Jr. (1997). Principles of cancer management: Chemotherapy. In V.J. DeVita Jr., S. Hellman & S.A. Rosenberg (Eds.), *Cancer: Principles and practice of oncology* (5th ed.). Philadelphia: Lippincott-Raven.

DeVita, V.J., Jr., Hellman, S., & Rosenberg, S.A. (Eds.). (2001). *Cancer: Principles and practice of oncology* (5th ed.). Philadelphia: Lippincott-Raven.

Dickinson, G.E. (1988). Death education for physicians. *Journal of Medical Education, 63,* 412.

Dodd, M.J. (1987). Efficacy of proactive information on self-care in radiation therapy patients. *Patient Education, 16,* 538–543.

Donovan, K., Sanson-Fisher, R.W., & Redman, S. (1989). Measuring quality of life in cancer patients. *Journal of Clinical Oncology, 7,* 959–968.

Dorrepaal, K.L., Aaronson, N.K., & van Dam, F.S. (1989). Pain experience and pain management among hospitalized cancer patients. A clinical study. *Cancer, 63,* 593–598.

Fawzy, F.I. (1994). The benefits of a short-term group intervention for cancer patients. *Advances, 10,* 17–19.

Fawzy, F.I., & Fawzy, N.W. (1994). A structured psychoeducational intervention for cancer patients. Special Section: A structured psychoeducational intervention for cancer patients. *General Hospital Psychiatry, 16,* 149–192.

Fawzy, F.I., Fawzy, N.W., Hyun, C.S., & Wheeler, J.G. (1996). Brief coping-oriented therapy for patients with malignant melanoma. In J.L. Spira (Ed.), *Group therapy for medically ill patients.* New York: Guilford.

Fawzy, F.I., Kemeny, M.E., Fawzy, N.W., Elashoff, R. et al. (1990). A structured psychiatric intervention for cancer patients: II. Changes over time in immunological measures. *Archives of General Psychiatry, 47,* 729–735.

Ferrell, B.R., & Dow, K.H. (1996). Portraits of cancer survivorship: A glimpse through the lens of survivors' eyes. *Cancer Practice, 4,* 76–80.

Fieler, V.K., & Borch, A. (1996). Results of a patient education project using a touch-screen computer. *Cancer Practice, 4,* 341–5.

Fincannon, J.L. (1995). Analysis of psychiatric referrals and interventions in an oncology population. *Oncology Nursing Forum, 22,* 87–92.

Foley, K.M. (1987). Cancer pain syndromes. *Journal of Pain & Symptom Management, 2* (2, Suppl.), 13–17.

Glajchen, M., Fitzmartin, R.D., Blum, D., & Swanton, R. (1995). Psychosocial barriers to cancer pain relief. *Cancer Practice, 3,* 76–82.

Golden, W.L., Gersh, W.D., & Robbins, D.M. (1992). *Psychological treatment of cancer patients: A cognitive-behavioral approach.* New York: Macmillan.

Gotay, C.C., Korn, E.L., McCabe, M.S., Moore, T.D., & Cheson, B.D. (1992). Quality-of-life assessment in cancer treatment protocols: Research issues in protocol development. *Journal of the National Cancer Institute, 84,* 575–579.

Gotay, C.C., & Stern, J.D. (1995). Assessment of psychological functioning in cancer patients. Special Issue: Psychosocial resource variables in cancer studies: Conceptual and measurement issues. *Journal of Psychosocial Oncology, 13*(1–2), 123–160.

Greenberg, D.B. (1998). Radiotherapy. In J.C. Holland (Ed.), *Psycho-oncology.* Oxford, UK: Oxford University Press.

Grond, S., Zech, D., Diefenbach, C., Radbruch, L., & Lehmann, K.A. (1996). Assessment of cancer pain: A prospective evaluation in 2266 cancer patients referred to a pain service. *Pain, 64,* 107–114.

Hardman, A., Maguire, P., & Crowther, D. (1989). The recognition of psychiatric morbidity on a medical oncology ward. *Journal of Psychosomatic Research, 33,* 235–239.

Hellman, S. (2001). Principles of cancer management: Radiation therapy. In V.J. DeVita Jr., S. Hellman & S.A. Rosenberg (Eds.), *Cancer: Principles and practice of oncology* (5th ed.). Philadelphia: Lippincott-Raven.

Holland, J.C. (1989). Clinical Course of Cancer. In J.C. Holland & J.H. Rowland (Eds.), *Handbook of psychooncology: Psychological care of the patient with cancer.* New York: Oxford University Press.

Holland, J.C. (1997). Preliminary guidelines for the treatment of distress. *Oncology, 11,* 109–114.

Holland, J.C. (1998). *Psycho-oncology.* Oxford, UK: Oxford University Press.

Holland, J.C., & Rowland, J.H. (Eds.). (1989). *Handbook of psychooncology: Psychological care of the patient with cancer.* New York: Oxford University Press.

Hopwood, P., & Maguire, G.P. (1988). Body image problems in cancer patients. Second Leeds Psychopathology Symposium: The psychopathology of body image (1986, Leeds, England). *British Journal of Psychiatry, 153*(Suppl. 2), 47–50.

Hu, D.S., & Silberfarb, P.M. (1991). Management of sleep problems in cancer patients. *Oncology, 5*(9), 23–27.

Ironson, G., Antoni, M., & Lutgendorf, S. (1995). Can psychological interventions affect immunity and survival? Present findings and suggested targets with a focus on cancer and HIV. *Mind/Body Medicine, 1,* 85–110.

Jacobs, J.R., Casiano, R.R., Schuller, D.E., Pajak, T.F., Laramore, G.E., & al-Sarraf, M. (1994). Chemotherapy as predictor of compliance. *Journal of Surgical Oncology, 55,* 143–148.

Jacobsen, P.B., Bovbjerg, D.H., & Redd, W.H. (1993). Anticipatory anxiety in women receiving chemotherapy for breast cancer. *Health Psychology, 12,* 469–475.

Jansen, C., Halliburton, P., Dibble, S., & Dodd, M.J. (1993). Family problems during cancer chemotherapy. *Oncology Nursing Forum, 20,* 689–694.

Jay, S.M., Elliott, C., & Varni, J.W. (1986). Acute and chronic pain in adults and children with cancer. *Journal of Consulting & Clinical Psychology, 54,* 601–607.

Jenkins, R.A., & Pargament, K.I. (1995). Religion and spirituality as resources for coping with cancer. Special Issue: Psychosocial resource variables in cancer studies: Conceptual and measurement issues. *Journal of Psychosocial Oncology, 13*(1–2), 51–74.

Johnson, J.E., Lauver, D.R., & Nail, L.M. (1989). Process of coping with radiation therapy. *Journal of Consulting & Clinical Psychology, 57,* 358–364.

Johnson, J.E., Nail, L.M., Lauver, D., King, K.B., & Keys, H. (1988). Reducing the negative impact of radiation therapy on functional status. *Cancer, 61,* 46–51.

Kaasa, S., Malt, U., Hagen, S., Wist, E., Moum, T., & Kvikstad, A. (1993). Psychological distress in cancer patients with advanced disease. *Radiotherapy & Oncology, 27,* 193–197.

Kanner, A.D., Coyne, J.C., Schaefer, C., & Lazarus, R.S. (1981). Comparison of two modes of stress measurement: Daily hassles and uplifts versus major life events. *Journal of Behavioral Medicine, 4,* 1–39.

Kastan, M.B., & Skapek, S.X. (2001). Molecular biology of cancer: The cell cycle. In V.J. DeVita Jr., S. Hellman & S.A. Rosenberg (Eds.), *Cancer: Principles and practice of oncology* (5th ed.) Philadelphia: Lippincott-Raven.

Kaye, J.M. (1987). Use of hypnosis in the treatment of cancer patients. *Journal of Psychosocial Oncology, 5*(2), 11–22.

Keitel, M.A., Cramer, S.H., & Zevon, M.A. (1990). Spouses of cancer patients: A review of the literature. *Journal of Counseling & Development, 69,* 163–166.

Kelly, B., Raphael, B., Smithers, M., Swanson, C. et al. (1995). Psychological responses to malignant melanoma: An investigation of traumatic stress reactions to life-threatening illness. *General Hospital Psychiatry, 17,* 126–134.

Kerns, R.D. (1995). Family assessment and intervention. In P. Nicassio & T. Smith (Eds.), *Managing chronic illness: A biopsychosocial perspective* (pp. 207–244). Washington, DC: American Psychological Association.

Kiecolt-Glaser, J.K., & Glaser, R. (1992). Psychoneuroimmunology: Can psychological interventions modulate immunity? *Journal of Consulting & Clinical Psychology, 60,* 569–575.

Knight, S.J., Chmiel, J.S., Kuzel, T., Sharp, L., Albers, M., Fine, R., Moran, E.M., Nadler, R.B., Sharifi, R., & Bennett, C.L. (1998). Quality of life in metastatic prostate cancer among men of lower socioeconomic status: Feasibility and criterion related validity of 3 measures. *Journal of Urology, 160,* 1765–1769.

Knight, S.J., Nathan, D.P., Siston, A.K., Kattan, M.W., Elstein, A.S., Collela, K.M., Wolf, M.S., Slimack, N.S., Bennett, C.L., & Golub, R.M. (2002). Pilot study of a utilities-based treatment decision intervention for prostate cancer patients. *Clinical Prostate Cancer, 1,* 105–114.

Koocher, G.P. (1986). Coping with a death from cancer. *Journal of Consulting & Clinical Psychology, 54,* 623–631.

Kurtz, M.E., Wyatt, G., & Kurtz, J.C. (1995). Psychological and sexual well-being, philosophical/spiritual views, and health habits of long-term cancer survivors. *Health Care for Women International, 16,* 253–262.

Lentz, R.J., & Ramsey, L.J. (1988). The psychologist consultant on the hospice team: One example of the model. *Hospice Journal, 4,* 55–66.

Lerman, C., & Croyle, R.T. (1995). Genetic testing for cancer predisposition: Behavioral science issues. *Journal of the National Cancer Institute Monographs* (17), 63–6.

Lerman, C., Rimer, B.K., & Engstrom, P.F. (1991). Cancer risk notification: Psychosocial and ethical implications. *Journal of Clinical Oncology, 9,* 1275–82.

Lerman, C., Schwartz, M.D., Miller, S.M., Daly, M., Sands, C., & Rimer, B.K. (1996). A randomized trial of breast cancer risk counseling: Interacting effects of counseling, educational level, and coping style. *Health Psychology, 15,* 75–83.

Lerman, C., Seay, J., Balshem, A., & Audrain, J. (1995). Interest in genetic testing among first-degree relatives of breast cancer patients. *American Journal of Medical Genetics, 57,* 385–392.

Levine, P.M., Silberfarb, P.M., & Lipowski, Z.J. (1978). Mental disorders in cancer patients: A study of 100 psychiatric referrals. *Cancer, 42,* 1385–1391.

Longman, A.J., Braden, C.J., & Mishel, M.H. (1996). Side effects burden in women with breast cancer. *Cancer Practice, 4,* 274–280.

Love, R.R., Leventhal, H., Easterling, D.V., & Nerenz, D.R. (1989). Side effects and emotional distress during cancer chemotherapy. *Cancer, 63,* 604–612.

Mahon, S.M., & Casperson, D.S. (1995). Psychosocial concerns associated with recurrent cancer. *Cancer Practice, 3*, 372–380.

Manne, S.L., Sabbioni, M., Bovbjerg, D.H., Jacobsen, P.B., Taylor, K.L., & Redd, W.H. (1994). Coping with chemotherapy for breast cancer. *Journal of Behavioral Medicine, 17*, 41–55.

Massie, M.J., Holland, J.C., & Breitbart, W. (1989). Common psychiatric disorders and their management. In J.C. Holland & J.H. Rowland (Eds.), *Handbook of psychooncology: Psychological care of the patient with cancer.* New York: Oxford University Press.

McDonough, E.M., Boyd, H.H., Varvares, M.A., & Maves, M.D. (1996). Relationship between psychological status and compliance in a sample of patients treated for cancer of the head and neck. *Head and Neck, 18*, 269–276.

McHorney, C.A., Ware, J.E., Jr., & Raczek, A.E. (1993). The MOS 36-Item Short-Form Health Survey (SF-36): II. Psychometric and clinical tests of validity in measuring physical and mental health constructs. *Medical Care, 31*, 247–263.

McNair, D.M., Lorr, M., & Droppleman, L.F. (1971). *Profile of Mood States manual.* San Diego: Educational and Industrial Testing Service.

Marcus, A.C., Garrett, K.M., Cella, D., Wenzel, L.B., Brady, M.J., Crane, L.A., McClatchey, M.W., Kluhsman, B.C., & Pate-Willig, M. (1998). Telephone counseling of breast cancer patients after treatment: A description of a randomized clinical trial. *Psychooncology, 7*, 470–482.

Meisenberg, B.R., Miller, W.E., McMillan, R., Callaghan, M., Sloan, C., Brehm, T., Kosty, M.P., Kroener, J., Longmire, R., Saven, A., & Piro, L.D. (1997). Outpatient high-dose chemotherapy with autologous stem-cell rescue for hematologic and nonhematologic malignancies. *Journal of Clinical Oncology, 15*, 11–17.

Mermelstein, H.T., & Holland, J.C. (1991). Psychotherapy by telephone: A therapeutic tool for cancer patients. *Psychosomatics, 32*, 407–412.

Meyer, T.J., & Mark, M.M. (1995). Effects of psychosocial interventions with adult cancer patients: A meta-analysis of randomized experiments. *Health Psychology, 14*, 101–108.

Meyers, C.A. (2000). Neurocognitive dysfunction in cancer patients. *Oncology, 14*, 75–81.

Minagawa, H., Uchitomi, Y., Yamawaki, S., & Ishitani, K. (1996). Psychiatric morbidity in terminally ill cancer patients. A prospective study. *Cancer, 78*, 1131–1137.

Moorey, S. (1996). When bad things happen to rational people: Cognitive therapy in adverse life circumstances. In P.M. Salkowskis (Ed.), *Frontiers of cognitive therapy* (pp. 450–469). New York: Guilford.

Moorey, S., & Greer, S. (1989). *Psychological therapy for patients with cancer: A new approach.* Washington, DC: American Psychiatric Press.

Moorey, S. & Greer, S. (2002). *Cognitive behavior therapy for people with cancer.* Oxford, UK: Oxford University Press.

Morrow, G.R. (1986). Effect of the cognitive hierarchy in the systematic desensitization treatment of anticipatory nausea in cancer patients: A component comparison with relaxation only, counseling, and no treatment. *Cognitive Therapy & Research, 10*, 421–446.

Moyer, A. (1997). Psychosocial outcomes of breast-conserving surgery versus mastectomy: A meta-analytic review. *Health Psychology, 16*, 284–298.

Mytko, J.J., Knight, S.J., Chastain, D., Mumby, P.B., Siston, A.K., & Williams, S. (1996). Coping strategies and psychological distress in cancer patients before autologous bone marrow transplant. *Journal of Clinical Psychology in Medical Settings, 3*, 355–366.

Mytko, J.J. & Knight, S.J. (1999). Body, mind, and spirit: Toward the integration of religiosity and spirituality in cancer quality of life research. *Psychooncology, 8*, 439–450.

Nezu, A.M., Nezu, C.M., & Faddis, S. (1998). *Helping cancer patients cope: A problem-solving approach.* Washington, DC: American Psychological Association.

National Comprehensive Cancer Network (1999). NCCN practice guidelines for the management of psychosocial distress. *Oncology, 13*, 113–147.

National Comprehensive Cancer Network (2002). *Distress management* (Version 1.2002). www.nccn.com

Newell, S.A., Sanson-Fisher, R.W., & Savolainen, N.J. (2002). Systematic review of psychological therapies for cancer patients: Overview and recommendations for future research. *Journal of the National Cancer Institute, 94*, 558–584.

Ofman, U.S., & Auchincloss, S.S. (1992). Sexual dysfunction in cancer patients. *Current Opinion in Oncology, 4*, 605–613.

Oktay, J.S., & Walter, C.A. (1991). *Breast cancer in the life course: Women's experiences.* New York: Springer Publishing Company.

Pasacreta, J.V., & Massie, M.J. (1990). Nurses' reports of psychiatric complications in patients with cancer. *Oncology Nursing Forum, 17*, 347–353.

Payne, S.A. (1992). A study of quality of life in cancer patients receiving palliative chemotherapy. *Social Science and Medicine, 35*, 1505–1509.

Pederson, L.M., & Valanis, B.G. (1988). The effects of breast cancer on the family: A review of the literature. *Journal of Psychosocial Oncology, 6*, 95–118.

Percy, C., Young, J.L., Jr., Muir, C., Ries, L., Hankey, B.F., Sobin, L.H., & Berg, J.W. (1995). Cancer. Introduction. *Cancer, 75* (1 Suppl.), 140–146.

Pinder, K.L., Ramirez, A.J., Black, M.E., Richards, M.A., Gregory, W.M., & Rubens, R.D. (1993). Psychiatric disorder in patients with advanced breast cancer: Prevalence and associated factors. *European Journal of Cancer, 29A*, 524–527.

Potts, R.G. (1996). Spirituality and the experience of cancer in an African-American community: Implications for psychosocial oncology. *Journal of Psychosocial Oncology, 14*, 1–19.

Rainey, L.C. (1985). Effects of preparatory patient education for radiation oncology patients. *Cancer, 56*, 1056–61.

Rawl, S.M., Given, B.A., Given, C.W., Champion, V.L., Kazachik, S.L., Kozachik, S.L., Barton, D., Emsley, C.L., & Williams, S.D. (2002). Intervention to improve psychological functioning for newly diagnosed patients with cancer. *Oncology Nursing Forum, 29*, 967–975.

Redd, W.H. (1989). Management of anticipatory nausea and vomiting. In J.C. Holland & J.H. Rowland (Eds.), *Handbook of psychooncology: Psychological care of the patient with cancer*. New York: Oxford University Press.

Redd, W.H. (1995). Behavioral research in cancer as a model for health psychology. *Health Psychology, 14*, 99–100.

Rimer, B., Levy, M.H., Keintz, M.K., Fox, L., Engstrom, P.F., & MacElwee, N. (1987). Enhancing cancer pain control regimens through patient education. *Patient Education and Counseling, 10*, 267–277.

Rosenberg, S.A. (2001a). Principles of cancer management: Biologic therapy. In V.J. DeVita Jr., S. Hellman & S.A. Rosenberg (Eds.), *Cancer: Principles and practice of oncology* (5th ed.). Philadelphia: Lippincott-Raven.

Rosenberg, S.A. (2001b). Principles of cancer management: Surgical oncology. In V.J. DeVita Jr., S. Hellman & S.A. Rosenberg (Eds.), *Cancer: Principles and practice of oncology* (5th ed.). Philadelphia: Lippincott-Raven.

Rowland, J.H. (1989). Developmental stage and adaptation: Adult model. In J.C. Holland & J.H. Rowland (Eds.), *Handbook of psychooncology: Psychological care of the patient with cancer*. New York: Oxford University Press.

Rowland, J.H., Holland, J.C., Chaglassian, T., & Kinne, D. (1993). Psychological response to breast reconstruction: Expectations for and impact on postmastectomy functioning. *Psychosomatics, 34*, 241–250.

Sarason, I.G., Johnson, J.H., & Siegel, J.M. (1978). Assessing the impact of life changes: Development of the life experiences survey. *Journal of Consulting and Clinical Psychology, 46*, 932–946.

Schag, C.A., Ganz, P.A., Polinsky, M.L., Fred, C., Hirji, K., & Petersen, L. (1993). Characteristics of women at risk for psychosocial distress in the year after breast cancer. *Journal of Clinical Oncology, 11*, 783–93.

Schag, C.A., Ganz, P.A., Wing, D.S., Sim, M.S., & Lee, J.J. (1994). Quality of life in adult survivors of lung, colon and prostate cancer. *Quality of Life Research, 3*, 127–141.

Schag, C.A., & Heinrich, R.L. (1989). Anxiety in medical situations: Adult cancer patients. *Journal of Clinical Psychology, 45*, 20–27.

Schag, C.A., & Heinrich, R.L. (1990). Development of a comprehensive quality of life measurement tool: CARES. *Oncology, 4*, 135–138.

Schain, W.S. (1990). Physician-patient communication about breast cancer. A challenge for the 1990s. *Surgical Clinics of North America, 70*, 917–936.

Scheier, M.F. & Carver, C.S. (2001). Adapting to cancer: The importance of hope and purpose. In A. Baum & B.L. Andersen (Eds.), *Psychosocial interventions for cancer*. Washington, DC: American Psychological Association.

Schipper, H., Clinch, J., McMurray, A., & Levitt, M. (1984). Measuring the quality of life of cancer patients: The Functional Living Index–Cancer: Development and validation. *Journal of Clinical Oncology, 2*, 472–483.

Schover, L.R. (1991). The impact of breast cancer on sexuality, body image, and intimate relationships. *Ca: A Cancer Journal for Clinicians, 41*, 112–120.

Schover, L.R. (1993). Sexual rehabilitation after treatment for prostate cancer. *Cancer, 71* (3 Suppl.), 1024–1030.

Schover, L.R., Fife, M., & Gershenson, D.M. (1989). Sexual dysfunction and treatment for early stage cervical cancer. *Cancer, 63*, 204–212.

Schover, L.R., & Jensen, S.B. (1988). *Sexuality and chronic illness: A comprehensive approach*. New York: Guilford.

Schumacher, K.L., Dodd, M.J., & Paul, S.M. (1993). The stress process in family caregivers of persons receiving chemotherapy. *Research in Nursing & Health, 16*, 395–404.

Silberfarb, P.M., Hauri, P.J., Oxman, T.E., & Lash, S. (1985). Insomnia in cancer patients. *Social Science & Medicine, 20*, 849–850.

Silberfarb, P.M., Hauri, P.J., Oxman, T.E., & Schnurr, P. (1993). Assessment of sleep in patients with lung cancer and breast cancer. *Journal of Clinical Oncology, 11*, 997–1004.

Silberfarb, P.M., Philibert, D., & Levine, P.M. (1980). Psychosocial aspects of neoplastic disease: II. Affective and cognitive effects of chemotherapy in cancer patients. *American Journal of Psychiatry, 137*, 597–601.

Siminoff, L.A. (1989). Cancer patient and physician communication: Progress and continuing problems. *Annals of Behavioral Medicine, 11*, 108–112.

Sobel, H.J., & Worden, J.W. (1982). *Helping cancer patients cope: A problem-solving intervention program for health care professionals.* New York: BMA Audio Cassettes, Division of Guilford Publications.

Spencer, L. (1994). How do nurses deal with their own grief when a patient dies on an intensive care unit, and what help can be given to enable them to overcome their grief effectively? *Journal of Advanced Nursing, 19*, 1141–1150.

Spiegel, D. (1985). Psychosocial interventions with cancer patients. *Journal of Psychosocial Oncology, 3*, 83–95.

Spiegel, D., Bloom, J.R., Kraemer, H.C., & Gottheil, E. (1989). Effect of psychosocial treatment on survival of patients with metastatic breast cancer. *Lancet, 2* (8668), 888–891.

Spiegel, D. & Classen, C. (2000). *Group therapy for cancer patients: A research-based handbook of psychosocial care.* New York: Basic Books.

Spielberger, C.D., Gorsuch, R.L., & Lushene, R. (1970). *State-Trait Anxiety Inventory manual.* Palo Alto: Consulting Psychologists Press.

Spira, J., & Spiegel, D. (1993). Group psychotherapy for the medically ill. In A. Stoudemire & B. Fogel (Eds.), *Psychiatric care of the medical patients* (2nd ed.). New York: Oxford University Press.

Spira, J.L. (1997). Existential group therapy for advanced breast cancer and other life-threatening illnesses. In J.L. Spira (Ed.), *Group therapy for medically ill patients.* New York: Guilford.

Spira, J.L. & Reed, G.M. (2002) Group psychotherapy for women with breast cancer. Washington, DC: American Psychological Association.

Spitzer, W.O., Dobson, A.J., Hall, J., Chesterman, E., Levi, J., Shepherd, R., Battista, R.N., & Catchlove, B.R. (1981). Measuring the quality of life of cancer patients: A concise QL-index for use by physicians. *Journal of Chronic Diseases, 34*, 585–597.

Stam, H.J., & Bultz, B.D. (1986). The treatment of severe insomnia in a cancer patient. *Journal of Behavior Therapy & Experimental Psychiatry, 17*, 33–37.

Stam, H.J., Bultz, B.D., & Pittman, C.A. (1986). Psychosocial problems and interventions in a referred sample of cancer patients. *Psychosomatic Medicine, 48*, 539–548.

Stanton, A.L., & Snider, P.R. (1993). Coping with a breast cancer diagnosis: A prospective study. *Health Psychology, 12*, 16–23.

Stefanek, M.E., Derogatis, L.P., & Shaw, A. (1987). Psychological distress among oncology outpatients. *Psychosomatics, 28*(10), 530–539.

Steptoe, A., Sutcliffe, I., Allen, B., & Coombes, C. (1991). Satisfaction with communication, medical knowledge, and coping style in patients with metastatic cancer. *Social Science & Medicine, 32*, 627–32.

Suinn, R.M. & VandenBos, G.R. (1999). *Cancer patients and their families: Reading on disease course, coping, and psychological interventions.* Washington, DC: American Psychological Association.

Swenson, J.R., & Dimsdale, J.E. (1989). Hidden grief reactions on a psychiatric consultation service. *Psychosomatics, 30*, 300–6.

Syrjala, K.L., Cummings, C., & Donaldson, G.W. (1992). Hypnosis or cognitive behavioral training for the reduction of pain and nausea during cancer treatment: A controlled clinical trial. *Pain, 48*, 137–146.

Syrjala, K.L., Donaldson, G.W., Davis, M.W., Kippes, M.E., & Carr, J.E. (1995). Relaxation and imagery and cognitive-behavioral training reduce pain during cancer treatment: A controlled clinical trial. *Pain, 63*, 189–198.

Taylor, E.J., Ferrell, B.R., Grant, M., & Cheyney, L. (1993). Managing cancer pain at home: The decisions and ethical conflicts of patients, family caregivers, and homecare nurses. *Oncology Nursing Forum, 20*, 919–927.

Taylor, S.E. (1979). Hospital patient behavior: Reactance, helplessness, or control? *Journal of Social Issues, 35*, 156–184.

Taylor, S.E., Lichtman, R.R., & Wood, J.V. (1984). Compliance with chemotherapy among breast cancer patients. *Health Psychology, 3*, 553–562.

Telch, C.F., & Telch, M.J. (1985). Psychological approaches for enhancing coping among cancer patients: A review. *Clinical Psychology Review, 5*, 325–344.

Thorne, S.E. (1988). Helpful and unhelpful communications in cancer care: The patient perspective. *Oncology Nursing Forum, 15*, 167–172.

Tierney, A.J., Taylor, J., & Closs, S.J. (1992). Knowledge, expectations and experiences of patients receiving chemotherapy for breast cancer. *Scandinavian Journal of Caring Sciences, 6*, 75–80.

Tovian, S.M. (1991). Integration of clinical psychology into adult and pediatric oncology programs. In J. Sweet, R. Rozensky & S. Tovian

(Eds.), *Clinical psychology in medical settings*. NY: Plenum.

Urguhart, J. (1996). Patient compliance with crucial drug regimens: Implications for prostate cancer. *European Urology, 29* (Suppl.), 124–131.

Vasterling, J., Jenkins, R.A., Tope, D.M., & Burish, T.G. (1993). Cognitive distraction and relaxation training for the control of side effects due to cancer chemotherapy. *Journal of Behavioral Medicine, 16*, 65–80.

Vinokur, A.D., Threatt, B.A., Vinokur-Kaplan, D., & Satariano, W.A. (1990). The process of recovery from breast cancer for younger and older patients. Changes during the first year. *Cancer, 65*, 1242–1254.

Weinberg, N., Schmale, J., Uken, J., & Wessel, K. (1996). Online help: Cancer patients participate in a computer-mediated support group. *Health & Social Work, 21*, 24–29.

Weisman, A.D. (1979a). *Coping with cancer*. New York: McGraw-Hill.

Weisman, A.D. (1979b). A model for psychosocial phasing in cancer. *General Hospital Psychiatry, 3*, 187–195.

Wellisch, D.K., Schain, W.S., Noone, R.B., & Little, J.W. (1985). Psychosocial correlates of immediate versus delayed construction of the breast. *Plastic and Reconstructive Surgery, 76*, 713–718.

Worden, J.W., & Weisman, A.D. (1984). Preventive psychosocial intervention with newly diagnosed cancer patients. *General Hospital Psychiatry, 6*, 243–249.

Worden, W.J. (1982). *Grief counseling and grief therapy: A handbook for the mental health practitioner*. New York: Springer Publishing Company.

World Health Organization (2002). *National cancer control programmes: Policies and managerial guidelines*. Geneva, Switzerland: Office of Publications, World Health Organization.

Wortman, C.B., & Dunkel-Schetter, C. (1979). Interpersonal relationships and cancer: A theoretical analysis. *Journal of Social Issues, 35*, 120–155.

Wyatt, G., & Friedman, L.L. (1996). Long-term female cancer survivors: Quality of life issues and clinical implications. *Cancer Nursing, 19*, 1–7.

Zabora, J., Brintzenhofeszoc, K., Curbow, B., Hooker, C., & Piantadosi, S. (2001). The prevalence of psychological distress by cancer site. *Psychooncology, 10*, 19–28.

Zigmond, A.S. & Snaith, R.P. (1983). The hospital anxiety and depression scale. *Acta Psychiatry Scand, 67*, 361–370.

Steven M. Tovian

13

Urological Disorders

The role of the clinical health psychologist in medical settings has expanded to include a wide range of medical conditions (Sweet, Rozensky & Tovian, 1991; Smith, Kendall & Keefe, 2002; Boll, Johnson, Perry & Rozensky, 2002). This chapter highlights the problem areas involving adult urological medicine. The reader may wish to consult the text by Tanagho and McAninch (1995) as a reference for medical issues. Specific problem areas discussed in this chapter involve urinary incontinence, erectile dysfunction, urethral syndrome, and briefly, prostatitis.

Biomedical Aspects

Urinary Incontinence

Anatomy and Physiology
The function of the lower urinary tract is maintained by a dual autonomic and somatic neural system. The urinary system is diagrammed in Figure 1. The bladder stores urine and provides propulsive force for voluntary voiding. The bladder is compliant, tolerating increasing urine volumes with little pressure increase. In addition to autonomic input, lower urinary tract activity is mediated by the afferent, or sensory, activity generated by the supportive pelvic floor muscles, which span the inferior surface of the bony pelvis. Unlike other skeletal muscles, these muscles are always active, except during urination and defecation, then this activity precipitously diminishes. In summary, the pelvic floor muscles function to support the bladder neck and other pelvic organs; close

off the urethra to prevent urine loss; inhibit smooth muscle contraction through spinal and supraspinal reflexes to prevent unwarranted urine loss; and relax to signal efficient bladder contraction when micturition is desired (Tries & Brubaker, 1996).

Definition
Incontinence is a symptom, not a disease (Orzeck & Ouslander, 1987), and can result from pathologic, anatomic, or physiologic conditions within the urinary system or elsewhere in the body. Urinary incontinence is a condition in which involuntary loss of urine can be a social or hygienic problem and is objectively demonstrable (Ory, Wyman & Yu, 1986). Many causes of urinary incontinence can be reversed, such as infection, atrophic vaginitis, acute confusional states, restrictions in mobility, fecal impaction, and the side effects of drugs. Longer term or permanent causes of urinary incontinence include diabetes, stroke, cerebral palsy, multiple sclerosis, prostate enlargement, prostate cancer, spinal cord injuries, and birth defects such as spinal bifida (American Association of Retired Persons and Simon Foundation for Continence, 1993). Depending on the underlying cause, the bladder may malfunction in different ways, resulting in several types of urinary incontinence.

Prevalence, Costs and Impact
It is estimated that approximately 13 million Americans suffer from urinary incontinence (Agency for Health Care Policy and Research (AHCPR), 1996). Urinary incontinence may be underreported because of the stigma attached to the disorder and because of the in-

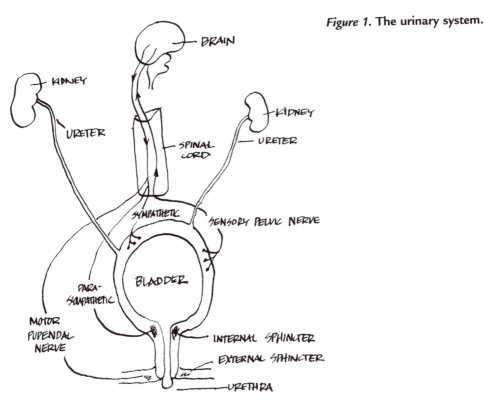

Figure 1. **The urinary system.**

herent difficulty in measuring its occurrence. Among the population between 15 and 64 years of age, the prevalence of urinary incontinence in men ranges from 1.5% to 5% and in women ranges from 10%–30% (AHCPR, 1996). The prevalence in the elderly (60 years and older) is approximately 15%–35% of non-institutionalized adults (70% are female); 53% of homebound elderly; 50% of 1.5 million nursing facility residents; with 11% reporting UI at admission to the hospital and 23% at discharge (AHCPR, 1996). The prevalence of UI in the younger population can be seen in studies where approximately 28% of 144 strenuous exercising females between the ages of 18–21 years, and 26% of 3,100 females between 30–59 years reported UI (Belar & Tovian, 2002).

Direct annual medical costs for caring for persons with UI is approximately $16.4 billion per year (APHCPR, 1996) with 11.2 billion spent in the community, 5.2 billion in nursing homes, an increase of 60% from previous estimates in 1990. The typical UI sufferer spends approximately $1,000–$3,000

annually on absorbent products. Adult undergarment sales exceeded $1.5 billion in 1996 and were projected to exceed $2 billion in 1999 (APHCPR, 1996). Also, urinary incontinence is associated with a reduction in self-esteem, circumscribed social interactions, decrease in quality of life, depression, and increasing dependence on caregivers, and it is aggravated with the effects of institutionalism and declining medical conditions (Tovian, Rozensky, Sloan & Slotnik, 1995; Tovian, 2002; Belar & Tovian, 2002).

Types

Urge incontinence or detrusor overactivity is the sudden and intense desire to urinate, with the inability to suppress the urge long enough to reach a toilet. Involuntary voiding is preceded by a warning of a few seconds to a few minutes. Leakage is periodic, but frequent, with a moderate-to-large volume. The term detrusor refers to the smooth muscle that composes the wall of the bladder, which contracts to expel urine. *Stress incontinence,* more common in women than in men, oc-

Table 1. Types of urinary incontinence.

Type	Definition
Urge	Detrusor overactivity with sudden and intense desire to urinate and inability to suppress urge
Stress	Physical stress on the abdomen causes excess pressure in the bladder
Overflow	Leakage of urine without the urge to void
Reflex	Complete absence of bladder control (Total)
Functional	Inability or unwillingness to use the toilet appropriately
Iatrogenic	Postsurgical or due to the effects of medication combinations
Complex	More than one type of incontinence occurring simultaneously (Mixed)

curs when physical stress on the abdomen (e. g., coughing, sneezing, and laughing) causes excess pressure in the bladder, which overrides the bladder's normal restraint. The volume leaked is small to moderate. *Overflow incontinence* is the leakage of small amounts of urine without the urge to void. This occurs when the weight of the urine in the bladder overcomes the outlet resistance, and the excess amount runs off, but the bladder remains full. *Total (reflex) incontinence* is a complete absence of bladder control, with either continuous or periodic leakage. When leakage is periodic, it is frequent, with a moderate volume. *Functional incontinence* is the loss of urine resulting from an inability or unwillingness to use the toilet appropriately. Factors that contribute to functional incontinence may include deficits of mobility, mental status, motivation or environmental barriers. *Iatrogenic incontinence* occurs after surgery or due to the effects of medication combinations. *Complex (mixed) incontinence* occurs when a person experiences simultaneously more than one type of incontinence. An example is the development of urge incontinence in someone with a history of stress incontinence (Resnick & Yalla, 1985; Orzeck & Ouslander, 1987; Burgio & Engel, 1987). The types of urinary incontinence are defined in Table 1.

Etiology

Urinary incontinence has many predisposing factors and is associated with impaired physiological or psychological functioning (Resnick & Yalla, 1985). Urinary incontinence af-

fects individuals of all ages but is most prevalent among the elderly. As a result, urinary incontinence is commonly and mistakenly attributed to the aging process. The elderly are more likely to have conditions that predispose them to incontinence or contribute to the causes of incontinence. For example, conditions such as decreased bladder capacity, decreased capacity of the urethral muscle to keep the bladder neck closed, increased frequency of bladder contractions, and increased postvoid residuals can contribute to urinary incontinence and are seen in the elderly (Burgio & Engel, 1987; American Association of Retired Persons and Simon Foundation for Continence, 1993). However, many of these conditions can be controlled or avoided when properly identified. Other risk factors include childbearing, directly related to the delivery experience and number of children delivered vaginally, weakening the muscles of the pelvic floor; prostate surgery, with removal of all or part of the prostate gland secondary to prostate cancer or benign prostatic hyperplasia; and disease processes such as multiple sclerosis, stroke, Parkinson's disease, and cerebral palsy. Additionally, birth defects affecting the bladder or nervous system (i. e., spinal bifida) can be associated with urinary incontinence (American Association of Retired Persons and Simon Foundation for Continence, 1993). Urinary incontinence is not a normal aspect of aging, nor is it irreversible. Some transient or temporary causes of urinary incontinence include delirium; urinary tract infection; vaginitis; use of pharmaceuticals (e. g., sedative hypnotics, diuretics); severe depression; excessive urine production; restricted mobility; and stool impaction (AHCPR, 1996).

Current Medical Treatments

Pharmacologic and Hormonal. Most drugs used in managing the varied causes of urinary incontinence target urge incontinence due to inhibited detrusor contractions. Detrusor instability is a condition where urine is lost due to an involuntary contraction or pressure rise in the bladder during filling associated with urge incontinence. This condition is not due to a neurological problem. For these patients, drugs that increase bladder capacity can be helpful. One risk, however, is the precipitation of urine retention. Examples of these agents include anticholinergics, such as propantheline, which can be effective but may produce side effects such as dry mouth, dry eyes, constipation, confusion, or glaucoma. Antispasmodics such as oxybutynin and flavoxate also have an anticholinergic activity with somewhat fewer side effects. Tricyclic antidepressants such as imipramine and doxepin have been used to control unstable bladder contractions as well. Calcium channel blockers such as nifedipine and terodiline have been shown to be effective in inhibiting unstable bladder contractions. Alpha adrenergic agonists such as ephedrine are often used in the treatment of stress incontinence. Because urinary incontinence increases in women with increasing age, and because menopause results in estrogen deficiency, estrogen replacement has been shown to be helpful in women with postmenopausal urge incontinence but not stress incontinence (AHCPR, 1996).

Surgery. Surgery is particularly effective in treatment of pure stress incontinence associated with dysfunction of the bladder neck. When incontinence in men is secondary to outflow obstruction and chronic retention is secondary to prostate enlargement, it is best treated with prostatectomy. When incontinence is due to intrinsic sphincter dysfunction, which may occur after the surgical trauma of radical prostatectomy or sphincter denervation, the compressive action of the sphincter is lost. An implantable prosthetic sphincter can restore this compression. Complications include erosion of the urethra, infection, and mechanical failure. Reoperations are frequently required. Urethral sling procedures pass a ribbon of fascia or artificial material beneath the urethra. The sling, fixed to the anterior body wall, serves to elevate and compress the urethra, restoring continence in 80 percent of patients. Bladder augmentation with isolated bowel segments will increase bladder capacity and vent excessive bladder pressure. This procedure is limited to certain specific bladder problems such as extreme contraction of the bladder due to neurological disease (AHCPR, 1996).

There are no simple procedures to control bladder instability or sensory urgency. When incontinence is due to a mixture of stress and urge, pharmacologic or behavioral treatment may be used in conjunction with surgery. Selection of surgical treatment depends upon the diagnosis and condition of the patient and the ability of the patient to heal and undergo rehabilitation. The severity of the symptoms must be considered in relation to the risk the patient must undertake. Finally, such factors as the durability of the treatment, efficacy, and the incidence of complications must also be considered in choosing any treatment option.

Erectile Dysfunction

Anatomy and Physiology

The penis contains three cylinders: Two corpora cavernosa and the corpus spongiosum, which houses the urethra. Each corpus cavernosa is supplied with blood by a cavernosa artery and is surrounded by the tunica albuginea, a fibrous, elastic sheath. The male genital organ is presented in Figure 2.

In the flaccid state, blood drains through the veins that transverse the tunica albuginea into the deep dorsal vein of the penis. The smooth muscle of the corpora cavernosa is maintained in a contracted state, exerting control over arterial blood flow to the penis. During sexual stimulation, activation of the autonomic nervous system results in relaxation of the smooth muscle, which allows di-

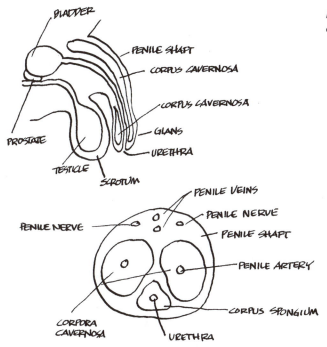

Figure 2. **Male internal genital organ.**

lation of the cavernosal arteries and arterioles and relaxation of the sinusoidal spaces, decreasing resistance to blood inflow.

After an initial drop in the intracorporeal pressure, blood inflow causes the pressure to rise. The expanding sinusoidal spaces compress the venules against the tunica albuginea and decrease venous outflow. Normally, restriction of venous outflow further increases intracorporeal pressure, and the penis lengthens and becomes rigid. The parasympathetic nerve pathways that control erection communicate with penile structures through the pelvic nerve, which lies adjacent to the rectum and prostate. Following ejaculation, the sympathetic nervous system promotes detumescence, with decreased arterial inflow, opening outflow routes and contraction of the sinusoidal spaces (Ackerman, Montague & Morgenstern, 1994).

Definition and Prevalence

Erectile dysfunction is defined as a persistent or recurrent, partial or complete, failure to attain or maintain sufficient penile erections for satisfactory sexual functioning to occur with subsequent marked distress and inter-personal difficulty (American Psychiatric Association, 1994). It is estimated that more than 10 million American men experience erectile dysfunction, with the prevalence of erectile dysfunction increasing with age as a result of physical and mental illnesses with concomitant prescription drug use that is common during the middle and later years of life. The incidence of erectile dysfunction is estimated to be found in at least 10% of the male population at age 50, 20% by age 60, 30% at age 70, and 40% at age 80 (Ackerman, 1992). Using a biopsychosocial model, erectile dysfunction is not seen as either organic or psychogenic, but rather is perceived as an interacting set of variables, requiring assessment of cognitive, behavioral, and interpersonal factors as well as physical factors for effective treatment. The psychological consequences of erectile dysfunction include depression, performance anxiety, and relationship distress (Ackerman, 1995; Ackerman & Carey, 1995).

Etiology

Erectile dysfunction can occur as a result of malfunction in any one or more of the physiological processes discussed previously. Vas-

Table 2. Factors associated with erectile dysfunction. Adapted from Ackerman, Montague & Morgenstern (1994).

Neurologic
  Epilepsy (including temporal lobe)
  Multiple sclerosis
  Peripheral neuropathy
  Spinal cord injury
  Stroke

Penile
  Trauma
  Peyronie's disease

Prostatic
  Prostatitis
  Prostate cancer treatment

Lifestyle
  Alcohol use
  Tobacco use
  Recreational & illicit drug use
    Cannabis
    Cocaine
    Heroin
    Lysergic acid diethylamide (LSD)
    Methadone HCl (Dolophine HCl)

Psychologic
  Anxiety
  Depression
  Psychosocial stress
  Marital discord
  Post traumatic stress

Endocrine
  Diabetes mellitus
  Increased estrogen
  Decreased testosterone

Vascular
  Atherosclerosis

Pharmacological agents
  Addictive substances
  Antihypertensive agents (beta-blockers, diuretics)
  Endocrine agents
  Psychotropic agents
  Antihypertensive agents
  Chemotherapy agents
  Histamine-receptor antagonists

cular inadequacy is the most frequent cause, and hormonal abnormality is the least likely cause, of erectile dysfunction. Neurological, structural and psychological factors are responsible for the remaining portion of male sexual difficulties (Ackerman, Montague & Morgenstern, 1994). The health psychologist needs to be aware of the many biological risk factors associated with erectile dysfunction. Diseases of the endocrine, vascular, and neurological systems should be carefully screened before or after any referral to the psychologist. Some common medical conditions that are associated with erectile dysfunction are presented in Table 2. Like urinary incontinence, erectile dysfunction is not a result of natural aging.

Many medications prescribed for various physical and psychiatric disorders can impair erectile functioning as well as sexual desire. Medications such as antihypertensive agents, anticholinergics, and drugs used in the treatment of psychiatric disorders (i.e., pheno-

thiazines, benzodiazepines, and antidepressants) can be associated with erectile dysfunction (Ackerman, 1995). Some medications associated with erectile dysfunction are also presented in Table 2.

Current Medical Treatments

Options for medical treatment will depend on the suspected cause of the erectile dysfunction. For example, testosterone replacement therapy is used when there is evidence of hormonal insufficiency. If the erectile dysfunction developed after medications were prescribed for a primary medical condition, cessation or substitution of those medications may be attempted. The FDA's 1998 approval of sildenafil citrate (Viagra), a selective inhibitor of chemicals that typically allow blood re-absorption from such areas as the corpus cavernosa in the penis, marked a new treatment for ED. The availability of the first oral agent that elicits penile erection before planned sexual intercourse revolutionized ED treatment enabling treatment for patients of various ages, ED severity and durations, and with numerous medical comorbidities. Sidenafil therapy is successful and well tolerated in 60% of patients with severe ED and 80% of patients with mid to moderate ED after approximately 8–10 attempts with the oral medication. Adverse side effects reported include headache, flushing, dizziness, and abnormal vision, including mild, transient color change, blurred vision, and/or increased sensitivity to light (Seidman, Roose, Menza, Shabsigh, & Rosen, 2001). Adequate education and follow-up are need to optimize the efficiency and safety of sildenafil therapy. Patients and their partners need to be advised that the agent is not effective in the absence of sexual stimulation and most effective when taken about 1 hour before sexual activity and not with food intake. Without adverse medical contraindications, clinical health psychologists will often find sildenafil as the first treatment attempt by physicians for ED. Ackerman, Montague and Morgenstern (1994) reviewed possible medicinal approaches with yohimbine HCl and Frental, and they concluded that these drugs provide nothing more than placebo effects at best. The authors also thoroughly describe and review additional medical options such as injection methods with papaverine HCl, vascular surgery, and both internal and external implant prosthesis. Surgical approaches attempt to correct vascular insufficiency by blocking venous return or increasing arterial inflow. Arterial reconstruction and bypass grafting can be considered to improve blood inflow. Intracavernous injection of vasoactive agents such as papaverine HCl are considered first-line therapy and can be self-administered. However, potential side effects such as painful erections, hypotension, and liver enzyme abnormalities have been reported. The reliability and effectiveness of penile implants have improved over the years and may be considered second-line therapies, should injections and vacuum devices (external vacuum chamber pulls blood into the penis producing an erection whereby an elastic is slipped on the base of the penis to maintain the erection after the chamber is removed) prove unsuccessful. Ackerman, Montague, and Morgenstern (1994) note that patients undergoing any invasive procedure will require adjunct psychological support and psychoeducational therapy to ensure success of these procedures. For more information about psychological assessment and intervention prior to invasive medical procedures and surgery, the reader may wish to consult Rozensky, Sweet and Tovian (1997) and Salmon (1992).

Urethral Syndrome

Symptoms and Prevalence

In women, urethral syndrome consists of urinary urgency and frequency, painful urination (dysuria), low back pain, and other voiding difficulties (i. e., weak stream and hesitancy) in the absence of definable organic pathology. Urethral syndrome accounts for over 5 million office visits per year in the United States (Scotti & Ostergard, 1984). The syndrome discussed here is either chronic or recurrent.

Etiology

Irritation in the urethra, particularly in the area of the external (striated) sphincter, is thought to be the cause of the urethral syndrome (Kellner, 1991). Most women with urethral syndrome have evidence of bacterial infection (15–75%). Even though there may be no evidence of concurrent infection, there is often histological evidence of previous infection in about 15% of samples studied (Scotti & Ostergard, 1984). Causes other than infections involving musculature and sphincter dysfunction have been suggested. Dynamic studies have shown spasticity of the smooth muscle sphincter may account for additional reports of urethral syndrome. In such cases, treatments with alpha-receptor-blocking drugs and/or surgical dilation procedures may be helpful (Bergman, Karram & Bhatia, 1989). A more thorough listing of causes and treatments of the urethral syndrome is presented in Table 3.

Table 3. Etiology and treatment of urethral syndrome.

Etiology	Treatment
Infection	Antibiotics
Obstruction (anatomic and spasm)	Dilatation
	Alpha blocker medication
	Benzodiazepines (Valium)
Chronic inflammatory urethritis	Dilatation Steroids
Neurologic	Anesthetic injections
Dermatologic	Estrogen and steroid creams
Allergic	Steroids
	Antihistamines
	Removal of allergic agents
Psychogenic	Psychotherapy

Current Medical Treatments

Since the etiology of urethral syndrome is obscure, medical treatment has been and remains very empirical. Antibiotics, bladder neck opening, internal urethrotomy, urethral dilation, local steroid injections, estrogens, general tranquilizers (i. e., Diazepam) have all been employed (Scotti & Ostergard, 1984). Since obstruction and infection are the most frequent potential etiologies, antibiotics (mainly tetracyclines) and urethral dilation have become the most popular treatment modalities (Kellner, 1991). Urethral syndrome based on psychogenic factors remains a diagnosis of exclusion of any physical disease.

Common Referral Issues

Working in urology, the health psychologist needs a thorough understanding of the nature of urological disorders, likely medical procedures (and their effects) involved in medical diagnosis and treatment, and medical influences on psychosocial and behavioral domains. Likewise, the urologist (and nursing staff) should be very familiar with the role of the health psychologist on the team and reasons for patient referral to the health psychologist.

Every effort must be made by the health psychologist to prepare the urologist to make timely, precise, relevant referrals as well as to adequately prepare the patient for psychological consultation. The latter may be accomplished when the urologist prepares the patient by: (a) emphasizing a team approach in treating his/her urological disorder, (b) identifying the consultant as a psychologist who has expertise in the areas of urological disorders; (c) emphasizing the urologist's positive past experience in working with the health psychologist; (d) noting that psychological consultation is routine for the specific problem in question; and (e) emphasizing that recommendations from the psychologist will be used by the urologist in more effectively managing patient care. It is most helpful, then, if the urologist can provide a positive rationale to the patient for referral to the health psychologist by noting the referral is needed to improve the outcome of medical care, to reduce stress or manage pain more effectively, to reduce reliance on certain medications, or to ascertain if additional factors may be worsening the patient's disorder.

For many patients, referral to the health psychologist infers weakness, incompetence, or emotional disturbance. Patients may feel the urologist believes his/her symptoms are exaggerated. Patient feelings of anger and abandonment may follow if he/she is not adequately prepared for the psychological consultation. Should such a patient follow through and enter the consultation, he/she may express anger, resentment, and defensiveness to the health psychologist. Such a patient may view the consultation as irrele-

> **Table 4.** Guidelines for possible referrals for psychological consultation in urology.
>
> 1. The patient's emotional response interferes with his/her ability to utilize appropriate treatment options or manage necessary medical procedures.
>
> 2. The patient's emotional response to the urological disorder interferes with his/her activities of daily living at home or work and/or curtails his/her usual sources of gratification.
>
> 3. The patient's emotional reaction to the urological disorder causes greater distress than the disorder would warrant or increases disorder-related impairments.
>
> 4. The patient reports his/her significant other is unable to cope with his/her urological disorder.
>
> 5. The patient is noncompliant with medical regimen.
>
> 6. The patient has a history of psychiatric disorders, suicide attempts, or substance abuse.
>
> 7. The patient is overly reliant on sleep, analgesic, or anxiolytic medications.
>
> 8. Prediction of patient's response to medical-surgical interventions.

vant to his/her urological disorder. Much time will then be spent redefining the purpose of the consultation, or worse, the results of the evaluation skewed by the patient's anger and defensiveness. To avoid this pitfall, the health psychologist may wish to revisit this issue early in the initial evaluation session by asking the patient, "When your urologist told you he/she was referring you for psychological consultation, what was your reaction? How do you feel now?" By posing this question early and with sensitivity and empathy, the health psychologist may facilitate rapport for the evaluation and later possible interventions. Guidelines for possible referrals are listed in Table 4.

Assessment

Urinary Incontinence

Psychological assessment with urinary incontinence includes characterization of the incontinence, identification of urine loss, and evaluating the emotional and behavioral responses to urinary incontinence and its causes, as well as a possible psychological treatment regimen, if appropriate (Tovian, 1996). The clinical health psychologist would do well to assess the adaptive tasks that must be accomplished by any medical patient (Moos, 1977). The assessment should

focus on: how the patient is coping with possible pain and incapacitation; the patient's coping style in response to special medical assessment and treatment procedures unique to urological disorders; and how this patient is developing and maintaining adequate relationships with the health care staff. In light of the nature of urinary incontinence, for example, any assessment should also focus on whether the patient is maintaining a reasonable emotional balance, preserving a satisfactory self image, and maintaining a sense of competence and mastery. Also, whether the patient is preserving relationships with family and friends, and how the patient may be preparing for an uncertain future need to be determined. The reader may wish to consult additional texts by Rozensky, Sweet and Tovian (1997), Nicassio and Smith (1995), and Keefe and Blumenthal (1982) on detailed aspects of psychological assessment in response to medical problems.

Behavioral and Psychological

Behavioral and psychological assessment of urinary incontinence should follow a physician's thorough medical examination. Burgio and Engel (1987) provided a thorough review of behavioral assessment techniques that can be used by the psychologist when working in collaboration with physicians and nurses in the area of urinary incontinence. Although the authors limit their dis-

Table 5. Bladder record. Adapted from Burgio and Engel (1987).

Name_____ Date_____

Instructions: (1) In the 1st column, mark the time every time you void
                 (2) In the 2nd or 3rd column, mark every time you accidentally
                     leaked urine
                 (3) Write "dry" if no accident occurred in the 2-hour interval

Time Interval	Urinated in toilet	Leaking accident	Large accident	Reason for accident	Reaction to accident
6– 8 AM					
8–10 AM					
10–12 AM					
12– 2 PM					
2– 4 PM					
4– 6 PM					
6– 8 PM					
8–10 PM					
10–12 PM					
Overnight					

Total number of pads or undergarments used today: _____

cussion to geriatric populations, their methods can be generalized to other populations as well. The authors used techniques involving interview guidelines, mental status evaluations, bladder records or symptom diaries, and assessment of mobility and toileting skills. Interview guidelines need to take into account antecedents of incontinence, descriptions of incontinent episodes, and the consequences of incontinence. As mentioned previously, there are different types of urinary incontinence, and each type may have its own unique antecedents and consequences for the patient. Bladder records or symptom diaries document patterns of urinary incontinence on a day-to-day basis. Records provide a source of data to diagnose causes of urinary incontinence and a means to assist in evaluating progress and treatment effectiveness. An example of a bladder record can be found in Table 5. Finally observations of mobility and assessment of toileting skills can be used to assess whether environmental barriers or physical handicapping conditions exacerbate or cause urinary incontinence.

Each individual who suffers from incontinence feels differently about it and reacts with varying degrees of emotional distress. Tovian (2002), Tovian, Rozensky, Sloan and Slotnik (1995), Tovian (1996), and Tovian and Rozensky (1985) have summarized numerous studies identifying the psychological reactions to urinary incontinence. Psychological responses such as depression, shame, and embarrassment from public accidents or possible odor, anxiety, agoraphobia, sexual dysfunction, irritability, frustration and anger have all been identified among incontinent patients and need to be assessed in the interview. Urinary incontinence results in changes in quality of life, with loss of self-esteem, possible loss of job, isolation, and increased dependency. Interviews with significant others and family members are recommended. Reactions of caregivers, institutional and home, can be assessed in keeping with the biopsychosocial model of assessment. Interview questions focusing on the impact of urinary incontinence, present and past means of coping including the outcomes of various strategies, evidence of past psychopathology, and possible problems with adherence and compliance need to be included.

Psychometric

Voiding habits and continence can be disrupted by depression or cognitive deficits, such as confusion, disorientation and memory impairment. Burgio and Engel (1987) recommend the use of the Mini-Mental Status Examination (MMSE; Folstein, Folstein & McHugh, 1975) and the Beck Depression Inventory (BDI; Beck, 1972), for example, to screen these areas. Referral to a neuropsychologist for a more thorough cognitive evaluation may be warranted.

Shumaker, Wyman, Uebersax, McClish and Fantl (1994) developed a life-impact assessment instrument specific to urinary incontinence in women, the Incontinence Impact Questionnaire (IIQ), and a symptom inventory, the Urogenital Distress Inventory (UDI), specific to symptoms associated with lower urinary tract and genital dysfunction. Data on the reliability, validity and sensitivity to change of these measures demonstrated they are psychometrically strong and they can be self-administered, as well. Uebersax, Wyman, Shumaker, McClish and Fantl (1995) further reduced the 30-item IIQ and the 19-item UDI to 7- and 6-item short forms, respectively, supporting the use of these instruments in clinical and research applications.

Psychophysiological

Biofeedback is the use of electronic or mechanical instrumentation to relay information to patients about physiological activity of their autonomic nervous system. Biofeedback aims to alter bladder dysfunction by teaching patients to change physiologic responses that mediate bladder control (Burgio & Engel, 1990). Display of this information, through auditory or visual displays forms the core of the biofeedback procedure (Schwartz, 1995). For women, a biofeedback device, called a perineometer, attaches by cable to a sensor that is inserted into the vagina. The sensor comes in contact with the pubococcygeus muscle and shows the strength of the muscle, the ability of the muscle to relax, and the level of control of that muscle through electromyographic (EMG) data (Burns, Mareck, Duttmar & Bullogh, 1985). Assessment procedures in biofeedback are discussed by Schwartz (1995) and with urinary incontinence by Tries and Eisman (1995). Use of biofeedback techniques requires specialized training in psychophysiology, electrical equipment, and bioelectric signal processing. The Biofeedback Certification Institute of America certifies therapists for practice in this area.

Erectile Dysfunction

Psychological and Behavioral

Ackerman (1992) noted the primary role of the health psychologist in the assessment of erectile dysfunction is to provide insights about patient behaviors, thoughts, affect, and psychosocial data through interview and assessment protocols. Screening for psychological dysfunction, substance abuse, cognitive distortions, personality disorders, or life stress events known to affect erectile dysfunction can be accomplished via interviews, self-monitoring diaries, and questionnaires. As with urinary incontinence, spouses or significant others should be interviewed individually or conjointly, whenever possible, to ascertain collaborative information regarding sexual performance and relationship factors.

Ackerman and Carey (1995) recommended a thorough evaluation of past and current erectile function (i. e., description of the presenting complaint and its duration, frequency, and nature of onset), once rapport has been established. Other relevant information includes masturbatory fantasies, sexual drive, sexual techniques, and sexual knowledge. Frequency and outcome attempts at intercourse should be reviewed, as well as coping effort for unsuccessful attempts. Questions pertaining to sexual orientation, sexual deviations, and past sexual abuse should be included. Occasionally, special treatment circumstances, such as vasoactive injection therapy or penile implant surgery require the psychologist to assess misconceptions, attitudes, or unrealistic expectations, to maximize treatment outcome.

The Miami Sexual Dysfunction Protocol

(MSDP; Ackerman, Helder & Antoni, 1989) is a broad, semistructured interview format designed for use in medical settings to help organize information taken from the sexual dysfunctional male and his partner. Another important skill that the psychologist brings to the evaluation of erectile dysfunction is the ability to elicit concise information regarding sexual functioning while creating a relaxed, trusting atmosphere (Ackerman & Carey, 1995). Having an organized protocol, such as the MSDP, helps to facilitate the collection of baseline data for clinical training and research purposes in a relaxed atmosphere.

Ackerman (1992) highlighted the importance of assessing the absence or presence of morning erections, quality of erections, and ejaculation ability. This may be completed by use of self-monitoring forms completed by the patient.

Psychometric

After the interviews are completed and rapport well-established and maintained, patients may complete psychological inventories such as the MMPI-2 (Butcher et al., 1989), Millon Behavioral Health Inventory (Millon et al., 1982), and/or the Beck Depression Inventory (BDI; Beck, 1992) in an effort to assess personality and coping styles and any affective disturbance. The careful assessment of depression, for example, is important, since recent research has demonstrated that clinical depression can inhibit erectile functioning (Ackerman, 1995). If the patient is married or reports a steady partner, the Locke-Wallace Marital Inventory (Locke & Wallace, 1959) or Dyadic Adjustment Scale (Spanier, 1976) can be administered conjointly to assess relationship factors (Ackerman, 1992).

Psychophysiological

As with all other urological disorders, prior to any referral to the health psychologists, all erectile dysfunction patients should undergo a medical and urological examination, including blood chemistry testing and specialized urodynamic studies. For example, the patient may return to the urologist for over-

night, in-hospital Rigiscan diagnostic monitoring. Rigiscan monitoring involves the assessment of erectile functioning, including rigidity and tumescence at the base and tip of the penis and duration of these events throughout the sleep cycle (Ackerman, 1992).

Prostatitis

Prostatitis is defined by painful, reduced urine flow in males secondary to inflammation of the prostate gland. Located just below the bladder, next to the rectum, the prostate gland is apple-shaped, with the urethra running through its center. if the prostate gland swells, the urethra is pinched off, obstructing the flow of urine and causing a reflux of urine, potentially damaging the kidneys (Tanagho & McAninch, 1995). Refer to Figure 2 for diagram of the male urinary system.

It is estimated well over 500,000 males experience prostatitis every year in the United States (Tanagho & McAninch, 1995). Prostatitis can occur at any age. There are several types of prostatitis, but all have similar symptoms: fever, urination problems, including burning or bleeding; decreased urine flow; steady pain in the lower back, pelvis or upper thighs. If bacteria or viruses enter the urethra and spread to the prostate, inflammation, or prostatitis, results. For younger men, prostatitis is usually caused by such a bacterial infection and will respond to antibiotics. However, in older men (over 50 years old), the prostate may enlarge to over 50% of its normal size secondary to the aging process, rather than infection. This latter type of prostatitis in older men is often treated with surgery, called transurethral resection (TUR), and involves trimming the gland down to normal size. About 20% of the men who have this operation experience impotence after surgery (Tanagho & McAninch, 1995). As was discussed in the previous section of this chapter on erectile dysfunction, clinical health psychologists can treat such males experiencing postsurgical impotence. Recent research has also established that symptoms of anxiety and depression, as well as psychosocial distress, impaired social function and suicide ideation often occur in patients diagnosed with prostatitis (Mehik, Hellstom, Sarpola, Lukkarinen, & Jarvelin, 2001).

Urethral Syndrome

Behavioral and Psychological

The urethral syndrome is a diagnosis of exclusion of treatable physical disease. A large proportion of women who seek medical treatment because of urethral symptoms have acute as well as chronic or recurrent infections that contribute to this syndrome. Women who are anxious or have other psychopathology and who have a tendency to perceive bodily sensations, either appear to be perceiving their urethral symptoms more or may be more distressed by these symptoms, or both. Anxiety may contribute to selective perception or induce hypochondriacal concerns (Keller, 1991).

The clinical interview is the core and most common method of gathering diagnostic information with urology patients, including those with urethral syndrome. The goal of the interview in urethral syndrome is to focus on the patient's report of specific thoughts, behaviors, emotions, and physiological responses that precede, accompany, and follow target symptoms, as well as on the environmental conditions and consequences associated with the symptoms. The interview can yield understanding of how symptoms of urethral syndrome vary intensity, frequency, and duration over time and circumstances, and the effects of past treatments. Elements of the mental status exam can be included in the interview.

Reiter, Shakerin, Gambone and Milburn (1991) studied 52 women with probable somatic cause of urological dysfunction and 47 women without somatic abnormality and a diagnosis of urethral syndrome. The authors found the psychosocial profile of women with urethral syndrome differed from that of women with somatic etiology and that previous sexual abuse was a significant predisposing risk for urethral syndrome. This study highlights the crucial need for evaluation of past sexual abuse and possible past traumatic stress for women with urethral syndrome.

As with urinary incontinence, behavioral assessment in urethral syndrome can involve self-monitoring of target symptoms, affect, cognitions, and behaviors related to the symptoms (i. e., pelvic or low back pain) as well as documenting the intensity, frequency, and duration of the target symptoms and associated responses.

Psychometric

Anxiety and concerns about health may exacerbate lower urinary tract symptoms of some urethral syndrome patients (Ratliff, Klutke, & McDougall, 1994) and induce these patients to seek medical care more often. Instruments such as the State-Trait Anxiety Inventory (STAI; Spielberger, Gorush & Lushene, 1970) may assist the health psychologist document anxiety. Instruments such as the Minnesota Multiphasic Personality Inventory-2 (MMPI-2; Butcher, Dahlstrom, Graham, Telleger & Kaemmer, 1989), normed with medical patients, the Psychological Adjustment to Illness Scale (PAIS; Derogatis, 1986), normed with renal patients, or the Millon Behavioral Health Inventory (MBHI; Millon, Green & Meagher, 1974) may help elucidate coping styles and overconcerns about health. Carson, Osborne and Segura (1979) studied 57 women with urethral syndrome. Using the MMPI as part of their psychosocial evaluation, they found a high correlation of these patients demonstrate a "classic V conversion" on Hypochondria (Hs), Hysteria (Hy), and Depression (D) scales which is consistent with other findings in research with chronic pain, lower back pain, and somatoform patients and supports the likelihood of psychophysiologic processes. If pain is a major symptom in the evaluation of the urethral syndrome patient, instruments such as the Pain Patient Profile (P-3; Tollison & Langley, 1995) and the West Haven-Yale Multidimensional Pain Inventory (WHYMPI; Kerns, Turk & Rudy, 1985) may be used. The reader may wish to consult Chapter 5 of this text for further discussion of pain assessment and treatment.

Urethral syndrome is not listed in DSM-IV (American Psychiatric Association, 1994). Because organic factors, particularly past or current infection, are found in a large pro-

Table 6. Recommended interview content for assessment in urological disorders.

For the patient:
- Attitude towards psychological referral and towards urological disorder.
- Details of the problem (precede, accompany, consequences of symptoms):
  · behavioral, affective, somatic, cognitive
  · interpersonal relations
  · history of medications, previous treatments, their outcome
- What makes symptoms worse/better
- Degree of impairment: social, occupational, leisure, familial
- Beliefs about origin, cause, course of symptoms
- Attitudes about healthcare personnel and treatment regimen
- With erectile dysfunction: Miami Sexual Dysfunction Protocol (MSDP; Ackerman et al., 1989)

For significant other:
- How is patient managing the urological disorder? How are you managing?
- What changes in family responsibilities do you think will be needed as a result of the patient's urological disorder?
- If symptoms persist for the patient, what are your plans for taking care of the problem over the long term?

Table 7. Recommended questionnaires for assessment in urological disorders.

Affect/Mood
  Beck Depression Inventory (BDI: Beck, 1972)
  State-Trait Anxiety Inventory (STAI: Spielberger et al., 1970)
  Brief Symptom Inventory (BSI: Derogatis, 1993)

Cognitive Functioning
  Mini-Mental Status Exam (MMSE: Folstein et al., 1975)

Personality and Coping Styles
  Millon Behavioral Health Inventory (MBHI: Millon, Green, & Meagher, 1982
  Minnesota Multiphasic Personality Inventory-2 (MMPI-2: Butcher et al., 1989)
  (use with medical population norms)

Psychological Adjustment to Illness
  Psychological Adjustment to Illness (PAIS: Derogatis, 1986)
  (use with renal patient norms)

Psychological Adjustment to Pain
  Pain Patient Profile (P-3: Tollison & Langley, 1995)
  West Haven-Yale Multidimension Pain Inventory (WHYMPI: Kerns et al., 1985)

Disorder-Specific Measures
  Urinary Incontinence:
  - Incontinence Impact Questionnaire (IIQ: Uebersax et al., 1995)
  - Urogenital Distress Inventory (UDI: Uebersax et al., 1995)
  Erectile Dysfunction:
  - Locke-Wallace Marital Inventory (Locke & Wallace, 1959)
  - Dyadic Adjustment Scale (Spanier, 1976)

portion of patients, it is inappropriate to classify this syndrome as an undifferentiated somatoform disorder unless urinary tract disease has been completely excluded by the urologist. If psychological factors appear to play a substantial role, the appropriate DSM-IV classification should be Psychological factors Affecting Physical Condition (316.00) and on Axis III, Urethral syndrome (Kellner, 1991).

In summary, one need not be wedded to a particular assessment strategy. Flexibility may be an asset. Tables 6 and 7 summarize the assessment approaches in urology.

Treatment

Thus far, this chapter has discussed biomedical aspects and assessment issues along several dimensions in the biopsychosocial model. At the end of the assessment process, the health psychologist should be aware of the patient's medical and psychosocial history, the referral question(s), the nature of the patient's problems, related environmental contributors (i. e., family and health care system), and the variety of resources available to the patient. The next step, then, is to translate these findings into some plan of intervention along a similar psychosocial framework. When choosing an intervention, the health psychologist must take into account the effects of any given intervention on other aspects of the biopsychosocial model; the appropriateness of the goals for any intervention; patient, family, and staff cooperation; and cost-effectiveness of the intervention (Belar & Deardorff, 1995).

Urinary Incontinence

The treatment of urinary incontinence falls with four areas: behavioral, pharmacologic, surgical, and supportive devices (including catheters and absorbent pads and garments). A combination of interventions may be used, depending on the patient's needs and physician's diagnosis. For this chapter, discussion focuses on the behavioral interventions that fall into the scope of practice of health psy-

chologists. Thorough reviews of all treatment options for urinary incontinence, including their risks, benefits, and outcome, are discussed in the *Clinical Practice Guidelines: Urinary Incontinence in Adults* (AHCPR, 1996).

Behavioral Techniques

Behavioral techniques include bladder training, habit training (timed voiding), prompted voiding, pelvic muscle exercises, and biofeedback. Behavioral techniques show improvement ranging from complete dryness to reductions of wetness (AHCPR, 1996). Behavioral techniques have no reported side effects, do not limit future treatment options, and can be used in combination with other therapies for urinary incontinence.

Some limitations, however, are noteworthy in published results determining the effectiveness of behavioral interventions with urinary incontinence. These include use of different outcome criteria, variability and frequency of treatment sessions, variability of comprehensiveness in training procedures, absence or variability in follow-up data, use of heterogeneous samples, and lack of standardized terminology for various behavioral techniques. These are important issues when considering future directions for health psychologists in research with urinary incontinence. Despite these limitations, behavioral interventions appear to be most effective for urge urinary incontinence and stress incontinence. Behavioral interventions are not effective for patients with overflow urinary incontinence (AHCPR, 1996).

Bladder training. Bladder training (also termed "bladder retraining") consists of three primary components: education, scheduled voiding, and positive reinforcement. The education program usually combines written, visual, and verbal instruction that addresses physiology and pathophysiology. The voiding schedule uses a progressively increased interval between mandatory voidings, with concomitant distraction or relaxation techniques. The person is taught to delay voiding consciously. If the patient is unable to delay voiding between schedules, one approach is to adjust the schedule and start the timing from the last void. Another option is to keep the prearranged schedule and disregard the unscheduled void between schedules. Finally, positive reinforcement is provided. More specific details regarding bladder-training programs, such as optional time involving voiding intervals, are available in the *Clinical Practice Guidelines: Urinary Incontinence in Adults* (AHCPR, 1996). Fantl et al. (1991), in a randomized controlled study, reported that 12% of the women who underwent bladder training became continent, and 75% improved to at least a 50% reduction in the number of incontinent episodes. This form of training has been used to manage urinary incontinence due to bladder instability. However, studies indicate that this training may also control stress incontinence (Tovian, 1996).

Habit training. Habit training, or timed voiding, is scheduled toileting on a planned basis. The goal is to keep the person dry by telling them to void at regular intervals. Attempts are made to match the voiding intervals to the person's natural voiding schedule. Unlike bladder training, there is no systematic effort to motivate the patient to delay voiding and resist urge. A review of numerous studies indicates improvement in patients with habit training (Tovian, 1966). In one controlled study on habit training, when 51 nursing home residents who were identified with an electronic monitoring device, Jarvis (1981) found that 86% of the participants improved their urinary incontinence over baseline levels, when compared with control groups.

Prompted voiding. Prompted voiding is a supplement to habit training and attempts to teach the incontinent person to discriminate their incontinence status and to request toileting assistance from caregivers. There are three elements to prompted voiding: monitoring (the person is checked by caregivers on a regular basis and asked to report if wet or dry), prompting (the person is asked or prompted to try to use the toilet), and reinforcement (the person is praised for maintaining continence and for attempting to toilet). Prompted voiding has been shown to be effective in dependent or cognitively impaired nursing home incontinent patients (Tovian, 1966).

Pelvic muscle exercises. Pelvic muscle exercises, also called "Kegel exercises," improve urethral resistance through active exercise of the pubococcygeus muscle. The exercises strengthen the voluntary periurethral and pelvic muscles. The contraction inherent in the exercise exerts a closing force on the urethra and increases muscle support to the pelvic visceral structures (AHCPR, 1996).

Pelvic muscle exercises have been shown to be effective with women with stress incontinence, with men after prostate surgery, and after multiple surgical repairs in women. This exercise is often coupled with pharmacologic therapy and biofeedback (AHCPR, 1996; Tovian, 1996).

Biofeedback. Tries and Brubaker (1996) critically reviewed 13 major studies using biofeedback and reported overwhelming effectiveness (overall 76–87% reduction in incontinent episodes) in the treatment of stress and urge incontinence, especially when used in conjunction with other behavioral techniques, as well as with surgical and pharmacological interventions. The samples studies by Tries and Brubaker were highly heterogeneous in terms of etiology, age, and sex. The authors concluded that on the basis of efficacy, low invasiveness, and cost effectiveness, biofeedback should be offered as an integral part of any multidisciplinary evaluation and treatment program.

Behavioral techniques in outpatient adults. Combined analyses were conducted on 22 studies that dealt with all behavioral interventions on outpatient basis (AHCPR, 1996). The studies were standardized along measures of efficacy, reflecting the percentage of wetness and dryness. Results indicated that the average percentage reduction in incontinence frequency at the end of behavioral treatments was 64.6%, with a 95% confidence interval range from 58.8% to 70.4%. Additional randomized controlled trials and a randomized but not controlled study, all with women in outpatient settings, suggested that behavioral techniques result in subjective cure/improvement rates of 70% to 77%, with improvements maintained for at least 6 months (AHCPR, 1996).

Behavioral techniques in the nursing home. The severity of urinary incontinence in nursing home residents is often aggravated by the effects of institutionalization, declining medical conditions, and inconsistent nursing care. Nevertheless, a similar combined analysis of 428 persons studied in nursing homes using habit training and prompted voiding (AHCPR, 1996) suggested that patients were dry 70% of the time at baseline, and this rose to 81% after behavioral treatments during daytime hours only. These techniques have the potential to reduce the costs and improve the quality of life for long-term-care patients, as well as to serve as an important place of intervention for health psychologists.

Additional Psychological Treatments

Self-help and patient education. Urinary tract infections (UTI) are common causes of prostatitis and urethral syndrome. Traditional treatment modalities utilize antibiotics and emphasize the treatment of these diseases after they have been acquired. An important future role of clinical heath psychologists working with physicians and nurses in urology may include reinforcing patient compliance to medical regimen and reinforcing self-care and cleanliness that would prevent future UTI.

"I Will Manage" is a Simon Foundation program based on the principles of self-help. It is hosted by both lay and professional persons. The program's format is designed to accomplish two goals: (a) to present practical multidisciplinary information on incontinence and (b) to encourage people to share their experiences and develop the confidence to make changes in their life ("I Will Manage" self-help groups, Simon Foundation for Continence, 1991). This patient education approach assumes that much of the psychosocial distress accompanying incontinence is largely a result of a lack of knowledge concerning incontinence, its causes and treat-

ment, and the health care system. Empirical evidence of the efficacy of this approach would be useful. Given the large psychosocial component of this self-help program, there is a defined role in which the psychologist may become involved.

Supportive group therapy. The second goal inherent in the self-help paradigm, that of encouraging people to share their experiences, is also important in another treatment modality, supportive group therapy. The effectiveness of supportive group therapy has been reviewed in the context of such medical problems as cancer (Telsch & Telsch, 1986) and cardiac surgery (Bond et al., 1979). The therapeutic mechanism of community and mutuality in group therapy would seem especially relevant to the social problems of urinary incontinent patient This therapeutic approach may also be useful for the needs of the home caregiver. To date, however, there have been no published studies of the effectiveness of supportive group therapy with urinary incontinent patients or their families.

Coping skills approach. The coping skills approach involves structured training in specific cognitive, behavioral, and affective competencies for managing the disruptive effects of urinary incontinence. The coping skills approach assumes that the distress experienced in managing the effects of illness and disability is partially due to a limited or ineffective skills repertoire. Rozensky and Tovian (1985) suggested the use of self-instruction techniques, which help individuals with urinary incontinence learn constructive self-talk and avoid negativistic thinking. Rozensky and Tovian also proposed assertiveness techniques and progressive relaxation approaches to be use by urinary incontinent patients in distressing social situations. For example, the use of covert reinforcement and structured exposure to feared situations could be applied to the problems of social withdrawal and social phobia seen among urinary incontinence patients in distressing social situations. Learning both cognitive and behavioral coping strategies may enhance adjustment

---

Table 8. Psychological interventions with urinary incontinence.

Behavioral Techniques
– Bladder training
– Habit training
– Prompt voiding
– Kegel exercises
– Biofeedback

Self-Help and Patient Education Group ("I Will Manage" — Simon Foundation)

Supportive Group Therapy

Coping Skills Training (Individual or Group)

---

by expanding coping repertoires, thereby increasing one's perception of control; a problem that is very relevant to the urinary incontinent patient. Among the coping skills area, Rozensky and Tovian also recommended stress inoculation training and problem-solving strategies. The coping skills techniques may be used in group or individual treatment formats. Lewin and Gonzales (1994) reported the successful use of systematic desensitization, for example, to eliminate urethral catheter dependence with a 69-year-old male with urge incontinence secondary to CVA. Psychological interventions with urinary incontinence are summarized in Table 8.

Erectile Dysfunction

Ackerman, Montague and Morgenstern (1994) outlined treatment options for erectile dysfunction. Treatment options will depend on the suspected cause of the erectile dysfunction, the quality of the patient's relationships, his premorbid sexual satisfaction, and his acceptance and mastery of any medical approach. If the causes are psychological or behavioral in nature, individual and/or sex therapy will be an important aspect or sole method of treatment. Readers are referred to comprehensive texts on sex therapy by Wincze and Carey (1991) and Schover and Jensen (1988). If relationship problems exist, conjoint therapy is recommended with or before sex therapy. For invasive therapeutic op-

Case Example

A 58-year-old married, postmenopausal mother of 6 was referred by her urologist with a diagnosis of stress and urge incontinence secondary to decreased capacity of the urethral muscle and bladder spasms. Treatment with oxybutynin and imipramine resulted in a "slight improvement" in baseline levels of incontinence. Her spouse reported the patient was gradually becoming more socially withdrawn, moody, with loss of self-esteem. Psychological evaluation confirmed the patient's depression over incontinence and her perceived loss of internal focus of control over her health. Her score on the BDI indicated high "moderate" depression. Her responses on the IIQ confirmed the negative impact of incontinence on domains of emotional health, social relations, and physical activity. Finally, her responses on the UDI supported urogenital irritative and stress symptoms rather than obstructive discomfort. Psychological treatment involved 10 sessions of EMG perineometer biofeedback training which reduced stress incontinence by 60% from baseline levels. Consultation with psychiatry indicated the need to increase imipramine dosage for depression. An additional 8 sessions of individual cognitive-behavioral psychotherapy focused on her depressive response to illness and social problem-solving skills related to the remaining urinary symptoms of incontinence. She and her husband were also referred to the "I Will Manage" self-help and patient education group. The patient's BDI score at the termination of psychotherapy fell in low "mild depression" range.

***Table 9.* Psychological interventions with erectile dysfunction.**

Conjoint therapy
- Relationship, communication skill training
- Sex therapy

Individual therapy
- Psychoeducational (post-invasive medical procedure)
- Cognitive/behavioral
- Sex therapy

chotherapy may be indicated. Problems such as performance anxiety, reduced orgasmic intensity, or relationship conflicts can emerge secondary to invasive medical procedures and often respond to cognitive-behavioral interventions (Ackerman & Carey, 1995). Psychological interventions with erectile dysfunction are listed in Table 9.

Urethral Syndrome

There are no adequately controlled studies in the literature to suggest the most appropriate psychological treatment of urethral syndrome. Kellner (1991) reported that diazepam was found to relieve symptoms in 13 of 15 women with urethral syndrome in several

tions such as injection methods, vascular surgery, implantable prosthesis, referral for adjunct psychoeducational and supportive psy-

Case Example

A 52-year-old married male with complaints of no erections during sex for the last 2 years was referred by his urologist for psychological consultation regarding his reaction to erectile dysfunction. The patient's reaction was characterized by increased hostility and withdrawal of affection and sex from his spouse of 27 years. The patient had been an insulin-dependent diabetic for the past 5 years. Medical evaluation revealed hormonal levels to be normal, no nocturnal erections, and, from the cavernosogram, penis blood flow but no leakage secondary to his diabetes. The patient rejected any recommendation of a penile implant or vacuum pump. He used paparverine injections for 6 months (6 times) and found erections satisfactory, but sex with his spouse remained unsatisfactory. Psychological evaluation with a conjoint interview and assessment with the Dyadic Adjustment Scale, revealed marital discord, with the patient appearing as rigid, critical, angry and controlling, while his spouse appeared passive, unassertive and quiet. Furthermore, it was revealed that the patient's erectile dysfunction clearly made him feel less masculine, exacerbating his vascular problems secondary to his diabetes. Sixteen sessions of conjoint marital therapy focusing on attitude restructuring, communication training, and sexual behavior change (using sensate focus skills) resulted in increased sexual activity, increased mutual sexual satisfaction, and decreased arguments from baseline levels.

Case Example

A 24-year-old single female, referred by her urologist, complained of intermittent urethral syndrome of 4 years' duration. After several initial bladder infections and an exclusion of any current infection, her urologist noted the patient was anxious and referred her for psychological consultation. The evaluation revealed subjective reports of bladder discomfort when in stressful situations at her part-time job and in graduate school with strong need to void urine. The patient was aware of always attempting to find seats near exits at lectures, movies, plays, and other crowded events. She feared she would become incontinent and this would be noticed by others. There was no evidence of previous psychiatric disorders. Psychometric evaluation revealed elevated state and trait anxiety scores on the STAI. The MBHI revealed sociable and cooperative personality styles in coping with medical illness as well as an elevation of the Somatic Anxiety Scale suggesting an over-concern with bodily functions and increased fear of pain and illness. The latter trait was confirmed in the initial interview. Fourteen subsequent sessions of individual psychotherapy focused on progressive muscle exercises, imagery, and desensitization to social anxiety in crowded places; and cognitive therapy focused on stress management and distortions regarding health and excessive fears about illness. Follow-up at 4 months after treatment revealed a 60% decrease in symptoms of urethral syndrome and an 80% reduction in the intensity of social anxiety.

uncontrolled studies. If organic causes of the syndrome are identified and treated, yet the symptoms persist, or if psychological factors (i. e., past sexual abuse) appear to play a substantial role, the patient should be referred for individual psychotherapy in accordance with treatment for psychophysiological or posttraumatic disorders. If the urethral symptoms occur predominately or only in certain places or situations, attempts may be made to treat them with cognitive-behavioral approaches, as with other phobias and anxiety disorders.

Professional Practice Issues

Scope of Services
The general purpose of integrating health psychology into urology programs is to enhance patient care. From the previous discussion, it is clear that the health psychologist can offer a full spectrum of services to multidisciplinary programs treating urological disorders. In addition to direct interventions involving individual assessment and psychotherapy in response to patients' psychological reactions to urological disorders, the clinical health psychologist can provide specialized interventions involving biofeedback and behavioral treatments to individuals, families, and professional caregivers, in medical settings and nursing homes. In addition to individual-treatment modalities, the clinical health psychologist can provide and supervise supportive and self-help group interventions to both patients and their families. As a member of a multidisciplinary health care team or in a specific urology program, the clinical health psychologist can also provide consultation in regular staff meetings to medical staff, regarding particular problems involving adherence to medical treatment or patient reactions to stressful medical procedures, often experienced with urology problems, such as urinary incontinence and erectile dysfunction.

Future Research
More extensive research is needed about the ways psychosocial factors affect and are affect-

ed by urological disorders. Additional research in areas described in this chapter would benefit from an emphasis on life-span perspectives and cultural diversity. However, because urological disorders are best understood in the context of a biopsychosocial model, more integrative research is needed to simultaneously examine relationships among biological markers of disease activity (e. g., functional incontinence), psychological parameters (e. g., coping patterns), and socioenvironmental parameters (e. g., social support). Psychologists working with urological disorders can no longer assume that a linear relationship exists between biology and behavior or culture and behavior (Belar & Tovian, 2002). For clinicians, empirically validated assessment instruments and treatments must be made widely known and implemented with urological disorders within the general health care system.

Program Development
In the changing health care milieu with managed care and capitated markets, the health psychologist based in or consulting with a urology program must have data on outcome parameters, quality assurance, and cost/effectiveness of his/her services. As outlined by Tovian (1991), some of these parameters may be reflected in the number of sessions and cost per specific intervention or evaluation (i. e., EMG biofeedback for stress incontinence), percent of patients indicating improvement on symptoms change scales, percent of inpatient consultations completed within 36 hours of receiving the referral, and number of unplanned terminations per intervention, to name a few. Adherence to ethical issues and avoidance of malpractice risks, especially relevant to health psychologists, must be followed (e. g., Belar & Deardorff, 1995).

Psychology and Surgery Interface
Health psychologists working in the tertiary field of urology will find themselves consulting with surgeons. In communicating with surgeons, written reports need to be prompt, concise, and free of psychological jargon. Reports should begin with a direct and concise

answer to the restated referral question, followed by brief and equally concise data to support that answer. Recommendations for specific interventions need to be stated succinctly and early in the report. Contraindications or specific medical interventions should be clearly noted, with evidence of potential problems delineated. Lengthy reports discussing test results are too often obscure to the surgeon and answer questions that are not asked but fail to answer those that are obvious (Adams, 1992; Ackerman, 1992).

The health psychologist working in urology needs to become familiar also with the surgical procedures used. A request to observe a surgical procedure, or "scrub" for a procedure, is an excellent way to demonstrate a willingness to learn firsthand about a given intervention, as well as to become a "member of the team." A health psychologist working in a surgical specialty such as urology needs to relate to both the nature of a surgeon's work and the patient's surgical experience, expectations, fears, and consequences (Adams, 1992).

Marketing Issues

In marketing services to relevant medical departments and professionals, the health psychologist must be aware of his or her training and experience with urological problems (Belar & Deardorff, 1995), as well as those sociopolitical issues that exist in any medical setting (Sweet et al., 1991; Frank, 1997). Establishing professional relationships with nurse-clinicians and physicians in urology may involve the psychologist's offering to present at medical grand rounds or notifying various medical staff about their interest and experience with urology patients. Major medical centers often have broad multidisciplinary programs that cross over various specialties, such as programs in geriatrics or women's health, for example, which can serve as a place for membership for a health psychologist interested in incontinence, for example.

Finally, as a result of their training and expertise, health psychologists can be instrumental in the necessary and increased efforts needed to inform and educate the public and public policy makers about urological problems. The public should be aware that a prob-

lem such as incontinence, for example, is not inevitable or shameful but is often treatable and always manageable. The psychology profession would appear to be a crucial link in any comprehensive, multidisciplinary attempts to design effective patient-education programs about the prevention, assessment, and treatment of urological problems such as urinary incontinence and erectile dysfunction. Given the approximately 4,000 psychologists employed as faculty in medical schools (Tovian, Rozensky, & Sweet, 2003), contributions from health psychologists would also appear to be crucial in efforts to educate other medical professionals about the psychological evaluation and treatment of those who suffer from urological dysfunctions.

References

Ackerman, M.D. (1992). Consultation with clinical urology: Expanded roles for health psychologists. *The Health Psychologist, 14,* 3–4.

Ackerman, M.D. (1995). Behavioral approaches to assessing erectile dysfunction. *The Behavior Therapist, 18,* 31–34.

Ackerman, M.D., & Carey, M.P. (1995). Psychology's role in the assessment of erectile dysfunction: Historical precedents, current knowledge, and methods. *Journal of Consulting and Clinical Psychology, 63,* 862–876.

Ackerman, M.D., Helder, L.H., & Antoni, M.H. (1989, March). *The Miami sexual dysfunction protocol.* Poster presented at the Tenth Annual Scientific Session of the Society of Behavioral Medicine, San Francisco.

Ackerman, M.D., Montague, D.K., & Morgenstern, S. (1994, March). Impotence: Help for erectile dysfunction. *Patient Care,* 22–56.

Adams, D.B. (1992). Medical and surgical interface: Problems with philosophy and nosology. *Psychotherapy Bulletin, 27*(2), 23–25.

Agency for Health Care Policy and Research, Public Health Service, U.S. Department of Health and Human Services. (1996, March). Urinary Incontinence Guideline Panel. *Urinary incontinence in adults: Clinical practice guidelines* (AHCPR Pub. No. 96–0682). Rockville, MD: Author.

American Association of Retired Persons and Simon Foundation for Continence (1993). *Promoting continence: Educating older Americans about incontinence.* Washington, DC: American Association of Retired Persons.

American Psychiatric Association (1994). *Diagnostic and statistical manual of mental disorders: 4th edition.* Washington, DC: Author.

Belar, C.D., & Deardorff, W.W. (1995). *Clinical health psychology in medical settings: A practitioner's guidebook.* Washington, DC: American Psychological Association.

Belar, C.D. & Tovian, S.M. (2002). Genitourinary diseases (Chapter 10). In T.J. Boll, S.B. Johnson, N.W. Perry, & R.H. Rozensky (Eds.), *Handbook of clinical health psychology: Volume I. Medical disorders and behavioral applications.* Washington, DC: American Psychological Association.

Bergman, A., Karram, M., & Bhatia, N.N. (1989). Urethral syndrome: A comparison of different treatment modalities. *Journal of Reproductive Medicine, 3,* 157–161.

Boll, T.J., Johnson, S.B., Perry, N.W., & Rozensky, R.H. (Eds.). (2002). *Handbook of clinical health psychology: Volume I. Medical disorders and behavioral applications.* Washington, DC: American Psychological Association.

Bond, G.R., Borman, L.D., Bankoff, E.A., Daiter, S., Lieberman, M.A., & Videka, L.M. (1979). The self-help mutual support group. In M.A. Lieberman & L.D. Borman (Eds.), *Self-help groups for coping with medical crisis* (pp. 489–526). San Francisco: Jossey-Bass.

Burgio, K.L., & Engel, B.T. (1990). Biofeedback-assisted behavioral training for elderly men and women. *Journal of the American Geriatrics Society, 38,* 338–340.

Burgio, K.L., & Engel, B.T. (1987), Urinary incontinence: Behavioral assessment and treatment. In L.L. Carstensen & B.A. Edelstein (Eds.), *Handbook of clinical gerontology* (pp. 252–266). New York: Pergamon.

Burns, P.A., Mareck, M.A., Duttmar, S.S., & Bullogh, B. (1985). Kegel exercises with biofeedback therapy for stress incontinence. *Nurse Practitioner, 4,* 28–33.

Butcher, J.N., Dahlstrom, N.G., Graham, J.R., Telleger, A., & Kaemmer, B. (1989). *Minnesota Multiphasic Personality Inventory (MMPI-2): Manual for administration and scoring.* Minneapolis: University of Minnesota.

Carson, C.C., Osborne, D., & Segura, J.W. (1979). Psychologic characteristics of patients with female urethral syndrome. *Journal of Clinical Psychology, 35,* 312–314.

Derogatis, L.R. (1986). The Psychosocial Adjustment to Illness Scale (PAIS). *Journal of Psychosomatic Research, 30,* 77–91.

Derogatis, L.R. (1993). *BSI: Administration, scoring and procedures manual for the Brief Symptom Inventory II* (3rd ed.). Minneapolis: National Computer Systems.

Fantl, J.A., Wyman, J.F., McClish, D.K., Harkins, S.W., Elswick, K.K., Taylor, J.R., Hunt, W.G., Dunn, L.J., & Bump, R.C. (1991). Efficacy of bladder training in older women with urinary incontinence. *Journal of the American Medical Association, 265,* 609–613.

Folstein, M.F., Folstein, S.E., & McHugh, P.R. (1975). Mini-mental state exam: A practical method for grading the cognitive state of patients for clinicians. *Journal of Psychiatric Research, 12,* 189–198.

Frank, R.G. (1997). Marketing at academic health centers. *Journal of Clinical Psychology in Medical Settings, 4,* 41–50.

Jarvis, G.J. (1981). A controlled trial of bladder drill and drug therapy in the management of detrusor instability. *British Journal of Urology, 53,* 565–566.

Keefe, F.J., & Blumenthal, J.A. (1982). *Assessment strategies in behavioral medicine.* New York: Grune & Stratton.

Kellner, R. (1991). *Psychosomatic syndromes and somatic symptoms.* Washington, DC: American Psychiatric Press.

Kerns, R.D., Turk, D.C., & Rudy, T.E. (1985). The West Haven-Yale Multidimensional Pain Inventory. *Pain, 23,* 345–356.

Lewin, L., & Gonzales, L.R. (1994). Treatment of urethral catheter dependence: A case study of intervention in the interdisciplinary geriatric setting. *Journal of Clinical Psychology in Medical Settings, 1,* 363–373.

Locke, H., & Wallace, K. (1959). Short marital adjustment and prediction tests: Their reliability and validity. *Marriage and Family Living, 21,* 251–255.

Mehik, A., Hellstrom, P., Sarpola, A., Lukkarinen, O., & Jarvelin, M. (2001). Fears, sexual disturbances and personality features in men with prostatitis: A population-based cross-sectional study in Finland. *British Journal of Urology International, 88,* 35–38.

Millon, T., Green, C.J., & Meagher, R.B. (1979). The MBHI: A new inventory for the psychodiagnostician in medical settings. *Professional Psychology, 10,* 529–539.

Moos, R.H. (1977). *Coping with physical illness.* New York: Plenum.

Nicassio, P.M., & Smith, T.W. (1995). *Managing chronic illness: A biopsychosocial perspective.* Washington, DC: American Psychological Association.

Ory, M.G., Wyman, J.F., & Yu, L.C. (1986). *Clinics in Geriatric Medicine, 2,* 657–671.

Orzeck, S., & Ouslander, J.G. (1987). Urinary incontinence: An overview of causes and treatment. *Journal of Enterostomal Therapy, 14,* 20–27.

Ratliff, T.L., Klutke, C.G., & McDougall, E.M. (1994). The etiology of interstitial cystitis. *Urology Clinics of North America, 21*, 1–5.

Reiter, R.C., Shakerin, L.R., Gambone, J.C., & Milburn, A.K. (1991). *American Journal of Obstetrics and Gynecology, 6*, 104–109.

Resnick, N.M., & Yalla, S.V. (1985). Management of urinary incontinence in the elderly. *The New England Journal of Medicine, 313*, 800–805.

Rozensky, R.H., Sweet, J.J., & Tovian, S.M. (1997). *Psychological assessment in medical settings.* New York: Plenum.

Rozensky, R.H., & Tovian, S.M. (1985). Strategies for a full life. In C.B. Gartely (Ed.), *Managing incontinence* (pp. 58–69). Ottowa, IL: Jameson Books.

Salmon, P. (1992). Psychological factors in surgical stress: Implications for management. *Clinical Psychology Review, 12*, 681–704.

Schover, L.R., & Jensen, S.B. (1988). *Sexuality and chronic illness: A comprehensive approach.* New York: Guilford.

Schwartz, M.S. (1995). *Biofeedback: A practitioner's guide.* New York: Guilford.

Scotti, R.J., & Ostergard, D.R. (1984). The urethral syndrome, *Clinical Obstetrics and Gynecology, 27*, 515–529.

Seideman, S.N., Roose, S.P., Menza, M.A., Shabsigh, R., & Rosen, R.C. (2001). Treatment of erectile dysfunction in depressed men. *American Journal of Psychiatry, 158*, 1623–1630.

Shumaker, S.A., Wyman, J.F., Uebersax, J.S., McClish, D.K., & Fantl, J.A. (1994). Health-related quality of life measures for women with urinary incontinence: The Incontinence Impact Questionnaire and The Urogenital Distress Inventory. *Quality of Life Research, 3*, 291–306.

Simon Foundation for Continence (1991). "I Will Manage" self-help groups. Simon Foundation, P.O. Box 815; Wilmette IL 60091.

Smith, T.W., Kendall, P.C., & Keefe, F.J. (2002). Behavioral medicine and clinical health psychology: Introduction to the special issue — A view from the decade of behavior. *Journal of Consulting and Clinical Psychology, 3*, 459–462.

Spanier, G.B. (1976). Measuring dyadic adjustment: New scales for assessing the quality of marriage and similar dyads. *Journal of Marriage and the Family, 38*, 15–28.

Spielberger, C.D., Gorush, R.L., & Lushene, R. (1970). *The State-Trait Anxiety Inventory manual.* Palo Alto, CA: Consulting Psychologists Press.

Sweet, J.J., Rozensky, R.H., & Tovian, S.M. (1991). *Handbook of clinical psychology in medical settings.* New York: Plenum.

Tanagho, E.A., & McAninch, J.W. (1995). *Smith's general urology* (14th ed.). Norwalk, CT: Appelton-Lange.

Telsch, C.F., & Telsch, M.J. (1985). Psychological approaches for enhancing coping among cancer patients: A review. *Clinical Psychology Review, 5*, 325–345.

Tollison, C.D., & Langley, J.C. (1995). *The Pain Patient Profile (P-3): Manual for administration and scoring.* Minneapolis: National Computer System.

Tovian, S.M. (1991). Integration of clinical psychology in adult and pediatric oncology programs. In J.J. Sweet, R.H. Rozensky & S.M. Tovian (Eds.), *Handbook of clinical psychology in medical settings* (pp. 331–352). New York: Plenum.

Tovian, S.M. (1996). Health psychology and the field of urology. In R.J. Resnick & R.H. Rozensky (Eds.), *Health psychology through the life span: Practice and research opportunities* (pp. 289–312). Washington, DC: American Psychological Association.

Tovian, S.M. (2002). Body image and urological disorders (Chapter 41). In T.F. Cash & T. Pruzinsky (Eds.), *Body image: A handbook of theoretical research and clinical practice.* New York: Guilford.

Tovian, S.M., Rozensky, R.H., & Sweet, J.J. (2003). A decade of clinical psychology in medical settings: The short longer view. *Journal of Clinical Psychology in Medical Settings, 10*, 3–18.

Tovian, S.M., & Rozensky, R.H. (1985). Building inner confidence. In C.B. Gartley (Ed.), *Managing incontinence* (pp. 48–57). Ottowa, IL: Jameson Books.

Tovian, S.M., Rozensky, R.H., Sloan, T.B., & Slotnik, G.M. (1995). Adult urinary incontinence: Assessment, intervention, and the role of clinical health psychology in program development. *Journal of Clinical Psychology in Medical Settings, 1*, 339–362.

Tries, J., & Eisman, E. (1995). Biofeedback for the treatment of urinary incontinence. In M.E. Schwartz (Ed.), *Biofeedback: A practitioner's guide* (pp. 597–631). New York: Guilford.

Tries, J., & Brubaker, L. (1996). Application of biofeedback in the treatment of urinary incontinence. *Professional Psychology: Research and Practice, 27*, 554–560.

Uebersax, J.S., Wyman, J.F., Shumaker, S.A., McClish, D.K., & Fantl, J.A. (1995). Short forms to assess life quality and symptom distress for urinary incontinence in women: The Incontinence Impact Questionnaire and the Urogenital Distress Inventory. *Neurology and Urodynamics, 14*, 131–139.

Wincze, J.P., & Carey, M.P. (1991) *Sexual dysfunction: A guide for assessment and treatment.* New York: Guilford.

Section III

Health and Illness – Community, Social, Spiritual, and Creative Involvement

Jean E. Rhodes

14

Family, Friends, and Community: The Role of Social Support in Promoting Health

Case Example
Immediately after learning of her lupus diagnosis, Robin turned to her older sister, Tonya, for comfort. Tonya had strongly urged Robin to make the appointment after witnessing her bouts with symptoms. As they returned from the hospital, Tonya assured Robin that things would be alright; that Robin was a fighter and would battle her way through this one too. Most of all, she reminded Robin that she wasn't alone—that Robin's husband and rich network of close friends would be there for her through thick or thin. This proved to be the case. Robin's husband was responsive to even the faintest of symptoms, and her sister and friends provided a steady source of laughs, distractions, conversation, and perspective. Over time, Robin discovered that her illness was, in fact, far more manageable than anticipated—partly attributable, she thought, to her caring network of support.

Indeed, a growing body of literature suggests that people with supportive family and friends remain in better health and recover better from physical and emotional distress than those who are less socially integrated (Hogan, Linden, & Najarian, 2002). Stansfeld and Marmot's (2002) recently reviewed epidemiological studies of social support and mortality and found convincing evidence for the association between social relationships and coronary heart disease, cardiovascular disease mortality, and deaths from accidents and suicide. Along similar lines, Reifman (1995), reviewed 13 longitudinal studies of heart disease and found that being married, or supported in other ways, was associated with survival or the lack of recurrence. More generally, House, Landis, and Umberson (1988) reviewed several large studies of support and health and concluded that the risk for mortality is higher among individuals with fewer supportive contacts. They concluded that "social relationships, or the relative lack thereof, constitute a major risk factor for health—rivalling the effects of well-established health risk factors such as cigarette smoking, blood lipids, obesity, and physical activity" (p. 541). Hogan et al. (2002) recently reviewed 100 studies and found evidence for the effectiveness of social support in promoting better long-term health outcomes. Along similar lines, Uchino, Cacioppo, and Kiecolt-Glaser (1996) reviewed over 80 studies and found that social support was reliably related to beneficial effects on the cardiovascular, endocrine, and immune systems. In addition to affecting an individual's health and mortality, support from family, friends and community members has been found to influence a myriad of other factors ranging from birth outcomes to the experience of psychological symptoms (Vaux, 1988). For example, it was found that women who had abnormal birth outcomes reported less support from husbands, mothers, and friends during their pregnancies and greater psychological distress. Taken together, the research literature provides compelling evidence for the links between social support and well-being. In the following sections, I will discuss social relationships as they relate to health. Within this context, I will address current issues and their implications for the fields of social support and health psychology.

Social Support Theory and Research

The term "social support" was first used in the mental health literature by community psychologists (e. g., Caplan, 1974; Albee, 1968) who noted its potential role in preventing and ameliorating psychological distress. Interest in linkages between social support and physical health rapidly emerged as medical researchers shifted their focus from single causes of acute diseases to multiple environmental (e. g., stress, psychosocial factors) and biological causes of chronic diseases (House et al., 1988). Within this context, two seminal reviews (Cassel, 1976; Cobb, 1976) established clear associations between social support and physical health. The authors drew from multiple human and animal studies to document the protective function of social support, highlighting the role of social relationships in moderating or buffering the potentially harmful effects of stress and other health hazards.

Hundreds of studies of social support have ensued, most of which have found positive associations between support and physical or emotional functioning (see Sarason, Pierce & Sarason, 1990; Vaux, 1988). Attempts have also been made to understand the psychological mechanisms that are responsible for the associations between social support and physiological functioning. Although a large number of studies have documented both the causes and effects of social support, Uchino et al. (1996) argue that most of these studies have not offered adequate empirical support for the underlying causal mechanisms. Thus, although health-related behaviors, stress, and depression clearly influence physiological processes, the major pathways by which social support influences physiological functioning

have yet to be determined (Cohen & Herbert, 1996; Uchino, et al., 1996).

Recurring Issues in the Field

In addition to questions regarding the underlying processes, many issues remain regarding the meaning and measurement of social support. One such issue concerns what is actually meant by the term "social support." Cobb (1976) has argued that social support is essentially information that an individual is loved, esteemed, and part of a network of communication and mutual obligation. More recently, however, researchers have presented more differentiated views of support. Barrera (1986), for example, has discussed the concepts of social embeddedness, perceived social support, and enacted support, arguing that these are distinct but related entities. Perceived support, for example, is the belief that support will be unconditionally available if needed (Sarason, Pierce & Sarason, 1990), whereas enacted support refers to the amount of support that is actually utilized within a given time frame. Vaux (1988) has called for the treatment of social support as a "metaconstruct" with separate subconstructs such as support network resources, support appraisals, and supportive behavior.

Similarly, researchers are increasingly advocating the differentiation of various types of social support, such as emotional support, information, advice, tangible assistance, and guidance. Attempts have been made to identify which types of support are most helpful for particular types of stressors (Barrera, 1986). For example, Seeman, Berkman, Blazer and Rowe (1994) have found that, among the various types of support, emotional support is the most consistent predictor of endocrine functioning.

Sources of Support

It is also important to consider the particular sources of support that are available to an individual. Help from a family member, a physician, a therapist, or close friends, for example, can mean vastly different things to an individual, and are thus likely to be differentially associated with health outcomes. In general, networks of family and friends are thought to be a more enduring source of support than the more formal support that is provided by professionals and through social interventions. Families are an important source of support to consider when assessing the effects of support on health, as family relationships are the earliest and often the most enduring of social ties. But even within the family, it is important to consider the influence of particular providers.

Spouses and partners, for example, are likely to be far more influential than more distant family members. Indeed, there is evidence to suggest that married individuals of both sexes have substantially lower mortality rates than those who remain single (Gove, Style & Hughes, 1990). It is, of course, important to consider the quality and type of marriage, particularly since unhappily married persons have more physical and psychological health problems than unmarried persons (Coyne & DeLongis, 1986). Moreover, gay, lesbian, and heterosexual married partners do not differ from one another in relationship satisfaction, underscoring the protective benefits of a range of intimate relationships (Kurdek & Schmitt, 1986).

Similarly, it is important to consider gender, particularly since men's health has been found to be even more favorably influenced by heterosexual marriage than is women's (Shachar, 1991). One factor that might account for this discrepancy is the greater tendency for wives to be burdened with housework, child care, and the provision of support to family members, even when they are employed full-time (Peplau, 1983). Oliker (1989) has argued that married women often form close friendships with other women, which help to maintain the stability of marriage by meeting the needs for intimacy.

More generally, friendship has been referred to as "the most widely diffused form of love" (Rollins, p. 318). Although both men and women place considerable value on their friendships, as noted above, there tend to be gender differences in the qualities of relationships. Women typically have a greater number of close friends than men and to have a more self-disclosing and helping orientation toward their friendships (Jones, Bloys & Woods, 1990). Men, on the other hand, usually spend more time sharing activities and interests with their friends. For both men and women, friendships tend to grow deeper and more complex over the course of the life span and are linked with psychological and physical wellbeing (Fox, Gibbs & Auerbach, 1985).

In addition to considering one's family and friends, it is important to consider the influence of community support on health. Sarason (1974) has referred to "the psychological sense of community," or the feeling that one is embedded in an extensive network of support, and has argued that the dissolution of communities is one of the most destructive forces in modern life. For example, increasing rates of urban crime and unemployment have led to increased social disorganization in lower-income, African American communities (Wilson, 1996). Nonetheless, the social networks in many such communities remain large and diverse, consisting of a wide array of kin and nonkin members who rely on one another for both tangible (e. g., money, transportation, services) and intangible (e. g., emotional assistance, advice, information) support (Taylor, Casten & Flickinger, 1993). Religious affiliation, which can facilitate access to social support and to promote social integration, has is associated with better adjustment to illness (Siegel, Anderman, & Schrimshaw, 2002). Although considerable health benefits are derived when community support is effectively mobilized (Uchino et al., 1996), it is also important to consider that some communities are less responsive than others. For example, traditional, insulated small towns, are often accepting (and helpful) only if members are of certain races, religions, ethnicities, and only if they follow strict rules of conduct. As Shafter and Anundsen (1993) remind us:

As tightly knit and stable as most old-style communities were, they were also homogeneous, suspicious of outsiders, socially and economically

stratified, emotionally stifling, and limited in opportunities for personal and professional development. So long as members belonged to the right
ethnic, religious, or racial groups—or stayed in
their place if they did not—and behaved within a
narrowly defined set of parameters, they could
count on strong community support. But if they
strayed too far outside the lines, their fellow community members might well shun or harass them
(p. 6).

Given the diversity that exists in most regions
of the U. S., there really exists no single vision
of community. Ultimately community is a
social construction, defined by the practices,
symbols, and associations of its members.

The Downside of Support

As I have discussed, most people think of
family, friend, and community member influences as extremely positive. Nonetheless,
these relationships can also be profoundly
negative. Indeed, there is growing recognition that social support has costs for those
who give and receive it (see Rook, 1990). Families, for example, provide the context for
some of the most severe violence in our society and for long-term patterns of abuse that
can seriously undermine the physical and
emotional well-being of adults.

A myriad of other, less extreme forms of relationship problems, such as disappointment, conflict, intrusiveness, and criticism
are also associated with negative outcomes
(Coyne & DeLongis, 1986; Lakey, Tardiff &
Drew, 1994; Rhodes & Woods, 1995). In fact,
some researchers have argued that adjustment to life stress may be more strongly influenced by relationship problems than by
the positive aspects of social support (Fiore,
Becker & Coppel, 1983; Rook, 1992) and that
strain can negatively impact physical health.
For example, after conducting a meta-analysis of social relationships and health, Herbert
and Cohen (1993) concluded that the negative aspects of social relationships may have
damaging effects on individuals' immune
system functioning.

Individuals suffering from chronic diseas-

es may be particularly susceptible to the negative aspects of support. Although family
members and friends may initially mobilize
positive support and assistance, they may
have difficulty remaining patient and sustaining this support over time (Clair, Fitzpatrick & La-Gory, 1995). Bolger, Foster, Vinokur and Nig (1996), for example, have
highlighted the ways in which severe health
problems can overwhelm significant others,
undermining their capacity to provide effective support. They interviewed one hundred
breast cancer patients and their significant
others at 4 and 10 months after diagnosis. Although significant others provided support
in response to patients' physical impairment,
they tended to withdraw support in response
to patients' emotional distress. The support
that was provided by significant others was
found to neither alleviate patients' distress
nor promote physical recovery.

Clearly, there are limits to the effectiveness
of close relationships in times of severe physical and emotional distress. In such cases, referrals to psychotherapy or alternative sources of support should be made. Fortunately,
there is evidence that supportive psychotherapeutic alliances can affect the course of disease, effectively reducing anxiety, depression
and often pain. Indeed, in three randomized
studies, Spiegel and his colleagues (Spiegel,
1996) found that psychotherapy resulted in
longer survival time for patients with breast
cancer, lymphoma, and malignant melanoma compared to controls. Along similar
lines, support groups can provide a crucial
context for individuals suffering from medical disorders to share their concerns and receive the validation and support that they
may not be receiving at home (McLean,
1995). There is even evidence that computer
bulletin board support groups can provide a
crucial supportive link to individuals with
health problems (Weinberg, Schmale, Uken
& Wessel, 1996).

Finally, there is some evidence that providing support can, in some instances, compromise one's health. Long-term care-giving,
such as providing in-home care for family
members with Alzheimer's diseaseor AIDS
has well-established negative effects on care-

givers' physical and mental health. People who provide such care are at increased risk for developing clinical depression and stress-related physical illnesses (Rook, 1990).

Summary and Implications

As can be seen from the above discussion, social support is a far more complex construct than one might initially assume. What one finds regarding the influence of family, friend, and community support may depend on the recipient's characteristics as well as the questions that are posed regarding the source, type, and intensity of support and strain. Nonetheless, there is ample evidence to suggest that social support serves an important role in promoting the well being of individuals.

Unfortunately, as evidenced from the above discussion, not everyone is embedded in a social network, and some relationships can actually be more problematic than helpful. In such instances, health psychologists can play an important role in improving individuals' social network resources. Practitioners can help clients to identify potential sources of support, and to develop the skills that are needed to actually mobilize and maintain that support. Within this context, a therapeutic relationship, or even can serve as a template for healthy, supportive relationships.

In addition to individual therapy, community-level interventions that are designed to enhance the social resources of individuals can be extremely helpful to individuals who may lack a network of strong social ties.

Unfortunately, many individuals do not have sufficient support available to them. Uchino et al., 1996). Similarly, declining neighborhood safety has led to social isolation and restricted opportunities for informal social contact. Thus, as House (1988, p. 544) points out, "just as we discover the importance of social relationships for health, and see an increasing need for them, their prevalence and availability may be declining." Young people, for example, are increasingly living in their lives without the caring support and guidance of adults. Shifting mar-

ital patterns, the entry of women into the workforce, overcrowded schools, and loss of community cohesiveness have dramatically reduced the availability of caring adults and restricted their opportunities for informal contact with youth. To address the needs of youth who lack attention from caring adults, people from a wide spectrum of disciplines and interests are turning to volunteer mentoring programs. Millions of youth are involved in mentoring programs, and the programs are continuing to expand (Rhodes, 2002).

In my research, I have shown that, when adolescents develop close connections with mentors, their ability to connect with other adults, especially their parents, also improves (Rhodes, Grossman, & Resch, 1999). This change is often noticed by both parents and program personnel. Through consistently warm and accepting interactions with their mentors, protégés can begin to recognize the enormous potential that exists in close relationships and to open themselves up more to the people around them. Heinz Kohut (1978) has argued that close relationships can be therapeutic, helping people realize "that the sustaining echo of empathic resonance is indeed available in the world." Consistent with this observation, Grossman and Tierney (1998) found that youth with mentors reported better relationships with both parents and peers than those in the control group, including greater feelings of trust and openness to deeper communication. Melanie Styles and Kristine Morrow (1995) concluded that the experience of a trusting and consistent mentor relationship led to better outcomes among youth. This is vividly demonstrated in the case study described below. As the adolescent's relationship with his mentor deepened, his defensiveness toward his peers softened. When he felt safe and accepted in the presence of a mentor, a fuller range of feelings and thoughts, and different ways of relating and being related to, began to grow.

Case Example
At age 12, Patrick Summers appeared to be headed straight for a criminal career. He was chronically on the brink of expulsion from

school for a pattern of fighting. Following a particularly aggressive encounter with a teen near his home, Patrick was temporarily placed in the care of an aunt and put under house arrest. Patrick was also referred to an in-school program called Refocus, designed for students with disciplinary problems. Despite his fighting and suspensions, Patrick's teachers also referred him to mentoring program in sixth grade. Most of the participants in the mentoring program had been identified by their teachers as likely to benefit from weekly, hour-long meetings with individual volunteers. Patrick was paired with Walter Pearson, a 59-year-old economics professor at the nearby university. Patrick seemed open to the relationship and won Walter over from the start. Within a few weeks the issue of Patrick's fighting came up. Although Walter admits to never having had a fistfight, he felt ready to tackle this problem. When Patrick confessed to him that he really did not want to fight, Walter suggested that Patrick consider telling himself, "I will not fight" every time he stepped through a doorway when entering or leaving a room. Walter also suggested wrestling as a means of channeling and controlling Patrick's physical responses. Since Patrick was responsive to the suggestion, Walter helped pave the way. The wrestling strategy seemed to work magic. "I don't know whether I want to take credit for this," Walter confides, "but as the year went on the fighting gradually decreased and things got better."

A growing body of research supports this observation. Mentoring relationships have been shown to positively influence a range of outcomes, including improvements in peer and parental relationships, academic achievement, and self-concept, as well as lower recidivism rates among juvenile delinquents and reductions in substance abuse (Grossman & Tierney, 1998; Rhodes, 2002). Given the importance of social support and the demographic shifts that have reduced the availability of family and neighborhood sources of support, it may be important to facilitate the development of close emotional bonds through supportive interventions.

In summary, it appears that support from family, friends, and community members serves an important role in promoting the well-being of individuals. As researchers and practitioners continue to explore the field of social support, we will face challenges in understanding the construct, delineating the optimal sources and types of support, and elucidating the underlying processes through which it produces health-protective effects. Although many conceptual issues remain to be resolved, we can at the very least have full confidence in the wisdom of California's Department of Mental Health slogan, "Friends are Good Medicine."

References

Albee, G.W. (1968). Conceptual models and manpower requirements in psychology. *American Psychologist, 23*, 317–320.

Barrera, M. (1986). Distinctions between social support concepts, measures, and models. *American Journal of Community Psychology, 14*, 413–445.

Bolger, N., Foster, M., Vinokur, A., & Nig, R. (1996). Close relationships and adjustments to a life crisis: The case of breast cancer. *Journal of Personality and Social Psychology, 70*, 283–294.

Caplan, G. (1974). *Support systems and community mental health*. New York: Behavioral Publications.

Cartenson, L.L. (1992). Social and emotional patterns in adulthood: Support for socioemotional selective theory. *Psychology and Aging, 7*, 331–338.

Cassel, J.C. (1976). The contribution of the social environment to host resistance. *American Journal of Epidemiology, 104*, 107–123.

Clair, J.M., Fitzpatrick, K.M., & La-Gory, M.E. (1995). The impact of psychosocial resources on caregiver burden and depression: Sociological variations in a gerontological theme. *Sociological Perspectives, 38*, 195–215.

Cobb, S. (1976). Social support as a moderator of life stress. *Psychosomatic Medicine, 38*, 300–314.

Cohen, S., & Herbert, T.B. (1996). Health psychology: Psychological factors and physical disease from the perspective of human psychoneuroimmunology. *Annual Review of Psychology, 47*, 113–142.

Coyne, J.C., & DeLongis, A. (1986). Going beyond social support: The role of social relationships in adaptation. *Journal of Consulting and Clinical Psychology, 54*, 456–460.

Fiore, J., Becker, J., & Coppel, D. (1983). Social network interactions: A buffer or a stress? *American Journal of Community Psychology, 11*, 423–429.

Fox, M., Gibbs, M., & Auerbach, D. (1985). Age and gender dimensions friendship. *Psychology of Women's Quarterly, 9*, 489–501.

Gove, W.R., Style, C.B., & Hughes, M. (1990). The effect of marriage on the well-being of adults: A theoretical analysis. *Journal of Family Issues, 11*, 4–35.

Herbert, T.B., & Cohen, S. (1993a). Stress and immunity in humans: A meta-analytic review. *Psychosomatic Medicine, 55*, 364–379.

Hogan, B.E., Linden, W., & Najarian, B. (2002). Social support interventions: Do they work? *Clinical Psychology Review, 22*(3), 381–440.

Homans, G.C. (1974). *Social behavior: Its elementary forms*. New York, NY: Harcourt Brace Jovanovich.

House, J.S., Landis, K.R., & Umberson, D. (1988). Social relationships and health. *Science, 241*, 540–544.

Jones, D.C., Bloys, N., & Woods, M. (1990). Sex roles and friendship patterns. *Sex Roles, 23*, 133–145.

Kohut, H. (1978). The psychoanalyst in the community of scholars. In P. Ornstein (Ed.), *The search for the self: Selected writings of Heinz Kohut* (pp. 685–724). New York: International Universities Press, 1978.

Kurdek, L., & Schmitt, P. (1986). Relationship quality of participants in heterosexual married, heterosexual cohabiting, gay, and lesbian relationships. *Journal of Personality and Social Psychology, 51*, 711–720.

Lakey, B., Tardiff, T.A., & Drew, J.B. (1994). Negative social interactions: Associations to social support, cognition, and psychological distress. *Journal of Social and Clinical Psychology, 13*, 42–62.

McLean, B. (1995). Social support, support groups, and breast cancer: A literature review. *Canadian Journal of Community Mental Health, 14*, 207–227.

NMHA (1995). *Getting started. The NMHA directory of model programs to prevent mental disorders and promote mental health*. Alexandria, VA: National Mental Health Association Publication Department.

Oliker, S.J. (1989). *Best friends and marriage: Exchange among women*. CA: University of California Press.

Peplau, L.A. (1983). Roles and gender. In H.H. Kelley, E. Berscheid, A. Christenson, J. Harvey & D. Peterson (Eds.), *Close relationships* (pp. 220–264). San Francisco: Freeman.

Reifman, A. (1995). Social relationships, recovery from illness, and survival: A literature review. *Annals of Behavioral Medicine, 17*, 124–131.

Rhodes, J.E., Grossman, J.B., & Resch, N.L. (2000). Agents of change: Pathways through which mentoring relationships influence adolescents' academic adjustment. *Child Development, 71*, 1662–1671.

Rhodes, J.E., & Woods, M. (1995). Comfort and conflict in the relationships of pregnant, minority adolescents: Social support as a moderator of social strain. *Journal of Community Psychology, 23*, 74–84.

Rollins, J.H. (1996). *Women's minds, women's bodies: The psychology of women in a biosocial context*. NJ: Prentice Hall.

Rook, K.S. (1990). Parallels in the study of social support and social strain. Special issue on social support and clinical psychology. *Journal of Social and Clinical Psychology, 9*, 118–132.

Rook, K.S. (1992). Detrimental aspects of social relationships: Taking stock of an emerging literature. In H.O.F. Veil & U. Baumann (Eds.). *The meaning and measurement of social support*. New York: Hemisphere.

Sarason, S.B. (1974). *The psychological sense of community*.

Sarason, B.R., Pierce, G.R., & Sarason, I.B. (1990). Social support: The sense of acceptance and the role of relationships. In B.R. Sarason, I.G. Sarason & G.R. Pierce (Eds.), *Social support: An interactional view* (pp. 95–128). New York: Wiley.

Seeman, T.E., Berkman, L.F., Blazer, D., & Rowe, J.W. (1994). Social ties and support and neuroendocrine function: The MacArthur studies of successful aging. *Annals of Behavioral Medicine, 16*, 95–106.

Shachar, R. (1991). His and her marital satisfaction: The double standard. *Sex Roles, 25*, 451–465.

Shafter, C.R., & Anundsen, K. (1993). *Creating communities anywhere: Finding support in a fragmented world*. New York: Putnam.

Siegel, K., Anderman, S.J., & Schrimshaw, E.W. (2001). Religion and coping with health-related stress. *Psychology & Health, 16*, 631–653.

Silverman, P.R. (1988). *Widow-to-widow*. New York: Springer-Verlag.

Spiegel, D. (1996). Cancer and depression. *British Journal of Psychiatry, 168*, 109–116.

Stansfeld, S. & Fuhrer, R. (2002). Social relations and coronary heart disease. In S. Stansfeld, & M.G. Marmot (Eds.), *Stress and the heart: Psychosocial pathways to coronary heart disease* (pp. 72–85). Willistton, VT: BMJ Books.

Styles, M.B., & Morrow, K.V. (1995). *Understanding How Youth and Elders Form Relationships: A Study of Four Linking Lifetimes Programs.* Philadelphia: Public/Private Ventures.

Taylor, R.D., Casten, R., & Flickinger, S.M. 1993). Influence of kinship social support on the parenting experiences and psychosocial adjustment of African-American adolescents. *Developmental Psychology, 29,* 382– 388.

Uchino, B.N., Cacioppo, J.T., & Kiecolt-Glaser, J.K. (1996). The relationship between social support and physiological processes: A review with emphasis on underlying mechanisms and im-

plications for health. *Psychological Bulletin, 19,* 488–531.

Vaux, A. (1988). *Social support: Theory, research, and intervention.* New York: Praeger.

Weinberg, N., Schmale, J., Uken, J., & Wessel, K. (1996). Online help: Cancer patients participate in a computer-mediated support group. *Health and Social Work, 21,* 24–29.

Wilson, W.J. (1996). *When work disappears: The world of the new urban poor.* New York: Knopf.

Randolph G. Potts

15

Spirituality, Religion, and the Experience of Illness

Attending to spiritual and psychological dimensions of the person in medical settings, may represent a "return" as well as an advance in the provision of clinical services. Religion, psychology and medicine confront forces that are not completely understood, and involve a relationship with a trained, socially sanctioned healer (Frank, 1982; Hiatt, 1986). Each addresses basic existential questions of life, death, illness, and the alleviation of suffering. Talk therapies using the power of the spoken word to promote healing have served as the cornerstone of traditional African healing systems. In traditional sub-Saharan healing systems, medicines are administered along with and are believed to derive some of their efficacy from the spiritual force of the spoken word, the "Nommo" (Jahn, 1990). The Ebers Papyrus, the oldest set of medical texts from ancient Egypt, indicates that when treating medical conditions, drugs and physical medicine are to be administered along with incantations and divine speech, "Mdw Ntr" (Carruthers, 1995; Nunn, 1996). Western medicine, psychology and religion were originally intertwined as well. Western medicine developed in religious contexts in which spiritual factors were seen as influencing health and illness. Physicians were members of the clergy and the church was the first to grant a medical license (Kuhn, 1988; McKee & Chappel, 1992). The original meaning of the term psychology was "the study of the soul," and appeared as a subdiscipline of pneumatology – the study of spiritual beings (Vande

Kemp, 1996). Biblical, Buddhist, Hindu, Islamic and other religious psychotherapies continue to flourish in many parts of the world (Rizvi, 1989; Epstein, 1995; Vande Kemp, 1996).

Influenced by successes in experimental physiology and breakthroughs in the medical sciences, Western medicine relinquished the holistic model for a biomedical model of health and disease. In contrast to the model in which nonmaterial factors were given equal attention, the biomedical focus was on specific microorganisms, cellular processes and organ systems. Despite the attention given to religion by William James and other prominent American psychologists, Western psychology has (re)constructed its modern identity as an empirical science unencumbered by the bonds of religion.

The biopsychosocial model upon which much of clinical health psychology is based integrates psychological and physiological dimensions of the person. A growing number of health professionals are exploring an expanded bio–psycho–socio–spiritual model for use in clinical practice (Kuhn, 1988). A substantial body of empirical literature is emerging that documents relationships between spirituality, religion and health (Chamberlain & Hall, 2000; Koenig, McCullough & Larson, 2001; Levin, 2001). During the past few years major peer-reviewed journals in medicine, psychology and public health have published articles on spirituality, religion and health (e. g., the *Journal of the American Medical Association*, the *American*

Journal of Psychiatry, the *American Psychologist*, the *Journal of Consulting and Clinical Psychology*, the *American Journal of Public Health*, and *Psycho-Oncology*). Special edited volumes of the *Journal of Health Psychology*, *Psychotherapy*, and the *Community Psychologist* have recently been devoted to this topic. The National Institute of Health and the National Institute on Aging have each convened conferences and funded research on links between religion and health. This burgeoning discourse on relationships known to be vital since antiquity opens new possibilities for integrative, culturally consonant and more efficacious clinical care.

Spirituality and Religion

Although the terms are often used interchangeably, and there may be some overlap in their meaning, spirituality and religion are not identical. Spirituality refers to the direct, personal experience of the sacred; the awareness of a higher power, a causal force beyond the material or rational, that operates in all aspects of existence. Spirituality has to do with the search for meaning and purpose in life, for life's ultimate significance (Mbiti, 1969; Ellison, 1983; Hiatt, 1986; Reed, 1992). A panel on spirituality and health convened by the National Institute of Healthcare Research (NIHR) defined spirituality as "the feelings, thoughts, experiences and behaviors that arise from a search for the sacred" (Larson, Swyers, & McCullough, 1997, p. 21). Religion can be defined as an established system of symbols, beliefs, communal rituals (liturgy), and texts (canons, scriptures, etc.) shared by a community of faith, designed to enhance the relationship with the sacred. Although religion provides a framework for the expression of spirituality, spirituality is " ... more basic than, prior to, and different from traditional expressions of religiosity" (Elkins, Hedstrom, Hughes, Leaf & Saunders, 1988, p. 6). Spirituality may motivate, direct, and transform one's specific religious involvement.

Spirituality and Religion in Health Psychology

Among several reasons why health psychologists should be prepared to address spiritual and religious issues in providing patient care are: (1) the importance of religious and spiritual issues in the lives of people generally (Bergin & Jensen, 1990), and medical patients particularly (Saudia, Kinney, Brown & Young-Ward, 1991), (2) research findings documenting salutary effects of religion and spirituality on the emotional well-being of medical patients (Harris et al., 1995; Chamberlain & Hall, 2000; Koenig, McCullough & Larson, 2001), (3) studies documenting the impact of religious practices on medical outcome (Chamberlain & Hall, 2000; Koenig, McCullough & Larson, 2001; Levin, 2001), and (4) new professional guidelines that call upon clinicians to develop competency in addressing religious issues in clinical practice.

Demographics of Faith

Religious and spiritual beliefs, practices, images and language are woven into the fabric of most societies. According to the World Almanac (1997, cited in Koenig, McCullough & Larson, 2001), globally there are 1.9 billion Christians, 1.1 billion Muslims, 781 million Hindus, 324 million Buddhists, and 14 million Jews. Other religious traditions, such as those originating in Africa, Asia and the Americas, are also widely practiced and have often influenced local practices of the five religions just listed. For example, the influences of the religion of the Yoruba, practiced by over 15 million people in Western Africa, can be seen in Afro–Caribbean religions such as Santería, Shango and Vodun, and Afro–Brazilian religions such as Condomblé and Macumba (Eliade & Couliano, 1991). It has been suggested that the centrality of spirituality in the African American experience is grounded in an African world-view (Jahn, 1990; Richards, 1990). Spirituality has been described as one of the most important dimensions of human experience for African Americans (Jones, 1986), and the most important "self-determined" component of psychological health and well-being (Edwards, 1987). Within the medical cultures of people of African descent, healing is seen as ultimately coming from God, and the specific healer (physician, pastor, priest, Santero, Babalawo, health psychologist, etc.) works as an instrument or agent of God in the healing process (Potts, 1996; Watson, 1984).

Similarly, religions originating in the Americas and Asia have had a transformative influence on certain Christian religious practices and belief systems. For example, the amalgamation of Mexican and Central American Indian belief systems with Catholicism has given rise to a spiritual outlook called the "Mestizo" world view (Ramírez, 1983; Cervantes & Ramírez, 1992). From a Mestizo perspective, as from a Hindu (Cavendish, 1980) or African (Mbiti, 1969) perspective, spirituality penetrates all phenomena, relationships, and experiences. McGuire (1988) describes how many middle-class suburbanites in the United States are now turning to Native American and East Asian religious systems which embrace this spiritual outlook.

Recent studies have documented the importance of religion in people's lives. Surveys in the United States have found that 95% of the population professes a belief in God (Hoge, 1996), and 93% identify with a religious group (Kosmin & Lachman, 1993). In a study by Bergin and Jensen (1990), it was found that 72% of the general population described religious faith as the most important influence in their lives. Similarly, a survey exploring the ultimate motives or guiding impetus in an East Asian context found that 93% of those surveyed believed in "spiritual pursuit aimed at union with the universal self" as the ultimate motive in life (Rangaswami, 1994).

Another population for whom religion and spirituality may take on a heightened significance transects all ethnic groups — people experiencing medical illnesses. The clinical relevance of religion and spirituality has often been given attention in pastoral counseling and nursing journals. "The importance of including spiritual care in nursing has been addressed in the literature for over 20 years" (Sodestrom & Martinson, 1987, p. 41). In a study of coping strategies of cancer patients, Sodestrom and Martinson found that, "The majority (88%) of patients used a variety of spiritual activities and resource people while coping with cancer" (p. 44). In a study of patients receiving treatment for coronary occlusive disease (Saudia, Kinney, Brown & Young-Ward, 1991), 96% of the patients indicated using prayer as a means of coping with the stress of cardiac surgery. Religious beliefs not only influence coping, but medical help seeking behaviors, medical treatment decisions (e. g., decisions about transfusions, transplants, or DNR orders), compliance with treatment protocols, and willingness to comply with recommendations for posttreatment dietary and lifestyle changes.

Sensitivity of care providers to the patient's religious or spiritual beliefs may enhance the therapeutic relationship and efficacy of clinical interventions. Bergin and Jensen (1990) found that most of the general population would prefer an approach to psychotherapy that was sensitive to a spiritual perspective. There is evidence that the effectiveness of psychotherapy with religious clients is augmented by the use of religious imagery (Propst, 1980), and the inclusion of religious materials in therapy (Azhart, Varma & Dharap, 1994; Propst, 1996). There is mounting empirical evidence that spirituality and religion often provide emotional comfort for medical patients and have beneficial effects on health outcome. For example, a review of 300 studies on relationships between religion, spirituality and health outcome by Chamberlain and Hall (2000), and an analysis of 1200 studies and 400 research reviews on these relationships by Koenig, McCullough and Larson (2001) found consistent evidence that religion and spirituality generally have ameliorating effects on emotional well-being and survival rates of medical patients.

Religion, Spirituality and Emotional Well-Being

Several studies have appeared during the past few years suggesting that religion and spirituality may provide cognitive and emotional benefits for medical patients. Koenig, McCullough and Larson (2001) reviewed 101 empirical studies that examined the relationship between religious involvement and depression, eight of which were clinical trials. In five of the eight clinical trials it was shown that depressed patients receiving religious interventions recovered significantly faster than subjects in control groups. In 60 (65%) of the 93 cross-sectional and prospective studies a significant positive relationship was found between religious involvement and lower rates of depression or depressive symptoms. Only four studies reported greater depression among the more religious. Similarly, reviews by Koenig, McCullough and Larson (2001), Chamberlain and Hall (2000), and Levin (2001), found religious and spiritual commitment to be associated with greater hope, optimism, self-esteem, sense of purpose and less anxiety.

Spirituality was found to be a source of emotional support in a study by Arzouman, Dudas, Ferrans, and Holm (1991) on the effect of chemotherapy on patient quality of life. Quality of life was measured in this study by a 35 item Quality of Life Index (QLI). The item with the highest satisfaction mean, as well as highest importance ranking, was "faith in God." "Patients stated that their personal faith helped them through the difficult times and that it was an important means of emotional support" (p. 893). Similarly, in another study of cancer patients, religious beliefs and activities were associated with lower levels of pain and greater happiness (Yates, Chalmer, St. James, Follansbee & McKegney, 1981).

In the study of patients receiving treatment for coronary occlusive disease mentioned above (Saudia et al., 1991), 70% of the patients who used prayer gave it the highest possible rating of helpfulness. "Findings suggest that prayer is perceived as a helpful, direct-action coping mechanism and warrants

support by health professionals" (p. 60). A study of heart transplant recipients found that those with strong religious beliefs and who participated in religious activities experienced better physical and emotional well being, fewer health worries, and showed better medical compliance (Harris et al., 1995). In a review of literature on burn patients, Sherrill and Larson (1988) found that when patients were given an opportunity to comment on what helps them cope, they frequently credited their religious faith or God.

It is important to note that some findings have suggested that religion may negatively affect coping with medical problems. For example, Baider and Sarell (1983) found that breast cancer patients in Israel who held fatalistic religious beliefs about their illness (and were mostly from non–European backgrounds) did not cope as well as those who embraced a more scientific view (and were mainly from European backgrounds).

Religion, Spirituality and Medical Outcome

Comprehensive reviews of research on effects of religious commitment on health are provided in Matthews, Larson and Barry (1993); Chamberlain and Hall (2000); Koenig, McCullough and Larson (2001); and Levin (2001). Studies reviewed indicate positive relationships between religious involvement and length of survival of medical patients, lower blood pressure, better immune system functioning, reduced likelihood of illness onset, and likelihood of recovery from illness. Koenig, McCullough and Larson (2001) found five studies on the relationship between religious involvement and immune system functioning, four epidemiological and one experimental. Better immune system functioning among more religious subjects was found in all five studies. Koenig and colleagues reviewed 101 quantitative studies on religiousness and mortality or length of survival. In 75% of the studies, those who were more religious survived longer. Only in one study did the less religious survive longer. In the research reviewed, the strongest predictor of longevity, as well as the strongest predictor of the prevention of illness onset is attendance at religious services.

Several studies suggest health benefits that may be more directly attributable to prayer. Seminal research by Benson (1979) found that the repetition of a prayer elicits a "relaxation response" characterized by a decrease in the activity of the sympathetic nervous system, and often resulting in fewer symptoms associated with anxiety such as headache, nausea, rashes, and diarrhea. More recent research has shown that prayer (and other "private religious activity") predicts longer survival among older adults (Helm, Hays, Flint, Koenig & Blazer, 2000). A study by Byrd (1988) examined the effects of intercessory prayer on patients in a hospital coronary care unit. In this randomized, double-blind study of 393 patients, each patient in the treatment group was assigned a group of "intercessors," unknown to the patient, who prayed daily for the patient's recovery. After 10 months, the hospital course for the treatment group was found to be significantly better than for the control group. Fewer patients in the treatment group experienced episodes of heart failure, required ventilatory support, antibiotics, or diuretics. A similar study was recently conducted investigating possible effects of intercessory prayer (along with three other "noetic" therapies) for patients undergoing percutaneous coronary intervention (PCI) for unstable coronary syndromes (Krucoff, et al., 2001). Although the findings were not statistically significant, there was a 25% to 30% reduction in adverse outcomes in patients treated with any type of noetic therapy. The lowest complication rates were found in patients who received intercessory prayer. Dossey (1993) has compiled results of studies on the impact of prayer on biological processes, including 56 controlled experiments.

In seeking explanations for how religious involvement may contribute to positive health outcomes, researchers have proposed several mechanisms:

- *Health behaviors*. Religious involvement often prohibits many health risk behaviors such as the use of alcohol, drugs and tobacco, violence, and risky sexual behaviors.

- *Social support*. Religious participation often includes fellowship, engagement in a community of others with shared beliefs, with opportunities for receiving and providing support. While social support and healthy behaviors have been shown to have a beneficial affect on health, neither explains more than 10% of the variance in the relationship between religion and health (George et al., 2000).

- *Meaning and purpose*. Religion and spirituality tend to provide a sense of meaning, coherence, and understanding of life purpose. Through religion or spirituality a person may construct a close personal relationship with the divine and a sense of vicarious or secondary control through this bond (Ellison & Levin, 1998). Of the mechanisms proposed to explain religion's affect on health, this one has received the most support (George et al., 2000), and overlaps with the following two.

- *Coping resources*. Religious involvement may provide a system of cognitive and behavioral responses to life events that reduce stress and promote health. Prayer and religious ways of framing life events may alter primary appraisals, buffer stress responses and thereby contribute to positive health outcomes (Ellison & Levin, 1998). Drawing upon one's spiritually enhancing beliefs and the support of others in one's community of faith may reduce "allostatic load", the major health costs associated with the physiological changes involved in recovery from chronic distress (Thoresen, 1999).

- *Positive emotions*. As discussed earlier, religious involvement has been shown to be associated with less depression and anxiety. Religion and spirituality are also associated with love, contentment, forgiveness and other emotions shown to effect a variety of physiological systems (Ellison & Levin, 1998).

- *Biospiritual energy*. Through private prayer, meditation or communal religious ritual there may be the activation of a super-empirical bioenergy (nonlocal consciousness, morphogenic field, psi effect, etc.) that is not fully discernable by our assessment tools and observations (Ellison & Levin,

1998; Levin, 2001). This vital energy may be better conceptualized in other healing systems, for example as *chi* (in Chinese healing systems), *ntu* (in Southern Africa), or *prana* and *kundalini* (in India).

New Professional Guidelines

The *Ethical Principals of Psychologists and Code of Conduct of the American Psychological Association* (APA, 1992) and the American Psychiatric Association Committee on Religion and Psychiatry (1990) call upon clinicians to develop a knowledge base and competency for addressing religious issues in clinical practice. Standard 1.08 of the APA Ethics Code includes religion among the significant dimensions of human diversity about which psychologists may need to obtain special training, consultation, or supervision, or make appropriate referrals in order to ensure the provision of competent services. The *Practice Guidelines for the Psychiatric Evaluation of Adults*, published by the American Psychiatric Association (1995) states that information on religious influences and beliefs should be collected as part of psychiatric evaluations.

Recommendations for Practice

Religious systems incorporate beliefs about illness, symbols, texts, communal and individual practices which may enable medical patients and their families to face illnesses with courage and hope. These same resources may also provide health psychologists with additional therapeutic tools that are more in accord with the patient's beliefs. A premise upon which health psychology is based is that emotional and immune system responses to illness appear to be mediated by personal constructions of illness, cognitions, and other central nervous system processes associated with the meaning of illness (Maier, Watkins & Fleshner, 1994). Consequently a focus in therapy is often the patient's assumptions, cognitions, or appraisals of the illness experience. The special relevance of religion in this context is that it serves just such an explanatory function, providing narratives, metaphors, and images that may inspire a sense of meaning, hope, and coherence in the face of what may otherwise seem to be senseless and unbearable. According to Pargament (1996), religion may provide a re-framing of the negative event, the individual, or the sacred. Within many religious traditions there are stories of suffering preceding spiritual growth, enlightenment, freedom, redemption, resurrection or some other beneficial transformation. In light of the pervasiveness of religious commitment, patients may be served best when therapists are able to integrate supportive elements of religious systems in clinical practice. Suggesting the appropriation of elements of religion within the practice of health psychology is not an attempt to "medicalize" the sacred (Csordas,

---

Table 1. **Recommendations for providing services to religious patients.**

Eight Recommendations (not "Commandments")

1. Obtain training in religious and cultural issues in health psychology
2. Conduct a spiritual assessment or take a religious history
3. Know when to refer to or consult with a religious professional or traditional healer
4. Know when to re-engage patient with religious systems of support
5. Explore patient's religious/spiritual sources of strength
6. Know when to offer new/alternative techniques or practices
7. Pray, meditate, share silence with patient
8. Be alert to countertransferences: Examine your own views on religion and spirituality

---

1987), but to find ways in which beliefs and practices with deep personal significance to the patient and demonstrated clinical benefits may be integrated in patient care. Toward this goal, the eight recommendations *(not Commandments!)* for clinical health psychology are presented and summarized in Table 1.

1. Training in Religious and Cultural Issues in Health Psychology

The first recommendation is that psychologists obtain training in religious and cultural issues in health psychology. The goal of such training would be for clinicians to become more skilled in finding therapeutic resources within religious and cultural belief systems — resources for enhancing the patient's ability to recover from illness, or find comfort when illness is chronic or death is imminent. Noting that psychologists rarely receive training in these areas, Shafranske and Malony (1996) propose a curriculum that would include the following modules: values in psychological treatment, psychology of religion, comparative religion, and working with religious issues. An example of the implementation of such a training program is the "Religious Beliefs Seminar" at Memorial Sloan–Kettering Cancer Center, in which trainees and staff members from psychiatry, social work, nursing, and the chaplaincy meet monthly to present and discuss issues pertaining to religion, culture, and health. McKee and Chappel (1992) note some innovative training programs that have clergy participate in hospital rounds with residents. At least 65 of the 126 medical schools in the United States now offer a course on religion, spirituality and medicine, up from only five schools in 1993 (Koenig, McCullough &Larson, 2001). For those working in settings which lack such

---

Table 2. **Resources on religion, psychology and illness.**

- The Link between Religion and Health: Psychoneuroimmunology and the Faith Factor. H.G. Koenig & H.J. Cohen (Eds.). (2002). Oxford University Press.
- Faith and Health: Psychological Perspectives. T.G. Plante & A.C. Sherman (Eds.). (2001). Guilford Press.
- God, Faith, and Health: Exploring the Spirituality-Healing Connection. J. Levin (2001). John Wiley & Sons.
- Handbook of Religion and Health. H.G. Koenig, M.E. McCullough, & D.B. Larson (Eds.). (2001). Oxford University Press.
- Realized Religion: Research on the Relationship between Religion and Health. T.J. Chamberlain & C.A. Hall (2000). Templeton Foundation Press.
- Measures of Religiosity. P.C. Hill & R.W. Hood, Jr. (Eds.). (1999). Religious Education Press.
- The Psychology of Religion and Coping. K.I. Pargament (1997). Guilford Press.
- The Faith Factor: Proof of the Healing Power of Prayer. D.A. Matthews & C. Clark (1999). Penguin.
- Is Religion Good for Your Health?: The Effects of Religion on Physical and Mental Health. H.G. Koenig (1997). Haworth Press

Resources on culture, religion and illness
- Cultural Competence in Health Care: A Practice Guide. A. Knights Rundle & M.R. Robinson (Eds.). (2002). Jossey-Bass.
- A Hospital Handbook on Multiculturalism and Religion: Practical Guidelines for Health Care Workers. N.A. Kirkwood (1999). Morehouse Publishing.
- Religion, Health and Suffering : A Cross-Cultural Study of Attitudes to Suffering and the Implications for Medicine in a Multi-Religious Society. J.R. Hinnells & R. Porter (Eds.). (1998). Kegan Paul International Limited.
- Transcultural Health Care: A Culturally Competent Approach (Book with Diskette). L.D. Purnell & B.J. Paulanka (Eds.). (1998). F.A. Davis Company

training opportunities, there are continuing education workshops available such as the one on "Psychotherapy with Religiously Committed Patients" which takes place at the annual convention of the American Psychological Association, sponsored by APA Division 36: Psychology of Religion. Table 2 contains resources for health psychologists who may want further information on spirituality, religion and illness.

Since religion is experienced and practiced quite differently in different cultural contexts, it is important that training address cultural variations in religious systems of belief. Such training is particularly valuable when the need arises to differentiate certain manifestations of religious experience from psychopathology, e. g., differentiating glossolalia ("speaking in tongues"), sin-byung in Korea or zar in North Africa and the Middle East (transmigration of souls; American Psychiatric Association, *Diagnostic and Statistical Manual of Mental Disorders, Fourth Edition,* 1994), susto in Central America and the Caribbean ("soul loss" brought about by a traumatic event; Rubel, O'Nell & Collado-Ardon, 1984), mystical experiences, or witnessing the Virgen de Guadeloupe (Cervantes & Ramírez, 1992), from episodes of delirium, seizure, or psychosis. It is not being suggested that health psychology assume the role of pastoral counseling or medical anthropology. Presently health psychology does not assume the role of cardiology or oncology, but psychologists in medical settings need to be knowledgeable of salient issues in these areas of medicine, and provide psychological services that are in accord with treatment provided in these medical disciplines. What is suggested here is that psychologists work to provide services which are congruent with the belief system of the client. To do so, therapists should know: (1) how to recognize religious themes or influences in the patient's presentation, (2) when and how to use elements of religious systems in therapy, (3) when it is important to refrain from addressing religious issues, and (4) when to refer or consult with a religious professional or traditional healer.

2. Spiritual Assessment and Religious History Taking

Assessment of religious orientation, affiliation, practices, and beliefs can provide useful information for constructing a treatment plan, informing the therapist of aspects of religious involvement which may serve as supports or obstacles for clinical interventions. The simple ascertainment of religious affiliation or frequency of church attendance does not provide an adequate account of patient spirituality or the role of religion in the patient's life. For example, many people with AIDS may feel estranged from organized re-

---

Table 3. **Questions for assessing spiritual and religious issues.**

1. Is there anything more important to you than regaining your health?
2. What is the most important thing in your life?
3. Upon what do you depend most when things go wrong?
4. What do you have faith in?
5. Has this illness influenced your faith?
6. For what are you most thankful?
7. Who have you forgiven? By whom have you been forgiven?
8. Do you participate in any religious activities? If so, which are most important to you?
9. Do you pray? If so, how important is prayer in your life?
10. Do you meditate?

ligion and avoid formal involvement due to doctrines which seem unsympathetic or punitive toward them, yet reveal a very strong spiritual life (Jenkins, 1995). Information is needed on religious affiliation and level of formal involvement, but also on the importance and specific meanings of religion and spirituality in the person's life.

Assessment may be composed of questions such as: "What role does religion, spirituality, or God play in your daily life?" "Has your religious faith been important in your experiences with illness or other crises? If so, how?" "Has your faith changed in some way since you have had your illness?" And, "Are there any religious practices that you have found particularly helpful?" Rizzuto (1996) recommends taking a "religious history" prior to beginning psychoanalytic treatment. Hodge (2001) has developed an instrument for obtaining a spiritual history, and also suggests obtaining a spiritual genogram. Malony

(1988) has developed a religious status interview, and Kuhn (1988) a spiritual inventory of the medically ill patient. Incorporating questions devised by Kuhn (1988) and Potts (1996), Table 3 provides a list of questions which might be used in a patient interview.

There are currently several instruments available for assessing religiosity and spirituality (see Table 4). A review of 125 measures of religion and spirituality is provided by Hill and Hood (1999). The instrument that has been most extensively used in research is the Religious Orientation Inventory (Allport & Ross, 1967), which contrasts an internal "intrinsic religious motivation" with a more socially influenced "extrinsic religious motivation." A third religious motivation — "quest" — is measured by Batson and Schoenrade (1991) in their Quest Scale. Quest religious motivation involves a search for resolution to religious conflict or doubt. The Spiritual Well-Being Scale (SWB; Ellison, 1983) and

Table 4. **Instruments for assessing religion or spirituality.**

Instrument	Authors	Description
Religious Orientation Inventory (ROI)	Allport & Ross (1967)	A self-report measure with intrinsic and extrinsic religious motivation subscales.
Quest Scale	Batson & Schoenrade (1991)	Measures quest religious motivation.
Spiritual Well-Being Scale (SWB)	Ellison (1983)	An instrument with subscales measuring religious well being and existential well being.
Spiritual Transcendence Scale (STS)	Piedmont (2000)	Measures spirituality as the sixth factor of personality.
Duke University Religious Index (DUREL)	Koenig, Meador, & Parkerson (1997)	Assesses dimensions of religiousness related to health outcomes.
Religious Coping Activities Scales	Pargament, Ensing, Falgout, Olsen, Reilly, Van Haitsma, & Warren (1990)	Assesses religious coping strategies.
Spiritual Experience Index (SEI)	Genia (1991)	Measures spiritual development from an object relations perspective.
Index of Core Spiritual Experiences (INSPIRIT)	Kass, Friedman, Leserman, Zuttermeister, & Benson (1991)	Measures appraisals of events which enhance spiritual convictions, and personal relationship with God.
Armstrong Measure of Spirituality (AMOS)	Armstrong (1996)	A measure of spirituality that acknowledges cultural differences and impact of spirituality on relationships.
Hassan Religiosity Scale	Hassan & Khalique (1981)	Ten item instrument for assessing Muslim or Hindu religiosity.

the Spiritual Experience Index (SEI; Genia, 1991) reveal a wide range of individual and family member beliefs and attitudes and are particularly well suited for clinical purposes. The SWB includes a subscale measuring a person's sense of life purpose, and another assessing a person's relationship with God. The SEI assesses spiritual development from an object relations perspective. In the context of the five factor model of personality, the Spiritual Transcendence Scale (STS; Piedmont, 2000) measures spirituality as the sixth factor of personality. The Duke University Religious Index (DUREL; Koenig, Meador, & Parkerson, 1997) provides a very brief assessment of major dimensions of religiousness that are related to health outcomes. An instrument developed specifically to assess African American spirituality is the Armstrong Measure of Spirituality (Armstrong, 1996). A ten item instrument for assessing Muslim or Hindu religiosity is the Hassan Religiosity Scale (Hassan & Khalique, 1981). An easily administered instrument for assessing religious coping strategies is the Religious Coping Activities Scales (Pargament et al., 1990). Obtaining a greater knowledge of the sacred in the patient's life, the patient's religious history, religious coping activities, and cultural/spiritual meanings of illness, contribute to more informed clinical decisions in regard to (1) integrating religious and spiritual resources within clinical interventions, (2) refraining from addressing religious issues in clinical interventions, and (3) consulting with or making referrals to religious professionals or traditional healers.

3. Working with Religious Professionals and Traditional Healers

There are several findings one may obtain through religious or spiritual assessment which might signal the need for consultation with or referral to a religious professional. For example, if it appears that the patient is mired in religious–oriented interpretations of illness which may exacerbate distress and suffering, consultation or referral may be warranted. Such distress evoking interpretations may include beliefs that one's illness is God's retribution for past sins, or punishment for a lack of faith. For medical patients the additional afflictions of religious self-condemnation, excessive guilt, or fears of damnation to an eternity in hell, may subvert health promoting medical and psychosocial interventions. Lovinger (1996) describes other markers of possible "religious pathology," and Meissner (1996) provides a discussion on "pathological beliefs." Contact with religious professionals would also be needed when spiritual assessment indicates other forms of severe crises of faith, "religious addiction" (Booth, 1991), or bitterness toward God.

Consultation with a religious professional or traditional healer may also be appropriate when one encounters a patient belief system which differs vastly from that of the therapist. Consultation is needed most when there is the risk that culturally or religiously sanctioned illness beliefs or behaviors may be misinterpreted clinically as idiosyncratic or pathological. For example, a patient may not only attribute illness to sin, but to a spell, hex, mal de ojo (evil eye), or brujería (witchcraft). In such instances, working with a traditional healer may be especially beneficial for the patient in that it expands the system of care to include forms of healing that are more in harmony with the patient's medical culture or what Good and Good (1980) refer to as the patient's "semantic illness network" — the specific cluster of personal and cultural meanings of the symptoms and the illness for the sufferer. It should be emphasized that interventions of traditional healers are not simply ancillary to those of psychologists. The work of the traditional healer may be considered the application of a culturally specific health psychology system. For example, practices such as curanderismo and espiritismo (traditional spiritually based healing practices in the Caribbean, Central and South America) incorporate forms of psychotherapy within multidimensional, holistic healing systems (Ramos-McKay, Comas-Díaz & Rivera, 1988; Cervantes & Ramírez, 1992). Richardson (1991) provides several important suggestions for working with traditional healers. These include recognizing that the patient or the patient's family may be instrumental in locating the traditional healer since such healers may often be accessible only by members of their community.

4. Re-engaging the Patient within Religious Systems of Support

During the course of the many challenges and changes in life brought about by major illnesses — the emotional trauma of learning the diagnosis, the disruption in the daily routines of the patient and family members due to hospitalizations, arranging outpatient treatments and special care in the home — the patient may have inadvertently become disengaged from involvement with a community of faith, or suspended spiritual practices which had been a source of strength and comfort in the past. In such cases it might be helpful to explore ways of reconnecting the patient with these religious sources of support.

Griffith, English and Mayfield (1980) and Jacobs (1990), described several practices and themes within African American churches which combine to provide therapeutic group experiences for participants. These practices include group prayer (at times specifically for those who are ill), testimonials (from those who have overcome illness or otherwise received God's blessings), scripture readings, singing of hymns, laying on of hands, sermons and communion, all within the fellowship of a community of faith which may also provide material supports such as food, transportation and financial support. Some of the themes presented in the readings, sermons and hymns include forgiveness, loving relationships, purpose in life, and finding hope, joy and reasons to be thankful in the midst of adversity. After exploring the patient's religious preferences and commitment, the health psychologist can work with the patient and family in developing a plan for resuming (or increasing) involvement with a community of faith. During and after contact with the health psychologist, churches or other religiously oriented groups may become long term sources of caring for the

patient, instrumental support for the family, and reinforcement of hope and sense of purpose for patient and family.

5. Explore the Patient's Religious/ Spiritual Sources of Strength

For many patients, the current medical condition may not be the first time that they or someone close to them has been confronted with a major illness. It is also possible that during previous encounters with illnesses or other life crises, spirituality or religion was a source of strength. If this is the case, a helpful intervention may be to ask about these experiences, and specifically explore what sustained the patient through adversity and provided hope. A goal of this intervention is to reconnect the patient with specific religious practices, objects, or themes which have provided comfort. Examples include finding ways for the patient to practice preferred forms of prayer, meditation, ablution, or communion; finding ways for the patient to hear specific religious music, hymns, or chants; and finding ways for the patient to have access to valued religious objects such as rosaries, religious art, or religious readings.

Sacred texts may serve as a particularly valuable therapeutic resource. The literatures of many religious traditions contain stories in which suffering ultimately leads to enlightenment, spiritual growth, freedom, redemption or some beneficial transformation. These literatures may contain stories of resurrection and transcendence of death itself. A recommended intervention is that of asking the patient to share passages from sacred texts or episodes in her or his own life of overcoming adversity through faith. Reading or recounting other stories of encounters with illness places the current affliction within a greater context in which it can be experienced as not so much a disruption of life but an integral part of life. These stories can make illness less terrifying, and can make us more keenly aware of possibilities in life which had previously been taken for granted. Religious reframing (Pargament, 1996) or constructing an account of one's illness experience as parallel to those found in sacred texts may instill a sense of meaning, coherence, and hope. The act of telling such stories (e. g., "testifying" in religious gatherings or sharing experiences in group therapy settings) may enhance the salutary power of these narratives. Inviting patients to (re)author their illness stories in preferred and more satisfying ways, acknowledging the transformative power of such stories, is at the heart of the relatively new approach to clinical practice that has become known as narrative therapy (Freedman & Combs, 1996; White & Epston, 1990).

6. Know When to Offer Alternative Techniques or Practices

There are several circumstances in which addressing religious themes would be unnecessary or harmful. Religious assessment may indicate that religion and spirituality are not significant influences in the life of a patient. As noted previously, there may be some patients for whom religious dogma or beliefs about illness present an additional source of distress. Assessment may also reveal that in spite of feelings of estrangement from formal religious involvement due to doctrines which seem punitive, some patients may still have a strong spiritual life. Although introducing religious topics would be contraindicated in cases such as these, there are a number of possibly appropriate interventions which have analogs in religious practices.

Some alternative interventions are typically within the repertoire of health psychologists and include meditation, visualization, guided imagery, and self-hypnosis training. Without involving images or messages of formal religion, these practices are often experienced as calming and comforting. Studies by Fawzy, Kemeny, Fawzy and Elashoff (1990), Spiegel, Bloom, Kraemer and Gottheil (1989) and others document the emotional and biomedical benefits of these practices for cancer patients. These practices may be offered to patients on an individual basis, but the cited

studies suggest that involvement in groups may provide enhanced or additional benefits. The experience of fellowship, sharing inspirational literature, and participating in helping others, contributed to the greater survival rates and other indicators of effectiveness of these psychosocial interventions.

7. Pray, Meditate, Share Silence

Perhaps one of the most comforting acts of a therapist in relationship with a religious patient facing severe illness is sharing a moment of prayer or silent meditation. Tan (1996) lists prayer among the three major examples of explicit integration of religious and spiritual resources in psychotherapy. The other two — referral to religious groups and the use of sacred texts — appear above in recommendations 4 and 5. Joining in prayer may be viewed as controversial, raising some important questions pertaining to standards for professional practice in health psychology. A major concern may be that sharing in prayer might place the therapist past the boundaries of professional competence, or beyond the defined professional role (APA, 1992). The decision to share in prayer with medical patients differs significantly from other recommendations for providing services to religiously committed patients in at least two ways. First, the use of prayer depends entirely upon the levels of comfort of both the therapist and patient. It should take place only after careful religious assessment, with the expressed consent of the patient, and with respect for the autonomy of the patient. Second, as emphasized by Payne et al. (1992) and Tan (1996), prayer is not to be used simply as a therapeutic "technique", e. g., for relieving anxiety. Prayer is appropriate in therapy when it is an authentic and meaningful part of both the therapist's and patient's way of life. Mindful of these considerations, the health psychologist may choose to incorporate prayer in her or his work by being present during prayer of a religious professional visiting the patient; joining in prayer with the patient's family; sharing a moment of prayer with the patient as a dyad, before or after psychotherapy; or sharing mo-

Case Example

Mr. Thomas was a 72-year-old African-American man diagnosed with advanced prostate cancer and receiving inpatient chemotherapy and radiation treatment. He was very quiet and had no visitors. He appeared depressed, irritable, and lethargic. He often refused meals and at times refused to respond to questions of physicians, nurses, and medical residents. These behaviors prompted a request for consultation with the psychology service.

I began by taking a psychosocial history which revealed several sources of distress. Mr. Thomas and his wife had lived together for 50 years in a small town 100 miles away from the large city where this hospital is located. Four years ago, his wife and daughter were in a car accident in which his daughter was killed and his wife paralyzed. Mr. Thomas moved to the city so that Mrs. Thomas would have greater access to more modern, comprehensive medical care. With relocation and involvement in care for his wife at home, he had become socially isolated. Mrs. Thomas died one year ago.

In taking a religious history I discovered that Mr. Thomas had also become isolated from his community of faith. In the town from which they had moved, Mr. and Mrs. Thomas were active members of a church. When asked about his faith and how it had served him through adversities in his life, Mr. Thomas provided several examples but spoke at greatest length about his experiences in World War II. "I survived when we landed on Normandy. I didn't know what to expect. I just heard shooting, everywhere. There were 40 thousand of us killed. They brought bulldozers to push the bodies into big holes. But God was with me then. He brought me through. You never know how many times each day he may save you. And I know he's with me now." Mr. Thomas went on to say that he had been a Deacon in his church, often visiting the sick and hospitalized members of his church. In my next meeting with Mr. Thomas I asked, "What would Deacon Thomas have said to you if he were sitting here where I am?" Mr. Thomas pondered this question for several minutes in silence, then sat up in his bed. Looking down at the side of his bed where I sat, he began by sharing from memory several biblical passages from the Gospels, the Book of Job, and the 23rd Psalm. He concluded with a testimony to his own faith saying, "I know that my God is the only doctor who has never lost a patient. But I want you to understand this too — The Lord did not put us here to stay, and when the time comes, we have got to leave. Our job is to be ready."

Inviting Mr. Thomas to revisit his role as Deacon in a Gestalt-like "empty hospital bed" exercise, revealed to him my recognition, respect and valuing of his role in comforting the sick. This acknowledgment of common vocation at times created moments of role reversal in therapy, during which Mr. Thomas enacted his role of Deacon, giving testimony to God's beneficence and healing. Originating in a town very close to that of Mr. Thomas, and sharing his ethnic and religious traditions, I felt very much "at home" in this familiar and satisfying place of listening and learning from an elder of my community.

In eliciting from Mr. Thomas the healing words and stories through which he had comforted others, it was evident that he was able to obtain some measure of this comfort and peace. It appeared in subsequent meetings that being recognized as a Deacon of his church, and not just a patient in the hospital, helped reactivate dormant resources which could fortify Mr. Thomas as he negotiates the difficulties of this illness. In a few days we were able to locate and retrieve from Mr. Thomas' home the Bible that he used and a lapel pin that he wore as a Deacon. Within a week, there were clear signs of an elevation in mood, a greater sense of calm, and willingness to interact with others on the unit. In meetings that followed we addressed his ministering to his wife during her final years, and how her loss and the loss of his daughter may have been even more painful than those he witnessed at Normandy. Mr. Thomas had been aware of the regularly scheduled support group meetings for men with cancer at the hospital, but had shown no interest in attending them in the past. He now says that he plans to find out if they can use the services of a Deacon.

ments of silent prayer and meditation during psychotherapy. The use of prayer and the explicit integration of religious resources in therapy calls upon the therapist to critically examine her or his own views on religion and spirituality.

8. Examining the Therapist's Own Views on Religion and Spirituality

Another major area for preliminary assessment prior to clinical intervention is the therapist's own views on religion and spirituality. In contrast with the majority of people receiving medical care, the dominant values in biomedical culture tend to exclude religious values (Bergin, 1980). Psychologists have been found to be among the least religious of all academicians (Jones, 1994), and the least religious of major psychotherapy provider groups (Bergin & Jensen, 1990). According to McKee and Chappel (1992) spirituality is neglected by care providers because of personal discomfort with the subject, and a belief that it has no place in the medical sciences. On the other hand, psychologists may choose to avoid religious issues out of awareness of certain rigid, closed (Meissner, 1996) religious teachings. Such religious systems may not only be rejecting and distrustful of psychology and empirical sciences, but of other religions whose teachings may vary from their own.

Divergences in belief systems between therapist and patient, especially if allowed to go unexamined, may pose some formidable clinical problems. Feelings and attitudes about religion, just as those about race, gender and sexual orientation are often deeply rooted in cultural beliefs and values. Clinical interventions are based upon an interpretive understanding of presenting problems. The therapist's interpretations and moment-to-moment responses in clinical transactions emanate not only from training and scientific research, but from the values imparted through professional socialization as they interact with her or his own cultural values and world view. Although ideally, the therapist and patient would collaborate in co-constructing meanings and realities of the illness experience, therapy relationships inevitably involve the transmission of values (Bergin, Payne & Richards, 1996), and the implicit values of the therapist tend to gain hegemony. A main component in training culturally competent clinicians for serving diverse populations is increasing their self-

awareness through exercises aimed at making implicit values more explicit. In addition to the study of comparative religious issues in health psychology (as discussed in recommendation 1 above), and studying literature on other dimensions of human diversity, a key module in diversity training involves experiential exploration of one's feelings and beliefs related to race, gender, stage of life, and religion through the use of video vignettes, enactments, and small group discussions (e. g., Pope-Davis, Prieto, Reynolds & Vasquez, 1994).

It is important for health psychologists to develop a greater awareness of their religious or anti-religious biases and associated countertransferences. Therapeutic use of self and quality of therapeutic relationships may be greatly enhanced as self-awareness grows along the various dimensions of human diversity which color our perceptions and influence our actions. Through greater self-awareness we may be better able to avoid being blinded to valuable resources in the patient's life by our own disbelief or different belief.

A Concluding Note

In the case example we can see how spiritual and religious assessment may simultaneously serve as an important intervention with the religious patient. The questions explored may affirm, validate and provide opportunities for expression of that which is most sacred in the patient's life. These assessments provide a window to what may prove to be major resources or obstacles to satisfying therapeutic relationships and successful treatments. As illustrated by the case with Mr. Thomas, testimonies and stories shared during religious history taking can have a revitalizing and inspiring impact on the health psychologist as well as the patient. It has been suggested that health care providers often benefit from listening to patients' stories in which comfort, peace, hope and meaning are extracted from experiences of illness and impending death (McQuellon & Hurt, 1993). As did Mr. Thomas, perhaps we recognize the very thin line, or rather natural alternation, between one's role as provider and recipient of healing words in our work of helping others (and ourselves) in the journey through illness.

References

Allport, G.W., & Ross, J.M. (1967). Personal religious orientation and prejudice. *Journal of Personality and Social Psychology, 5*(4), 432–443.

American Psychiatric Association (1995). American Psychiatric Association practice guidelines for the psychiatric evaluation of adults. *American Journal of Psychiatry, 152*(suppl), 64–80.

American Psychiatric Association. (1994). *Diagnostic and statistical manual of mental disorders: Fourth edition.* Washington, DC: Author.

American Psychiatric Association Committee on Religion and Psychiatry. (1990). Guidelines regarding possible conflict between psychiatrists' religious commitments and psychiatric practice. *American Journal of Psychiatry, 147,* 542.

American Psychological Association. (1992). Ethical principles of psychologists and code of conduct. *American Psychologist, 47,* 1597–1611.

Armstrong, T.D. (1996). Exploring spirituality: The development of the Armstrong Measure of Spirituality. In R.L. Jones (Ed.), *Handbook of tests and measurements for black populations. Volume 2.* Hampton, VA: Cobb & Henry.

Arzouman, J.M.R., Dudas, S., Ferrans, C.E., & Holm, K. (1991). Quality of life of patients with sarcoma postchemotherapy. *Oncology Nursing Forum, 18*(5), 889–894.

Azhart, M.A., Varma, S.L., & Dharap, A.S. (1994). Religious psychotherapy in anxiety disorder patients. *Acta Psychiatrica Scandinavica, 90,* 1–3.

Baider, L., & Sarell, M. (1983). Perceptions and causal attributions of Israeli women with breast cancer concerning their illness: The effects of ethnicity and religiosity. *Psychotherapy and Psychosomatics, 39,* 136–143.

Batson, C.D., & Schoenrade, P.A. (1991). Measuring religion as quest. *Journal for the Scientific Study of Religion, 30,* 416–430.

Benson, H. (1979). *The mind/body effect: How behavioral medicine can show you the way to better health.* New York: Simon and Schuster.

Bergin, A.E. (1980). Psychotherapy and religious values. *Journal of Consulting and Clinical Psychology, 48*(1), 95–105.

Bergin, A.E., & Jensen, J. (1990). Religiosity of psychotherapists: A national survey. *Psychotherapy, 27,* 3–7.

Bergin, A.E., Payne, I.R., & Richards, P.S. (1996). Values in psychotherapy. In E.P. Shafranske (Ed.), *Religion and the clinical practice of psychology* (pp. 297–325). Washington, DC: American Psychological Association.

Booth, L. (1991). *When God becomes a drug: Breaking the chains of religious addiction and abuse.* New York: Perigee Books.

Byrd, R.C. (1988). Positive therapeutic effects of intercessory prayer in a coronary care unit population. *Southern Medical Journal, 81*(7), 60–65.

Cassileth, B.R., Lusk, E.J., Miller, D.S., Brown, L.L., & Miller, C. (1985). Psychosocial correlates of survival in advanced malignant disease? *New England Journal of Medicine, 312*(24), 1551–1555.

Carruthers, J.H. (1995). *Mdw ntr: Divine speech.* London: Karnak House.

Cavendish, R. (1980). *The great religions.* New York: Arco Publishing.

Cervantes, J.M., & Ramírez, O. (1992). Spirituality and family dynamics in psychotherapy with Latino children. In L.A. Vargas & J.D. Koss-Chioino (Eds.), *Working with culture: Psychotherapeutic interventions with ethnic minority children and adolescents* (pp. 103–128). San Francisco: Jossey-Bass.

Chamberlain, T.J., & Hall, C.A. (2000). *Realized religion: Research on the relationship between religion and health.* Philadelphia, PA: Templeton Foundation Press.

Connors, G.J., Tonigan, J.S., & Miller, W.R. (1996). Measure of religious background and behavior for use in behavior change research. *Psychology of Addictive Behaviors, 10*(2), 90–96.

Csordas, T.J. (1987). Health and the holy in African and African American spirit possession. *Social Science and Medicine, 24*(1), 1–11.

Dossey, L. (1993). *Healing words: The power of prayer and the practice of medicine.* San Francisco: Harper Collins.

Edwards, K.L. (1987). Exploratory study of Black psychological health. *Journal of Religion and Health, 26,* 73–80.

Eliade, M., & Couliano, I.P. (1991). *The Eliade guide to world religions.* San Francisco: Harper San Francisco.

Elkins, D.N., Hedstrom, L.J., Hughes, L.L., Leaf, J.A., & Saunders, C. (1988). Toward a humanistic-phenomenological spirituality: Definition, description, and measurement. *Journal of Humanistic Psychology, 28*(4), 5–18.

Ellison, C.W. (1983). Spiritual well-being: Conceptualization and measurement. *Journal of Psychology and Theology, 11*(4), 330–340.

Ellison, C.G., & Levin, S.L. (1998). The religion-health connection: Evidence, theory, and future directions. *Health Education and Behavior, 25,* 700–720.

Epstein, M. (1995). *Thoughts without a thinker: Psychotherapy from a Buddhist perspective.* New York: Basic Books.

Fawzy, F.I., Kemeny, M.E., Fawzy, N.W., & Elashoff, R. (1990). A structured psychiatric intervention for cancer patients: Changes over time in immunological measures. *Archives of General Psychiatry, 47*(8), 729– 735.

Frank, J.D. (1982). Therapeutic components shared by all psychotherapies. In J.H. Harvey & M.M. Parks (Eds.), *Psychotherapy research and behavior change.* Washington, DC: American Psychological Association.

Freedman, J., & Combs, G. (1996). *Narrative therapy. The social construction of preferred realities.* New York: Norton.

Genia, V. (1995). *Counseling and psychotherapy of religious clients: A developmental approach.* Westport, CT: Praeger.

Genia, V. (1991). The Spiritual Experience Index: A measure of spiritual maturity. *Journal of Religion and Health, 30,* 337–347.

George, L.K., Larson, D.B., Koenig, H.G., & McCullough, M.E. (2000). Spirituality and health: What we know, what we need to know. *Journal of Social and Clinical Psychology, 19,* 102–116.

Good, B.J., & Good, M.D. (1980). The meaning of symptoms: A cultural hermeneutic model for clinical practice. In L. Eisenberg & A. Kleinman (Eds.), *The relevance of social science for medicine* (pp. 165–196). Boston: Reidel.

Griffith, E.E.H., English, T., & Mayfield, V. (1980). Possession, prayer, and testimony: Therapeutic aspects of the Wednesday night meeting in a Black church. *Psychiatry, 43,* 120–128.

Harris, R.C., Dew, M.A., Lee, A., Amaya, M., Buches, L., Reetz, D., & Coleman, G. (1995). The role of religion in heart-transplant recipients' long-term health and well-being. *Journal of Religion and Health, 34*(1), 17–32.

Hassan, M.K., & Khalique, A. (1981). Religiosity and its correlates in college students. *Journal of Psychological Research, 25,* 129–136.

Helm, H., Hays, J.C., Flint, E., Koenig, H.G., & Blazer, D.G. (2000). Effects of private religious activity on mortality of elderly disabled and nondisabled adults. *Journal of Gerontology, 55A,* M400–M405.

Hiatt, J.F. (1986). Spirituality, medicine, and healing. *Southern Medical Journal, 79*(6), 736–743.

Hill, P.C., & Hood, R.W., Jr. (1999). *Measures of religiosity.* Birmingham, AL: Religious Education Press.

Hodge, D. (2001). Spiritual assessment: A review of major qualitative methods and a new framework for assessing spirituality. *Social Work, 46*(3), 203–214.

Hoge, D.R. (1996). Religion in America: The demographics of belief and affiliation. In E.P. Shafranske (Ed.), *Religion and the clinical practice of psychology* (pp. 21–42). Washington, DC: American Psychological Association.

Hood, R.W., Jr., Spilka, B., Hunsberger, B., & Gorsuch, R. (1996). *The psychology of religion: An empirical approach* (2nd ed.). New York: Guilford.

Jacobs, C.F. (1990). Healing and prophesy in the Black spiritual churches: A need for re-examination. *Medical Anthropology, 12,* 349–370.

Jahn, J. (1990). *Muntu: African culture and the western world.* New York: Grove.

Jenkins, R.A. (1995). Religion and HIV: Implications for research and intervention. *Journal of Social Issues, 51*(2), 131–144.

Jones, J. (1986). Racism: A cultural analysis of the problem. In J.F. Dovidio & S.L. Gaertner (Eds.), *Prejudice, discrimination, and racism* (pp. 279–314). New York: Academic.

Jones, S.L. (1994). A constructive relationship for religion with the science and profession of psychology. *American Psychologist, 49,* 184–199.

Kass, J.D., Friedman, R., Leserman, J., Zuttermeister, P.C., & Benson, H. (1991). Health outcomes and a new index of spiritual experience. *Journal for the Scientific Study of Religion, 30* (2), 203–211.

Kelly, E.W., Jr. (1995). *Spirituality and religion in counseling and psychotherapy: Diversity in theory and practice.* Washington, DC: American Counseling Association.

Koenig, H.G., McCullough, M.E., & Larson, D.B. (2001). *Handbook of religion and health.* New York: Oxford University Press.

Koenig, H.G., Meador, K.G., & Parkerson, G. (1997). Religion index for psychiatric research. *American Journal of Psychiatry, 154,* 885–886.

Kosmin, B., & Lachman, S. (1993). *One nation under God. Religion in contemporary American society.* New York: Crown.

Krucoff, M.W., Crater, S.W., Green, C.L., Maas, A.C., Seskevich, J.E., Lane, J.D., Loeffler, K.A., Morris, K., Bashore, T.M., & Koenig, H.G. (2001). Integrative noetic therapies as adjuncts to percutaneous intervention during unstable coronary syndromes: The monitoring and actualization of noetic trainings (MANTRA) feasibility pilot. *American Heart Journal, 142,* 760–797.

Kuhn, C.C. (1988). A spiritual inventory of the medically ill patient. *Psychiatric Medicine, 6*(2), 87–100.

Larson, D.B., Swyers, J.P., & McCullough, M.E. (1997). *Scientific Research on Spirituality and Health: A Consensus Report*. Rockville, MD: National Institute on Healthcare Research.

Levin, J. (2001). *God, faith, and health: Exploring the spirituality-healing connection*. New York: John Wiley & Sons.

Lovinger, R.J. (1996). Considering the religious dimension in assessment and treatment. In E.P. Shafranske (Ed.), *Religion and the clinical practice of psychology* (pp. 327–364). Washington, DC: American Psychological Association.

Maier, S.F., Watkins, L.R., & Fleshner, M. (1994). Psychoneuroimmunology: The interface between behavior, brain, and immunity. *American Psychologist, 49*(12), 1004–1017.

Malony, H.N. (1988). The clinical assessment of optimal religious functioning. *Review of Religious Research, 30*, 2–17.

Matthews, D.A., Larson, D.B., & Barry, C.P. (1995). *The faith factor: An annotated bibliography of clinical research on spiritual subjects. Volume I*. Rockville, MD: National Institute for Mental Healthcare Research.

Mbiti, J.S. (1969). *African religions and philosophies*. Garden City, NY: Anchor.

McGuire, M.B. (1988). *Ritual healing in suburban America*. New Brunswick, NJ: Rutgers University Press.

McKee, D.D., & Chappel, J.N. (1992). Spirituality and medical practice. *The Journal of Family Practice, 35*(2), 201–208.

McQuellon, R.P., & Hurt, G. (1993). The healing power of cancer stories. *Journal of Psychosocial Oncology, 11*(4), 95–108.

Meissner, W.W. (1996). The pathology of beliefs and the beliefs of pathology. In E.P. Shafranske (Ed.), *Religion and the clinical practice of psychology* (pp. 241–267). Washington, DC: American Psychological Association.

Nunn, J.F. (1996). *Ancient Egyptian medicine*. Norman, OK: University of Oklahoma Press.

Oxman, T.E., Freeman, D.H., & Manheimer, E.D. (1995). Lack of social participation or religious strength and comfort as risk factors for death after cardiac surgery in the elderly. *Psychosomatic Medicine, 57*, 5– 15.

Pargament, K.I. (1996). Religious methods of coping: Resources for the conservation and transformation of significance. In E.P. Shafranske (Ed.), *Religion and the clinical practice of psychology* (pp. 215–239). Washington, DC: American Psychological Association.

Pargament, K.I. (1997). *The psychology of religion and coping*. New York: Guilford.

Pargament, K.I., Ensing, D.S., Falgout, K., Olsen, H., Reilly, B., Van Haitsma, K., & Warren, R. (1990). God help me: Religious coping efforts as predictors of the outcomes to significant negative life events. *American Journal of Community Psychology, 18*(6), 793–824.

Payne, I.R., Bergin, A.E., & Loftus, P.E. (1992). A review of attempts to integrate spiritual and standard psychotherapy techniques. *Journal of Psychotherapy Integration, 2*, 171–192.

Piedmont, R.L. (2001). Spiritual transcendence and the scientific study of spirituality. *Journal of Rehabilitation, 67*, 4–14.

Plante, T.G. & Sherman, A.C. (Eds.). (2001). *Faith and health: Psychological perspectives*. New York: Guilford Press.

Pope-Davis, D.B., Reynolds, A.L., & Vasquez, L.A. (1994). *Multicultural counseling: Issues of diversity. A video workbook* (for multicultural counseling video #2). Iowa City, IA: University of Iowa.

Potts, R.G. (1996). Spirituality and the experience of cancer in an African–American community: Implications for psychosocial oncology. *Journal of Psychosocial Oncology, 14*(1), 1–19.

Propst, L.R. (1980). The comparative efficacy of religious and nonreligious imagery for the treatment of mild depression in religious individuals. *Cognitive Therapy and Research, 4*, 167–178.

Propst, L.R. (1996). Cognitive-behavioral therapy and the religious person. In E.P. Shafranske (Ed.), *Religion and the clinical practice of psychology* (pp. 391–407). Washington, DC: American Psychological Association.

Propst, L.R., Ostrom, R., Watkins, P., Dean, T., & Mashburn, D. (1992). Comparative efficacy of religious and nonreligious cognitive–behavioral therapy for the treatment of clinical depression in religious individuals. *Journal of Consulting and Clinical Psychology, 60*, 94–103.

Ramírez, M. (1983). *Psychology of the Americas: Mestizo perspectives on personality and mental health*. New York: Pergamon.

Ramos-McKay, J.M., Comas-Díaz, L., & Rivera, L.A. (1988). Puerto Ricans. In L. Comas-Díaz & E.E.H. Griffith (Eds.), *Clinical guidelines in cross-cultural mental health* (pp. 204–232). New York: Wiley.

Rangaswami, K. (1994). Self-actualization and beyond: Union with universal self, the highest motive from Indian perspective. *Indian Journal of Clinical Psychology, 21*(2), 45–50.

Reed, P.G. (1992). An emerging paradigm for the investigation of spirituality in nursing. *Research in Nursing and Health, 15*, 349–357.

Richards, D. (1990). The implications of African American spirituality. In M.K. Asante & K.W.

Asante (Eds.), *African culture: The rhythms of unity*. Trenton, NJ: Africa World.

Richards, P.S., & Bergin, A.E. (1997). *A spiritual strategy for counseling and psychotherapy*. Washington, DC: American Psychological Association.

Richardson, B.L. (1991). Utilizing the resources of the African American church: Strategies for counseling professionals. In C.C. Lee & B.L. Richardson (Eds.), *Multicultural issues in counseling: New approaches to diversity* (pp. 65–75). Alexandria, VA: American Counseling Association.

Rizzuto, A. (1996). Psychoanalytic treatment and the religious person. In E.P. Shafranske (Ed.), *Religion and the clinical practice of psychology* (pp. 433–460). Washington, DC: American Psychological Association

Rizvi, S.A.A. (1989). *Muslim tradition in psychotherapy and modern trends*. Lahore, Pakistan: Institute of Islamic Culture.

Rubel, A., O'Nell, C., & Collado-Ardon, R. (1984). *Susto: A folk illness*. Berkeley: University of California Press.

Saudia, T.L., Kinney, M.R., Brown, K.C., & Young-Ward, L. (1991). Health locus of control and helpfulness of prayer. *Heart & Lung, 20*(1), 60–65.

Saur, M.S., & Saur, W.G. (1992). Images of God: A study of psychoanalyzed adults. In M. Finn & J. Gartner (Eds.), *Object relations theory and religion: Clinical applications* (pp. 129–140). Westport, CT: Praeger Publishers.

Shafranske, E.P., & Malony, H.N. (1996). Religion and the clinical practice of psychology: A case for inclusion. In E.P. Shafranske (Ed.), *Religion and the clinical practice of psychology* (pp. 561–586). Washington, DC: American Psychological Association.

Sherrill, K.A., & Larson, D.B. (1988). Adult burn patients: The role of religion in recovery. *Southern Medical Journal, 81*(7), 821–825.

Sodestrom, K.E., & Martinson, I.M. (1987). Patients' spiritual coping strategies: A study of nurse and patient perspectives. *Oncology Nursing Forum, 14*(2), 41–45.

Spiegel, D., Bloom, J.R., Kraemer, H.C., & Gottheil, E. (1989). Effect of psychosocial treatment on survival of patients with metastatic breast cancer. *Lancet, 2,* 888–891.

Steere, D.A. (1997). *Spiritual presence in psychotherapy: A guide to caregivers*. New York: Brunner/Mazel.

Tan, S. (1996). Religion in clinical practice: Implicit and explicit integration. In E.P. Shafranske (Ed.), *Religion and the clinical practice of psychology* (pp. 365–387). Washington, DC: American Psychological Association

Thoresen, C.E. (1999). Spirituality and health: Is there a relationship? *Journal of Health Psychology, 4,* 291–300

Vande Kemp, H. (1996). Historical perspective: Religion and clinical psychology in America. In E.P. Shafranske (Ed.), *Religion and the clinical practice of psychology* (pp. 71–112). Washington, DC: American Psychological Association

Watson, W.H. (1984). Introduction. In W.H. Watson (Ed.), *Black folk medicine: The therapeutic significance of faith and trust* (pp. 1–15). New Brunswick, NJ: Transaction Books.

White, M., & Epston, D. (1990). *Narrative means to therapeutic ends*. New York: Norton.

Yates, J., Chalmer, B., St. James, P., Follansbee, M., & McKegney, F. (1981). Religion in patients with advanced cancer. *Medical and Pediatric Oncology, 9,* 121–128.

Janet K. Long

16

Medical Art Therapy: Using Imagery and Visual Expression in Healing

Imagery exercises for healing are now commonly used in the fields of health psychology and medicine. This chapter will explore the addition of art therapy in the production and application of personal imagery in healing: concretizing and transforming physical states using art processes.

Uses of the imagination in healing are as old as the most ancient shamanic cultures. The power of the human psyche to produce both negative and positive images that have dramatic impact upon health has been explored in modern studies on stress and mind-body healing (Achterberg, 1985; Rossi, 1986). Medical art therapy approaches have been used in formal practice since the 1970's (Long, Chapman, Appleton, Abrams, & Palmer, 1989; Long, 1994, 2001; Anand & Anand, 1997; Packman et al., 1998; Mal-chiodi (Ed.), 1998, 1999; Koepher, 2000; Luzzatto, & Gabriel, 2000; Chapman et al., 2001). Medical art therapy is an approach to healing that draws upon ancient and modern traditions, wherein process imagery produced in the mind of the client/patient is translated to the page through drawing, painting or collage media, or sculpted into three-dimensional forms. This art forms a living record of the person's internal and external experience of the symptom, illness or chronic condition. Transforming a negative somatic picture held in the mind of the client to a creative and positive artistic experience, holding special metaphoric meaning, is the essence of this art

therapy approach (Long, 1989, 1994, 1995, 1996, 1997, 2001).

This chapter begins with a discussion of a developmental perspective, clarifying differences in the graphic and conceptual abilities between pediatric and adult clients seen in hospital outpatient and inpatient settings. The processes of metaphoric thinking and symbol formation are then explored using different historical references. This author's use of medical art therapy interventions with cancer, arthritis and migraine patients will then focus on the structure and process of patients developing imagery and artwork for symptom reduction and healing. A summary of this work, noting further applications, concludes the chapter.

Developmental Considerations

Kagin and Lusebrink (1978) developed The Expressive Therapies Continuum, the most inclusive developmental paradigm for understanding art expression and its relationship to activating creativity throughout the lifespan. This paradigm combines information from neurological research on how the human brain processes imagery with sensory-motor-integration, cognitive, psychosocial, and self psychology theories of human development (Lusebrink, 1990):

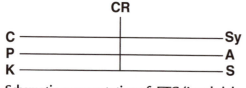

Schematic representation of ETC (Lusebrink, 1990, p. 92)

Starting from the bottom at the first level on the continuum, Kinesthetic-Sensory (K/S), all humans explore the nature of art materials and the objects around them in a merged and rhythmic fashion: moving all parts of the body and using all the senses to explore themselves through the texture and color of the art media. A sense of relaxation and stability are achieved at this level. Imagine a child freely moving the paints across a piece of fingerpaint paper, delighting in the slick and easy way the paint connects with the hands and glides onto the paper. Details are not important to the child, only the bodily expression of the movement of paint onto the paper.

The second level on the Expressive Therapies Continuum, Perceptual-Affective (P/A), reflects the person's abilities to explore the structural properties, the form, of art media, and to modify this form with feeling. An inner dialog develops between the person and the art media, reflective of the inner organization of the person as he/she discovers the natural boundaries of self and other (symbolically, the art materials). The person experiences less merging with the materials and begins to develop some reflective distance, the ability to observe self in action. Some clients are unable to experience affect in this process; a few being diagnosed with alexithymia. The clinician's challenge is to start at the Kinesthetic-Sensory level of experience with these clients, giving them the developmental, neurological support they need before proceeding with more demanding art therapy exercises.

The third level of the Expressive Therapies Continuum is the Cognitive-Symbolic Level (C/Sy). While engaged in the cognitive aspect of this level, the person is using analytic, logical, sequential thought while operating and acting on the art materials. Verbalization is added to this problem-solving mode, giving the person greater reflective distance and the opportunity to use art therapy experience to symbolically transform internal states. Intuition plays a significant role in the symbolic aspect of this level, allowing for the realization of symbols. Intuitive concept formation leads to the experience of meaning in the artwork, deepening the entire bodily experience for the client artist. The ability to separate self from other more effortlessly reflects the inner psychic ability of the client to be both regressive and progressive in the expression of the illness through the art media.

The final and fourth level of this continuum, The Creative Level (CR), demonstrates the ultimate in human ability: to synthesize experience through the creative process, the individual bridges inner and outer psychic realities to achieve resolution and a creative product that represents an awareness of inner physiological states and symbolic symptom transformation. The creative process experienced at this level translates into physiological responses in the autonomic nervous, endocrine and immune systems of a client, evidenced by a healing effect (Achterberg, 1985; Rossi, 1986).

To illustrate this paradigm in a practical way, imagine a four-year-old child showing his/her therapist a scribbled design on paper made with a thick red crayon, saying, "You see, my head and stomach hurt just like this!" The therapist asks the child to show again what the hurt looks like; the child scribbles in a tangled fashion with the red crayon on the white paper. Now the therapist instructs the child to imagine the red lines getting smoothed out, de-tangled; so the child is taught to gradually make smoother and smoother red lines on several pieces of white paper. The therapist asks the child to now imagine (with closed eyes, if possible) these smoother lines being inside his/her head and stomach; further, the therapist asks the child to think of a color that would be soothing and pleasant. The child opens his/her eyes and draws the smoother lines in this new color. The therapist again asks the child to now imagine this new color drawn in the smoothest lines and place this image inside his/her head and stomach. Children are usually able to visualize the suggested transplantation of symbols. The therapist again asks the child to tell how the pain feels after each imagic shift. Most children learn this way to transform pain over time using repetitions of this changing imagic process. By using all of the levels on the continuum, even a child at the scribble stage of graphic development (Lowenfeld, 1970) can give form and feeling to the sensory experience of the pain and learn simple cognitive and symbolic ways to transform the pain experience. This example also shows the visualization capability of this four year old, the ability to learn self-hypnotic, autogenic (pre-verbal) methods for self-awareness using art media. (The child unable to learn this method is usually not atuned to visual thinking, is emotionally blocked, or has organic impairment.)

Understanding the stages of graphic art development is useful for those treating medical clients, not only those working with children but also for those clinicians screening for regression and/or organicity in their adult clients (Uhlin, 1984; Rubin, 1978; Drachnik, 1995). For example, adults will regress to early stages of graphic development during emotional and physiological stress and illness. Adults with organic signs will sometimes use the random scribble patterns of a young child to represent objects, the lines repeating themselves (perseveration) and not meeting or forming recognizable shapes.

Basically, the first stage of graphic development begins at 12 to 18 months when a child is able to hold a drawing tool and scribble randomly and uncontrollably across a sheet of paper. When playing with clay, pounding and pinching and smearing this wet media delights and stimulates the child. A lack of eye-hand coordination is apparent in this stage.

Between 18 and 24 months of age, the child has the beginning of visual-motor control and proceeds to wave a crayon back and forth on the paper in a push-pull motion, the "swing scribble" (Pasto, 1964). In clay, he/she is able to make a snake-like coil. And between 24 and 30 months of age, the child can make a "circular form" in his/her scribble, and has

the motor ability to make a round ball from a lump of clay. By 36 months, the child is able to experiment with figure-ground relationships by scribbling vertical and horizontal lines across the page and "naming" them. And by the time the child reaches 3 1/2 years, he/she is able to make and name sun and radial shapes, and combine coils and balls of clay to sculpt decorative forms.

At about 4 years old, the child makes a cognitive and emotional leap and creates his/her first figure, drawing a circle with features and stick-like arms and legs coming out of this circle-body (a "tadpole" figure). The ability to control his/her shapes delights the child, and other shapes like triangles, crosses, squares and rectangles are soon to fill out the repertory in drawings and clay figures. From 4 ½ to 6 ½ years old, "pre-schematic" development is achieved: The child can perceive figures in motion on a line, use colors realistically, make up stories about his/her artwork, and generally use the same symbolic form for the same subject each time.

From 6 ½ to 9 years of age, the "schematic" stage is entered: A baseline is consistent in drawings and many new objects in the child's environment are represented – trees, houses, people with well-defined bodies (head, features, neck, torso, arms and legs in the correct places, with details of clothes, etc.), clouds and sun in the sky, and so forth. Art has become a nonverbal form of language. By 9 years and up, depth perception appears; people can be drawn in action, positioned in a landscape so that there is the illusion of depth. There is now overlapping of figure-ground elements and the child is capable of inventing details and designs that are individual favorites.

By 12 years old, children can think and work abstractly and with problem-solving ability with art materials and can be trained in the techniques of drawing, painting, collage-assemblage, and sculpture. The artwork develops from very realistic to highly abstract features and tells the stories of the budding adolescent's interests and obsessions. Some adults show that they have not reached this level, but are rather stuck in the schematic stage (parallel to the cognitive level of concrete operations).

Metaphoric Thinking and Symbol Formation

Medical art therapy draws upon each client's developmental and idiosyncratic abilities to represent and metamorphize inner experience using visualization and art experience. From a dynamic point of view, art and free spontaneous creative expression can aid in the release of unconscious, repressed emotions and conflicts that may be too threatening to discuss (Naumberg, 1966). The art process is a means of sublimation and catharsis; art making is equated with ego building (Kramer, 1979). Symbols serve as the connection between reality and human thought and fantasy. Through making visual images the capacity to symbolize is developed (Wilson, 1987). The ability to symbolize is a link to other complex mental representations (images, fantasies, thoughts, concepts, intuitions and dreams).

Children operate out of the developmental schema presented in the section above (Rosal, 1996), but they also have specific preferences regarding choices of art media. They might be limited by age-appropriate skill level, but nevertheless use imaginative ingenuity to describe and transform symptoms and learn new coping skills.

Older adolescents and adults possess a full range of established abilities, but sometimes need to develop a facility for imaginative thinking. By starting at the Kinesthetic-Sensory Level of activity, the therapist is able to guide the adult client into imaginative play. For example, the therapist asks his/her client to choose a colored marker, and with eyes closed, scribble with a big continuous line on an 18 × 24 inch piece of white drawing paper for a few seconds. The client then is instructed to open his/her eyes and look at the scribble from each of the four sides of the drawing. The therapist asks, "What do you see in this scribble? You may see something from each vantage point, but now choose one image out of the these to develop into a picture. You can use all the colors here to enhance your image." This scribble projection technique (Betensky, 1973) opens the world of imaginary possibilities to an adult not facile, or simply out of practice, using projective visual abilities. After such warm-up art exercises, the therapist usually has a more cooperative, risk-taking client, with whom to move toward exploring the sensations and personal experiences of his/her illness. If a client still says, "I can't draw," then the therapist can use preformed media, such as magazine photo collage or sandplay, to encourage the client into the visual expression of his/her inner and outer experiences.

Art materials are transformers. As soon as you set a marker to paper and draw something, you have transformed nothing into something. As soon as a client draws a red tangle of lines to represent a headache, he/she has externalized the inner sensation and can then reflect on the image. The very act of doing this gives the client the needed distance to use other faculties to further describe or change the tangled lines.

The metaphoric power of taking these steps toward transforming the pain or discomfort into some other form and feeling is an ancient human capacity (Arnheim, 1974). Our relatively big visual cortex, connecting to our other brain centers, directly accesses the central, autonomic and somatic nervous systems (Achterberg & Lawlis, 1980; Achterberg, 1985). Thus, we can directly influence the functioning of our bodies via the process of making images to positively alter pain signals and dysfunctional patterns of illness. The ability to turn on needed neurotransmitters, change the path of pain, and change the chemistry of pain seems to be a human capacity.

Metaphoric thinking connects us to this very human capacity to heal ourselves. Just as meditation allows the body to lower vital rates of breathing and heart rate for deep restorative rest, so imagery allows us to alter our state of consciousness and access our somatic reality at the deepest level for healing (Achterberg, 1985; Rossi, 1986; Weil, 1995; Lusebrink & Long, 1998).

Rossi (1986) emphasizes state-dependent memory and learning modalities in mind-body communication: imagery and behavior are vitally linked with sensation (perception) and identity (actualization process), which are linked to emotion (representation and psychophysiological processes) and cognitive awareness (self-reflective and psychosynthetic processes). Using this model, Rossi integrates the study of how information is internally transmitted, transduced (changes form), and is sometimes "stuck" in a state-bound form (i. e., cellular memory of the injury, trauma, experience of an illness) so that it becomes what a person labels the symptom or problem. He equates this to C.G. Jung's process of depth psychology, where the "transcendent function" integrates conscious and unconscious elements. When Jung's patients became overwhelmed with emotions, he would sometimes have them draw a picture of their feelings. Once the feelings were expressed in the form of imagery, the patient was encouraged to use active imagination and let the images speak to one another (Jung, 1960, pp. 67–91). Once this dialog could take place, the patient was well embarked on the process of reconciling different aspects of his/her dissociated (repressed) psyche (Jung, 1960, pp. 81–83). In this process, the patient gains possession of the misdirected energy, letting fantasy and imagery be allowed the freest possible play, clarifying affect and its content, and creating new internal pathways of understanding (knowing).

Medical Art Therapy with Cancer Patients

Cancer patients deal with the impact of their illness in varying ways: pragmatic acceptance, surrender, or a fighting determination to beat the odds and survive. Life-threatening illness brings to the fore all the coping skills the person possesses. Inner struggles to maintain hope while enduring surgeries and treatments, manifest themselves in many ways. Fortunately, the progressive cancer centers at major hospitals incorporate psychological support for patients, including individual and group art therapy sessions.

Adults have abstract conceptual skills to express the impact of the cancer on their daily lives and to portray the physiological effects cancer has exerted on their bodies. They can also conceptualize and express the struggle of their immune system (Achterberg, 1985) to fight the cancer cells and restore balance using "helper" cells. Using imagery and visual expression to portray this thematic material is both natural and effective for many patients.

I first start working with adults by having them tell me the story of their cancer: how it was discovered; how they have responded to their treatment and to the health professionals with whom they have sought help; how they feel at the present time; how they have managed in their daily lives; how this illness has impacted their work lives and their home lives; what sort of support system is in place or not; what pain or discomfort they have experienced in the past and now; what ways of thinking or feeling seem to have helped them through the illness so far; and what activities they find pleasant and comforting now. After the client tells me this story, I explain to him/her that creating imagery in art therapy becomes easier after some relaxation training.

I will illustrate a simple relaxation method. I ask the client to sit or lie in a very comfortable position, and explain that I will guide him/her through a visual scanning of the body. As they breathe and allow their body to rest heavily onto the chair or couch, they are asked to notice any sensation or tension in each area of their body, from head to feet. They are asked if these sensations have any certain feeling or words or shapes or colors that appear as they focus their attention on each area. They are reminded to breathe easily and allow any images to appear as their attention now floats from area to area. As the client opens his/her eyes, I ask him/her to "Open your eyes, and tell me anything you noticed during this relaxation experience."

This recounting is usually done first in words and then in drawing or painting media. Each person chooses the art media that seems easiest and begins to create the image(s) that came into awareness. This spontaneous art may reflect pain, tension, or any

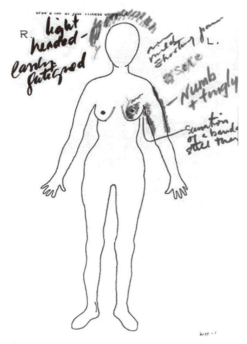

Figure 1.

Figure 2.

other sensation felt in the body, or an emotion. This free art assignment gives me the opportunity to observe each client's energy level, approach to doing something novel, interaction style, thinking style, and affective state. It also begins to give me a diagnostic picture of how this person is coping with his/her illness.

If the person needs more structure, I ask him/her to draw the outline of his/her body and to map in the sensations and images using colors and shapes. Some people need the structure of a predrawn body outline (these are sometimes standard printouts in pain clinics and cancer centers).

Figure 1 shows the use of a predrawn body outline by a 55-year-old professional woman. She did this drawing in her first medical art therapy session three weeks after having breast cancer surgery (lumpectomy). As she notes on the paper, she feels light-headed, is easily fatigued, and uses the color orange to map in the "mild, shocking pain" and the underarm sensation of a "bandage still there." She uses blue and purple markers to map in the predominant "numb and tingly" sensa-

tion in the inside area of her left breast, the actual site of the surgery. Figure 2 is her free drawing revealing how the diagnosis of cancer and the surgery has affected her life. She stands in the middle of the drawing, with her two grown children at each side. Lots of questions rim her head, along with heartfelt feelings for friends who have given her support. She notes at the top of the page "play, art, rest and fun," the activities she wants to enact in her life now. At the bottom of the page she deals with the "good news" that her type of cancer has a 90% chance of not recurring in five years. On the left side of the paper, she reveals how scared she feels about the upcoming radiation treatments. And on the right side of the page she draws about her financial worries, as she has just quit a stressful job and will need to find other work when her temporary disability payments stop. In this first session, her first two drawings tell the story of her terror, fatigue, pain, anticipatory fear, support system, and pragmatic concerns brought to consciousness, expressed and reflected upon in the drawings. She felt relieved in seeing all her experience organized in the

Figure 3.

Figure 4.

Figure 5.

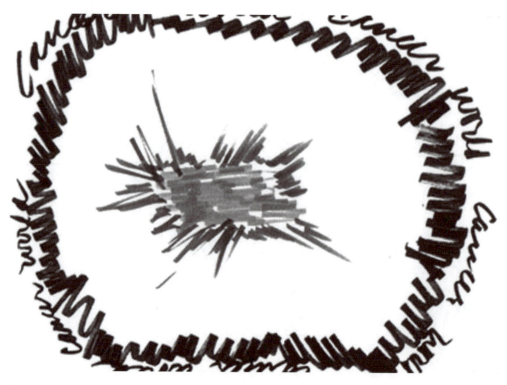

Figure 6.

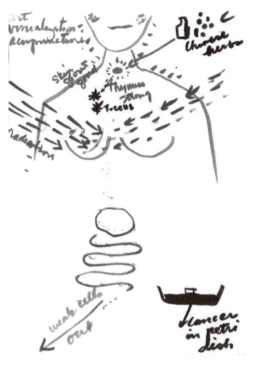

drawings; she now wanted to start healing the wound in her breast and also healing the stressful quality of her life.

During the next three sessions, this client was able to begin the healing process. In Figure 3, she uses the watercolor markers to draw a circle of good energy around her healing breast. And in Figure 4, she likens rebuilding her life after the cancer surgery to the period in her life when her husband left her home to be with another woman, resulting in divorce. Figure 5 shows her mending her heart again, handling the onset of radiation treatments, learning to rest while she looks for new work, and spending more time with family and friends. All of these images were reinforced and augmented through hypnotic relaxation and creating worlds in the sandtray.

In the three following sessions she was able to contrast the depressive feelings she was experiencing during the radiation treatments, Figure 6, with the positive visualization meditations that became her daily routine, Figures

Figure 7.

Figure 8.

7, 8, 9, and 10. In Figure 7 she is asked to draw her immune system, and represents her strong thymus gland and T-cells fighting against the cancer cells remaining after the surgery. She also includes the radiation, Chinese herbs, acupuncture, positive visualization and art therapy she is receiving to help this fight. The weak cells are being excreted from her body. To reframe her fears about receiving the radiation treatments, she liked the idea of drawing into a scratch-board, revealing the fluorescent orange lines underneath, Figure 8, representing the radiation targeting any cancer cells present in her breast. Her visualizations became much more specific as she educated herself about the cells in her body: Figure 9 shows a T-cell injecting "poison" into a cancer cell, the cancer cell being hollowed out as the T-cell "sucks the life out of it" and the dead cancer cell with the "T-cells on top." Her next drawing, Figure 10, shows the same process happening in full color inside her breast (using pink, orange, green, blue and yellow soft pastels). The affective quality of both her diagrams and self drawings helped her form a positive picture of the "fight" against cancer becoming her psychic reality, which in turn helped her better cope with the healing process and the side-effects from the radiation treatment.

Some children under the ages of 9 to 12 find drawing their illness and pain onto a body map very frightening. These children think that by drawing the cancer and their pain onto a self representation that the drawing will "make it so," i. e., that drawing it makes it real, maybe worse, and overwhelming (unchangeable). Some adults also reject drawing the illness for the same reason. These adults, rather that focusing their attention on internal states, need to express thoughts and feelings regarding their illness using more concrete and external symbols and imagery.

One 6-year-old boy with acute lymphocytic leukemia (ALL), referred from a local children's hospital for medical art therapy, overcame his trauma-related depression and anxiety by drawing and sculpting animals that were both wounded and heroically triumphant. Some of these symbols were created after invasive procedures, e. g., lumbar punctures and catheter or shunt placements. As shown in Figure 11, this is a drawing of a sphinx figure, a cross between a dragon and a dinosaur, with an anchor in his upper chest. This symbolic drawing of his own shunt being anchored in his chest, allowed this child to express feelings about the wound and his rage at being ill with cancer (fire coming from the creature's mouth). It is also an archetypal statement about his survival instincts in the face of terminal illness (this was his second round of chemotherapy since being rediagnosed after a period of remission).

To help this child cope better with painful, invasive procedures, he was given choices about creating distraction objects/toys to use before, during, and after upcoming procedures. This boy loved making art and chose to make Native American motif rattles. The first rattle, Figure 12, was made from a dried gourd that had a rounded top and a cylindrical bottom. This child painted designs and a snake on the top part, and used the bottom part as a handle. This rattle was made in one session, after which it was brought to every medical appointment by this boy. He played his rattle instrument before, during, and after procedures, and taught the nurses and doctors that this positive therapeutic distraction tool was a far better way to cope with the chemotherapy and other "pokes." After a few months using this rattle, he made another one out of a dried piece of sea kelp that had a pod on its end. In his sandtrays, this boy had used many animal helper figures to help battle many evil forces, so he chose the tiger as the animal he painted onto the round kelp pod, Figure 13. He decided that this rattle was going to be about "power," later understanding this to be *his* power to cope and to overcome the cancer cells invading his body. He put about a cup of dried corn into the long tail of the kelp (to create the rattle sound), and glued the end shut using a snail seashell. Then he painted other animals onto this long piece and glued a piece of leather in the middle for a handgrip. Later he added a bone and stone necklace and a feather sash to his rattle (Figure 13a). This rattle was

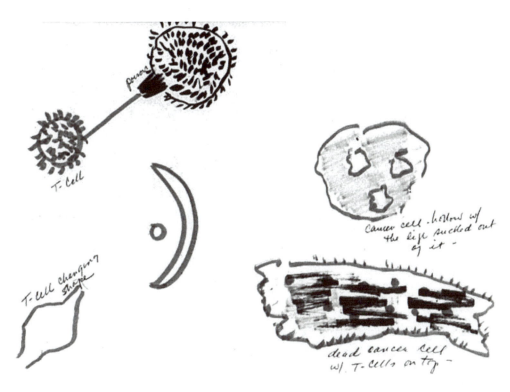

Figure 9.

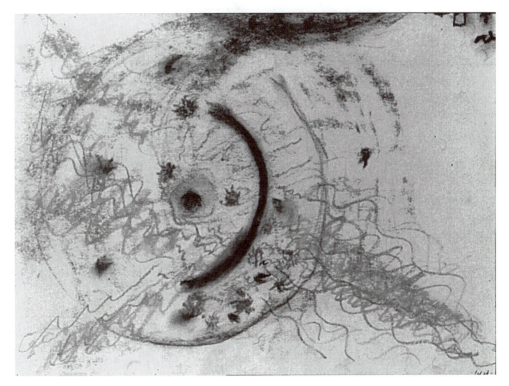

Figure 10.

Figure 11.

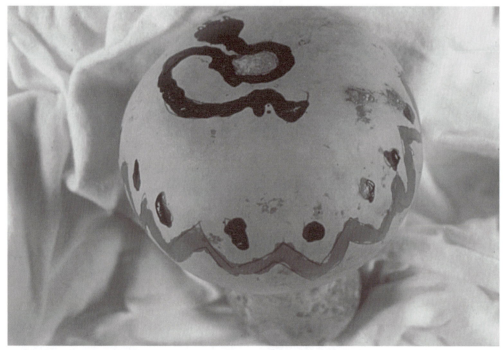

Figure 12.

Figure 13.

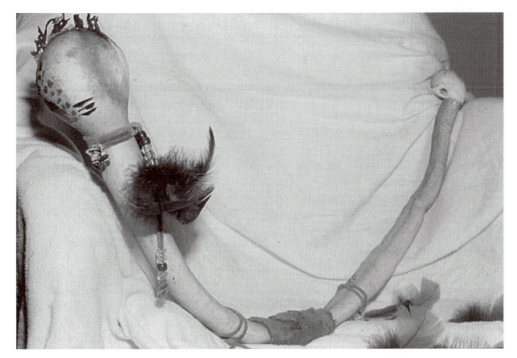

Figure 13a.

brought to many medical appointments, but most of the time was hung over his bed, he told me, for "protection."

Making a series of artworks provides a container for transformation. This child became less depressed and anxious as a result of weekly art therapy sessions where he was joined by the therapist in the free expression of his inner life. Concrete, knowable symbols became his talisman for weathering his illness. Identifying with strong characters allowed him to master the victim role and identify with the victorious. This is illustrated in Figures 14 and 15, where he draws characters modeled after those in his comic books: The creature (14) with huge teeth, fierce enough "to eat your heart out," and the hero figure (15) "ready to fight evil for true justice." This boy went into remission again after drawing these heroic comic-like figures on their quests, drawings that were predictive of changes in this boy's fight over cancer.

Many children experiencing cancer treatment need more than verbally based support and desensitization to help cope with procedures (Long & Sedberry, 1994). For example: A 7-year-old girl, after her cancer was in remission, needed a follow-up MRI procedure but was so terrified of the MRI machine that she refused to lay in it. As part of the art therapy session, we visited the MRI machine, recorded its sound, took a polaroid photo of it, and returned to the therapy office to enact a baby doll having this test. She chose the baby doll and constructed an MRI machine from cardboard, plexiglas, construction paper and markers (Figure 16). She play-acted the doll having the test inside the machine, playing the recording we had made. Then she learned how to transfer this play in a self-hypnotic manner to herself, imagining that she was in the machine, that she was a little nervous but nonetheless could lay still like the doll while the test took place. This form of desensitization using play and art supplies is a very effective method to lessen the anticipatory fear for children. Figure 17 shows other types of play therapy equipment used to prepare children for surgery, procedures and tests.

Medical Art Therapy with Arthritis Patients

Whether the arthritis sufferer is diagnosed with osteoarthritis (OA) or rheumatoid arthritis (RA), the imagery for the illness seems to be locked, painful, red, swollen and stiff joints and surrounding tissue. During periods of inflammation, the hot, sharp fire quality of sensation in the tissues predominates the conscious awareness of the patient. When the fire is put out, stiffness and dull pain returns and the person goes back to his/her accommodating behaviors.

After she had tried six years of arthritis treatments at a nearby medical center (drugs for pain, physical therapy, gold injections, cortico-steroid and chlorambicil injections and tablets), a 79-year-old woman with rheumatoid arthritis was referred for medical art therapy. This woman was house-bound at that time, unable to leave her apartment without a great deal of help. She wanted desperately to stay independent, to keep her apartment and not to be forced by the crippling nature of her illness into an intermediate care facility.

I began to make weekly home visits to her small apartment to do medical art therapy. She was very motivated to try this new treatment modality; she had always enjoyed viewing art in museums and in books, and one of her daughters and a granddaughter were trained painters. She also enjoyed making copper enamel dishes and tile-mosaic objects at the senior center before her illness kept her from leaving home. Having this positive belief system about the value of art made her introduction to art therapy processes easy.

We set up a cardtable near her front window so that she could make art between our sessions when she felt the urge. She chose watercolor markers, crayons, oil pastels, and notebook-size white drawing paper as her art supplies. She drew five images in her first session describing how her body felt with intractable RA pain. The first image was of a five-pointed star, a symbol for herself, with red hot pain inside, and an outer layer of blue

Figure 14.

Figure 15.

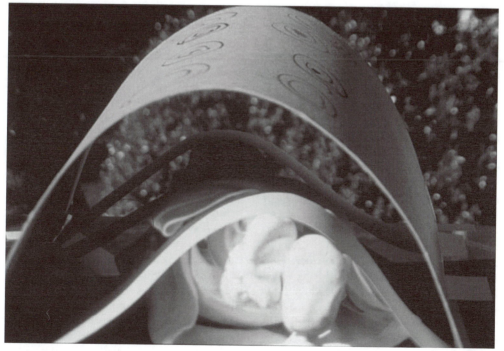

Figure 16.

Figure 17.

numbness that was interrupted by black poking lines, "needling" pain. A little patch of green grass was drawn under the star, "A small feeling of comforting nature," she told me.

She then drew several images of how she did not like the effects of taking drugs, saying, "They fuzz up my head; I like to keep my head clear." One drawing showed a person whose body was filled with the hot molten lava from the center of the earth. She said of this drawing, "This is how deep the pain comes from, up from the center of the earth into my body."

The symbolic nature of this drawing also referred to her life story, that of being a refugee, a widow with two daughters to raise, making her way to this country during WWII and making an independent start here. This was a very strong woman who was not accustomed to being sick and lying in bed with pain much of the day.

The hand-drawn, full-body pain map came after these other descriptive drawings, Figure 18. She drew the worst pain areas in thick red crayon and the lesser pain areas in light red crayon. Since there were so many painful regions in her body, I asked her if she would like to address all these areas together, or whether she would like to more fully represent a few pain areas. She chose the pain in her shoulders and her feet to "work on first," as the pain in these areas prevented her from putting on a coat or wearing shoes. Her drawing of the pressured, hot pain in her shoulders and feet can be seen in Figure 19. She told me she had tried rubbing old-fashioned liniment into these areas, even wrapping them in soft wool, but without positive results. Figure 20 shows her shoulder areas with the liniment on, plus the pressured feeling portrayed as big talons gripping each of her shoulders. Using an active imagination fantasy, I guided her to imagine what sort of bird belonged to those big talons. She spent the remainder of the session drawing a larger version of the "purple monster" she experienced as the pressured pain in her shoulders, Figure 21. I asked her to visualize this image when she was resting

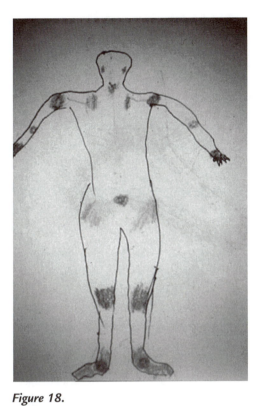

Figure 18.

Figure 19.

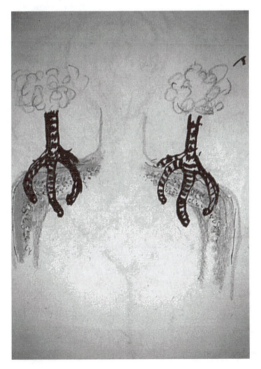

Figure 20.

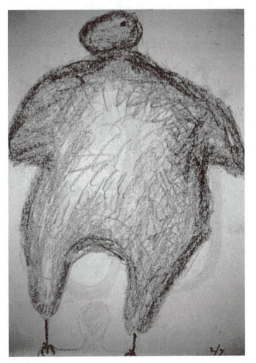

Figure 21.

Figure 22.

during the next week, letting any image appear that might be able to guide her in dealing with this "monster" pain. When I returned the following week on my home visit, she showed me how she had "electrocuted" the monster, causing him to fall apart and leave her shoulders, the drawing in Figure 22. Using her creativity and visual imagination, she had unconsciously used the red bolt of energy coming from the ground to electrocute (do away with) the symbol of her pain. Portraying and revisualizing this fiery resolution, her solution for ridding herself of the hot-pressured pain, had a most powerful psychological and physiological outcome: Her pain gradually left her shoulders and she experienced little pain after a few weeks. I was as surprised as she was that utilizing process imagery in art therapy could bring about such a reduction in pain symptoms.

We continued using this method on each area of pain in her body, from her feet to her

Figure 23.

hands. Over a ten-month period, the RA pain and discomfort diminished to the point where she could learn to use a padded cane to walk, with her shoes on; she could wear sweaters, coats and dress warmly to go outside; she could sit in the sun and enjoy nature once again.

She stayed in therapy for another year, working on many frustrations, as well as teaching herself to do 5 × 7 inch watercolor paintings of scenes from her past (e. g., her homeland, and visits to Mt. Shasta and Hawaii) that brought up pleasant, peaceful feelings. The last watercolor painting she completed as we terminated art therapy sessions, (Figure 23), are three people in a boat observing the sunset. She said that the art therapy experience was the only time during any form of treatment that she felt "heard and seen." The support offered to chronic patients in hour-long sessions where they express and create visions of illness and wellness seems paramount to enhancing the healing process.

Art Therapy and Psychophysical Integration

The combination of medical art therapy experiences and gentle bodywork (the Trager Approach to Psychophysical Integration) seem to have the greatest positive effects for the juvenile arthritis patients seen by our interdisciplinary pain team over the past ten years at Children's Hospital Oakland. Learning simple relaxation exercises and drawing descriptive and pain-reducing images also help these younger patients. Envisioning themselves as stronger and in less pain helps children cope with arthritic joint disease. "Stronger" in many cases means going to school and accomplishing reachable goals.

Children and young teenagers seem to need validation that their pain is "real." By mapping the pain and specifically describing the nature of their pain (e. g., hot, stabbing, sharp, continuous, or dull, hurting all the time) and visualizing the pain-reduction process imagery produced in art, these children

can learn an easier and more graphic way how to protect their joints and experience reduced levels of pain.

Figure 24 shows the hand-drawn body in pain by a 13-year-old girl seen at the pain clinic. She has used red and blue markers to draw her arthritic pain, and has added a color code with descriptive words to explain the specific sensations she feels. She is asked to draw a "pain scale, where *10* is the most pain she has experienced and *1* is the least pain she has had." She decides to draw a thermometer-style pain scale, giving each of the gradations of pain, from *1* to *10*, a color to signify the feeling of pain at each level, Figure 25. She is then taught a self-hypnotic method to help lower the pain: "In your mind's eye, see the number and color that goes with the discomfort you have right now. Now, imagine the number and color just below this level; see if you can let this color go to the area of your body that needs your special attention. As you see this color, imagine the level of discomfort changing, lessening. Now imagine the color just below that color on the scale, again allowing this color to be in the areas that still need attention; see if the pain is even lower than before" . . ., etc. Actively influencing the level of pain in this manner gives some control back to the child. Areas of pain are revisualized and redrawn in the subsequent sessions, Figure 26, and the self-hypnotic procedure is reinvented based on the repetitive trying-out of the method at home. After five such sessions, this teenager was able to draw herself feeling much better, feeling some mastery over the pain, Figure 27.

This multidisciplinary approach (the Trager Approach, art therapy and self-hypnotic visualization created from the child's process imagery in the art) has not only been the treatment of choice for young arthritis patients in our pain clinic but also for others with autoimmune and post-viral-infection symptoms of pain. Pediatricians now send patients to us knowing that this multi-faceted treatment regime cuts down on seeing them with frequent requests for medication and more diagnostic tests.

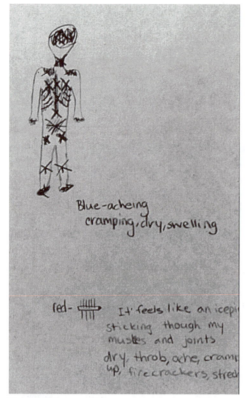

Blue-acheing
cramping, dry, swelling

red- |||| It feels like an icepi
          sticking though my
          musles and joints
          dry, throb, ache, cramp
          up, firecrackers, strech

Figure 24.

4/45: In pain all the time

every
day

—10
—9
—8
↑
low
—7
—6
—5
—4
—3
—2
—1
—0

Figure 25.

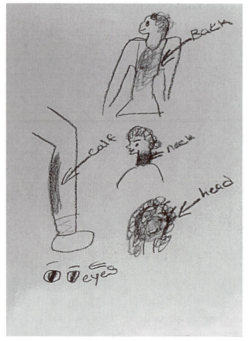

BaKK

calf   neck

head

eyes

Figure 26.

B-Pretty G
Y-Perfe
G-magnie-
cent
P-sour

Figure 27.

Medical Art Therapy with Migraine Patients

The self-hypnotic method described above of using imagery produced in artworks to help patients reduce their experience of pain, can also be taught to children, adolescents and adults suffering from migraine. Symptomatology in migraine syndrome varies greatly among sufferers. Similar pain scale imagery can be produced by patients, but upon deeper probing by the therapist the complexity of the pain problem may involve exploring the psychodynamics of the patient and his/her family (Long, 1997a). Two examples of this dynamic approach with an 8-year-old girl and a 42-year-old woman will be presented here.

A pale, withdrawn girl of 8 years was brought in for therapy by her troubled mother. The mother and father both suffered from migraine, both having similar head and stomach upset to this girl. The family situation was tense, the parents raising three children on very little money while the mother attended college. The parents were at odds regarding parenting styles with their children. The father was much more rigid and authoritarian than the mother, and the children were confused and experienced split loyalty when interacting with each parent. More tension was experienced in the household while this middle child went through medical evaluation for her intense migraine pain. Diagnostic testing found nothing anomalous and drug therapy failed to lower this child's pain. The medical bills put more financial pressure on the family and this girl was made aware of this by her parents. During some therapy interviews with the mother and the father, this child was blamed for "all the problems in the family." It was easier for the parents to scapegoat this child with migraine than to face the problems of daily life present for this couple and family. Therapy consisted of individual sessions with the child, mother-child sessions, and family sessions.

This girl took three months to warm up to the therapeutic process. She was emotionally guarded and so reductive in her thought processes that even describing the pain or talking about school or home experiences was very difficult for her. Rapport building involved her taking the lead in free art expression, and the therapist respecting her pacing. Finally she revealed herself to be merged with her mother's pain, perfectionistic and internally pressured at school (an A student whose teacher was concerned about her general level of distress), and the victim of her father's rage and frustration.

She soon could grasp and imaginatively draw metaphors for her migraine pain: a pain scale, Figure 28, and a devil sticking a pitchfork into her head and stomach, Figure 29. After twenty therapy sessions and fruitless trials of analgesic and antidepressant medications, she chose colored modeling clay as art media. In the clay, she sculpted two painful red bodies, animal companions, a variety of foods, an exotic lady on a pedestal with a fruit bowl on her head, and finally a solid red hand, Figure 30. This hand belonged to her father. Her rage toward her father was expressed by throwing balls of the modeling clay against the solid door in the therapy room. She was allowed to sublimate her pain in this way, showing a release of her body tension and her psychic pain. Family therapy was continued, and even though the troubled home situation stayed somewhat tense, this child's migraine pain became more manageable.

In a similarly complex case with a 42-year-old woman, understanding and working through some personal and family issues helped tackle the presenting problem of migraine pain. This woman was pursuing an academic career when she became disabled with headaches. Her mother had been an institutionalized schizophrenic during her childhood, and she was shuffled back and forth to relative's houses while her mother was in hospital. She had no father, and felt responsible for her mother, even though her mother was either mean to her or ignored her. She felt guilty about her academic success, while feeling "depressed and angry that (she) had no social life." The migraine pain paralyzed her going forward with her life. Again, no diagnostic tests, medications, or rest had helped in the slightest reduce her pain.

Figure 28.

Figure 29.

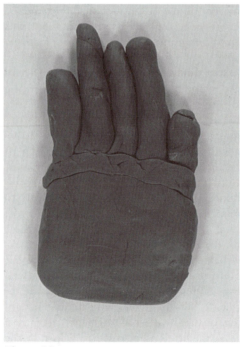

Figure 30.

She produced an entire portfolio of water-color paintings of her pain during three months of weekly art therapy sessions. Figure 31 is an example of her early paintings, always in the color black, always of pictographic arrows coming into her head. When she began talking more about her relationship with her mother, she came up with metaphoric imagery parallel to the surfacing feelings: Figure 32 shows her as a container-vase, trying to let out the bad energy; and Figure 33 shows her head as a pressure cooker. The pressure cooker image became a transformative symbol to her; she made the connection between the pressure cooker, the feelings that she had been carrying all her life toward her mother and herself, and the pain in her head.

Working on problems of identity formation and how these manifested in her adult life, she began to symbolize the migraine pain as energy states and painted these in many colors onto mask forms. Each mask form was made of white watercolor paper and was de-

Figure 31.

Figure 32.

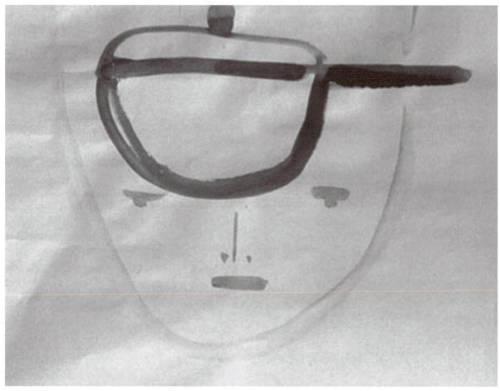

Figure 33.

Figure 34.

Figure 35.

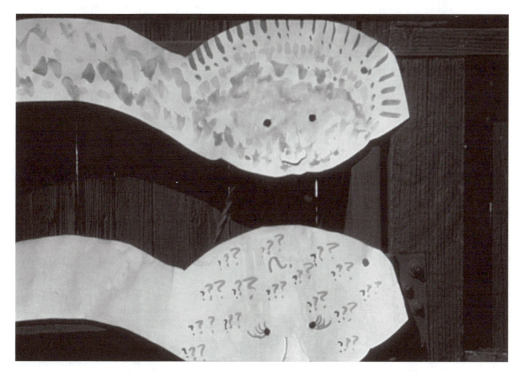

Figure 36.

signed to be wrapped around her entire head. She first painted a series of masks representing the worst pain (Figure 34), followed by a series representing ever changing, lessening pain (Figure 35), and finished with two masks which began to explore and question current identity issues (e. g., her gender identity; her identity as a woman in the academic world; her relationships with other people) (Figure 36). When she finished each mask, she would wrap it around her head and walk around, looking in the mirror to see her reflection, and dialoguing with herself about the meaning of her pain. This dramatic existential exercise helped her differentiate herself from her mother and from her pain.

Conclusion

Medical art therapy draws upon the formal principles of past and current art, art therapy and image formation theorists, the research of physiological psychologists and other scientists exploring the workings of the human brain, and the studies of mind-body practitioners. It is both a hybrid discipline and a new form of clinical therapy. The intent of the author has been to highlight the theoretical inspiration and foundation for this work, and to illustrate the practice of medical art therapy using actual clinical cases. The author hopes that Medical Art Therapy will stand as an accepted form of experiential treatment in the field of health psychology.

The human mind has the ability to create a path away from illness and pain using imaginative processes made tangible and interactive through works of art. This statement may seem too global to some, but after observing patients over the past twenty-five years transform their symptoms and live more vital and pain free lives I have come to accept the value of this approach to healing. The nonverbal and preverbal nature of negative and positive imagery about illness and symptom patterns held in the human mind-body seems to need the clinical interventions of medical art therapy methods.

The next steps in evolving the use of art in healing seem to be laid out in the current approaches to wellness and mind-body, integrative medicine. Preventive programs help children and adults to learn inner guidance techniques that enhance health and enable better coping skills when faced with illness. Helping parents guide their children through illness, pain and upsets (physical and emotional) using simple art therapy exercises is this author's challenge for prevention that will hopefully have lifelong benefits (Long, 1997b).

Since September 11, 2001, many art therapists all over the United States responded to the tragedy in New York City by offering victims and their family members art therapy services. A whole issue of *Art Therapy, Journal of the American Art Therapy Association* (Volume 18, Number 4, 2001) is dedicated to the work of these art therapists and to future research in the field of art therapy. Many of us have treated traumatic injury and grief using principles of psychiatric and medical art therapy (e. g., Tinnin & Gantt, 2000; Chapman et al., 2001; Long, 2002). As the world becomes more dangerous, access to the creative arts therapies for healing traumatic effects of disasters seems advantageous. Medical art therapy's new frontier will include this work.

References

Achterberg, J. (1985). *Imagery in healing: Shamanism and modern medicine.* Boston: New Sciences Library.

Achterberg, J., & Lawlis, J.F. (1980). *Bridges of the bodymind: Behavioral approaches to health care.* Champaign, IL: Institute for Personality and Ability Testing.

Anand, S.A., & Anand, V.K. (1997). Art therapy with laryngectomy patients. *Art Therapy, 14*(2), 109–117.

Arnheim, R. (1974). *Art and visual perception* (rev. ed.). Berkeley: University of California Press.

Betensky, M. (1973). *Self-discovery through self-expression.* Springfield, IL: Charles C. Thomas.

Chapman, L.M., Morabito, D., Ladakakos, C., Schrier, H., & Knudsen, M. (2001). The effectiveness of art therapy interventions in reducing P-T-S-D (PTSD) symptoms in pediatric trauma patients. *Art Therapy, 18*(2), 100–104.

Drachnik, C. (1995). *Interpreting metaphors in chil-*

dren's drawings: A manual. Burlingame, CA: Abbeygate Press.

Jung, C.G. (1960). *The structure and dynamics of the psyche. Vol. III. The collected works of C.G. Jung.* Translated by R.F.C. Hull. Bollingen Series XX. Princeton: Princeton University Press.

Kagin, S.L., & Lusebrink, V.B. (1978). The Expressive Therapies Continuum. *Art Psychotherapy, 5*(4), 171–179.

Koepfer, S.R. (2000). Drawing on the spirit: embracing spirituality in pediatrics and pediatric art therapy. *Art Therapy, 17*(3), 188–194.

Kramer, E. (1979). *Childhood and art therapy.* New York: Schocken.

Long, J., Chapman, L., Appleton, V., Abrams, E., & Palmer, S. (1989). Innovations in medical art therapy: Defining the field. *Proceedings of the 20th Annual American Art Therapy Association Conference* (p. 84). Mundelein, IL: AATA.

Long, J.K. (1994). Medical art therapy in California: The history and practical context of this therapeutic field. *Section 3, Position Paper of the Northern and Southern Art Therapy Associations to the California Legislature.* California State Congress Hearing, June 26.

Long, J., & Sedberry, D. (1994). *Pain reduction in pediatric oncology: Integrating medical art therapy, hypnotherapy and play therapy.* Poster Session, Third International Symposium on Pediatric Pain: Children and Pain: Integrating Science and Care. Philadelphia, PA.

Long, J.K. (1995). Establishing medical art therapy in a new outpatient pediatric pain management service. *Proceedings of the 26th Annual American Art Therapy Association Conference* (p. 97). Mundelein, IL: AATA.

Long, J.K. (1989, 1996). *Innovations in medical art therapy.* Unpublished manuscript.

Long, J.K. (1997a). *Medical art therapy in the treatment of migraine.* Paper presented at the Fourth International Symposium on Pediatric Pain, Helsinki, Finland.

Long, J.K. (1997b). *Helping your child through illness, pain and upset using simple art exercises: A manual for parents and workbook for children.* Unpublished manuscript.

Long, J.K. (2001). Art therapy: a process of healing. *MS Connection,* #3, 4–6. National Multiple Sclerosis Society Journal, Northern California Chapter.

Long, J.K. (2001). Treating pediatric trauma cases using art therapy: complementary medical and psychiatric perspectives. *Proceedings of the 32nd Annual American Art Therapy Association Conference* (p. 83). Mundelein, Il: AATA.

Long, J.K. (2002). *"Ronny: Medical art therapy in complementary medicine."* Independent Video.

Lowenfeld, V., & Brittain, W.L. (1970). *Creative and mental growth* (5th ed.). New York: Macmillan.

Lusebrink, V.B. (1990). *Imagery and visual expression in therapy.* New York: Plenum Press.

Lusebrink, V.B., & Long, J.K. (1998). Comparison of brief art therapy and sandtray therapy with breast cancer patients. *Proceedings of the 29th Annual American Art Therapy Association Conference* (p. 164). Mundelein, IL: AATA.

Luzzatto, P., & Gabriel, B. (2000). The creative journey: A model for short-term group art therapy with posttreatment cancer patients. *Art Therapy, 17*(4), 265–269.

Malchiodi, C. (Ed.) (1998). *Medical art therapy with children.* London: Jessica Kingsley Pub.

Malchiodi, C. (Ed.) (1999). *Medical art therapy with adults.* London: Jessica Kingsley Pub.

Naumberg, M. (1966). *Dynamically oriented art therapy: Its principles and practice.* New York: Grune and Stratton.

Packman, W.L., Crittenden, M.R., Rieger Fischer J.B., Cowan, M.J., Long, J.K., Gruenert, C., Schaeffer, E., & Bongar, B. (1998). The kinetic family drawing with donor and nondonor siblings of pediatric bone marrow transplant patients. *Art Therapy, 15*(3), 177–184.

Pasto, T.A. (1964). *The space-frame experience in art.* New York: A.S. Barnes.

Rosal, M.L. (1996). *Approaches to art therapy with children.* Burlingame, CA: Abbeygate Press.

Rossi, E.L. (1986). *The psychobiology of mind-body healing: New concepts of therapeutic hypnosis.* New York: W.W. Norton.

Rubin, J.A. (1978). *Child art therapy: Understanding and helping children grow through art.* New York: Van Nostrand Reinhold.

Tinnin, L.W., & Gantt, L. (2000). *The Trauma Recovery Institute Treatment Manual.* Morgantown, WV: Gargoyle Press.

Uhlin, D.M., & Chiara, E. (1984). *Art for exceptional children* (3rd ed.). Dubuque, IA: Wm. C. Brown.

Weil, A. (1995). *Spontaneous healing.* New York: Alfred P. Knopf.

Wilson, L. (1987). Symbolism and art therapy: Theory and clinical practice. In J.A. Rubin (Ed.), *Approaches to art therapy: Theory and technique* (pp. 44–62). New York: Brunner/Mazel.

Marian L. Fitzgibbon & Lisa A. P. Sánchez-Johnsen

17

Reduction of Health Risk in Ethnic Minority Populations*

Introduction

Incidence of chronic disorders, including cardiovascular disease (CVD), diabetes, hypertension, and some cancers, are higher among certain ethnic minority groups than Whites in the United States (e. g., Flegal, Carroll, Ogden, & Johnson, 2002; Haynes & Smedley, 1999; National Cancer Institute, 1999, 2001; Smedley, Stith, & Nelson, 2002). In addition, research suggests that certain ethnic minority groups, such as Latinas/os and Blacks engage in fewer health risk reduction behaviors, have higher smoking rates, and consume diets higher in fat and lower in fiber when compared to Whites (Center for Disease Control & Prevention, 2001; National Cancer Institute, 1999, 2000, 2001; Smedley et al., 2002). In the face of increasing evidence linking lifestyle and genetic factors with CVD, hypertension, diabetes, and cancer risk, the health of ethnic minorities represents one of the most pressing public health issues confronting the United States today (e. g., Smedley et al., 2002).

Obesity [Body Mass Index (BMI) ≥ 30 kg/m²] (NHLBI, 1998) and overweight (BMI ≥ 25 < 30) (NHBLI, 1998) have been associated with all of the above-mentioned chronic disorders (Flegal et al., 2002) and the prevalence of overweight has shown a striking increase in the United States over the past decade (Flegal et al., 2002; Ogden, Flegal, Carroll, & Johnson, 2002). Moreover, Mexican-American and Black women have higher rates of overweight than White women (Flegal et al., 2002). For example, among women ages 40–59, 79.3% of Mexican American and 81.5% of Blacks are overweight, compared to 61% of Whites (Flegal et al., 2002). Similar trends have been noted among ethnic minority youth in the United States (Ogden et al., 2002). Specifically, 6–17 year-old Black girls had the highest prevalence of overweight, and White girls had the lowest prevalence (Ogden et al., 2002).

Researchers and health care providers are challenged to understand reasons behind the high rates of chronic disorders among ethnic minorities. Clearly, prevention of overweight would favorably impact the variety of chronic diseases associated with increasing overweight (e. g., Field, Barnoya & Colditz, 2002). Given the extreme difficulty involved in weight loss and weight loss maintenance (e. g., Perri & Corsica, 2002; Wing & Klem, 2002), prevention efforts are crucial (Wadden & Osei, 2002).

Despite the high prevalence rates of chronic disorders among ethnic minorities, few prevention and intervention efforts include ethnic minorities (Giuliano et al., 2000; Haynes & Smedley, 1999; NIH, 2002). For ex-

---

* Although the terms "Latinas/os" and "Blacks" will be used throughout this chapter, the authors acknowledge that there is great heterogeneity within these ethnis groups. Latinas/os refers to anyone whose ethnic origins can be traced to Central America, South America, the Caribbean, or Spain, while the term "Blacks" refers to those whose ethnic origins can be traced to the Black ethnic groups of Africa and/or who self-identify as African-American.

ample, in some of the large scale prevention trials conducted by the National Cancer Institute, less than 2% of the participants were Black, and even smaller percentages of individuals were from other ethnic groups (Haynes & Smedley, 1999). Moreover, ethnic minority populations have historically not participated in clinical trials at rates proportional to participation among middle and upper-middle income Whites (Giuliano et al., 2000; Haynes & Smedley, 1999; NIH, 2002). Nevertheless, in recent years, NIH has made significant gains in increasing representations of ethnic minority women in both of its intramural and extramural research programs (NIH, 2002). During fiscal year 1999, 14% of females who participated in extramural research were Black non-Latino, 18% were Asian and Pacific Islander, 7% were Latina; and .07% were American Indian and Alaskan Native. In contrast, White women (non-Latina) represented 54% of all females enrolled in extramural research funded by NIH (Pinn, Roth, Hartmuller, Bates, & Fanning, 2001). Given their low participation in prevention and treatment studies (Haynes & Smedley, 1999), the recruitment of ethnic minorities and development of culturally competent programs have recently received increased attention (e. g., Alcalay, Alvarado, Balcazar, Newman, & Huerta, 1999; Fitzgibbon, Gapstur, & Knight, 2002; Fitzgibbon, Prewitt, Blackman, Simon, Luke, Keys, Avellone, & Singh, 1998; Fitzgibbon, Stolley, Dyer, VanHorn, & Kaufer-Christoffel, 2002; Harris, Ahluwalia, Okuyemi, Turner, Woods, Resinow, & Backinger, 2001; Mau, Glanz, Severino, Grove, Johnson, & Curb, 2001). However, data also suggests that recruitment and program development strategies used for non-minority populations are often unsuccessful when used with ethnic minority populations (Harris et al., 2001; Haynes & Smedley, 1999). The goal of this chapter is to present successful strategies for the recruitment of low-income Latina and African American women for CVD and cancer risk reduction studies and the development of culturally competent programs to address the specific needs of these populations.

The chapter will be divided into three sec-tions. The first section will describe a theoretical model guiding the recruitment and implementation of the programs. The second section will describe some logistical considerations for recruitment and retention success and challenges to be anticipated. The third section will discuss the key elements related to effective program development and implementation.

1. Theoretical Model

Stages of Change

Dietary interventions may be more successful when based on theory and research related to health behavior change (Glanz, Rimmer & Lewis, 2002; Kristal, Glanz, Curry, & Patterson, 1999).

The stages of change model developed as part of a broader theoretical model of intentional behavior change, called the Transtheoretical Model (Prochaska & DiClemente, 1992), and has shown promise as a framework for dietary behavior change interventions (e. g., Greene, Rossi, Rossi, Velicer, Fava, & Prochaska, 1999; Kristal, Glanz, Curry, & Patterson, 1999; Mau et al., 2001; Schorling, 1995). The stages of change model was initially conceptualized as a framework to study addictive behaviors. Research on smoking cessation showed that smokers could be categorized into various stages according to their motivation to stop smoking. The stages have been identified as: precontemplation, contemplation, preparation, action, and maintenance (Jeffery, French, & Rothman, 1999). Individuals in the *precontemplation* stage have no intention of changing in the near future. They may even be unaware that a problem exists. Resistance to any change is the main aspect of this stage. *Contemplation* is the stage where individuals are aware there is a problem and are thinking of doing something about it. However, they have not yet made the commitment to take any behavioral action. Individuals in this stage struggle over the pros and cons of changing the behavior (Prochaska & DiClemente, 1992). In the *preparation* stage, individuals begin to take small steps toward changing the behavior. They usually intend to take action in the very near future. The *action* stage is where individuals begin to actually change the behavior in measurable ways. This usually requires a great deal of time, energy, and perseverance. Finally, the *maintenance* stage is where individuals work to prevent relapse and identify the processes that have worked to help sustain their change (Prochaska, DiClemente & Norcross, 1992).

This model has been used successfully with other problems such as alcohol abuse (DiClemente, Bellino & Neavins, 1999), crack cocaine (Siegal, Rapp, & Saha, 2001), weight loss (Jeffery, French, & Rothman, 1999), and exercise (e. g., Cardinal, 1997; Sarkin, Johnson, Prochaska, & Prochaska, 2001; Schumann, Nigg, Rossi, Joedan, Norman, Garber, Riebe, & Benisovich, 2002; Suminski & Petosa, 2002). Overall, the results of these studies suggest that this model can be instrumental in promoting change across an array of problem behaviors. Recently, the stages of change model has been used with several ethnic minority populations (i. e., Davis, 2000; Mau et al., 2001; Suris, Trapp, DiClemente, & Cousins, 1998). For example, Scholaring (1995) found that the predictors of stages of change for 556 Black smokers were the same as those found in other populations. Stages of change were also significantly correlated with dietary intake (fat and fiber) and physical activity in a sample of Native Hawaiians (Mau et al., 2001).

Changes in eating patterns, like other entrenched behavior patterns, involve numerous steps and adaptations over time toward permanent change. People naturally differ in their readiness for change and the behaviors they utilize to make those changes (Glanz et al., 2002).

Although the bulk of dietary change research using the stages of change model has focused on changing dietary habits to lose weight, recently there have been studies that have examined the predictors of selecting low fat diets (e. g., Mau et al., 2001) and increasing dietary fiber (Mau et al., 2001). Dietary change interventions present unique challenges to researchers because the main focus of the interventions are replacement and modification, not cessation, as in smoking or

drug abuse. Therefore, dietary change is fundamentally different from substance abuse (Jeffery et al., 1999; Kristal et al., 1999). Several recent studies have examined the stages of change model as it relates to dietary changes. For example, in a cohort of 11, 237 worksite employees, Glanz and colleagues (1998) found that changes in dietary stage of change were associated with decreases in fat intake and increases in fiber, fruit, and vegetable intake. Kristal and colleagues also found that stage of change at follow-up was also associated with dietary change (Kristal, Glanz, Tilley & Li, 2000). These authors suggested that the most effective interventions should focus on continued change among those in the action and maintenance stages, as well as helping to move people out of preaction stages (Kristal, Glanz, Tilley, & Li, 2000). Prochaska and colleagues (1992) have speculated that progression from contemplation to action is necessary if behavior is to change. They found that individuals who moved toward the action stage early in an intervention were more likely to succeed. For example, in an intensive program for smoking cessation, 94% of individuals who were in the action or preparation stage were not smoking at the 6-month follow-up. The intensive program had no substantial effect on patients who entered the program in the precontemplation or contemplation stages (Ockene, Ockene, & Kristellar, 1988). Overall, behavioral change programs seem to be more effective when individuals enter them in the preparation and action stages, rather than the precontemplation and contemplation stages. This strongly supports the value of matching the stage with key intervention strategies.

Processes of Change

The stages of change reflect a dimension that suggests movement along a continuum. Although the movement toward permanent change is seldom a linear progression, the stages of change model describes a structure that suggests intentions and behaviors will change over time. As interventions were developed to facilitate behavior change, it became apparent that there was a subset of processes that were used in different stages. Individuals use different processes as they attempt to exert more control over their behavior. Ten processes of change were first identified by Prochaska (1979). They include two global constructs: experiential processes and behavioral processes (Prochaska, 1979).

The experiential processes include: consciousness raising, dramatic relief, environmental re-evaluation, self-evaluation, and social liberation (Prochaska, 1979). *Consciousness raising* is increasing information about the problem and being open to confrontations or interpretations related to the problem behavior. *Dramatic relief* occurs as individuals are able to express feelings about the problem and formulate possible solutions. *Environmental re-evaluation* is the process of assessing how the problem affects the environment. *Self-evaluation* is an assessment of how one feels and thinks about oneself in relation to the problem. Finally, *Social liberation* is the process of increasing alternatives so as not to engage in the problem behavior.

The behavioral processes include: counterconditioning, helping relationships, reinforcement management, self-liberation, and stimulus control (Prochaska, 1979). *Counterconditioning* refers to the substitution of alternative positive behaviors for problem behaviors. *Helping relationships* refers to the process of becoming more open to social and familial support. *Reinforcement management* is a process where individuals reward themselves for making positive changes. *Self-liberation* occurs as individuals begin to believe they have the ability to change. Lastly, *stimulus control* refers to the restructuring of the environment to avoid the problem behavior. Research suggests that at each stage, one or a combination of processes can be utilized.

From Theory to Application: Processes within Stages

The analysis of the stages of change theory and its empirical foundations can help to profile what strategies can be helpful at ascertain stages in the change process. For example, individuals in the precontemplation stage use fewer processes than those in other stages. They spend less time evaluating their problem and do not seek out ways to better manage their environment and to control the behavior (Prochaska et al., 1992). Those in the contemplation stage seek out more information and are more open to consciousness raising techniques (Prochaska & DiClemente,1984). For example, we found that many of the Black parents in our program had less knowledge about the caloric and fat content of foods than we initially anticipated, but they were highly interested in nutrition information. Individuals in the contemplation stage also begin to look at how their problem affects their environment. The more central the problem becomes, the more they are ready to re-evaluate themselves. In the preparation stage, individuals start to take small steps toward action and begin to utilize stimulus control techniques to control the environment. This use of stimulus control or environmental management can greatly affect the ability to sustain self-regulatory behavior. We found that many people entered our program skeptical about their ability to make behavioral changes related to diet and exercise. They voiced a desire to change, but felt they lacked the requisite skills. We found these people, most likely in the preparation stage, to be the most amenable to coping strategies that could assist in change.

In the action stage there is an increase in the use of self-liberation or self-efficacy. In other words, individuals show an increase in their ability to feel they control their environment. During this stage there is also more successful use of counterconditioning and stimulus control. Additionally, there is more reliance on support and understanding from important others (Prochaska & DiClemente, 1992). However, this type of support would probably not be beneficial in the earlier stages, but only when the person has made the decision to change (e. g., preparation, action).

The culmination of change is seen in the maintenance stage. This involves building on the processes that have worked during the previous stages. Individuals in this stage make assessments of what coping responses have been successful. As in the action stage,

Table 1. **Linkage of conceptual stages of change model and intervention.**

Stage	Characteristics	Intervention
Precontemplation	No intent to change in the near future; unaware that a problem exists Resistance to change	1. Educational materials 2. Availability of interventionist to respond to possible questions regarding behavior change
Contemplation	Aware of problem; thinking of taking action Not yet committed to change	1. Educational materials 2. Discuss pros and cons of behavior change 3. Clarify misinformation regarding behavior change 4. Work toward improving insight
Preparation	Begin to take small steps toward change; intend to take action in the near future	1. Support small changes 2. Organize environment to avoid high-risk situations
Action	Behavior changing in measurable ways	1. Continue support 2. Discuss options for increased social support 3. Continue environmental management 4. Reinforce insight already gained about the importance of behavior change
Maintenance	Working to prevent relapse and continue successful problem solving strategies	1. Continue support 2. Reinforce networks of support 3. Continue to identify and develop coping strategies to reduce relapses 4. Reinforce that a lapse is not a relapse and that change is often cyclical, not linear.

using stimulus control and counterconditioning seem to be among the most effective strategies. The key to more success toward permanent change is to utilize the correct processes during the appropriate stage. A mismatch between stage and process can be detrimental. For example, it may be futile to teach stimulus control skills to someone in an earlier stage (precontemplation, contemplation). These strategies may only be helpful for someone who has reached the preparation or action stages. At that time they may show more willingness to reduce the intake of high fat foods through less exposure to these foods in the home and the avoidance of places that are associated with high-fat foods (e. g., fast food restaurants). Table 1 depicts the potential links between stage, characteristics, and intervention strategies.

The interaction between processes and the stages of change model has only recently been applied to dietary interventions. Some of these intervention studies have attempted to identify differences between individuals who are successful at making long-term dietary changes and relapsers. Successful maintainers of a low fat diet monitor their body weight regularly, exercise regularly, and monitor fat intake (McGuire, Wing, Klem, Lang, & Hill, 1999; Wing & Klem, 2002). Results have also shown that people successful at maintaining change use various cognitive skills such as problem solving and cognitive restructuring (Marlatt & Gordon, 1980). Particularly in the action and maintenance stages, individuals need to be very aware of high-risk situations and plan strategies to cope with situations that could lead to relapse. Frequency of contact with a therapist and degree of support received from family members can dramatically affect one's ability to make dietary changes (Mau et al., 2001; Wing & Jeffery, 1999). For example, in a recent study, Wing and Jeffery (1999) assigned participants to either a standard behavior therapy or behavior therapy with social support training. At 6-month follow-up, participants who were recruited with family and friends and received social support training maintained 66% of their initial weight losses. In contrast, participants who entered the study alone and received standard behavior therapy maintained only 24% of their initial weight losses (Wing & Jeffery, 1999). Finally, the dynamic process involved in the stages of change model views lapses as a natural part of the change process. To avoid relapse, the key is to develop effective responses to situations associated with relapse. This seems to be critical for successful maintenance (e. g., Cooper & Fairburn, 2002; Perri, 2002).

The theoretical underpinning of the stages of change model and corresponding processes help to guide our understanding of how diverse people are in their motivation and ability to make permanent changes toward a healthier lifestyle. However, in addition to a theoretical grounding in behavior change, there are many practical obstacles in the implementation of a successful intervention. The following section will illustrate several of the strategies utilized and challenges that arose during the implementation of our dietary change interventions with Latinas/os and Blacks.

2. Logistical Considerations

Recruitment Strategies

Choosing a setting. A substantial barrier for low income, inner-city individuals to participate in prevention programs is transportation to the program and safety related to that travel (Brown, Fouad, Basen-Engquist, & Tortolero-Luna, 2000; Haynes & Smedley, 1999). It is very important that the setting be in a safe area that is easily accessible (NHLBI, 1998) and preferably within walking distance from the

participants' homes. In addition to easy accessibility, programs must be in a familiar location. Even if transportation is provided, participants are less likely to attend if the setting is unfamiliar. In one of our earlier programs in a Black inner city community, we initiated a "field-trip" to a local nutrition center. This center had a state of the art "mock" grocery store, and we thought this would be a beneficial and fun experience for the participants. We provided transportation to and from the nutrition center, which was a 5-minute bus ride from our program site. To our surprise, very few participants came on the trip. We asked several participants why they had not come, and we were told it was because the neighborhood was "unfamiliar" to them.

Given the needs for safety and easy accessibility, it may also be necessary to consider multiple sites. For example, we found it necessary to offer a program for Black families in two sites on either side of an inner city housing complex. This was helpful in that participants did not have to cross high crime areas in order to attend. When we only had one site, we were told by potential participants they wanted to come to the program, but to attend would require that they cross "gang lines." Mothers were naturally unwilling to put their children in an unsafe situation, so they didn't attend. This is obviously not a consideration for many interventions, but it is one that needs to be considered when implementing a program in an inner city or higher crime neighborhood.

Community relations. In our experience, attempt to recruit participants from local health facilities and doctor's offices proved unsuccessful. Our initial attempts at recruitment at one of the local health facilities was dismal. Individuals who came to the clinic primarily came with very ill children and were usually not interested in a discussion of our program. Since they did not know or have a relationship with us, there was no compelling reason to listen to find out more about our program, much less attend. Several researchers have also noted that in order to increase the recruitment and retention of ethnic minorities, it is essential to become involved in the community by establishing relationships with neighborhood residents, community leaders, and community organizations, as well as involving community members in the research from the beginning to the end of the project (Fitzgibbon et al., 1998; Giuliano et al., 2000).

As our relationships with community members developed, we were better able to use these avenues to recruit participants. For example, we recruited Black children and parents from local after-school literacy programs. We presented the goals of our prevention program to parents who attended orientation sessions for the literacy program. We also sent mailings to all of the parents who had children enrolled in these programs, and these mailings were followed up with phone calls. Furthermore, we established relationships with individuals from the community who later conducted canvassing in the neighborhoods. Trust and knowledge that we were conducting a program for them rather than merely taking information from them was the key ingredient for attendance for many of the participants. For some, the personal relationship, rather than the content of the curriculum, was a more essential component for involvement. Our study coordinator had particularly close relationships with many of the women in the program. When she needed to schedule someone for a specific appointment, and they were not at home, she had permission to call a sister, mother, or neighbor. If a child could not get to the program with a parent, the coordinator would call a neighbor whom she had met that could then facilitate the child's attendance to the program.

Neighborhood peer leaders. In many neighborhoods where it may be unsafe for researchers to do neighborhood canvassing, it is essential to develop relationships with individuals who are trusted in the community (Fitzgibbon et al., 1998; Giuliano, 2000). Peer leaders participated in our programs to aid in recruitment and also to enhance attendance. Programs utilizing a peer approach have reported positive changes (Perry & Grant, 1991). Peers are unique in their ability to influence peer group behavior because they are part of the group and are credible role models (Perry, 1989). Inclusion of peers has been shown to be an effective means of preventing high-risk behavior (Tobler, 1986).

Recruitment Challenges

Fear of exploitation. There are several barriers to effective recruitment of low-income ethnic minorities in prevention studies (e. g., Fitzgibbon et al., 1998; Haynes & Smedley, 1999). One of the most frequently cited reasons for nonparticipation in research is the fear of exploitation by researchers (Blumenthal, Sung, Coates, Williams & Lift, 1995). The large media attention to the infamous Tuskegee Study of untreated syphilis among Black males has led many minorities, particularly Blacks, to believe that they would be treated unfairly in any research endeavor (Haynes & Smedley, 1999). One of our experiences underscores this problem. To promote our program among the Cabrini-Green neighborhood, the principal investigator agreed to do a radio interview on a Black radio station in the Chicago area. Individuals were asked to call in and ask questions about the program. To our surprise, one caller called and strongly suggested that the aim of this program was to give the children harmful chemicals and use them as "guinea pigs." All efforts to allay his fear and state that our goals were to reduce fat in the diet and to increase exercise were ignored. To compound the problem, it appeared that the radio commentator agreed more with the caller than with the principal investigator.

Additionally, among low-income individuals, day-to-day living is often stressful and difficult. Many ethnic minority women have multiple obligations, such as wife, mother, employee, family caregiver, student, or church and community volunteer (Brown et al., 2000). All of these obligations may limit their time for additional activities and therefore, prevention is deemed a low priority. For example, some of the women who came to the program were handling problems with drug-addicted older children or friends. Some were caring for children of siblings who were unable to care for their own children. Given these day-to-day stressors, healthcare may only become important when there is a presence of symptoms (Blumenthal et al., 1995). Researchers need to be sensitive and knowledgeable about the population being recruited and develop effective and culturally competent skills to engage diverse ethnic minority groups.

Random assignment. An important and often difficult problem to handle is how to manage random assignment. Random assignment to an active intervention or a control group is usually a foreign concept and is often interpreted as, "Why should I participate if I might not get anything out of it?" and "Why is her family getting something and mine isn't?" An additional commonly cited structural barrier for Latinos is fear of not knowing whether they are in the experimental treatment or the control group (Giuliano et al., 2000). Moreover, random assignment of the family is problematic in communities where the traditional nuclear family is rare. Researchers need to be aware of and inquire about the extended family. Otherwise, one sister and her children may be assigned to the treatment group and another sister and her children may be assigned to the control group. We encountered this situation, and it led to confusion because one family in the control group thought if they missed their session they could attend the treatment group session that was deliberately held on a different day to avoid contamination.

Retention Efforts

Weekly contact calls. In order to keep people engaged in our program, it was necessary to call on a weekly basis and remind individuals of the session day and time. Our experience was that this personal contact raised the program as a priority. One staff-person realized that she was able to contact people most efficiently during the hours when the O.J. Simpson trial was being broadcast. She and the participant would spend some time chatting about the developments of the trial before she reminded her of a health screen-

ing visit or weekly class. Although discussions of personal family problems would be considered intrusive by some people, many of the participants began to feel comfortable talking with the intervention staff about their lives. Therefore, it became important to ask and follow-up on issues raised during previous phone calls.

Multiple incentives. Several researchers have noted that incentives can increase the recruitment and retention of ethnic minorities (i. e., Brown et al., 2000; Giuliano et al., 2000). In our CVD risk reduction projects, we used incentives such as food coupons for the parents and prizes for the children to improve attendance. We found that food coupons were effective but that monetary compensation was the most effective. In another project, during the last 12 weeks of the 20-week breast cancer risk reduction program for Black women, we offered incentives (either a small indoor electric grill or a walkman radio) for women who attended 4 biweekly classes during weeks 12-16 and another incentive (either a pedometer or a walkman radio) for women who attended 4 biweekly classes during weeks 16–20. Moreover, regardless of whether participants were randomized to the treatment or control group, all women received a free 20-week YMCA membership as part of their participation in our program.

Program announcement letters. Weekly program announcement letters were sent out to inform participants of the topic for the following week. In this way, we sought to inform participants and to keep them connected with the program. Although the program was held at the same time and day each week, several mothers would not send their child if they did not receive a reminder letter or phone call.

Peer leaders. In our cardiovascular risk reduction program, we used older students from the community as teaching assistants and to help with program promotion. We felt these students were especially important because of their familiarity with the culture, neighborhood, and participants. In one case, the "most popular" peer leader was a student who had been in the program during our initial year and wished to continue after she had become too old for inclusion. She became a natural example of the fun and engaging nature of the program.

Retention Challenges

Transient populations. Financial instability, unemployment, and immigration status are problems in low income and certain ethnic minority communities (Giuliano et al., 2000) and may lead to frequent relocations. Therefore, the key for participation is often the engagement of the extended family, rather than the individual. The traditional concept of the nuclear family is often not applicable in inner city settings. For example, we had one extended family that included three sisters, a grandmother, and 10 children. One of the participants left for a period of time to enter a drug-rehabilitation program. During that time, another family member, with whom they were living, brought the children.

Gang activity. Any intervention needs to be held in a safe setting, however this does not diminish the presence of gangs in many inner city neighborhoods, nor the allure they hold for many children. For example, during the program one boy abruptly stopped coming. We heard that he had relatives in a gang and was under pressure to join. It was unclear if he had joined the gang or if it became unsafe for him to walk to the program because he was under continued pressure to join the gang.

Poverty-related stress. For many ethnic minorities, poverty is a major structural barrier to participating in research (Giuliano et al., 2000). Lack of telephones, financial problems, and unemployment are only some of the impediments that can affect motivation to stay engaged in a health risk reduction program. In order to improve the ability to track participants, multiple phone numbers and addresses of family and close friends should be collected.

3. Effective Program Development and Implementation

Culture Specific Curriculum

Focus groups. Focus groups are a necessary part of curriculum development in order to better understand the subtleties of a population. We found on several occasions that ideas we thought were innovative and stimulating were not received well among the potential participants. For example, we developed an exercise video in conjunction with some of our participants. We thought that women would want a back-drop of a beach or an exotic location. We received a resounding "no" when we presented this idea to the participants. They told us that they wanted a video that looked like they were exercising in their own living room. They expressed that videos with thin models filmed on exotic locations made them feel uncomfortable and intimidated about exercising. Additionally, we conducted focus groups to assess the level of embarrassment or anxiety that low-income Latinas might have with breast self-exam (BSE) and learning to touch breast models. To our surprise, the women voiced no anxiety and were enthusiastic and motivated to learn more about BSE.

It is important to understand the heterogeneity among minority populations. We have found that literacy and education level are crucial factors to consider when planning an intervention. During the focus groups, specific questions such as the amount of reading material that can be read easily and the format in which the reading material can be best presented are important. If this is not done and material is developed without this input, participants may not spontaneously admit that the level of reading is beyond their capacity. They simply will not engage in the program. If development of the curriculum is not done with the detailed consideration of the target population, it is not only problematic, but potentially useless.

Inclusion of ethnic foods. Including cultural preferences for food is an important component of developing a culturally competent program (Kumanyika, 2002; NHLBI, 1998). The inclusion of foods that are specific to the culture of participants makes the curriculum more relevant and increases the likelihood that they will integrate the aims of the intervention outside of the sessions. During focus groups, it is important to ask about foods that are commonly eaten and typical preparation methods. When we first began to conduct health screenings, we brought snack foods that we liked. We were soon told that these foods were not the same foods that the participants normally ate. In addition, we tried to integrate new, "healthier" foods into our curriculum. Often we were told that these foods would not be eaten. Thus, our intervention became more successful when we altered the fat and fiber content of foods that were commonly eaten.

Consideration of Acculturation, Ethnic Identity, and Religion. Members of ethnic minority groups also differ with respect to their degree of adopting mainstream American diets versus more traditional diets; the degree to which they identify with their own ethnic group; and the degree to which they adopt religious practices and customs. For example, several studies have found that more acculturated Latinas/os consume more dietary fat and fewer fruits and vegetables than less acculturated Latinas/os. Therefore, it appears that level of acculturation has a significant relationship with dietary intake (Satia-About, Patterson, Neuhouser, & Elder, 2002).

In addition to dietary acculturation and ethnic identity, it is also important to consider religious customs when designing culturally competent interventions. During a recent dietary/exercise/breast health intervention, one of our Black participants commented that she would not be able to experiment with any of the recipes that we distributed that day because of her Jewish religious dietary customs and the fact that she was also a vegetarian. Therefore, we recommend that researchers assess level of acculturation, ethnic identity, and religious dietary patterns, and tailor their interventions to incorporate these variables.

Community interventionists. Although this is not always possible, the inclusion of interventionists that are familiar with the participant's culture and language can be an important part of building rapport and trust (Ayala et al., 2001; Giuliano et al., 2000). For example, one study with Mexican girls and their families included the use of "promotoras", Spanish-speaking volunteer change agents from their Mexican community who received training on how to communicate nutrition messages to their neighbors. Promotoras provided informational, instrumental, and emotional support to the participants (Ayala et al., 2001).

Focus groups can also help assess the need of participants to have interventionists that are similar to them in language and ethnicity. We have asked questions such as, "If we cannot provide both, would you rather have someone be of your same ethnicity or speak your language?" We were most often told that the language was more important than the ethnicity.

Curriculum for High Risk Populations

Health beliefs and obesity. The empirical literature supports the premise that Latina and Black women have less weight concerns, less body dissatisfaction, and more favorable attitudes toward overweight and obesity than White women (Fitzgibbon, Blackman, & Avellone, 2000; Johnsen et al. 2002; Striegel-Moore & Smolak, 2002). The lower prevalence of restrictive eating and less rigid body image ideals may result in lower rates of anorexia and bulimia nervosa in minority women when compared to Whites (Striegel-Moore & Smolak, 2002). Some authors have conceptualized eating disorders as "culture-bound syndromes" in which eating disorders are described as a problem that exits among predominantly White females in Western, industrialized societies (Paniagua, 2000; Striegel-Moore & Smolak, 2002). However, the relative lack of emphasis on weight concerns in certain ethnic minority groups may also foster the development and maintenance of obesity (Flynn & Fitzgibbon, 1998). Clearly, rates of obesity are higher among Black women than among White women. Moreover, the development and maintenance of obesity may contribute to health problems. Because of the recalcitrant nature of obesity, once Black women recognize a health problem related to their obesity, they may be less likely to achieve and maintain any significant weight loss.

Body image. Body image is a complex construct and can take many forms, including affective, cognitive, behavioral, and perceptual features (Thompson, Heinberg, Altabe, & Tantleff-Dunn, 1999). Researchers have hypothesized that those who internalize and adopt the Western culture's beauty ideal of a thin body yet simultaneously fail to achieve that ideal tend to experience body image dissatisfaction (Smolak & Striegel-Moore, 2001). Consistent research has shown that the body image held by Blacks is heavier and less narrowly defined than that of Whites and that Black women report less weight dissatisfaction than Whites (i. e., Flynn & Fitzgibbon, 1998). Moreover, White women tend to experience body dissatisfaction at a lower BMI and below the criteria for overweight than Latina and Black women, who do not report body discrepancy until they were overweight (Fitzgibbon, Blackman, & Avellone, 2000). In general, it appears that Black women may have a more flexible definition of beauty and their bodies. In other words, it may not be that Black women prefer heavier bodies as much as they do not perceive themselves as unattractive because they are overweight. Weight also appears to be only one aspect of attractiveness. Participants told us that men in their lives liked women with "meat on their bones". Beauty may also encompass grooming and attention to dress (Parker et al., 1995). This definition of beauty may allow Black women to feel good about their bodies even thought they are overweight (Abrams, Alien, & Gray, 1993; Parker et al., 1995). Some data suggest that Black

women may reject the thin ideal because it is a White standard of beauty (Allan, Mayo & Michel, 1993). This rejection of a standard that is physically impossible for most individuals (Brownell & Rodin, 1994; Harris, 1994) may be a healthy response to a physiologically unattainable standard. Although the prevalence of obesity among Latina women resembles that for Black women, Latinas report a significantly lower ideal body image than Blacks (Fitzgibbon et al., 1998). We can speculate that the disparity between actual and ideal body weight poses a dilemma for some Latinas, who may aspire to be thinner, but may not be able to attain or maintain weight within a normal range (Fitzgibbon et al., 1998).

Issues related to health beliefs and differing standards of beauty must be recognized and integrated into any health risk reduction intervention for minority populations. It is important to stress healthy eating and exercise in the service of health risk reduction and never to advocate restrictive eating or deprivation.

Conclusions

We have attempted to present the theoretical underpinnings, logistical considerations, and effective intervention strategies that contribute to a better understanding of the mechanisms and processes toward permanent health risk reduction behavior. Converging theory, data, and "hands on" experience indicate that tailoring interventions to an individual's readiness to change can increase the chances of success (Mau et al., 2001). However, the pattern of change is varied and is usually a cyclical process rather than a linear one. Additionally, specific considerations need to be addressed when working with ethnic minority or economically disadvantaged populations.

In individuals for whom every day existence related to food and shelter is of concern, health care is often only a priority when symptoms develop. Therefore, preventive health and health risk reduction programs are necessary. There are several important aspects to successful programs. Recruitment and retention of participants often need more attention and resources than commonly occur. Programs also need to be engaging and culturally competent. In addition, close ties to the community are an essential ingredient for a successful intervention. Finally, adequate trust and stability need to be established in order to overcome some of the biases inherent in intervening with populations less familiar with the positive benefits of research programs.

References

Abrams, K.K., Alien, L.R., & Gray, J.J. (1993). Disordered eating attitudes and behaviors, psychological adjustment, and ethnic identity: A comparison of black and white female college students. *International Journal of Eating Disorders, 14*, 49–57.

Alcalay, R., Alvarado, M., Balcazar, H., Newman, E., & Huerta, E. (1999). Salud para su Corazon: A community-based Latino cardiovascular disease prevention and outreach model. *Journal of Community Health, 24*(5), 359–379.

Allan, J.D., Mayo, K., & Michel, Y. (1993). Body size values of white and black women. *Research in Nursing & Health, 16*, 323–333.

Ayala, G.X., Elder, J.P., Campbell, N.R., Engelberg, M., Olson, S., Moreno, C., & Serrano, V. (2001). Nutrition communication for a Latino community: Formative research foundations. *Family & Community Health, 24*(3), 72–87.

Blumenthal, D.S., Sung, J., Coates, R., Williams, J., & Lift, J. (1995). Recruitment and retention of subjects for a longitudinal cancer prevention study in an inner-city black community. *Health Services Research, 30*, 197–205.

Brown, M.N., Bases-Engquist, K., & Tortolero-Luna, G. (2000). Recruitment and retention of minority women in cancer screening, prevention, and treatment trials. *Annals of Epidemiology, 10*(8 supplement), 13s–21s.

Brownell, K.D., &. Rodin, J. (1994). The dieting maelstrom. Is it possible and advisable to lose weight? *American Psychologist, 49*, 781–791.

Cardinal, B.J. (1997). Construct validity of stages of change for exercise behavior. *American Journal of Health Promotion, 12*(1), 68–74.

Center for Disease Control & Prevention (2001). Cigarette smoking among adults, United States, 1999. *Morbidity and Mortality Weekly Report, 50*(40), 869–73.

Cooper, Z., & Fairburn, C.G. (2002). Cognitive-behavioral treatment of obesity. In T.A. Wadden & A.J. Stunkard (Eds.), *Handbook of obesity treatment* (pp. 465–479). New York: Guilford Press.

Davis, L. (2000). Exercise and dietary behaviors in African American elders: Stages of change in efficacy expectancies. *ABNF Journal, 11*(3), 56–58.

DiClemente, C.C., Bellino, L.E., & Neavins, T.M. (1999). Motivation for change and alcoholism treatment. *Alcohol Research & Health: the Journal of the National Institute on Alcohol Abuse & Alcoholism, 23*(2), 86–92.

Field, A.E., Barnoya, J., & Colditz, G.A. (2002). Epidemiology and health and economic consequences of obesity. In T.A. Wadden & A.J. Stunkard (Eds.), *Handbook of obesity treatment* (pp. 3–18). New York: Guilford Press.

Fitzgibbon, M.L., Blackman, L.R., & Avellone, M.E. (2000). The relationship between body image discrepancy and body mass index across ethnic groups. *Obesity Research, 8*(8), 582–589.

Fitzgibbon, M.L., Gapstur, S.M., & Knight, S.J. (2003). Mujeres Felices por ser Saludables: A breast cancer risk reduction program for Latino Women. Design and baseline descriptions. *Preventive Medicine, 36*, 536–546.

Fitzgibbon, M.L., Prewitt, T.E., Blackman, L.R., Simon, P., Luke, A., Keys, L.C., Avellone, M.E., & Singh, V. (1998). Quantitative assessment of recruitment efforts for prevention trials in two diverse Black populations. *Preventive Medicine, 27*, 838–845.

Fitzgibbon, M., Spring, B., Avellone, M., Blackman, L., Pingitore, G., & Stolley, M. (1998). Correlates of binge eating in Hispanic, Black and White women. *International Journal of Eating Disorders, 24*, 43–52.

Fitzgibbon, M.L., Stolley, M.R., Dyer, A.R., VanHorn, L., & Kaufer-Christoffel, K. (2002). A community-based obesity prevention program for minority children: Rationale and study design for Hip-Hop to Health, Jr. *Preventive Medicine, 34*, 289–297.

Flegal, K.M., Carroll, M.D., Ogden, C.L., & Johnson, C.L. (2002). Prevalence and trends in obesity among U.S. adults, 1999–2000. *Journal of the American Medical Association, 288*(14), 1723–1727.

Flynn, K.J., & Fitzgibbon, M.L. (1998). Body images ad obesity risk among Black females: A review of the literature. *Annals of Behavioral Medicine, 20*(1), 13–24.

Giuliano, A.R., Mokuau, N., Hughes, C., Tortolero-Luna, G., Risendal, B., Ho, R., Prewitt, T.E.,

& McCaskill-Stevens, W.J. (2000). Participation of minorities in cancer research: The influence of structural, cultural, and linguistic factors. *Annals of Epidemiology, 10*, 22s–34s.

Glanz, K., Patterson, R.E., Kristal, A.R., Feng, Z., Linnan, L., Heimendinger, J., & Hebert, J.R. (1998). Impact of work site health promotion on stages of dietary change: The Working Well Trial. *Health Education & Behavior, 25*(4), 448–463.

Glanz, K., Rimmer, B.K., & Lewis, F.M. (2002). *Health behavior and health education: Theory, research, and practice* (Third Edition). San Francisco: Jossey-Bass, Inc.

Greene, G.W., Rossi, S.R., Rossi, J.S., Velicer, W.F., Fava, J.L., & Prochaska, J.O. (1999). Dietary applications of the stages of change model. *Journal of the American Dietetic Association, 99*(6), 673–678.

Harris, K.J., Ahluwalia, J., Okuyemi, K.S., Turner, J.R., Woods, M.N., Backinger, C., & Resnicow, K. (2001). Addressing cultural sensitivity in a smoking cessation intervention: Development of the Kick that Swope Project. *Journal of Community Psychology, 29*(4), 447–458.

Harris, S.M. (1994). Racial differences in predictors of college women's body image attitudes. *Women 6: Health, 21*, 89–104.

Haynes, M.A., & Smedley, B.D. (1999). *The unequal burden of cancer: An assessment of NIH research and programs for ethnic minorities and the underserved.* Washington, DC: National Academy Press.

Jeffery, R.W., French, S.A., & Rothman, A.J. (1999). Stage of change as a predictor of success in weight control in adult women. *Health Psychology, 18*(5), 543–546.

Johnsen, L., Spring, B., Pingitore, R., Sommerfeld, B.K., & MacKirnan, D. (2002). Smoking as subculture: Influence on Hispanic and non-Hispanic White women's attitudes toward smoking and obesity. *Health Psychology, 21*(3), 279–287.

Kristal, A.R., Glanz, K., Curry, S.J., & Patterson, R.E. (1999). How can stages of change be best used in dietary interventions? *American Dietetic Association, 99*(6), 679–684.

Kristal, A.R., Glanz, K., Tilley, B.C., & Li, S. (2000). Mediating factors in dietary change: Understanding the impact of a worksite nutrition intervention. *Health Education & Behavior, 27*(1), 112–125.

Kumanyika, S.K. (2002). Obesity treatment in minorities. In T.A. Wadden & A.J. Stunkard (Eds.), *Handbook of obesity treatment* (pp. 447–464). New York: Guilford Press.

Marlatt, G.A., & Gordon, J.R. (1980). Determinants of relapse: Implications for the maintenance of behavior change. In R.O. Davidson &. S.M. Davidson (Eds.), *Behavioral medicine: Changing health lifestyles* (pp. 410–445). New York: Brunner/Mazel.

Mau, M.K., Glanz, K., Severino, R., Grove, J.S., Johnson, B., & Curb, J.D. (2001). Mediators of lifestyle behavior change in Native Hawaiians: Initial findings from the Native Hawaiian Diabetes Intervention Program. *Diabetes Care, 24*(10), 1770–1775.

McGuire, M.T., Wing, R.R., Klem, M.L., Lang, W., & Hill, J.O. (1999). What predicts weight regain in a group of successful weight losers? *Journal of Consulting and Clinical Psychology, 67*(2), 177–185.

National Cancer Institute (1999). *Cancer facts: Questions and answers about cigarette smoking and cancer.* Bethesda, MD: National Cancer Institute.

National Cancer Institute (2000). *Cancer facts: Obesity and cancer.* Bethesda, MD: National Cancer Institute.

National Cancer Institute (2001). *What you need to know about cancer.* Bethesda, MD: National Cancer Institute.

NHLBI, Expert Panel of the Identification, Evaluation, and Treatment of Overweight and Obesity in Adults (1998). Clinical guidelines on the identification, evaluation, and treatment of overweight and obesity in adults: The evidence report. *Obesity Research, 6*(supplement), 51S–209S.

National Institutes of Health (2002). *Women of Color Health Data Book.* Bethesda, MD: Office of Research on Women's Health, NIH.

Ockene, J., Ockene, I., & Kristellar, J. (1988). *The coronary artery smoking intervention study.* Worcester, MA: National Heart Lung Blood Institute.

Ogden, C.L., Flegal, K.M., Carroll, M.D., & Johnson, C.L. (2002). Prevalence and trends in Overweight among US children and adolescents, 1999–2000. *JAMA, 288*(14), 1728–1732.

Paniagua, F.A. (2000). Culture-bound syndromes, cultural variations, and psychopathology. In I. Cuellar & F.A. Paniagua (Eds.), *Handbook of multicultural mental health* (pp. 142–170). San Diego: Academic Press.

Parker, S., Nichter, M., Nichter, M., Vuckovic, N., Sims, C., & Rienbaugh, C. (1995). Body image and weight concerns among African-American and White adolescent females: Differences that make a difference. *Human Organization, 54*, 103–114.

Perri, M.G. (2002). Improving maintenance in behavioral treatment. In C.G. Fairburn & K.D. Brownell (Eds), *Eating disorders and obesity* (pp. 593–598). New York: Guilford Press.

Perri, M.G., & Corsica, J. (2002). Improving the maintenance of weight lost in behavioral treatment of obesity. In T.A. Wadden & A.J. Stunkard (Eds.). *Handbook of obesity treatment* (pp. 357–379). New York: Guilford Press.

Perry, C.L. (1989). Prevention of alcohol use and abuse in adolescence: Teacher vs. peer-led intervention. *Crisis, 10,* 52–61.

Perry, C.L., & Grant, M. (1991). A cross-cultural pilot study on alcoholic education and young people. *World Health Statistics Quarterly, 44,* 70–73.

Pinn, V.W., Roth, C., Hartmuller, V.W., Bates, A., & Fanning, L. (2001). *Monitoring adherence to the NIH policy on the inclusion of women and minorities as subjects in clinical research.* Comprehensive report (Fiscal Year 1998 & 1999 Tracking Data). Bethesda, MD: National Institutes of Health.

Prochaska, J.O. (1979). *Systems of psychotherapy: A transtheoretical analysis.* Homewood, IL: Dorsey Press.

Prochaska, J.O., & DiClemente, C.C. (1984). *The transtheoretical approach: Crossing traditional boundaries of change.* Homewood, IL: Dorsey Press.

Prochaska, J.O., & DiClemente, C.C. (1992). Stages of change in the modification of problem behaviors. In M. Hersen, R.M. Eisler, & P.M. Miller (Eds.), *Progress in behavior modification* (pp. 184–214). Sycamore, IL: Sycamore Press.

Prochaska, J.O., DiClemente, C.C., & Norcross, J.C. (1992). In search of how people change: Applications to addictive behaviors. *American Psychologist, 47,* 1102–1114.

Sarkin, J.A., Johnson, S.S., Prochaska, J.O., & Prochaska, J.M. (2001). Applying the transtheoretical model to regular moderate exercise in an overweight population: Validation of a stages of change measure. *Preventive Medicine, 33,* 462–469.

Satia-About, J., Patterson, R.E., Neuhouser, M.L., & Elder, J. (2002). Dietary acculturation: Applications to nutrition research and dietetics. *Journal of the American Dietetic Association, 102*(8), 1105–1118.

Schorling, J.B. (1995). The stages of change of rural African-American smokers. *American Journal of Preventive Medicine, 11,* 170–177.

Schumann, A., Nigg, C.R., Rossi, J.S., Jordan, P.J., Norman, G.J., Garber, C.E., Riebe, D., & Benisovich, S.V. (2002). Construct validity of the stages of change of exercise adoption for different intensities of physical activity in four samples of differing age groups. *American Journal of Health Promotion, 16*(5), 280–287.

Siegal, H.A., Rapp, R.C., & Saha, P. (2001). Measuring readiness for change among crack cocaine users: A descriptive analysis. *Substance Use and Misuse, 36*(6–7), 687–700.

Smedley, B.D., Stith, A.Y., & Nelson, A.R. (2002). *Unequal treatment: Confronting racial and ethnic disparities in health care.* Washington, DC: National Academy of Sciences.

Smolak, L., & Striegel-Moore, R. (2001). Challenging the myth of the golden girl: Ethnicity and eating disorders. In R.H. Striegel-Moore & L. Smolak (Eds.), *Eating disorders: Innovations in research and practice* (pp. 111–132). Washington, DC: American Psychological Association.

Striegel-Moore, S., & Smolak, L. (2002). Gender, ethnicity, and eating disorders. In C.G. Fairburn & K.D. Brownell (Eds), *Eating disorders and obesity* (pp. 251–255). New York: Guilford Press.

Suminski, R.R., & Petosa, R. (2002). Stages of change among ethnically diverse college students. *Journal of American College Health, 51*(1), 26–31.

Suris, A.M., Trapp, M.C., DiClemente, C.C., & Cousins, J. (1998). Application of the transtheoretical model of behavior change for obesity in Mexican American women. *Addictive Behaviors, 23*(5), 655–668.

Thompson, J.K., Heinberg, L.J., Altabe, M., & Tantleff-Dunn, S. (1999). *Exacting beauty: Theory, assessment, and treatment of body image disturbance.* Washington, DC: American Psychological Association.

Tobler, N. (1986). Meta-analysis of 143 adolescent drug programs: Quantitative outcome results of program participants compared to a control or comparison group. *Journal of Consulting and Clinical Psychology, 54,* 416–423.

Wadden, T.A., & Osei, S. (2002). The treatment of obesity: An overview. In T.A. Wadden & A.J. Stunkard (Eds.), *Handbook of obesity treatment* (pp. 229–248). New York: Guilford Press.

Wilson, D.B., Sargent, R., & Dias, J. (1994). Racial differences in selection of ideal body size by adolescent females. *Obesity Research, 2,* 38–43.

Wing, R.R., & Jeffery, R.W. (1999). Benefits of recruiting participants with friends and increasing social support for weight loss and maintenance. *Journal of Consulting & Clinical Psychology, 67*(1), 132–138.

Wing, R.R., & Klem, M. (2002). Characteristics of successful weight maintainers. In C.G. Fairburn & K.D. Brownell (Eds), *Eating disorders and obesity* (pp. 588–592). New York: Guilford Press.

Author Index

Author Index

Striegel-Moore, R. 352, 353, 356
Striegel-Moore, R.H. 356
Striegel-Moore, S. 356
Strosahl, K. 14, 24
Strub, R.L. 64, 74
Strunk, R.C. 66, 71
Stuart, S. 231
Studd, J. 216, 230
Stuifbergen, A.K. 192, 207
Stump, N. 66, 74
Stunkard, A.J. 354, 355, 356
Sturdevant, R. 165
Style, C.B. 291, 295
Styles, M.B. 293, 295
Styra, R. 201
Suarez, T. 181
Suchman, A.L. 44, 53
Sudler, N. 162
Sudler, N.C 24
Sudler, N.C. 21, 65, 72
Suess, W.M. 66, 74
Suinn, R.M. 20, 25, 260
Sullivan, R. 46, 53
Suminski, R.R. 345, 356
Sung, J. 349, 354
Superko, H.R. 44, 53
Suris, A.M. 345, 356
Surridge, D. 188, 189, 207
Surwit, R.S. 126, 127, 137, 138
Sutcliffe, I. 247, 260
Sutphen, J. 161
Sutthent, R. 182
Svebak, S. 97, 163
Svedfund, J. 155, 165
Svedlund, J. 159, 162, 165
Swan, G.E. 42, 56
Swanson, C. 239, 257
Swanton, R. 247, 256
Sweet, J. 260
Sweet, J.J. 10, 24, 57, 263, 269, 271, 283, 285
Swenson, J.R. 242, 260
Swenson, W. 165
Switala, J. 165
Swyers, J.P. 298, 313
Syralia, K.L. 246
Syrjala, K.L 260
Syrjala, K.L. 88, 92, 99, 246, 260
Szurszewski, J. 161

T
Tabrizi, K. 48, 49, 56
Taghavi, E. 231
Takayanage, S. 254
Talajic, M. 42, 51, 54

Tally, N. 162
Tan, S. 308, 314
Tanagho, E.A. 263, 274, 285
Tanaka-Matsumi, J. 19, 20, 25
Tancredi, L. 120, 138
Tansey, C. 190, 205
Tantleff-Dunn, S. 353, 356
Tardiff, T.A. 292, 295
Tariot, P. 202
Tarter, R. 148, 165
Tarter, R.E. 138
Tas, M. 200
Taylor, A. 165
Taylor, A.G. 126, 135
Taylor, C.B. 93, 97
Taylor, D. 56
Taylor, E.J. 240, 260
Taylor, J. 241, 260
Taylor, J.L. 199
Taylor, J.R 284
Taylor, K.L. 258
Taylor, M. 165
Taylor, R.D. 291, 296
Taylor, S.E. 192, 207, 240, 241, 260
Tearnan, B.H. 85, 99, 246, 255
Teasdale, J.D. 108, 116
Tedesco, L.A. 110, 115
Telch, C.F. 246, 260
Telch, M.J. 246, 260
Tellegen, A. 284
Telleger, A. 275
Telsch, C.F. 279, 285
Telsch, M.J. 279, 285
Ten Brinke, A. 65
TenBrinke, A. 74
Teng, E.L. 40, 41, 56
Tennant, C. 160
Tennen, H. 23, 192, 199, 224, 230
Ter Horst, G. 104, 114
Teutsch, S. 66, 71
Therneau, T.M. 230
Thom, A. 104, 115, 116
Thomas, R.J. 53
Thomas, S.A. 41, 56
Thomas, W. 136
Thompson, A. 202
Thompson, A.J. 188, 202, 207
Thompson, B. 163
Thompson, D.G. 9, 10
Thompson, D.S. 185, 190, 202
Thompson, G. 159, 162
Thompson, J.K. 353, 356
Thompson, L. 42, 54
Thompson, L.W. 202

Subject Index